# Understanding Occupational and Organizational Psychology

Lynne Millward

 SAGE Publications

London ● Thousand Oaks ● New Delhi

This book is dedicated to all my students, past, present and future,
and to Rick, Oli and D'Arcy, of course!

SAGE Publications Ltd
1 Oliver's Yard
55 City Road
London EC1Y 1SP

SAGE Publications Inc.
2455 Teller Road
Thousand Oaks, California 91320

SAGE Publications India Pvt Ltd
B-42, Panchsheel Enclave
Post Box 4109
New Delhi 110 017

**British Library Cataloguing in Publication data**

A catalogue record for this book is available
from the British Library

ISBN 0-7619-4133-9
ISBN 0-7619-4134-7 (pbk)

**Library of Congress Control Number available**

Typeset by C&M Digitals (P) Ltd., Chennai, India
Printed in Great Britain by TJ International, Padstow, Cornwall

# Contents

# Acknowledgements

In writing this book I have also been aided and inspired by other writers on occupational and organizational psychology, especially Neil Anderson, Rob Briner, Chris Brotherton, Cathy Cassell, Nik Chmiel, Cary Cooper, Christine Doyle, Adrian Furnham, Alex Haslam, Peter Herriot, Gerard Hodgkinson, Jennifer Kidd, Denise Rousseau, Paul Sparrow, Phyllis Tharanou, and Peter Wall. I am profoundly indebted to them all for helping me to find my way through the subject. Special thanks to Peter Herriot, who has always been a source of much material, inspiration, and opportunity, and especially for consistently believing in me and what I am doing. Peter, you are the best scientist-practitioner role model I have ever met!

I must also gracefully thank all my students, past and present (from 1995–2004), for their engagement with the course and its material, for their ideas, suggestions and feedback on early drafts of this book, and for their enthusiasm, encouragement and belief in the importance of this very large project. A special thanks to all the students in cohort 2003–2004 at the University of Surrey who fed me encouragement and support and also afforded me the space to do the last run on the book at the final delivery phase. Extra big thanks to Emma Laverick for organizing all her friends to do all the references for me at the last minute despite many other of her own commitments, to Joanna Blackford for getting the referencing process kick-started, and to Jacquie Pearce for always offering to help in any way she can, despite being just as busy as me juggling work and family commitments. You have all been stars. Particular thanks must also go to Joanne Marriot, Olivia Kyriakidou, Julie Gore and Adrian Banks for advice, support, inspiration, and practical help in gathering material and reading drafts.

Special thanks to my academic colleagues Mark Cropley, Dora Brown, Chris Fife-Schaw, David Uzzell, John Groeger, Caroline Bailey (even though she deserted ship to go off to Australia, for which I nonetheless forgive her), Emma Russell, Adrian Banks, Jennifer Brown and Carol Harris-Lees for their unending support and belief in me, and particularly Mark and Dora who, despite having to put up with me being quite 'stressy' (the word my son uses to describe me sometimes!) for a while, have never failed to be there for me. I endeavour always to be able to *be* the same for you too. Mark and Dora, you have been amazing friends to me, thank you. I would also like to give special thanks to Ros Gilbert (my departmental mum) and Ann Drever for looking after me and going that extra mile to provide help and support, warmth and encouragement (even if, at times, you did have to curse me for not doing something I should have been doing). Thank you for being behind me, and for all those lovely cups of coffee, Ann. Thanks also to Julie Earl for always smiling, always paying an interest, always being supportive, and for proofing some of the modules, and to Patricia Yehia for helping me out with the children during the odd child-care crisis when I had a meeting to go to. I am also indebted to Karen Bryan in EIHMS who has given me time, practical support, invaluable mentorship, involved me in projects, and provided rare collegiality and a genuine interest in what I can contribute. And finally, Emre Ogzen for providing useful feedback on early drafts and for looking after Oli during those awful in-set days that creep up on you when you least want them to. We will all miss him when he goes off to set up his own department of psychology in Turkey but are looking forward to some fun Turkish holidays!

Big enormous gargantuan thanks also to Michael Carmichael at Sage for his patience with me over a long period of time, for always having a solution up his sleeve when you think there isn't one, for practical help and advice and for being so incredibly supportive and behind me every step of the way. And at my delivery stage, you too delivered your own baby! I must also express my appreciation to the copyeditor Sarah Price, who did all the copyediting (no mean feat!) with extreme diligence and a deep understanding of the readers' needs. Thank you Michael and thank you Sarah. Thanks also to Fabienne Pedroletti, the Production Editor at Sage, as well as Fern Bryant, the proofreader.

Finally, in trying to find the words to thank my family, I ashamedly struggle! Thank you to my mum and dad for being proud of me, even though they might not really understand what I do. Thank you also to my parents-in-law, Tony and Audrey, for allowing me the time and space to get on with it all, and to Clare, Ian, Isabelle and Lucy for looking after D'Arcy, my daughter, as if she were their own. Thank you to my son, Oli, who is now 10, for appreciating why I might not be able to come and watch his district cricket at the weekend because I have work to do, for keeping my feet firmly on the ground, for showing an interest in what I am doing and why, for telling me off for working too much, and for simply being himself. Oli, you are lovely and I am very proud of you. One day you will play cricket for England and I will be there to wash your smelly old kit, regardless! And to my daughter, D'Arcy, who has been the best distraction ever; and though she is only two and a bit, I cannot ever imagine life without her, flitting around like a pretty little fairy, full of spirit, energy and innocence, bossing everyone around and keeping them all on their toes! Last but not least, thank you to Rick for putting up with me neglecting my wifely role and responsibilities, talking too much shop, for buying too many 'ready meals', for giving me a cuddle when I most need it, and for generally loving and having faith in me, especially when I am low.

Lynne Millward
May 2004

# Preface

This book has evolved in response to my MSc students' pleas over the last 10 years for an all-encompassing text, addressing the syllabus requirements for the Level 1 Knowledge criterion for membership of the British Psychological Society (BPS) Division of Occupational Psychology (DOP). The main objective, then, is to provide a comprehensive resource from which to derive a 'big picture' of the overall subject domain (the boundaries of which are fuzzy and also perhaps open to debate and dispute, but this can be a strength of the discipline); to obtain a sound basic understanding of the key issues, theories, concepts, methods, evidence and practice implications of each of the eight BPS-prescribed competences; to develop a critical and reflective stance on this material; to appreciate the importance and relevance of theory to the formulation of an issue; to facilitate the process of bridging the gap between theory and practice; and to inspire further reading, reflection and research.

Perhaps I should also confess that it reflects in no small part my own need to be able to 'grasp' the essentials of the discipline. At times in my teaching and project supervision, I have only just been one little step beyond some of my students (and in some aspects of the subject, maybe even one or two steps behind them). The experience and expertise they have brought to their course, the challenge of the questions and issues they have raised, the cases and examples they have brought to bear, their contribution to class discussions and seminars, the analytic pieces and practical assignments they have delivered, and their sheer enthusiasm for the subject have keep me going, and in large part, really the material in this book is a product of their minds as much as my own. Hence some due acknowledgement and credit must be given to my students, who in their own learning and development have facilitated my learning and development.

Thus, on one level it was easy to write this book because I live and breathe its material daily in the course of my work, and have engaged with probably all of its contents at some point over the years. On another level, it has been a very difficult, insecure and chaotic task of trying to catch and contain (if it ever could be) a constantly moving, ever expanding, knowledge and practice domain. This is by no means a criticism. On the contrary, it is refreshing and exciting to see how the knowledge base and its practice implications have evolved and are still very much evolving. Perhaps it is a lesson for us all here, in the, perhaps futile, attempt to capture the essential knowledge base of anything! Effectively, this textbook is really only the product of my own sense-making efforts. But hopefully it will nonetheless raise or inspire different kinds of questions, challenge some assumptions and help others 'make sense' of the discipline.

On this note, and with an important caveat here, I may not have done justice to some aspects of occupational and organizational psychology in which I do not myself specialize, or practice. I have the benefit of colleagues whose knowledge and skills complement my own, and I hope to have done justice to their contributions in this book. I have also strived to appropriately contextualize the subject matter, within a broader historic, economic and political framework. For instance, the topic of training and development can be seen in the context of a broader learning metaphor prevalent in society as a whole, where economic progress and survival is said to depend on intellectual capital.

Whilst this book addresses directly the needs of masters or diploma students in occupational psychology, it will also provide an invaluable source of specialist material for many other audiences including final-year undergraduates taking an option in occupational psychology, business and HR students taking options in occupational psychology, work psychology, organizational psychology and organizational behaviour and for practitioners wishing to keep abreast of the knowledge base in the field or to acquire the BPS Level 1 requirement for DOP entry through independent study.

The textbook addresses the DOP requirements one by one in a self-contained way, although it makes every effort to cross-fertilize and cross-reference across different subjects in the syllabus in an integrated and coherent way. It begins with a primarily 'personnel' stance (Chapters 1–3), moving on to look at the organization and the individual in the organization (Chapters 4–6), and ends with work and work environment (Chapters 7–8). There are perhaps some things that I have not covered at all that I should have done, such as the interface between work and people via the particular physical arrangements of their work (for example, open-plan, singular offices). There is a growing psychology of facilities management, which is a topic claimed mainly by environmental psychology. Whilst it is easy to argue that where it belongs does not matter, it might equally be argued that I should have addressed the human issues arising from different physical arrangements in the workplace – but I had to stop somewhere!

There are indeed – as became increasingly apparent to me in writing this book – very many fine lines that can be drawn between occupational psychology and other disciplines when it comes to focusing on a particular work issue or problem. For instance, environmental psychology can inform us of theories and concepts to understand why different types of attitude and behaviour can be found across different types of office structure and layout. Other fine lines include cross-over into counselling and clinical psychology (for example, in the counselling, development, and coaching domains of occupational psychology), into social psychology (for example, group, team and leadership processes, attitude and behaviour change), developmental psychology (for example, career development), cognitive and socio-cognitive psychology (across all domains of occupational psychology), ergonomics (for example, human–machine interaction), health psychology (for example, occupational health), dispositional psychology (again, across all domains of occupational psychology) and even neuro-cognitive psychology (for example, neural network models of motivation).

It might therefore even be a bit futile to claim a distinct knowledge base for occupational psychology, because of so many other overlapping claims on the topics it addresses. This does not mean that what occupational psychology does is not distinctive. It is perhaps in the 'practice' of occupational psychology that we see our discipline most clearly, and, in so doing, draw on the knowledge base of literally any field of psychology so long as it can help shed light on a problem or issue, or soundly and accountably inform our interventions. If the aims of the occupational psychologist are to simultaneously increase effectiveness (of the individual, group and organization) and to improve the job satisfaction and well-being of the individual, what limits are there to be drawn on what theories and methods we use so long as they are appropriately grounded and used in a reflexive and self-critical way?

It is increasingly being argued that occupational and organizational psychology should reflect on itself and its knowledge base, the ideology and epistemology that underwrites it. This is clearly beginning to happen, as individual workers are modelled more as proactive shapers of their own destiny as much as they are shaped by external factors, as postmodernism alerts us to the highly constructed nature of reality. Whilst only a few of us in the field have ventured completely into postmodernist thinking, research and practice, most of us are nonetheless mindful of the critical importance of perception and interpretation, as well as individual needs, interests and identities, as core to understanding workplace attitudes and behaviours.

This moves us away from the assumption that we can tweak features of work and the work environment (for example, job design interventions, introduction of new technologies) and automatically see a benefit in human terms. On the contrary, it is clear that determinist thinking and practice has had its day and we are no longer so fixed on identifying the predictors of this, that and the other work-relevant criterion, but more concerned with looking at mechanisms and processes, and seeking explanations for what we see and find. I see a definite trend away from conventional scientific research (modelled on the experimental paradigm) to looking at the processes *in situ*, using more creative field-sensitive methods that are equally scientific, but more ecologically valid, and yielding new insights from 'ground up' that can be used to develop theory as well as new ways of practising. Research on stress, emotion and coping is perhaps one of the champion domains in this respect (for example, using diaries, introducing longitudinal designs), and there is a growing field of career psychology and organizational development psychology, within what is called the language or narrative mode, espousing new ways of investigating, interpreting and intervening.

This does not mean that we should abandon our experiments or our more conventional methods, since these clearly do still have a very important place in our science, but that they yield findings that need to be 'reality checked' in the field, just as much as what we find in the field may need to be dissected, tested and analysed for generalizability purposes. For instance, in the training domain, the concept of mental model has become significant and has generalizability potential across the discipline for understanding, for example, effective teamwork, organizational change, human–machine interaction and so on. This is a topic for cognitive science to get its teeth into as much as the practitioner, and can be equally validly considered in experimental as well as field contexts. My close colleague Adrian Banks calls the experimental and quasi-experimental angle a 'micro-world' scenario enabling ideas to be tested in a fairly controlled way, but which will also facilitate its application to and testing in the field. Hence, all types of research can be entertained in occupational and organizational psychology across micro-worlds, to simulations, to real world.

The burgeoning use of qualitative and other more field-sensitive methods of investigation is exciting, but may require a form of 'cognitive switching' across different epistemological mindsets. Some would say that it is antithetical to the idea of an epistemological framework to be able to 'switch' back and forth between, say, positivism and postmodernism; but maybe there are instances – certainly in the practice of occupational psychology – where you do have to do exactly that. Pure, maybe not, but appropriate to the situation at hand, nonetheless; and this does not mean that we undermine our scientific integrity either, when we do switch thinking modes. I have a project right now which requires that I look at the issue (of women's career development in Housing Associations) from both a conventional positivist, as well as a more social constructionist, perspective, harnessing relevant theory and evidence accordingly. The pragmatist in me therefore says, 'don't put the cart before the horse', adopt the most appropriate thinking and practice mode or modes (if you can integrate them coherently into a defensible evidence-based approach) required for the issue at hand.

This textbook will reflect these activities in the way it presents and addresses particular topics and through the provision of cases and examples. It should be used primarily as a resource, prompting and inspiring further reading and research, as well as ideas for dissertations, for problem formulation and the creative application of knowledge to various problem situations. A scientist-practitioner approach built on a problem-solving model will be reflected throughout. That is, how to describe and formulate practical problems arising from the world of work using existing theory and research; how to pursue evidence-based practice; how to design problem solutions or management interventions that are theory-driven and testable through evaluation; and how to 'use' knowledge in a critical and constructive and skilled manner in various client situations. I have sought to represent only material from credible rather than popularist sources, adopting a position of the pragmatic scientist (see Introduction and Overview), and, in so doing, have also tried to reflect on the relevance of the more pedantic side of the discipline and its technical advice.

The current book is designed specifically to address the BPS syllabus as a broad overview and resource, rather than an exhaustive treatise on the subject or its component parts. Complementary recommended texts include: *Work Psychology* by Arnold, Robertson, and Cooper (1995); Adrian Furnham's (1997) book, *The Psychology of Behaviour at Work*, which is a brilliant source book with a very useful managerial practice slant, whilst nonetheless firmly rooted in the theoretical and empirical literature; Nik Chmiel's (2000) edited text called *Work and Organizational Psychology*, which provides a collection of more specialist works offered by experts in their field, which are key sources for more detailed follow-up on particular issues or subject areas; and Christine Doyle's (2003) book, *Work and Organizational Psychology*, which takes a very challenging – maybe also somewhat cheeky – stance on the field, providing legitimate licence as well as an inspiration to move beyond what the discipline thinks it knows to address what in actual fact it really does know. I have also derived much from reading Chris Brotherton's (1999) application of social psychological thinking to management science; and from Haslam's (2004) book using a social identity approach, which provide a theoretical basis in social psychology for integrating knowledge across many different but important aspects of organizational psychology, enabling the coherent formulation of many different problem issues and considerations arising in this field and a basis for informed practice.

One other important resource to 'attach' to this textbook is Cathy Cassell and Gillian Symon's recently published second edition of a book called *Essential Guide to Qualitative*

*Methods in Organizational Psychology* (2004), which really does offer an *essential tool book* for all occupational psychologists, whether in research and/or practice, as well as providing another way of thinking about what we do, why and how.

This book is a rather more pedestrian view of the field than presented by my afore-mentioned colleagues, although I do not hesitate to offer my views or to provide my own insights and suggestions where appropriate or relevant. No knowledge of psychology is assumed, although the book is written at the level of a final-year undergraduate student. The text will take the reader to the level of thinking required by the full-fledged scientist-practitioner able to apply knowledge in an informed and critical and profes-sional manner to practical situations. Reference is made to the companion website, **www.sagepub.co.uk/millward**, throughout the book as a crucial source of additional detail, supporting case examples, exercises and activities, and other support material, including measures and other practical resources for both research and practice.

Each chapter is self-contained and does not depend on prior reading. However, cross-reference is made to themes, issues and topics arising across modules to facilitate lateral thinking and to furnish a bigger thematic picture of the knowledge base of occupa-tional psychology. In my view some general themes do emerge across the book, and the reader is encouraged to cross-fertilize accordingly. These themes are:

- a change to a model of the individual as a sense-making, proactive processor of infor-mation, and thus a challenge to the assumption that employee experiences and behaviours are 'determined'; parallel to this is the heightened attention to the idea of the self-regulating, self-managed, constantly learning and developing individual;
- a heightened interest and relevance to occupational psychology of the disposi-tional (individual difference) perspective;
- increased attention to the cognitive and meta-cognitive processes involved in accounting for behaviour;
- increased use of more ecologically sensitive research designs and methods of data collection, including, in particular, the use of more qualitative methods; parallel to this is an increase in research reflexivity;
- increased attention to the need to understand and explain, rather than just predict;
- increased salience of the research–practice gap and the need to close it;
- increased use of theories and insights from other disciplinary knowledge bases;
- increased attention to the employee voice;
- increased attention to emotional experiences and processes;
- increased reference to postmodern thinking.

Other important themes pertaining more to content include the constructs of:

- learning;
- development;
- knowledge;
- experience and expertise;
- self-regulation;
- reconciling group/organizational and individual interests;

- sense-making;
- change;
- balance;
- exchange.

Finally, you are not intended to read this book from cover to cover or from Chapter 1 through to Chapter 8; it is intended for you to dip in and out of, as suits your needs and interests. I hope you find it useful.

## Using the Website

The companion website, **www.sagepub.co.uk/millward**, provides an essential complement to the text by providing the following additional material:

- elaboration or further detail on an issue, a piece of research or a discussion issue;
- resources in the form of measures and other tools for research and practice;
- a source of self-reflection through the provision of exercises and activities designed to illustrate certain points and to bring concepts and theoretical issues alive;
- examples of contemporary research and ideas for further dissertation research purposes;
- practical case examples for illustrative purposes, to aid understanding and to consolidate the text.

The material is organized consecutively by chapter. Whilst reference is made in particular to the website at certain key points throughout the text, the reader is encouraged to surf the website to explore its contents and to use it iteratively in combination with the text as a form of learning support.

## Postscript

Please contact me by email [l.purvis@surrey.ac.uk] if you have any comment arising from reading all or any section of this textbook, or if you have feedback or suggestions for improving it.

# List of Abbreviations

**16PF** – Sixteen Personality Factors
**AART** – Applicant Attribution-Reaction Theory
**ACTA** – Applied Cognitive Task Analysis
**ASR** – Automatic Speech Recognition
**BARS** – Behaviourally Anchored Rating Scales
**BDI** – Behavioural Description Interview
**BOS** – Behavioural Observation Scales
**BPR** – Business Process Re-engineering
**BPS** – British Psychological Society
**BTEC** – Business and Technology Education Council
**BTRI** – Belbin Team Role Inventory
**C2 Organization** – Control and Command Organization
**CATs** – Cognitive Ability Tests
**CBI** – Confederation of British Industry
**CCS** – Cynbernetic Coping Scale
**CDM** – Classical Decision Making
**CEO** – Chief Executive Officer
**CEST** – Cognitive-Experiential Self-Theory
**CIS-R** – Revised Clinical Interview Schedule
**CIT** – Critical Incident Technique
**COPE** – Coping Styles Measure
**CRE** – Commission for Racial Equality
**C/R ratio** – Control/Response Ratio
**CRT** – Cognitive Resource Theory
**CSCW** – Computer-Supported Cooperative Work
**CSE** – Core Self-Evaluations
**CSUQ** – Computer System Usability Questionnaire
**CTA** – Cognitive Task Analysis
**DAT** – Differential Aptitude Test
**DoH** – UK Department of Health
**DOP** – Division of Occupational Psychology
**DoT** – UK Department of Transport
**DSM** – Diagnostic and Statistical Manual for Mental Disorders
**EAP** – Employee Assistance Programme
**EC** – European Commission
**EEC** – European Economic Community

**EID** – Ecological Interface Design
**EL** – Emotional Labour
**ELM** – Elaboration Likelihood Model
**EPQ** – Eysenck Personality Questionnaire
**FFM** – Five Factor Measures
**FOR** – Frame of Reference Training
**GAS** – General Adaptation Syndrome
**GCSEs** – General Certificate of Secondary Education
**GEMS** – Generic Error Modelling System Approach
**GHQ** – General Health Questionnaire
**GMA** – General Mental Ability
**GNS** – Growth-Need-Strength
**HAVS** – Hand–Arm Vibration Syndrome
**HCI** – Human–Computer Interaction
**HMD** – Head-Mounted Display
**HPI** – Hogan Personality Inventory
**HR** – Human Relations
**HRA** – Human Reliability Analysis
**HRM** – Human Resource Management
**H & S** – Health and Safety Regulations
**HSE** – UK Health and Safety Executive
**ICL** – International Classification of Diseases
**IR** – Industrial Relations
**IT** – Information Technology
**ITB** – Industry Training Boards
**IWAF** – Informal Work Accommodations to Family Life
**JCM** – Job Characteristics Model
**JDS** – Job Diagnostic Survey
**KSA** – Knowledge, Skill and Ability
**LB** – Learning Bay
**LEC** – Local Enterprise Company
**LMX** – Leader Member Exchange
**LPC** – Least Preferred Co-Worker
**MCI** – Management Charter Initiative
**MPS** – Motivating Potential
**MSFS** – Multiple Source Feedback Systems
**MSMR Feedback System** – Multi-Source-Multi-Rater Feedback System
**MSQ** – Minnesota Satisfaction Questionnaire
**MSS** – Mixed Standard Scales
**NA** – Negative Affect
**NCB** – National Coal Board
**NCVQ** – National Council for Vocational Qualifications
**NDM** – Naturalistic Decision Making
**NEC** – Network Enabled Capability
**NEO-PI** – Big Five Personality Tests

**NHS** – UK National Health Service
**Non-FFM** – non Five-Factor Measures
**NPE** – Negative Psychological Effects
**NTA** – National Training Award
**NVQ** – National Vocational Qualification
**OA** – Organizational Analysis
**OAR** – Overall Assessment Rating
**OC** – Organizational Commitment
**OCB** – Organizational Citizenship Behaviour
**OCQ** – Organizational Commitment Questionnaire
**OD** – Organizational Development
**OID** – Organizational Identification
**OPQ** – Occupational Personality Questionnaire
**OSI** – Occupational Stress Indicator
**PA** – Performance Appraisal
**PAI** – Post Appraisal Development Interview
**PAS** – Probabilistic Safety Analysis
**PMI** – Performance Management Indicator
**PMS** – Performance Management Strategy
**POB** – Presocial Organizational Behaviour
**POS** – Perceived Organizational Support
**PPQ** – Professional Personality Questionnaire
**QUIS** – Questionnaire User Interaction Satisfaction
**RBS** – Royal Bank of Scotland
**RG** – Repertory Grid
**RJP** – Realistic Job Preview
**SDS** – Self-Directed Search
**SM** – Scientific Management
**SMEs** – Subject Matter Experts
**SMIs** – Stress Management Interventions
**STS** – Socio-Technical Systems
**TAM** – Technology Accepetance Model
**TB** – Team Building
**TEC** – Training and Enterprise Council
**T-Group** – Therapy Group
**TNA** – Training Needs Analysis
**TQM** – Total Quality Management
**VDU** – Visual Display Unit
**VE** – Virtual Environment
**VIE Theory** – Valence, Instrumentality, Expectancy Theory
**WAB** – Weighted Application Blank
**WCCL** – Ways of Coping Checklist

# Introduction and Overview: Occupational Psychology – Paradigms, Perspectives and Practice

## What is Occupational Psychology?

The Division of Occupational Psychology (DUP) of the British Psychological Society (BPS) argues that the purpose of occupational psychology is to facilitate 'change towards improved work and working conditions', and is based, in the words of Brotherton (1996: 50) on 'a thoroughgoing analysis of the psychological factors of work in its many forms'. In particular, the aims of the occupational psychologist are to:

- increase the effectiveness of the organization or group;
- to improve the job satisfaction of the individual.

Until recently, the work of the 'occupational psychologist' has been largely tactical involving, for instance, individual assessment, vocational guidance and choice, and training. Contemporary contributions of the occupational psychologist, however, have extended into more *strategic* 'organizational level' roles (for example, change management). This new architectural profile has created imperatives for psychologists to become more business minded and context sensitive.

Recently there has been much debate about whether the British Psychological Society's (BPS) Division of Occupational Psychology (DOP) should change its name (Brotherton, 1996). This debate is underpinned by the argument that the term 'occupational psychology' no longer reflects the activities in which practitioners are engaged. However, no clear name preference has yet been agreed by members of the Division. The equivalent role in Europe is known as 'work and organizational psychology' and in the USA as 'industrial and organizational psychology'.

The BPS recognizes that the remit of the occupational psychologist is broad, overlapping with other fields such as management science, organizational science and human resource management. The work undertaken by occupational psychologists is listed as follows (BPS, 2004):

- *Organizational development consultancy* – involving problem diagnosis, coupled with the design, implementation and evaluation of solutions geared to improving organizational effectiveness and/or to improving an organization's ability to cope during periods of change or development. This may involve helping a company to develop a new vision of itself and evolve a supporting culture, helping an organization to 'analyse' its structures, processes and behaviours to identify 'blocks' to its success and take steps to overcome them, and/or helping leaders and managers to acquire the necessary communication and interpersonal skills to effect change or to become more effective in their role.
- *Group work including team development* – involving problem diagnosis in team contexts coupled with the design and implementation of 'development' solutions.

- *Training* – involving the identification of training needs, the development of instructional programmes, training implementation and evaluation.
- *Assessment* – helping with the assessment and selection of new recruits and with developing efficient and effective ways of pursuing performance appraisals.
- *Vocational guidance and counselling* – helping individuals to make informed and self-aware job/career choices, cope with job loss (through redundancy/early retirement and so on) and to cope with the stresses and strains of their work.
- *Ergonomics* – involving the investigation and management of the interface between individuals and their workplace environments, and designing interventions that promote health, safety and well-being.
- *Research* – all practitioners are encouraged to adopt a research-based approach to intervention, but research can also be pursued on a more full-time basis to help develop the 'science' of the discipline.

Occupational psychologists work in the public and private sectors as either full-time occupational psychologists, as managers (particularly within Human Resources groups), as trainers, organizational consultants or career counsellors. There is a growing demand for occupational psychologists in the UK, as indicated by the increased number of jobs appearing in professional memoranda and other advertising media. The qualifications and skills of the occupational psychologist are also highly transportable in a global market.

## How Do You Become an Occupational Psychologist?

The achievement of chartered status in occupational psychology signals that the practitioner adheres to recognized BPS standards of professional competence to practise independently and without supervision. Chartered status protects the public, and serves as a seal of assurance, and a guarantee. Moreover, chartering provides a mechanism for monitoring and continuously improving professional standards (Division of Occupational Psychology, 2003).

There are three steps towards becoming chartered in occupational psychology: Level 1 (knowledge and understanding), Level 2 (practical experience) and Level 3 (independent but supervised practice). There are eight competences categorized into four broad areas of professional contribution (Study Box 0.1), comparable with the three broad European criteria: work psychology, personnel psychology and organizational psychology.

---

**Study Box 0.1**

**The eight core competences in four broad categories**

**The individual**
Selection and assessment (Chapter 1)
Performance appraisal and career development (Chapter 3)
Workplace counselling and personal development (Chapter 6)

---

**Study Box 0.1    Continued**

**Training**
 Training (Chapter 2)

**The organization**
 Employee relations and motivation (Chapter 4)
 Organizational development and change (Chapter 5)

**Work and work environment**
 Human–machine interaction (Chapter 7)
 Design of work and work environments: Health and safety (Chapter 8)

---

The current text addresses all of these competences in the form of modular chapters. There are two routes to acquiring Level 1 (knowledge in eight competence areas): completing an accredited masters course in occupational psychology or via the BPS qualifying exam. The achievement of Level 1 provides affiliate status within the DOP. Affiliates are then supervised 'on the job' for a minimum of two years to attain evidence of practice in their chosen areas (Level 2 and Level 3). Attainment of Levels 2 and 3 affords eligibility for full membership of the DOP. For achievement of Level 2, skills may be developed through:

- practical work pursued during an accredited masters programme (and any relevant work completed during an undergraduate occupational psychology course);
- working alongside an experienced practitioner; and
- attending workshops or practical skills based training courses.

Trainees are required to keep a 'logbook' in which details are provided of skills acquired and implemented, backed up with 'evidence' (for example, client letters, client reports, materials developed, progress/feedback reports; see Brotherton, 1996 for details).

To achieve Level 3, affiliates must provide evidence of the generic problem-solving and project-management skills required of all professional consultancy practice, as well as a full appreciation of ethical issues involved. The generic problem-solving model involves the following steps:

1  identification of a client's needs/problems;
2  analysing those needs/problems;
3  formulating solutions (that is, identifying and selecting solutions);
4  implementing solutions; and
5  evaluating outcomes.

Ballantyne and Hind (1995: 8) explain how 'knowledge, skills and expertise' in the eight areas of competence can be translated into 'job requirements and behaviours'. They elaborate on the problem-solving model by identifying and explaining the skill requirements on a more detailed and concrete (that is, less abstract) level. They assume two broad sets of consultancy skills:

1   inventing solutions and initiating action;
2   indirect influencing – that is, adequately persuasive or assertive, to be able to 'read the situation', including the political realities.

To enact these skills, they advocate five other critical 'personal competencies':

- *Diagnosis* – objectivity (dispassionate and value-free empirical diagnosis), curiosity (including reluctance to form conclusions without adequate information), conceptualization and analysis (ability to detect patterns in a wide variety of data since most problems are multi-causal and 'messy').
- *Solution orientation* – focus on solutions and action orientation. This requires imagination, including divergent thinking and the ability to visualize the implementation; courage and conviction, and the ability to present information that people often do not want to hear, based on expert knowledge.
- *Communications* – listening, presentation skills, intervening to provide focus.
- *Skills acquisition* – qualifications (appreciation, understanding, practised, expert) and real-world learning (including being up-to-date in the field).
- *Personal considerations* – initiative, energy, self-motivation, self-awareness, self-criticism, ethical standards, optimism.

## Paradigms and Perspectives

Hollway (1991) was the first to have examined the economic and political conditions of 'a psychology of work', which shaped its character in the form of an applied science and a 'profession'. These conditions can be most appropriately illustrated with reference to three dominant perspectives underwriting all research and practice in occupational psychology (scientific management, human relations, contingency approach). These perspectives (which are meta-theoretical) help situate the discipline. They are *paradigmatic* in that they circumscribe the way we 'see' and 'conceptualize' the workplace situation and its problems.

These perspectives framed not only the evolution of occupational and organizational psychology, but also management science and other forms of organizational science. The need for management and for a science of management evolved alongside the need for 'occupational psychology', both being fundamentally concerned with addressing the issue of employee regulation and control and with the need to *reconcile individual and organizational interest*, in pursuit of corporate efficiency and effectiveness (Argyris, 1962; Barnard, 1938).

Management science, however, takes the organization as its starting point whilst occupational and organizational psychology begins and ends with the individual. Whilst organizations cannot survive without individuals, we nonetheless need to situate our understanding of individuals and their needs and interests in an organizational context (Herriot, 1992). If we do not, we risk losing sight of the organization's needs, needs with which individuals must cooperate if they are to survive as employees.

## Scientific management

As a school of thinking, scientific management (SM) dominated during the early part of the 20th century. In its broadest sense, SM is concerned with optimizing the efficiency and effectiveness of the production process. The basic assumptions of the paradigm were first proposed by F.W. Taylor in his 1912 paper, 'Scientific management', along with proposed methods for maximizing 'the output of each man and each machine' (Taylor, 1947: 27; Study Box 0.2).

---

### Study Box 0.2

#### Assumptions of scientific management

- Jobs/tasks can be objectively studied to determine the optimum method for doing them.
- Money is the prime motivator for all workers.
- Ergonomic requirements are of greatest importance when designing a workplace.
- An individual's skills, abilities and knowledge and the job's requirements must be matched to guarantee efficiency.
- Workers should not be consulted with respect to working practices and job efficiency – such matters should be decided upon by management.

---

Underpinning SM was what Taylor termed 'the task idea' (Taylor, 1947: 64), involving detailed analysis of task requirements – that is, precisely what is to be done and how. In his seminal paper, Taylor outlines the practical ways in which his theory could be utilized, citing a number of specific jobs (including bricklaying, shovelling and pig-iron handling) whose efficiency had been significantly improved by application of so-called objective, scientific observational and analytical principles (Study Box 0.3).

---

### Study Box 0.3

#### 'The science of shovelling ...'

Taylor described the science of shovelling at the Bethlehem Steel Works, involving the following steps:

1 Establishing that the job could be objectively analysed and set against specific indicators of performance (total load shovelled per day).
2 Selecting two 'first class shovellers' from the workforce and observing their shovelling technique, load per shovel, and so on, for a given period.
3 Identifying the most efficient techniques and methods used by the first-class shovellers.

*(Continued)*

---

**Study Box 0.3   Continued**

4   Establishing realistic 'load per day' targets for any shoveller within the workforce, given that they applied the techniques demonstrated by the first-class shovellers.
5   Offering all shovellers a 60 percent increase in wages if they were able to achieve these targets (with training) and threatening shovellers with the sack if they were unable to meet the targets.

---

SM was not novel or new to the industrial realm. The idea that scientific principles could be applied to work was emphasized by the three 'great thinkers' Fahol, Taylor and Weber. All advocated that organizations could be made more efficient via structure, order, logic and rules. Taylor merely formalized what was already an integral part of the tried and tested 'way of working' of the time, at least in the manufacturing domain (Taylor, 1947). It has been argued that the principle of task rationalization, standardization and systematization was evident in the production domain as far back as 1830 (Hollway, 1991: 17–18). What Taylor did was to articulate the principles in a more 'scientific' way. In so doing, he succeeded in accrediting SM with both legitimacy and esteem in parallel with the growth of science generally. It took foothold thus.

Seen in an historical perspective (Hollway, 1991), the consequences of SM were several:

- *It created a need for management*: control of the work process was transferred from worker to management, 'the de-skilling of labour produced a new management class to deal with the problem of control' (Hollway, 1991: 19). Prior to this, workers operated in the tradition of craftsmanship, at their own personal discretion, controlled only by the unwritten agreements inherent to the traditional 'master-servant relationship'. In this tradition, workers were merely 'overlooked' rather than actively supervised or managed. SM, with its emphasis on 'standardisation', 'precise planning' and 'procedure', changed all of that.
- *It directed attention away from 'the workforce' to the individual worker as an integral part of a divide-and-rule policy*. A criticism of the 'individualism' inherent to SM was in its power to 'destroy the solidarity and co-operative spirit of the group' which is 'incompatible with and destructive of unions' (Hoxie, 1915: 15–19). Ironically, it is this focus on the individual worker that provided fertile ground for applications of psychology (for example, 'fitting the man to the job').

SM was criticized as having good intentions but, in practice, not being at all conducive to optimal production. On the contrary, the Hoxie (1915) report documented a notable increase in 'unproductive' workers attributed to what was described as an *over-regulation* of the workforce (that is, the worker as an industrial tool). Lack of productivity was largely attributed to 'output restriction' due to dissatisfaction with the terms and conditions of employment. The dramatic increase in union membership witnessed during the SM era was symptomatic of poor industrial relations and employee disgruntlement, creating the now renowned 'industrial relations' problem, originating from the resistance of workers (that is, as evident in unrest, sabotage and/or restriction of output) to being controlled. The problem of 'control of output' thus became more than ever salient.

---

**Study Box 0.4**

**The industrial psychologist**

SM viewed workers as 'factory hands' and held a model of human nature as 'rational economic'. The industrial psychologist's goal was to increase efficiency (from a largely management-led perspective). Fatigue research balanced the tension between the need to increase productivity and the need to ensure employee welfare. Despite this, the introduction of the 'time and motion' approach to labour research (Moorrees, 1933) served to foster the feeling that the industrial psychologist was there to 'speed things up'. Whilst this psycho-physical approach to the worker held sway for a long time, it was soon complemented by a humanistic concern with working conditions that pre-dated the formal introduction of the human relations paradigm. This enabled industrial psychology to distance itself from charges of 'efficiency engineering' by becoming instrumental to the promotion of a 'welfare spirit' (Moorrees, 1933: 155).

---

Prominent aspects of SM originating from the now almost bedrock principle of 'mutual adaptation of the task and the worker' are evident in contemporary approaches to selection (which is heavily reliant on psychometric assessment), training and job/equipment design (Chapter's 1, 2 and 7 respectively). Thus, despite the paradigm shift in thinking and focus with regards to the 'problem of output regulation', SM was never entirely displaced as a philosophy of work design and organization.

### Human relations

Progressing from the stark objectivity of SM theory, the human relations (HR) movement developed in the 1930s, partly as a reaction to the classic Hawthorne Studies (Roethlisberger & Dickson, 1939) and partly as a reflection of the 'softer' attitudes towards management that were beginning to take hold (Child, 1977; Study Box 0.5).

---

**Study Box 0.5**

**Assumptions underpinning Human Relations theory**

- Interpersonal relations can be the most important determinant of productivity.
- Social-psychological factors outweigh monetary incentives.
- Workers are more responsive to peer values than to those of management.
- Workers have an inherent need for meaningful work units, informal social relations and participative management styles at work.

Evidence for the tenets of HR thinking can be seen in the work of researchers like Roethlisberger and Dickson (1939), and Barnard (1938). The former had originally set out to analyse the work practices and relative efficiency of a number of departments within the AT&T-owned Hawthorne production plant in Chicago. After conducting numerous experiments and following years of reflection on the ambiguous results, they developed a new set of hypotheses for which they found much firmer support (Study Box 0.6).

### Study Box 0.6

### The Hawthorne experiments

Using interviews (rather than observation), Roethlisberger and Dickson (1939) established that within some divisions of the Hawthorne plant, *group processes* were the major influence on productivity and morale. Established work-team groups had developed their own production norms over time. When one of their number, or a newly introduced team-member, failed to conform to these norms (by under- or over-producing), they would be pressured into conformity by the rest of the group (through sabotage, threats, or physical violence). Thus, the mechanistic worker proposed by Taylor was now seen as a social and sentient creature, with a socially-dependent set of needs and motivations. This was consistent with the Elton Mayo philosophy of loyalty, solidarity and communal ties, as well as the work of Barnard (1938) on the cooperative organization as a social system, both writers suggesting a cooperative, harmonious, altruistic organization to be the most productive (see Chapter 4 for more on this).

The Hawthorne experiments provided formal scientific recognition of the need for a more employee-centred approach to output regulation and as the target for management intervention (but see also Carey, 1967 for a criticism of the 'scientific' status of the experiments). However, the HR movement did not displace SM entirely, it merely complemented it by emphasizing the need for 'maintenance crews' for the *human* side of the industrial operation (Hollway, 1991).

Interestingly, it was not 'group' considerations that were uppermost for psychologists. The focus of attention became less the group than the satisfaction of the individual worker with 'attitudes and sentiments' that 'cannot be modified by logic alone' (Roethlisberger, 1964: 15, 31; Study Box 0.7). Whilst the group was seen as the source of worker satisfaction, it was the individual *in* the group and the interface of the individual employee with management (that is, psychological and interpersonal considerations) that figured more prominently as the focus of organizational intervention (for example, Roethlisberger & Dickson, 1939). This legitimized practices such as interpersonal skills training (particularly for supervisors who began to be seen as critical to the morale of the workgroup or team) and employee counselling, as well as research on job satisfaction and employee motivation (Study Box 0.8).

---

**Study Box 0.7**

### McGregor's (1964) 'Human Side of Enterprise'

The conventional view of the manager's task in harnessing human energy to organizational requirements can be stated broadly in terms of three propositions, sometimes known as Theory X:

1  Management is responsible for organizing the elements of the productive enterprise (money, materials, people, equipment and so on) in the interest of economic ends.
2  With respect to people, this is a process of directing their efforts, motivating them, controlling their actions, modifying their behaviour to fit the needs of the organization.
3  Without this active intervention by management, people would be passive – even resistant – to organizational needs. They must therefore be persuaded, rewarded, punished, controlled – their activities must be directed.

The human side of the economic enterprise has in part been fashioned from such propositions and beliefs; conventional organizational structures, managerial policies and practices, and so on, reflect these assumptions. Nowadays, it is generally assumed that people are, on the contrary, not all of such ilk, and may be intrinsically motivated by some if not all of their work, and respond better to facilitation rather than control (Theory Y). Indeed, handing some control over to the employee can motivate even the most reticent and resistant person by furnishing them with a sense of ownership and responsibility (see Chapter 4 on self-regulation theories of motivation). Unfortunately, some managers still operate with Theory X.

---

The knock-on effect of this, however, was to attribute the source of all workplace problems to the individual and his or her 'personal situation' (Roethlisberger & Dickson, 1939: 358). This facilitated what Hollway (1991) calls the formulation of an implicit distinction between 'objective information' and 'emotional significance', suggesting a dismissal of the factual legitimacy of worker sentiment. The locus of the output regulation problem was hence placed firmly in the 'psychological well-being' of the individual, thereby deflecting attention away from the conditions of work and of organizational life. Echoes of this remain today in debate about 'whose' responsibility is stress and the individualistic nature of most organizational interventions (see Chapters 6 and 8). It was nonetheless conceded at the time that the conditions of work, particularly the 'social' conditions (that is, the opportunity to interact), could compensate for psychological problems created by 'repetitive work' (for example, Mayo, 1933).

---

**Study Box 0.8**

**Interpersonal skills training**

Roethlisberger (1964: 523) describes the activities of the Harvard Business School, commissioned by the Ford Foundation to design and implement a training programme to instruct people in HR training and research. The intention was to encourage supervisors to treat the sentient worker with respect. Nonetheless, the approach taken was essentially behaviourist (that is, geared to interpersonal skill development) and thus largely antithetical to the HR ethos. Argyris (1962) later introduced a more 'experiential' element to the HR training package, arguing that training should be geared to penetrating deep into the individual to harness change. He emphasized the need to address the 'emotional' as well as 'intellectual' side of learning. In doing this, he also highlighted the problem of 'authenticity' of change in the 'humanistic' direction. This, Argyris (1962: 154) said, can only be achieved by ascertaining the 'personal directives' underpinning behaviour, and harnessing them accordingly.

---

However, HR did begin to take on a different shade as the emphasis moved from individuals to organizations, and the engineering of change at this level.

### Contingency approach

The prescriptive nature of both the SM and HR movements, both of which advocated inflexible organizational forms and processes which would be effective regardless of the internal or external situation, was superseded by open systems theories (such as socio-technical systems theory) and contingency theory (a meta-theory based on Fiedler's 1967 premise that all organizational systems and processes are contingent upon other systems and processes) during the 1950s and 1960s (see the discussion of leadership in Chapter 4 which clearly illustrates this principle). These theories suggested that, rather than being fixed and immovable entities, organizations need to adapt and change according to the needs of the market, and of the workforce, to achieve high productivity and morale. Whilst this approach, almost by definition, precludes the application of general principles, the following hold for most examples of open system and contingency-based approaches:

- Companies should be organized and managed depending on their specific circumstances.
- No single strategy will work under all sets of internal and external conditions.
- Workers have complex needs, expectations and motivators, which are dependent on their specific situation and on individual-level factors.

The upsurge in technology which took place from the 1930s to the 1950s across Europe led to a call for new theories to assist in the implementation of new technologies within the workplace. Organizations, rather than being seen as 'closed' and removed from the outside world and marketplace, began to be regarded as 'open' and interactive with external factors (Argyris, 1971). Trist and Bamforth's (1951) work with the National Coal Board (NCB) was some of the first research to herald this paradigm shift (see Chapters 4 and 7 for more on this). The NCB had developed a number of mining machines to supersede traditional coal-face mining, thereby shifting the traditional, craft-based way of working towards a manufacturing approach. Whilst these machines were intended to reduce labour costs and improve productivity, the NCB failed to address the vital social issues that faced the miners, who had previously worked in groups, with a fair amount of autonomy and self-regulation. By separating miners and reducing their independence, the vast leaps in productivity that had been expected were not apparent.

Subsequent work by the Tavistock Institute led to new ways of reorganizing work, increasing collective responsibility and developing self-regulating work groups, through an appreciation of the interactive nature of social and technological aspects of work. The legacy of this approach is now in the concept of the autonomous work group (or self-managed team; see Chapter 4) rather than in developments in the way technological intervention is managed (which remains largely uninformed by these insights; see Chapter 7).

Lawrence and Lorsch (1967) were the first to formally propose contingency theory as integrating both internal organizational factors and the external market, social and economic environment. By using the example of three different companies, each successful within their own industry, they showed that organizational success was almost entirely dependent on the effective management of the 'complex sets of interrelationships among internal organizational states and processes and external organizational demands'. These examples were illustrations of the importance of an *integrative* approach to organizational development and action, rather than as templates for action.

We are still to some extent operating within this perspective today, but things are changing with the tide of postmodernism and we are at the brink of either a 'new scientific paradigm' (Symon & Cassell, 1998) or a new 'hybrid' perspective on work, the employee, the organization and the role of the psychologist either heavily influenced by postmodern thinking, whilst maintaining a foot in the door of the traditional positivist approach (for example, stress research), or firmly rooted in positivism whilst nonetheless permeated with *postmodern*-like thinking (for example, selection and assessment psychology, training, performance appraisal). This does not mean that positivism has been displaced. On the contrary, observers on this matter reckon that most research and practice in 'work psychology' is still firmly entrenched in positivist thinking (Johnson & Cassell, 2001: 126). Whether it will ever be completely superseded is a matter for the crystal ball.

## Epistemological Reflections: Critical Theory and Postmodernism

Critical theory denotes all approaches to work adopting a radical stance on contemporary society with particular interest in the investigation of marginalization, exploitation and asymmetrical power relations. Postmodernism is derived from this critical tradition and pertains at a more abstract level to a set of philosophical approaches to contemporary social and organizational life. Common to all those operating within the postmodernism school is the philosophical assumption that people and reality are 'constructed', that language (especially 'narrative') is central to the construction process, that contemporary life is fluid and 'hyper-real', and that there is an inextricable link between power and the production of knowledge (Alvesson & Deetz, 1996: 192–193; Study Box 0.9). This philosophy is radically different from 'the epistemological orthodoxy of work psychology' (Johnson & Cassell, 2001: 128).

## Study Box 0.9

### From positivism to postmodernism

To precisely define postmodernism is antithetical to its philosophy, which assumes no single reality or correct view, espousing indeterminacy. It is more easily understood by what it is now, and that is its rejection of positivism (Johnson & Cassell, 2001: 131). Positivism, a term introduced by Comte (1853), assumes that there is an objective reality that can be accurately represented by the neutrality of science, using rational inquiry. This was a product of a broader philosophy of 'empiricism' (for example, Descartes, Locke) that evolved from the so-called Enlightenment that grew out of a critique of 'metaphysical dogmatism'. Whilst, historically, this was seminal to the launch of rational science as we know it today postmodernist critiques (which started sweeping society around the 1980s) began to point out the consequence for the human sciences was to 'exclude human subjectivity' from legitimate consideration, non-reflexively imposing the same determinist paradigm on the human and social sciences as for the natural sciences. Whilst positivism has been attacked as a paradigm for both the natural and the social sciences now for almost a century, it nonetheless remains the dominant lens through which questions are asked, and the way they are answered. Postmodernism has been expressed in psychology generally through two main avenues of critique: social constructivism (Berger & Luckman, 1967), and methodological movements towards the use of more interpretative qualitative techniques to access human subjectivity (for example, Henwood & Pidgeon, 1992).

Social constructivism assumes that there is no objective science; all data is interpreted. Any scientific account of something will not therefore uncover universal truths, it will be a local construction derived from the linguistic traditions of the discipline, professional agendas and interests and world-views. *In essence this implies that the researcher is constructing the phenomenon under scrutiny which is itself also a product of social construction.* This has raised the importance of so-called researcher reflexivity, which requires that the scientist is mindful of their own 'logics' as not immutable, and to examine their own impact on the data they obtain. Recently postmodernism has taken a 'linguistic turn' (Johnson & Cassell, 2001: 131). The argument here is that it is through our linguistic representations that we create reality, so what counts as truth is a 'changeable socio-linguistic artefact' (p. 132). In short, postmodernism embraces diversity and, as such, is concerned with deriving knowledge of 'socially contingent understandings' (p. 132). Our science then is effectively a narrative, and our understanding of things like motivation and personality is 'rhetorically produced', evolving into a set of discourses about the phenomena in question.

This critical approach can only be understood in the context of positivism as 'status quo', which here (for the sake of an argument) I will call the discourse of 'modernism'. Within this discourse, people (and nature generally) are 'instrumentalized'. In the organizational world, this discourse gave birth to 'management' through rational-instrumental means. Yet the costs of this are becoming apparent in organizational life, as rational-instrumental means of control are said to have become increasingly strained. With the eclipse of the manufacturing sector by the growth of the service sector, the means–end chain of control (as signified by the term 'bureaucracy') has become long, unwieldy and highly complex to the point where the costs of management control have become far greater than can be gained in added value (Alvesson & Deetz, 1996). According to critical postmodernism, 'something fundamental has gone awry' that more technical/instrumental solutions 'will not fix' (p. 195). Instrumental reasoning is productive to a point, but without being coupled with 'practical reasoning' (which aims at politically, ethically informed judgement) has led to (pp. 203–204):

- Constrained work conditions where intrinsic work qualities (for example, creativity, meaningfulness, development) have been subordinated to instrumental values.
- The development and reinforcement of asymmetrical social relations between experts (including the management elite) and non-experts. The role of non-experts or 'troops' is to subordinate themselves to experts (as 'strategists'), and to implement corporate strategy.
- Gender bias in terms of styles of reasoning, asymmetrical social relations and political priorities.
- Extensive control of employees' mindsets and freezing of social realities.
- Far-reaching control of employees, consumers and society generally through the mass media, and by promulgating the money code as a priority yardstick for values.
- Destruction of the natural environment through increased pollution.

What is the significance of this critique for occupational psychology? Alvesson (cited in Alvesson & Deetz, 1996: 202) notes how the metaphor of organizations as 'technocracies' has given rise to mystification and cultural doping. Specifically, he argues that 'expertise' has generated passivity among the non-experts, and that instrumentalism has engineered values and definitions of reality that have weakened, or even denied, low-level (that is, marginalized groups) contributions to the negotiation of workplace reality (in the guise of value-free neutrality). Moreover, instrumentalism has generated a form of hegemony insofar as the codes of formal power and money dominate workplace reality.

Organizations that have recognized the tension between instrumental (that is, as expressed through intention to maximize output) and practical (that is, as expressed through attempts to eliminate repression and repressive practices) reason have avoided resolution by advocating an optimal management strategy in combination with strategies that encourage employee well-being and afford opportunities for their development as well as high productivity. Such strategies include those known as 'job enrichment' and an emphasis on 'corporate culture' (both discussed in Chapter 5). In this way, note Alvesson & Deetz (1996: 192, 204), 'the political is transformed into the technical, and thereby subordinated to instrumentalism ... the objects for management control are decreasingly labour power and behaviour and increasingly the mind-power and subjectivities of employees'.

In practice, postmodernism translates into a philosophically based research perspective which assumes the following:

- the centrality of discourse as the main focus of study;
- fragmented identities and subjective reality (that is, the unitary individual as 'object' is not a viable metaphor in postmodern thinking);
- an emphasis on 'multiple voices' (for example, women, ethnic minorities, disabled employees) rather than all-encompassing theoretical narratives that do not take account of diversity;
- a connection between knowledge and power (see, for example, Hollway, 1991 on the relationship between power and the construction of knowledge in occupational and organizational psychology).

This research perspective contrasts fundamentally with that of positivism and as such has met with resistance from some quarters of occupational psychology, in part due to the absence of 'empirical work' conducted. Recent attempts have been made to render the approach more empirical by grounding critical analysis 'in the field' but, as noted by Alvesson and Deetz (1996: 212), there is still a lot more to do to render the approach more acceptable. They advocate that one way of using postmodernism and critical theory is as 'meta-theory' from which to draw insights and encourage reflexivity in the research process as opposed to using it as a theory for guiding and interpreting empirical work. Alternatively, one could restrict its use to the study of language and communicative practices in 'real' social settings as advocated by discourse and conversational analysts.

The study of linguistic practices in an organizational setting is one way in which postmodernist thinking is beginning to filter into occupational and organizational psychology (for example, Marshall, 1994), though as yet the take-up of this philosophy within the discipline is not common. Others, like Hollway (1991) and Mills and Tancred (1992), have adopted a more macro-analytic 'critical' stance on the study of work and organizational life, both of which provide an important challenge to the mainstream positivistic paradigm. As for the linguistic approach, these frameworks have yet to be seriously reflected upon in the discipline of occupational and organizational psychology. In reflecting on the role of narrative in studies of culture, some caution should be advised against the subjugation of the subjective to linguistic practices, since postmodernism argues that human subjectivity is determined as an outcome of power.

The implications for occupational psychology are that strictly there is no phenomenon 'out there' to be objectively described and understood, independently of researchers (Johnson & Cassell, 2001; Study Box 0.10). In allowing participants to voice their perspectives, and in abandoning the traditional search for one truth, the social constructionist approach assumes no one size fits all; it sees organizations as communities of collaborating individuals, rather than simply engaged in economic activity. The consequence of this is an empowerment of the employee perspective (Cloke, 2004).

---

**Study Box 0.10**

### Social constructionism in IBM

Bradley (2002) describes the IBM experience of taking on a social constructionist approach to its corporate existence. In the early 1990s, IBM recognized that its rapidly decline in business profits was, in large part, due to the inability of the organization to capture and share new knowledge and ways of doing from employees' experiences, and, hence, each new project was resorting to traditional, largely redundant processes, necessitating re-learning. To address this problem in the first instance, the organization set up unstructured databases, in the attempt to capture lessons learnt and experiences gained in an objective manner with a view to generalizability across projects. However, after 18 months, it became obvious that there was negligible reuse of this information, due to the so-called 'objectivity' and 'generalizability' of the information. Employees were unable to find relevant information because the information had been stripped of its context. Without the context, employees were unable to judge its usefulness or transferability. IBM reacted to this with a paradigm shift. Taking a socialconstructionist approach to knowledge management, they abandoned the database and set up processes to support and facilitate employee creation and sharing in a more meaningful and useful way. By empowering employees to own this process, the results soon became tangible, with both processes and systems being constantly revised and improved based on lessons learnt, and profits rising.

---

Whilst there is some evidence of take-up in occupational psychology of postmodernist assumptions, they are generally being assimilated to a modernist paradigm. For instance, understanding the employee perspective on selection (Chapter 1), training (Chapter 2), career development (Chapters 3 and 6), and on change (Chapter 5) has become important to the research agenda. The voice of employees is thus being brought to the forefront of our understandings of occupational and organizational life.

Some areas of occupational psychology have taken the linguistic turn completely. For example, in the area of organizational development and change, the concept of narrative has become important to organizational analysis, including recognition of the value of metaphor for understanding employee world-views (Study Box 0.11). Career psychology has also taken up a narrative approach. However, other areas of occupational psychology reflect a more hybrid weak social constructionist approach ranging from very weak (for example, in motivation and training psychology it is increasingly recognized that the employee is a proactive self-regulating individual whose perceptions and interpretations are key to understanding attitudes and behaviours) to weak (for example, adopting a sensemaking approach to understanding how employees construct their psychological contracts).

## Study Box 0.11

### Morgan's metaphors

Morgan (1997) argues that the concept of 'metaphor' can be used as an intervention tool insofar as it can help in 'reading' a situation. Instead of imposing a metaphor or theory on the situation, which is the most common way to approach a problem situation in an organizational context, one can try to see what kind of 'theories' or metaphors are in use by members of an organization. Thus, one way to understand what is going on in organizations is to explore the 'metaphors' used by people to describe events, since it is these that help construct and shape the reality of the situation for members of the organization (Tsoukas, 1991). Indeed, researchers are beginning to find the application of the metaphor perspective to be useful and revealing in many different organizational contexts – for example, understanding group development, as a tool for achieving organizational transformation and to understand culture (Srivastva & Cooperrider, 1990). Pascale, Millemann and Gioja (2000) use metaphor deliberately to explain organizations to managers (for example, 'the 800-pound gorilla that impaired performance and stifled change was culture' and a protracted analogy with medicine and vital 'signs').

One trend, however, that has become discernible over the last few years is the increased use of qualitative methods, more attention to the way context influences experience and constructions, and to the fact that some things simply cannot be measured using standard psychometric techniques (for example, coping strategies). A good example of this is in arguments being voiced in research on stress and coping for more ecologically sensitive, qualitative and quantitative methods to understand stress and coping processes (Chapter 8). In this field in particular, an increased number of studies are appearing in prestige journals (for example, *Journal of Occupational and Organizational Psychology*, *Journal of Applied Psychology*) using more context-sensitive designs and methods of data collection (for example, diaries). A recent second edition of a book providing the 'essential guide' to the use of qualitative methods in occupational and organizational psychology (Cassell & Symon, 2004) is testimony to developments on this front.

Postmodernism is also not without critics. Whilst the abandonment of searching for the 'truth' and attempting to represent multiple perspectives coherently can be applauded, it can be argued that if there is no reality independent of perception then, in principle, no perspective is ever wrong. In a situation of disagreement, then, or when faced with a multitude of alternatives, it is unclear how to proceed as there is no independent means of adjudication. From a practical point of view, however, interventions must be chosen and justified, *somehow*.

Nonetheless, postmodernism does place in check the historically over-technical nature of occupational psychology, which has often put the emphasis on technical precision and prediction, at the cost of understanding and explaining. Selection psychology and performance appraisal psychology are prime examples of this, bringing charges on psychologists for being mere 'technicians' (Chapters 1 and 3). Whilst in a postmodern era any perspective is a viable one so long as it is acknowledged that it is not *the* only correct way of seeing things and intervening, the great divide between academic advice and practical reality in the way organizations conduct selection and performance appraisal suggests that perhaps psychologists need to reflect on their contributions in this area. Occupational psychologists may create a rod for their own back when they become too 'pedantic' about their science at the cost of its relevance (Anderson, Herriot, & Hodgkinson, 2001; see below).

Thus, postmodernism can be seen to create an important imperative for occupational psychologists to be critically reflective in both their research and their practice.

## Research and Practice – The Great Divide

Several occupational psychologists, in the UK and abroad, have criticized the discipline for exacerbating the research–practice divide (Anderson et al., 2001; Tharenou, 2001a). Whilst the history of the discipline is rooted in the principle of informed relevant practice (see earlier discussion of paradigms on occupational psychology), Anderson et al. (2001) argue that there has been a breakdown in the scientist–practitioner relationship due to advances in methodological and technical rigour at the expense of relevance. They call this 'pedantic science', which dominates all high status journals in the field, meaning that the majority of work is too technical, incomprehensible to all but specialist researchers.

At the other end of the scale, however, an increased tendency towards *popularist science* is emerging, perhaps in response to the esoteric nature of much occupational research (for example, mantras on managerial competences). This work is characterized mainly by its prescriptive, non-empirical, non-theoretical basis.

Anderson et al. (2001: 41) advocate that we undertake what they call 'pragmatic science' that is 'both theoretically and methodologically rigorous on the one hand, and socially relevant on the other'. That is, pragmatic science has both rigour and relevance. They argue that the only way this can be achieved is through a systematic process of 'stakeholder realignment'. How best to do this is thus an important and serious question for the occupational psychologist, whether in research and/or practice.

The BPS is a strong advocate of the scientist–practitioner approach to both research and practice (Study Box 0.12). This requires that to secure chartered status as an occupational psychologist, the trainee must demonstrate the ability to operate with both rigour and relevance. Unfortunately, there are all too few trainees who see the 'rigour' side of the equation as a hurdle to be overcome in achieving their goal. The current text in combination with its associated website are designed in complement to demonstrate how both theory and practice are an inextricable part of what it means to be an occupational psychologist in today's society, by encouraging a self-reflexive stance.

---

**Study Box 0.12**

**The scientist–practitioner**

The 'scientist-practitioner' model highlights the role of research in the practice of applied research on at least three different levels:

1  *Research as a formal activity* pursued in the form of a specific project with a clear beginning and a clear end (for example, a project on 'leadership and its role in organizational change').
2  *Research-based practice* – that is, drawing on the knowledge base of the discipline in an informed and critical way (for example, drawing on the 'leadership' literature in the design and implementation of a leadership development process).
3  Application of knowledge, experience and skill using the *research-process* – that is, systematic practice based on inquiry, a process of hypothesis formulation and testing, and model development.

---

## Practice ...

Strictly, an understanding of the workplace, its organizations and its people requires more than just the application of psychology. Psychology can help us to describe and explain what makes people and organizations 'tick', but does not throw much light on how they are contextualized in a wider economic, political and legal sense. People and organizations do not operate in a vacuum. As psychologists, we thus need to be able to take a step back to reflect on our discipline and its accountability to society, and as part of a much broader interdisciplinary nexus of understanding than we might ordinarily appreciate. The workplace is a microcosm of society and to this extent we need to understand not just 'individuals' and 'organizations' (or collectivities) but also *individuals in their interface with organizations,* which in turn interface with other organizations in *society as a whole.*

This does not mean to say that as psychologists we should become jacks-of-all-trades and masters of none (although the multi-disciplinary *breadth* of occupational psychology as a discipline can be overwhelming at times). It means that we need to be *accountable* in our role as psychologists, recognizing not just our contributions and their potential, but also the *limits of our contributions*. We may need to draw on 'understandings' of the workplace and 'expertise' derived from other disciplines, such as sociology, anthropology and economics, in order to be able to explain some workplace phenomena (for example, culture), processes (for example, change) and problems (for example, turnover, absenteeism). This does not 'dilute' what we do; on the contrary, it strengthens our position. By collaborating with others, and recognizing the highly complex, interdisciplinary character of the workplace, the 'value' of psychology can be more appropriately harnessed and its contribution optimized.

In today's business climate, the cultivation and management of knowledge occupies a prominent place (Herriot, 1992). Psychology can contribute to knowledge creation and use, and by forging 'strategic alliances' with other disciplines, it is in a better position to promote the development of individual and corporate competence. By collaborating with other disciplines, psychology can not only achieve greater efficiency and quality in its own contribution, it can help in the *creation of new value* (that is, by promoting cross-fertilization and the integration of knowledge).

Unfortunately, psychology is yet to fully appreciate its role in the process of value-creation. It has been (and still is) largely pursued in a piecemeal and practitioner-driven fashion, with little overarching coherence or focus. The history of occupational and organizational psychology is problem-built – that is, evolving from a need to address performance shortfalls – but this does not preclude either the need for theory or research.

The inextricable link between knowledge and practice in occupational and organizational psychology is best illustrated by the fact that the British 'answers' to these questions are likely to be different from the American 'answers', and both different still from the Asian and the European answers. Perhaps this serves to highlight the critical importance of factoring 'context' into our understanding of occupational and organizational life. That is, different 'practical' conditions mean that different answers have evolved to address them. Moreover, context should not be seen as separate from the individual, something 'out there' to be captured in the form of an independent variable so that 'its' impact can be monitored. Context and person are inextricably linked through action (Frese & Zapf, 1994). Psychology has yet to properly reckon with the fundamentally *contextual nature of attitudes and behaviours*.

To date, however, 'work psychology' inclines to be 'a hotchpotch of different theoretical assumptions and concepts' which 'makes for some inconsistent and conflicting precepts underpinning practice' (Hollway, 1991: 9). Maybe within the postmodern era this is now just a fact of life for the occupational psychologist (that is, theoretical and methodological pluralism).

## Summary

- The discipline of 'occupational and organizational psychology' has economic and political origins. It is largely problem-centred and practitioner-driven. There is currently little theoretical or heuristic coherence within the field, and, until recently, little attempt at critical analysis or reflection on the part of the profession of occupational psychology on the contribution it makes to our understanding of individual and corporate well-being and success.
- The pursuit of occupational and organizational psychology has tended to be piecemeal and thus difficult to distil or integrate. Its knowledge base is thin and has largely evolved independently of other organizational studies (for example, management science, sociology of organizations, organizational analysis). Its primary focus on the individual means that we tend to examine him or her in an organizational and societal vacuum.
- Occupational and organizational psychology emerged as a means of addressing problems of employee regulation and control arising from scientific management,

and evolved more significantly during the reign of the human relations movement. Both scientific management and human relations 'thinking' still dominate in some aspects of psychology and management science, although their use is now more 'contingency based'. Contingency approaches now prevail, and this reflects in the number of 'contingency-type' theories that have emerged in recent years.

- Theory is important because it helps to organize our thinking in relation to organizational life, but at the same time it is important to be aware of the 'partial' role that theory has. More attempt at horizontal integration is required to strengthen the theoretical basis of occupational and organizational psychology. To a certain extent, the plethora of theories and models available to draw upon in our attempts to understand organizational life prevents us from engaging in linear thinking and keeps us open to alternatives. However, there is a point at which fragmentation is not useful for the interventionist.
- One of the biggest issues within the study of organizations is that of how to reconcile organizational and individual interests.
- There is some move in occupational psychology towards acknowledging the importance of the employee's voice, the role of context and the need to use more ecologically sensitive methods of investigation.
- The influence of postmodernism has been to introduce a linguistic paradigm into some areas of occupational and organizational psychology, but at the very least it has created an imperative for both researchers and practitioners to reflect on their language and their practices as only one way of seeing and doing things.
- Arguments are appearing for a closing of the research–practice divide, which is believed to have widened across a deep ocean with pedantic (irrelevant, highly technical) science on the one hand, and a popularist (relevant but lacking theoretical and methodological rigour) approach on the other. The call is for occupational psychologists to strive for both rigour and relevance in both their research and their practice, to be pragmatic scientists.
- Occupational psychologists can do this by trying to realign the stakeholders, and being constantly reflective.

## Recommended Reading

Anderson, N.R., Herriot, P., & Hodgkinson, G.P. (2001). The practitioner–research divide in industrial, work and organizational (IWO) psychology. *Journal of Occupational and Organizational Psychology*, 74(4), 391–411

Cassell, C., & Symon, G. (Eds) (2004). *Essential guide to qualitative methods in organizational research*. London: Sage

Hollway, W. (1991). *Work psychology and organizational behaviour*. London: Sage

Johnson, P., & Cassell, C. (2001). Epistemology and work psychology: New agendas. *Journal of Occupational and Organizational Psychology*, 74(2), 125–144.

# 1 Selection and Assessment

© 2000 Randy Glasbergen.
www.glasbergen.com

'I hate to criticize, but you've only been
employed here for two days and you're
already three weeks behind in your work.'

## Preface

Selection and assessment are seminal topics within occupational psychology. Early interest was driven by the need to select good military personnel. By the mid 1950s, the field was criticized for being overly technical, lacking theoretical insight. Cynicism was compounded by Equal Opportunity arguments that many of the favoured measures discriminated against minority groups. Recent recognition of the strategic potential of selection to enhance organizational performance reinvigorated the field. However, some critics note that many of the most sophisticated selection techniques still await construct-validation. Progress may be held back by practitioners seduced by complex selection procedures regardless of conceptual integrity and irrespective of predictive power. Beliefs about validity are not the same as actual validity. Unfortunately, technical rather than psychological considerations still prevail. Moreover, the criterion (or 'to be predicted') domain is relatively impoverished, making it difficult to be clear about exactly how different selection methods work in performance terms. This is especially problematic where commonly the criterion domain is continuously shifting through changing job and organizational demands. This has prompted some to suggest that 'job-specific criteria' are no longer appropriate to selection relative to more general and transferable skills, qualities and competences relevant to economic survival today. There is also a 'coming of age' of research on the applicant perspective on selection processes and, in particular, the dynamics of selection as a vehicle for understanding the early stages of the employment relationship. This interest assumes a model of the applicant as a subjectively active participant in the selection process rather than as a passive and quantifiable resource to be measured and 'slotted' into a job. The first part of this chapter describes the conventional 'organizational perspective' on the selection system, explains the selection validation paradigm, asks questions about fairness, and also explores the relatively ill-studied criterion domain. The second part examines the reliability and validity of different selection techniques or predictors (interviews, tests and so on). The third part looks at the 'applicant perspective' on selection.

## Learning Objectives

Studying the contents of this chapter will enable you to:

1   describe the personnel selection system and its component parts;
2   describe and explain the selection validation paradigm with particular reference to the concepts of reliability and validity;
3   provide a rationale for validity generalization and generalizability theory in the context of selection;
4   describe the problem of the criterion in selection research;
5   discuss fairness issues arising from selection practices drawing on equal opportunities policy;
6   compare and contrast the reliability and validity of commonly used selection techniques and methods;
7   describe and debate the features of each different technique or method, including problems of implementation and issues of fairness;
8   critically consider the active role played by the applicant in the selection process, and in particular the selection process as a connecting mechanism at the point of entry into an employment relationship;
9   compare and contrast the organizational perspective with the applicant perspective on selection;
10   identify future theoretical and practical challenges in the field of selection and assessment research.

### Case Study 1.1: Daewoo Cars

Daewoo Cars began recruiting in 1994 starting with its management team. Job profiles were drawn up by a consulting company (involving job analysis and person specification) and then advertised locally. Each advert generated 800 enquiries. Information packs contained details about Daewoo Cars, its place within the Daewoo Group, its philosophy for selling cars, its pay and reward system, opportunities for training and development, details about job purpose and accountabilities and instructions for completing the application questionnaire.

Application involved self-assessment of breadth and depth of experience in seven major categories: motor trade, finance and insurance, retail trade, budget and staff management, information technology, dealing with the public and working patterns. From this data, Daewoo's computer system was able to screen applicants. Daewoo's Human Resources department then examined all 'above the line' applications, selecting a proportion of them for interview, typically four or five for each vacancy. Applicants also answered questions on issues such as 'customer service', success through team effort and sales success in previous jobs. In the first of two rounds of interviews, agency personnel trained in competency-based interviewing conducted rigorous 45-minute interviews, scoring each competence on a five-point scale. Around half of the applicants from this stage went on to a second interview with members of Daewoo's staff, either Human Resources or line management (or for more senior roles, regional managers). Second interviews were more traditional, looking at applicants' personalities, presentation and interpersonal skills in interviews lasting up to an hour. About half of the applicants interviewed at this stage received an offer. References were checked on job acceptance as means of factual verification.

IDS Study 581, July 1995.

# Part 1: The Organizational Perspective on the Selection System

The Daewoo case study illustrates the conventional practice of selection from an 'organizational perspective' (Anderson, 2004; Guion, 1998). The selection process assumes that the systematic assessment of the ability or potential of a person to meet a particular set of job criteria can be precisely evaluated. This should enable a forecast or *prediction* to be made about the suitability of a person for a particular job. This process has a number of advantages relative to a purely intuitive approach. First, it describes a step-by-step procedure for ensuring that selection practice is 'objective' and thus also 'fair' and open to empirical verification. Second, it offers both practitioners and researchers a model of best practice against which to evaluate the success of a selection intervention.

The larger the selection ratio (number of applicants to number of vacancies), the more discriminating the selection strategy will need to be. A selection device known to be reliable and valid with respect to a particular outcome criterion can be used to select from even a small applicant pool (for example, cognitive ability test for a senior management position). The cost of a selection error will depend on the job. If poor performance could irreparably damage the company (for example, finance director) then the cost of a mistake will be high.

## The Selection Validation Paradigm

The above selection process is framed by 'the selection validation' approach, the prevailing model in recruitment science. It assumes that the key to predicting performance is to identify a job-relevant outcome *criterion or criteria* and a predictor that will generate evidence with good discriminating power against the criterion. In this instance, predictors are the methods of assessment. Measures can be both psychometric (standardized and reliant on a statistical metric to produce a score), and non-psychometric (for example, interviews, references). It is generally agreed the more *psychometric* the measurement method, the more precise the forecasts. In practice, both forms of selection devices are commonly used to obtain applicant evidence.

Adequate description and explanation of the selection validation paradigm requires the introduction of two key psychometric concepts: reliability and validity.

## Reliability

Reliability is the extent to which a measurement tool yields a consistent score or set of scores. A highly reliable measure produces the same or similar readings over time for the same thing, like a tape measurement of the length and width of a table. Measurement of physical objects or phenomena using precisely calibrated measures (rulers, thermometers, scales) is less open to error than the measurement of abstract constructs. Scope for variation across different instances of *psychological measurement* is enormous, arising from test factors (for example, item difficulty level), person factors (for example, motivational state), and the circumstances surrounding the measurement process (for example, test conditions).

The *reliability index* is the result of a *correlation* (*r*) between two or more sets of readings from the same source, using the same tool either immediately or after a short delay. Parallel readings may be derived by splitting the test on an odd–even basis (split-half technique) or by using alternate versions of the test (alternate forms). High reliability does not imply correctness. A measure of intelligence may produce a consistent score for the same person over time, but does it really measure intelligence?

## Validity

Validity indicates whether a measure is *right* for the purpose. High reliability is no guarantee of high validity, although low reliability is a sure indicator of low validity. There are four main ways of assessing validity (Study Box 1.1). Each type of validity provides an important perspective on a measure. A measure with high construct validity may not necessarily have good criterion-related validity. For instance, a test of 'extroversion' may be construct-valid (various measures converge in their description of an extravert person as sociable, outgoing, articulate), yet possess dubious criterion validity in the context of job performance. On the other hand, a test with high criterion validity (a test of clerical skills predicts the performance of clerical staff on the job) may nonetheless be low on construct validity (different components of the test do not yield internally consistent results). Indeed any conclusions drawn about predictive validity may not be easily explained. In short, validity of one kind does not necessarily imply validity of another.

## Study Box 1.1

### Types of validity

#### *Construct validity*

Constructs are inferences about psychological phenomena that cannot be directly measured (for example, conscientiousness) so they have to be translated into concrete attitude or behavioural (that is, operational) terms that can be measured (for example, attention to detail, organized, reliable, precise). The test of construct validity is to determine whether the *indirect* measure is indeed a true indicator of the supposed construct. Estimating this begins with a theory about how the 'construct' operates or displays itself. Another way to assess construct validity is to compare test scores from different supposed measures of commitment. The scores should converge. However, debates are inevitable surrounding what measures should converge and why. Recent controversies have arisen over the use of particular techniques like confirmatory factor analysis for ascertaining construct validity (see Lievens & Klimoski, 2001).

#### *Content validity*

This refers to the representation of a measure. A measure of cognitive ability should cover the entire range of attitudes and behaviours considered theoretically relevant to the construct. This may be a matter of expert judgement. If the content in question pertains to a well-defined set of behaviours (for example, number manipulation, spatial configuration and manipulation, fluency of word use, speed of information processing), it is easier to describe the construct in empirical terms (for example, convergent or divergent thinking ability).

#### *Criterion-related validity*

This pertains to whether the measurement tool can account for significant variance in the 'criterion'. A valid test of cognitive ability, for example, should yield a score that predicts job success. There are two ways of assessing criterion validity: *predictive* and *concurrent*. Predictive validity involves testing *job applicants* and then comparing their scores with supervisor ratings of on-the-job performance at some later point. Concurrent validity, by contrast, involves testing *job incumbents* and then correlating the results with supervisor ratings of on-the-job performance.

#### *Face validity*

This refers to whether a measure *appears* relevant to the test domain. Some tests are more obviously job relevant (for example, work samples involving concrete tasks) and others are not (for example, personality tests). The importance of face validity is not so much for selection validation, rather for *how applicants react* to the assessments they face. Applicant perceptions about test relevance and meaning are critical to their opinions about fair assessment (see Study Box 1.14 later in this chapter). It is crucial to have a defensible criterion against which to gauge each predictor. Nonetheless the issue is a contentious one, leading some to argue that face validity is an important public relations consideration, if only from the standpoint of what it implies for the development of a relationship of 'trust' between employee and employer (Herriot, 2001).

## Selection validation

Selection validation is synonymous with criterion validity which concerns the appropriateness of a particular selection device for making accurate forecasts about future job performance. A number of conditions need to be specified under which performance forecasting works best. In the initial prediction validation exercise, applicants should *not* be hired on the basis of their test scores. If the test score is valid, it is difficult to obtain a true assessment of this from pre-selected applicants because the criterion measure is unlikely to yield performance data variable enough to make fine discriminations. This is called the *restriction of range problem*. However, in practice it may be burdensome to put applicants through a costly assessment process (for example, work sample test) that is strictly *not* used for selection decisions. This, coupled with a tendency to rely on early performance information to make applicant judgements, accounts for why concurrent validation techniques are more popular (Study Box 1.1). Concurrent techniques have less forecasting potential, but are better than no validation at all.

The most often used index of criterion validity is the *validity coefficient* describing the relationship between a predictor (x) and a criterion (y) measure assessed by *correlation (r)*. The higher the correlation (expressed from –1 to +1), the higher the strength of the association. Correlation expresses an association, not a causal relationship. A high cognitive ability score *predicts* but does not necessarily cause high performance. Many other factors like effort and disposition could contribute to this association.

Validity coefficients derived from the correlation of test scores with criterion measures are only one form of evidence. Guion (1998: 114) describes validity as an inference about how confident we can be in attributing meaning to scores, built from various sources of evidence. Other forms of evidence include judgements about test construction procedures. Was there a clear idea of the attribute to be measured? Are the *mechanics* of the measure consistent with the way the attribute has been defined? For instance, it would not be possible to obtain a valid measure of divergent thinking style from a problem-solving puzzle with only one correct solution. Similarly, the *content* of the test should have a logical association with the attribute being measured. If the attribute is multi-dimensional does the content of the measure reflect this? Kline (1986) said that if the original item pool was derived from theoretical and empirical insight, it may be reasonable to infer that the scores are a valid indicator of the attribute in question.

Hakel (1986) adds that the validity of the criterion is also crucial to interpretations of the validity coefficient. He notes many instances of over-prediction attributable to invalid criterion measures, especially those that are heavily reliant on subjective judgements about a job incumbent. A supervisor may, for example, unwittingly rate highly cooperative employees as 'better' than those who are relatively non-cooperative. Performance measurement will thus be confounded by a measure of cooperation. Many inappropriate conclusions may result from assuming the measure of performance is sound.

In short, criterion validity statements cannot be accepted in a vacuum. Questions of construct and content validity of the selection device coupled with consideration of the validity of the criterion measure are also required. In practice, the selection validation paradigm is heavily data driven rather than theoretically informed (Robertson & Smith, 2001; Salgado, 1999).

## Validity Generalization and Meta-analysis

Validity generalization involves controlling the impact of multiple sources of error on test scores to produce truer estimates of validity (Hunter & Schmidt, 2000; Study Box 1.2). Hunter and Schmidt argue that validity generalization is necessary to empirical integration, providing a more substantial factual foundation on which to build theory. The rationale is that firmer conclusions can be derived from cumulative generalizable research rather than from isolated 'local' validation studies. Unfortunately, many researchers favour local validity studies in the belief that validity is situation specific. Traditionally, empirical work has been synthesized by 'narrative' review. However, contradictory results make the task of coherent synthesis difficult, yielding only vague or ambivalent conclusions. On the down side, reviewing only selected studies may produce definitive but only partial conclusions.

---

### Study Box 1.2

#### Validity generalization

The techniques of validity generalization are too complex to describe here. Many debates exist about the mathematics and mechanics. All, however, involve some form of meta-analysis. Sources of error may arise from unreliability of the predictor and/or criterion measures, sampling strategies and characteristics, and 'restriction of range'. The combined effect of errors arising from such sources can substantially reduce the overall validity coefficient. For example, the average observed validity for cognitive ability tests in predicting job performance increases from 0.20 to 0.75 when effects attributable to measurement artefacts are controlled (Hunter & Schmidt, 2000). This finding has substantial theoretical as well as practical importance. The general rule of thumb is that uncorrected validity coefficients are dubious; an important point when evaluating claims made by test publishers. Authoritative sources of advice and guidance on meta-analysis for the statistical synthesis of selection research are provided by Hunter and Schmidt (2000), and more recently Landy (2003).

---

Meta-analysis has had a profound impact on selection research. It has enabled the examination of cumulative evidence on alternative predictors of performance, assessment of test fairness and of the moderating impact of individual differences. Schmidt and Hunter (1998) recently found, for instance, that general mental ability (GMA) predicts performance in all jobs for many different types of sample (for example, minority and majority groups) and across many different geographical regions. Salgado et al.

(2003) demonstrate that this finding is generalizable across data obtained from 10 EC states across 12 different occupational categories including those not often represented in meta-analysis (for example, management, professionals, blue-collar workers).

For practical purposes, the reasons why GMA predicts performance are not important. However, meta-analysis designed to test alternative theoretical explanations suggests that GMA predicts performance because it predicts learning and skill mastery. Other generalizable findings produced by meta-analysis afford strong support for this interpretation. For instance, the association between GMA and job performance is consistently moderated by *job complexity* (Salgado et al., 2003). Moreover, the performance of occupational categories theoretically associated with job complexity (for example, management, professionals) is more strongly predicted by GMA than the performance of, say, blue-collar workers whose jobs are less overtly 'cognitive' (Salgado et al., 2003). Finally, GMA consistently explains more variance in training success (which presupposes a high degree of learning and skill mastery) than job performance (Ree & Carretta, 1996). Thus, although meta-analysis is not a theoretical tool it can be used to build and/or test theory.

Until recently, meta-analysis has rarely been used for theoretical work. Schuler and Guldin (1991: 215) argue that whilst it *is* important to ascertain the heuristic value of a diagnostic device, the ultimate aim is to develop a theory of performance. Viswesvaran (1993) was the first to take up this challenge (see also, Viswesvaran & Ones, 2000) and more recently, Schmidt and Hunter (2004). Refer to Chapter 3, Part 1 for details of performance theory.

## Selection Criteria

The aim of assessment in selection is to form a 'valid' inference about probable levels of performance against a particular job-specific criterion. Unfortunately, practicalities may dictate which of the many criterion constructs it is viable to investigate. Measures obtained in this way are, in the words of Robertson and Smith (2001: 447), 'often incomplete, irrelevant or seriously contaminated by artefacts'. Even when the process of ascertaining and measuring selection criteria is systematic, the problem remains of how to synthesize and integrate findings across a complex multi-dimensional, multi-level performance domain (Robertson & Smith, 2001: 448, Table 1).

Many debates exist in association with the now renowned 'criterion problem' (Guion, 1998), a problem spanning the performance literature generally, and arising in particular in connection with performance evaluation and appraisal (see Chapter 3, Part 1 for discussion). In the field of selection, researchers have been charged with predictor preoccupation at the expense of understanding the criterion domain. Many now advocate that progress in personnel selection depends on the development of a stronger theoretical basis for *both* predictor and criterion research (Schmitt & Chan, 1998).

It is generally agreed that the criterion should be derived from a judicious combination of performance theory and systematic job analysis. For selection purposes, job analysis should enable the identification of those characteristics that typify the best person for a job, and that predict not only current but future job performance. In more theoretical terms, 'job analysis should contribute to the development of prediction models in order to predict performance' (Algera & Greuter, 1989: 8).

Thus, selection based on job analysis should yield valid results so long as job demands remain constant: '... valid selection methods will be seen to have one element in common – a relationship to job content' (Smith & George, 1992: 57). Content-oriented methods require the rational and systematic linking of predictors and criteria on a concrete point-by-point basis which is 'valid, practical and defensible in court'. These methods include the classic work sample (Pannone, 1994) and the situational interview (Latham & Saari, 1984). If, on the other hand, job demands do not or are unlikely to remain constant, detailed content-oriented job analysis is almost nonsensical. Robertson and Smith (2001) add that choice of method should be informed by the formation of plausible hypotheses about relevant criterion characteristics. If this involves looking at team- or organizational-level 'criteria', then so be it.

Overall, it is clear that progress in our understanding of how to produce sound selection decisions depends fundamentally on being able to 'clarify what we want to explain' (Salgado, 1999: 38). In Salgado's words, we therefore urgently need to develop a 'theory of work behaviour in which performance constructs are well defined and assessed' (1999: 38). Whilst recent reviews suggest that there has been an increase in attention to theoretical issues with respect to criterion issues (for example, Viswesvaran & Ones, 2000), we are still a long way off from being able to achieve this goal. Moreover, many are now suggesting that the concept of the isolated 'job' is no longer viable in contemporary organizational life, and that a higher order of abilities and skills operating at team and organizational level should be undertaken to ascertain the most appropriate criteria for selection (for example, Ployhart & Schneider, 2002).

Mavericks amongst us will also question whether all job criteria are known and measurable and, even if they are, whether 'ratings' would capture them and whether they would be stable enough to justify being measured at all (for example, de Wolff & van den Bosch, 1998).

## Job Descriptions and Personnel Specification Techniques

### Job description

A job description outlines the principal responsibilities and tasks associated with a particular job derived from job analysis. Ironically, job descriptions are often used as the starting point *for* job analysis (Study Box 1.3), yet they rarely reflect practical reality, particularly for continually changing jobs (Hough & Oswald, 2000).

---

**Study Box 1.3**

**What is job analysis?**

Job analysis can be described as 'any systematic procedure for obtaining detailed and objective information about a job, task, or role that will be performed or is currently being performed' (Pearn & Kandola, 1993). Although essentially a job analysis involves the breaking down of a job into its component activities and requirements, it can be conducted at several levels of analysis. Traditionally, job analysis has been approached from a task-oriented engineering stance, describing the objectives of the job, the technologies used plus the physical, mechanical and social demands of the job. Nowadays, as well as providing information about specific tasks, job content, and the work environment (a work- or *task-oriented approach*), job analysis can be used to identify the knowledge, skills, abilities and personal attributes necessary for an individual to perform a job successfully (a person or *worker-oriented approach*) (Sandberg, 2000). Note also that job analysis provides the basis not only for selection but for training, performance evaluation, ergonomics and many other personnel functions. For detailed review of various job analysis techniques and methods, and guidelines on how to conduct a simple job analysis, see **www.sagepub.co.uk/millward**.

---

Tate (1994) says that the job description is inadequate for introducing applicants to a job and advocates combining it with a *realistic job preview* (see below). Moreover, given the contemporary climate of constant change, it is unlikely that any job will remain the 'bounded' entity (denoting readily identifiable tasks with definite end points) it could once have been assumed. This may require a new way of thinking about jobs and job description, particularly for legal purposes (Hough & Oswald, 2000). Also, at the managerial/professional level someone may be employed to fulfil objectives or agendas as opposed to specific tasks. In such instances, Cascio (1995) says that what can often remain is something more 'person-like' than 'job-like', insofar as the job (as a set of objectives or agendas) is idiosyncratically defined and enacted. Yet, traditionally, job analysis does not account for variations in the overlap between job and person factors. Wichroski (1994) similarly raises the issue of *emotional labour* as well as *rational labour*, referring to the *way* work is accomplished as opposed to simply *what* one is to do.

On the other hand, Darrah (1994) argues that decomposing jobs into discrete tasks, skill and person-attribute components can isolate work from its broader context. This has prompted some to suggest that the appropriate analytic unit is 'the workplace' rather than 'the job' (for example, De Wolff & van den Bosch, 1998). Others argue for a more team-level analysis (for example, Ployhart & Schneider, 2002). Robertson and Smith (2001) lament, however, that in practice, the contextual aspects of the job are largely ignored.

### *Person specification*

The person or job *specification* details the knowledge, skills, abilities, experience, and attributes or attitudes required to perform the job effectively. There is no logical deductive way of transforming task characteristics into person characteristics or behaviours, even though it is central to the production of selection criteria. Schuler (1989) describes this as 'the missing link' in job analysis, arguing moreover that task and task components may not be completely independent of the job incumbent.

One commonly used tool for generating person specifications is known as the '7-Point Plan' (Boydell, 1970), comprising: physical make-up, attainments, general intelligence, special aptitudes, interests, dispositions and home circumstances. Each set of information is classified as essential or desirable to successful job performance. However, personnel specifications of this kind have been criticized for depicting the ideal rather than clarifying how each aspect of the proposed specification links with performance.

There is a dearth of research on the predictive value of person specifications. Contemporary efforts to identify the personal characteristics involved in a job are either competence driven (that is, What must someone be able to do?) or have conflated 'personal characteristics' with personality.

Fleishman and Quaintance (1984) offered a taxonomy of job analysis techniques that could provide a basis for constructing both a job description and person specification. Thus, the *behavioural description* (what exactly is done) and *task characteristics* (external to the individual, like working conditions and tools) can inform the job description. The *behavioural requirement* (what exactly is required) and the *ability requirement* (what abilities and attributes are required), on the other hand, can inform the person specification (which is arguably not singularly reducible to 'personality').

## Part 1 Summary

- The selection process involves the systematic assessment of applicants using carefully chosen measurement methods (or predictors) for making statistically sound predictions about future job performance. The more rigorous the selection process, the more verifiable and accountable the selection decisions.
- Technical considerations prevail at the expense of theoretical (for example, construct validity of predictor or criterion domain) issues, though increased attention to theoretical (and epistemological) considerations is recently being witnessed.

# Part 2: The Validity and Reliability of Selection Techniques

With regard to the literature on selection techniques, Robertson and Smith (2001: 442) note that little has changed since their review of 1987 except 'the increased confidence that researchers have in the validity of most personnel selection methods'. In 1987 they noted an increased interest in the situational interview (Latham & Saari, 1984), increased use of biodata forms of evidence gathering, and the development of accomplishment records (Hough, 1984).

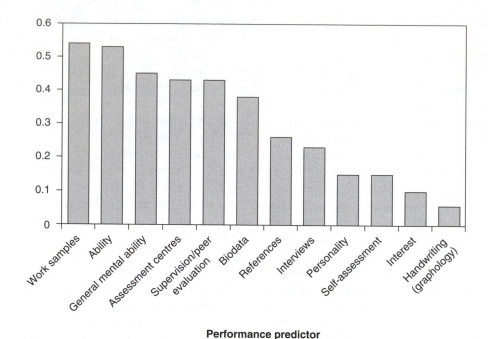

**Performance predictor**

**Figure 1.1**   Validity coefficients of workplace performance predictors

Since then, however, Robertson and Smith (2001) point to the huge growth in the use of personality testing, a trend also highlighted by Salgado (1999). The field, however, can also be said to have witnessed a growth in computer-assisted testing techniques (Bartram, 2001), the use of projective tests (Carson & Gilliard, 1993), integrity testing (Ones, Viswesvaran, & Schmidt, 1993), and in the use of biodata (Mount, Witt, & Barrick, 2000). Other small developments include interest in physiological measurement (for example, evoked potentials correlate with cognitive ability) and the use of computer-generated virtual reality simulations (Salgado, 1999). It is not yet clear whether these developments add anything in terms of predictive power over and above what can be achieved by an ability test and, as such, it is difficult to justify the extra resource cost this would incur.

The bulk of the literature on selection techniques concerns their reliability and predictive validity, much of which is now available in summary form based on narrative reviews (for example, Robertson & Smith, 2001; Salgado, 1999), and meta-analysis (for example, Schmidt & Hunter, 1998). From the latter are derived clear, quantifiable estimates of validity coefficients for many different types of 'predictor'. Figure 1.1 provides a summary of coefficients derived from Schmidt and Hunter's (1998) meta-analysis. However, all reviews afford remarkably similar conclusions.

It is now well established that ability tests (or the '*g*' factor) and work samples provide the best predictions of performance, accounting for 50 percent or more criterion variance. Schmidt and Hunter (1998) have further demonstrated the feasibility of combining two predictors (for example, cognitive ability and work sample, cognitive ability and structured interviews) to obtain even higher validity coefficients (r = 0.60–0.65).

However, little is known about how different predictors interrelate, nor about the gains in validity that might be expected by combining particular predictors. Limitations on this are posed by technical and statistical constraints within meta-analysis making it difficult to look at the 'combined' effect of particular predictors. Yet, clearly, it is more usual for selection systems to include multiple methods of selection, and so the practical question of which methods add unique non-overlapping predictive power is an important one for future research (Robertson & Smith, 2001: 463).

## Choice of Assessment

According to Wernimont and Campbell (1968), a good predictor will 'sample' future job-relevant behaviours (criterion-relevant). In practice, choice of assessment is often down to what people like doing and feel comfortable with. Indeed, choice of technique has tended to be 'excessively *ad hoc* and atheoretical' (Guion, 1998: 114). Smith and George (1992) note a high association between beliefs about validity and frequency of use, but no association between this and the true validity of the method. It seems that the more complex the method the more seductive it may seem to the practitioner, irrespective of its job relevance or validity.

Findings, from an international perspective, indicate that method selection is a lot down to 'local' cultural factors rather than universal 'best practice' guidelines (Huo, Huang & Napier, 2002; Study Box 1.4).

### Study Box 1.4

#### International methods of selection

Huo et al. (2002) report finding more divergence than convergence in recruitment practices across the world influenced by locally determined cultural considerations. Different cultures value different applicant attributes and have different beliefs about how best to assess them. For example, in France and Belgium there is a greater reliance on tests than in UK, Germany and Holland, who are more likely to use assessment centres and Spain, Greece and China, who use generally less structured approaches. US companies report the heaviest use of integrity testing. However, there may also tend to be as much divergence within countries as between them. Taking into consideration local cultural factors is a critical consideration for multi-national companies otherwise using 'globally standardized' strategies for recruitment and selection. Local applicants may react negatively to strategies and methods that they are not familiar with or that do not align with their own cultural beliefs and values.

Increased test use has crucial implications for ethical standards and controls, prompted in part by the highly 'commercial' nature of much test development and marketing. The attraction of tests is that they yield *numbers,* which can engender an *illusion of objectivity*. However, tests can and have been misused to justify many inappropriate selection decisions (Porteous, 1997). This has prompted the BPS to regulate test use in all practical contexts. A predetermined level of competence in ability (Level A) and personality (Level B) testing must now be demonstrated before tests can be licensed for use by a particular individual. These efforts have been reinforced by UK legislation on fair selection and equal opportunity, and publication by the Institute of Personnel Management of a strict Code of Practice on Occupational Testing.

## Non-Psychometric Predictors

### References/curricula vitae

Reference checks are widely used sources of applicant evidence in the UK (for example, on past job behaviours/experiences) despite problems of restriction of range, leniency, low predictive validity, and low inter-rater reliability (Shackelton & Newell, 1997). Salgado (1999) quotes predictive validity coefficients ranging between 0.14 and 0.26. Anderson and Shackleton (1996) advocate the use of references limited to a factual check on the biographical claims made in application forms and curricula vitae (CVs).

Continued reliance on reference material – due in part to convenience and low cost – suggests that researchers should nonetheless be looking for ways of improving validity (Shackleton & Newell, 1997; Smith & George, 1992). Smith and George (1992) note the importance of the point-to-point correspondence model for obtaining and using reference material, whereby references are sought on a criterion-specific basis.

Others argue for structuring references in the form of systematic ratings of 'personality' (for example, supervisor ratings), which have been shown to increase the predictive validity of reference checks (for example, Mount, Barrick, & Strauss, 1994). However, studies like these are often conducted using hypothetical profiles rather than actual job resumes, which produce very different kinds of judgements. For instance, Fritzsche and Brannick (2002) found that judgements of hypothetical profiles were more favourable, predictable and consistent than judgements of actual CVs. When judging actual CVs, assessors may place more weight on negative information and/or whatever is salient (that is, ratings are highly unreliable). Judging actual CVs is also far more complex.

Some say that the difficulty with securing valid references and CVs is perhaps more to do with the lack of theory guiding their use. Bright and Hutton (2000) found that CVs written in the form of competency statements were more likely to be associated with being selected for interview, suggesting that selectors pay particular attention to information about what the applicant can do from the language they use. There is clearly scope for much more research on how CV information is used and in what form it is most valid.

### Graphology

Graphology involves evaluating the character of individuals from samples of their handwriting. Despite the extremely low criterion-related validity of the characters identified from handwriting analysis, graphological means of personnel assessment are popular in France (Anderson & Shackleton, 1996). Rafaeli and Klimoski (1983) found that whilst graphologists tend to agree fairly well amongst each other on their character assessments of particular people, their judgements do not tally well with those made by those who know the individual well, like supervisors. Given that peer and supervisor evaluations are fairly good predictors of performance at work (for example, Gaugler, Rosenthal, Thornton & Bentson, 1987), these findings somewhat undermine the credibility of graphologists as valid assessors of character.

More damning are the findings obtained by Ben-Shakhar et al. (1986), who in one study presented graphologists with eight employment categories coupled with the scripts of 40 successful professionals. The results were no better than a randomized arrangement would have obtained. It is also important to note that graphology is commonly (and across widely different cultures) likely to be perceived as unfair (Moscoso & Salgado, 2004).

## Interviews

The use of interviews continues unabated. Keenan (1995) reported that all 536 organizations in his UK sample used interviews – either alone or as part of a multiple assessment procedure. McDaniel, Whetzel, Schmidt and Maurer (1994: 599) define the interview as a 'procedure designed to predict future job performance on the basis of applicants' oral responses to oral enquiries'. Guion (1998), however, cautions against this generic definition because it assumes that interviews are monolithic entities like tests. There are many different forms of interview with some achieving predictive validity coefficients comparable to ability tests (for example, situational interviews). Moreover, different types of interview (for example, structured/unstructured, conventional/behaviour-based) may assess very different competences and skills (Huffcutt, Conway, Roth, & Stone, 2001; Moscoso, 2000).

The clearest boundary can be drawn between the traditional unstructured and more structured forms of interview (for example, criterion-based behavioural interviewing, situational interviewing) (Salgado, 1999). Traditionally, interviews are used merely to form a global impression about applicant job suitability including whether they would 'fit in'. In the typical 'unstructured' interview, much time is spent telling the applicant about the job and organization and getting a feel for the person, rather than asking them job-related questions (Porteous, 1997). Research has consistently confirmed that the low reliability and validity of the traditional interview might be due to a lack of standardization when eliciting and interpreting applicant information (for example, Mayfield, 1964; Ulrich and Trumbo, 1965; Wright, 1969).

By contrast, structured interviews (see Moscoso, 2000 for a review) involve a series of job-related questions with pre-determined answers consistently applied across all interviews for a particular job (that is, standardization of questions, question sequence, interview length, and so on). Indeed, meta-analyses show that significant improvements in validity can be gained by *structuring* the interview (McDaniel et al., 1994; Moscoso, 2000). The situational interview is an example of a highly structured interview format that has consistently yielded figures indicating a high predictive validity.

For example, Salgado (1999) reports an average (corrected) coefficient of 0.50 (see also Schmidt & Hunter, 1998, whose meta-analysis yielded a coefficient of 0.51 for structured interviews generally; Example Box 1.1).

Latham and Saari (1984) obtained initial evidence for the high validity of the situational interview in two studies. One, using a sample of clerical staff, showed that the data derived from interviews was independently verifiable through observation by supervisors and peers. The other involved 349 entry-level utility people in a news print mill and confirmed that situational interviews were significantly correlated with performance on the job. Such evidence demonstrates the discriminative power achieved by a close correspondence between selection criteria and job performance criteria, as well as the reliability of behaviour-based scoring techniques. However, not everyone speaks highly of the situational interview (Gabris & Rock, 1991).

---

### Example Box 1.1

### The situational interview

The situational interview (Latham, Saari, Russell, & Campion, 1980) assumes that intentions and behaviour are related. A job analysis using the critical incident technique (CIT) identifies the behaviours critical to effective performance on the job. This is then translated into a question about a hypothetical but job-relevant situation. A scoring guide is developed for evaluating an interviewee's response to each question by providing exemplars of behavioural responses to that question. An example of a situational question taken from Latham and Saari (1984: 571) is as follows:

> For the past week you have been consistently getting the jobs that are the most time-consuming (for example, poor handwriting, complex statistical work). You know its nobody's fault because you have been taking the jobs in priority order. You have just picked your fourth job of the day and it's another 'loser'. What would you do?

Interviewees offer unstructured responses that are then scored against benchmark answers. The benchmark answers for the example question are: 1 = Thumb through the pile and take another job (poor); 3 = Complain but do the job anyway (average); and 5 = Take the job without complaining and do it (good).

---

Interestingly, research also shows that board interviews involving multiple raters of the same set of applicants are no more valid than comparably structured one-to-one interviews, despite their considerably higher administrative costs (Conway, Jako, & Goodman, 1995). Recently, it has been suggested that previous research involving the aggregation of scores across individual raters does not do justice to the validity of individual ratings from each member of the panel (Herriot, 2003). This would imply that it is perhaps better to obtain individual ratings from panel members before discussion rather than asking them to aggregate their ratings into one overall consensual score.

In other words, the process of discussion in itself can substantially distort the consensual score through conformity and polarization effects. Herriott is surprised that none of the group literature has been sourced as the basis for understanding how collective decisions are made either in panel interview or assessment centre contexts (see also Lievens & Klimoski, 2001). The limited research that has been conducted suggests that assessors are sometimes reluctant to share information that could otherwise be crucial to selection decisions, and that sometimes there is an undue focus in discussion on the negative. In the Netherlands, Zaal (1998) says that this problem of distortion in post-assessment centre 'wash up' sessions is overcome by using external advisors who are usually psychologists.

---

### Example Box 1.2

#### The behavioural description interview

The behavioural description interview (BDI) is a variant of the situational interview (Janz, 1982). However, whereas the situational interview invites applicants to respond to questions in the light of how they *might* behave, the BDI requires examination of how the applicant *actually behaved* in the past when encountering similar incidents (assuming that past behaviour predicts future behaviour). Janz (1982) showed that the BDI could obtain validity coefficients of 0.54, on a par with the situational interview. However, recent reviews cite lower figures than this. For instance Salgado (1999) reports an average validity coefficient for the BDI of 0.39 (compared with 0.50 for the situational interview).

---

Whilst 'it is generally recognized that structured interviews are preferable to informal ones, ... no consensus exists about *how much* structure is needed' (Daniel & Valencia, 1991: 128). There are potentially many different degrees of interview structure, though researchers have tended to focus on only the two extremes (structured, unstructured) in their validity studies. Huffcutt and Arthur (1994) examined the findings from 114 different studies involving interviews for entry-level jobs, and broke the interview structure down into four different levels. Their findings strongly showed that interview validity systematically increases with increased structure, but that there is a point at which additional structure yields little or no incremental validity.

McDaniel et al. (1994) proposed that an important way forward in interview research is to ascertain what exactly it is that interviews are measuring. They suggest that, like paper-and-pencil tests, selection interviews may tap different kinds of construct (for example, interpersonal sensitivity and competence, verbal ability, motivation). Many studies have found that ratings derived from structured interviews correlate highly with scores on ability tests (for example, Ree & Carretta, 1996). It is now generally accepted that some 'ability' and/or 'knowledge' component is being accessed by the structured interview (for example, Robertson & Smith, 2001; Moscoso, 2000). On the other hand, figures such as that reported by Schmidt and Hunter (1998) of 0.63 for a combined selection method involving structured interviews and cognitive ability tests, suggest that the former is also adding some 'incremental' validity (that is, explanatory power not accounted for by ability or related constructs).

Some have suggested that interviews are nothing more than tests of social skill. However, Schmidt and Hunter (1998) say that interviews measure a mixed bag of experience, ability, and personality (especially conscientiousness). The answer may hinge in part on the nature of the job. For example, the job may require considerable face-to-face contact (for example, sales clerks), hence the interview can be used as a means of assessing the critical social skills needed for this. Other jobs (for example, pilot) may be more heavily dependent on cognitive and psychomotor skills (Schuler, 1989). Robertson and Smith (2001) advocate that more research should be conducted on the role of intentions, goals and expectancies and other similarly future-oriented variables in the selection interview, all of which are known predictors of work behaviour. Raising some caution to this, however, are the substantially lower validity figures reported for the use of 'future-oriented' questions in the situational interview (0.39) than for 'past-oriented' questions (0.51) (Robertson & Smith, 2001).

Schuler's (1989) multi-modal approach to interviews openly acknowledges that different components of an interview serve different functions. He advocates the use of the interview as a forum in which to pose situational questions, to investigate self-presentation, to obtain biographical data, and to ask vocational questions. As cautioned by Van Iddekinge, Raymark, Eidson and Attenweiler (2003), it is inappropriate in this instance to talk about 'the construct-validity' of interviews, as each component will tap different forms of evidence.

In practice, there is tension between increasing structure (that is, to enhance validity) and maintaining good public relations (that is, avoiding adverse reaction). Whilst the unstructured interview may be charged with being overly personal, the highly structured interview may create adverse reaction because it is perceived as 'depersonalizing'. Overall, applicants demonstrate a distinct preference for the unstructured over the structured interview (for example, Hough & Oswald, 2000). Also, the less structured the interview, the more symbolic opportunity there is for the applicant to get a feel for the organization and its culture (via the interviewer), enabling more realistic acceptance decisions (for example, Anderson, 2001; Herriot, 2003). Selectors may also prefer to use a less structured style affording them more autonomy and ownership.

The public relations issue also arises in association with the increasingly popular telephone interview. Silvester and colleagues caution against assuming that telephone interviews are more convenient substitutes for the face-to-face interview. In their research, those interviewed by telephone received significantly *lower* ratings than those interviewed face-to-face and perceived themselves to be disadvantaged by it (Silvester, Anderson, Haddleton, Cunningham-Snell, & Gibb, 2001). It was speculated that this finding is due to a heightened focus of selectors on *what* is said rather than *the way* it is said by interviewees. In support of this, Silvester and Anderson (2003) found that personal attributions of success (from which can be inferred a sense of responsibility) were associated with higher ratings only for applicants who were interviewed by telephone rather than conventionally. Such findings suggest that using the telephone creates a different *interpersonal dynamic* that must be taken into consideration in the selection decision.

### Biodata

Biodata refers to *biographical information,* or descriptions of individuals' life histories using a retrospective, quasi-longitudinal, self-report format (see Drakeley, 1989 for examples of biodata forms). The technique evolved from Goldsmith's 'weighted application blank' (WAB) (Furnham, 1997: 177–180, for a review). Goldsmith showed how success at selling life insurance could be predicted from certain biographical information (for example, aged 30–40, 12 years' education, sales experience).

Nowadays biodata forms typically comprise multiple-choice items assessing factual (demographic information, work experiences) and sometimes also attitudinal (interests, motivations, expectations) factors (Study Box 1.5). These items are often referred to as 'hard' and 'soft' items respectively, in that the former are potentially verifiable whereas the latter are not (Drakeley, 1989: 440).

---

**Study Box 1.5**

### Taxonomy of biodata items

Asher's (1972) eight dimensions are commonly used as the basis for constructing items.

- *External Events* (for example, 'What kinds of sporting activities did you engage in at school?') versus *internal* cognition/feelings (for example, 'How did you feel about taking on the role of team captain?')
- *What one* has *done* (for example, 'How *did you* deal with parental criticism?') versus *what one is inclined to do* (for example, 'How *would you* deal with a friend who had betrayed your trust?').
- *Domain specific* (for example, 'As a child did you paint much?') versus *general* (for example, 'What kinds of things did you tend to get involved in as a child?').
- *Factual* (for example, 'At what age did you start nursery school?') versus *evaluated events* (for example, 'What do you think you gained from your nursery education?').
- *What one remembers well* (for example, 'When did you learn to swim?') versus *what one speculates about* (for example, 'If you had had the opportunity, do you think that you would have … ?')
- *Actual* (for example, 'What kind of science projects did you do at school?') versus *hypothetical* behaviour (for example, 'If you had been encouraged to pursue a science route at school do you think you would have enjoyed it?')
- *Past* (for example, 'What grades did you get in your final year exams?') versus *future* (for example, 'What grades do you think you will get in your final year exams?')
- *Verifiable items* (for example, 'Who was your last employer?') versus *non-verifiable items* (for example, 'How did you get on with your colleagues/peers?').

*(Continued)*

> ### Study Box 1.5   Continued
>
> It is debatable whether these dimensions refer to distinct forms of item content (Stokes & Reddy, 1992). Typically, item construction is pragmatic, with reference to sources like the 'catalogue of life history items' (Glennon, Albright, & Owens, 1966) as opposed to systematic research. Mumford and Stokes (1992) advise that the first step is to specify precisely the criterion of interest and then work back to identify items that may discriminate between successful and unsuccessful people against that criterion.

Retest reliability for biodata is high even after five years, especially for hard items (pertaining to a discrete verifiable behaviour) issued in a multiple-choice format (Mumford & Stokes, 1992). Ironically though, it is the 'soft' items that may have the most predictive power. Hunter and Hunter (1984) obtained a coefficient of 0.37 for biodata generally with respect to overall job performance. Subsequent findings confirm this picture, with coefficients ranging from 0.25 to 0.38 (Stokes & Reddy, 1992). Russell, Mattson, Devlin and Atwater (1990) amassed evidence suggesting that the predictive power of biodata scales is attributed to them being highly pertinent to job performance.

Opinion is divided, however, about the ultimate value of all types of biodata methods, particularly empirically keyed biographical data scales comprising only those items that discriminate between people against a criterion (Stokes & Reddy, 1992). This approach has been criticized for being situation specific rather than facilitating generalization (Schmidt & Hunter, 1998). Moreover, empirically keyed formats are time-consuming and labour-intensive to administer, score and interpret (Furnham, 1997).

Rothstein, Erwin, Schmidt, Owens & Sparks (1990) claim that biodata pioneers intended that it *should* be potentially generalizable (for example, Levine & Zachert, 1951). They constructed an item pool tapping two 'generalizable' constructs: self-concept evaluation and work value orientation. Both constructs yielded highly reliable and valid findings across 79 organizations. Thus items selected on conceptual as well as on empirical grounds have generalizability potential (Carlson, Scullen, Schmidt, Rothstein, & Erwin, 1999).

However, evidence suggests that there is shrinkage of validity over time, due to changes in policy, practice and societal attitudes, and that biodata forms need to be continually revalidated. The 'shelf life' is said to be around three to five years (Drakeley, 1989: 451). A charge of cultural relativity has also been made, and that a biodata key developed within one cultural and social group is unlikely to be valid for another group against the same criteria unless the developmental trajectories of individuals are the same (Dalessio, Crosby & McManus, 1996). Others like Rothstein et al. (1990) find little evidence for differential validity as a function of ethnic group membership. Likewise, evidence for the moderating impact of gender on the validity of biodata is mixed (Bliesener, 1996). The advantages and disadvantages of biodata are comprehensively reviewed by Furnham (1997: 186–187).

Contemporary research on biodata centres on the debate about whether it assesses anything over and above cognitive ability, personality and vocational interest (Study Box 1.6). There is growing evidence, however, for the incremental validity of 'biodata analogues' of personality constructs (for example, Mount, Witt, & Barrick, 2000). Notwithstanding this, it is generally agreed that the use of biodata needs to be more theoretically inspired. Mael and Ashforth (1995), for example, used social identity theory to investigate the extent to which biographical data predisposed new recruits to identify with the US Army. Biodata correlates of organizational identification ($N = 2535$ male recruits) were: pursuit of outdoor activities; a dependable, non-delinquent lifestyle; preference for group attachments; and diligent involvement in intellectual pastimes. This biodata analogue of identification was a strong predictor of attrition from the US Army over a 24-month period.

---

### Study Box 1.6

#### Vocational interest 'analogues'

Wilkinson (1997) constructed a biodata inventory with reference to the vocational interest literature. Biodata factors significantly predicted each of Holland's (1973) six vocational types (Chapter 3, Part 2). For example, the biography of someone who has 'realistic' vocational interests is characterized by maturity, low educational achievement, numerical/mathematical orientation, social/artistic and creative, non-professional parents, and male. The findings suggest that differences in vocational interest indicate different life experiences, not different effects of the same life experiences. These findings also confirm the analogue potential of biodata and demonstrate that validity generalization is possible (across differences in gender, age, occupation and situation) given a carefully defined and appropriate criterion, and a relevant bank of questions.

---

One potential route to conceptualization is offered by the 'ecology model' which enables 'causal influence and developmental markers' to be 'systematically specified' (Stokes & Reddy, 1992: 294). Stokes and Reddy (1992) report that many adolescent subgroups identifiable from biodata items follow clearly defined 'paths' into adulthood (that is, *continuity* in personality, interests and goals). Discontinuity could be traced to intervening life experiences (for example, failure to get an aspired-to job).

The ecology model suggests that development is a process whereby individuals bring their past to all situations, including all intellectual, personality and social resources. Time and energy are limited resources so individuals make choices about what to do and how to do it based on what has worked before (for example, via 'filtering' and 'choice' mechanisms). Differential characteristics emerge and are maintained by the life choices people make. The choices people make thus begin to form *developmental trajectories* that can be predicted from past patterns of activity and resources.

However, the construct and predictive validity of particular developmental trajectories has yet to be determined. Moreover, Drakeley (1989: 447) has pointed out that the 'person classification' approach inherent to the model is 'too general to account adequately for the relationship between biodata predictors and specific job criteria'. Drakeley (1989) also criticizes the model for being derived from work primarily involving 'classification' of North American university students and thus not generalizable across the general population.

## Psychometric Tests

A test can be defined as a standardized measure of aptitude, knowledge, ability or performance administered and scored using fixed rules and procedures. A *psychological* test measures any kind of psychological phenomenon and may or may not have been developed using 'psychometric' principles. A *psychometric* test is constructed in accordance with various rules, most of them statistical. All psychometric tests are scaled using a finely graded numerical system and a set of statistical formulae to ensure reliability and validity.

Most psychometric tests are also norm-referenced such that the range and distribution of scores obtained for many different types of sample (graduates, managerial, manual, professional) provide group-specific norms against which to compare an individual's score. The scores for a managerial applicant, for example, are examined with reference to the most closely matching set of norms (that is, managerial). The norm-referenced nature of psychometric tests is critical to their practical use. Reference to norms can also demonstrate whether the test is 'transportable' from one context to another. For example, it is only fairly recently that UK norms for the well-known and much-used US-developed 16 Personality Factors Test (16PF) have become available.

All psychometric tests should be developed on the basis of hypotheses about the nature of various psychological constructs. However, there are many different theoretical angles adopted in both the ability and personality domain, making it difficult to compare the relative viability of different tests. Some tests are more theoretically based than others, so the constructs on which they are built vary in clarity and substance.

### Cognitive ability tests

Cognitive ability tests (CATs) can be classified somewhat arbitrarily as achievement tests, specific aptitude tests and intelligence tests (Study Box 1.7). An important distinction needs to be made, however, between GMA (all-encompassing 'intelligence') and specific abilities (domain specific aptitudes and abilities). Schmidt (2002) defines GMA as any measure that combines two, three or more specific aptitudes or any measure that includes a variety of items across a range of ability domains (for example, visual, verbal, spatial). GMA is found to be consistently high on criterion-related validity for a whole range of jobs (supervisory, managerial and professional) and occupations (in the UK, USA and across the European Community (EC)), attaining validities on average around 0.53 (Schmidt & Hunter, 1998; for the EC data, see Salgado et al., 2003).

It is also beyond dispute now that 'weighted combinations of specific aptitudes tailored to individual jobs do not predict job performance better than general mental ability ("g") alone' (Schmidt & Hunter, 2004).

From their now classic review of hundreds of studies, Hunter and Hunter (1984: 80) stated unequivocally that 'there is no job for which cognitive ability does not predict training success … and job proficiency'. Twenty years on, this conclusion has been consistently verified (Robertson & Smith, 2001; Salgado, 1999; Salgado et al., 2003). Schmidt and Hunter (2004) have in fact begun to develop a theory of job performance that explicates the central role of general mental ability or 'g' in the workplace. Literally 100 years ago, Spearman (1904) said as much and, intuitively, it makes everyday sense (see, for example, Schularios & Lockyer (1999) on lay models of job performance).

---

## Study Box 1.7

### Cognitive ability tests

#### *Achievement tests*

Achievement tests tap current knowledge or proficiency in a particular ability domain, usually as a function of education or training. Examples include GCSEs (ordinary and advanced), National Vocational Qualifications, Bachelor of Arts/ Science, and professional examinations.

#### *Specific aptitude tests*

Aptitude tests look at what one is capable of doing in the future, usually in specific domains like mechanical aptitude, verbal and numerical aptitude and psychomotor ability. In practice, it is difficult to distinguish between achievement and aptitude. Examples include the Differential Aptitude Test (DAT), the Computer Aptitude Battery and The General Clerical Test.

#### *Intelligence tests*

These tests tap GMA indicative of overall capability for acquiring and using knowledge. Examples include omnibus tests like the NFER Nelson Tests of General Ability and the Ravens Progressive Matrices. The use of intelligence testing has generated much social and political debate, at the centre of which is the question of what exactly 'intelligence' is (Schmidt & Hunter, 2004).

---

The idea nonetheless of using only an ability test score to select someone is highly controversial, underpinned by moral as well as legal debate (Murphy, Cronin & Tam, 2003). For years it has been consistently argued that ability testing does *not* produce differentially unfair predictions for different groups of people (that is, ability testing is more or less equally accurate in discriminating ability within as well as across different groups). Recently, however, there are findings suggesting that ability testing is *unfair* to minority groups, with over 60 percent of Blacks (relative to 10 percent of

Whites) likely to be *incorrectly rejected* for a job (Chung-Yan & Cranshaw, 2002; see below). This finding is set to cast the legal and moral debate into a completely different landscape.

Some maintain that many jobs, especially managerial jobs, presuppose 'tacit' knowledge or action-oriented 'know how' rather than ability per se (Sternberg & Wagner, 1995), 'emotional intelligence' (ability to perceive, understand and manage emotion) (Goleman, 1996) and at least some level of commitment (Meyer & Allen, 1997). The importance of tacit knowledge is said to be especially important to nursing, and has been demonstrated to explain more variance in performance on certain nursing tasks than 'explicit' formal knowledge (for example, Herbig, Bussing, & Ewert, 2001).

On the other hand, reviews show that tests of tacit knowledge, emotional intelligence and 'practical' intelligence do not produce better predictive validities than CATs; nor do they add any unique incremental validity (Salgado, 1999). For instance, tacit knowledge (or practical intelligence) is typically measured using problem-solving tasks (for example, using a 'situational inventory') (Motowidlo & Tippins, 1993), performance on which is consistently found to be highly correlated with 'g' (McDaniel et al., 1997). It is now commonly said that tacit knowledge and practical intelligence are just different ways of referring to 'job knowledge' (Schmidt & Hunter, 1993). It is also difficult to ignore the reality of increased *cognitive demand* in today's technologically complex, 'more for less', fast-paced/'just in time', consumer-oriented economic world. Findings derived from construct validation research, involving interviews and assessment centres in particular, suggest that irrespective of what these methods intend to assess (criterion-based dimensions), GMA can account for substantial proportions of variance in the overall applicant rating (for example, Collins, Schmidt, Sanchez-Ku, Thomas, McDaniel & Le, 2003; Moscoso, 2000). Thus, it seems that we cannot really get away from the fact that GMA does matter to performance, perhaps more than we care to realize.

In conclusion, the 'fact' that GMA is a robust, generalizable predictor of performance must be balanced with deeper psychological considerations when making decisions about whether to use CATs as part of a selection process (Rynes & Cable, 2003). For instance, recruiters and applicants are consistently found to have little faith in CATs, which may evoke negative applicant reactions (for example, evaluation apprehension, perceived job irrelevance) (Klingner & Schuler, 2004). Added to this are recent findings indicating the potential for adverse impact by systematically excluding particular groups of applicants from valid consideration (Chung-Yan & Cranshaw, 2002). This has prompted some to develop *latent* intelligence tests presented as work samples (for example, Klingner & Schuler, 2004). These are potentially costly to develop because they 'sample' work pertinent to particular occupational groups or jobs. Face-valid intelligence test hybrids of this kind, however, may signal one constructive way forward on the issue of how to balance efficiency needs with legal imperatives and psychological concerns.

One suggestion is that school/college grades could constitute a form of evidence about cognitive ability. Predictive validity coefficients of 0.32 have been obtained against job performance for grade information (for example, Roth, BeVier, Switzer, & Schippmann, 1996). However, some applicants would object to this on grounds that it pins them too much to their past, and does not reflect their current ability. Using grades as a substitute for CATs could thus raise even more questions and challenges than answers.

## Personality inventories

Whilst there are many (sometimes wildly) different perspectives on personality (Pervin, 1997), selection science assumes that personality is comprised of stable traits and dispositions. There are many different types of personality measure, each assuming a certain number of traits and trait structures. Cattell's (1965) work led to the development of the now renowned 16PF test (Cattell, Eber & Tatsuoka, 1970), one of the most widely used measure of personality in the occupational context (Brindle & Ridgeway, 1995). A contrary view is provided by the Eysenck Personality Questionnaire (EPQ; Eysenck, 1982) that assumes a *three-factor* personality model: extroversion/introversion, neuroticism/stability, and psychoticism. The proposed psycho-neurological basis of the EPQ has been validated mainly using clinical samples.

The contemporary view is that there are five super-ordinate trait dimensions (the so-called 'big five') on which all people can be described (Costa & McCrae, 1990): extroversion, agreeableness, conscientiousness, emotional stability and openness to experience (or intellect). The NEO-PI is the test of this model, although other operational formats have since also been advocated (Rust, 1999). Many of the tests used by companies for selection purposes have been developed for commercial purposes. The Occupational Personality Questionnaire (OPQ) (Saville, Holdsworth, Nyfield, Cramp, & Mabey, 1984) is one such tool. The OPQ is second to the 16PF in popularity for occupational testing (Brindle & Ridgeway, 1995), although the rapidly growing interest in, and use of, the Hogan Personality Inventory (HPI) is set to override this (Impara, Plake & Spies, 2004). HPI is specifically designed to predict organizational success by providing 'a comprehensive evaluation of a person's strengths and shortcomings with regard to social and occupational goals' (Hogan & Hogan, 1995). The HPI is based on the Big Five model (its primary scales measuring: even tempered, ambitious, sociable, agreeable, conforming, inquisitive, and continuous learning), and has been extensively validated. Its occupational scales measure service orientation, stress tolerance, sales potential, clerical potential, managerial potential and reliability.

Ferguson, Payne and Anderson (1994: 224) argue that the onus is on the test publisher 'to provide a theoretical validation of their measures and to test a number of competing structural hypotheses underlying their scales'.

A less well known, hitherto 'hidden' *non-commercial* inventory called the Professional Personality Questionnaire (PPQ) has also been recently uncovered. The PPQ was developed for occupational purposes by the late Paul Kline and one of his PhD students (Kline & Lapham, 1992). Based on the Big Five model, the dimensions assessed are: insecurity versus confidence, conscientiousness versus carelessness, introversion versus extraversion, tough versus tender minded, and conventional versus unconventional. The measure also includes a scale assessing inaccuracy and inconsistency in responding (invalidity scale).

In the past, the use of personality tests for occupational selection has been heavily attacked. For example, Blinkhorn and Johnson (1990) argued that using personality tests can delude people into assuming they offer a comprehensive picture of a person, and also 'overly objectify' the person. The anti-personality debate was also fuelled by findings such as those obtained by Schmitt, Gooding, Noe and Kirsch (1984), revealing average validities of only 0.15 (derived from a meta-analysis of 62 studies) for the relationship between personality and performance. Whilst others have since obtained slightly more promising findings, few until recently would dispute the conclusion that non-work related selection tools are relatively poor predictors of job success relative to structured interviews and ability tests and should be treated with caution (Robertson & Smith, 2001).

However, renewed interest in personality testing has been spawned by findings demonstrating that the more rational the use of personality tests in selection, the greater their criterion-related validity. For instance, Tett and Guterman (2000) obtained an average corrected validity of 0.24 for studies testing a priori hypotheses about associations between personality and job criteria. Consistent with this, Barrick and Mount (1991) obtained a corrected average validity of 0.22 for 'conscientiousness' across five occupational samples (professionals, police, managers, skilled/semi-skilled, and sales), and against three criteria (job proficiency, training proficiency and personnel data).

Recent meta-analyses point to an even higher predictive validity for 'conscientiousness' of around 0.30 (for example, Schmidt & Hunter, 1998). Ones and Viswesvaran (1996) argue that this finding is not surprising really in that the conscientious person is more likely to spend time on assigned tasks, acquire greater job knowledge, set goals autonomously and persist in achieving them, go beyond role requirements and avoid being counterproductive. Others add that traits like conscientiousness (coupled with integrity, see below) predict in particular the more contextual and motivational aspects of performance extremely well (for example, Fisher & Boyle, 1997). While, indeed, intentional distortion does and can occur in item responding, it has no consequential impact on validity (Salgado, 2003). Most would nevertheless advocate the use of some kind of 'social desirability' screening measure, to minimize distortion likelihood.

Empirical debate now centres more on whether broad or narrow measures of personality are most appropriate, rather than whether they should be used at all. Some like Ones and Viswesvaran (1996) advocate a 'broad' approach (for example, the Big Five or similar) on theoretical grounds, whilst others like Schneider, Hough and Dunnette (1996) advocate a more criterion-specific approach (Study Box 1.8). Salgado (1999) takes a more pragmatic line in arguing that the final choice should depend on exactly what is being predicted.

## Study Box 1.8

### The trait activation model

Tett and colleagues (Tett & Guterman, 2000; Tett & Burnett, 2003; Tett, Steele, & Beauregard, 2003) have evolved what they call a 'trait activation' model of selection methods. They describe different selection methods as affording different opportunities for trait expression. To the extent that different methods cue the same trait-relevant behaviours, there will be cross-method consistency in assessor ratings. The challenge for selectors is to be able to describe the situational cues of different selection methods a priori. For example, an in-tray exercise requiring close attention to detail will cue conscientiousness, whilst a group discussion exercise may cue extroversion.

Caution is due nonetheless in that even the highest obtained validities for personality tests are low, relative to those obtained by other tools, suggesting they should therefore only be used on rational (a priori) grounds and in combination with other methods (Hurtz & Donovan, 2000). Moreover, a recent meta-analysis published by Salgado (2003) has demonstrated that the predictive power of 'conscientiousness' is heavily dependent on the type of measure used. Synthesizing findings from across Europe as well as the USA, Salgado obtained a corrected criterion validity for conscientiousness of only 0.18 when measured using non five-factor (non-FFM) means of personality assessment, compared with 0.28 across studies using five-factor (FFM) measures. Salgado attributes this to the lower construct validity of the non-FFM relative to the FFM measures. There is also some evidence for differential group validities in the personality domain for male and female employees (Baron & Janman, 1996). Others have found significant criterion-related personality differentials across members of different socio-economic classes and ethnic backgrounds (Salgado, 1999). These findings advise both gender and cultural sensitivity when using personality descriptors as a basis for selection.

Other less conventional methods of personality assessment are also available, including the so-called projective test (Study Box 1.9).

---

### Study Box 1.9

**Alternative tests of personality**

#### *Objective personality tests*

Cattell (1965) constructed miniature behavioural situations affording observation of responses to particular stimuli (for example, speed of reaction). Thus, so-called *objective* personality tests do not rely on self-report and applicants are not aware of the relationship between their behaviour and the personality characteristics being measured.

#### *Projective Tests*

Projective tests involve the completion of a structured task that affords applicants the opportunity to 'project' themselves into it without them knowing. This rules out the influence of self-presentational strategies and does not require the applicant to be articulate. For instance, the *sentence completion process* involves presenting people with a sentence fragment to complete. The content of the fragment can be altered to fit occupational, clinical and other requirements (for example, 'When I do not get results …', 'My biggest asset …' and 'Sometimes I worry about …'). A widely used 'sentence completion' measure in personnel selection is the Miner Sentence Completion (MSC) scale (Miner, 1964). Carson and Gilliard (1993) reviewed strong evidence for the construct validity of the MSC scale in an occupational setting as a measure of 'motivation to manage'. This was positively correlated with 'conscientiousness', 'extroversion' and managerial performance ratings.

## Integrity testing

Integrity testing concerns the assessment of honesty, and ultimately the forecasting of employee dishonesty (Camara & Schneider, 1995). There are three types of integrity testing: overt measures of integrity, personality-oriented methods, and clinical measures like the 'galvanic skin response', an indicator of increased physiological arousal. Overt integrity tests may deal with attitudes towards theft and other forms of dishonesty, including admissions of theft and other illegal activity. Questions like, 'If you knew that your best friend had taken small change out of the till, what would you do?' are then validated against a broad range of criteria like absenteeism, sabotage, turnover and theft. Jones, Joy, Werner and Orbon (1991) found that 23 percent of employees hired by a company scored below the pre-determined cut-off point on an 'honesty' test; 44 percent of these were indeed found to be *counter-productive employees*. The issue of theft measurement is by definition more problematic. It is estimated that on average 30 to 44 percent of all employees engage in theft of some kind in the workplace. In practice, only 3 to 5 percent of dishonest employees are ever detected (Jones, Slora & Boye, 1990).

Similar problems of measurement are found when attempting to validate personality-based measures of integrity that rely on the empirical keying of standard personality test items against counter-productivity criteria (that is, theft, absenteeism, poor performance, sabotage). High validity coefficients have been reported for criteria based on self-report, but not for criteria like 'detected theft' (Sackett & Harris, 1984). There are many disagreements about the value of integrity testing, and also its ethical status. Some argue that the construct of integrity is vague and ill-defined, and that there is no compelling evidence for its criterion-related validity (Camara & Schneider, 1995). Others argue that it may be inextricably linked with 'conscientiousness' (for example, Ones & Viswesvaran, 1996).

Camara and Schneider (1995) fear that integrity testing might signal an unacceptable breach of ethical standards. Other concerns include misclassification, high selection thresholds and adverse impact on applicants screened out by integrity test results, coupled with the fact that anyone can use them. By contrast, Ones, Viswesvaran and Schmidt (1995) point to good construct and criterion validities, suggesting promising results that should not be ignored. Indeed, recent meta-analyses put the predictive validity coefficients at around 0.41 (for example, Schmidt & Hunter, 1998). Moreover, there is growing evidence for the incremental validity of personality-based integrity testing over 'g', together achieving a validity coefficient as high as 0.65 (Robertson & Smith, 2001).

## Computer-assisted testing

In the past, most tests involved 'paper-and-pencil', with the occasional test of actual performance (for example, manual dexterity). It is now commonplace to computerize test administration and also (more controversially) test interpretation. New types of tests have also been developed that capitalize on software and hardware advances within the information technology (IT) industry and are compatible with psychometric theory (for example, adaptive testing). For example, it is possible to make tests dynamic: a test item can move, rotate, change, and so on, in real time. Moreover, tests can also permit the analysis of the *processes* underpinning item response (Bartram, 2001).

Comprehensive reviews of the computer-assisted testing literature all concur that computerized tests correlate highly with their traditional paper and pencil equivalents, and are generally as valid (Bartram, 2001). However, there are several issues to consider before computer-assisted testing can be considered satisfactory in psychometric terms. These are the issues of:

- *equivalence* – ensuring reliability and validity of computer-based tests is the same as for the equivalent paper-based version;
- *interpretation* – use of computers to provide immediate feedback lays open the possibility of misdirection, misuse and mistaken decisions;
- *ethicality* – transcending national boundaries and guidelines brings with it the danger of unrestricted, under-informed and dangerous pseudo-psychometric tools to be instantly sold and transported to an unprotected audience.

In short, the advent of technology-led testing has its dark side. Who is ensuring that standards are maintained? How do you counter the unwarranted impression of objectivity and accuracy ascribed to computers? How do you stop the encouragement of the transfer of the practitioner's identity from skilled interpreter to mere technician?

## Assessment Centres

Assessment centres have long been both the US and European method of choice in the government sector (Zaal, 1998), but have recently become popular in the business sector for assessing suitability across a whole range of jobs. The key features of an assessment centre are that they are designed to produce behavioural evidence, employ a variety of techniques for eliciting evidence, assess several applicants at once on several criteria and involve several trained assessors. This multi-method, multi-trait assessment technique has a rich military history, originally designed to identify officer potential. Nowadays assessment centres are used not only for selection, but also to aid promotion decisions, to identify management potential, to diagnose training and development needs and for human resource planning generally. Example Box 1.3 illustrates the multi-trait, multi-method principle for the selection of maintenance engineers.

---

**Example Box 1.3**

**Multi–trait, multi–method grid**

| Criteria | Method of Assessment | | | | |
|---|---|---|---|---|---|
| | Technical interview | Behavioural interview | Group discussion | Ability test | Applied test |
| Teamworking | | ? | ? | | |
| Problem solving | ? | ? | ? | ? | ? |
| Time management | | | ? | ? | ? |
| Innovation | ? | ? | | | ? |
| Technical competence | ? | | | ? | ? |
| Commercial awareness | ? | ? | | | |

*(Continued)*

---

The matrix or grid method enables practitioners to ensure that each criterion is assessed by a minimum of two exercises/tests.

### Technical interview

Evidence for the technical knowledge a maintenance engineer should possess, for example, 'What do you understand by manufacturing engineering at XXX?', 'What are the pros and cons of a just-in-time policy?'

### Behavioural interview

Evidence on prior history of work and how one would behave in certain situations. Example 'situational questions' include, 'Give me an example of any problem you have faced and tell me how you went about solving it.'

### Group discussion

Evidence on cooperation with others to achieve a common goal, and the ability to draw on and build on the contributions of others. Positive indicators include 'tries to keep involved' and 'asks for clarification from others'. Negative indicators include 'focuses attention on only one or two other members in the group', 'directive/ authoritarian style'.

### Ability test

A verbal ability test measuring ability to understand and work with verbal concepts. A numerical ability test to assess ability to reason with numbers. A spatial ability test to assess ability to visualize objects in 3D and to manipulate them mentally.

### Applied test

Applicants are asked to handle a simulated breakdown and to write a report. Problem-solving technique is observed and understanding of the processes performed is assessed.

---

### The predictive validity of assessment centres

The validity coefficients obtained for specific assessment centres vary from between –0.25 to 0.78 (Gaugler et al., 1987), suggesting much situation-specific variability in the value of the assessment centre. Indeed the reality of the assessment centre technique is that it has many different types of operational form and procedure (Sackett, 1987). Gaugler et al. (1987) cite a corrected mean coefficient (for sampling error, restriction of range, and criterion unreliability) of 0.37 (a figure since confirmed by Schmidt & Hunter, 1998). It is generally agreed that this is a low overall validity for a multi-method approach, especially given that structured interviews alone can obtain validities of up to 0.57 (Hough & Oswald, 2000; Huffcutt & Arthur, 1994). Indeed, it is consistently noted that the overall assessment rating (OAR) validity often does not exceed the validity of individual component parts of an assessment centre (for example, tests, interviews; see, for example, Jones, Herriot, Long, & Drakeley, 1991).

Higher validities are generally obtained for assessment of *potential* rather than *performance* ratings. Notably, Chan (1996) obtained a predictive validity coefficient of 0.59 for potential (and promotion) compared to only 0.06 for performance ratings. Gaugler et al. (1987) also identified other significant moderators of validity, including group composition, type and range of assessment technique and assessor training and status (manager, psychologist). All of these moderators have since been investigated in detail and are now well-established considerations to be acknowledged when designing assessment centres (Lievens & Klimoski, 2001; Zaal, 1998).

## The rating process

It has been suggested that variability in the validity of assessment centres may be due to 'process loss' – that is, data may be lost during the rating process (see Lievens & Klimoski, 2001). In their efforts to improve the validity of an otherwise well-established assessment centre (at the Admirality Interviewing Board), Jones, Herriot, Long & Drakeley (1991) hypothesized that assessors were not making the best use of assessment information. They cite findings showing that even though the assessment centre may involve ratings on up to 10 different dimensions, most assessors only use about three of these. Also, assessors can implicitly attach too much weight to the dimensions of least importance to the criterion. Moreover, if discussion is permitted amongst assessors on arriving at the overall rating, group pressures can come into play. Despite the sophistication of Jones et al.'s (1991) efforts to address these rating considerations (for instance, by reducing the number of dimensions to be considered), no improvement in overall validity was observed.

Close examination of the data by Jones et al. suggested that assessors were using different criteria to form their assessments. Klimoski and Brickner (1987) identified three potential bases on which assessors form their judgements: anticipation of how future superiors might evaluate applicants, heavy reliance on present ('in situ') and past actual performance as a predictor of future performance, and heavy reliance on information about an individual's intellectual functioning. The use of 'anticipatory' criteria may reflect areas of broad organizational concern, such as the ability to cope with professional training, leadership potential and the likelihood of meeting standards of general conduct. The use of past and present performance as a basis for judgements may reflect a preference for weighting 'samples' of behaviour (evidence of past and present behaviour) more heavily in judgements than 'signs' of potential behaviour ascertained by abstract means. Moreover, present behaviour can also be tested for consistency against verifiable records of past behaviour.

To examine the moderating effect of the assessor and the use of implicit criteria as the basis of assessment, Sagie and Magnezy (1997) compared the construct validity of assessment centre ratings made by psychologists against those made by managers. They tested a one-factor, two-factor and five-factor model of construct-validity based on assessor ratings. They found that the two-factor solution fitted the ratings of managers whilst the five-factor solution fitted the ratings of psychologists. The two-factor solution suggested that managers based their ratings on two global dimensions: performance and interpersonal skill. The five-factor solution, however, reflected all of the dimensions intended for use within the assessment centre. Sagie and Magnezy (1997) argue that this finding is a reflection of reality. In practice, managers are often required to make *integrative evaluations* of applicants, summarizing diverse information into a composite score. Psychologists, however, are more likely to use dimensions in a valid and uniquely discriminating way.

The use of 'implicit' criteria in the assessment process contributes to what is known as 'criterion contamination' (Gaugler et al., 1987: 504). Other findings are available demonstrating that assessors use only a few dimensions to derive their overall ratings and that, more often than not, overall ratings are dominated by a single factor or 'halo effect' (Sagie & Magnezy, 1997). Chan (1996), for instance, has suggested that assessors may make judgements on the basis of promotion potential, including whether they think an applicant will engage in *extra-role behaviours* (do more, and apply more effort, than is contractually required), and if not, whether they will 'perform' well on the job. This kind of basis for decision making has been termed 'policy capturing' (Schmitt, 1989), and, whilst it might increase the criterion validity of the assessment centre, it will fundamentally interfere with the 'here and now' task of finely rating performance against assessment criteria (Lievens & Klimoski, 2001; Study Box 1.10).

Findings indeed suggest that ratings for different dimensions within the same exercises are usually highly correlated (that is, low discriminant validity) whilst cross-exercise consistency across ratings of dimensions is low (Lievens & Klimoski, 2001). Moreover, when ratings are factored, a strong 'exercise' effect is observed (Robertson & Smith, 2001). This 'exercise' effect has since been the focus of much attention in assessment centre research.

In reviewing the literature on the 'exercise effect', Zaal (1998) says that we need to study the nature of exercises in detail to understand what they are measuring. The same skills, he notes, may not be manifest in the same way in different situations. However, the way in which they manifest is not entirely arbitrary either, suggesting that there are elements of cross-exercise validity. In other words, the meaning of particular behavioural dimensions or skills is not just situationally determined. Zaal (1998) cites evidence for some generalizability of particular behavioural dimensions, like communication skills, across exercises. The problem is, he adds, different situations may afford different opportunities for particular skills to be demonstrated and this may cloud the generalizability issue. Zaal contemplates the recommendation of some to use 'exercises' as the basis for rating (as a sample of work behaviour) rather than try to pin ratings down to particular behavioural dimensions (or 'signs'). This would give people an overall performance effectiveness rating for each exercise. However, Zaal argues that ratings would still be loaded highly with situational variance and does not address (merely pushes under the carpet) the need to really get to grips with the complex interaction between competencies and situations.

In short, it is clear that irrespective of the technical sophistication of the assessment centre, it may not necessarily generate the evidence intended, in part because we do not know enough about what we are trying to assess (Jones et al., 1991; Chan, 1996). Zaal (1998) suggested that the focus of rating should be exclusively on operational definitions rather than dimensions or constructs. Operational definitions may take the form of behavioural statements derived directly from job analysis. Assessment techniques or exercises should then be selected for their power to elicit the required behavioural evidence. Behaviour-based assessment methods are indeed now commonplace. Lievens and Klimoski (2001) add, however, that the exercises must afford the opportunity to actually demonstrate the required behaviours. Many exercises, they say, are selected for face validity rather than for their capacity to 'expose behaviour'. Norton and Edinger (1978) claimed, moreover, that the validity of assessment centres is based on how closely *as a whole* the exercise resembles the job in question. Accordingly, he argued for the focus on *broad* rather than specific rating criteria, consistent with what assessors are naturally inclined to do. Recent 'best practice' guidelines reiterate this advice to use fewer conceptually distinct dimensions (for example, Hough & Oswald, 2000). What these broad-based dimensions will look like exactly is unclear.

---

### Study Box 1.10

#### Models of rating in the assessment centre

##### Rational model

- *Assumptions*: Data driven, assumes people can 'attend to detailed behaviour … classify these many specific pieces of factual information into distinct categories, and to form relatively objective and accurate judgements' (Lievens & Klimoski, 2001: 90). No limits are assumed in what assessors can achieve.
- *Implications*: Assessor training for increased accuracy in rating precise behavioural indicators; heighten motivation for increased accuracy by increasing accountability for decisions made. One suggestion is to 'ipsitarize' the rating process, involving a compulsory division of ratings of different qualities of the same person to avoid halo effects (Zaal, 1998).

##### Limited capacity model

- *Assumptions*: People are not always able to meet cognitive demands of rating process – for example, behavioural flow is rapid and precise ratings are difficult to obtain, inferential leaps are required to translate behavioural ratings into dimensional ratings and for quantification.
- *Implications*: Reduce cognitive overload by limiting the number of dimensions to be rated; use behavioural checklists, increase ratio assessor/applicant, use video technology.

##### Expert model

- *Assumptions*: Professional assessors have well-established cognitive structures that guide attention, categorization, integration and recall.
- *Implications*: Use psychologist assessors, provide frame of reference training (that is, furnish people with a mental framework to help them assign behaviour to dimensions and judge performance levels).

Issues also arise from the way evidence is discussed and collated in collective rating situations. When discussing the concept of the panel interview earlier, the distinct lack of evidence on how assessors integrate 'assessment' information was noted (Lievens & Klimoski, 2001). The literature on group dynamics should throw some light on this, but surprisingly little work has been done looking at the normative structure of assessment centre teams and the dynamics of integrating evidence (Herriot, 2003).

### Content validity

Norton and Edinger (1978) say that the content validity of exercises and exercise-based ratings are more relevant to performance prediction than trait or dimension-based ratings. They argue that an assessment centre exercise is justified as job-relevant to the extent that it meets five conditions:

1  A behaviourally defined test content domain is identified (for example, in-tray exercise assessing the ability to prioritize and to balance short-term and long-term managerial considerations), which is unambiguously defined (specifying exactly what will constitute evidence for the ability to prioritize and so on), and relevant to the job.
2  A job-content domain external to the test-content domain is identified (for example, managerial job requires prioritizing on a daily basis and the ability to balance short-term and long-term considerations).
3  Qualified judges must agree that the content domain has been adequately sampled (for example, 'does the in-tray exercise elicit the exact behaviours of interest?').
4  Applicant responses must be reliably observed and evaluated ('how will performance on in-tray exercises be evaluated?').
5  Score variance must be clearly attributable to the content of the exercise rather than irrelevant sources ('how far does the in-tray enable the valid discrimination between applicants in their ability to prioritize, and so on?').

Russell and Domm (1995) conducted two field studies in which they controlled the basis for rating applicants. Criterion-related validities were indeed higher for *task-based* rather than trait-based ratings. The greater validity of exercises over dimensions is a consistent finding. McCredie and Shackleton (1994), however, note that for development purposes, ratings based on exercises or tasks alone may not be acceptable as the sole basis for giving feedback. Most people require some sort of dimension-specific feedback as a pointer for future action.

The way that applicants react to the selection process is only a recent consideration. Research shows that applicants' immediate reactions to assessment centres are consistently positive, attributing this mainly to their face validity (Lievens & Klimoski, 2001). Whilst assessment centres are costly to run (especially if they do not add explanatory power over and above the use of a single ability test and/or situational interview), they clearly do fulfil a good public relations function. In the words of de Wolff and van den Bosch (1998), they allow for some degree of implicit 'harmonisation' of individual and organizational needs and goals.

# Alternative Techniques

## Work samples

Work samples are said to be one of the most appropriate means of selection because of the 'point-to-point correspondence' between the job and the assessment scenario (Smith & George, 1992). It is an *analogous* test (as opposed to an analytical test) designed to replicate the key activities of a job. Work samples are relatively easy to construct for manual jobs (for example, bricklaying, electrical wiring), clerical jobs (for example, typing) or those involving contact with clients (for example, role play dealing with a complaint). For more managerial/intellectual type jobs work samples may be built around specific and identifiable concrete tasks (for example, writing a report, dealing with the in-tray). They can be used to assess both performance and 'trainability' potential.

A modified work sample or 'low-fidelity simulation technique' has been proposed by Motowidlo, Dunnette and Carter (1990) that elicits *hypothetical* rather than actual work behaviour. The simulation involves the presentation of descriptions of particular work scenarios, and applicants are required to indicate their most and least likely responses. Motowidlo et al. (1990) obtained correlations between work sample scores and independent on-the-job ratings ranging from 0.28 to 0.37 for 120 managers. However, this kind of work sample is said to be more appropriate to the assessment of broad management potential than of performance in any one particular task (Smith & George, 1992).

A prime example of a work sample test is the 'in-tray' exercise (Example Box 1.4). One potential problem with the use of in-tray exercises is the heavy reliance of organizations on 'off-the-shelf' packages. Porteous (1997: 131) also cautions against thinking that 'just getting someone to do something constitutes a test'. Just like any other test, a work sample needs to be carefully constructed and validated. The most valid work samples not only correspond with a particular task, but also capture some of its contextual features (Robertson & Kandola, 1982): the issue of psychological fidelity (context mapping) is just as important as physical fidelity (content mapping). How much fidelity is required remains unclear. A basic rule of thumb is to ensure that the work sample is as 'complex' and 'ambiguous' as the task itself, but the downside here is that the 'sample' cannot then be 'transferred' across jobs (unless jobs are similar). On the other hand, they provide a good source of 'realistic job preview' for the applicant (see below).

Porteous (1997) says that because reliable and valid work samples are time-consuming and costly to construct, administer and score, they are of most value when used in the last stages of a selection process. The strength of the well-designed work sample is illustrated by the findings of Palmer, Boyles, Veres and Hill (1972), who developed work simulation tests of filing and proofreading and validated them using a pencil-and-paper clerical selection test. In two validation studies (one concurrent and one predictive) the work sample tests were highly correlated with scores on the selection test, and also with supervisor ratings of performance.

---

**Example Box 1.4**

**The in-tray (in-basket) exercise**

The in-tray (or in-basket) exercise samples the typical contents of an executive's in-tray, providing the applicant with a variety of everyday problems in written form (letters, memoranda, notes, reports, telephone messages), both expected and unexpected and requiring immediate decision and action (Gill, 1979). Applicants are provided with in-tray contents under standardized conditions (instructions, company information and its organization and the role to be played) in a fixed time (about 90 minutes). During this time applicants are required to prioritize the different tasks and record their decisions and actions for the most important ones *as if they were really doing the job*.

   Schippman, Prien and Katz (1990) concluded from their exhaustive review that in-tray scores have 'moderate' (0.20–0.30) criterion-related validity. Little if any agreement exists, however, on what in-trays are measuring. Two main factors determine the content of a particular in-tray: management position and level of interruption. One practical problem is the time it takes to construct an in-tray exercise that is both relevant and representative of the task in question. The scoring of in-tray exercises is also problematic as there is no standard procedure for this.

---

### Group exercises and business simulations

The group exercise (and its variant, the business simulation) is at the heart of the assessment centre technique, allowing the observation of applicants interacting with each other (Thornton & Mueller-Hanson, 2004). The *leaderless group discussion* is an especially popular method involving applicants attempting to reach consensus on an otherwise contentious issue. Other exercises involve *assigned roles,* where applicants are each required to represent a particular point of view when, for example, competing for limited resources or arguing a case. Simulations provide examples of a more task-focused exercise in which applicants may be required to make decisions under pressure and to achieve a specified business outcome within a limited time span, under various constraints.

   Group exercises are scored by trained assessors and observers, achieving reasonable levels of inter-rater reliability. Robertson and Kandola (1982) report an uncorrected criterion validity of 0.34 for the group exercise. The difficulty in constructing any simulation is in adequately representing the particulars of the task (or task context) whilst also ensuring some standardization (cross-task validity generalization) (Thornton & Mueller-Hanson, 2004). The latter is easier to achieve for jobs like management, which involve some generic components (for example, ability to assimilate new information quickly and use it to make decisions, set priorities in the face of conflicting demands and incomplete information, and how to get a job done within minimal resources).

   Most organizations rely on 'off-the-shelf' group exercises and simulations available in the test publishing market, each standardized for a particular assessment purpose.

Baron and Janman (1996) note the scope within group exercises for wide variation in the performance of applicants, depending on group composition and the tenor of internal group dynamics. Most researchers have found that applicant reactions to group exercises and simulations are very positive, particularly those with a business-related content (Rynes & Connerley, 1993).

### Realistic job previews

The realistic job preview (RJP) exposes applicants to *representative* samples of the job (Wanous, 1973). Whilst some doubt the validity of the RJP (for example, Guzzo, Jette, & Katzell, 1985), most accept that it has validity for applicant screening (see Premack & Wanous, 1985, for a meta-analysis of 21 RJP experiments). Premack and Wanous (1985) attribute the validity of RJPs to the tempering of initial job expectations, facilitating a more balanced and realistic consideration of the job. Others argue more broadly that RJP aids work adjustment via a 'matching' process of self to job (Vandenberg & Scarpello, 1990) using Lofquist and Dawis's (1969) theory of work adjustment.

Previews can be presented on videotape, through observation and/or job shadowing. They can be structured or unstructured, intensive or extensive and either descriptive or evaluative (Wanous, 1973). The decision about how much opportunity is given for evaluation is critical, because of the risk of putting applicants off completely. It is generally agreed, however, that a balanced preview opportunity is more appropriate on ethical grounds than a one-sided and overly positive one that can defeat the object (Taylor, 1994; Example Box 1.5).

---

**Example Box 1.5**

#### The truck driving experience

Taylor (1994) illustrates how the heavy physical and mental demands faced by truck drivers are seldom comprehended by applicants until they actually do the job. This may account for the high turnover rate in long-haul companies. His study involved the implementation of a realistic job preview programme in a long-haul company with over 1500 drivers and an annual turnover of 207 percent. One year later, the annual turnover rate had decreased substantially to 150 percent. Perceived accuracy of the realistic job preview was also significantly linked with job satisfaction among drivers with no previous driving experience prior to joining the company.

---

## Selection Decisions

Selection decisions can be informed in several ways. Evidence from a battery of test scores taken from multiple predictors can either be integrated into a single indicator or each predictor score can be examined separately. Predictors may be differentially weighted or each applicant may be required to achieve a minimal 'cut off' score on all. Alternatively, selection decisions can be made in stages during an intensive period of training. For instance, military helicopter pilots must pass many progressively harder assessments with only one chance of achieving the minimum score. The gruelling nature of this approach is defensible when considering the military significance of the decisions made. Medical training is of a similar ilk.

Decisions can also be informed statistically. The relative 'predictive' power of various selection scores can be identified using regression techniques. Regression analysis assumes that if the scores on one variable are known (the predictor), it should also be possible to predict scores on another (the criterion). The criterion variable may be a composite of supervisory ratings of job performance. The predictors may be scores on a test of cognitive ability, a measure of leadership ability, a measure of communication skills and a measure of commercial awareness. In principle, a low score on one predictor can be offset or compensated for by a high score on another. Weightings can also be introduced. If, for example, it is known that scores from one predictor (for example, CATs) are substantially more valid than those from another (for example, interview ratings) then the former can be weighted proportionately higher in the selection decision.

In practice, selection decisions are often made in group or team situations and, as such, require consideration of underlying group dynamics – for example, conformity pressures, polarization (see earlier discussion about panel interviews, and Herriot, 2003).

## The fairness issue

**When is selection unfair?**   Whilst the prime goal of personnel selection is to select those whose predicted performance is the best, there is another goal of Equal Opportunity (Schmitt, 1989). The use of psychometric tests can, in principle, objectify the recruitment process. Equal Opportunity advocates have, however, noted that many of the most commonly used tests yield lower scores for minority than for majority group members. Moreover, many tests are developed using majority group members as samples, thereby introducing a bias in favour of benchmark norms that do not adequately represent minority groups.

Legal charges incurred for the unfair use of tests have prompted considerable research on the differential validity of tests across different social subgroups. Whilst test use is not necessarily unfair to an individual, it may be unfair on the minority group as a whole. Research has shown that there are, indeed, sizeable differences between the means of minority and majority groups for many types of selection instrument (for example, Schmitt and Noe, 1986). Fewer members of a minority group may thus be recruited than would otherwise be the case. The real issue, however, is said not to be the mean difference, but the *differential prediction of job performance*.

A test is said to be biased when 'the criterion score predicted from the common regression line is consistently too high or too low for members of the sub-group' (Cleary, 1986: 35). Thus, if the regression lines for different subgroups are not equal, then each person will receive a statistically fair predicted criterion score only if separate regression lines are used for the two groups. This so-called 'Cleary rule' is widely accepted in legal circles as the most appropriate assessment of test bias. This, however, rests heavily on the assumption of an unbiased criterion measure.

---

**Case Study 1.2: 'Equal Opportunities'**

Eight Asian guards working at Paddington Station sat, along with other applicants, various aptitude and 'safety' tests with a view to becoming train drivers. Of the 25 applicants who sat the tests, however, only four white applicants were successful. The eight Asian guard applicants complained of discrimination and applied to the Commission for Racial Equality (CRE), thus initiating an industrial tribunal. At the eleventh hour British Rail agreed to a settlement, the terms of which were to improve their selection procedure, review its equal opportunities policy to bring it into line with the CRE's Code of Practice, and consider positive action training as provided for in the Race Relations Act.

---

*Criterion bias or true differences*   Criterion bias denotes the systematic or consistent measurement of something other than the performance criterion. Kraiger and Ford (1985) reported from two large meta-analyses that white employees seem to perform better than black employees on most job performance criteria, except when the assessors are black. These differences are particularly significant when there are a small number of minority group members being rated. On both subjective and objective criteria, the biggest difference between racial groups arises in cognitive performance measures. These findings suggest that some differences arising on the criterion measure may actually be job relevant rather than biased. Decisions arising from this of course raise a major conflict between productivity goals and those of Equal Opportunity. In the words of Schmitt (1989: 139), 'a procedure which produces the best possible employees and is fair to the individuals of both groups in the sense that the expectation or prediction of their job performance matches their actual performance, will result in the hiring of a very small proportion of minority group members'.

Recently, however, a major challenge has been levelled on this conclusion. Chung-Yan and Cranshaw (2002) convincingly demonstrate how 56–69 percent of Blacks would be *incorrectly* eliminated from job consideration (relative to 10 percent of Whites) using the Thorndike (1971) 'intercept' rule rather than the Cleary (1986) 'differential prediction' (regression line) rule. Simply put, this rule states that a test is biased if the difference in the predictor score is greater than the difference in the criterion score. Chung-Yan and Cranshaw (2002) report that a 1SD (one standard deviation) difference in predictor score amounted to a one-third of a SD Black/White difference on the criterion measure, a fraction reduced to one-tenth when the performance criterion is objective rather than subjective. They argue that not taking this into consideration would lead to an unacceptably high 'false rejection' rate among minority applicants which selectors must be accountable for.

These findings are strong enough to suggest that researchers should be examining the presence and meaning of subgroup differences on both predictor and criterion rather than making the assumption that CATs are a valid reflection of actual ability. Chung-Yan and Cranshaw (2002: 504) end on a big cautionary note in association with the use of CATs (and tests of any kind): '... if they are to be used at all ... only in combination with other information collected about the job candidate prior to this'. Scrutinize the psychometric properties of the predictor and the criterion, take into consideration legal guidelines and organizational values, and bear in mind that *diversity* can be a core company asset.

**Minority recruitment**   Little research exists on effective minority recruitment. However, several factors known to be important to how selection procedures impact on minority recruitment rates are minority representation in the applicant pool, the proportion of the applicant pool selected, test validity, and the standard deviation of job performance in financial terms. High test validity and high proportions of minority applicants can to some extent overcome the conflict between the need to select those whose expected performance is highest, and adequate representation of those from lower performing subgroups.

One problem is that attracting enough qualified applicants to match or exceed the proportion of subgroup representation in the general population may require an extensive and very costly recruitment drive. Moreover, by fulfilling Equal Opportunity quotas, a substantial performance differential may arise between different subgroups recruited into an organization. This may raise the issue of reverse discrimination. Humphreys (1986) argued that there is nothing a test constructor can do (except bad psychometric practice) to reduce criterion bias. Discarding particular items may reduce reliability and validity of the test and distract attention from the cause of differences in criterion performance. Others argue that the general ability of minority applicants in actual performance terms (rather than test terms) may be seriously underestimated (Chung-Yan & Cranshaw, 2002).

### Utility analysis

Calculating the value of a particular selection technique using business terminology is controversial. In 1979, Schmidt, Hunter, McKenzie and Muldrow showed that the financial utility of a selection method could be assessed against variations in job performance. It is possible to estimate, for instance, the relative value of different types of selection procedure by calculating the exact improvements expected in both performance and financial terms. It is likewise possible to cost out the performance worth of individuals. Cascio (1991) summarizes various techniques of utility analysis and discusses its value in promoting defensible selection strategies.

The advantage of 'utility-speak' is that it facilitates bottom-line decision making by personnel practitioners. Indeed, a growth in the requirement to produce utility estimates can be envisaged as a way of backing up selection (and related) decisions. However, definitions of 'utility' are highly contestable, as are the assumptions underpinning some utility models (for example, a linear relationship between performance and its economic value to the company; Cascio & Morris, 1990).

Many different cost estimation tools are now available. The practical value of these is, however, limited in that the estimates produced are highly variable and provide a very limited perspective on selection. Anderson et al. (2001) argue that research on utility has lapsed into what they call 'pedantic science'. The ever-increasing myopic preoccupation, they say, with the 'minutae of formulaic expressions' (p. 395) has undermined the practical value of utility analysis, making the term 'utility' somewhat meaningless. Dipboye, Smith and Howell (1999: 454) also caution against using scientific techniques to make 'socially irresponsible behaviour look like wise business practice, particularly if no attempt is made to factor in social costs'.

## Part 2 Summary and Conclusions

- Issues of predictive validity have prevailed in the study of 'predictors' at the cost of understanding how or why, leading some to criticize selection psychology as blind prediction.
- GMA (as opposed to specific abilities) is the most powerful and generalizable single predictor of performance.
- Situational interviews and work samples can attain validities on a par with GMA (suggesting that they measure similar things), and both conscientiousness and integrity (personality-based integrity) are also pretty good predictors of performance, injecting personality measurement with renewed contemporary vigour.
- Assessment centres work well, but not as well as singular predictors like GMA, making it difficult to justify the costs in efficiency terms.
- Contemporary research is increasingly focusing on the construct validity of, especially, interviews and assessment centres. This effort raises methodological and statistical, as well as conceptual, challenges. Evidence suggests that interviews and assessment centres measure a mixed bag of constructs including ability, personality, job knowledge, experience and skill.
- The better the predictor the more adverse the applicant reaction: applicants prefer the unstructured interview over testing or other highly structured methods (situational, behavioural interview). The assessment centre is also well liked, because it provides the opportunity to demonstrate actual work skills. Findings highlight the important symbolic function of selection, hitherto clouded by prediction-based efficiency imperatives.
- Computer-based testing has opened up new testing possibilities, but also new ethical issues.
- Findings must also be coupled with Equal Opportunity considerations including the possibility of false rejection of minority group members based on measures of GMA. Efficiency needs must be reconciled with public relations and Equal Opportunity considerations.
- Little work is available on *how* or *why* particular methods of selection are chosen. Evidence suggests a strong impact of national and local cultural factors.
- Utility research is a good example of how technical preoccupations can undermine practical applicability.

# Part 3: The Applicant Perspective on Selection

In a definitive article of 1989, Peter Herriot drew attention to the symbolic function of interviews as a vehicle for negotiating role expectations and establishing the foundations of a 'psychological contract' between employer and employee. Critics from European quarters were also concerned about the overly technical focus of conventional selection science (for example, de Wolff, 1989). In parallel, Rousseau (1989, 1995) had begun to afford the selection process a crucial role in conveying messages (implicitly and explicitly) about organizational obligations and expectations. However, until recently (Anderson, 2004) only a handful of researchers (for example, Anderson & Ostroff, 1997; Millward & Cropley, 2003; Rynes, 1993; Wanous, 1980) have systematically pursued this alternative line of thinking about selection processes.

Most of the research on 'applicant reactions' has also been assimilated to a 'public relations' perspective on selection, the central concern of which is to design reliable and valid assessment processes that do not incite 'adverse reaction' (to avoid the likelihood of litigation). This consideration of the applicant subjective perspective on selection has thus been somewhat transplanted onto an otherwise prediction-oriented approach in which technical concerns predominate. The former, indeed, does not sit easily within an approach that seeks to eradicate subjectivity as the source of all error and bias from an otherwise highly objective selection process (Study Box 1.11).

Thus, whilst research on applicant reactions has grown, it has largely been driven by pragmatic (and legal) rather than theoretical concerns (Anderson, Born, & Cunningham-Snell, 2001). In a landmark special issue on 'applicant perspectives' in the *International Journal of Selection and Assessment*, Anderson (2004: 1) notes how the applicant 'side' of selection has been 'shrouded' (that is, '*the dark side of the moon*'). Reaction research, Anderson (2003) says, has 'patchy' coverage, is driven by 'dustbowl empiricism' (atheoretical), 'myopically focused' on only immediate level outcomes, and mainly based on student samples.

---

**Study Box 1.11**

**Micro-analytic perspective on selection**

*Non-verbal behaviour in interviews*

Laboratory and field studies consistently show that non-verbal cues influence only the strength of applicant evaluations not their direction (positive or negative), indicating that in the main it is *verbal* rather than non-verbal content that affects interviewer judgements (Anderson, 1991). Judgements of social skill in particular are facilitated by non-verbal cues like applicant air-time, and the use of gestures.

**Study Box 1.11    Continued**

## Decision making

Research on decision making has identified biases in interviewer judgements. Findings show that:

- judgements are more likely to be influenced by *negative* than positive information;
- interviewers form impressions early in the interview which they then seek to confirm and favour applicants with whom they perceive themselves to be similar ('similar-to-me' effect) and whom they find attractive;
- judgements of any one particular applicant are influenced by the quality of preceding applicants in the interview sequence.

Research on rater bias relies heavily on the 'hypothetical applicant' method involving 'paper people', though notably similar findings are reported from field studies (Gallois, Callan, & Palmar, 1992).

### Applicant characteristics

Studies have looked at non-job-relevant characteristics that influence interviewer judgement. For instance, there is evidence for an interviewer sex bias. The chances of a female being offered a job is also moderated by the extent to which they create a masculine or feminine impression (Van Vianen & Van Schie, 1995). Moreover, whether a masculine or feminine impression is perceived more or less favourably may depend on the job being sought. Thus, Buttner and McNally (1996) found that assertive tactics used by females applying for a stereotypically 'feminine' job were not well received, limiting their chances of job acceptance. The same tactics used by females applying for a stereotypically masculine job, however, increased their chances.

### Attributions

An attribution is a *causal explanation* for an event most commonly classified as: internal/external, stable/unstable, and general/specific (Silvester, 1997). The pattern of attributions used by applicants to explain their successes and failures is of interest for the clues it affords the interviewer about motivation (Case Study 1.3). For example, attributing failure to unstable, internal and controllable factors (for example, 'I failed my exam because I didn't work hard enough') gives the impression of someone who takes responsibility. Struthers, Colwill and Perry (1992) argue that impressions like this can have a strong influence on hiring decisions. Indeed, Kacmar, Delery, and Ferris (1992) found that applicants who used internal attributions (self-focused impression tactics) were rated higher, received more recommendations for a job offer, and received fewer rejections from 80 university business students than when they used other-focused tactics.

Gilliland's (1993; Gilliland & Chan, 2001) seminal work on the perceived justice of selection processes is one rare exception to this (Study Box 1.12). The 'perceived justice' construct is now core to other important theoretical developments in connection with the applicant perspective (Bell, Ryan, & Wiechmann, 2004; Derous, De Witte, & Stroobants, 2003; Harris, Lievens, & Van Hoye, 2004; Truxillo, Steiner, & Gilliland, 2004).

---

**Study Box 1.12**

### Perceived justice in selection practices

Gilliland (1993) proposed a model of perceived procedural justice as a basis for understanding and investigating applicant reactions. Procedural justice has been defined as 'the perceived fairness of process and procedures used to make decisions' (Herriot, 1995). Perceived fairness is, in turn, associated with reactions both during and after hiring (for example, job acceptance, litigation, 'talking up' the organization) as well as self-perception (for example, self-efficacy). Gilliland and Chan (2001) proposed six procedural justice rules of selection:

- *Interpersonal sensitivity* – extent selectors are perceived warm and empathic.
- *Informativeness* – perceived quality and quantity of information regarding selection task and procedures.
- *Two way communication* – extent applicants perceive they are given an opportunity to ask questions and have some control over the selection process.
- *Career/job relevance* – perceived relevance of the selection process.
- *Bias suppression* – perceived extent to which procedures are standardized and the genuine implementation of Equal Opportunity principles.
- *Opportunity to perform* – perceived extent to which an applicant has had the opportunity to demonstrate their abilities.

Gilliland (1993) found interpersonal sensitivity to be the most important procedural justice item. Subsequent work has confirmed this, and also the critical importance of job/career relevance (Gilliland & Chan, 2001; Higuera, 2001; Moscoso & Salgado, 2004; Schmitt, Oswald, Kim, Gillespie, & Ramsay, 2004). Looking closely at the impact on perceived fairness of particular techniques, it would seem that interviews, CVs and work samples are the most positively perceived (Moscoso & Salgado, 2004). It is also becoming increasingly clear that judgements of fairness may be substantially accounted for by the outcome (accepted, rejected), rather than the process per se (Ryan & Ployhart, 2000). This has been termed the 'self-serving bias,' because it involves the denigration of test fairness as a protection against the impact of poor performance on self-esteem (Schmitt et al., 2004). However, they argue from their findings that perceived relevance of the selection procedure can counter this in some instances.

Research on outcomes has been more equivocal, with findings indicating a consistent impact of perceived fairness on so-called 'soft' indicators like satisfaction, but a less definitive impact on 'hard' indicators like job acceptance and performance (Ryan & Ployhart, 2000). This has prompted Gilliland and colleagues to ascertain more precisely *when* (that is, the 'boundary conditions') selection fairness matters (Truxillo, Steiner, & Gilliland, 2004). In pursuit of this, they argue (2004: 45) that much more conceptual work needs to be done looking at the meaning of fairness

## Study Box 1.12    Continued

(that is, 'the essence of what fairness really is and thus what the outcomes are likely to be'). Most outcome research has used self-report ratings of relative fairness rather than gross *un*fairness, and does not afford consideration of the 'threshold' between the two. Nor is it clear what the relevant outcomes are exactly. Possible mediators of the experience of perceived fairness include fairness expectations (Bell, Ryan, & Weichmann, 2004), familiarity with/beliefs about particular selection methods, and individual and group/demographic differences in unfairness tolerance (Viswesvaran & Ones, 2004). Van Vianen, Taris, Scholten and Schinkel (2004) have also demonstrated the importance of looking at the impact of different aspects of the selection process (for example, feedback content and delivery) on perceived fairness. Moderators of whether perceived unfairness leads to particular outcomes include the costs of taking legal action, social support, cultural norms and individual differences.

Conceptual and methodological issues aside, it is clear that 'selection fairness really does matter' (Truxillo et al., 2004: 51). There is also considerable 'cross cultural consistency' in the perceived justice of particular selection techniques (Moscoso & Salgado, 2004). Some argue that justice perceptions (and expectations) are critical to understanding discrimination experiences, not just in selection but more generally (including promotion; Harris, Lievens, & Van Hoye, 2004).

## Case Study 1.3: Attributions as a 'psychometric barometer' of motivation

In a rare field study, Silvester (1997) analysed 35 real-life job interview transcripts (15 applicants to a law firm and 20 applicants to a distribution company) using the Leeds Attribution Coding System. Interviewers from the law firm were personnel staff and senior partners. A total of 1967 attributions were identified: 25.7 percent for negative events, 64.4 percent for positive events. To analyse the influence of attribution style on interviewer evaluations, applicants were categorized into 'good', 'poor' or 'midrange' using original interviewer ratings. The results showed that successful and unsuccessful applicants made significantly different kinds of attributions. Across both companies, applicants who were rated 'good' tended to make significantly *more stable and personal attributions for negative events* (but not positive events) than 'poor' applicants did. Silvester (1997) explained these findings using a self-presentational model in that applicants who attribute failure to stable and personal events afford an impression of taking responsibility. However, the possibility remains that different types of attribution style will have a different meaning for interviewers, depending on both the job and the type of occupation/industry it represents. Thus, whether a stable or unstable attribution for negative events is construed as good or bad may depend on whether it is an attribution style congruent with that expected.

Advocates of a genuinely 'subjective' approach (as opposed to the 'subjective-must-imply-error' approach) view 'selection as a two way interactive and inter-subjective process' (Herriot, 2002). Selection techniques and practices are said not to be 'neutral predictors', but 'interventive affectors of applicant expectations, attitudes and on the job behaviours' (Anderson, 2001: 90). One of the ways in which they perform this symbolic function is by allowing both individual and organization (via assessor) to form impressions of each other. Rynes (1993) has pointed out that applicant decisions are likely to be substantially affected by their impressions of an organization. Such impressions are fundamental to 'organizational reputation', especially if applicants have experienced negative treatment (perceived as unprofessional or unfair) (see Chapter 5 on the impact of corporate image and identity on employee motivation). Yet, surprisingly, research on applicant (as opposed to assessor) impression formation has been a highly neglected consideration (Anderson, 2001: 90; Ryan & Ployhart, 2001).

Anderson and Ostroff (1997: 427) describe the symbolic function of the selection process as 'socialisation impact'. All selection techniques to varying degrees, they argue, have *unavoidable* (that is, whether we like it or not) socialization impact across five domains: information provision, preference impact, expectational impact, attitudinal impact and behavioural impact. Attitudinal impact is interactively influenced by information, preference and expectational impact, whilst behavioural impact is interactively influenced by all of these impacts (Anderson, 2001: 87–89):

- *Information provision* – information conveyed (intentionally or not) will be 'interpreted by applicants as unconditional and contractually binding', irrespective of whether or not message delivery and receipt is accurate (p. 87). Drawing on Rousseau's work on the psychological contract (1995), Anderson (2001: 88) proposes that applicants may read 'promises and obligations into the contextual information provided during selection'. This may explain why it is so common for employees to perceive that their contract has been violated (that is, mismatch of expectations against reality) after a short while in the job (Rousseau, 1993).
- *Preference impact* – applicants' acceptance of job offers will be influenced by perceptions of preference impact (that is, reactions to/preference for certain selection methods), influenced in turn by job availability, organizational image, and job attractiveness (p. 88). For instance, if a company has an image of a 'good place to work' (Rynes, 1993) (for example, career prospects, development opportunities), this could override the impact of the selection technique (that is, applicants may tolerate an otherwise 'adverse' experience if they felt it was for a good cause). Applicants who are insecure about their job prospects might also accept a job offer regardless of their selection experience perhaps because they have been job hunting for a while, and/or they are insecure about their job prospects.
- *Expectational impact* – applicants are 'actively predisposed' towards inferring 'multiple, varied, and enduring expectations of the future work relationship' (Anderson, 2001: 88) even if this means 'extending, embellishing and extrapolating' from limited information (see Case Study 1.4). Rynes (1993) has also suggested that early information may help form applicant impressions used thereafter as anchors for subsequent information. This raises questions about the symbolic significance of both the phasing (for example, assessment centre for initial screening, one-to-one

interview later) and sequencing (for example, test first, interview last) of the selection process. In association with justice perceptions, Truxillo et al. (2004: 48) argue that 'early fairness episodes … will have the greatest impact on the general fairness judgement, which will in turn, influence the lense through which the person perceives the organization'. Even the job advert may unwittingly create expectations.

Anderson (2001) adds that different selection methods have varying degrees of impact across all five domains and that there will be individual differences in the perceived impact of the same method (for example, some may enjoy the experience of an assessment centre because it gives them the opportunity to demonstrate their skills – and stand out from the crowd – whilst others may experience 'performance anxiety'). Key questions include how applicants obtain information and how this impacts on them, how expectations are inferred and on what basis, and what accounts for individual differences in preference impact.

---

**Case Study 1.4: Nanny study**

Millward and Cropley (2003) conducted three studies (one exploratory, one concurrent between-group, post-only and one prospective between-group, time-series) to investigate processes of psychological contracting in the context of interviews conducted by parents looking for a live-in nanny to care for their children. The two experimental studies examined the frequency, character (explicit, implicit) and content (relational, transactional) of spontaneous discussions about mutual expectations (using a coding scheme evolved from the exploratory work) within two types of employment interview: 23 first time nanny–employer pairs and 16 experienced nanny–employer pairs. The focus was on the consequences of these features of interviews for (a) perceptions of mutual trust, mutual understanding and perceived reciprocity at post-interview; and (b) selection decisions. The findings showed that clarity of expectations (experience) was associated with an increased likelihood of time spent referring to or discussing expectations, whether explicitly or implicitly, but did not induce a more explicit discussion of these expectations. Instead, clarity predicted an increased likelihood of discussing expectations 'implicitly', especially relational considerations. Generally speaking, relational material was discussed more implicitly than explicitly. Also, what was discussed (relational, transactional) predicted feelings of mutual trust, not the explicit or implicit nature of the discussion. Nonetheless, implicit discussion did mediate the association between discussion of relational material, mutual understanding and perceptions of reciprocity. Finally, post-interview outcomes (mutual understanding, trust and reciprocity) mediated selection decisions, not the explicit or implicit nature of the discussion. Whilst the findings are clearly sample and context specific, they are consistent enough to point to the important role played by implicit communication in psychological contract formation.

---

The applicant perspective on selection is not supposed to be an alternative to the selection validation perspective; on the contrary, it provides an essential complement. In Anderson's words (2001: 84), 'while it is nonsensical to claim that selection techniques do *not* act as predictors, it is equally nonsensical to claim that this is *all* that they do'. The selection validation approach has 'a wealth of empirical support for its practical recommendations' spanning 80 years or so, but asking additional questions about the symbolic functions of selection affords a more 'ecologically comprehensive view of selection' (see also Chan & Schmitt, 2004). Moreover, it seems only reasonable to acknowledge the *active* part played by the applicant in the selection process.

Within this perspective on selection, it is also important to acknowledge that applicants may seek out self-defining employment in which they receive self-verifying feedback. Niendethal and colleagues (Niedenthal, Cantor, & Kihlstrom, 1985), for instance, have shown that 'individuals imagine the typical person who would be found in each of the situation options ... then compare the defining traits of the prototypes with those of him or herself and select the product, situation or institution associated with the greatest similarity between the self and the prototypic person-in-situation' (Setterlund & Niedenthal, 1993: 269–270). Self-to-prototype matching is likely to be used when choices have implications for others' beliefs about one's identity – especially choices laden with personal and social meaning as in the job/career context.

However, it is important to recognize that the internalization of prototype value sets may result in an idealized (and not realistic) perception of the group (and the self). Mabey (1986) found that the higher the initial applicant expectations, the greater the reality shock and the lower their job satisfaction and commitment. In such instances, expectations could be 'reality' checked through the so-called RJP (Premack & Wanous, 1985; see earlier in this chapter for details of this method). Notably, Premack and Wanous (1985) found that RJP was associated with reduced turnover only for those employees who took up 'complex jobs' (military recruits and insurance representatives) rather than 'simple' jobs (for example, telephone operators) which makes sense given that the former are more likely than the latter to be vulnerable to identity-relevant stereotypes (but see Study Box 1.13).

Clearly, a critical issue for future research is to examine how applicant intentions and ideals are translated into actual job decisions. For some people, these choices will be perceived as 'limited' (see Chapter 3, Part 2) depending on various other anticipatory socialization processes (in turn bound up with socio-economic background, educational opportunities, parental expectation and such like). Rynes and Cable (2003) remind us that job choices may in some cases involve 'serious opportunity costs' and that we need to emphasize more the broader context in which recruitment occurs.

---

### Study Box 1.13

#### Realistic job preview

The primary concern of RJP is employee retention rather than applicant attraction, the belief being that recruitment strategies designed to attract applicants can promulgate a largely fictitious representation of the job and the organization. The intention of the RJP is to aid the self-to-organization matching process (Wanous, 1980). Research, however, has tended to focus on job acceptance rather than applicant decision-making processes, such that matching theory has not been properly tested. A possibility also exists that the RJP has an *adverse impact* on applicants,

| **Study Box 1.13    Continued** |
| --- |

turning them away from the job, and hence serving a screening or *drop-out* function (Rynes, 1993). Bretz and Judge (1998) found that pre-entry organizational attraction can decrease with exposure to job/organizational drawbacks, but whether this is the process underlying withdrawal from a selection process is a different issue. Moreover, whilst drop-outs may not be well-matched to either the job or the organization, this has yet to be directly demonstrated. Others argue that RJP that involve exposure to both unfavourable and favourable information (that is, provide a realistically balanced exposure) *increases* the likelihood of positive outcomes (Meglino, Ravlin, & De Nisi, 2001). Herriot (2002, 2004) conceptualizes the selection process as a mutual matching process on the part of both selector and applicant, underpinned by an identity dynamic. He proposes that with a perceived incongruence of identity on the part of both parties (for example, selector does not perceive the applicant to 'fit' the prevailing organizational identity and/or applicant perceives his or her own identity is threatened or incompatible with their perceptions of organizational identity), will mean that withdrawal of either party from the selection process is likely. Research needs to examine applicant perceptions and expectations prior to, and immediately following, realistic compared with traditional methods of selection, to ascertain the relative impact of RJP at the *process level*. It might be that those who withdraw following a RJP are those who have more attractive job alternatives to contemplate, whilst those who pursue the job regardless may not be quite as 'employable'. The benefits of a realistic as opposed to traditional job preview have been merely inferred rather than actually observed (Rynes, 1993). It could be that any effect a RJP has can be attributed to actual job and organizational characteristics as opposed to the preview process itself. One of the problems in assessing the impact of 'realistic' and 'traditional' selection methods is that neither concept has been well defined in the literature and their differential content is not specified. This means that the boundary between realistic and traditional previews is fuzzy. When does a method stop being 'traditional' and become 'realistic'? It is not clear also why traditional selection methods are unrealistic. Does 'realistic' mean accurate?

Research on applicant reactions has also taken on new conceptual turns within the genuinely *subjective* model of selection. Apart from theoretical developments in the field of justice perception (Study Box 1.12), Ployhart and Harold (2004) have proposed the applicant attribution-reaction theory (AART), whilst Herriot (2004) draws on social identity theory. AART proposes that applicant reactions (emotional, cognitive, behavioural) are 'fundamentally driven by an attributional process' (Ployhart & Harold, 2004). In other words, perceived fairness is not in itself an *explanation* of applicant reactions; it is a consequence of attribution processes. This is one reason why 'outcomes' (acceptance, rejection) may affect justice perceptions in a self-serving way – that is, the 'cause' of failure is attributed to the selection process (Study Box 1.11).

By contrast, Herriot (2004) sees social identity as driving applicant reactions. Specifically, he argues that all parties to the exchange process bring with them various identities, some chronically more salient than others in a work context (for example, professional identity) and others heightened in salience through the selection encounter itself. For instance, an intrusive personal question asked as part of a biographical means of assessment might raise the salience of a gender identity that an applicant may feel is unjustifiably evoked (non-work relevant) in the context of an interview. This would explain why biographical formats often evoke adverse reaction (for example, Smither, Reilly, Millsap, Pearlman, & Stoffey, 1993).

Herriot (2004) says that negative reactions including exit from a selection encounter are likely to occur because of a perceived incongruence between applicant identity and job/organizational perception. Evidence from studies on organizational identity confirms that perceptions of self-organization fit and self-job fit are positively related to subsequent job and organizational satisfaction (for example, Saks & Ashforth, 2002). Applicant (and recruiter) preference for unstructured over structured interviews makes sense given the increased opportunity this affords for identities to be matched. Recruiters, as representatives of the organization, may be judged accordingly (Connerley & Rynes, 1997). On the other side, Zedeck and Kafry (1977) report how recruiters may implicitly use a 'similar-to-me' rule when making judgements about applicant suitability, which has been called 'policy capturing'. The same implicit rule may be used by applicants in making their own decisions.

Moreover, if an applicant has already 'matched' his or her identity to that of the organization (anticipatory self-organizational fit), specific selection experiences may make no difference at all to post-selection attitudes and behaviours (Turban, 2001). Consistent with the idea of a confirmatory bias in operation, Turban (2001) found that applicants who withdrew early from a selection encounter were more likely to have reported feeling negative about the organization beforehand. The big downside of self-to-organization and organization-to-applicant matching is the increased organizational homogeneity (and lack of diversity) it implicates (see Herriot, 2002 for a discussion of problems associated with this 'attraction – attrition' process).

On a broader level, Chan and Schmitt (2004) offer what they call a 'construct oriented' approach to research on applicant reactions comprising the following dimensions:

- *Making explicit the nature and specificity of different dimensions of reaction* – to date, only three main theoretical dimensions have been studied: perceived relevance (face validity), perceived fairness and the outcomes of applicant reactions. Chan and Schmitt advocate expanding this 'construct space' to include test-taking motivation and perceived performance.

- *Looking at change in applicant reactions (either in level or nature)* – this links to research demonstrating that 'outcomes' retrospectively impact on perceptions of fairness (Study Box 1.12) and, theoretically, would enable some of the 'causes' of applicant reactions to be more precisely identified. Anderson (2003) has criticized reaction research generally for only considering 'immediate level' outcomes (the so-called 'feel good/feel bad' factor).

- *Identifying the precise antecedents of particular reactions, including applicant characteristics as well as method factors* – Derous and colleagues (Derous, Bom, & De Witte, 2004; Derous et al., 2003) have evolved a 'social process' model (and measurement method) building on Schuler's (1993) 'social validity' approach to selection. Core to this is an assumption that applicants bring with them certain *general beliefs* about how they wish and expect to be treated during the selection encounter. These beliefs, they argue, are broader than those underpinning justice perceptions and expectations, and reflect past experiences of the selection process (Study Box 1.14). Herriot (2004) says that applicants may bring with them organizational perceptions derived from word-of-mouth endorsement (or criticism), and other vicarious sources, that determine how positively or negatively disposed they are to the selection process (see earlier).

---

**Study Box 1.14**

### The social process model of the selection encounter

Using multi-dimensional scaling methods, Derous and colleagues (2003, 2004) demonstrate how general beliefs about selection treatment can be described across two main bipolar dimensions (differentiation-shared, task-relational):

- *differentiation* concerns the extent to which personal privacy is respected and humane (warm, personalized) treatment is experienced;
- *shared* pertains to being treated with objectivity and equality;
- *task* refers to the technical qualities of selection including selector competence;
- *relational* denotes attention to candidate needs for respectful treatment, feedback, information/transparency.

Using the 'Social Process Questionnaire on Selection', Derous et al. (2003, 2004) report a negative relationship between the number of prior selection experiences and applicant qualitative evaluation of previous treatment, a positive relationship between the qualitative evaluation of previous treatment and expectations of forthcoming treatment and a positive relationship between expectations and motivation to apply. Limitations of this approach include the lack of attention to individual differences, use of student samples and its cross-sectional (rather than longitudinal) nature.

---

- *The question of whether (and if so, under what conditions) certain reactions (for example, perceived job irrelevance) have certain motivation impact* – for example, performing less well in the associated test.
- *Clarifying the criterion domain when investigating the outcomes of applicant reactions* – to date, most reaction research is myopically focused on 'immediate level reactions' (Anderson, 2003). Chan and Schmitt (2004) recommend a taxonomy of outcome criteria as follows: withdrawal from the selection process, job performance, personal outcomes (for example, self-efficacy), and organizational perceptions (for example, organizational reputation; Study Box 1.15).
- *Looking at reactions to 'technological innovations' in the testing domain* (see Anderson, 2003) – these may uncover different reactions, antecedents and outcomes. Innovations in computer-based testing include Internet-based testing, telephone interviews; video-based situational judgement tests, and virtual reality technology.

Studies report a phenomenal growth amongst large multi-nationals in the use of Internet-based testing in particular (for example, Bartram, 2001). Whilst reactions to Internet-based testing are said to be largely positive, some concern has arisen about the potential for 'e-loaded adverse impact' arising from socio-demographic differences in accessibility of the Internet.

- *Closer attention to methodological and data analysis issues* – these may involve the use of experimental designs and also meta-analysis. Particular attention needs to be addressed to process issues including mediator (factors which connect or provide a route of association to other factors) and moderator (factors which change observed associations) relationships. For example, justice expectations may provide a through route (mediate) to the association between justice perceptions and adverse reaction, whilst the 'outcome' of a selection process can be said to increase (moderate) the association between justice perceptions and adverse reaction.

---

### Study Box 1.15

#### Negative psychological effects

The concept of 'negative psychological effects' (NPEs) looks at the impact of selection processes on employee well-being and mental health (Anderson, 2004; Ryan & Ployhart, 2000) addressing, in addition, experiences of mistreatment and rejection (Schinkel, van Dierndonck, & Anderson, 2004). On moral and ethical grounds alone, anticipating and managing the psychological consequences of rejection are increasingly becoming part of the professional agenda. Schinkel, van Dierndonck and Anderson (2004), for instance, investigated the impact of rejection both with and without performance feedback on 'core self-evaluations'. Consistent with findings obtained by Ilgen and Davis (2000), rejected applicants provided with feedback were more significantly negatively affected than those who were not given feedback. Variation in perceived justice made no difference to this finding. The practical implications of this finding are potentially difficult to justify (that is, do not provide feedback when rejecting an applicant), because applicants may argue that they have a basic legal right to know on what grounds they have been excluded. NPEs could have long term undermining consequences for job confidence. If the job is an internal post and/or involves an upward move (that is, promotion), the impact on the individuals' relationship with the organization could be profound.

---

Derous and colleagues (Derous, De Witte, & Stroobants, 2003) remind us that both applicants and selectors shape the selection encounter and that, to this extent, we must also consider the part played by the assessor/recruiter in, for example, selecting particular methods of assessment and managing information provision and expectations (as opposed to focusing exclusively on biases in their judgements and decisions). Such an avenue of investigation may seem 'daunting', potentially plagued with methodological if not conceptual difficulties (Herriot, 2002, 2004; but see Case Study 1.4 for an example of two-way research), but the benefits for increased ecological validity of the final selection outcome (from both applicant and recruiter point of view) would be enormous (Herriot, 2001).

## Part 3 Summary and Conclusions

- The applicant perspective heralds growing respect for the needs, concerns, reactions and basic dignity of the assessed individual (or group member). Until recently, research on applicant reactions was side-lined as a necessary but bothersome consideration, driven mainly by legal and ethical imperative rather than a genuine interest.
- Contemporary work on applicant reactions is more construct-driven. The approach to selection as an inter-subjective encounter, involving interaction and negotiation, changes the epistemology underpinning selection research, away from seeing social factors as sources of error (undermining objectivity and rationality) towards one that recognizes the central role played by these factors in an ecologically valid selection process.
- No research has yet looked at how selectors model and enact the selection encounter, how they make sense of and use applicant evidence and how they contribute to the formation of psychological contracts.

## Research Challenges

- examining the decision-making strategies and other judgement processes of assessors;
- developing and testing a conceptual framework for integrating job analysis techniques with selection and assessment principles;
- linking selection validation issues to a theory of performance, and adopting a more conceptually driven approach to performance prediction;
- conducting meta-analyses of the selection literature that are built on the testing of hypotheses about the relationship between predictor and criterion;
- elucidating the concept of 'job';
- examining the construct validity of job analysis techniques, including the impact of job perceptions and schemas (implicit criteria) and their influence on job analysis and performance ratings;
- the process of 'method' selection and the issue of 'point-to-point correspondence';
- the construct validity of interviews – is it simply another means of assessing 'personality' or 'social intelligence' or 'g'?
- the *construct validity* of biographical selection methods;
- the 'interfacing' role of the selection system, and its *social psychological dynamics*;
- the role of the 'realistic job preview' in anticipatory socialization;
- the role of *content validity* as a moderator of applicant performance during assessment procedures;
- the interaction between *dimensions and constructs* in selection procedures;
- the role of *implicit stereotypes or prototypes* in applicant selection via the assessment centre;

- the role of *justice perceptions* on job acceptance, and also psychological contract formation during the selection process;
- looking more closely at the so-called 'g' factor of cognitive ability as a predictor of performance and, in particular, how and why it might vary across persons as well as distilling its subcomponents.

## Recommended Reading

Anderson, N. (2001). Towards a theory of socialization impact: Selection as pre-entry socialization. *International Journal of Selection and Assessment,* 9(1/2), 84–91.

Anderson, N., & Herriot, P. (Eds) (1997). *International handbook of assessment and selection.* London: Wiley.

Guion, R.M. (1998). *Assessment, measurement and prediction for personnel decisions.* Mahwah, NJ: Erlbaum.

Herriot, P. (2002). Selection and self: Selection as a social process. *European Journal of Work and Organizational Psychology,* 11(4), 385–402.

Robertson, I.T., & Smith, M. (2001). Personnel selection. *Journal of Occupational and Organizational Psychology*, 74, 441–472.

Salgado, J.F. (1999). Personnel selection methods. In C.L. Cooper, & I.T. Robertson (Eds), *International review of industrial and organizational psychology.* Vol. 14. Chichester: Wiley.

# 2 Training

## Preface

Training can be defined as 'the systematic acquisition of attitudes, concepts, knowledge, rules or skills that result in improved performance at work' (Goldstein, 1991: 508). Training is necessary to keep abreast of rapid economic, organizational and technological change, and the need to compete in world markets. Work today is infinitely more cognitively complex and the tempo is fast. The foremost question for the contemporary organization is not 'how should the organization be structured to effectively achieve its task' but '*how can the task be most optimally performed in the circumstances*?' 'Smart' systems reconfigure for the occasion (that is, 'just-in-time'). This requires cognitive superiority (that is, high situation awareness, effective knowledge management, self-regulating strategies and processes, initiative taking/risk management, and people management) which requires an appropriate investment in the *cognitive infrastructure or human capital* of an organization.

Such shifts in human capital requirements are said to have outpaced society's ability to cope with the educational and training demands they pose. The conventional 'instructional' model of training has been criticized for assuming the organization is a relatively stable system with knowledge, skill and ability (KSA) requirements that can be easily mapped, and because it treats the trainee as a passive recipient of 'instruction' who, after a period of off-site training, can then be slotted neatly back into the system.

Management psychology is, however, paving the way for a paradigm shift as new models of the organization (for example, 'the learning organization', 'the knowing organization', 'the self-organizing organization') and of the learner (for example, 'self-regulating', 'sense-making') are emerging. In the instructional model, trainee characteristics are treated as critical 'moderators' or 'mediators' of the training process, but the new epistemology pictures the learner as actively constructing the learning environment as much as vice versa. In this framework, learning is a situated and highly contextualized activity, heralding new ways of designing and delivering training involving proactive inquiry and self-evaluation. The 'planned on the job training' movement (versus 'sitting with Nellie') holds an important key to preparing the workforce for the 21st century. Necessarily this puts less accent on classroom-based off-site learning, emphasizing instead the importance of retaining situational fidelity in the learning process. From this perspective, 'transfer of training' is a problem created by the instructional paradigm, in its archetypical *off-site* mode. The reality is that the majority of training is conducted off-site, although inspiration for a more 'on-site' model is emerging from the German concept of 'learning bay'.

These developments, however, are in tension with an increasingly classroom-based educational paradigm in which previously vocational domains are rendered more 'theoretical' (for example, nursing, building, mechanics). The responsibility resides with the individual to translate theory into practice. Attempts to facilitate this comes from professional initiatives emphasizing 'evidence-based practice' and 'reflective practice' involving the systematic application of problem-solving strategies. Teaching students how to use different 'learning strategies' is part of this general model of educational preparation although, notably, these ideas are now also being harnessed to understand how to optimize the transfer of training (and learning processes more generally) in occupational settings. It is a *continuous learning capability* that is of most value to organizations in today's competitive world.

Contemporary debate at the macro-level concerns whether centralized regulation is required, whether education and training should be prescribed (teacher-led) or self-initiated (trainee-led) and whether it should be integrated into the workplace or within institutions separate from the workplace (Reid & Barrington, 1997: 44–45). These tensions are reflected in the political drive towards standardization, coupled with cultural emphasis on self-development.

Micro-level considerations concern the learning process itself, and how to most effectively design training programmes to optimize this. Contemporary research increasingly draws on cognitive and motivational concepts to understand the interaction between person and environment in the learning process. The psychology of training is nonetheless a largely theoretical field, and, to date, the introduction of cognitive and motivational constructs has been quite piecemeal rather than offering a coherent basis for research and practice. Theoretical developments informing team training in a military context are an exception to this. The concept of mental model is central to these developments, and is arguably one that has a more generic potential to inform training research and practice of all kinds.

Part 1 of this chapter reviews the training system in an historical and political context. Part 2 describes 'the training system'. Part 3 compares different models of training, whilst Part 4 examines training as a learning process using instructional theory. Part 5 looks in detail at the transfer of training problem and Part 6 covers the topic of training evaluation.

## Learning Objectives

Studying the contents of this chapter will enable you to:

1 discuss the history of training in a social, educational, economic and political context with particular reference to the long-standing education/training divide;
2 debate the critical role played by 'learning' to the survival of the contemporary organization and, in particular, what psychology can contribute in both theory and practice;
3 compare and contrast different training models, and produce a rationale for the overriding prevalence of the instructional model in the psychology of training;
4 explain the training system from an instructional point of view, and the steps involved in a comprehensive need assessment;
5 explain instructional theory (the instructional model) and its application of learning theory;
6 assess the contribution made by the introduction of cognitive and motivational concepts to our understanding of the learning process and how it can be optimized;
7 explain the transfer of training problem; identify common 'blocks' to transfer and ways in which they might be overcome in the context of contemporary movements towards integrating 'training' more closely with workplace learning initiatives;
8 debate the concept of 'learning how to learn' and its practical implications for instructional style and practice in the context of a framework in which person and environment are assumed to reciprocally interact;
9 debate the aims of, and approaches to, training evaluation and associated methodological problems.

# Part 1: The Historical Context of Training

## The Education/Training Divide

Debate on the extent to which the government should regulate and standardize training began with the Carr Report in 1958, a largely reactionary and prescriptive treatise advocating a 'leave it to industry' approach. In the 1964 White paper on industrial training (HMSO, 1964), the Government was forced to admit the need to intervene, advocating a common policy on occupational training. In practice, the consequence of this was not greater coordination or coherence, but ever increasing industry-specific fragmentation. Quasi-autonomous Industry Training Boards (ITBs) were established to govern training practices (Training Act, 1964), but national standards were never established. Each ITB operated fairly independently and, moreover, ITBs were not representative of all industrial and business sectors. They were also rejected by some industries as state interference. In 1973, ITBs were thus disbanded.

The 1950s pattern of crisis-driven political reform characterized by the rhetoric of national integration and standardization and a reality of local fragmentation, duplication and dispute repeats itself until well into the 1990s, when training continued to be a marginalized (non-educational) industry and trade-specific activity, attracting little political, organizational or public interest.

The gap between vocational training and education thus became ever wider, with the former accorded second class 'technical' status and the latter the exclusive province of aspiring managers or professionals (Finegold & Soskice, 1990). Training in organizations continued to have little or no national recognition (and many people were excluded from it), remained industry-specific and ill-funded, and was underpinned by a short-term reactionary perspective. Even the Confederation of British Industry, though enjoying a virtual monopoly in its influence over business, has until recently taken a laissez-faire approach to training.

Vocational education has also been haphazardly conducted, the responsibility of many different institutions (for example, City & Guilds, Business & Technology Education Council (BTEC), various professional institutions) with reference to a wide range of different standards.

## Towards a more Integrated Education and Training System

In 1996, the Dearing Report proposed a common national vocational qualification (NVQ) structure including equal status for vocational and academic qualifications (Study Box 2.1).

---

### Study Box 2.1

**Recent national training initiatives**

#### *NVQ*

NVQs are competence-based, nationally approved qualifications designed to establish 'occupational standards' reflecting real workplace needs within the industries for which they are relevant. By the end of 1995, over 600 NVQs were recognized, applying to more than 500 different occupations, awarded by independent organizations like City & Guilds or BTEC. NVQs address 11 areas of competence (engineering, manufacturing, health/social care, transportation, construction, tending animals/plants/land, business services, developing/extending knowledge and skills, communicating, providing goods and services, extracting and providing natural resources) at each of five different standards (from Level 1, covering routine operative-type skills to Level 5, involving competence in complex techniques, responsibility, and autonomy).

#### *Training and Enterprise Councils (TECs) and Local Enterprise Companies (LECs)*

Employer-led bodies established in 1990, TECs and LECs manage the national training schemes locally (including Youth Training and Training for Work), and promote skill development in response to local need. They have the power to dispense government

---

**Study Box 2.1   Continued**

funds, to manage Training Credit Schemes (vouchers exchanged for approved training), Career Development Loans and the Investors in People initiative (awarded to companies that have met certain specified training standards). Youth Training is designed for school-leavers involved in planned supervised work experience, coupled with attendance at college classes leading to the award of NVQ Level 2 (for example, hairdressing, catering, engineering, mechanics). One of the problems facing employers, however, is that many school-leavers exhibit low levels of literacy.

*Source*: NCVQ (1991) and the Dearing Report (Dearing, 1996).

---

**Study Box 2.2**

**Investors in People**

For Investors in People, the IIP standard stipulates the following criteria must be met:

1   Commitment by top management to the development of employees to achieve corporate objectives – that is, the business plan must incorporate employee development intentions.
2   Regular reviews of employee training and development need.
3   Specification of resources available for training and development.
4   Training and development begins with recruitment and is an ongoing employee development issue requiring regular training needs assessment.
5   Training and development procedures and practices are regularly and systematically evaluated.

In a rare and important evaluation of the long-term impact of Investors in People on organizational performance involving over 120 companies, Tamkin, Hillage, Cummings, Bates, Barber and Tacker (2000) found that 'there is no sudden benefit'. Benefits take time to evolve and must be actively initiated, embedded within the organization and maintained. Organizations that reap the most benefits see Investors in People as the first step in the process of improved profitability, beginning with good management leading to positive staff attitudes, better performance and higher customer satisfaction. These organizations see their workforce ('human capital') as their key resources where cost is a consideration, but not the primary driver of business strategy.

---

Parallel educational initiatives include the establishment of the National Curriculum for Schools (integral to which is the aim of 'economic and industrial understanding') as well as Careers Education and Guidance. Central to government and educational policy is the development of a Key Skills programme, embedded into the national qualification system (Dench, Perryman, & Giles, 1998). These skills (communication, application of numbers, IT, working with others, improving own learning and performance and problem solving) are said to be key to one's ability to operate in the workplace. This programme has also heralded a notable increase in attention to the importance of managing the school-to-work transition (for example, Lent & Worthington, 2000) as well as vocational development in general (for example, Magnuson & Starr, 2000).

Vocational learning is also being progressively integrated into degree-level courses prompted by an Enterprise in Higher Education initiative. Many national attempts have also been made to bring vocational education and training into the core business arena, by fostering employer commitment to training activity. These attempts include Investors in People (Study Box 2.2), the National Training Awards (NTAs), the Life-Long Learning movements (Study Box 2.3) and the Management Charter Initiative (MCI) involving the establishment of management standards and an associated Code of Practice.

The MCI has issued a comprehensive list of management standards, forming the basis of accredited NVQs up to Level 5 (Reid & Barrington, 1997: 445). Whilst the idea has been controversial, companies like British Airways and British Aerospace adopted it apparently to good effect (Harrison, 1989: 6). Support for the MCI initiative came from the Confederation of British Industry, the Department of Education and the Trade Unions Congress, and the delivered MCI-competencies now comprise national management standards incorporated into National Training Targets. Some have, however, criticized the MCI for being unable to adequately capture the complexities of management across different types of organization and industry. The skill needs of managers are also rapidly changing in line with changing business needs (Hirsh & Carter, 2000). One issue in particular continues to be a source of debate and that concerns the value of generic as opposed to specialist knowledge and skill, with the weight of opinion moving more in favour of context-specific education and training (Kettley & Strebler, 1997).

---

### Study Box 2.3

#### Contemporary 'learning' movements

##### *The continuous development movement*

This espouses the importance of integrating learning with work and promoting continuous self-development.

##### *The learning organization*

Argyris and Schon (2002) define the learning organization as one that facilitates the learning of all its members and continually transforms itself in line with business strategy and objectives. The concept of the learning organization is a total cultural solution for an organization and requires a completely different approach to the way training is organized. Nowadays, a learning organization also engages in systematic 'knowledge management' (Hatchuel, LeMasson, & Weil, 2002).

---

**Study Box 2.3   Continued**

### The learning society

In 1991, and later in 1996, the Royal Society of Arts championed the ideal of a 'learning society', the ambit of which encompasses learning in general, the concept of the learning organization and the idea of a 'knowledge economy' (knowledge as a key source of competitiveness in a world market). Learning ability is now a key employability criterion (Contu, Grey, & Ortenblad, 2003).

### Lifelong learning

The EU's 'Year of Lifelong Learning' (1996) prompted the UK Government to identify priority areas requiring action on the learning front.

---

Advantages of the NVQ framework include its 'transparency', 'portability' (people can move about in the NVQ system) and consistency of standards. Disadvantages arise from the prescriptive nature of the standards perhaps more appropriate for lower level routine work than for work requiring autonomous thinking, responsibility, creativity and rapid adjustment to change (for example, Fleming, 1991). Even for lower level jobs, each standard needs constant updating via a functionally minute job analysis (Steedman & Hawkins, 1994). Others have also noted the ever increasing need of organizations for multi-skilled workers (for example, Mafi, 2001).

Marks (1996) has also pointed out the variation in standards generated by lead bodies, and the lack of attention given to comparability across occupational standards for different industries at the same NVQ level. Debate continues in particular over the potentially limited usefulness of company- or industry-specific competency frameworks for management development and also their relevance as a source of leverage for improving organizational performance (for example, Hayes, Rose-Quirie, & Allinson, 2001). Other criticisms pertain to the inaccessible language of NVQs, and the burdensome nature in which the NVQ systems require implementation. Finally, questions remain for how academic degrees will be aligned with NVQ structures.

Despite the criticisms, a recent Institute of Employment Studies survey found that the use of competence based management training is increasing (Strebler, Robinson, & Bevan, 2002). Most companies explained their use of competences to improve the link between skill supply and business needs, to assist in the identification of training needs and designing training. Interestingly, however, companies were generally in favour of internally generated competence frameworks.

## Training as Human Resource Management Strategy

The low priority conventionally assigned to training activity by organizations (Manpower Services Commission, 1987) has cast training practitioners in largely reactive roles. Since the introduction of the integrated national training scheme along with over 100 government and EEC-led schemes offering support for training, organizations have, however, seriously begun to review their training policy. It is now consistently argued that training is no longer a remedial or peripheral option but an essential and intrinsic part of Human Resource Management (HRM) strategies for enhancing organizational competitiveness (Yamnill & McLean, 2001).

A Confederation of British Industry report (CBI, 1989) argued that successful training policy in an organizational context is:

- supported by appropriate infrastructure;
- reconciles employee training and development needs with corporate objectives;
- manages employee attitudes and motivation (Case Study 2.1);
- addresses future as well as existing skill requirements;
- has high status because it produces results.

---

**Case Study 2.1: Training for attitude**

MMS, a company that manufactures pharmaceutical products sold on prescription, formed a mission statement expressing an intention to produce medicines of the highest quality. The fulfilment of this mission required 'highly skilled and adaptable employees ... operating in a rapidly changing technological and market environment' (McKenna & Beech, 1995: 163). In addition to restructuring (delayering, setting up autonomous business units, team approach), a shift in attitudes was believed to be required towards 'adaptability' and 'continuous improvement'. The company identified 12 competencies considered essential to the achievement of this mission, and designed development centres geared to diagnosing employee development needs in the light of organizational changes and then addressing them.

---

The recent HRM rhetoric of training challenges traditional distinctions between training (short-term, skill-based), education (long-term, knowledge-based) and development (process of progressing) (Wexley & Latham, 2002). It also requires a revision of the classic definition of training as a fundamentally 'individual-level' activity (acquiring individual knowledge and skill), towards one that recognizes its 'organizational-level' significance (fostering learning consistent with organizational objectives). The latter affords the training function a strategic role whereby the trainer (an expert in his/her own right) acts as consultant to the organization (for example, analysis of training needs, creation of training solutions to corporate problems).

The issue of how training is defined is more than just semantic; it has critical implications for how training is conceptualized and practised. Whilst training is viewed from a 'system perspective' (see Part 2 of this chapter), it is the individual-level definition that has tended to dominate theory and practice in the training domain.

Training theory is couched in learning theory (for example, Gagne, 1974) rather than in a theory of organizational functioning (Handy, 1987). The use of learning theory is not in itself problematic. What *is* problematic is the lack of systematic consideration addressed to the organizational context of training (De Jong, Thijssen, & Versloot, 2001; Wexley & Latham, 2002). Movements towards linking learning with organizational-level considerations are emerging, but the contribution of psychology to these developments has yet to be fully realized.

A communique in the *Training and Development Journal* (1991) argued for a new agenda for training to address the following questions: Where has the organization been? What is the history and previous business growth like? Where is the organization going? What are its plans? What personnel does it need and what knowledge, skills, attitudes do they require? How is it going to get there? What are its short-term business objectives? What priority areas need tackling? How will the organization know if it is successful? What performance measures will it have? How will it assess its performance? Do trainers have the necessary power bases from which to implement organizational change?

## Part 1 Summary and Conclusions

- The education/training divide is a recurrent problem that society has, and is trying to bridge. Organizations are harnessing a philosophy of learning that has raised the business profile of education, and blurred the boundaries between education and training. The 'learning' principle has thus become a key integrating force and training is no longer seen as a reactive activity but a key business strategy.
- Educational concepts have entered the language and practice of training (for example, learning strategies, self-regulated learning), whilst training concepts have also begun to impact on the language and practice of education (for example, skills initiatives in higher education).

## Part 2: The Systems Approach

A systematic approach to training presupposes a training cycle involving the identification of training needs, specification of training objectives, careful design of training programmes, their implementation and their evaluation (McGhee & Thayer, 1961). A research orientation underwrites this cycle. Goldstein (1993) conceptualized training as an *instructional system* (or subsystem) within a larger organizational and societal system (Study Box 2.5; see also Patrick, 2000 for a comprehensive review of the systems approach to training).

---

**Study Box 2.4**

**Assumptions of the systems approach**

- Uses feedback to continually modify instructional processes: training is never a finished product, it is continually adapting to the situation and its requirements.
- Recognizes the complex interaction among components of a system; concerned with total system.
- System and systematic analysis provides a frame of reference for training practice.
- The training system is part of a larger set of interacting systems – for example, corporate policies, personnel selection, and management philosophy. The criteria for evaluating training are never absolute. Changes in management philosophy, organizational structure or culture, changes in technology, contracts or the design of work, reward and appraisal systems, the actions of competitors, the state of the market, selection practices and attitudes towards training can all profoundly impact on the training system.

---

The instructional model prescribes an analysis of organizational as well as individual level training needs, both providing input to the design of training environments and to the establishment of evaluation criteria. The training environment is more than a set of tools and techniques, but a forum in which choices are made as to which objectives to achieve and how, and also for whom, and by whom. Attention to the training environment also includes consideration of the learning principles that support the acquisition and transfer of learned behaviour.

## Training Needs Analysis

A thorough analysis of training needs (TNA) is a fundamental prerequisite for training design, yet ironically is the most neglected component of the cycle. It is logical to assume that training is best used to address specific needs. Yet organizations often 'put the cart before the horse', designing training to accommodate a new training technology or to match what the competition is doing, rather than customizing their training strategies. There is no substitute for systematic organization-specific TNA. Job names may not differ but their content might, if not the performance context.

Since the classic work of McGhee and Thayer (1961), TNA can be described at three levels: organizational, task and person. Whilst there has been some refinements of these three basic approaches (for example, Goldstein, 1991, 1993; Goldstein & Ford, 2002), the same principles underpin them.

### *Needs analysis as a diagnostic intervention*

***Establishing organizational commitment and support***  Goldstein and Ford (2002) describe TNA as a diagnostic intervention, conducted as a research-based exercise. Like any thorough diagnostic exercise, the process can be highly invasive and potentially disruptive. This could seriously undermine both the quantity and quality of information obtained (Breakwell & Millward, 1995). Goldstein and Ford (2002) thus propose an essential first step in what amounts to a six-step process of TNA (Figure 2.1). This is to establish organizational commitment and support, underpinned by mutual trust and respect and the adoption of a collaborative approach.

**Step 1   Establishing organizational commitment and support**

- Establish relationships with senior management and other key personnel
- Form a liaison team

**Step 2   Organizational analysis**

- Specify goals
- Determine training climate
- Identify external and legal constraints
- Identify resources

**Step 3   Requirement analysis**

- Determine target jobs for TNA
- Determine methods
- Determine participants
- Determine points of contact and their key responsibilities
- Anticipate problems
- Develop a protocol

**Step 4   Needs assessment (Task and knowledge–skill–ability or KSA analysis)**

- Specify tasks
- Cluster tasks
- Analyse KSAs
- Link KSAs to tasks

**Step 5   Person analysis**

**Step 6   Input to and design of training environment, and training evaluation**

**Figure 2.1**   The six-step approach to TNA

McGhee and Thayer (1961) argued that it is not necessary to wait for a performance problem to develop. By asking what produces training needs (for example, where new jobs are created or old jobs are redesigned, when new employees are hired, when the organization changes in some way), future needs of the organization and its employees can also be anticipated.

*Organizational analysis (OA)*   TNA begins by assessing how well the organization is doing. Where is training required?, What are the goals?, What are the obstacles to these goals?, What are the staff discrepancies?, How can training fill the gaps?, Where are the inefficiencies in the system?, and Where are the areas of future change and technological demand? The issue of OA is undoubtedly complex with no hard and fast rules. Goldstein (1993) advises four steps: specify training goals, determine training climate, identify legal constraints and determine resources (Study Box 2.5). Latham (1988) also advocates a *demographic analysis* to identify the needs of different populations of workers (for example, minority groups, female/part-time workers, temporary workers).

---

### Study Box 2.5

#### Organizational analysis of training needs

##### Training goals

Latham (1988) describes three types of goals: (1) training goal is clear and methods of training exist, but whether goals have been appropriately met or not requires evaluation; (2) training goal is clear but method is not obvious (for example, customer complaints indicate a need for training); and (3) training goal and methods are unclear (for example, implementation of changes to adopt a new corporate culture).

##### Training climate

Goldstein (1993) laments the lack of either conceptual or empirical work on training climate, in particular aspects that facilitate or inhibit transfer of learning from training to performance environment.

##### Legal constraints

Legal constraints can operate either *vertically* (for example, industry-specific legal regulations) or *horizontally* (for example, Equal Opportunity rules and regulations).

##### Identification of resources

What *human* (personnel planning and projection of future requirements) and *physical* (equipment, financial) resources are available for training?

---

*Requirement analysis*   Requirement analysis involves identifying the target job(s) to be assessed, how the data is to be collected, who is going to be involved in providing the critical data, ascertaining the key points of contact and their responsibilities, anticipating problems and developing a TNA protocol. OA may highlight all target jobs to be assessed (for example, job changes, structural changes, technological changes, legal requirements).

The purpose is to obtain *accurate, valid* and *reliable information* so 'it is important to develop a method of collecting needs assessment information in a manner that least biases the quality and accuracy of the information ... Each method has unique characteristics that can affect the kind and quality of information obtained' (Goldstein, 1993: 47). Methods include interviews, observation, survey, tests, records, consulting subject matter experts (SMEs), work samples and focus groups. Obtaining multiple perspectives can also reveal *alternative viewpoints* (job incumbents, immediate supervisors). In deciding on which method to use, who to sample and how to handle the information, it is also important to decide on the *level of analysis*. Different units or groups in the organization may have very different views.

The project protocol will incorporate estimated timescales, points of contact and so on. As for any other sound piece of applied research, the protocol should be highly standardized, ensuring both project accountability and future comparability and replicability of the TNA exercise.

***Task analysis***   Task analysis is integral to job analysis. Task analysis for TNA or 'job training analysis' (Reid & Barrington, 1997: 281) identifies exactly what KSAs and attitudes an employee should have in order to perform well at the job in question. Analysing all tasks is, however, potentially very costly and time-consuming. Thus, unless there is good reason, only the core or critical tasks (for example, problem tasks) are identified and analysed in detail. Exhaustive analysis is considered necessary if the trainee is unfamiliar with the majority of their tasks, or if tasks are difficult to learn and/or the cost of error is unacceptably high, and where time and resources are available or where the job is closely prescribed (for example, a surgical operation).

The approach taken will depend on the exact job in question and the circumstances under which a training need may have arisen. The task statement should describe all the essential activities of a job including the results to be accomplished, the tools and equipment and materials used, as well as the requirements of the worker. Task element analysis involves the breakdown of a task into smaller subcomponents and their critical KSA and attitude requirements. Various researchers have offered procedures and other analytical techniques for conducting task analysis (see Goldstein, 1993).

Two constructs of particular relevance to task analysis include 'technical error' (identification of where error is most likely to occur or 'critical' task moments) and 'situational constraint' (identification of the kind of physical and psychological conditions in which trainees will apply what they have learned). Psychological fidelity is especially important. This enables training conditions to be created that set the stage for the acquisition of all relevant KSAs. This can be aided by various techniques including 'stages and key points analysis', 'manual skills analysis', 'job learning analysis', 'faults analysis', 'benchmarking' and 'critical incidents technique' (Reid & Barrington, 1997; Study Box 2.6). For more on task analysis, see **www.sagepub.co.uk/millward**.

---

**Study Box 2.6**

**Analytical techniques for identifying critical features of a job or task**

- *Stages and key points analysis* – involves pinpointing what needs to be done at each stage of a task to advance the job and identifying aspects of the task that need emphasizing.
- *Manual skills analysis* – the exact physical movements of the experienced worker are observed and recorded (for example, fish filleting).
- *Faults analysis* – identification of where faults are most likely to occur in the process of performing a job (occurring in procedure, product, service), particularly costly faults.
- *Job learning analysis* – focuses on the learning processes involved in task completion. Pearn and Kandola (1993) describe nine broad categories of learning skill (defined as skills used to increase other skills and knowledge): physical skills; complex procedures; checking, assessing, discriminating; memorizing facts and other types of information; ordering, prioritizing and planning; looking ahead; diagnosing, analysing, solving; interpreting or using written, pictorial or diagrammatic material; and adapting to new ideas or systems.

---

### Person analysis

Identifying individual needs for training requires 'person analysis'. Questions include whether necessary KSAs are prerequisite to entering the job, whether they can be learned on the job, or whether their acquisition depends on appropriately tailored training. Reid and Barrington (1997: 311) argue that person analysis should also take into consideration what skills/knowledge/personal attributes are likely to be rewarded. Assessing the training needs of new employees is a different consideration. It may involve assessment of *trainability potential* (that is, evaluation of likely performance in training; Downs & Perry, 1987).

Most of the other protocols available for the pursuit of TNA are variations of the above (for example, Reid & Barrington, 1997: 297). All are largely descriptive and prescriptive, geared to maximizing both scientific substance (reliability, validity and accuracy) and also organizational commitment and support.

### Competence analysis

The term 'competence' is now an integral part of personnel and training rhetoric such that the use of jargon, like KSAs (or even 'learning objectives'), no longer seems legitimate or acceptable. The National Council for Vocational Qualification (NCVQ) (1991) defines a competence as the ability to perform 'whole' work roles to the standards expected in employment in real working environments. This approach to job analysis for training purposes thus switches the emphasis from input (KSAs) to output (achievements) using *functional job analysis* techniques (Study Box 2.7).

## Study Box 2.7

### Functional job analysis

Functional job analysis involves analysing the key purpose of the overall area of competence (for example, generic management). The question posed is: What needs to happen for this purpose to be achieved? (for example, breadth of awareness to be well-informed, incisiveness, imagination, organization, drive, self-confidence, sensitivity, cooperativeness, patience; Woodruff, 2000). The same question is repeated so that the functions and subfunctions are broken down into their constituent elements, each accompanied by performance criteria or indicators. Elements and criteria are stated with precision, affording unambiguous interpretation by different users (for example, awarding bodies, assessors, trainers and candidates), yet not so detailed that they pertain only to a specific task or job, specific employer or organization, location or set of equipment. For example, 'organization' is defined as 'identifies priorities, thinks back from deadline, identifies elements of tasks, schedules elements, anticipates resource needs, allocates resources to tasks, sets staff objectives, manages own and others' time' (Woodruff, 2000). Performance criteria are required to specify a critical outcome by defining what has to be done for the relevant function to be successfully achieved.

The idea of transferable competencies is attractive. Unfortunately, too heavy a reliance on the competence framework developed by the NVQ system may incline one to think that a comprehensive TNA is no longer necessary. The derivation of competencies is currently a purely rational exercise without empirical substantiation. Of generic frameworks, it is critical to ask whether the competencies acquired are actually relevant (Woodruff, 2000).

### *Special training needs*

The design of training also requires a review of global training demands. For instance, technological advancement has created a need for the 'knowledge worker' (Bhatt, 2001). Some have argued that in a world of continuous change, the future of work depends critically on 'learning ability', putting the accent on higher order thinking skills, flexibility and quickly learning new skills to an appropriate standard (Hatchuel, Le Masson, & Weil, 2002; Rowley, 2002).

Some have also argued that with the growing accent on team-based working, people need to be trained specifically in the skills of 'team work' and, accordingly, some useful pointers for conducting a team-level needs analysis are emerging (Marks, Sabella, Burke, & Zaccaro, 2002).

Globalization has also raised the salience of diversity management, and for many organizations this is now imperative (Adler, 2002). Increasingly, organizations are operating in the global arena, with people, goods, and services coming from, and going to, many different countries; and the types, frequency, and number of intercultural contacts in organizations are increasing greatly around the world. Diversity training may entail, for instance, training in the appreciation of ethnic and racial diversity (or 'race relations competence') and/or in the skills of cross-cultural communication and management.

The Institute of Employment Studies review of the impact of racism awareness and cultural diversity within training practice concluded that diversity training can work, but too many organizations take a 'sheep dip' approach without lasting impact (Tamkin & Pollard, 2002; see **www.sagepub.co.uk/millward** for review and case studies). The concept of *cultural intelligence* has emerged in association with training for cross-cultural working, defined as the ability to function effectively in a diverse context (Offermann & Phan, 2002). The concept is, however, in need of a theory, and currently lacks empirical foundation.

Three other diversity considerations also arise in connection with demographic changes: older workers, female returns and disabled workers. Older workers now make up a sizeable proportion of the labour market relative to entry-level workers. Downsizing practices during organizational streamlining initiatives meant that many 'older' workers (aged between 40 and 55) were encouraged to retire early or were simply made redundant. However, despite stereotypes about the older worker degenerating cognitively, there is no evidence that age per se affects the capacity of the older worker to be trained in new skills or their ability to adapt to change (Ali & Davies, 2003). Indeed, the wisdom of older workers is increasingly being recognized and harnessed as critical to competitiveness in a world where, increasingly, 'knowledge means power'; older workers may hold implicit organizational wisdom that is impossible to replace (Kodz, Kersley, & Bates, 1999; Rowley, 2002).

The second diversity consideration pertains to the increased number of women returning to work after a career break. Though qualified, some may lack confidence and may need skill updates. Many will seek to combine work with domestic/familial responsibilities, often meaning that they are only available part-time. All of these factors make for a unique set of training and development needs (Kodz, Harper & Dench, 2002).

Regarding the disabled worker, the UK Disability Discrimination Act (1995) imposes a legal responsibility on an employer to make 'reasonable adjustments' to accommodate disability which may have training implications. For example, modifications may need to be made to training methods, materials and instructional techniques generally (Brothen, Warnbach, & Hansen, 2002). There may be instances where this requirement clashes with Health and Safety regulations, but in cases where Health and Safety considerations arise, usually the issue is not sufficiently clear cut to justify outright exclusion (for example, dyslexia in nursing) (Millward, Bryan, Collins, & Everatt, 2004).

Finally, training for re-entry into work after a period of illness-induced absence is of long-standing political concern. Being out of work can become a way of life, creating a sense of isolation from the commercial world and even difficulty with contemplating re-assimilation. Re-entry programmes require attention to motivational and attitudinal factors as well as job skills (Luzzo, 2000).

## Part 2 Summary and Conclusions

- The systems approach sees training as a strategic intervention addressing gaps in KSA and attitude between organizational requirement and the human capital available in fulfilment of these requirements. It is also a pre-emptive intervention that can enable strategic preparation for future KSA requirements.
- A prescriptive research-based model of TNA is described. Central to implementation is the importance of cultivating participation in and ownership of the needs analysis at different levels of the organization. Well-researched aspects of needs analysis pertain to the task level involving job analysis. Person-level analysis is inextricably linked with the appraisal process.
- Organizations, however, tend to short-circuit on their needs analysis, relying instead on 'off-the-shelf' training packages. Others taking a more bespoke approach are increasingly relying on the ill-founded notion of 'competency' to organize TNA.
- Generic training needs across all contemporary organizations include the need to develop learning skills, to address the requirements of minority populations (females who have returned to work after a career break, ageing workers and disabled workers) and to prepare for working in a diverse, multi-cultural employment arena.
- There is a heightening awareness of the need to think less about training for particular jobs, and more for particular types of work (including teamwork). Methods of ascertaining the KSA requirements of teamwork are emerging.

# Part 3: Models of Training

There have been three decades of pleas to develop a theoretical basis for training. In 1961, McGhee and Thayer (p. ix) cautioned that until organizational 'training is submitted to systematic and carefully controlled research and evaluation, management will continue to use a tool of unknown worth, or worse yet, jump from bandwagon to bandwagon'. Whilst there is some attempt to bring theory to bear on some aspects of training (for example, learning theory, motivation theory), this has not rendered the training domain any more coherent. On the contrary, the approach has been piecemeal and unwieldy, making it a difficult field to distil let alone being able to draw out a clear set of practical implications for training design and delivery (Haccoun & Saks, 1998; Salas & Cannon-Bowers, 2001). However, five different 'models' (approaches or perspectives) of training can be described, each with their own distinctive psychology: *instructional, apprenticeship, inquiry, self-evaluation* and *situational learning*. Each model assumes a particular type of learning process, and as such also presupposes a different role for both trainer and trainee (De Jong, Thijssen & Versloot, 2001; Table 2.1):

Table 2.1  *Models of training and their role assumptions*

| Model | Trainer role | Trainee role |
| --- | --- | --- |
| Instruction | Shape skills using behavioural methods | Compliant, blank slate |
| Apprenticeship | Role modelling | Observe/Participate |
| Inquiry | Facilitate/Guide | Explore/Take risks |
| Self-evaluation | Coaching/Goal setting | Self-reflection |
| Situated learning | Collaborator | Task performance, dialogue and social reflection |

## Instructional Model

This is sometimes called the 'industry training model' because it is rooted in the mass skills training initiative after World War II, built from behavioural reinforcement principles. Initially training was conducted on-site, by designated instructors following a standardized training protocol derived from a detailed task analysis (Dooley, 1945; and see above). Later, instructional training was mainly undertaken off-site as a corrective activity (and marginalized accordingly). The emphasis in this model is on skill demonstration followed by guided acquisition through practice, reinforcement and performance testing. Whilst the language of behaviour has since been replaced by the language of cognition, it is still the instructional model that prevails today in the training (Jacobs & Jones, 1995).

This model is, however, increasingly being criticized as perpetuating a false and unjustifiable divide between 'learning' and 'working' (Mafi, 2001), hence the revival of 'on-site' training methods (Jacobs & Russ-Eft, 2001), including modified versions of the apprenticeship model (Dehnbostel, 2001).

## Apprenticeship Model

This model derives from the traditional craft paradigm and involves the transmission of skills by an expert (or master) to the apprentice through a modelling process over a sometimes lengthy period of time (Lave & Wenger, 1991). The apprentice works alongside the master on real work projects, and is socialized into the language and practice of a particular community of work (Sfard, 1998). Learning thus occurs informally as well as formally, the assumption being that practical situated experience is fundamental to the training process. Formal learning may initially involve working on peripheral work activities, moving gradually onto more core work activities with 'training' undertaken through example, assignments, recognition and feedback.

The perceived association between regularized apprenticeships in 16th century England and servantry contributed to the apprenticeship's decline as a method of training in the UK during the 19th century. However, World War I brought a mass demand for highly skilled craftsmen, heralding a revival in apprenticeships. Nevertheless, similar weaknesses inherent in the Elizabethan system (and which contributed to its failure in the 19th century) were identifiable in the revived post-World War I model (Study Box 2.8).

**Study Box 2.8**

**The 'Rip Van Winkle' approach to apprenticeship**

Wexley (1984) outlines seven main characteristics of the traditional apprenticeship system:

1　It generally lasted for five years, whatever the trade.
2　There was certification of the qualified craftsman.
3　It was governed by rigid age limits.
4　There was no theoretical or academic requirement in the process of apprenticeship.
5　There was no central or national control of the apprenticeship process, no consistency in standards or regular evaluation or inspection, no entry requirements or check on training practices. It varied from highly structured and sophisticated (for example, production shops in engineering companies) to unstructured and haphazard (for example, shadowing a skilled craftsman).
6　It focused on one craft.
7　It was wedded to the present and was largely job oriented.

The apprenticeship model has recently made a comeback, though in a more 'planned' form called 'structured on-the-job training', as many organizations reckon with the need to decentralize and re-contextualize the learning process (Dehnbostel, 2001; Jacobs & Jones, 1995; Johnson & Pratt, 1998; Case Study 2.2).

**Case Study 2.2: Learning bays in German manufacturing companies**

*Learning bays* describe a training method commonly used in German industry as a part of a coordinated network of learning (vocation school, corporate training centre, learning by doing in the workplace and learning bays; Dehnbostel, 2001). The concept arose from a decentralized learning project in two Daimler plants. The learning bay (LB) has a double infrastructure of a normal workplace (including all necessary resources) and a learning zone (comprising a range of learning facilities). For instance, in DaimlerChrysler, a group of four to six apprentices spend about six weeks in one LB during the last 18 months of a three-and-a-half year apprenticeship. Apprentices do the same work as the skilled workers but in a controlled environment with a trainer. Each apprentice job rotates within each LB so that they acquire competence on all key tasks including team leadership. The planning, doing and checking of assignments is performed by the group collectively on both a content and a process (including personal attitudes) level. The trainer creates a semi-autonomous learning environment to encourage self-managed problem-oriented learning, which includes setting objectives for the content of learning but mainly also by acting as consultant as well as role model. The LB can also be a site for initiating innovation of new work processes and arrangements. The theoretical basis of the concept of learning bay builds on the principles of experiential learning (see Inquiry Model and Self-Evaluation Model below).

Professional training, especially clinical (medical, dental, nursing and allied professions) training has arguably always comprised elements of the apprenticeship model (Sinclair, 1997). Nonetheless, little is formally known about the learning processes involved from either a practitioner or trainee perspective. Interestingly, there is some research suggesting that what medical students perceive as learning may not always tally with their teachers' perceptions (Ten Cate et al., 2004). This is perhaps indicative of the typically ad hoc and largely opportunistic nature of most on-site 'medical training'.

Conventionally, medical skills (for example, *procedural knowledge*) training (after an extensive period of acquiring theoretical or *declarative knowledge*) is undertaken through a planned series of rotations (akin to those involved in a graduate management scheme) designed to facilitate the acquisition of generic medical skills across the entire clinical range. In practice, medical students thus experience a range of 'apprenticeships' attached to different teams (for example, led by a consultant) where learning may be largely opportunistic and in association with a variety of 'teachers' (including students at a more advanced stage in their learning). Later, more specialized internships may be undertaken within particular clinical domains and attachments to particular consultants (as 'masters of their trade') become more important, especially in association with surgical training (which is more classically undertaken as a form of 'apprenticeship').

However, medical students who are cast in the teaching role 'on the job' may not have had any formal training in 'training skills' or in systematically managing the learning process (Ten Cate et al., 2004). Learning is largely trainee driven (involving mainly observation) and depends fundamentally on the character and quality of the role model (Kenny, Mann, & MacLeod, 2003). Kenny et al. (2003) find the literature on role modelling in the medical education literature largely descriptive (differentiating between 'good' and 'bad' role models) rather than addressing the crucial cognitive and motivational factors involved in the modelling process. They nonetheless emphasize the critical part played by role modelling as a primary source of medical training not only for the imparting of essential clinical skills, but also in professional socialization (or 'character formation'), but caution that its ad hoc non-regulated nature could be highly problematic for the trainee (if, for instance, the trainee is repeatedly humiliated by his or her professional mentor or if his or her experience with a particular mentor is highly eccentric).

Sinclair (1997) also found that learning through 'apprenticeship' in the medical profession is heavily reliant on the dissemination of 'stories' (in the form of myths and legends) about particular consultants, rather than formal training. Also, in practice, medical students may become apprenticed not to the 'master' him or herself (the elusive consultant), but one of the master's higher order 'servants' (for example, the consultant's registrar), and more informally (which often remains only implicit and unacknowledged), may also learn a great deal from senior nursing staff.

Unfortunately, little is known about how skills are learned *in context* whether during medical training (Bannister, Hilliard, Regehr, & Lingaard, 2003) or organizational training in general (Jacobs & Jones, 1995; Salas & Cannon-Bowers, 2001). Some recent attempts have been made amongst medical educators to develop 'learning models' to facilitate a more systematic undertaking of training on-the-job (for example, Ten Cate et al., 2004) and 'skills training' in particular is increasingly being held to account (for example, Hoffman & Donaldson, 2004). It is generally agreed that classroom-based learning (often involving virtual reality simulators) must be coupled with 'structured clinical experience' across a range of clinical scenarios, graded in level of difficulty and systematically assessed (to increase performance accountability; for example, Schaefer, 2004).

In the service domain, learning 'on the job' is equivalent to 'doing the job', which adds a critically different dimension to the learning process. In their research on 'on-site' clinical training, Hoffman and Donaldson (2004) found that the quality of patient coupled with pressures of time affected the interpretative and reflective processes of team-members, created role conflicts (for example, teacher/practitioner, learner/practitioner) and generally disrupted teaching and learning processes. On a more positive note, Rafiq et al. (2004) report on a new technological application (digital video capture, robotics, video teleconferencing, and intranet transmission) in surgical training to support consultants during 'real time' in their training of 'apprenticed' surgeons.

Another related issue arising in recent years in association with professional training in general, and medical training in particular, concerns the viability of 'accelerated' learning (Talbot, 2004). Whilst the optimal length of medical training remains undetermined, most recommend a slow incubation process facilitated by reflection on experience (akin to what has been called the 'hidden curriculum' in professional training). Talbot (2004) applies the metaphor of 'good wine' needing time to 'mature' and cautions against the movement towards 'accelerated' professional training. Indeed, accelerated training is now an option within many different 'professions' but raises important questions about the quality of learning.

## Inquiry Model

The inquiry model assigns the trainee a more active role, with the trainer recast as facilitator. Faced with a task, trainees actively collect information relevant to this task and learning arises through reflecting on this. Theoretically, this model is rooted in the notion of experiential learning and action learning (Farnham, 1994). Basically, this model involves learning by doing and, in particular, by problem solving. Training objectives are framed (as in the apprenticeship model) as broad tasks to be mastered rather than skills to be learned. The trainee is empowered to get on with the task, and is expected to be able to justify his or her approach to the task in an informed and reflective way. Relevant information and tools are available to resource inquiry-based learning, and the trainer takes a 'tutoring' or facilitating role in guiding, supporting, monitoring quality and providing challenges.

Learning from experience, however, 'can be messy, difficult and often lengthy' (Mafi, 2001: 489), which may put organizations off any serious use of the inquiry model in an organizational context. On the other hand, it is increasingly being realized that highly regulated off-site training does not furnish 'performance ready' employees, able to keep apace with the demands of continuous change (Carnevale, 1992). The McDonald's metaphor might not inspire much faith in a training system built on the 'quick and dirty' take-away principle, but there is an important (and perhaps unfortunate) reality check nonetheless in Mafi's (2001: 491, italics in original) words: 'there is a need to increase the trainee's contact with real problems, in real time, and in real organizational settings, *forcing trainees to apply the learning as quickly as possible.'* Providing training on an 'expedited basis' does not, however, mean that the design process is circumvented; on the contrary, it requires even more careful attention to design and delivery considerations.

Management training in particular has become a critical issue in the on-site/off-site training debate, the inquiry-based approach being central to these consideration. Companies are responding to these imperatives by interconnecting classroom-based case studies with 'real-life' learning on the job through action learning principles (involving the presentation of novel scenarios for which there are no performance scripts, challenging assignments and individual responsibility and accountability through having to make real decisions that matter; see Mafi, 2001 for best practice examples). Evidence suggests that building a planned cycle of action and reflection into the management training process in actual job situations (involving active coaching) facilitates transfer of training (for example, Robinson & Wick, 1992).

Whilst some 'on-the-job' training is usually built into most formal management programmes, this may be merely 'tagged on' to classroom-based learning rather than systematically integrated into it. This will require that close attention be addressed to the context in which this learning is most appropriately couched (without unwittingly creating a transfer of learning problem as opposed to facilitating it), to the methods of training delivery (for example, inductive learning through active inquiry balanced with deductive learning where trainers provide the material to be learned) and the role of the trainer (for example, the need for on-site coaching and mentoring) (Study Box 2.9).

---

### Study Box 2.9

#### Coaching

There are many different 'models' of coaching, but it is generally agreed that the effective coach actively *involves* the learner in the process of skill acquisition. Integrating the results of many observational taxonomies of effective 'coach behaviour', Douge and Hastie (1993) elaborate on this as follows:

- provides frequent and constructive feedback with numerous prompts and hustles;
- provides high levels of correction and reinstruction;
- uses high levels of questioning and clarifying;
- is predominantly engaged in instruction;
- manages the training environment to achieve considerable order.

However, more recent views are that coaching is substantially more complex than this, and that part of what makes a coach effective is his or her ability to adapt to the requirements of the individual situation, and that there is a critical and hitherto somewhat elusive 'relationship' component. The concept of coaching, especially executive coaching, is now a hot topic in the contemporary organization (Carter, 2002; see Chapter 6) but whether it does actually improve performance remains to be properly investigated (for example, Kampa-Kokesch & Anderson, 2001).

The principle of inquiry-based learning has nonetheless found a small foothold in the mainstream occupational training literature in the form of 'error training'. Whilst the instructional model actively discourages errors (with training designed to increase the likelihood of 'success' experiences to maximize opportunity for positive feedback), some say that this does not facilitate the development of exploratory (innovative) behaviours, nor the appropriate self-regulatory strategies required to avoid errors or mistakes in the future (Gully, Payne, Koles, & Whiteman, 2002). By contrast, error encouragement training allows trainees to experiment, and to reinterpret errors as a learning opportunity (Dormann & Frese, 1994).

Initial evidence from Frese and colleagues points to the added value of error training over error avoidance training insofar as it encourages active learning, a higher level of information processing and efficacy, which is itself an important predictor of whether learning is transferred from training to work environment. Gully et al.'s (2002) findings, however, note that error encouragement training may not be suited to all trainees, particularly those who are highly conscientious (who may suffer too much frustration and anxiety) and/or who do not have a prerequisite level of cognitive ability to be able to learn from their errors. In their study, only trainees with a high level of cognitive ability and who were relatively 'open to experience' benefited from error training. Gully et al. point to the need for more research to explore the mechanisms by which error training (and other similar, discovery-based learning activities) could optimize learning (for example, learning orientation).

There are clearly very real limits to the extent to which inquiry-based learning opportunities (see below) can be facilitated in some practical settings like medicine. A considerable literature, for instance, has emerged within the medical training literature on how to strike an appropriate balance between learning 'for real' and the *ethics* of doing so on live patients (for example, Flanagan, Nestel, & Joseph, 2004). It is now common to find papers evaluating the relative effectiveness of high-fidelity computer-based virtual reality simulation methods as a basis for learning important medical skills (for example, airway management, gastro-intestinal endoscopy; see, for example, Schaefer, 2004) as a quasi-clinical 'safe' alternative to on-site inquiry-based training.

## Self-Evaluation Model

A variant of the inquiry model, the self-evaluation model encourages reflective thought through professional supervision or mentorship (Pajak, 1993). The trainee sets goals, seeks feedback and reflects on his or her performance continually whilst the trainer facilitates this process. The role of formal training is downplayed in this model.

One way to conceptualize the self-evaluation model is using the concept of 'andragogy' (Knowles, 1972). Andragogy is learner-centred in that the learner has a monopoly over what is learned and how, which contrasts with pedagogy which is instructor-centred (that is, the teacher has a monopoly over what is learned and how). Andragogy assumes that the learner is primarily self-directed, problem-oriented, motivated by internal satisfiers like self-esteem and recognition and needing to be involved in the learning process. Mezirow's (1985) 'Charter for Andragogy', in particular, specifies a way of fostering self-direction through challenge and critical awareness (Study Box 2.10).

Ideological critiques note the implicit barriers to inclusion within this particular learning philosophy (Contu, Grey, & Ortenblad, 2003). Elen and Lowyck (1999) nonetheless illustrate how andragogical learning principles can be effectively built into design strategy. The onus is on educational and training institutions to make active attempts to identify and overcome cultural and social barriers to participation in learning events.

---

### Study Box 2.10

### The Charter for Andragogy

- Progressively decrease the dependency of the learner on the educator/instructor.
- Help the learner to understand the use of learning resources including how to engage others in reciprocal learning.
- Assist in self-diagnosis of learning needs (including helping people become aware of how cultural and/or organizational factors might have influenced these).
- Assist learners to assume increasing responsibility for their own learning.
- Foster decision making and perspective taking by appreciating the choices available.
- Encourage the use of 'criteria' for personal benchmarking and a self-corrective approach.
- Facilitate problem solving and a self-reflexive approach.
- Reinforce learner self-concept and self-esteem by providing progressive mastery experiences (to promote self-efficacy) and a supportive climate with feedback to encourage genuine efforts to change, including the willingness to take personal risks and the inclination to avoid making competitive or critical judgements about oneself.
- Emphasize the use of experiential and participative methods.

---

One of the most important features of andragogy as conceived by Brookfield (1986), Mezirow (1985), and Tennant (1988) is that it describes an approach to learning that links education with personal development. Contemporary writers argue that progress in training design in the 21st century will depend fundamentally on the ability to factor in 'person' considerations at both a theoretical and practical level (Spector, 2002).

The concept of 'reflection' is central to formulations of training in which self-evaluation is said to be the critical medium of learning. Reflective practice is now inextricably built into many professional training programmes as a central mechanism for self-directed learning (and continuous professional development; for example, Dornan, Scherper, & Boshuizen, 2003). However, surprisingly little is known about what this involves, whether it is indeed an effective way of learning, and, if it is, how it can be most effectively 'facilitated'.

The concept of 'learning styles' suggests that there are individual differences in 'reflective tendencies'. Kolb (1984: 38) defines learning as 'the process whereby knowledge is created through the transformation of experience', a process that is not identical for everyone. He talks of 'styles' of learning that operate as 'organised ways of automatically processing' the information one encounters on a day-to-day basis. They are not fixed, but adaptive states evolved from past experience of 'what works'. Different styles arise from relative degrees of emphasis on concrete experience and reflective observation as a means of apprehending reality, in combination with either abstract conceptualization and/or active experimentation as ways of transforming this reality (Study Box 2.11).

---

### Study Box 2.11

#### Kolb's learning styles

Kolb (1984) argues that each mode of gathering and processing experience combines to form a learning style as follows (measured using the Learning Style Inventory):

- *divergers* – reflect on specific experiences from various different perspectives (combines 'concrete experience' and 'reflective observation');
- *assimilators* – develop a theoretical framework on the basis of reflection (combines 'reflective observation' and 'abstract conceptualization');
- *accommodators* – use the results of testing as the basis for new learning (combines 'concrete experience' and 'active experimentation').

In a study of over 200 management undergraduates, Loo (2004) found little evidence for Kolb's proposed association between learning preferences and learning styles. He found, on the contrary, wide individual differences in learning preference within each 'style' and small differences in learning preference mean scores. Clearly, the conceptual and empirical relationship between learning style, learning strategy (practical learning inclinations) and cognitive style (modes of information processing) also needs to be clarified (see below).

---

The concept of self-reflection as a learning strategy has not been systematically explored and remains very much assumption based. Research needs to look at the possibility of different types of reflection (intentional/unintentional, internal/interpersonal) to explore the content of reflection (positive, negative), its underlying mechanisms (for example, meta-cognitive) and consequences. Moreover, self-reflection needs to be distinguished from concepts like 'rumination' (which denotes a form of cognitive perseveration with intrusive subjective consequences; Cropley & Millward, 2004). Jordan and Millward (2004) used diaries to investigate everyday reflective tendencies amongst mental health professionals. All engaged in substantial reflection daily (although there were wide individual differences), in part created by the requirements of the diary. However, of particular interest were differences in the type of reflection engaged in. For instance, internally oriented self-reflection was coupled with interpersonal reflection (reflective discussion with others) and ruminative reflection was also common. Joireman, Parrott and Hammersla's (2002) argument for a distinction between self-rumination and self-reflection is consistent with these findings. They note how self-rumination can involve focusing on bad aspects of self, which in turn creates anxiety and poor self-image. In learning terms, this type of reflection could seriously inhibit performance. The learning implications of these different types and foci of reflection have yet to be systematically investigated.

## The Situated Learning Model

Situated learning pertains to an epistemology of knowledge, thinking and learning from a social constructionist perspective (Lave & Wenger, 1991; Stein, 2001). It begins with a challenge to the assumption of conventional training approaches that cognition is independent of the context in which it occurs. This assumption is rooted in a general philosophy of situated cognition (for example, Brown, Collins, & Duguid, 1989). Rather, the situated learning principle assumes that the physical and social context in which an activity takes place is an integral part of that activity and, in turn, this activity is an integral part of the learning. How an individual learns and the situation in which the information is learned are inextricably one and the same thing. Social interaction (with people and artefacts of the situation) is a key mechanism of learning, where knowledge is acquired through a process of collaboration and critical reflection (Study Box 2.12).

From the situated learning perspective, trainees acquire (that is, construct) job knowledge from engaging with the task and entire task context (the 'ultimate authentic situation'; Stein, 2001: 416). Learning is not haphazard but structured by the imperatives created by the task. However, an important element of situated learning is the role of experts (the practice community) who, through action and dialogue, define what constitutes legitimate knowledge.

---

**Study Box 2.12**

**Situated learning constructs**

*Content*

Learning content (*what* is learned) is embedded in tasks (incorporating social norms about the most appropriate way to accomplish the task) and is acquired by doing those tasks, and also by discussing and reflecting with others on the meaning of this experience. Trainees experience what works and what does not (as opposed to extracting knowledge *from* the situation).

## Study Box 2.12    Continued

### Context

Context describes the values, beliefs, socio-cultural and environmental cues through which the trainee masters job content; it constitutes the background for content interpretation. Context encompasses power relations, politics, competing priorities, and so on, and defines the application of knowledge and skill.

### Work community

Whilst context shapes how content is interpreted, the work community shapes the learning experience itself. It denotes the distributed knowledge of experience, providing a setting for social interaction. Community provides the opportunity to observe, engage in dialogue and internalize accepted ways of doing things. In Stein's (2001: 419) words, 'by engaging in reflection on experience and through sharing of everyday work stories, trainees and trainers construct job knowledge'. This resonates with the finding reported earlier of medical trainees learning 'the trade' in part through myths and legends (Sinclair, 1997).

The practical implications of the situated learning model (which also comprises elements of inquiry and reflection) are that learning should take place within the complexity and ambiguity of performing actual job tasks, through immersion in the daily life of an organization (Stein, 2001). Whilst trainers may also provide explicit training through lectures or demonstrations, trainees will only come to 'own' this knowledge through insights garnered through reflective conversations with other. This requires trainers to become attuned to the 'environmental cues guiding task performance, the thought processes involved in action taken and the consequences' (Stein, 2001: 419). *Reflective debriefing* of this kind is now common within the professions (for example, Dornan, Scherper & Boshuizen, 2003) and, in the form of 'after action reviews', is also built into military training (Roddy, 2004).

In conventional training models, trainers are considered merely as 'transmitters of established ideas'. However, the situated learning approach necessitates a different conceptualization of the trainer's role as collaborator in the learning process. Initially, trainers select situations that will engage the trainee but must also provide guidance on how to master the situation. Later, as trainees become more able to 'stand alone', the role of the trainer may become more facilitative (for example, encouraging reflection, helping trainees become aware of contextual cues, continually assessing trainee development). The skill of the trainer is to judge when it is most appropriate to start 'fading' out their involvement and to do so in a meaningfully successive way (Atkinson, Renkl, & Merrill, 2003; see Study Box 2.13). Trainers and trainees collaborate in developing problem-solving strategies such that learning is situated in the performing not the teaching. To this extent, knowledge is relational and particularistic.

This conceptualization of the trainer's role focuses in particular on the character and quality of the relationship evolved with the trainee, as a constantly changing inextricably linked part of the learning process. Stein (2001: 421) refers to the idea of 'cognitive apprenticeship' as a fruitful means of applying a situated learning approach to training (Study Box 2.13).

---

### Study Box 2.13

### Cognitive apprenticeship

Cognitive apprenticeship (Brant, Farmer, & Buckmaster, 1993) comprises the following integrated use of techniques: modelling, coaching and scaffolding, articulation, reflection and exploration. The instructor 'models' the appropriate behaviour or skill and then proceeds to coach the trainee using observation and feedback. Once the trainee has a good grasp of what to do, the instructor takes on less the role of coach and more the role of 'scaffolder' (providing suggestions, hints and so on). Effectively, the scaffolding role is a means of weaning the trainee from their dependence on the instructor. The trainee is invited to articulate what they are doing and why, in a way similar to that required for 'verbal protocol analysis' – that is, a means of accessing the current state of the mental model guiding performance (Ford & Kraiger, 1995: 17). Illustrating the importance of 'prompts' like verbal protocol analysis, Atkinson et al. (2003) found that skills do not reliably generalize to 'far-transfer' tasks (tasks further removed from the training situation) purely through 'fading out' the trainer's role, unless trainees are encouraged through strategic prompting to reflect on and identify the underlying principles. In the final stage of cognitive apprenticeship, the trainee is then required to reflect on what they have done and what they could have done better and to explore new applications of what they have learned.

---

Evidence for the idea of 'ownership' of the learning process and its outcomes can be derived from research on the benefits of empowerment on job knowledge (Leach, Wall, & Jackson, 2003). Empowerment involves the delegation of responsibility down the hierarchy to increase the decision-making authority of an employee with respect to their primary task. It may also be a term used to refer to a feeling of being empowered (that is, perceived efficacy).

The idea that empowerment promotes knowledge acquisition is central to the work design literature. The assumption is that empowerment facilitates 'cognitive growth ... through the transfer of knowledge among individuals who might not otherwise share information' (Wagner, Leana, Locke, & Schweiger, 1997). Action theory (Frese & Zapf, 1994) sees empowerment as a form of 'control' that is itself a facilitator of learning. Wagner and colleagues (1997) tested these assumptions with a sample of operators of complex manufacturing technology (using a knowledge elicitation interview) and confirmed that especially for novice operators, there was a substantial knowledge gain (fault management knowledge, in particular) after an empowerment initiative combined with improvements in self-efficacy. Whilst it is difficult to say for sure whether this knowledge gain was directly attributable to the empowerment initiative, Leach et al. (2003: 49) argue that enhanced decision-making responsibility can build on an employee's existing knowledge, skill and experience, and to this extent can 'unlock knowledge' as much as facilitate knowledge acquisition. As such they note that 'empowerment represents … a plausible alternative or complement to formal off the job training'.

These findings are consistent also with the concept of the 'learning bay' (which also embodies an empowerment initiative; Case Study 2.3) within a more planned version of the 'apprenticeship model', and with other on-site training initiatives that encourage inquiry and self-reflection (Jacobs & Jones, 1995; Johnson & Pratt, 1998).

## Part 3 Summary and Conclusions

- Five different 'models' of training can be described, each with a distinctive set of epistemological assumptions about the nature of the learning process and its most effective management: the instructional model (experimental psychology), apprenticeship model (action theory), the inquiry and the self-evaluation model (experiential psychology), and the situational model (social constructionism).
- The importance of *on-site* training and the *active* role of the trainee in the learning process are assumptions strongly defended by all models. All except the instructional model emphasize the importance of *informal* as well as formal 'on-site' training opportunity. The apprenticeship model integrates considerations from all models (instruction, inquiry, self-reflection, situated learning).
- The instructional model remains the dominant framework for 'organizational training', but evidence suggests that alternative forms of learning (inquiry-based, self-reflection) are being assimilated into this framework. Consideration of the cognitive and motivational factors involved in the learning process is now central to instructional theory.

## Part 4: Instructional Theory

Within the psychology of training, training design has been largely addressed from within the *instructional model* (Part 3), hinging fundamentally on the determination of content-valid training objectives derived from a valid and reliable TNA (Goldstein, 1993: 79). Two essential psychological considerations arise from this:

1  how to optimize learning during the training process;
2  how to maximize retention and transfer of learning to the place of work.

The second consideration assumes that training is conducted 'off-site' in a specially constructed learning environment (Haccoun & Saks, 1998). 'Instructional theory' is a theory about how to 'design instructional environments' using the principles of learning.

# What is Instructional Theory?

The aim of instruction is to provide an optimal learning environment, that is, to manage learning (Bass & Vaughan, 1967). Specifically, instructional theory demonstrates *how* this can be done through the careful manipulation of external instructional events (Gagne, Briggs, & Wager, 1992: 7), especially the 'conditions of learning'. Early work on instructional theory was underwritten by stimulus–response learning principles. Thus, a stimulus (instructional context and medium) is followed by a response (trainee behaviour) that is then rehearsed (practice) and reinforced (knowledge of results and feedback) (Bass & Vaughan, 1967: 7). Nowadays, consideration of how a new behaviour or skill can be shaped by external stimuli is coupled with consideration of how to optimize the learning process cognitively within the individual, through the appropriate arrangement of instructional events (Ford & Kraiger, 1995; Goldstein, 1993).

Gagne et al. (1992) talk of macro-level behavioural learning principles and micro-level cognitive learning processes.

## Micro-cognitive learning processes

Micro-cognitive learning processes refer to the information processes involved in the act of learning (Gagne & Driscoll, 1988; Study Box 2.14).

---

### Study Box 2.14

### Micro-processes of learning

The kinds of processes presumed to occur during any learning act are (Gagne et al., 1992: 188–189):

- *attention* – determines the extent and nature of reception of stimulation;
- *selective perception* – transforms stimulation into features or patterns (sometimes called pattern recognition);
- *cognitive rehearsal* – maintains and renews information stored in short-term memory; aids transfer to long-term memory;
- *semantic encoding* – prepares information for long-term storage;
- *retrieval* (and search) – returns stored information to working memory or to a response generator;
- *response organization* – selects and organizes performance;
- *feedback* – provides information about performance and sets processes of reinforcement into play;
- *executive control processes (or meta-cognition)* – selects and activates cognitives strategies; can modify any or all of the processes described above – for example, the role of expectancies can influence how an event is perceived, encoded, retrieved and used.

The model puts accent in particular on how to design instruction to optimally harness memory processes. For example, information is most likely to be meaningfully processed when presented in chunks (similar information is presented together), by forming images (certain metaphors evoke an entire image array) and when emphasis is given (raising salience by forming contrasts). Retention and retrieval are critical to learning. Knowledge of how information can be forgotten is important since instruction can be designed to prevent this. For instance, meaningful information is retained for longer than that which has been rote learned (Bass & Vaughan, 1967).

Instances of learning interference have also been documented – including the interference between new learning and old (proactive inhibition), and old learning by new (retroactive inhibition). Instructional design can aim to minimize inhibition or interference of this kind, for example, by forging explicit and meaningful links between old and new information. In short, Gagne, Briggs, and Wager (1992: 11) point out that to be effective, instruction must be able to influence the micro-processes of learning.

## The macro-principles

*The repetition principle*   Repetition involves rehearsal or practice. Various different types of learning curve (the rate of increase or decrease of learning with time, as a function of practice) can be described. If the task is easy, a negatively accelerated curve is likely, describing an instance of rapid learning until a plateau is reached and mastery is attained. Thereafter, further practice may reach a point of diminishing returns. For complex tasks, a slower and more accumulative process is more likely, with some acceleration in the later stages (reflecting a slow beginning followed by more rapid progress later on).

In reality, learning curves are never as smooth as such descriptions might suggest. They can vary widely depending on: (a) the specific schedule of practice; (b) the instructional medium; (c) the extent to which guidance is given; (d) the nature of the task; and (e) the state of trainee readiness (Bass & Vaughan, 1967). Whatever the shape of the learning curve, it is now well established that a response must be repeated for sustained learning to occur. There are some instances, however, where repetition may not improve learning due to motivational decline (for example, Driskell, Willis, & Cooper, 1992).

The issue of temporal spacing also arises in connection with practice schedules – that is, distributed (spread over time) or massed (intensive). Donovan and Radosevich (1999) synthesized the results from 63 studies on this issue using meta-analysis, and found that individuals in spaced practice conditions performed significantly higher than those in massed practice conditions. However, a more detailed analysis revealed that whether spaced or massed practice is superior depends fundamentally on the nature of the task as well as the interval between 'spaced' practice conditions. In general, distributed practice seems to be better for ensuring learning efficiency (particularly when considering total overall workload). Massed practice is better where temporal efficiency is more important than learning efficiency, particularly for short learning assignments and for assimilating largely familiar information (for example, last-minute revision). Qualifiers include the capability and experience of trainees, coupled with task difficulty (Salas & Cannon-Bowers, 2001).

***The reinforcement principle***　The principle of reinforcement (or instrumental conditioning) presupposes an initial behavioural response that can be either strengthened or weakened depending on its consequences. Early formulations of training within the instructional model were built on precise 'operant principles' – for example, programmed learning, teaching machines (Nord, 1969). A behaviour that is contingent on certain consequences (reward, avoidance of punishment) is self-reinforcing and will be maintained (Skinner, 1957). If the contingencies of reinforcement change (for example, there are no longer any rewards) the behaviour is extinguished because it is no longer instrumental. Formally defined then, reinforcement is a rewarding stimulus that follows a behaviour (or operant) and thereby increases the likelihood of it occurring again.

In the stimulus–response model of reinforcement, the learner is modelled as blindly attempting to obtain a reward and to avoid punishment through trial-and-error. In practice, the precision required to apply operant principles (that is, making the outcome immediately contingent on a specific behaviour) is difficult to sustain. Evaluation studies of operant training methods have failed to provide support for its superiority over more unstructured methods (Latham, Millman, & Miedema, 1998).

The socio-cognitive model (Bandura, 1977), however, assumes that action consequences *inform* the individual (knowledge of results) about whether modification is needed (Study Box 2.15). This results in the evolution of a behavioural chain where successful completion of one component acts as a cognitive cue for successful performance of the next (successive approximation). Expectations of success (outcome expectancy) also acquire self-regulatory power by building self-efficacy (Study Box 2.16). A task can also be symbolically represented or modelled, making it possible to learn *vicariously* from the successes and failures of others through observation and imitation. This formulation of the training process has moved instructional psychology away from a predominantly experimental approach towards the integrative application of insights derived from cognitive, social, clinical, counselling and also sports psychology (Haccoun & Saks, 1998).

---

### Study Box 2.15

#### Feedback

Feedback refers to a process of issuing reward of either an intrinsic (for example, praise), or extrinsic kind (for example, recommendation for promotion), whilst knowledge of results refers to the content of the feedback. Feedback must be accurately perceived (for example, errors must be recognized, as must be the connection between what happened and its consequences) and accepted for it to be of use to a learner/trainee. Neither can feedback be taken for granted, particularly if it is negative (Ilgen & Davis, 2000). Recent research suggests that there are differences in 'feedback seeking'

## Study Box 2.15    Continued

on the part of trainees, perhaps in part a function of their goal orientation (learning or performance oriented). Learning-oriented trainees are more likely to seek and respond constructively to feedback whilst performance-oriented trainees who are preoccupied with proving themselves are less likely to seek and respond well to feedback (Tuckey, Brewer, & Williamson, 2002). Emotional blocks to learning can be erected by repeated experiences of failure and an inappropriate use of feedback to judge performance rather than to facilitate learning (Downs, 1996). Optimal use of extrinsic feedback is that which does not put pressure on a trainee/learner to perform, but which facilitates learning through the provision of intermittent success experiences. Additionally, too much augmented feedback during the instructional process can engender dependency. Independence can be fostered by gradually reducing the amount of feedback, calling attention to intrinsic cues and developing the cognitive strategies required for independent functioning (Bass & Vaughan, 1967).

## Study Box 2.16

### Self-efficacy

Self-efficacy pertains to the conviction one holds of one's ability to successfully execute the behaviour required to produce particular outcomes, assuming a perceived link between action (for example, 'if I study hard' ...) and outcome (for example, 'I will get the grades I need to get into medical school'). Perceptions of self-efficacy are specific to a particular behavioural domain (for example, academic, vocational, social, family). They determine choice of behavioural settings and activities, the amount of effort individuals are ready to expend, and how long they persist in the face of obstacles. Wood and Bandura (1989) highlight the importance of mastery experiences for building self-efficacy, including the experience of success, coupled also with the observation of models proficient in overcoming blocks to success, even failure. Feedback and encouragement must be realistic, facilitating the investment of greater effort rather than either disillusionment (for example, through repeated failure experiences) or complacency (for example, through repeated success experiences).

Research consistently highlights the positive impact of self-efficacy on various different training outcomes, including the likelihood of transfer of learning to job performance (Ford, Smith, Weissbein, Gully, & Salas, 1998; Haccoun & Saks, 1998; Kraiger, Ford, & Salas, 1993; Latham et al., 1998). However, we know very little about how and when best to influence self-efficacy during the training process. For instance, we know that pre-training efficacy perceptions can mediate and moderate training effectiveness, in which case it would be of benefit to enhance efficacy during the skill acquisition process to ensure successive 'success' experiences. On the other hand, too much feedback could distract the trainee or create undue performance anxiety at the early stages of skill acquisition when cognitive resources are dedicated to the learning itself (Anderson, 1982). If post-training efficacy for transfer is low, the trainee may need additional on-site support and mentorship to facilitate

*(Continued)*

---

**Study Box 2.16   Continued**

continued task rehearsal and its subsequent performance application (Haccoun & Saks, 1998). Experiential learning is generally found to be most conducive to building efficacy for both acquisition and transfer (Bretz & Thompsett, 1997; see 'Managing Training Motivation' later in this chapter).

---

**Study Box 2.17**

### Cognitive and behavioural modelling

Cognitive and behavioural modelling describes a process by which we learn vicariously rather than through direct experiences (Bandura, 1977). This is also called 'mastery modelling' (Goldstein & Sorcher, 1974), and involves:

1   the trainer bringing the attention of the trainees to key learning points;
2   showing a videotape or film that depicts the enactment of the learning points (for example, behaving assertively as opposed to aggressively);
3   discussing the modelled behaviour;
4   role playing the behaviour in the presence of the other trainees and the instructor;
5   trainees receiving feedback (for example, praise) for successful enactment of the desired behaviour; and
6   trainees discussing how they will transfer what they have learned to work.

Goldstein and Sorcher (1974) reported on several studies that supported the use of this particular technique in improving managers' skills, orienting new employees, teaching job skills and handling discrimination complaints, respectively. However, not much is known about what aspects of behavioural modelling are effective, or why. Gagne et al. (1992) speculate that its effectiveness could be due to the individualized focus of the technique (trainees generate their own personal learning points, and feedback on performance is individually tailored). Gist and Mitchell (1992) suggest that trainees may 'cognitively model' (visualize) themselves performing an activity as a form of vicarious learning. There is an extensive literature on 'visualization' strategies in sports psychology that could fruitfully be harnessed to understand this modelling process. Increased interest in recent years in the training/learning benefits of having an on-site mentor may provide renewed impetus for research into the processes involved in modelling and its effectiveness as a training strategy (Latham, Millman & Miedena, 1998).

## Instructional Analysis

Gagne et al. (1992) emphasize that identifying all component skills required to reach a particular instructional goal is not in itself a sufficient basis for instructional design.

Tasks and their capability requirements must be classified in terms of particular learning outcomes. A first step in the process of inferring learning outcomes is to produce an instructional map for each particular task, the KSAs that the tasks pre-suppose, and then to classify tasks by identifying the capability requirements they have in common.

### Infer learning outcomes

The design of instruction works backwards from outcomes before considering instructional strategy and methods. Gagne et al. (1992) and Gagne (1974) describe five categories of learning outcome: verbal information, intellectual skills, cognitive strategies, motor skills, and attitudes.

***Verbal information*** This pertains to the 'facts' associated with a learning domain (declarative knowledge). Information is organized in 'schemas' or 'knowledge structures' that can strongly influence how new information is understood and assimilated. Schemata can be prototypes of concepts (for example, a leader, teamwork), schemata of action (for example, driving), or scripts reflecting a sequence of events (for example, flying a plane, problem solving). They can also take the form of plans or goals.

***Intellectual skills*** These denote the concepts, rules and principles (procedural knowledge) associated with problem solving and other higher-order thinking domains, such as forming abstractions and applying them to a variety of structured situations (for example, linguistic rules and their application). Most rules form 'learning hierarchies' where some intellectual skills are prerequisite to others and must be integrated or combined. Learning a foreign language, for instance, requires learning elementary discriminations and concepts (for example, word-sounds, basic terms and phrases) before learning the rules governing the formation of elaborate sentences.

Instructional events can be designed to facilitate the development of cognitive schemas by providing 'organizing schemes or frames' in the form of a cue (either verbal, quantitative, or graphic) that brings into salience relevant existing knowledge, to which new material can be related (Merrill, 2002). The organizer helps focus attention on important features of a task or learning process, and moreover can facilitate active assimilation and integration of new information with old. An example is described by Mayer (1988), who produced diagrammatic representations of the functional structure of a computer (a so-called 'advanced organizer'), which successfully aided learning during a computer programming course.

***Cognitive strategies*** Cognitive strategies allow one to learn, think, and solve problems. Whilst intellectual skills pertain to how people deal with structured problems, cognitive strategies are concerned with the solving of novel problems. They are self-regulatory, pertaining to how individuals learn how to learn, how to remember, and how to engage in reflective and analytical thought (Gagne, 1974: 138). They involve executive control over processes of semantic encoding (for example, forming images of the material to be learned), retrieval (for example, mnemonic systems) and also problem-solving capabilities (for example, searching for deep meaning, flexibility of approach and ability to synthesize material). 'Experts' can be so named by their ability to apply more effective and efficient cognitive strategies to a task than the 'novice' (Ford & Kraiger, 1995).

Elen and Lowyck (1999) argue that the instructional design process should incorporate a fine-grained analysis of how particular trainees think about instruction, how this influences their information processing in instructional environments, and also their use of various forms of instructional support (see Study Box 2.19). Recently, there has been a heightened interest in the concept of 'cognitive style' as an important means of understanding individual differences in information processing (Hodgkinson & Sadler-Smith, 2003).

---

### Study Box 2.18

#### Meta-cognition

Flavell (1979) talked of meta-cognition as an 'executive ability' enabling an individual to select and regulate the employment of particular intellectual skills and cognitive strategies – that is, planning, monitoring and revising goal appropriate behaviour (Ford & Kraiger, 1995: 8). An example is the application of study skills and strategies (for example, reading for meaning, power reading, note-taking strategies, assignment planning, essay writing, mind mapping). It is generally found that meta-cognition is acquired through experience and practice in relation to specific tasks, which is then generalized in its applicability to other tasks. Learners or trainees can be encouraged to engage in self-monitoring by testing and providing themselves with diagnostic feedback on what they tried, why it did/did not work, and what could be done instead. This is consistent with the self-evaluation model described earlier. Schmidt and Ford (2003) found that learners who reported greater levels of meta-cognitive activity during a meta-cognitive training intervention gained more declarative knowledge, performed better on a skill-based measure and had higher levels of self-efficacy. Meta-cognitive activity also partially mediated the relationship between goal orientation and learning outcomes in that the meta-cognitive intervention was only beneficial for non-avoidant learners (but not for highly avoidant learners). These findings suggest that meta-cognitive activity may be suited to some learners more than others. Consistent with this, Gully, Payne, Koles and Whiteman (2002) found that error training (designed to facilitate meta-cognitive thinking) was responded to favourably only by those with a higher level of cognitive ability.

---

*Cognitive style* describes variation in the extent to which an individual relies on 'intuition' or 'analysis' (Hayes, Allinson, Hudson & Keasey, 2003; Sadler-Smith, Spicer, & Tsang, 2000). Intuition pertains to an information-processing mode that is deep, automatic (that is, beyond conscious control), primarily non-verbal, permeated with affect and holistic/associational, enabling people to 'cut through vast quantities of information' (Hodgkinson & Sadler-Smith, 2003: 246). Analysis, on the other hand, denotes a more controlled conscious mode of processing involving detailed analysis and is primarily verbal, relatively affect free and intentional (see also Epstein's 'cognitive-experiential self-theory' (CEST) (Epstein, Pacini, Denes-Raj, Heier, 1996; Study Box 2.19).

Hodgkinson and Maule (2002) propose a dual process theory of strategic decision making in which lower salience considerations are processed relatively automatically whilst higher salience considerations are processed in analytic detail. Individuals high on need for cognition, internal locus of control and need for achievement are expected to be more likely to process information in an analytic way.

---

### Study Box 2.19

#### Cognitive style

Disagreement exists as to whether intuition and analysis denote two separate and distinct processing modes (that can independently vary; Hodkinson & Sadler-Smith, 2003) or one bipolar dimension (which assumes that they are inversely related; Hayes, Allinson, Hudson, & Keasey, 2003). All provide a good case nonetheless for the complementary nature of each style of information processing, with intuition facilitating 'faster decisions', whilst the use of analysis ensures that no vitally important information is overlooked. The key skill, say Hodgkinson and Sadler-Smith (2003), is not so much in the use of one style or another, but in the ability to 'switch' cognitive style as required by the situation (which is a meta-cognitive ability).

---

To date there has been no research on the implications of cognitive style for training, but it may provide a focus for learning (that is, ability to cognitively switch mode as required by a situation) and/or as a framework for instructional design (for example, designing instruction to harness both modes of processing).

*Motor skills* These refer to psychomotor activities where practice predictably results in a gradual improvement with time. The distinction between fine and gross muscular activity is also important. A gross motor act involves the whole body (for example, swimming), whilst a fine motor act involves certain aspects of the body and requires precision (for example, writing). Most useful motor skills are open-looped (relying on external feedback), with some controlled in part by intellectual plans (or 'executive routines'), as distinct from muscular feedback like piano playing or typewriting. Individual motor skills often occur within larger units of motor activity called procedures, the acquisition of which requires the integration of part skills (for example, breaking an egg, cutting up vegetables, rolling out pastry) into more complex and skilled procedures (for example, producing a three-course meal for six people) (Study Box 2.20).

---

**Study Box 2.20**

**Whole- versus part-task learning**

Progressive part-task training involves new components being combined with previously taught components in each successive phase of training. Whether to pursue whole- or part-task learning depends crucially on how complex the task is and also how it is internally structured and organized. Whole-task training is more efficient when the task is highly organized and complex (for example, driving). The part method, however, is superior to whole-task training with tasks high in complexity but low in internal organization (for example, cooking) (Blum & Naylor, 1968). Recent on-site training initiatives advocate 'whole-task' learning particularly for professional work (for example, Maran & Glavin, 2003).

---

Motor skills require active production coupled with repeated practice to attain precision, and also feedback (corrective information). The accepted model of skill acquisition describes a three-stage process (Anderson, 1982) as follows: (1) acquisition of declarative knowledge (facts, theoretical knowledge); (2) a period of integration where cognitive and motor processes become orchestrated into a coherent response to perform the task; and (3) a stage of acquiring a more automated (less conscious) form of procedural knowledge.

This model has also been applied to skill acquisition not just in the motor domain, but also in the cognitive domain. At each stage, progressively less cognitive resource is required to enact the task (Kanfer & Ackerman, 1989). Setting performance goals will also only improve performance to the extent that attention is freed up from the task itself as setting goals competes for cognitive attention. To this extent, goal setting at the early stages of skill acquisition may undermine learning, whilst goal setting at the later more automated stages can enhance performance (now known as *resource allocation theory*, Latham et al., 1998).

There are instances where automated processing with respect to a particular skill will constitute an instructional objective (Shiffrin & Schneider, 1977). Automation frees up attention capacity and facilitates progress during the learning process as tasks requiring more controlled processing can be simultaneously pursued. For example, tasks like radar signal detection require long periods of time watching and infrequent signal occurrence and are prone to a vigilance decrement over time. This can be overcome to the extent that the signal detection skill is automated, thereby reducing the degree of conscious attention required to perform the task effectively. Automaticity can be ensured by coupling stimulus (for example, radar signal) and response (for example, signal detection) over multiple trials during a training programme to produce 'overlearning' (Driskell, Willis, & Cooper, 1992). Some task components may, however, always require full attention and self-regulatory capacity.

***Attitudes***   Attitudes do not directly determine behaviour, but they delimit certain possibilities for action, making some types of behaviour more or less probable (that is, a 'response tendency'). An example would be an 'attitude of precision' towards a task or an 'attitude of care' with respect to client welfare. Most attitudes are learned incidentally rather than as a result of planned instruction, although an organization may wish to instil particular attitudes as a means of enabling employees to adapt to a particular working environment and/or as a vehicle for ensuring that they perform in accordance with expectation. The emotional side of educational and training curricula is a critical yet highly neglected consideration (Martin & Reigeluth, 1999).

## Instructional Strategy

### The conditions of learning

Instructional strategy involves developing a plan for how trainees can be assisted in the learning process. It maps out the learning objective(s), the instructional programme, instructional activities or events, the material to be used, the exercises or tasks to be employed, and the means of monitoring progress. Gagne et al. (1992: 10) argue that there are established ways in which learning can be optimized within an instructional delivery system: engaging and maintaining attention, eliciting performance, stimulating recall of past experience, providing feedback, enhancing retention and transfer. A detailed review of the conditions of learning pertinent to each particular category of learning outcome is provided by Gagne, Briggs and Wager (1992).

In a nutshell, Merrill (2002) argues that effective instruction involves: (1) activating existing relevant knowledge; (2) demonstration of knowledge and skill to the learner; (3) providing opportunity for the learner to apply the new knowledge and skill; and (4) providing an opportunity for the learner to integrate this new knowledge and skill into everyday life. Refer to **www.sagepub.co.uk/millward** for suggestions on how to apply instructional design principles in practice, including a brief review of different training methods.

## Managing Training Motivation

Noe (1986) was one of the first to point out that managing motivation to learn is a critical part of the instructional process. The relationship between cognitive and motivational factors in a training context are potentially highly complex but this is a research area that is rapidly gaining momentum (Colquitt, LePine, & Noe, 2000; Patrick, 2000). Noe (1986) defined motivation to learn simply as a desire to learn the content of a training programme. Research has since consistently demonstrated a positive association between motivation to learn and learning across both cognitive and skill-based outcomes (Colquitt & Simmering, 1998). Motivation to learn also predicts the likelihood of active participation in training and development events (Salas, Cannon-Bowers, Rhodenizer, & Bowers, 1999; Tharanou, 2001b). In itself, however, the concept of 'motivation to learn' explains nothing about why it is that some people are more motivated than others.

Noe (1986) identified four main antecedents of motivation to learn: job attitudes, reactions to feedback, contextual factors, and individual perceptions of self-efficacy or expectancy (that is, effort-performance contingencies). Whilst efficacy (a personal estimate of one's ability to do something) and expectancy (a probabilistic judgement about effort–outcome associations) denote different constructs, they are both equally strongly related to motivation to learn (Study Box 2.16). However, listing the potential antecedents is one thing, explaining how they work in accounting for differences in motivation to learn is another.

Mathieu, Tannenbaum, and Salas (1992) argued that trainees will be more motivated to learn to the extent that they can see an 'instrumental' relationship between their effort and actual learning progress (that is, expectancy) and where the outcomes that can be attained from such progress are valued (that is, valence). Motivation is built out of a belief that one can achieve particular outcomes coupled with the value placed on these outcomes. This formulation is now known as '*motivation through expectation*' and draws on valence-instrumentality-expectancy (VIE) theory (Mathieu & Martineau, 1997). Expectancies with respect to particular learning outcomes are likely to arise as a result of prior behaviour (for example, previous success/failure experiences) coupled with a preference for achieving some kinds of outcomes over others (for example, promotion, increased income, self-esteem, confidence).

Mathieu and Martineau (1997) argued that the VIE approach puts motivation to learn within a broader 'motivational framework' in which efficacy perceptions are still central, but where incentives are also recognized to play a role. The latter is an important consideration that puts the motivation issue into context where the outcomes of training may really matter to an employee (that is, are rewarded by the organization).

The key role played by expectancy in motivation to learn (and, thus, also in predicting successful learning) raises important questions about whether expectancy is open to manipulation during a training event. Where do 'expectancy' beliefs come from? Do trainees bring them to the training situation (that is, pre-existing individual differences) or can they be developed during the training process (that is, by creating the appropriate motivational arrangements)? Research suggests that poor progress (or negative feedback) during a training event *can* decrease self-efficacy levels (for example, Gist & Mitchell, 1992), suggesting that expectancy beliefs may, at least in part, be task and context dependent. In the words of Lee and Klein (2000: 1176), 'an individual's level of self-efficacy can be expected to change over time as new information and experience are acquired through direct experience with the task, performance feedback, and other factors'.

However, there is also research demonstrating that negative performance feedback does not always undermine expectancy: it depends fundamentally on *how* the trainee *characteristically* responds to feedback (Colquitt & Simmering, 1998). For instance, conscientiousness is associated with strong expectancy beliefs (that is, perceiving a link between effort and performance) that resist change in the face of difficulties (McCrae & Costa, 1987) and predicts goal commitment and training perseverance (irrespective of feedback tone), as well as higher performance levels on learning tests (Colquitt & Simmering, 1998). On the other hand, several studies have found that conscientiousness is associated with self-deceptive tendencies that inhibit learning

(Colquitt, LePine, & Noe, 2000; Lee & Klein, 2000) because of an unrealistically positive self-image intolerant to incongruent performance feedback. Consistent with this, Gully, Payne, Koles and Whiteman (2002) found that conscientiousness had a negative effect on self-efficacy during 'error encouragement' training (Study Box 2.21). Lee and Klein (2000) found that learning was inhibited by self-deceptive tendencies especially at the early stages of training, with the effect tapering off at a later stage. They argued that 'providing early feedback that is overly positive ... in an effort to foster self-efficacy could, in fact, inhibit learning by failure to provide the information necessary to disconfirm an unrealistic self-image' (p. 1179).

---

### Study Box 2.21

#### Error training

Sitkin (1992) has cautioned that 'failing to fail' can restrict some individuals from exploring alternatives and may perpetuate incorrect assumptions, maybe even lead to complacency. Nordstrom, Wendland and Williams (1998) found that trainees encouraged to make errors and to reframe negative information experienced increased competency and enhanced intrinsic motivation. This type of error encouragement environment is akin to 'discovery learning' (Smith, Ford, & Koslowski, 1997), and is consistent with the key principles of action theory (Frese & Zapf, 1994; see Chapter 4 for details).

---

The impact of conscientiousness on learning may depend in part on goal orientation. Learning-oriented individuals (motivated to learn new skills) for instance, hold strong expectancy beliefs and tend to react positively and constructively to challenge, achieving higher levels of actual learning during a training event. Conversely, performance-oriented individuals (motivation to meet normative standards) are more likely to react negatively to poor progress during a training event and to experience actual performance problems (Colquitt & Simmering, 1998; Dweck, Hong, & Chiu, 1993). Unlike conscientiousness which is a trait-like state, goal orientation is dependent in part on situational cues (Kraiger, Ford, & Salas, 1993). For instance, a learning orientation could be fostered by creating a training environment encouraging experimentation to infer and learn rules, principles, and learning strategies for effective performance. The alternative for those who are particularly sensitive to poor performance feedback is to slow the rate of learning and minimize the likelihood of difficulty, error or failure during the training process, and perhaps also to increase the perceived value of training outcomes by establishing appropriate incentives (Colquitt & Simmering, 1998).

Overall, such findings indicate the powerful part played by individual differences in accounting for whether 'expectancy beliefs' will be enhanced or undermined by performance feedback during a training event, with direct consequences for actual achievement levels.

Criticisms of the VIE approach to learning motivation allude to its complexity, its assumptions of rationality and of seeking to maximize satisfying returns (Tharanou, 2001b). The VIE approach has nonetheless inspired enormous research and has furnished the training literature with some theoretical substance. Moreover, it is clear that instrumentality beliefs do have something important to say about training motivation. Tharanou (2001b) found in particular that the 'instrumentality' component of VIE theory accounted for most variance in whether employees opted to participate in an organization's training and development activities. That is, 'an employee's participation in training and development is greater if she or he expects that the skills and knowledge gained from training are instrumental for gaining extrinsic outcomes' (p. 617). Contrary to previous work, neither 'valence' or 'expectancy' beliefs added anything unique to this explanatory model, suggesting to Tharanou that motivation to learn may simply be an instrumentality issue, with expectancy and valence considerations largely subordinated to this.

Also noteworthy is Tharanou's (2001b) finding that motivation to learn was also enhanced by supervisor support for training. The significance of local supervisory support (over and above other job, individual and organizational variables) in moderating the association between motivation to learn and participation in training is consistent with other findings (Noe, 1996). Supervisor support may be inextricably linked with the perceived instrumentality of training insofar as supervisors are usually the local providers of valued outcomes.

Another important source of motivational impetus is afforded by goal setting (Locke & Latham, 1990). Setting goals not only focuses the allocation of cognitive resources, it generates energy by creating aspiration. Goals that are specific and challenging (in both laboratory and field contexts) are substantially more effective than easy goals, do your best goals or no goals at all. Locke and Latham (1990) argue that the benefit of goal setting arises because goals direct and mobilize energy expenditure consistently over time (persistence) and, in so doing, motivate the individual to develop relevant strategies for goal attainment. Where individuals have not set their own goals, they must at least accept and be committed to those presupposed by the instructional event (see Chapter 4 for a detailed review of the goal setting literature).

Kanfer and Ackerman (1989), however, showed that early goal setting can in some instances impede learning on some tasks (for example, simulated air traffic control tasks). Specifically, they found that setting a specific outcome goal during stages one and two of the learning process (acquisition of declarative knowledge and knowledge compilation) hindered skill acquisition because it poses too high a cognitive demand before trainees really understand what the task is all about. In short, the effectiveness of goal setting in a training context is moderated by 'resource allocation' processes at different stages in the learning process. When learning has become proceduralized (or automated), attention demands are reduced and can be focused on achieving specific performance goals. Resource allocation theory, however, remains to be fully tested and explored in relation to goal setting (Latham et al., 1998).

For goal setting to work, trainees also need to believe that what they do (the effort they make, the changes they work on, the skills they acquire) will have the desired consequences. This links the notion of goal also with VIE theory. The beliefs of individuals with respect to their capabilities (perceptions of self-efficacy), coupled with the ability to represent, invest in, and 'mentally practice' the attainment of future goals, are also important (Merrill, 2002; Morin & Latham, 2000; Noe, 1986; Wood & Bandura, 1989; Study Box 2.17).

## Part 4 Summary and Conclusions

- Instructional theory systematically prescribes a way of designing and delivering training grounded in learning theory. It was initially underwritten by behaviourist thinking, but is now strongly grounded in cognitive psychology and more recently also socio-cognitive theory.
- Evidence for the empirical and practical viability of socio-cognitive constructs like expectancy, self-efficacy and goal setting in a training context is now substantial, but questions remain as to the most appropriate way to 'manage' cognitive motivational phenomena like this in the design and delivery of a training event.
- There is a growing emphasis on the role of the trainee in the learning and training process and in understanding, in particular, the way 'trainee characteristics' (including pre-existing personality, motives, cognitive style and ability) mediate or moderate the learning process.
- Instructional theory espouses tight regulation and control of all components of a training event to optimize learning outcomes. Whilst elements of 'inquiry based learning' (for example, error training) and the importance of 'self-reflection' (that is, to encourage meta-cognitive understanding and strategy use) have become assimilated into the instructional model, they have been somewhat dissociated from their epistemological basis and to this extent may not necessarily be used with conceptual authenticity.

# Part 5: Transfer of Training

## Types of Transfer

On the 'input' side of training, positive transfer occurs when existing skills and knowledge influence how easily a new task is mastered. This can be facilitated by helping trainees to forge explicit links between relevant past learning and new learning events (from old to new task, or from part to whole task; Annett & Sparrow, 1985: 122). If what is learned has a more general use (for example, cognitive strategies) this may have a broad transfer effect. If the learning is task specific then it is unlikely to transfer beyond this, other than to tasks having similar (if not identical) capability requirements. Negative transfer refers to interference by a previously learned skill on new learning. For example, intrusion errors occur when a procedure from one skill somehow becomes incorrectly triggered in the performance of another skill. For example, people may incorrectly apply a 'solution rule' to new problems because it had been successfully used with previous problems.

At the 'output' side, a trainee also has to transfer skills developed during training to performance on the job. Thorndike & Woodworth (1901) proposed that transfer is possible between tasks that require the same skills or skill components ('identical elements'). That is, transfer is determined by the extent to which two tasks 'share common methods, principles, procedures, associations and even given rise to the same attitudes'. Thus, trainees provided with opportunities to practice on the actual tasks they will be required to perform on the job will transfer their learning more effectively.

Contemporary thinking assumes that fidelity between task and task environment (in both stimulus conditions and response requirement) should not just be physical but also psychological (Goldstein, 1993). Physical fidelity refers to the actual properties of equipment and the environment, whilst psychological or functional fidelity refers to: (1) the conditions established (the equipment acts like the real equipment); and (2) the behavioural requirements of a task or task situation. In practice, physical and psychological fidelity work in tandem to reproduce true performance conditions (physical fidelity may provide an important psychological cue).

Even given identical elements, lack of positive transfer is common in association with cognitive tasks. For instance, thinking and problem-solving skills that are expected to generalize to a range of situations often fail to do so. This may arise out of a tendency (by instructors and trainees alike) to 'compartmentalize' learning (Annett & Sparrow, 1985: 118), and also from a lack of understanding of how skill and knowledge bases inter-relate in the job context (Ford & Kraiger, 1995). This has been dubbed 'the surprising specificity of transfer' (Gray & Orasanu, 1987) and, more recently, 'the performance overhead' incurred by the need to re-conceptualize the new task as one involving common skills (Speelman & Kirsner, 2001). Specificity appears to be a transfer condition, even for skill domains, with a strongly generalizable potential like problem solving, and with respect to the application of general principles (for example, translating general principles of fault finding into action). However, not even the transfer of *specific* heuristics is guaranteed (Ford & Kraiger, 1995).

## Reasons for Lack of Transfer

### Lack of awareness by trainees

If the learner does not perceive the training and transfer situation as similar, he or she will not 'transfer' the learning. Even if a rationale is offered concerning the range of situations to which a skill is applicable, transfer may not necessarily occur. This has led to the proposal that people need to be trained in how to select, monitor and regulate their high-level thought processes (Ford & Kraiger, 1995).

### Contextualized knowledge and skills

Knowledge and skill are highly context dependent, which enables the trained person to react fluently and quickly. The cost, however, is lack of transferability. This has led to the idea of 'contextual knowledge' (that is, appreciation of when and when not to use trained skills; for example, Tennyson, 1999), which can be facilitated by 'contextual interference' (that is, increasing the variability and variety of examples provided during training). Ford and Kraiger (1995: 25) describe this as 'embedded training'. Thus, if a person has to fly six types of aircraft, training and subsequent transfer will be more successful to the extent this variety is captured in the training.

Different transfer requirements can change dramatically both the skills to be trained and how training is designed. For instance, with respect to fault-finding skills, a major problem concerns how to train people to deal with novel faults. Truly novel faults require the person to develop a new method(s) for tackling them, which is outside of that person's existing skill repertoire. Training, then, has to enable a fault finder to identify not only when an existing method is insufficient, but also how to devise a new and more appropriate method. This applies to training in any novel task in which solutions cannot be pre-defined, and some innovation and improvisation is required.

## Lack of an appropriate mental model

Ford and Kraiger (1995) argue that instructional design should be geared to acquiring mental models appropriate to competent performance on a particular task or task set. Those trained to use conceptual models outperformed those trained using traditional behavioural techniques on a recall and creative problem-solving task. For example, the fire fighter may develop a 'mental model' for handling a particular type of road traffic accident or for dealing with a small localized domestic fire, a model comprising several submodels or plans. A mental model constitutes a mapping between the object modelled and the model (Moray, 1997). A mental model pertains to a mechanism of description, explanation and prediction rather than merely to a knowledge structure.

Annett and Sparrow (1985) argue that learning involves the acquisition of a new mental model. If a new model (driving a lorry) is similar to an existing one (for example, driving a car) positive transfer is likely, although intrusion errors may occur. If the overall model is different (for example, problem diagnosis versus driving a car) then it is unlikely that the individual will automatically be aware that one of the subskills employed within the plan (for example, observational skills, diagnostic skills) is relevant to a new task (Speelman & Kirsner, 2001).

The notion of mental model is attractive, yet still relatively under-researched as a transfer concept or even as an instructional focus or tool (Ford & Kraiger, 1995; van Merrienboer & Kirschner, 2001), although there is a growing research interest in the idea of 'cross-training' as an instructional strategy for enhancing knowledge of the interpersonal activities of other team members based on the concept of 'shared mental model' (Volpe, Cannon-Bowers, Salas, & Spector, 1996; Study Box 2.22). The difficulty in using the concept of mental model for training purposes lies in ascertaining what the crucial similarities are within a particular model, and more importantly at what level of generality they should operate for positive transfer to occur. The relationship between mental models and meta-cognition also remains to be clarified. The effectiveness of transfer, for instance, may depend heavily on self-assessment skills and the systematic allocation of attention (Morin & Latham, 2000).

---

**Study Box 2.22**

**Shared mental models and the 'cross-training' strategy**

The idea of a shared mental model in team or collective contexts is that it facilitates coordination because it presupposes that individual members have some shared understanding of the team purpose and characteristics, connections and linkages, roles and behavioural patterns required to fulfil its objectives. Individual members may have different models of the team task, team members and team member inter-actions and the team's interface with relevant artefacts/equipment (Volpe et al., 1996). Cross-training harnesses the idea of a team interaction model containing process knowledge about how members should work with each other on a particular task including what should happen next (Volpe et al., 1996). The aim of team training is to increase the degree of 'sharedness' within the mental model (for example, simi-lar expectations regarding roles and responsibilities of team members). Evidence suggests that mental model similarity in the team interaction domain improves coor-dination processes, which improves team performance overall (Mathieu, Heffner, Goodwin, Salas, & Cannon-Bowers, 2000). Cross-training, in particular, is designed to increase team members' inter-role knowledge. There are three different levels of training, each of which builds on the other: *positional clarification* (verbal presentation of information about team-mates' jobs through lecture or discussion), *positional modelling* (verbal discussion and observation of each others' roles), and *positional rotation* (hands-on approach to learning by role rotation). Studies conducted so far indicate that cross-training holds much promise for building shared mental models and improving team performance (Volpe et al., 1996; Cannon-Bowers, Salas, Blickensderfer, & Bowers, 1998; Marks, Sabella, Burke, & Zaccaro, 2002). Questions remain about the depth of cross-training required to improve team performance, and especially whether full positional rotation is a necessary prerequisite for this. To some extent this raises issues about how much similarity across mental models is needed for it to constitute a 'shared' mental model. Other mental models relevant to team per-formance include 'team situation awareness' but methodological issues have also arisen concerning, for example, the best way of measuring 'sharedness' (Cooke, Kiekel, Salas, Bowers, Stout, & Cannon-Bowers, 2003).

---

### Negative transfer climate

Goldstein (1993) argues that for positive transfer to occur, an instructional system that provides opportunities for the maintenance of trainees' learned behaviour in the work organization is required. One important factor in this respect is *transfer climate*. It is consistently found that trainees in work environments that support them in the appli-cation of what they had learned exhibit significantly more transfer behaviour than those in units with a negative transfer climate irrespective of the amount learned (for example, Cheng & Ho, 2001). The support of managers and also co-workers is partic-ularly key to a positive transfer climate (Gumuseli & Ergin, 2002).

Ford and Kraiger (1995) recommend that a balance is sought between the acquisition of task-specific skills and strategies and the acquisition of necessary self-monitoring skills appropriate to their application and transfer back to the workplace. The latter can be promoted by situational assessment and taking steps to prevent 'relapse' in the transfer situation. In the classic relapse prevention approach, people are required to identify and describe those situations likely to prompt relapse and also (and perhaps most importantly) to consider various means of coping with them (Latham et al., 1998).

## Trainee Learning Strategies

What trainees bring to the process of instruction that can increase the likelihood of transfer is of increasing interest (Warr & Allan, 1998). Downs (1996: 79) argues that the end product of all training is 'to help learners develop better learning skills to enable them to be responsive and adaptable to learning needs'. This is especially relevant to today's increasing emphasis on creating a 'learning' impetus in organizations as a means of securing competitive advantage through the leverage of new knowledge and skill on a 'just-in-time' basis (Pearn, Roderick, & Mulrooney, 1995).

Individuals vary widely in their use of different learning strategies, including how efficiently they use them (Warr & Allan, 1998). Patrick (2000) describes the skilled learner as similar to experts in other domains insofar as they decide what to attend to, select appropriate strategies and monitor and regulate their own cognitive processes. He says, nonetheless, that learning skills can be developed with the help of the instructor, using what Rigney (1978; cited in Weinstein & Mayer, 1986) calls 'orienting tasks' that 'nudge' the trainee to use a particular cognitive strategy (for example, note-taking, summarizing, re-reading, reviewing, and so on; see Weinstein & Mayer, 1986 for a review).

Drawing on educational psychology, Warr and Allan (1998) identify, describe and review in detail two different categories of learning strategy: cognitive (for example, rehearsal, organization, elaboration) and behavioural (for example, help-seeking, practical application), amounting to six different 'strategies'. Subsequent empirical work by Warr and Downing (2000) involving occupational (rather than educational) samples obtained support for five of these six strategies using a self-report questionnaire with 'organization' and 'elaboration' loading on one factor which they called 'active reflection'. However, Holman, Epitropaki and Fernie (2001) obtained a six-factor solution, although not consistent with the theoretical structure originally postulated by Warr and Allan (1998). In their solution, two factors comprising both organization and elaboration items were discerned, one labelled 'extrinsic work reflection' (that is, how reflection occurs) and the other 'intrinsic work reflection' (that is, the content of the reflection). Holman et al. (2001) argue for research on a wider range of learning strategies (including self-regulatory strategies) involving occupational samples and that looks, in particular, at their implications for training design, training outcomes and training transfer.

On the issue of self-regulation, Downs and Perry (1987) have shown that many people have a negative attitude towards learning, and may even be learning 'blocked' due to traumatic learning experiences in the past. Negative learning attitudes can arise from self-perception (for example, 'I have a poor memory', 'I'm easily distracted', 'I'm no good at learning') and/or from the experience of failure generally (for example,

'I worry about keeping up with others', 'I feel shown up when I make mistakes in front of others').

Downs (1996) says that learning to learn is facilitated by 'learners trying out new ways' (p. 90), whereby learners are encouraged to ask questions, are left alone to work things out and are encouraged to identify and correct their own mistakes. Warr and Allan (1998) argue that 'by identifying which strategies are associated with success in specific types of learning, it will be possible to attempt practical improvement through strategy training and also to expand understanding of the processes of learning themselves' (p. 219).

## Part 5 Summary and Conclusions

- Transfer of training pertains to how pre-existing skills and knowledge can facilitate the learning of new knowledge and skills, but most research has focused on how what is learned can be most effectively transferred to performance on the job. This issue has arisen to the extent that training occurs 'off-site', in a different environment to that of performance (that is, training environment). On-site training rarely poses a transfer problem, because learning and performing are both one and the same thing.
- The artificial divide created between learning and performing is problematic as organizations strive to make learning (and knowledge capture and creation) core to their everyday business activities. Responses to this have been to consider alternative modes of learning that are more *situated* (on-site) and which also *assign more responsibility to the learner*.
- Facilitators of transfer include the design of a training environment which is a realistic (high-fidelity) simulation of the performance environment, enabling learners to acquire the appropriate self-regulatory strategies and where the transfer environment is appropriately supportive. 'Transferable' skills are now an employability criterion.

# Part 6: Training Evaluation

Tamkin, Yarnall and Kerrin (2002) describe training evaluation as 'a bit like eating five portions of fruit and vegetables a day'. That is, 'everyone knows they are supposed to be doing it, everyone says they are planning to do it better in the future and few people admit to having got it right' (p. 1). Clearly, training is supposed to make a difference, to bring about changes to both individuals and organizations. Yet, very little training evaluation is actually carried out, and when it is, it will usually be limited to the convenient but largely inconsequential assessment of trainee reactions (Schott, Grzondziel, & Hillebrandt, 2001) – despite the availability of many well-established evaluation methods (Breakwell & Millward, 1995). A lot of training is therefore conducted on 'faith' rather than clear analysis. This is particularly surprising given today's economic preoccupation with accountability and bottom-line 'results'.

## Training Effectiveness

There have been seven noteworthy systematic reviews of the organizational training literature dating from 1971 to 2003: Campbell (1971); Goldstein (1980); Wexley (1984); Latham (1988); Tannenbaum and Yukl (1992); Salas and Cannon-Bowers (2001); Arthur, Bennett, Edens and Bell (2003) and one pertaining to management training in particular: Burke and Day (1986). With only two exceptions (Arthur et al., 2003; Burke & Day, 1986), these reviews are based on a narrative rather than statistical synthesis of relevant material.

Arthur et al. (2003) reported a sample-weighted effect size for mainly the off-site training of individuals (rather than teams) of 0.60 to 0.63 (depending on the criterion), which they interpreted as a medium to large effect size. Reviews, indeed, consistently suggest that effectiveness depends on the criterion used against which to measure effectiveness (for example, learning or behaviour criteria). In particular, Arthur et al. found that there was a subsequent decrease in effect size the more distal the criterion from the training event. Thus, reactions are the most proximal criteria, followed by 'learning', but the 'behavioural' or performance criteria and especially the organizational criteria denote increasingly distal indicators of training effectiveness. This makes sense given the now renowned problems of transferring training to the work environment. The more distal the criterion (behaviour, results), the more likely it is that 'other' factors moderate the relationship between the training event and its impact on outcomes including performance opportunity and the transfer climate (Colquitt, Le Pine, & Noe, 2000).

Arthur et al. (2003) also found that the content of training was an important moderator of effectiveness. Using Wexley and Latham's (2002) skill taxonomy they found that the largest effect sizes (against learning and behavioural criteria) were associated with training that was concerned with both cognitive and interpersonal skill components followed by psychomotor skills. For results criteria, the largest effect size was obtained for training involving interpersonal skills. Finally, the training method used also moderated training effectiveness, but no particular method was found to be especially superior for training a particular skill. Most surprising was the robust effect obtained for lectures 'which contrary to their poor public image, appeared to be quite effective in training several types of skills and tasks' (Arthur et al., 2003: 243).

Factors also known to be influential, though not included in Arthur et al.'s (2003) meta-analysis, include trainer skill and also trainee variables like self-efficacy (Mathieu, Martineau, & Tannenbaum, 1993), cognitive ability (Warr & Bunce, 1995), motivation (Colquitt et al., 2000; Tharanou, 2001b) and goal orientation (Colquitt & Simmering, 1998).

Difficulties associated with performing systematic meta-analysis of the kind reported by Arthur et al. (2003) is the absence of certain types of evaluation studies (for example, on-site evaluation studies are rare) and the incompleteness of the reporting (for example, absence of information about whether a training event has been designed on the basis of a comprehensive TNA).

## The Science and Practice of Evaluation

Goldstein (1993) defines evaluation as the systematic collection of descriptive and judgemental information necessary to make effective training decisions related to the selection, adoption, value, and modification of various instructional activities.

In the absence of a coherent theoretical basis for the design and delivery process, the approach taken to evaluation is largely impact oriented, rather than addressing questions about 'how' or 'why' (Latham et al., 1998; Arthur et al., 2003). Within this pragmatic framework, training is classified as an 'experimental intervention' designed to change behaviour (that is, performance enhancement), the success of which can in principle be assessed using the 'scientific method'. The question of validity is central to this method of establishing whether training is effective and requires the use of rigorous research designs to determine what changes, if any, have occurred during training (Study Box 2.23).

The scientific integrity of the research design is undoubtedly important, determining both the type and quality of results obtained. However, 'it is difficult to envisage being able to capture the subtleties and complexities of real-life phenomena in a truly experimental way' (Breakwell & Millward, 1995: 31). Arguably, a tightly designed evaluation study will produce findings with limited generalizability potential. Haccoun and Saks (1998) talk of a compromise in the form of an 'internal referencing strategy' involving a pre- and post-intervention comparison of the content of learning derived directly from the training programme relative to 'germane' content that has not otherwise been covered.

It is generally agreed that the techniques of evaluation must be sound but also 'manageable in their levels of complexity and sophistication' (Spilsbury, 1995: 3). It is also clear, however, that both more and better evaluation is needed and that progress may be hindered in part by a difficulty in bridging the gap between espoused 'best practice' and the practical reality of trying to define and measure 'impact' at different levels of analysis (Haccoun & Saks, 1998; Case Study 2.3).

---

**Case Study 2.3: Best practice organizations**

In 1994, Xerox adopted the Kirpatrick model as the basis for its systematic attempt to demonstrate the impact of their learning and development services. Links to business impact were inextricably built into training strategy (from TNA, through design and delivery). Self-assessed competence standards were established and used strictly as a development tool. Training is self-managed with trainees using a learning resource guide to aid them in the planning process. Ernst and Young see evaluation as a tool to sustain change whilst Motorola has established an evaluation unit within its training function. IBM will only offer training courses in their catalogue of resources if its 'value added impact' has been demonstrated at both job and business levels of analysis.

Source: Ernst & Young (2004)

Goldstein (1993) says that the biggest threat to the integrity of a research design is not planning for evaluation before a training intervention is implemented. In practice, evaluation may be seen as a political tool used for rationalizing decisions that have already been made rather than to inform the decision-making process. Pulley (1994) describes evaluation as necessarily 'responsive', focusing on what the organization needs to know and in what context.

---

**Study Box 2.23**

### Validity issues in evaluation science

The design used for evaluation purposes must address the following questions:

1  Has change occurred in the expected direction, and if so, how real is the change observed? (*training validity*)
2  Did learning transfer into real changes in performance on the job? (*transfer validity*)
3  Is needs assessment appropriately addressed by the training (*content validity*)
4  Can the changes discerned be attributed to the intervention? (*internal validity*)
5  How likely is it that similar changes will occur for different participants in the same intervention? In Goldstein's (1993: 589) words, 'how *dangerous* is it to generalise results from the previous training programme to a new group of trainees in the same organization?' (*intra-organizational external validity*)
6  How likely is it that similar changes will occur for different participants in the same intervention in a different organization? Can a training programme validated in one organization be validly implemented in another? (*inter-organizational external validity*)

#### Threats to internal validity

These threats arise from circumstances where the results of a training intervention may be attributed to sources of explanation over and above that of the intervention per se. Such threats include *corresponding events* (between the first and second phases of measurement offering an alternative explanation of the results), *pre-testing* (pre-testing sensitizes participants), *statistical regression* (when trainees are chosen because of their extreme scores on a measure), *differential selection of participants* (where biases in choice of comparison group afford group differences simply because the groups were different in the first place), *experimental mortality* (differential loss from experimental and control groups means that sample characteristics may alter in favour of an impression that the experimental group worked better than it did) and *leakage of treatments* (if members of the experimental and control groups know each other they could talk about what is happening during the training intervention and thus leak out the 'treatment').

#### Threats to external validity

Threats to external validity are nearly always a matter of inference and thus cannot be definitively specified. Internal validity is a pre-requisite for external validity since the changes obtained must be valid for the group in question before they can be transferred. Threats include:

*(Continued)*

---

**Study Box 2.23   Continued**

- *reactivity* (different samples of participants may be differentially sensitive to the instructional procedures);
- *interaction of selection procedures and experimental treatments* (sample characteristics determine generalizability);
- *reactive effects of experimental settings* (procedures used in experimental settings may limit the generalizability of a study, including awareness of being a participant in an experimental intervention, the enthusiasm of the instructors, social interactions during the training intervention, and feedback on results); and
- *multiple-treatment interference* (where it is difficult to ascertain a single-treatment effect in a multiple-treatment situation, for instance, the isolated effect of lectures in a training intervention comprising role-plays and audio-visual input).

---

## Establishing the Criteria of Effectiveness

Goldstein (1993) says that criterion development is a fundamental first step in the conduct of any training evaluation exercise (Study Box 2.24).

---

**Study Box 2.24**

**Criterion development**

Two different measurement bases can be distinguished: *criterion-referenced* and *norm-referenced*. Criterion-referenced measures depend on an absolute standard against which to compare results, whereas norm-referenced measures are associated with relative (that is, group-specific) standards. In the former, an instructional objective provides an example of how a benchmark of achievement might be specified. In the latter, the capabilities of trainees (for example, management trainees) may be compared with those found to be typical of a particular group (for example, MBA students). Goldstein (1991) argues that such conclusions are not useful as they are too global and abstracted from organizational life. They do not, for instance, provide much information about individual capabilities or enable specific problems to be identified either in the design or conduct of the training. Hence, most advise focusing attention on developing criterion-referenced rather than norm-referenced evaluation measures. Goldstein (1993) says that the prime task in *criterion development* is to establish exactly what would constitute a measure of success for a particular training programme.

---

Whilst there are now several models of training evaluation available (for example, Day, Arthur, & Gettman, 2001) the Kirpatrick (1976) four-level model of training evaluation is the most frequently cited and used basis for developing evaluation criteria:

- *Reactions* – self-report measures of satisfaction.
- *Learning* – typically assessed using pencil-and-paper tests and performance tests.
- *Job behaviour or performance* – (see also Chapter 3, Part 1: Performance and Performance Appraisal) assessing the extent to which trainees have 'transferred' their learning into job terms, typically on the basis of supervisor ratings.
- *Organization* (for example, 'local' organizational effects include improvements to quality and quantity or production, safety, damage to equipment, absenteeism, turnover, attitudes towards work, running costs, improvements in work methods). Phillips (1990) added a fifth level called 'return on investment' (or ultimate monetary value).

Critical to this criterion model (and other similar models of training evaluation) is an assumption that the achievement of each particular 'level of change' is a prerequisite to change at the next level of analysis. However, whilst each level of change may be a necessary condition for the next, it is unlikely to be *sufficient* for subsequent change to come about. Whilst learning and behaviour criteria are 'conceptually linked', no empirical relationship between them has been demonstrated (Arthur et al., 2003). Problems simply in transferring what has been learned to everyday performance (as discussed earlier) illustrates just some of the complexities involved in mapping the pathway between the two. Other proposed associations, such as between reactions and learning and between individual level performance and organizational level performance, are no easier to contemplate.

Research tells us that there is no association between 'training satisfaction' and learning or between reactions and subsequent behaviour change (Arthur et al., 2003; Tamkin et al., 2002). In fact, there is no association between any of the training criteria within the Kirpatrick model (Alliger, Tannenbaum, Bennett, Traver, & Shotland, 1997). One of the difficulties with 'testing' the Kirpatrick model is that the psychological mechanisms connecting one level of change with another have never really been properly described or explained. Research suggests that if there is a link between reactions and learning, it is far more complex than previous models have presupposed. Mathieu, Tannenbaum, and Salas (1992) found that reactions moderated the relationship between training motivation and learning. When reactions were positive, there was a stronger association between motivation and learning than when reactions were negative. Evidence like this suggests that affective reactions may well constitute an important pre-condition of successful learning, but that there is still an awful lot of work to be done to unravel the precise nature of this link. In the absence of theory, this could also lapse into a bit of a tail chasing exercise.

One way forward is to look more closely at the concept of trainee reaction. Kraiger, Ford and Salas (1993), in particular, have questioned the definition and measurement of reactions in purely affective terms. They argue that reactions are likely to be multi-dimensional, comprising cognitive (for example, self-efficacy beliefs) and motivational (for example, motivation to transfer) as well as affective components. Along similar lines, Alliger et al. (1997) have demonstrated the explanatory significance of what they call 'utility' reactions (for example, 'I found it useful') over and above affect-based reactions, in the pathway to learning. The notion of 'utility' resonates with models of motivation in which the idea of 'perceived instrumentality' is central (Haccoun, 1997;

Tharanou, 2001b). This would afford the prediction that trainees who report reacting to the content of training as 'instrumental' to the attainment of valued goals are more likely to have learned something.

Another theoretical basis for looking at trainee reactions and their links with learning is provided by the concept of self-efficacy. As a well-established predictor of performance during training and other performance-relevant domains, self-efficacy could justifiably be used as a sound, reaction-based, 'can-do' indicator of immediate training success. Self-efficacy also predicts persistence, and, as such, could provide an important psychological mechanism linking learning with real performance change (see earlier). In short, socio-cognitive insights could be used to furnish our understanding of how one level of change may 'connect' with another, and highlight, in particular, the benefits of expanding the criterion domain concerned with 'reaction' to incorporate cognitive and motivational constructs.

Unfortunately, training evaluation is mainly undertaken myopically with reference only to the 'feel good' criterion, as if this provides the fundamental pretext for change (Arthur et al., 2003). Yet clearly, reactions are not a surrogate measure of either learning or behaviour change (Tannenbaum & Yukl, 1992). Meta-analyses point to almost exclusively positive post-training reactions. Hence the often facetious use of the term 'happy form' in association with reaction-level questionnaires is perhaps not far off the reality. On a more methodological note, the ceiling effect in association with reaction data also renders it rather meaningless in statistical terms, because there is no real variance to explore in relation to other variables.

## Operational Problems in the Criterion Domain

Practical problems in conducting training evaluation arise from methodological debates about appropriate measurement of learning and of performance. For instance, evaluations of 'learning outcome' are commonly criticized as overly superficial (for example, assessments of declarative knowledge involving whether trainees can repeat what they have learned) rather than of 'true' learning. This may be attributable in part to a lack of understanding about how learning manifests and is most appropriately assessed.

Haccoun and Saks (1998) argue that a better indicator of true learning is procedural (not, declarative) knowledge, meaning the extent to which a trainee can demonstrate their learning in performance terms ('know-how'). An example of how the latter can be assessed is provided by Ostroff (1991) in the form of a situational interview, akin to that developed for selection purposes (Chapter 1). In the situational interview, trainees would be asked to contemplate a series of vignettes designed to assess their likely course of action. Leach et al. (2003) also report on their use of a 'knowledge elicitation interview' to assess the impact of an empowerment initiative on job knowledge, but assessments like this might be considered too time-consuming and costly to develop.

At the level of job behaviour, there are well-established difficulties (and controversies) surrounding performance modelling and measurement (see Chapter 3) including the fact that trainees often disperse to distant locations after training. Some have advocated the design of creative measurement solutions like those recently introduced into the performance appraisal process (for example, 360-degree appraisal) involving a convergence of performance ratings from self, peers, subordinates and managers/supervisors, to overcome the otherwise heavy (and inappropriate) reliance on self-report (Haccoun, 1997).

There are, however, conceptual and methodological issues arising specifically in association with evaluating post-training performance concerning how to measure subtle changes in skill manifest in job behaviour as well as what constitutes a reasonable time span across which learning will have begun to really make an impact on performance. Clearly, training cannot in itself develop expertise; this requires extensive practice over time (Talbot, 2004). The question of post-training duration is important, and the boundary between novice and expert may impose a false dichotomy onto an otherwise more gradual and staged process of acquiring mastery. The assessment of behaviour change may require sensitivity to temporal issues, based on an understanding of the way skills are acquired and at what stage a trainee can be considered to have successfully learned enough to make a real difference in performance terms.

At a departmental and organizational level, performance generally is also dependent on so many different factors that the task of pinpointing variance attributable to the training intervention may be difficult, if not impossible. Generally, cost-effectiveness studies of training are rare and poor in quality. Time-lag between the intervention and its effects may also pose difficulties in answering questions about financial return on investment. Methods of translating soft psychological outcomes into hard financial terms are also controversial (Pulley, 1994).

## Process Considerations in Training Evaluation

On a more complex theoretical level, the training evaluator may also wish to answer questions like 'which training method worked best for which participant?' (that is, *aptitude/treatment interaction effect*) and 'which training intervention worked the best and why?' These kinds of questions also impact fundamentally on the type of design employed to evaluate training effectiveness. For example, when looking at interactions between trainee attributes and the type of intervention used, measures of trainee differences (for example, self-efficacy, learning style) can be built into evaluation designs. These questions arise in connection with the process of training rather than its outcomes (Scriven, 1967).

The multi-level criterion-based approach to evaluation described above necessarily requires attention to the psychological processes or mechanisms involved in connecting one level (for example, reactions) with another (that is, learning, and behaviour change) (Haccoun & Saks, 1998). Process evaluation can help provide an *explanatory basis* for both the development and evaluation of a training programme. For instance, a socio-cognitive approach to training would focus the design, delivery and evaluation of training against criteria such as self-efficacy. Within this framework, it would be possible to assess which particular aspects of the delivery process are particularly efficacy enhancing (or undermining) so that these can be most effectively managed.

## Part 6 Summary and Conclusions

- The training evaluation literature is highly prescriptive, lacking a theoretical basis. Most evaluation looks only at the immediate affective reactions of trainees (that is, satisfaction) as if this were an automatic pretext for learning and behaviour change.
- Whilst trainee reactions are consistently positive, this does not necessarily imply successful learning, and likewise learning does not necessarily furnish real performance change, in part because of 'transfer' problems and in part owing to difficulties pinpointing the exact performance impact learning should have.
- Organizational-level considerations are remote from the intervention, making it difficult to establish precise causal links. Evaluation in a field setting using stringent experimental designs may compromise ecological validity.
- Recent efforts to conceptualize reaction incorporate cognitive (for example, self-efficacy) and motivational (for example, training motivation) as well as affective criteria, which promise more explanatory and predictive power. Process research addresses more precise questions about 'why' a particular training method is more effective than another.

## Research Challenges

- methods of TNA that take the 'future' into consideration;
- training needs analysis at the team level;
- cognitive and behavioural modelling processes;
- on-site training including apprenticeship processes;
- self-regulated learning, especially reflective practice as a training/learning method;
- role of discovery and errors in learning;
- self-efficacy as a mediator/moderator of training success and transfer;
- the notion of 'competence' as the basis for training and learning;
- the role of training in the cultivation of the 'learning culture' and 'learning organization';
- training impact evaluation beyond the impressionistic and attitudinal level;
- the integration of 'training' with 'development' considerations;
- understanding and promoting training motivation;
- detailed comparison of 'on-the-job' relative to 'off-the-job' training;
- the application of insights from cognitive psychology (for example, mental models) to training design and evaluation;
- the application of theories of motivation as means of understanding the learning process from the perspective of the trainee;
- understanding of the contribution made by concepts like cognitive style and learning style to the learning/training process;
- learning strategies;
- challenging the epistemology of training and development psychology, by contemplating the types of questions afforded by a sense-making perspective and their implications for training design.

# 3

# Performance Appraisal and Career Development

'Cheshire-Puss,' said Alice, 'Would you tell me, please, which way I ought to go from here?'
'That depends a good deal on where you want to get to,' said the Cat.
'I don't care much where …' said Alice.
'Then it doesn't matter which way you go,' said the Cat.
'… so long as I get somewhere,' Alice added as an explanation.
'Oh, you're sure to do that,' said the Cat, 'if only you walk long enough.'

(Lewis Carroll. *Alice's Adventures in Wonderland*)

## Preface

Nowadays the terms 'performance appraisal' (PA) and 'performance management' are used synonymously. Both involve measuring employee performance, generating information central to decisions about the recruitment, use and maintenance of human resources. The increase in *formality* of performance management in recent years parallels the market imperative to rationalize organizational functioning in order to maintain competitive advantage. Accordingly, PA has become a strategic-level system consideration involving a set of practices (rather than just an 'annual review') linked with business policy. Historically, PA was linked with bonus- and merit-awarding schemes, was fundamentally *evaluative* and afforded little scope for feedback. Research in the field was primarily motivated to refine the instruments of appraisal and performance measurement. However, by the 1960s, progress was limited, the research–practice gap seemed to widen and researchers became despondent. Appraisal instrumentation is today still plagued with issues of reliability, validity and relevance and the theory–practice gap remains. Most employees remain dissatisfied with their appraisal schemes. Contemporary research has broadened to encompass motivational and relational factors, including *context* and *process* as well as *content* considerations. Context issues concern both *distal* (that is, cultural) and proximal (that is, relationship between appraiser and the appraised) factors surrounding performance appraisal. The issue of performance reward is inextricably linked with this broadened research agenda.

   Part 1 of this chapter looks at the appraisal system in an organizational context. It addresses criterion conceptualization, as well as various issues arising from the practice of appraisal, including its social context, the relationship between appraiser and the appraised, appraiser values and goals, appraisal style, mechanical issues concerning feedback delivery, feedback reactions and appraisal effectiveness. Nowadays, the issue of 'career development' is inextricably linked with 'development issues' arising from performance appraisal. However, little systematic attention has been paid to this aspect of appraisal. Part 2 discusses the concepts of career and career development within a career management system. A classic incentive for optimal performance is the prospect of promotion. However, organizational flattening has limited promotional opportunities. Many organizations are increasingly aware of the need to rethink their approach to careers, to develop new strategies for facilitating employee responsibility for their careers and to create a supportive development-oriented culture. It is argued that career theories must account for this new 'career culture', integral to which is the possibility of non-conventional 'minority' group careers (that is, involving non-white and/or blue-collar and/or female and/or disabled members).

# Part 1: Performance and Performance Appraisal

## Learning Objectives

Studying the contents of Part 1 will enable you to:

1 debate contemporary approaches to performance appraisal and their associated methodologies, with particular attention to the theory and practice surrounding multi-source feedback systems;
2 discuss the content or focus of PA, including performance conceptualization and measurement;
3 identify and discuss the strengths and weaknesses of different types of PA techniques;
4 discuss the concept of feedback and consider in particular employee reactions to negative feedback and the implications of this for feedback delivery systems;
5 situate appraisal systems in an organizational context and discuss potential tensions arising from the need to reconcile performance evaluation with a developmental orientation;
6 discuss the design, implementation and evaluation of an employee appraisal system.

## Overview of the Performance Appraisal System

Contemporary PA denotes *a set of practices* often integral to a much broader performance management strategy (PMS) involving performance assessment, development and reward (Fletcher, 2001; Williams & Fletcher, 1998; Case Study 3.1). It is no longer appropriate to see it merely as an 'event' undertaken annually by a line manager with little or no employee involvement. Nowadays, PA is seen as a crucial medium not only for managing individual-level performance, but for *integrating* this with corporate-level performance considerations (Case Study 3.1). Managing this complex interface is thus fundamental to understanding the strategic role played by the contemporary PA system. Career management may be inextricably linked with this insofar as the concept of 'career' may afford a critical interface concept in the effort to reconcile individual and organizational level interests and goals (Millward & Kyriakidou, 2004a).

In practice, appraisal evokes many emotions, mostly ego defensive, and not only for the appraised. Accountability dilemmas also surround the appraiser. Bluntly, Drenth (1998: 59) wonders whether appraisal would be better undertaken outside a formal system of evaluation involving impersonal tick box type performance ratings, but concludes that most employees (both appraiser and appraised) appreciate a *system* of some kind for reassurance, if nothing else, of 'fair' performance comparison. The use of appraisal systems is now widespread in the USA, the UK and Northern Europe in general.

In parallel, there has been a move away from the somewhat decontextualized preoccupation with measurement matters towards looking more closely at the social and cultural context of PA, including relational processes (between appraiser and appraisee) as well as its fundamental role in managing *performance motivation* (that is, its effectiveness) (Keeping & Levy, 2000). Growing interest in examining employee reactions towards their appraisal systems is part of this trend. However, existing research suggests that 'reactions' are not good (for example, Fletcher, 2004), which is highly problematic for effective performance management.

The appraisal system can be discussed in terms of the goals, the content, the appraisal process (performance measurement, feedback delivery) and the context of appraisal. The topic of *multi-source feedback systems* will be addressed in the context of developmental appraisal (Fletcher & Baldry, 2001; Case Study 3.1).

---

### Case Study 3.1: Performance enhancement

Kent Police, in partnership with the Home Office, Police Standards Unit (PSU), are developing at local level a performance framework based on quantitative 'points' weightings. The weightings enable measurement of work quality, whilst driving business towards priorities set at both national and local level. The 'points' weightings system contains three core elements:

- *weightings* – for intelligence information, arrests, initial investigation, case files and disposals;
- *enhancement* – points for target offenders, hotspots, national & local priorities;
- *penalties* – for substandard work and poor service provision.

The regime is based on the principle that success is achieved through improved 'quality' of service delivery, and the provision of performance indicators that are meaningful, understandable and motivational (MUM) to police and public alike. The system is highly flexible, as it is easily transferable to other forces/agencies and offers opportunity for 'real time' monitoring/development of performance at team/individual level. Another objective is to provide immediate identification and delivery of staff development needs. For more detail, see **www.sagepub.co.uk/millward.**

# The Goals of the Appraisal System

It has been a long-standing concern to detach appraisal discussion from formal 'evaluation' on which matters of pay may also be contingent. Many argue that it is not possible to reconcile *regulatory goals* with *developmental goals:* each presupposes distinctly different *assumptions*, *attitudes* and *skills* for effective implementation (Study Box 3.1). Others note that separating evaluative and developmental activity is pointless, because employees may nonetheless link them subjectively together such that their artificial separation could be interpreted as deceitful (Boswell & Boudreau, 2001).

---

### Study Box 3.1

#### Evaluative and development appraisals

*Evaluative appraisal* involves a *retrospective analysis* of performance (both positive and negative), most often using quantitative techniques (for example, supervisor ratings) and tied to performance-related pay, to enable objectively fair judgements on which defensible Human Resource Management (HRM) decisions (for example, promotion, transfer, pay, dismissal) can be made. A *development-oriented appraisal*, by contrast, aims to identify and build on *future aspirations and involves goal setting*. Unlike the evaluative appraisal, the well-conducted development appraisal is performed in a facilitative manner, inviting self-appraisal of personal strengths and limitations. However, evaluative appraisal is not necessarily antithetical to development and can, on the contrary, facilitate the take-up of development activity, especially when evaluations are made by subordinates (Brutus, London, & Martineau, 1999).

Fletcher (2002) nonetheless raises some important considerations for a system of appraisal with both an evaluative and a developmental focus. For instance, the uptake of a developmental activity is usually optional, but an appraisal system is mandatory. Development is, by definition, ongoing whilst appraisal is normally an annual exercise, so does this mean that development will also be a 'one-off' affair, whose ratings matter to development rather than appraisal? Are peer ratings a fair source of performance evidence on which to make rewards contingent? Who is responsible for follow-up? In practice, the most influential factor in the attempt to reconcile evaluative with developmental activity is the implication of linking 'development' with pay. Early research on this issue suggested that linking pay with appraisal processes can undermine the quality of the interaction between the appraiser and the appraised. Today, the economic climate may be such that 'development' (or the outcomes of development in the form of increased human capital) is a key performance criterion, to be systematically cultivated and rewarded. The reality may thus be one of being appraised and rewarded *for* our developmental capabilities.

---

Early advocates of the developmental approach involved the employee in performance planning within a single appraisal system (for example, Graves, 1982), a trend that continues fairly much unabated (Drenth, 1998; Fletcher & Baldry, 2001). 'Appraisal' and 'development' are now also often used synonymously, particularly in the application of multi-source multi-rater (MSMR) feedback systems as discussed below (Fletcher & Baldry, 2001; Fletcher, 2004).

Drenth (1998: 61) says that appraisals have a 'multi-purpose' character (for example, performance measurement and improvement, remuneration, human resource planning, identifying potential, criterion for validation of selection methods and training outcomes) and that whilst conceptually its operational objectives can be delineated, in practice they fundamentally overlap (that is, both involve comparative evaluation, feedback and an emphasis on improvement) (Drenth, 1998; Study Box 3.2).

---

**Study Box 3.2**

### Assessment of potential

Drenth (1998: 62) says that the use of appraisal for the identification of potential 'is another story altogether'. The aim of this type of appraisal is to anticipate future developments from current behaviours, looking in particular at 'behavioural constants' like personality and other personal competencies. The important issue for this type of appraisal is its predictive power (that is, how effective is it in accurately identifying future potential?). In a longitudinal study, Russell (2001) found, for example, that 'people oriented' competency ratings were strongly predictive of the subsequent performance of 98 senior executives. The competency rating format in this instance was to 'forecast candidates' future job performance in executive positions' (p. 562).

---

However, in practical terms, Drenth (1998: 68) says that there must be serious attempts to 'disentangle all kinds of undesirable confusions ... becoming an issue' to employees because of mismatched expectations (for example, the appraiser's need to provide an objective evaluation against a desire on the part of the appraised for a constructive developmental discussion about the future).

The issue of *organizational accountability* has recently become an important psychometric consideration (for example, impact on appraiser motivation for accuracy) (Mero, Motowidlo, & Alexandra, 2003), but arguably this also has important consequences for how appraisers manage the tension between evaluative and developmental goals, and for the ongoing relationship between appraiser and appraised (for example, the need to produce accurate assessments whilst also maintaining good leader-member relations) (Murphy & Cleveland, 1995; Murphy, Cleveland, Skattebo, & Kinney, 2004).

Research on appraisal processes has largely been undertaken in an interpersonal vacuum, so recent work on the motives and goals of both appraiser and the appraised puts the performance evaluation process back into perspective.

## Part 1 Summary (I) and Conclusions

• The appraisal system denotes a set of practices comprising both evaluative and developmental elements, goals that may sometimes be difficult to reconcile. Development is itself also becoming a focus of evaluation.

- Most of the appraisal literature is about the psychometrics of performance measurement but there is a growing interest in looking at the interpersonal context of appraisal (from the perspective of both appraiser and the appraised) in an organizational framework.

## The Content or Focus of Appraisal

This section looks at the *criterion issue* (that is, what constitutes performance), and then considers the focus of appraisal (that is, *performance content*).

### The criterion issue

The statement of Bechtoldt (1947: 1257) that there is 'no subject of greater importance than the criterion to be used in evaluating performance' remains as relevant today as ever. A criterion is an operational definition of performance that is quantifiable, which is distinct from a performance dimension (Bailey, 1983; Study Box 3.3).

---

**Study Box 3.3**

**Criteria versus dimensions**

Criteria and dimensions are terms often inappropriately used interchangeably in the performance measurement literature.

- *Dimension* – a singular and independent characteristic, but not necessarily theoretically singular; a unidimensional measure can tap into a very complex psychological attribute (for example, intelligence). Dimensions are abstractions from reality or scientific artefacts, generally the product of techniques such as factor analysis. At the measurement level, dimensions *describe* the performance domain (for example, cognitive ability, decision making) and afford comparison and prediction.
- *Criterion* – 'a canon or standard' against which performance is evaluated as effective or ineffective. Performance criteria can cross over dimensions, delineating the 'ideal' or 'evaluative standard' (for example, a certain level of cognitive ability and/or psychomotor ability). Sometimes criteria are used to signal the variable to be observed (that is, the performance dimensions) as well as the accepted or desired level at which it should be observed.

---

Bailey (1983: 55) advocates that the first step in criterion development is to ascertain the dimensions that appropriately summarize performance information. Dimensional analysis reduces 'descriptions of performance phenomena to the lowest possible dimensionality whilst maintaining optimal power for explaining variance'. Choice of dimensions is ultimately down to relevance of the dimensions to *actual job performance.* Unfortunately, the reality is that most performance criteria used for research purposes depend heavily on what data source is most conveniently available (selection validation, appraisal processes, training evaluation) rather than theoretically derived (Robertson & Smith, 2001; see Chapters 1 and 2).

---

### Study Box 3.4

#### Issues central to the criterion debate (see also Chapter 1)

##### Multiple versus composite criteria

Thorndike (1949) talked of the *ultimate criterion*, a standard requiring a single measure to optimally summarize all relevant performance requirements. This presupposes a *general performance factor* underpinning all variations in performance. (for example, Guion, 1961). Critics advocate the use of multiple criteria to reflect the real-world complexity of performance (for example, Dunnette, 1963). Some, however, argue that in practice, performance is assessed in terms of an employee's overall worth even when subcriteria are available (Murphy, Jako, & Anhalt, 1993).

##### Dynamic versus static criteria

Should criteria be fixed or dynamic, reflecting fluctuations in performance? Deadrick and Madigan (1990) found that the performance of sewing machine operators shifted continually over a six-month period: criterion measures valid at one time may not be equally valid at another. Others note an 'impressive' degree of criterion stability (for example, Hanges, Schneider, & Niles, 1990: 666). Hofmann, Jacobs and Baratta (1993) say that the controversy is less to do with the fact of change than how to detect it and at what level (for example, *group- or individual-level change*).

##### Behavioural versus personal criteria

Dispositional criteria assume consistency across situations and time whilst behavioural criteria pertain to what an employee does, a product of specific environmental conditions. Bailey (1983: 54) says that behavioural criteria are more realistic and context sensitive. However, dispositional criteria may be a more appropriate basis for appraising potential (Study Box 3.2).

##### Scale independence of criteria

Some argue that each criterion should be measured by a single independent scale, while others say that criterion *interdependence* is inevitable. A 'good' performer will tend to be 'good' in a variety of ways, and thus at least moderate correlation is expected even between otherwise unrelated performance dimensions.

##### Who determines the performance criteria?

Some argue that SMEs (for example, job incumbents, supervisors, and so on) should determine performance criteria, whilst others say it is a task for an independent specialist. There is growing support for appraisers to generate the criteria, to increase their understanding of, and commitment to, the appraisal process.

Issues central to the criterion debate 20 years ago and still relevant today are outlined in Study Box 3.4 (Bailey, 1983: 52–55). The performance criterion must also be practical (available, plausible, and acceptable to users), useful (serves its purpose) and fair in its discrimination of employees (Dipboye, Smith, & Howell, 1999). Usefulness depends on appraisal objectives. In practice, the criteria used for appraisal are not always the ones that employees see as the most important (Pettijohn, Parker, Pettijohn, & Kent, 2001).

### The focus of appraisal – the performance concept

Until 1970, there was no systematic attempt to conceptualize performance per se, and to this day it is only Campbell and colleagues (Campbell, 1991; Campbell, 1999; Campbell, McCloy, Oppler, & Sager, 1993) who have produced anything substantial on this topic. Few, however, have since made any formal reference to this work, although theoretical interest in performance is beginning to accumulate a broader and more sustained attention (Borman, 1991; Pulakos, Arad, Donovan, & Plamondon, 2000; Schmidt & Hunter, 2004; Vance, Coovert, MacCallum, & Hedge, 1989; Viswesvaran, 1993).

Campbell (1991) defined performance as *the value attributed to particular behaviours by an organization that leads to the attainment of important organizational goals*. Performance is thus behaviour in the context of a job, position or role imbued with value because of what it leads to. Performance is the act itself (for example, preparing a tender document), not its outcomes (for example, the tender document), which may not reflect the unique contributions of an employee.

The act of performing may not be directly observable (for example, decision making) but can nonetheless be assessed independently of its outcomes (Campbell, 1991: 695). Campbell also differentiates performance from effectiveness ('evaluation of the results of performance') and productivity ('the ratio of effectiveness to the cost of achieving that level of effectiveness').

**Performance modelling**   Attempts to model the content and structure of job performance are still, in the words of Campbell (1991: 704), a 'virtual desert', reflecting the bias in favour of developing predictor models. Campbell (1991) says that performance modelling should begin by identifying core *performance components* or behaviours, distinguishable from performance determinants (also Campbell et al., 1993: 35; Campbell, 1999).

*Campbell's competence model*   Campbell models performance as a multi-component hierarchical construct. At the most general level he describes eight *latent* higher order components (Study Box 3.5). Not every job will presuppose all eight components. Moreover, each component will vary in content and in the way it is expressed at the lower order across different jobs.

Campbell (1991) emphasizes that each of the eight components requires construct-validation. For example, peer leadership is differentiated from supervisory leadership, even though they comprise similar behaviours (for example, goal setting, coaching). The difference is the object of their focus, and also their determinants. The content and structure of the lower-order factors comprising each of the eight factors also require elucidation. For instance, effort could be reduced to its physical, cognitive and motivational aspects.

Recently, Campbell (1999) and others (for example, Pulakos et al., 2000) have suggested that another important component not included in the original taxonomy pertains to how well individuals adapt to new conditions or job requirements, a consideration of growing importance in today's constantly changing work environment. Pulakos et al. (2000) refer to this in the shorthand as *adaptive performance* (Study Box 3.6).

---

### Study Box 3.5

#### The eight components in Campbell's performance taxonomy

- *job-specific task proficiency* – the substantive or technical tasks core to the job, independent of motivational inclinations;
- *non-job-specific task proficiency* – common tasks required of nearly everyone, not specific to any one job (for example, attending meetings, dealing with co-workers and so on);
- *written and oral communication* – formal presentations, reports, letters, memos, for example;
- *demonstrating effort* – degree of commitment, despite all odds;
- *maintaining personal discipline* – refraining from negative behaviours such as absenteeism, substance abuse, rule infraction, and so on;
- *facilitating peer and team performance* – supporting peers, helping them and providing training, coupled with commitment to group goals and the facilitation of effective team functioning;
- *supervision* – proficiency at influencing the performance of employees through face-to-face interaction and influence (that is, supervisory leadership);
- *management/administration* – for example, articulating goals for the department or organization, organizing people, problem solving, controlling expenditure, obtaining resources.

---

### Study Box 3.6

#### Adaptive performance

Pulakos et al. (2000) content analysed over 1000 critical incidents from 21 different jobs ($N = 1619$) to clarify the concept of adaptive performance and then tested its validity using the 'Job Adaptability Inventory' across 24 different jobs representing 15 of 23 major occupational categories in the US Standard Occupational Classification System. Six different facets of adaptive performance were identified, more or less relevant to all jobs, although Pulakos et al. recognize that their generalizability must be evaluated further (2000: 617):

*(Continued)*

---

**Study Box 3.6    Continued**

- *solving problems creatively* – solving atypical, ill-defined and complex problems as they arise;
- *dealing with uncertain and unpredictable work situations* – efficiently switching orientation or focus as appropriate and taking reasonable action in spite of ambiguity;
- *learning work tasks, technologies, and procedures* – learning new ways to perform a job or learning different skill sets or tasks to retool for a new job or career;
- *demonstrating interpersonal adaptability* – especially with the shift to a more service-oriented economy, demonstrating interpersonal flexibility, adjusting interpersonal style to achieve a goal to work more effectively within a particular team and being responsive and flexible are now critical skills;
- *demonstrating cultural adaptability* – includes being able to adapt to cultural demands within a company or in a new country; this may involve learning a new language, norms and values and successfully integrating into a new culture (see Chapter 2);
- *demonstrating physically-oriented adaptability* – for instance, adapting to heat, noise, uncomfortable climates and difficult environments quickly and effectively; this is inextricably linked with global working.

---

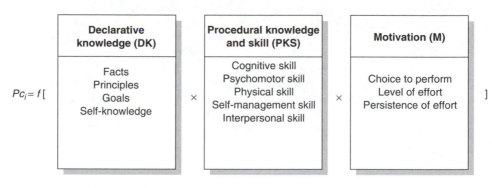

$Pc_i = f\,[$ 

| Declarative knowledge (DK) | | Procedural knowledge and skill (PKS) | | Motivation (M) |
|---|---|---|---|---|
| Facts<br>Principles<br>Goals<br>Self-knowledge | × | Cognitive skill<br>Psychomotor skill<br>Physical skill<br>Self-management skill<br>Interpersonal skill | × | Choice to perform<br>Level of effort<br>Persistence of effort |

$]$

$i = 1, 2, \ldots k$ performance components

**Campbell's Functional Equation:**

$PC_1$ (performance component) $= f\,[DK \times PKS \times M]$

**Figure 3.1**    Campbell's performance model

*Source:* Campbell (1991: 707)

Campbell (1991) also outlines three determinants of performance variation: declarative knowledge, procedural knowledge and skill, and motivation (Figure 3.1; see also Chapter 2). *Declarative knowledge* denotes knowledge about facts and things, understanding of the requirements of a task and self-awareness in relation to the task and its requirements. *Procedural knowledge and skill* is attained when knowing what to do is successfully combined with knowing how to do it – for example, skill in self-management. *Motivation* is defined as the combination of choice to expend effort (direction), of level of effort to expend (amplitude) and of persistence in the expenditure of that effort (duration), and is a direct determinant of performance. These three determinants together comprise Campbell's functional equation. The precise functional form, as Campbell (1991: 706) puts it, is not known and perhaps even unknowable.

Campbell, however, offers two testable propositions. Performance will not occur unless: (1) there is motivation to perform at some level of effort for a specified time; and (2) there is some threshold level of procedural knowledge and skill. Declarative knowledge is also assumed to be prerequisite for procedural skill, and the predictors of the three performance determinants are likely to be different for different jobs.

Campbell's performance model is a *competence* model in that it describes the higher order abstract components or structure of performance. Whilst some evidence can be cited for this model using US Army data, its various components require more precise specification and its operational implications are still largely unclear (Campbell, 1999). Evidence from McCloy, Campbell and Cudeck (1994) confirmed that some degree of declarative knowledge, procedural knowledge and motivation was necessary for nine different occupational categories, despite wide variation in job content. This and other findings afford good initial support for the validity of the model (e.g., Campbell et al., 1993; McCloy et al., 1994). Work by Campbell and colleagues on testing and refining the performance model continues unabated (Borman, Walter, Campbell, & Pulakos, 2001; Campbell, Houston, & Oppler, 2001).

Hackett (2002) argues that the value of Campbell's model is in its multi-dimensional view of performance accounting not just for task-focused performance per se, but also motivational and contextual aspects (see also Rotundo & Sackett, 2002). It is these 'contextual' aspects of performance that have attracted more attention in recent years than job performance per se.

**Contextual performance**   Borman (1991) argues for expanding the criterion domain to include elements of contextual performance beyond formal task requirements. Many extra-role activities pursued by employees, whilst not formally recognized, are nonetheless critical to organizational effectiveness. They describe two main areas of 'contextual performance': organizational citizenship behaviour (OCB) and prosocial organizational behaviour (POB). The concept of OCB derives from the extensive conceptual and empirical work of Smith, Organ and Near (1983), and comprises two dimensions: *altruism* (spontaneous day-to-day prosocial behaviours helping others to perform more effectively) and *conscientiousness* (generalized compliance with organizational rules and procedures). Altruism describes OCB towards individuals whilst conscientiousness describes OCB towards the organization.

The concept of POB is not dissimilar to OCB, although it is said to include other aspects of 'contextual performance'. Brief and Motowidlo (1986: 711) describe it as behaviour intended to promote the welfare of the individual, group and organization. POB can be role prescribed, or beyond the call of the core tasks, and includes assisting co-workers with job-related or personal matters, complying with organizational values and policies, suggesting organizational improvements, applying extra effort to the job, staying with the organization during hard times and representing the organization favourably to outsiders. Related concepts include 'civic virtue' (that is, responsible participation in the political life of an organization), 'loyalty' (that is, defending the organization; Graham, 1986) and 'courtesy' (for example, preparing secretaries in advance for a significant work load; Organ, 1998).

All of the above activities support 'the organizational, social and psychological environment in which the technical core must function' (Borman, 1991), and unlike task activities, are common across most if not all jobs. Rotundo and Sackett (2002: 68) caution that perhaps we should not discuss these other important aspects of performance in literally 'contextual' terms because 'the same behaviour may be in-role or rewarded in one organization and extra-role in another'. Regardless of the situation, they say, the behaviour is the same. Hence they use the term 'citizenship performance' to refer to behaviour that contributes to organizational goals. So far, however, arguments for forging a link between contextual performance dimensions and organizational effectiveness are conceptual rather than empirical.

Rotundo and Sackett (2002) also maintain that 'counterproductive performance' should be integral to discussions about citizenship including 'downtime behaviour' and personal deviance, all of which pertain to voluntary behaviour that can harm organizational well-being. Campbell (1999) has since also argued that all of these citizenship considerations can be easily integrated as subfactors into his eight-factor model (for example, personal discipline, demonstrating effort, non-specific job proficiency).

*Blumberg and Pringle's (1982) performance variation model*  Blumberg and Pringle (1982) advocate a general model of work performance, addressing the issue of performance variation more explicitly than Campbell by focusing on *performance in practice*. Performance comprises three components: opportunity, capacity and willingness to perform (Figure 3.2).

The Blumberg–Pringle model assumes individual and environmental factors interact to produce a particular level and quality of work performance. Environmental factors are the *opportunity* component of the model (for example, job design, working conditions, communication, group membership and leadership). *Capacity to perform* pertains to physical, physiological, and knowledge/skill variables like age, education, energy, health and ability. The *motivation* component signals willingness and includes individual characteristics, values, attitudes, perceptions and motivation. Together, opportunity (O), capacity (C), and willingness (W) combine to produce work performance, where performance = $f(O \times C \times W)$. That is, given two people with equal ability, the model predicts that the one with the greatest level of energy will have the greater capacity to perform. However, the components themselves are believed to work multiplicatively in that some level of each should be present for performance to occur at all.

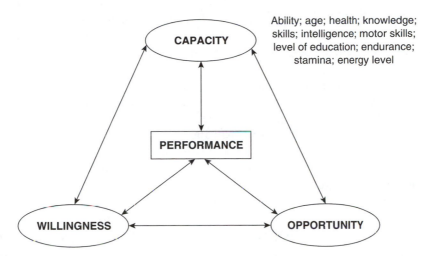

**Figure 3.2** Blumberg and Pringle's performance model

As indicated in Figure 3.2, the components are believed to interact such that a favourable environment, for example, may increase levels of willingness, and so on. Examples of the kind of environmental variables relevant to performance differences include task preparation, budgetary support, time availability, tools and equipment, materials and supplies, job-related information, and so on – all of which have a largely constraining effect. One attraction of the Blumberg–Pringle model is that it accounts for both person (competence-based) and situational factors (Russell, 2001). What it does not do, however, is clarify or explain the relational rules linking person and situation factors.

Both the Blumberg–Pringle and the Campbell model aim to capture performance in a generalizable way (that is, across broad job families), rather than in the context of a particular organization. Some argue against constructing generic performance models applicable across all jobs, because of the measurement problems associated with the so-called 'positive manifold' (where different job dimensions are highly inter-correlated; for example, Viswesvaran & Ones, 2000). Campbell and colleagues (Campbell, 1999) have long acknowledged across their eight different dimensions of performance positively correlated.

Although there is currently no consensus on the meaning or source of shared variance across different performance dimensions, research has begun to directly tackle this issue. Viswesvaran, Schmidt, and Ones (2002) ruled out the halo effect as a potential explanation for inflated correlation across different performance dimensions, advocating a 'general factor in job performance' over and above this. Recent work looking at how performance can be described at a construct level has yielded some important insights into what this general factor might constitute.

*Evolving a construct model of performance*　Another theoretical approach to performance begins by measuring performance in the context of specific tasks. The aim is to identify a 'nomological network' of constructs 'that provides meaning to the measures' (Landy, 2003). This network will include predictor and criterion constructs. Effectively, a nomological network is a measurement model that links observed variables to underlying constructs and describes the structural relationship (pathways) between these constructs.

Beginning with a 'general model of job performance' (that is, experience, capability, supervisor support) for three task categories pertinent to the job of jet engine mechanic, Vance et al. (1989: 447), found that task ratings (derived from supervisor, self and peers) was significantly predicted by capability (itself linked with training performance) and experience across all three tasks. They argued that this kind of measurement modelling can facilitate 'a more efficient linking of task characteristics, performance requirements, and capabilities' (p. 454) and should also include other predictor variables. The development of task taxonomies could provide a crucial starting point for this (Fleishman & Quaintance, 1984).

Within this same basic framework, it has been consistently demonstrated that general mental ability, defined as the ability to learn (GMA), is very strongly correlated with job performance (Schmidt & Hunter, 2004). Moreover, meta-analyses (of selection- validation studies in particular), comprising both cross-sectional and longitudinal studies, have shown that GMA predicts job performance more strongly than any other trait, including specific aptitude(s) (see Chapter 1). The more highly the measure of GMA loads on the 'g' factor, the larger the correlations. Until fairly recently, it was believed that the shelf-life of GMA was largely over after formal schooling and that it had little if anything to do with real-world performance. These beliefs have since been strongly refuted, the unweighted average (across meta-analyses) validity of GMA being 0.55 for performance on the job and 0.63 for training performance (see Schmidt & Hunter, 2004 for a review).

Some have argued that the more experienced the employee, the less relevance GMA has to job performance, and whilst many single studies do demonstrate that experience does matter to performance, meta-analyses demonstrate that the predictive validity of experience overall is *not* significant relative to GMA. It is GMA that 'turns experience into higher job knowledge and hence higher performance' (Hunter & Schmidt, 1996: 455).

Findings pointing to a 'general performance factor' do not imply that job performance is unidimensional, since in practice any one job can be analysed into various component dimensions like those postulated by Campbell and colleagues (Campbell, 1999). However, this does not preclude one from deriving what Schmidt and Hunter (2004: 170) call 'a composite index of job performance'. Moreover, component models remain purely *descriptive*, whilst the identification of underlying constructs is moving towards the development of an *explanation for performance*. For instance, causal analyses show that the major effect of GMA on job performance is mediated by *job knowledge*: those higher on GMA acquire more knowledge and faster (p. 170). The greater the level of job complexity (degree of reasoning, judgement and planning), the greater the requirement for GMA, and even jobs low in complexity engage more GMA than is perhaps typically assumed (see also Hunter & Schmidt, 1996).

In view of an attempt to provide an explanation for performance, it is also becoming increasingly clear that the 'conscientiousness' component of the Big Five model (see Chapter 1) consistently predicts job and training performance, especially when assessed by others (Schmidt & Hunter, 2004). Importantly, conscientiousness is not correlated with GMA and predicts performance over and above GMA (though not as much as GMA; Schmidt & Hunter, 1998). Other work has demonstrated that personality-based integrity tests are also strong predictors of job performance (stronger than conciousness, although they may to some extent incorporate it; Ones, Vivswesvaran, & Schmidt, 1993).

In Schmidt and Hunter's (2004: 170) words, together these findings suggest that 'GMA and conscientiousness affect performance on all job performance dimensions is almost certainly part of the explanation' for general job performance.

## Part 1 Summary (II) and Conclusions

- The performance domain is relatively ill researched and understood, although sub-stantive contributions are emerging. Campbell's multi-component competence-based performance model explains the basis on which performance is possible. The dimen-sion of 'adaptive performance' has been recently incorporated into this model.
- Blumberg and Pringle's model examines 'operational performance', taking into consideration external and contextual influences on performance.
- Recent contributions include research on contextual performance, attempts to develop performance constructs from measurement models of performance on par-ticular tasks and from other literature on life outcomes, of which occupational out-comes (performance, training success, achievements) are a critical part.
- Some argue that performance is underpinned by a generic construct signifying a mix of general mental ability and conscientiousness or integrity.
- Manifest performance, however, is explained by a combination of personal and situational factors (including opportunity, support and other people). Performance outcomes may thus not be entirely down to the performance of an individual.

## Performance Measurement

In the practice of performance measurement there are no absolutes and no guarantees. Measures can be subjective (for example, rating scales) or objective, referring to the use of formalized performance tests such as work samples, job knowledge tests, and so on, and other quantifiable sources of data (for example, sales figures, productivity levels) denoting the 'outcomes' of performance rather than performance per se (Campbell, 1999). Issues surrounding performance measurement are primarily psychometric (that is, ensuring reliability and validity) (see Chapter 1).

## Performance ratings

Employee rating systems have a history going back to the 1930s. Ratings can provide a fairly *direct measure of individual performance*, and are preferable to narrative evaluations that do not enable fine performance discriminations. Meta-analytic integrations of studies on rating reliability indicate an average reliability of 0.55 for supervisor ratings (which is higher than for peer ratings; Viswesvaran, Schmidt & Ones, 2002). The idea of quantification is attractive to organizations, particularly in the absence of clear-cut performance end points.

Recently some have cautioned that measures of reliability that rely heavily on inter-rater correlations are inappropriate because of the implicit assumption made that all raters are motivated to be accurate, have access to the same employee information and use it in the same way to form an evaluation (Murphy & De Shon, 2000; Study Box 3.7). On the contrary, we must *expect* systematic differences (rather than random error) across raters in what they observe and how they make sense of it, especially across raters from different sources (for example, supervisor versus peer ratings; Murphy & Cleveland, 1995). This 'ecological perspective' on ratings competes with the assumptions of classical test theory.

---

### Study Box 3.7

**Systematic or random error across performance ratings**

Using a policy-capturing framework, Rotundo and Sackett (2002) found differences between managers in how much weight they put on task, citizenship and counter-productive behaviours in their performance ratings. Most weight overall was placed on task performance, but otherwise there was no 'common policy' in rating tendencies. Rating policies could be grouped into three clusters reflecting *implicit policies about what really matters to performance*: task performance, counter-productive behaviour, and both task- and counter-productive behaviour. Murphy and Cleveland (1995) likewise found a systematic association between 'rater goals' and rating behaviours, goals which may not always coincide with organizational goals (for example, encouraging or motivating future performance rather than accuracy), linked with implicit theories about the consequences of evaluation for employee motivation (for example, belief that giving high ratings demonstrates support versus belief that rigorous evaluation will provide a challenging impetus for change) reflecting in a general tendency towards either leniency or stringent accuracy. Meaningful variation in rater goals appears to be independent of external incentives (Murphy, Cleveland, Skattebo, & Kinney, 2004). Goals may change over time depending on the particular purpose to which the evaluative information is being used and on general attitudes to the organization (for example, trust in the appraisal process).

---

## Rating reliability and validity

Reliability and validity or accuracy is by no means a trivial issue for appraisal. Decisions based on appraisal information can have fundamental life implications for employees (for example, promotion, increased salary). Yet the way appraisals are conducted, and the reliability and validity of the information generated, is ironically the weakest link in the decision-making chain (Fletcher, 2001, 2002, 2004). Like selection, appraisal information may adversely influence job or career opportunities for certain people or groups. It can be used implicitly as a selection device to 'streamline' someone for promotion, demotion or even termination.

Scullen, Mount and Goff (2000) found that up to 62 percent of variation in performance ratings was attributable to *idiosyncratic rating tendencies* (Study Box 3.8). Explanations for these tendencies include reference to generic cognitive processes (for example, categorization processes, attribution processes), motivational factors (for example, rater goals), and individual differences (for example, conscientiousness, self-monitoring tendencies, goal orientation).

---

### Study Box 3.8

#### Idiosyncratic rating tendencies

##### *Restriction of range errors*

Overly severe, overly lenient, central tendency or average rating ('play safe') tendency gives rise to ratings in a restricted range across the distribution (for example, 'ceiling' and 'floor' effects). Leniency is the most common range error (Jawahar, 2001).

##### *Illusory halo*

Reliance on global impressions (halos) that frame and integrate evaluations into one overarching judgement gives rise to perceptions of an 'illusory correlation' between otherwise different dimensions of performance. This may be triggered by traits on which an individual is deemed 'conspicuously good or especially bad' or by a general good or bad impression (Drenth, 1998: 79). Accordingly, halos are positive (high–high–high and so on) or negative (low–low–low and so on). The halo effect is more likely when the performance dimension is unfamiliar, not clearly defined, and/or difficult to observe. Recent research, however, advocates caution to the assumption that the 'halo' effect is necessarily always biased or inaccurate. Supervisor ratings, it is said, generally consist of 'global impressions', but this halo may reflect a genuine assessment of overall performance (Jackson & Furnham, 2001). Jackson and Furnham (2001: 23) point out, however, that appraisals based on global ratings are an insufficient basis for either decision making or constructive feedback (that is, do not provide detailed behaviour-specific feedback, may be perceived unfair) and whilst 'accurate', are nonetheless 'flawed'.

##### *Similarity, attraction and liking errors*

*Similar-to-me errors* where raters use their own personal characteristics as a benchmark to judge someone, giving preferential evaluations to those perceived 'similar'

*(Continued)*

---

| Study Box 3.8   Continued |

(Strauss, Barrick, & Connerley, 2001). Perceived similarity predicts physical attractive-ness and personal liking and/or familiarity, which, in turn, systematically enhances rat-ings, although liking can increase attention to an employee, thereby contributing to improved performance (Lefkowitz, 2000). This raises the important overlooked fact that the pre-existing relationship (and anticipated post-appraisal relationship) is likely to have a profound impact on the final appraisal result (Drenth, 1998).

### Assimilation/contrast effects

Assimilation refers to the use of a category standard or prototype as a basis for eval-uation (for example, the sacrificial angel image of a nurse). The employee may be evaluated as better or worse on a particular performance dimension depending on stereotypical features of the assigned category. Contrast effects occur when two average employees are nonetheless rated as radically different, depending on the group norm. If the performance norm for A is very low, A's performance *by contrast* may be evaluated quite high relative to peers, whilst if the performance norm for B is high, B's performance *by contrast* may be rated that much lower. Thus A and B receive different evaluations despite similar levels of actual performance (Kravitz & Balzer, 1992).

### Other errors

These include *first impression error* (when early encounters with a person weigh dis-proportionately high in evaluations), *systematic distortion* (assumptions made about what behaviours should go together as a product of rater's 'implicit performance the-ories'), and the *negativity effect* (when more weight in placed on negative informa-tion than on positive or neutral information). Errors in ratings make it difficult to compare the evaluations of one rater with another with respect to the same individ-ual or set of individuals. A score of 5 on a scale used by a 'lenient' rater may be equivalent in meaning to a 3 or at most a 4 for a 'severe' rater. Converting both sets of ratings to the same standard scale (that is, z-scores) will render them compara-ble statistically, but not in real-life terms.

---

The *cognitive perspective* has aspired to develop a 'theory of ratings' that explains how people form their performance ratings (Landy & Farr, 1980: 285). One explanation refers to the use of cognitive representations (knowledge structures) in which perfor-mance information is assimilated on an informal and continuous basis and attribution processes (for example, how much of the cause of performance can be attributed inter-nally or externally) when making formal evaluations. Through a process of cognitive representation, a transformed version of the original set of information becomes 'amenable to mental manipulation and storage into memory' (Kinicki, Hom, Trost, & Wade, 1995: 354). Research suggests that this model can be supported in its basic elements (for example, Woehr & Feldman, 1993: 239).

Woehr and Feldman (1993) show in particular that whilst the relationship between specific information and subsequent judgement in appraisal systems depends on the presence or absence of *previously formed evaluations*, there are also *contextual factors* involved that influence the final judgement (for example, the purpose of appraisal). Evidence suggests, however, that we are generally prone to locate the causes of performance internally rather than looking at the circumstances surrounding performance (the fundamental attribution error), although those familiar with the job and its environs are less prone to this than less experienced appraisers (DeNisi & Peters, 1996).

Another inextricably linked cognitive explanation points to the categorization processes used in processing performance-related information, especially at the encoding stage (Barnes, 2001). Categories (which can comprise performance prototypes and/or group stereotypes) are selected to make sense of the appraised behaviour via a matching process (for example, hard working). These may be called 'folk theories' of performance (for example, Barnes, 2001). When performance information is recalled, the category but not specific behavioural instance is automatically retrieved unless an unexpected or otherwise noteworthy behaviour is observed, in which case a more active re-construal process may be occasioned. Kulik and Ambrose (1993) note that the latter is more likely when appraisers are faced with providing a negative evaluation, particularly in the light of concerns about discrimination and employee grievance. Perceptions of accountability (that is, being required to justify and defend one's evaluation) may pose pressure for a more considered performance evaluation process (Jawahar, 2001; Murphy et al., 2004).

Both cognitive explanations draw heavily on the person perception literature and both assume some form of knowledge structure in which performance information is represented (either in an individuated or categorical form). The more ambiguous the meaning of someone's behaviour, the more open to interpretation and the use of pre-existing knowledge structures to organize performance information (that is, signifying a loss of behavioural detail). This may account for why it is easier for raters to provide a global evaluation than a finely discriminated set of behavioural ratings (Jackson & Furnham, 2001; see Study Box 3.9).

## Study Box 3.9

### Frame of reference 'accuracy' training

Various suggestions for improving the accuracy of appraisal ratings include 'frame of reference' (FOR) training (for example, Bernardin & Buckley, 1981; Goodstone & Lopez, 2001). In FOR training, raters are taught to properly categorize and assess behaviour (that is, correctly assign them to dimensions). The rationale is that whilst raters tend to forget many of the specific individual behaviours they have observed, they nonetheless provide accurate ratings overall, suggesting that they retain 'correct on-line impressions' which are then accessed for purposes of rating (as opposed to specific behaviours). Formal evaluation of how successful FOR training is relative to other training methods in yielding more accurate and reliable performance assessments is yet to be undertaken. Moreover, FOR training is potentially highly resource consuming and could potentially demoralize the assessors. Some thus note that training of any kind in performance assessment can enhance rating quality (for example, Goodstone & Lopez, 2001).

Finally, there is growing respect for individual differences in appraisal tendencies and how these interact with organizational and interpersonal considerations. For instance, Jawahar (2001) has demonstrated the impact of differences in self-monitoring inclination using Snyder's (1987) approach. High self-monitors are said to be adept at deciphering social expectations and cues, and tend to adjust their behaviour accordingly to maximize approval and minimize disapproval for their actions and decisions. Jawahar (2001) found that high self-monitors produced substantially less accurate ratings than low self-monitors, particularly under conditions of high accountability. This tendency inclines high self-monitors to be especially lenient in their performance ratings (for example, to maximize the approval of subordinates and/or to ratify themselves in the eyes of superiors as good managers). Other suggested factors on which individuals can vary are conscientiousness and goal orientation (oriented to pay attention to strengths or weaknesses; for example, Murphy et al., 2004).

The idea that certain dimensions are easier to rate than others (perhaps because they are more readily observed or more clearly associated with particular evaluative standards; Wohlers & London, 1989) has generally not been upheld (Viswesvaran et al., 2002).

## Rating systems

There are many different kinds of rating system, from the simple to the elaborate (reviews by Borman, 1991; Drenth, 1998; Study Box 3.10). Rating formats can be broadly classified as individual or comparative. In the former, the lone employee is the focus of evaluation; in the latter, the employee is compared with their peers. In practice, individual methods still involve some form of implicit comparison. Individual-oriented rating formats are also sometimes described as formats with absolute standards, as they compare the individual against a set of criteria. The production of different rating formats is primarily motivated by improved accuracy.

---

### Study Box 3.10

**Rating formats used for evaluating employee performance**

*Graphic scales (Paterson, 1922–23 cited in Borman, 1991)*

Employees are rated from low to high along a set of unidimensional scales depicting various performance characteristics, for example, leadership ability. Scales vary in how they are anchored – for example, 1 to 5; 1 to 7 – where anchors may or may not be explicitly labelled (for example, 'low' to 'high'). Some scales also include verbal designations for the mid-points of the continuum (for example, very poor, poor, average, good, very good). The biggest problem for these scales is 'restriction of range' (for example, leniency, severity).

## Study Box 3.10    Continued

### Comparison formats

Examples are rank order, paired comparisons, forced distribution. These assume an identifiable performance distribution along which employees can be differentially located (for example, r*ank ordering* employees from highest to lowest on specific performance dimensions). Ranking affords little scope for precise feedback however. Moreover, the distance between ranks may not be equal, thus exactly how much one is better than X or worse than Y is not easy to ascertain. *Paired comparison* involves comparing each employee with every other employee, on overall performance. The number of comparisons may be large, and assumes day-to-day contact with employees. *Forced distribution* entails sorting a large number of employees into categories determined by a particular distribution, typically the 'normal distribution'. An example is 'the best 10 percent of the group', 'the next best 20 percent of the group', 'the middle 40 percent', 'the next lower 20 percent' and, finally, 'the worst 10 percent of the group'. However, the meaning and use of lower-level categories may be problematic.

### Checklist methods

These techniques – weighted or forced-choice – present a set of descriptive statements of behaviour directly tied to a particular job. In the *weighted* version, either the best or the typical behaviour of the employee is described using as many items as necessary. Example items include 'regularly sets vague and unrealistic program goals', and 'develops work schedules that allow for completion of projects'. Items are weighted although this is hidden to the rater. The *forced-choice* version is designed to overcome bias arising from guessing the item weights. Two or more behavioural statements are grouped together describing behaviours similar in levels of desirability. The rater then selects one of the two behaviours in a set to describe the behaviour of an employee.

### Behaviourally anchored rating scales (BARS)

BARS evolved from work using the Critical Incident Technique (CIT) (Flanagan, 1954; Chapter 1) by Smith and Kendall (1963), who argued that rating scales should be anchored with behavioural examples signifying different levels of effectiveness on a particular dimension. The task is to match the performance of the individual to the behavioural anchors on the scale, and to assign them a numerical weighting accordingly. Users can participate in developing them, thereby creating a sense of ownership, ensuring the credibility of the format and reducing ambiguity in the rating process.

### Behavioural observation scales (BOS)

BOS were developed by Latham and Wexley (1977), and also rely on 'critical behaviours'. Unlike BARS, BOS evaluate the statements generated according to their frequency of occurrence in employee behaviour. Response categories can be defined verbally (for example, never, sometimes, always) and/or numerically (for example, 5 percent, 50 percent, 75 percent).

*(Continued)*

## Study Box 3.10   Continued

### *Mixed standard scales (MSS)*

MSS are a variation on the BARS (Borman, 1991). They comprise three behavioural statements similar to behavioural anchors for each performance dimension (referring to highly effective, highly ineffective and average behaviour respectively). The statements are randomly arranged along the scale, the task being to indicate whether employee performance is better than, worse than, or at about the same level as, the performance described. The mixing of the standards is designed to minimize halo and leniency errors.

Contemporary rating systems have moved away from the traditional emphasis on trait evaluation (for example, appearance, conscientiousness) to behavioural evaluation (see **www.sagepub.co.uk/millward** for examples of rating scales). This behavioural focus reflects a concern about the dubious reliability and validity of judgements about 'traits'. As Drenth (1998: 64) puts it, 'the concepts used are often situation dependent and not unequivocally defined' (see also Tett & Guterman, 2000). Also, one could score 'excellent' on every item, yet still not be performing well. Moreover, feedback discussions that become deeply 'personal' can lead to 'irritation, defensiveness, denial or a sort of passive resignation', which is clearly not a justifiable basis for facilitating performance improvement (Drenth, 1998: 64).

Nowadays, behaviour-anchored appraisal is considered much more useful, unless trait-based ratings can be directly tied to the job and/or the appraisal is about 'potential performance' where the emphasis will inevitably shift to trait-like personal constants such as people orientation, analytic strategy, locus of control/attribution style (Study Box 3.2). In instances of appraisal for promotion purposes, there is always a tension between selecting for 'current' requirement relative to 'future' requirement, and in particular between the need to maintain organizational continuity whilst also allowing for innovation and change. Formal appraisal, though, is generally not the only source of evidence for identifying potential, typically complemented by the use of development centres, biographical information and/or responses to ability tests and personality inventories (see Chapter 1 on assessment centres). For all appraisal purposes, Drenth (1998: 67) says that:

> Somehow a path has to be steered between the Scylla of excessive tangibility and the Charybdis of excessive abstraction … one does not, as it were, dive so deeply into the personality structure that one loses touch with reality, neither does one stay so near the surface that one becomes lost in irrelevant details.

Contemporary reviews have, however, cast doubt on the supposed psychometric superiority of behaviour formats over global/comparative ratings for more conventional appraisal purposes. Evidence suggests that the latter can, in some instances, be more accurate (reliable and valid) than multi-component behavioural measures (for example, Jackson & Furnham, 2001). However, an important consideration here is that global/comparative scales do not provide a precise basis for delivering constructive 'behavioural' feedback (Tziner & Kopelman, 2002). There may also be contingencies under which one method is better than another.

***Objective criteria***   Objective criteria refer to tangible outcomes often obtained from personnel data such as turnover, absenteeism, production rates, job level, salary, sales volume, disciplinary cases and other similarly countable records (see **www.sagepub. co.uk/millward** for a review). So-called objective measures have intuitive appeal, and are thus perceived 'fair'. However, outcome criteria may only tap a very small proportion of job performance, and may in many ways be very unfair (for example, sales performance across a company may vary widely by geographical region because of opportunity differences).

Outcome measures may also be overemphasized to the neglect of less measurable, but equally, if not more, important aspects of performance. For instance, accent on the measurement of speed and efficiency in dealing with client complaints or difficulties may cloud issues of quality and customer service. If, as in Accident and Emergency departments in the UK hospitals, performance is assessed by patient throughput, employees may resort to shortcuts in patient care or neglect the intangibles of care. Objective performance pressures (for example, sales targets in brokerage firms) may also promulgate informal practices that are unethical or even illegal.

In short, objective outcome data can be useful, but Borman (1991) and others (for example, Drenth, 1998) have cautioned that it is almost always deficient and/or contaminated (**www.sagepub.co.uk/millward**).

## Part 1 Summary (III) and Conclusions

- The performance measurement literature is dominated by considerations of reliability and accuracy or validity, and remains uninformed by performance theory.
- It is generally agreed that performance ratings are the most appropriate source of employee evaluation relative to free-form methods and objective measures of outcome.
- Efforts have been largely directed towards developing the most appropriate rating format which is inextricably linked with attempts to eliminate or reduce rating error or bias.
- Different source of rater error have been described but there is a growing move towards differentiating between error and systematic differences in ratings arising from rater characteristics and goals (for example, the appraiser is not always motivated towards accuracy because he or she has other goals in mind like employee motivation). Findings suggest that raters hold implicit or folk theories of performance that guide their rating behaviour.

## The Conduct of Appraisal

Appraisal can be described as a job that managers 'love to hate' (Pettijohn et al., 2001).

## The developmental function

Clearly, the purpose of the appraisal will influence how it is conducted (Fletcher, 2001, 2004). Appraisal for administrative purposes is found to be generally more lenient than that conducted for research purposes because of the politics of the evaluation process. Appraisals for development purposes, on the other hand, are more likely to differentiate between employees than ratings because there is no evaluative comeback on either the appraiser or the appraised.

The emphasis on accuracy in comparing different sources of ratings has been criticized for losing sight of the developmental functions of appraisal. Indeed, a key function of the appraisal interview is to provide feedback to facilitate performance improvement (London & Smither, 1995). Thus, some argue, albeit controversially, that the main practical concern within appraisal is not whether ratings are accurate, but user accept-ability and/or usefulness in meeting individual and organizational goals (Pettijohn et al., 2001). Surveys have documented a steady increase since the 1990s in the use of so-called Multiple-Source Feedback Sysems (MSFS), often more popularly known as 360-degree appraisal, suggesting that 'developmental' issues are becoming a more inte-gral part of the practice of at least *management* appraisal (Fletcher & Baldry, 2001; Fletcher, 2004). These systems involve the manager being rated on various behavioural dimensions by one or more bosses, peers, subordinates and sometime also customers (Study Box 3.11).

There is disagreement on how to interpret differences in ratings obtained from dif-ferent sources (lack of convergence; Facteau & Bartholomew, 2001). Whilst there are often big discrepancies between raters from different sources, the issue of whether this reflects error or a valid difference is another question. Facteau and Bartholomew (2001) found evidence suggesting a common performance conceptualization across ratings from different sources, suggesting that they provide different *but ecologically valid* perspectives on performance. Such findings, though, may not be generalizable across all instruments and rating dimensions. There may be instances where a differ-ent interpretation of the same performance construct may underlie rating discrepan-cies, raising caution to the use of multi-source ratings for other than developmental purposes. Ash (1994) found that managers would only endorse 360-degree appraisals for developmental purposes (for example, feedback on leadership style), rather than for determining bonuses or merit.

One of the benefits of incorporating self-appraisal into the appraisal scheme is not for increased accuracy, but to promote a constructive dialogue between employee and organization (Case Study 3.2). It is generally agreed that employees who are involved in the appraisal process are more likely to respond favourably to the appraisal system and its goals (Fletcher, 2004). Bailey and Austin (2002) also found evidence for the beneficial effects of different sources of feedback on managers' beliefs about their ability to apply what they had learned from a 360-degree appraisal to their role. Specifically, peer ratings were associated with an increase in managers' beliefs, whilst subordinate ratings were associated with general feelings of personal mastery.

## Study Box 3.11

### Source of appraisal

#### *Supervisors*

Experienced supervisors are able usually to detect performance variations reasonably reliably, unless an employee works independently. Employees also generally construe supervisor evaluations as more useful than from other sources. Supervisors can also feel unable or uncomfortable in the evaluator role.

#### *Peers*

Peers are witness to the day-to-day performance of each other and generally respond well to peer appraisal for development but not administrative purposes (for example, pay/merit award) when negative peer feedback can undermine working relations. Peer evaluations generally obtain high reliabilities and are also valid predictors of future performance, although why is unclear. Peer evaluations also often agree well with those of the supervisor (Fletcher & Baldry, 2001).

#### *Upward appraisals*

Employees are well placed to comment on the leadership and/or managerial abilities of their supervisors/managers, although they may lack the experience and language necessary to make fine-grained evaluations. However, employees are only likely to be party to the behaviour of their supervisors in performance domains in which they are directly involved (for example, team meetings, work scheduling). Wohlers, Hall and London (1995) found that agreement between employee and supervisor was high when they had a 'close' working relationship. Resistance to subordinate appraisal among managers is common, although Antonioni (1994) found that managers were more willing to accept appraisals from subordinates in a system of accountability (for example, where feedback is obtained from specific individuals) than in a system of anonymity. Subordinate ratings can facilitate manager take-up of developmental activity (Brutus, London, & Martineau, 1999).

#### *Self-ratings*

Self-appraisal is often central to employee development programmes, affording the employee an opportunity to evaluate their own needs for improvement, independently of supervisor assessments. Self-appraisals often disagree with peer and supervisor evaluations (more lenient, less discriminating), particularly for white-collar employees (that is, managerial, professional). Jones and Fletcher (2002), however, argue that the quality of self-appraisals can be improved (less halo and leniency) by constructing positively toned (unbalanced) rating scales of 'behavioural elements' (rather than global competencies). Self-appraisals can also be moderated by accountability pressures (Sedikides, Herbst, Hardin, & Dardis, 2002). There is mounting evidence, however, for the usefulness of self-appraisals for enhancing the motivational and developmental impact of appraisal feedback (Fletcher, 2004).

---

### Case Study 3.2: A self-appraisal scheme

Huddart (1994) reports on a pilot scheme at Michelin (the tyre manufacturer) involving self-appraisal as a means of empowering employees, enhancing teamwork and raising quality consciousness. The scheme involved 30 employees, each required to complete self-appraisals forms evaluating themselves against criteria like 'productivity', 'quality', 'teamwork', 'safety' and 'commitment'. The appraisal forms were used to frame discussion with managers. Managers, in being freed from form filling, felt much more able to spend time communicating with employees. Employees who participated in the self-appraisal scheme were forthcoming with self-criticism, more so in fact than if managers had conducted the appraisal. The pilot scheme was considered a success and plans made to formalize it on a company-wide basis. Recent research confirms the performance enhancing consequences of training in self-appraisal and other self-management techniques (for example, Frayne & Geringer, 2000). Others caution against the idea that empowerment is an absolute general recipe for performance improvement; it depends on whether there is a climate of opportunity in which truly empowered behaviour can flourish (for example, Wall & Jackson, 1995).

---

## Developmental feedback

> Appraising others is, and will remain, a sensitive matter, especially if this appraisal is negative, and this has to be communicated to the person in question. This may activate all kinds of psychological mechanisms (resistance, denial, aggression, discouragement) in the person appraised which can seriously upset the relationship between the assessor and the assessed. (Drenth, 1998: 59)

The post-appraisal development interview (PAI) is a forum to enable each employee to get feedback as to how well he or she is doing in the opinion of the manager, and to give the manager and employee an opportunity to discuss how the employee can improve performance (Wexley, 1984: 167).

The assumption underpinning this is that feedback will lead to performance improvement, particularly if the feedback is discrepant from self-perception (Locke, 1997). However, this hypothesis of a feedback–performance improvement link mediated by discrepant self-perception has obtained mixed support (Fletcher & Baldry, 2001). Whilst there is some evidence for the increased congruence of self and other perceptions over time after an appraisal intervention (for example, Bailey & Fletcher, 2002), whether discrepant self-perception is the key mechanism for leveraging change is another issue. There are clearly many other mediators and moderators at stake (Study Box 3.12).

Moreover, incongruence may not matter to an individual who does not trust the source of the discrepant appraisal and/or does not accept it as a personal benchmark for change. As Kuhl (1994) notes, the discrepant perception must pertain to a desired goal, and must be achievable relative to one's current position (moderately discrepant), otherwise it will not evoke the appropriate self-regulatory action. In this instance, it is surprising that researchers have not sought inspiration from the more general literature on behaviour change including goal setting theory and self-regulation theory (see Chapter 4).

The success of the developmental appraisal directly hinges on the extent that feedback recipients react favourably, and respond to feedback constructively (Maurer, Mitchell, & Barbeite, 2002). However, research shows that feedback commonly has only negative consequences (for example, Walker & Smither, 1999) In a rare longitudinal study reported by Maurer et al. (2002), no direct association was found between feedback and subsequent development attitudes and activities. In this study, *workplace support* was more predictive of developmental activity. Even MSFS that have generally beneficial effects may not be 100 percent successful in yielding performance improvement. In a rare longitudinal study of managers from a large UK-based financial institution, Bailey and Austin (2002) showed that around one in four were perceived by their manager to have decreased in effectiveness following feedback.

Research has focused on two main sources of explanation for why negative feedback may not lead to positive change: characteristics of the feedback and feedback context, and the role of individual differences (for example, variation in self-monitoring inclinations, feedback seeking and self-efficacy). Feedback, for example, can be positive or negative in tone and can be delivered in various ways. Ilgen and Davis (2000) distinguished between negative feedback and criticism insofar as the former is offered constructively (job-relevant, future-oriented, maintaining self-esteem), whilst the latter is judgement-ridden and undermining. Many have found that negative feedback delivered constructively can promote greater performance benefits than positive feedback (for example, Atwater, Waldman, Atwater & Cartier, 2000).

---

### Study Box 3.12

#### The role of self-awareness in developmental performance improvement

Wohlers and London (1989) propose that disagreement of others' ratings with self-ratings provides an impetus for behavioural change (see also Brutus et al., 1999). Fletcher (1997) elaborates on this proposition using the concept of self-awareness or the degree to which individuals see themselves as others see them. Defined in this way, evidence suggests that self-awareness is positively associated with performance. Formulating the self-awareness-performance link, London (1993) argues from within a symbolic interaction perspective that people derive information about themselves and others from what others say and do. London says that people integrate feedback into self-concept by judging its accuracy and realism. Once feedback is internalized people interpret its content in relation to their current beliefs (or schemas). Feedback consistent with schemas is accepted automatically, whilst feedback that is inconsistent prompts either a reinterpretation of the feedback or an altered frame of reference. Based on research on MSMR feedback systems, London and Smither (1995) look at how feedback helps people understand how they are seen by others and how it enables them to identify areas for performance improvement. The degree of perceived goal–performance discrepancy is moderated by: self-enhancement propensity, feedback-seeking propensity, self-monitoring tendency and rating format. Number of raters, their credibility and value of the behaviours evaluated (that is, behaviours that matter to the organization) also impact on goal–performance discrepancies. The likelihood of acting on this is affected by self-efficacy, outcome expectancies and impression management tendencies.

Another issue concerns the specificity of feedback. It is generally assumed in the development literature that the more specific the feedback, the greater the performance benefits (for example, Gomez-Mejia, Balkin, & Cardy, 2001). Findings, however, suggest that this is 'not always' the case. Goodman, Wood and Hendrickx (2004) found that the performance benefit arising from specific feedback was short-lived. They explain that this occurs because precise pedantic feedback can create performance dependency, which in turn discourages self-regulatory exploration (see also Chapter 2).

Others have also suggested that the improvement potential of feedback depends heavily on 'the healthiness' of the interpersonal relationship between supervisor or manager and the focal employee (Wexley, 1984: 168). Feedback from a good manager can have a greater impact on future performance than from any other source (Sala & Dwight, 2002). On the other hand, a manager who does not believe in the value of appraisal can undermine the effectiveness of an otherwise well-designed scheme (Harris, Lievens & Van Hoye, 2004).

On the issue of individual differences, Yammarino and Atwater (2001) argue that the relative favourability of feedback (vis-à-vis self-assessment) interacts with self-efficacy to determine its differential performance effect. Self-efficacy denotes a belief in the possibility of skill improvement. Maurer and colleagues (Maurer, 2001; Maurer et al., 2002) argue that those who under-estimate their capability relative to others' perceptions of them may accept they have developmental needs, but only those whose self-efficacy is high are likely to do anything about it. Self-efficacy can also impact on whether individuals desire and seek performance feedback (Tuckey, Brewer & Williamson, 2002).

Furnham (1997) reports that 360-degree appraisals can work well under the following conditions: a trust in staff to be honest, fair and constructive; real commitment to the notion of communication as a two-way process; and that the ratings of subordinates are taken seriously and acted upon. Indeed, many practical and political issues can arise from the implementation of 360-degree appraisals (that is, training, experience, adequate job knowledge, rewarding weak managers for political reasons) in non-conducive cultures (Antonioni, 1994).

However, PA continues to be seen as something negative and to be feared rather than as an opportunity for two-way dialogue and developmental advancement. Significant senior management commitment and support is required for not just the rhetoric of appraisal, but also its full-blown implementation (Church & Waclawski, 2001). Research consistently points to the importance of the so-called 'feedback environment' and in particular cultural support for development as a critical factor in predicting take-up of developmental activity post-feedback (Maurer et al., 2002).

Line managers may also need to be involved in deliberations concerning the appraisal system (Church & Waclawski, 2001; Fletcher, 2004). Indeed, the new system needs to 'become a way of life for employees'. This may require reward systems that ensure that managers are appropriately trained and supported to evaluate their employees accurately, and are able to provide them with constructive feedback. The lack of acceptance of appraisal systems is associated with poorly designed appraisal forms; the use of irrelevant performance items; insufficient time devoted to preparation and completion of forms or training; feedback deficiencies; little impetus to act as a result of an appraisal; unreliable judgements; and minimal target setting (Church & Waclawski, 2001).

## The post-appraisal interview

... appraisal involves the interaction of two adult individuals.

(Drenth, 1998: 81)

There is little guidance in the literature on how to conduct an effective PAI involving the provision of feedback, other than from Wexley (1984; see **www.sagepub.co. uk/millward** for details).

Fletcher (2001) laments the relative absence of research on the appraisal interview relative to that on the selection interview. Wexley (1984) argues that the role of the PAI should be to *review issues that have already been discussed* by the supervisor with the employee during appraisal, rather than to introduce them fresh. In practice, however, appraisal may happen only once a year, with many supervisors/managers delaying or even resisting conducting appraisals altogether because they feel uncomfortable in this role. If, coupled with this, employees anticipate criticism, the appraisal may end up being a highly tense non-constructive affair (Fried, Tiegs & Bellamy, 1992).

Cederblom (1982) cautions that, in the final analysis, the effectiveness of an appraisal interview depends on employee characteristics (expectations and performance level), management characteristics (usual style of management), the nature of the employee/manager relationship (confidence in each other) and organizational characteristics (decision-making structures and processes) (Fried et al., 1992).

For example, there are instances where a pay-dominated appraisal is culturally expected (for example, the market trading division of an investment bank), affording a vehicle for transmitting values about acceptable behaviour as well as a basis for promotion (Tziner, Latham, Price, & Haccoun, 1996). Clearly, appraisal of any kind can be used strategically to link personal and corporate objectives. In a development-oriented culture, there may be less emphasis on evaluation and more on feedback as a management tool (for example, IBM), although there is nonetheless the facility to use them to determine merit pay.

Overall, the issue of performance measurement, appraisal and management is a highly political one. Cullen (1999) notes a general neglect of contextual considerations in the analysis of performance and its measurement, advocating more analytic consideration to the possibility of performance as a social construct.

A recent report from the Institute for Employment Studies says that many performance appraisal systems are failing, having limited impact on personal or business success. Their investigation revealed that appraisal systems are frequently 'stale, artificial and loaded with bureaucracy', and dreaded by all (Strebler, Robinson, & Bevan, 2002).

## Appraisal effectiveness

Whilst the effectiveness of appraisal systems can be judged against the same psychometric criteria (reliability, validity) used to ascertain the relative effectiveness of predictors in a selection process, it is increasingly recognized that understanding employee reactions is in fact critical to the validity and effectiveness of a PA system

(Keeping & Levy, 2000). The appraisal process may be technically sound, but if, for example, it is perceived unfair, accuracy is irrelevant (Cardy & Dobbins, 1994). The issue is hence one of identifying and assessing those employee reactions that really matter to the acceptability of an appraisal system. Typical reaction foci include satisfaction (with the interview, the system and the ratings), perceived fairness (of the ratings, the system, procedural and distributive justice), perceived utility (that is, instrumental value) and perceived accuracy.

Lack of acceptance is associated with poorly designed appraisal forms; the use of irrelevant performance items (lack of ecological validity); insufficient time devoted to preparation and completion of forms or training; feedback deficiencies; little impetus to do anything as a result of an appraisal; unreliable judgements; and little target setting (McKenna & Beech, 1995: 126). Lack of acceptance is particularly likely to be associated with an appraisal system *imposed* for administrative purposes alone, particularly if it does not inspire confidence in managers (Fried et al., 1992). Some would say that rater participation is more important at the appraisal development stage than employee participation, with employee participation ('employee voice') more appropriate to PAI procedures (Roberts & Pavlak, 1996).

Several examples of how negative reactions to PA can seriously undermine its effectiveness have begun to emerge. Kluger and DeNisi (1998) report that in more than one-third of cases they reviewed, PA feedback resulted in a *performance decrement* because employees feel *discouraged* and *de-motivated*. Atwater et al. (2000) report that negative 360-degree feedback (that is, lower than expected) delivered in a confidential developmental context was not seen as either useful or accurate, giving rise to anger and discouragement. Such reactions can substantially undermine employee commitment to appraisal. They argue that research should look closely at both feedback content and process to identify ways in which negative impacts come about and how they can be minimized (Study Box 3.13). For instance, providing 'normative data' (against which one's performance is compared) may induce a strong performance orientation in which 'standards' become an overriding defensive preoccupation relative to learning and improving.

Interestingly, Brett and Atwater (2001) found that employees with a pre-existing learning orientation (versus performance orientation) reflected more constructively on the usefulness of the feedback, suggesting that there is an important *temporal dimension* to the way in which people react to PA. Also, negative reactions can dissipate over time, suggesting that one important additional temporal dimension to take into consideration is the possibility of being treated differently by supervisors as a result of the performance feedback.

---

### Study Box 3.13

#### A 'reaction' research agenda

Brett and Atwater (2001: 941) raise some important questions for further research on employee reactions to PA feedback:

---

**Study Box 3.13    Continued**

- What negative behaviours and repercussions accompany negative feedback?
- Do negative reactions dissipate over time? If so, how long do they last? If not, what factors account for this?
- What individual difference factors (for example, goal orientation, self-efficacy, attribution style, social norms, personality, negative affectivity) can help under stand reactions to feedback?
- What role is played by feedback format (for example, numeric, narrative, behaviour based) in creating negative reactions, and how can it be designed to increase perceived accuracy and usefulness? Across four different evaluation studies, Tziner and Kopelman (2002) found that a behavioural observation-based rating format yielded the most positive reactions to feedback.
- What can be done during (PA) and after (developmental follow-up) the feedback delivery process to minimize negative reactions and foster a developmental orientation?
- Are some people leaving PA feeling so negative that this impacts on organizational attitudes and behaviours more generally?

There is some suggestion, too, that whether the source of feedback is direct or indirect (for example, clients, co-workers, objective records) is also important to perceptions of accuracy and utility (for example, Uggerslev & Sulsky, 2002).

---

In their review of the reaction literature, Cawley et al. (1998) note inconsistencies and confounds associated with the measurement of all criteria except perceived utility, as well as the difficulty of ruling out the impact of global affective tendencies on self-report measures. They note that problems of measurement can, in part, be attributed to the *a*theoretical nature of the research. Cardy and Dobbins (1994) argued that, whilst reactions may vary empirically across different 'foci', they are expressions nonetheless of a more latent higher order construct. Testing this proposition, Keeping and Levy (2000), however, found that their reaction data (satisfaction with system, satisfaction with interview, distributive justice, procedural justice, perceived utility and perceived accuracy) was more appropriately modelled with distinct, albeit interrelated, constructs. This does not rule out the likelihood of an overarching 'reaction construct' but suggests that a more hierarchical conceptualization is more appropriate.

Makin et al. (1996: 197) identify three gaps in the PA process: training, objectives and culture. In the instance of a *training gap,* the appraisal system is introduced on the assumption that employees have all the skills (rating skills, feedback skills) they need. An *objectives gap* arises where managers often try to sell the idea of appraisal on the basis of staff development, yet most start with ratings that employees then associate with appraisal. Ratings are also associated with administrative requirements including disciplinary, which mean that sometimes they can degenerate into exactly this. A *culture gap* arises when the appraisal scheme does not 'fit' into the organization's culture. The introduction of an employee developmental scheme and appraisal system within a hierarchical and authoritarian structure is likely to be highly problematic, as would a highly evaluative and administrative scheme.

Overall, whilst the importance and usefulness of appraisals has been questioned (Nelson, 2000), their use for administrative, developmental and legal reasons is likely to continue unabated (Kald & Nilsson, 2000). However, regardless of psychometric soundness, an appraisal system will ultimately be unsuccessful if it is not accepted and supported by its users (Fletcher, 2004).

It is strange that development appraisal has not yet entered the literature on career management (Drenth, 1998).

## Part 1 Summary (IV) and Conclusions

- Application of MSFS is on the increase, but research on post-appraisal feedback processes and consequences suggests that, far from achieving positive developmental outcomes, there is often no effect and worse, sometimes even a performance decrement.
- The assumption that leverage for change can be secured through highlighting a discrepancy between self and other perceptions in relation to performance has received no strong support. Attempts to formulate this mediating mechanism using the concept of self-awareness have been partially successful in accounting for variation in developmental uptake. However, it is clear that the issue is far more complex than this.
- Little guidance is available on how appraisers should conduct a post-appraisal development interview.
- There is a trade-off between psychometric precision and usefulness in systems requiring some form of performance measurement. It is generally assumed that appraisal systems work well so long as they are perceived acceptable.

## Research Challenges

- test Campbell's performance model across a range of task and occupational domains, including the concept of adaptive performance;
- investigate the implicit performance theories used by appraisers;
- explore the viability of the idea of a general performance factor and, in particular, explore the underlying nomological network of constructs (including ability and personality) that may account for this;
- examine the subjective link between the evaluative and developmental functions of appraisal in the eyes of both appraisers and the appraised;
- test theoretical propositions regarding the role of self-awareness in accounting for post-appraisal developmental change;

- explore the relationship between developmental feedback and the uptake of developmental activity and potential mediators (for example, self-efficacy, goal orientation) and moderators (for example, support for development) of this;
- explore developmental reactions to different sources of feedback (subordinate, peer, boss, customer);
- examine appraisal interview processes in their *dyadic* and behavioural form to see what actually happens and compare this with the perceptions and interpretations of all parties involved in the dialogue;
- investigate employee reactions to appraisal from an 'organizational justice' perspective.

# Part 2: Career Development and Occupational Choice

## Learning Objectives

Studying the contents of Part 2 will enable you to:

1   examine the career concept in both objective and subjective terms;
2   explain the key factors guiding career considerations in both theory and practice (adult development, individual differences, career patterns, job transition, career stress, life role, career motivation, and so on);
3   describe and evaluate the concept of career from five different perspectives: developmental, behaviourist/social learning, differentialist, decision making, structural;
4   explain why new ways of defining and examining 'careers' are required in the light of organizational change, the increased economic profile of women and of other minority group members;
5   suggest ways in which individual and organizational interests can be reconciled.

## A Taxonomy of Career Facets

The literature on careers is multi-disciplinary, multi-level, and difficult to distil. From an occupational and organizational perspective, Boerlijst (1998: 284–286) argues for a 'facet' model of careers to aid clarity of focus, investigation and intervention (Study Box 3.14). Accordingly, he defines a career as a 'sequence of successive positions as ascertained by an *observing agency* (self and/or other) that a *career occupant* has held or acquired within a certain period of time on *aspect variables that have a certain relevancy* to a certain *context*' like role, position, status or other externally verifiable markers. Career development, on the other hand, he says pertains to the *interventions* of a person or body geared to the application of *determinants* (self-originated and/or externally originated) for the influencing of the career consistent with policy objectives (p. 284).

Study Box 3.14

**Career facets**

- *Career occupations – individual* idiosyncratic careers ('true to life', biographical) and *categorical* (or modal) careers of members of groups (for example, managers). Some categorical careers are antithetical to contemporary requirements for versatility (that is, prevailing expectations pertaining to a particular category of career can inhibit flexibility).
- *Context –* all careers arise in a context, each with its own requirements. Participation in different contexts may create conflict (for example, work and family life).
- *Career aspects and their contextual relevance –* that is, position, role, activities.
- *Career dynamics –* time and change of position, indicated not just by the passing of time, but the significance of certain events (subjective time).
- *Career observers –* external objective career described by others and internal career described by self.
- *Career determinants and career theory –* career predictors/determinants inner derived/outwardly originated.
- *Career policy –* internal policy of individual (goals, objectives), and external (organizational objectives) and super-ordinate policy for particular categorical careers.

This definition of career and career development accommodate both objective and subjective facets of career, the time dimension (historically and prospectively) and the importance of understanding how careers arise, unfold and become successful within particular contexts. It also emphasizes that careers are not confined to managerial or white-collar occupations and may include self-employment and other non-conventional career phenomena (for example, part-time working). The following discussion will look in detail at these facets of career under three main headings: 'Objective and Subjective Facets of Career', 'Career Determinants and Theory', and 'Career Management'.

## Objective and Subjective Facets of 'Career'

> Careers are normative in that they are constraining and limit choices of action. But careers are also cognitive in that they are understood, experienced and used.
>
> (Evetts, 1996: 4)

Until recently, an individual's career has been largely 'owned' by the organization, thus implying that 'having a career' is something accredited to the individual. In this context, the term 'career' is used as a metaphor for upward progression in a public and positional sense (denoting increased status, power and recognition). This so-called 'objective' or external career is reflected in the use of structural terms like 'career ladder', 'promotion', and 'demotion'. Such a career is typically the prerogative of managers and professionals, thereby restricting the applicability of the career concept. Here 'success' constitutes upward progression through a series of related jobs (Boerlijst, 1998). An 'objective' career may be either entirely dependent on progression within an organization ('locals'), or dependent on a profession or occupation which may involve movement from one organization to another ('cosmopolitans') (Gouldner, 1957). Movement may involve a change of job or simply increased responsibility within the same job.

By contrast, the career concept may be used subjectively to describe a developmental experience. In its more restricted 'occupational' sense, the subjective perspective recognizes that people can have meaningful careers in a non-hierarchical sense (Heslin, 2003). Success is subjectively defined rather than associated with formal stamps of recognition and prestige. Many jobs – particularly service jobs – often involve 'career scripts' (that is, interpretative schemes and norms) and 'social identities' (associated with professionalization and marketability across organizational and geographical boundaries) independent of the control of any one particular organization (Arnold, 1997; Hall & Mirvis, 1995; Herriot & Pemberton, 1995). Arthur (2000) refers to this as the 'boundaryless career'.

In recent years, switching 'occupations' has become more commonplace, perhaps redundancy initiated (and funded by redundancy pay-outs), and/or prompted by a mid-life realization that subjective criteria (satisfaction, quality of life, self-fulfilment) are in some ways as important, if not more important, than objective career criteria (Eby & Buch, 1995).

Occupational members can construct careers, in terms of movement between work settings, by mobility across geographical space, and by increasing job mastery. Some argue that the career concept is in fact largely retrospective, and used for making sense of one's past and future in relation to the present (Pahl, 1995; Study Box 3.15).

---

### Study Box 3.15

#### Subjective careers

Nowadays, dealing with transition is an inextricable part of working life, let alone 'a career'. New career configurations, some of which are heavily transition-bound, require increased ability to cope with potential disruption to security or continuity (Riverin-Simard, 2000). With increased life longevity and the increase in retirement age, there is a strong trend towards career change with many people entertaining two if not three or four different careers throughout their working life (Teixeira & Gomes, 2000).

Nicholson's (1987) model of the transition cycle depicts the career as cyclical. Four transitions are proposed: *preparation* (anticipatory socialization of a general rather than job-specific kind; expectations may be unrealistic), *encounter* (sense making marked by change from previous roles), *adjustment* (personal and role development reduces person-job misfit) and *stabilization* (increased commitment to the organization, personalizing the job). Any form of transition is preparation for the next one. Moreover, the cycles may short-circuit each other. Adjustment, for example, may be interrupted by the preparation and encounter stages of a new cycle. In addition, experiences at one stage will strongly influence what happens at later stages. For instance, inappropriate/inadequate preparation will increase the amount of adjustment required.

*(Continued)*

> **Study Box 3.15   Continued**
>
> Louis (1981) offers a model for understanding the 'encounter' phase of transition, and in particular the experience of s*urprise* (from co-workers, the nature of work, atmosphere, performance requirement, decision-making processes, personal reactions, supervision, lifestyle implications and learning opportunities). Arnold (1985) found co-workers to be the most common source of the surprising experience in his study of graduate newcomers. Newcomers actively 'make sense' of the new encounter with respect to their expectations and, in so doing, rely heavily on the interpretations of others.

The idea of a subjective career has raised the issue of what constitutes career success and how it can be measured (Heslin, 2003). Various self-report measures have been developed alluding to potential subjective success indicators like *career insight, identity* and *resilience* (London & Mone, 1987), *career satisfaction* (Millward, Flyn, & Anderton, 2004), *occupational self-efficacy* (Koumoundourou, 2004) and *career entrenchment* (Bedeian, 2002), and other methods have been ventured as a means of elucidating the subjective career (for example, *The Intelligent Careers Card Sort*; Wnuk & Amundson, 2002). All of these postulate various subjective criteria as meaningful ways of ascertaining success (for example, career efficacy, career satisfaction). Subjective career success is, it is argued, largely self-referential, defined against one's own personal goals and aspirations (Arnold, 1997).

Nonetheless, when people are freely invited to reflect on how they know or judge the extent to which their career is successful in these terms, they invariably also evoke other more externally verifiable reference criteria (for example, satisfaction with income relevant to peers). Drawing on social comparison theory (Festinger, 1954), Heslin (2003) found that other-reference success criteria accounted for 12 percent of variance in perceived career success among his sample of MBA students. Research like this demonstrates that people make sense of their careers with reference to both self-referential and objective criteria. Findings, however, also suggest that both self-esteem and the availability of objective benchmarks moderate the comparison process in that people with low esteem are more negative about their success, especially in the absence of externally verifiable criteria (Suls, Lemos, & Lockett Stewart, 2002). It is viable to argue, then, that features of the traditional objective career to a large extent still frame the subjective career (Guest & Mackenzie, 1996).

Whilst most writers on careers tend to focus on one or other viewpoint, the fundamental duality of the concept has long been recognized (Goffman, 1961). As Goffman (1961: 127) put it, one side is 'linked to internal matters held dearly and closely, such as an image of self or felt identity: the other side concerns official position … and is part of a publicly accessible institutional complex'. For many employees, personal development and career success *are* still synonymous with hierarchical promotion, especially where opportunities for promotion imply higher earnings, status and authority (Arnold, 1997; Guest & Mackenzie, 1996).

The term 'status passage' also illustrates the inseparability of objective and subjective aspects of career, and its significance for understanding the way people 'interface' with society and its institutions. A status passage signals a change in 'identity' experienced upon a transition in social role. If the social role is meaningful in structural terms (that is, denoting expectations and prescriptions for behaviour), internalization of the role links the experience of the individual with its ascribed organizational meaning (Becker & Straus, 1956). Thus, careers are not entirely the making of the individual, since they are necessarily limited by 'contextual possibilities' (Barley, 1989: 51).

---

**Study Box 3.16**

### Organizational changes impacting on the notion of 'career'

| Economic, political and organizational changes | Organizational implications | Individual implications |
|---|---|---|
| Increased use of the core/complementary employment model | Leaner organizations, contracting out of 'peripheral' operations/ functions, different types of contract    Need to train 'flexible' and 'multi-skilled' core employees | Minimal job security, succession problems, need to be 'flexible' (for example, to be relocated, multi-skilled)    Few career prospects for 'peripheral' employees; more opportunities for obtaining a 'career portfolio' |
| Decentralization | Flattening of organizational structures | Little opportunity for upward progression, more horizontal mobility, increased need to develop 'social networks' and 'interpersonal skills' to negotiate new structures and cultures |
| Decline in the manufacturing sector in parallel with rise in the service sector | Greater need for knowledge workers and 'professionals' | Increased need to train, retrain and self-educate |
| Demographic changes | Growing use of female workers and 'older' workers, less young people entering labour market | Increased opportunity for women and for older workers |
| Technological advancement | Increased need for technical specialists | Increased need for 'technical' skills |

Nonetheless, the flattening of management pyramids means that fewer employees are likely to enjoy 'orderly' and predictable career paths structured by the organization (Guest & Mackenzie, 1996; Herriot & Pemberton, 1996; Study Box 3.16). The shift from manufacturing to service work also relies heavily on organization-independent knowledge and skill. The contemporary career is indeed less the responsibility of the organization and more *the responsibility of the individual career aspirant* (Maurer, 2001). In essence, the 'new' employment relationship asks an individual to recognize that their career is about self-development and self-management, and to show commitment to the organization for as long as the organization can demonstrate its continued encouragement and support (Holbeche, 2003).

One of the implicit assumptions made within the contemporary career literature is that transition is not only inevitable but a good thing. In dealing with transition and adapting to new job requirements, 'development' occurs, even if the transition was imposed by job transfer (rather the self-initiated). Transition can be anxiety-inducing and potentially highly stressful, so 'a career' in this sense arguably requires enormous determination and resilience (London & Mone, 1987; Study Box 3.17).

---

### Study Box 3.17

#### Career motivation

London and Mone's (1987) theory of career motivation postulates three aspects of career self-concept: identity ('who am I?' in relation to career), resilience (dealing with barriers and disruptions without becoming demotivated) and self-insight (knowledge of strengths and limitations, goals and values). Arnold (1997) says that these three constructs may denote 'personal resources' rather than motivation per se (defined as a driving force to manage one's career). Grzeda and Prince (1997), however, found that each construct within this model relates in the expected way to other variables. For instance, resilience correlates with self-reported autonomy and perseverance. Nonetheless, there is no direct evidence that 'career motivation' measured in this way predicts career success. Resilience it would seem may denote self-efficacy (Betz, 2000), and as such plays a crucial role in career development by increasing the likelihood of initiation and persistence of developmental behaviour in the face of obstacles and uncertainty (Maurer, 2001). Recent findings also suggest that career commitment may be a better predictor of work outcomes than organizational commitment (Blustein & Noumair, 1996). See also Blustein and Noumair (1996) for a comprehensive review of identity considerations in career development theory and practice and Brutus, Ruderman, Ohlott and McCauley (2000) for discussion on the role of self-esteem in the context of job challenge.

---

## Part 2 Summary (I) and Conclusions

- Career concepts have expanded beyond the managerial domain, accommodating subjective as well as objective aspects. Correspondingly, research has begun to explore internally generated facets of subjective careers that facilitate personal success (for example, efficacy, resilience, self-insight, self-motivation).

- Whilst individuals can take ownership and responsibility for their career, it is increasingly acknowledged that subjective careers derive meaning from context and may to varying extents still refer to externally verifiable criteria (status markers, formal roles, positions and achievements).

## Career Determinants and Theories

There is no shortage of theory on careers, which is not the property of any one disciplinary view (Arthur, Hall, & Lawrence, 1989). However, until recently and with the exception of Schein's approach to organizational careers, very little theory has been used to inform an understanding of careers in an 'organizational context'. This may in part be because only managers (and professionals) had 'careers', the focus of a distinct management development literature (Tharanou, 1997; Study Box 3.18). Nowadays, careers are more likely to be supra-organizational (that is, independent of any one organization), and new ways of formulating these more individually owned careers are beginning to emerge (for example, London & Mone, 1987). Arthur (2000) and Brotherton (1999), for instance, talk of the portfolio career developed through cultivating networks and gaining access to others' knowledge and resources.

---

**Study Box 3.18**

### Predictors of management success

Attempts to explain management success (in the traditional sense of the objective upward management career) have been mainly empirical and lack theoretical substance. Reviewing this literature, Tharanou (1997) identifies the following key predictors:

- Large informal social networks involving close ties. Understanding of networking processes is currently very limited. One key question for research is whether networks are selective, reciprocal, milked only at certain times of need or on an ongoing basis.
- High cognitive ability.
- Investing in education, training and development.
- Working long hours full-time.
- Making geographical job moves (although there is some inconsistency here concerning the impact of frequent job moves and whether these moves should occur within or across organizations).

---

Theories of career development and occupational choice derive from six different perspectives: developmental, behaviourist, differentialist, decision-making, structural and organizational. Each perspective is only briefly reviewed here. The review should be undertaken in the context of critiques raising concerns about the relevance of classic career theories to the analysis of the contemporary career (for example, Arthur, 2000; Brotherton, 1999; Savickas, 2002).

## *Developmental Perspective – Super's (1980) vocational self-concept*

Ginzberg and colleagues pioneered the application of developmental thinking to the career concept (Ginzberg, Ginsberg, Axelrad & Herma, 1951; Ginzberg, 1972). Career (as occupational development) denotes the evolution of a positive self-concept which may occur through a series of stages or phases. In Ginzberg's model, development begins with simplistic ideals, ending with a realistic choice of job or career at around the age of 17. It is now common, however, to take a *life-span* view consistent with Super's (1990) 'theory of vocational self-concept development'. Super depicts career development as a process of implementing and testing vocational self-concept in the context of various roles (for example, parent, worker, spouse), across different life-theatres (for example, home, school, community, work). The work role, in particular, affords the opportunity to establish an identity as competent and valued (Study Box 3.19).

Super's analysis situates career in life-space generally (but see suggested revisions by Herr, 1997). It is perhaps in this over-inclusive aspect that the theory loses some of its heuristic and explanatory power. Moreover, the idea of occupational self-concept lacks explanatory power, being merely a descriptive term denoting progression through roles. The benefit of the analysis is in recognition that whilst careers are unique to individuals, they are nonetheless circumscribed by role expectations and various life-stage considerations.

---

### Study Box 3.19

#### The centrality of self in careers

The concept of self is central to the analysis and management of careers in an occupational and organizational context (Blustein & Noumair, 1996). Arguably, the self-concept could provide the core construct linking developmental appraisal with career management (for example, Fletcher & Baldry, 2001). It is generally agreed that self-insight is a prerequisite for effective decision making in a career context and a key predictor of career success (London & Mone, 1987). This requires regular self-assessment, and the opportunity to benchmark these assessments against self in the past, organizational and co-worker expectations, as well as the aspired to or possible self (projected image of self in the future against personal goals). Theories of decision making underestimate the role of self in weighing up alternative options, and making vocational choices (see below). Caution is due, however, in assuming a stable sense of self to be assessed and articulated when self theories highlight that self-concept comprises many different sometimes inconsistent identities. These identities vary in salience across different contexts and reflect varying levels of cognitive and emotional investment in these contexts (Haslam, 2004; see Chapter 4). Sometimes these inconsistencies manifest in equivocation during decision making about which value or interest to pursue (for example, work versus family priorities may compete; Arnold, 1997). Contemporary identity research conducted within the postmodern framework emphasizes that self is becoming increasingly fragmented, such that it is not possible to talk of 'the self' in any coherent or stable sense (for example, Alvesson, 2001).

The developmental approach has been criticized for overemphasizing autonomy, without consideration of either emotional blocks or structural constraints surrounding career decision making. Its strength, though, lies in its emphasis on lifestyle, its recognition of the importance of work/family dynamics and other life-space considerations, and of career as a life-long process with no clear end point (Sekaran, 1986). Schein (1978) described how adults often see mid-life as the opportunity to reassess their dreams and to establish whether career progress is consistent with them, to assess the kinds of work/family trade-offs and personal sacrifices one has made.

Another approach to development harnesses the idea that 'adult development' can be understood in terms of its own series of 'cognitive stages' – for example, early adulthood, age 30 transition, mid-life transition (for example, Levinson et al., 1978). Researchers acknowledge, however, that stage theories are now somewhat out of synch with reality (characterized by multiple job and career changes). Cognitive theories have likewise been criticized for insensitivity to organizational context. Boerlijst (1998: 281) argues that a more appropriate way of conceptualizing adult development is as a succession of entirely person-related actions and reactions of that person in relation to the circles in which he or she moves. He says that the classification of development into stages is a complex matter for any single individual as virtually any social context imposes its 'stage' requirements.

Some maintain, in fact, that *general theories of development* are unlikely to enlighten our understanding of the individual life span in career terms, advocating a more personal, phenomenological approach (for example, Flum & Blustein, 2000; Savickas, 2002).

Attempts to integrate developmental thinking into an organizational context are limited. It is clear nonetheless that organizations have a central and pervasive part to play in the way 'careers' unfold (Levinson et al., 1978), even in today's short-term organizational climate. In the words of Herriot (1992: 9) 'there is ... little point in idealistic notions of individual fulfilment outside of organizational frameworks'. As Strauss (1959) put it, we need to uphold our identities in 'open court'. The organization might also be described as the best available setting in which individuals can do this, but in today's society, organizations compete for an individual's cognitive and emotional investment rather than vice versa (Herriot, 2001).

## The behaviourist perspective

In the late 1970s, career theories were heavily influenced by the application of social learning theory to the issue of occupational choice (for example, Krumboltz, Mitchell, & Jones, 1976). This approach is closely associated with Bandura's (1977) work, proposing that people learn from the consequences of their own behaviour (instrumental reinforcement) and from their observation of other people's behaviour (behavioural modelling). In this tradition, Krumboltz et al. (1976) pay particular attention to influences on career decisions posed by 'learning experiences'. *Instrumental learning* arises from consequences of such feedback from others, and the observable results of one's own action (Krumboltz et al., 1976: 73). *Associative learning* occurs when an individual pairs one factor or situation with another (for example, particular occupations become associated with particular feelings and thoughts). Individuals tend to form generalizations about occupations from a few examples: often the first associations formed are long lasting (for example, a nurse as 'ministering angel'), and most often highly inappropriate!

Krumboltz et al. hypothesize that an individual is more likely to express a preference for a particular occupation, job or field of work if he or she has:

- been positively reinforced, and/or observed a valued model (parent, sibling) being reinforced for engaging in activities known to be associated with the success in a particular line of work (for example, 'my mum is a doctor');
- been consistently positively reinforced by a valued person who models or advocates engaging in activities associated with a particular line of work;
- been exposed to positive words and images associated with a particular occupation (for example, medicine associated with power, status and prestige).

The social learning perspective might seem highly mechanistic and difficult to fathom. However, evidence does exist for the power of association to dictate the images people hold about particular occupations or fields of work (Dutton, Dukerich, & Harquail, 1994). Many career decisions are made without valid or reliable information, with reference only to abstractions derived from observing others.

The value of the social learning approach is in highlighting the basis of decisions, often in abstractions and ideals that are not consistent with reality. In being provided with information and 'preview' experiences, an individual may at least have the opportunity to road test their learned preferences and assumptions (Helwig, 2001; see Realistic Job Preview in Chapter 1). The theory also points at the relevance of 'modelling' experiences (vicarious learning opportunities) to the way in which careers are pursued in organizational contexts (the role of the 'mentor'). It is in this connection that the concept of career self-efficacy derives importance (Anderson & Betz, 2001).

### The differentialist perspective – Holland's theory

The differentialist approach assumes that optimal career outcomes for both individual and organization are facilitated by ensuring a basic congruence between individual characteristics and job/organizational demands (Parsons, 1909). Examples of theories within this framework include Dawis and Lofquist's (1984) theory of work adjustment, Williamson's trait factor theory (1972), Rodger's (1968) seven-point plan and Holland's (for example, 1973, 1997) theory of vocational choice. The latter is the most often cited of these theories. In 1959, Holland (based on his experience of career counselling) argued that individuals develop preferred methods for dealing with environmental tasks called 'vocational orientations' or 'types' (Study Box 3.20). The more closely an individual resembles a particular vocational type, the more likely he or she is to exhibit the associated traits and behaviours. Knowledge of vocational type is used to 'pair' the individual with a particular environment, with a view to 'optimizing' the match between them. The theory proposes that 'other things being equal', the better the match between type and environment, the more beneficial the outcome.

Each 'type' is the product of an interaction between a variety of cultural, familial and personal factors, and indicates a preference for some activities over others (that is, an occupational interest). The evolution of particular occupational interests frames thinking (for example, self-expectations), feeling (for example, satisfaction) and behaving (for example, seeking out particular types of activity, experience and people). Each person's 'type' is unique since it denotes a particular pattern of resemblance against all six different vocational categories (which in principle affords 720 different vocational orientations or patterns).

---

**Study Box 3.20**

### Holland's orientation categories

- *Motoric orientation ('realistic')* – enjoyment of activities requiring physical strength, aggressive action, motor coordination and skill, a preference for dealing with concrete problems and for 'acting out' rather than 'thinking through'.
- *Intellectual orientation ('investigative')* – task-oriented but prefer to 'think through' rather than to 'act out' problems, marked by a need to organize and understand the world, and a preference for activities involving ideas and thought rather than dealing with people and things.
- *Supportive orientation ('social')* – prefer teaching and/or therapeutic roles, reflecting a desire for contact with and feedback from others, in a structured and safe environment.
- *Conforming orientation ('conventional')* – prefer structured verbal and numerical activity, and subordinate roles, achieving their goals through conformity, in particular via the rules and regulations of a job.
- *Persuasive orientation ('enterprising')* – prefer to use their verbal skills in situations affording opportunity for selling and/or leading others, avoid structured situations and also those requiring intellectual effort, preferring the challenge of ambiguity and the need to rely on their social skills.
- *Esthetic orientation ('artistic')* – prefer indirect relationships with others, dealing with them through self-expression. Avoid situations requiring interpersonal interaction, a high degree of structuring or physical skill.

---

People vary in how well defined their orientations are. The stronger the orientation the greater it will predict career choice. In the 1970s, Holland proposed that individuals seek congruence between their vocational interests and the environments in which they work (Holland, 1973). It was argued that congruent individuals should be more satisfied and less likely to change their work environment than incongruent individuals. Incongruence can be a major cause of stress and dissatisfaction that the individual is motivated to rectify and evidence does indeed show that people search for environments that support their salient traits (for example, Holland & Nichols, 1964; Hogan & Hogan, 1995). More recently, Holland (1997) has emphasized that the model does not assume a static matching process: on the contrary, it is a dynamic interaction process.

Vocational type is gauged by an inventory (Vocational Preference Inventory, The Strong Vocational Interest Blank, and The Self-Directed Search; Holland, Fritzsche, & Powell, 1997), in combination with job experiences, educational background and an assessment of leisure interest all ascertained by interview or biographical questionnaire. The 'environment' can also be classified and assessed (Position Classification Inventory) into the same set of six types, according to the 'type' that predominates therein (Gottfredson & Holland, 1996) as people of similar vocational types tend to congregate together in environments congruent with their interests, dispositions and competence.

Most of the research within this framework has looked to establish the construct validity of the 'vocational types'. Holland (1996) has presented strong support for the predicted 'personality' associations (for example, academic aptitudes and interests, self-ratings, non-academic interests and achievements, extra-curricular activity) for each vocational type. However, the concept of 'congruence' is more problematic (Study Box 3.21).

---

### Study Box 3.21

#### 'The congruence problem'

In a recent comprehensive and incisive critique of Holland's congruence proposition, Arnold (2004) finds little evidence to support the link predicted between congruence and vocational outcomes (see also Tinsley, 2000). To account for this, Arnold (2004) identifies 14 possible reasons why this may be the case, under three main headings: theory, research and the world (that is, the theory lacks ecological validity):

#### *Theory*

1   *Does Holland's theory validly reflect the structure of vocational interests?* Arnold (2004) concludes that evidence does support the idea of six vocational types arranged as predicted in a circumplex though not necessarily equally spaced (p. 98).

2   *Does the theory omit some key constructs?* Whilst scores on the six types do correlate significantly with scores on personality tests, Arnold (2004: 99) says, 'Holland vocational personality types fail to capture some individual differences that are important to some people's vocational choices', such as goals and values (for example, career salience). Arnold says that the latter may moderate the impact of congruence on vocational outcomes.

3   *Does the theory overlook the main effects of environment and person?* Arnold (2004: 100) says it does. He cites evidence demonstrating how some environments can have a universally consistent impact on the people who experience them (for example, moderate variety will stave off boredom for most people) and likewise, that individual differences may influence behaviour across nearly all environments (for example, conscientiousness). Holland's theory also omits some important features of the environment likely to facilitate satisfaction and performance (for example, variety, feedback).

| **Study Box 3.21   Continued** |
| --- |

4  *Occupation is not an adequate conceptualization of environment.* Arnold (2004: 101) says that whilst Holland does not assume that occupations are the only important aspect of an environment, the dominant focus nonetheless is occupation.

5  *The separation of person and environments is artificial.* Arnold (2004: 101–102) says that individuals can create their own environments as much as vice versa. Although Holland does acknowledge that people can adjust their micro-environments to suit them, there is insufficient appreciation within the theory of the inseparability of person and environment.

6  *The three-letter coding scheme of people and environments is inadequate*: (a) it does not indicate how far apart the codes are (for example, RCI: Realistic (R), Conventional (C), Investigative (I)); (b) the overall magnitude of scores is not accounted for; and (c) the lower three type scores are disregarded.

### Research

7  *Environmental measurement is not precise enough*: (a) the same occupational title may mean different things to different people; (b) people may not report their full job title; and (c) there may be common method variance in the description of job and environment.

8  *Poor choices of outcome variable.* Most studies have used satisfaction as the outcome but there are many different correlates of satisfaction (Tinsley, 2000). There have been no proper tests of the congruence hypothesis in relation to attitudes (for example, commitment) or performance.

9  Congruence studies may suffer from restricted range. Arnold (2004: 105) says that there is no strong evidence that this is a viable explanation for why the congruence hypothesis has not obtained much support.

10  *Over-reliance on cross-sectional and between subject designs* rather than longitudinal studies.

11  *Suboptimal measurement and statistical analysis of congruence.*

### The world

12  *Few people may be in seriously incongruent environments.* If the numbers are small, qualitative research may be more appropriate and, indeed, *qualitative* forms of assessment are increasingly being advocated in the career counselling literature (for example, McMahon & Patton, 2002; see Chapter 6).

13  *Innovation and flexibility is increasingly valued.*

14  *Job demands frequently change.*

Herriot and Pemberton (1996) see congruence as fundamentally a process of social negotiation, by which organizations and individuals adjust their expectations of each other (Study Box 3.22). Congruence of this negotiated kind is likely to be 'workable' rather than denoting a perfect fit, and is likely to be in need of re-negotiation with time. Limited attention has also been given to the way various socio-economic factors (including considerations of gender and race) interact with the congruence issue.

---

**Study Box 3.22**

**The process of adjustment**

The issue of adjustment is central to the analysis of career. Various writers highlight the reciprocal nature of adjustment: the individual can adapt in response to the demands of the environment (for example, changes in personal values, skills and outlook), but can also manipulate the environment to suit individual needs (for example, the way work is performed) (Nicholson, 1987). For example, an individual can change roles by imposing their unique identities on them. Jones (1986) found that differences in self-efficacy moderated the effect of induction on adjustment, whilst Crites (1971) argued that ability to cope with anxiety is central.

---

It is generally agreed that the typology could be more tightly linked with personality and also values, and that the theory generally requires more attention to contextual as well as dispositional factors. In this vein, Arnold (2004) suggests that it would perhaps be more appropriate to change the theory from being focused on person-occupation fit to person-job fit, particularly in that people are more inclined these days to think *job* rather than *occupation*. On the other hand, Holland's theory may be most optimally viewed as one pertaining to the outcomes of vocational rather than job choice (which may be better explained by values).

## The Decision-making Perspective

All career theory either implicitly or explicitly makes statements about career decision making. Some have argued, however, that a career is no more or less than a series of decisions. Tiederman, O'Hara and Baruch (1963), for example, offered a three-stage model of the decision-making process: (1) 'anticipation' (and exploration including visualizing oneself at work); (2) 'crystallization' (assessing personal values against possible occupations, weighing up potential pros and cons); and (3) 'stabilization' (final choice and action). However, this approach assumes that individuals can make rational and informed 'choices' from a range of alternatives, whilst in reality decisions may be strongly fielded by emotion (Kidd, 2004).

Knefelkamp and Slepitza (1976) describe a model of career decision making built around adult identity concerns. Accordingly, it is assumed that individuals have to deal with various – and progressively more complex – cognitive-developmental tasks to achieve a satisfactory vocational identity. Tasks include movement from external to internal locus of control (signifying less reliance on others' views), the ability to self-examine, to assume responsibility and to take on new roles. However, no explanation is offered for how an individual progresses through proposed developmental sequences. The empirical basis of the theory is weak (interviews and observations with 35 students in career development classes), and no mention is made of the gender composition of the sample, how it was chosen nor the analytical procedures used to derive the 'stages'. The focus of the theory is student centred, without consideration of its application to non-student samples (early school age, middle and later work life) or non-androcentric populations (male-dominated, middle-class, educated). Such theories do, however, frame intervention with a valuable cautionary note. Career intervention at school and college age tends to be 'information' driven, yet clearly students will use this information in very different ways depending on their 'developmental' readiness (Hopson & Hayes, 1972). Evidence also suggests that decision-making models can be readily used in career guidance (Jackson, Arnold, Nicholson & Watts, 2000). However, the theory lacks applicability to non-student samples at critical decision points (for example, induced by redundancy, job change, marriage, and so on).

Attention to the decision-making side of career development is of particular relevance to the contemporary organizational world characterized by continual change and transition. The opening up of multiple potential career pathways heightens the importance of individual career choices and decisions. Recent work has focused on decision making within a career self-management model applicable across both educational and occupational settings (for example, King, 2001). The growth in reliance on computer-based methods of career planning is integral to this self-management emphasis, both of which are now heavily factored into contemporary thinking about careers (Reile & Harris-Bowlsbey, 2000).

### *Structuralist perspective – Roberts' (1977) theory of opportunity structures*

Most of the careers literature takes either the individual or the organization as its starting point, without respect for the economic and political environment of decision making, or the actual pursuit of careers. Roberts (1977) argues that taken in its broader context, the concept of 'occupational choice' is meaningless: people can only take what is available. Job preferences are not mere matters of individual taste but are determined by a system of stratification and opportunity. Aspirations can best be understood not as preliminaries to decisive occupational choices, but as products of anticipatory socialization (Study Box 3.23).

Vocational guidance cannot change the employment realities of society or create opportunities for personal growth and development. Thus careers work, argues Roberts, should concentrate on practical employment problems. This analysis highlights the importance of putting careers into an opportunity structure that may pose limits on the kinds of choices made, and then realized, by young people in western society (Banks et al.,1992). A structural analysis can also be applied to organizations insofar as they evolve their own *opportunity structures* (Tharanou, 1997) that delimit the career development possibilities, particularly of female (Evetts, 1996; Nicholson, 1995) and non-white employees (Swanson & Woitke, 1997). These opportunity structures mirror those in society generally. The danger with developmental theories is that they overestimate the importance and scope of the individual's range of occupational choice, encourage the adoption of unrealistic aims and fail to target resources to the areas of greatest need.

> ### Study Box 3.23
>
> **Reality shock**
>
> Anticipatory socialization describes the expectations formed by people prior to entering a job and/or organization (Feldman, 1976). Two aspects are of particular relevance to careers: *realism* (extent to which individuals have a realistic image of what it is like to work in a particular job or organization), and *congruence* (extent to which organizational and individual interests are reconciled). The extent to which 'realism' permeates a set of expectations is indicative of how successful an individual has been in their information search. Unfortunately, organizations are rarely explicit about what a job is really going to be like. This can engender 'reality shock'. Many trainees in the professions, for example, enter the field with strong ideals that are shattered by harsh encounters with reality (Ondrack, 1975). Schein (1978) argues that all who enter the workplace for the first time operate with 'ideals' about what they want to do and why, and that a major developmental task in this early career period involves coming to terms with reality (Chapter 1).

### Organizational theories

Schein's (1978) theory offers the most well-known analysis of the organizational career as movement within an organization. He distinguishes between 'structural' variables (that is, stable elements of the organization) and 'process' variables (socialization of the individual by the organization and organizational innovation by the individual). Individuals can move up, across functions or into the centrality of their role. Movement is controlled by boundaries. Boundaries vary in their degree of permeability, and also in their filtering properties (the rules governing boundary negotiation). Career is thus a sequence of 'boundary passages'. Schein's analysis predicts that an individual is most vulnerable to socialization pressures just before and just after a boundary passage experience. Innovation will occur only if the individual is secure (that is, has achieved centrality and acceptance) in their role. Innovation close to a boundary will be resisted. In general, socialization will be more prevalent in the early stages of a career, and the process of innovation more prevalent late in the career, but both processes occur at all stages.

This analysis assumes only one type of organization (static, hierarchical) and merely *describes* the kind of movement that an individual can make, rather than offering a testable explanation of progression across a boundary. Gunzol (1989) argued that people may not wish to pursue the career model upheld by the organization, seeking something more consistent with personal requirements. Others may abandon the career concept altogether, seeing their job as something merely necessary for survival.

The concept of boundary is nonetheless useful to the analysis of careers. Although Schein (1978) conceptualizes a boundary in structural and normative terms, it is also a fundamentally psychological concept. The possibility that individuals can be blocked from career progression by the boundaries they perceive (for example, the 'glass ceiling' in the case of female professionals and executives) is an important issue

(Nicholson, 1995). Schein's (1978) theory has been criticized for its focus on the 'managerial career', although this is by definition typical of 'organization-centred' theories of career. Schein does at least consider the role of the individual in shaping the organizational career, although he does not look at the career experience per se (Study Box 3.24).

---

**Study Box 3.24**

**Schein's (1990) career anchors**

Schein (1990) argued that people enter work with particular career anchors summarizing their hopes and expectations, occupational interests, values and skills, which constrain their career decisions. Five career anchors (assumed to provide a stable basis for self-evaluation particularly during times of change) were proposed: technical-functional competence, managerial competence, security and stability, creativity, and autonomy/independence. The small size and select nature of the sample (well-educated, career-oriented) on which this analysis is based has been strongly criticized. Despite this, it is clear that individuals do bring various 'career orientations' with them to the workplace involving expectations crucial to understanding how individuals interface with the institutions that afford them career opportunities (Herriot, 1992). The role of values in accounting for variation in career outcomes has increased in importance because of ever widening choice coupled with the inextricable link found today between career choice and personal development (for example, Patton & Creed, 2001).

---

## Career 'Stories'

A postmodern analysis of careers may be more able to accommodate contemporary workplace realities than classic career theory (Patton & Creed, 2001) on the assumption that people and reality are 'constructed' (Alvesson & Deetz, 1996: 192–193). Constructivist theory offers an alternative philosophical and psychological framework (rather than a set of techniques) for career development and counselling based on a holistic approach that emphasizes the self-organizing principles underlying human experience (Peavy, 1997; Study Box 3.25). It is often observed, for instance, that people do not necessarily lack information, but the ability to use it (that is, they do not feel empowered, in part due to a lack of knowledge about themselves in relation to the world of work). In practice, this translates into a philosophically-based perspective that assumes the following:

- the centrality of discourse as the main focus of study: understanding of self-organizing processes is obtained by listening carefully to the words and phrases used when people relate their stories;
- fragmented identities and subjective reality (that is, the unitary individual as 'object' is not a viable metaphor in postmodern thinking);

- an emphasis on 'multiple voices' (for example, women, ethnic minorities, disabled employees) rather than all-encompassing theoretical narratives that do not take account of diversity;
- a connection between knowledge and power (Hollway, 1991).

One translation of this otherwise abstract somewhat meta-theoretical approach is in the form of 'narrative psychology': the idea that life can be analysed as a series of 'scripts' and 'stories' (for example, White, 1995).

---

**Study Box 3.25**

**Constructivist career concepts**

- There are multiple realities and thus no one right way to think, feel or act.
- Humans are 'self-organizing', not a bundle of traits and behaviours. Life is a story or set of stories evolving autobiographically and under continual narrative revision.
- Individuals 'construct' themselves through their interpretations and actions. Society is increasingly calling for people to be proactive and reflective.
- Self is 'polyphonic' – that is, it has several voices.
- People are 'meaning makers' who use language and action to create meaning out of everyday life. The most important personal meanings are relational derived through interactions with others and the world.
- Empowerment requires critical reflection of the assumptions underpinning everyday action.

---

It is easy to see how this might be applied to the notion of a career as a life-story, currently and continually in authorship, where meaning and continuity is retrospectively constructed and where multiple 'plots' and 'endings' are possible. Recent developments on career counselling have taken up this line of thinking more systematically (for example, Peavy, 1997; Savickas, 2002).

The concept of 'possible selves' (Markus & Nurius, 1987) may be especially useful within a narrative approach to careers (Meara, Day, Chalk, & Phelps, 1995). The possible self represents an individual's ideas of what they might become, what they would like to become, and what they are afraid of becoming. Markus and Nurius (1987) argue that possible selves focus and energize in the pursuit of goals, provide an interpretative context for the contemporary view of self, and afford meaning and coherence to decisions – past, present and future.

## Part 2 Summary (II) and Conclusions

- Career theories pertaining in particular to understanding careers in an occupational and organizational context are reviewed. Developmental theories emphasize the life-span dimension and the evolution of self within a life-space framework.

- Behaviourist and social learning theory focuses on learning processes and, in particular, the influence of the formative years on vocational choice. Decision-making theories explore the cognitive mechanisms involved in making a career choice, and differentialist theories concern themselves with the idea of a good career decision involving a successful matching of people to appropriately personality-congruent occupations and jobs.
- Organizational theories have looked at how people negotiate boundaries in organizational contexts and point to the importance of understanding how the self deals with transition. Postmodern contributions to understanding careers as socially constructed phenomena (retrospectively and prospectively) are also emerging. The idea of self-narrative is central to this.
- Across all career theories the concept of self is an important connecting thread.

## Career Management

Conventionally, careers were the province of management, synonymous with upward succession planning (Boerlijst, 1998; Tharanou, 1997). In the contemporary 'now-you-see-it-now-you-don't' economic climate, long-term projections are no longer possible (Study Box 3.18), prompting a move towards conceptualizing careers in subjective terms (Noe, 1996). Organizations nonetheless furnish the career with an important source of meaning and context, and, moreover, it is becoming increasingly apparent that the 'career' concept might hold the key to reconciling individual and organizational goals (Herriot & Pemberton, 1995; Millward & Kyriakidou, 2004a). Expectations of 'development' are now an integral part of many employee psychological contracts (Herriot, 2001) and development potential is becoming a valuable organizational asset (that is, a form of human capital) in the so-called knowledge economy (Hatchuel, Le Masson, & Weil, 2002). The resurgence of organizational interest in career management is thus based on the assumption that an organization can gain strategic leverage from this. In Boerlijst's (1998: 275) words:

> career steering could lead to the creation of a pool of flexible human ingenuity and accumulated experience, which the organization can draw on in changing circumstances and which it can count on in the planning and execution of strategic policy.

Yet as organizations increase in complexity and their external environments become more uncertain, it is unrealistic to expect them to take complete charge of employee careers (Ornstein & Isabella, 1993). This puts individuals in a double bind. Whilst many will appreciate that the shelf-life of their formative education is long past, few really know how to manage their own careers either. Many organizations are thus becoming increasingly aware of the need to rethink their approach to careers, and to develop systematic strategies for career management without undermining individual career ownership or excluding non-executive staff from its privilege (Jackson, Arnold, Nicholson, & Watts, 2000; Kirk, Downey, Duckett, & Woody, 2000).

Arnold (1997: 3) defines career management as 'attempts to influence the careers of one or more people'. In contemporary approaches to career management, career development is understood to be the responsibility of both individual and organization. Thus, the organization's responsibility in this instance is to facilitate subjective ownership and responsibility through the provision of an organizational infrastructure such as self-development and career planning programmes, and by making available alternative development options (Study Box 3.26).

---

**Study Box 3.26**

### Career management activities

- *Career audits* – of expectations and beliefs, as well as tests/questionnaires/exercises to promote 'self-insight' (Boerlijst, 1998: 289).
- *Career counselling and interviews* – to negotiate individual and organizational expectations.
- *Job shadowing and mentoring* – where a more experienced person advises or guides the development of a less experienced one. There is some tension here, however, between the formal mentoring scheme and the spontaneity of informal mentoring relationships, but the former need not preclude the latter. The mentoring concept has been subject to close scrutiny in recent years with attention not just to the impact of having mentors, but to the particular features of the mentoring relationship that are most conducive to success (in both objective and subjective terms; for example, Peluchette & Jeanquart, 2000). It is generally agreed that mentoring is conducive to careers, although it is often difficult to trace back career success solely to this because it may occur in the context of other equally conducive developmental activities (but see Gibb, 2003 for some caveats and qualifiers). The ultimate consideration here is that mentoring must be 'managed well' to be effective.
- *Executive coaching* – an interactive process designed to help individuals develop rapidly (Carter, 2002; Chan & Latham, 2004).
- *Job rotation* – in a career context, designed to expand skills and knowledge as well as motivate (Campion, Cheraskin, & Stevens, 1994). Campion et al. (1994) found that the developmental benefits outweighed the costs associated with the time taken to master the new job (and the loss of expertise from the previous job). There is a need for research, however, on what precisely are the 'developmental ingredients' of job rotation schemes.
- *Cross-training* – a strategy for enhancing knowledge of the interpersonal activities of other team members involving, in its purest form, temporarily taking on the role of others (Volpe, Cannon-Bowers, Salas, & Spector, 1996)
- *Systematic management of relocation and/or job transition* – to ensure satisfactory adjustment for the employee and his/her family.
- *Provision of a variety of contracts and systems* – geared to individual needs (part-time, job-share, career breaks, flexi-time, cafeteria benefits, paternity leave, phased retirement, secondment, and creche facilities).
- *Computer-aided career management information systems* – comprising occupational information (for example, jobs, positions available) and career development information (that is, for purposes of interpretation of needs, interests, attitudes and aspirations) (see Boerlijst, 1998 for a review).

Unfortunately, systematic career management in the new era is only patchily undertaken and has no theoretical or empirical basis (Arnold, 1997). In a rare attempt to conceptualize 'the career management challenge', Herriot (1992) argues that organizations can facilitate career development through the practice of psychological contracting. In the days of the 'job-for-life', a balance of exchange was achieved by guaranteeing security of tenure and career prospects in return for loyalty, commitment and good performance. The contemporary organization however requires 'flexibility', 'technical competence', and 'mobility' coupled with heightened expectations of 'commitment'. The key human resource task, then, is to explicitly ascertain individual needs and expectations and to reconcile them with organizational expectations.

Psychological contracting, says Herriot (1992), implies reciprocity in that the organization and the individual must take each other's needs and viewpoints into consideration. Pre-conditions include the perception of some common ground between organizational and individual interest, and a reasonably accurate perception of what these mutual interests are. Unfortunately, employees and their organizations are largely in the dark about what each other want (Herriot, 2001). Successful psychological contracting requires a culture of collaboration and respect for diversity and differences in values, expectations, skills potential and contribution (see Herriot, Hirsh, & Reilly, 1998 for examples of successful career contracting in an industry setting).

Herriot's (1992) analysis of careers integrates both objective and subjective notions of career, appreciates that the needs of both parties are liable to change, and sees the reconciliation of individual and organizational expectations as a reciprocal process. However, it assumes that all employees have the necessary self-insight and wherewithal (and power) to negotiate a career contract with the organization (King, 2001). Moreover, it depends on the ability of an organization to persuade its employees that nowadays a successful career depends more on 'skill mastery, transferability, flexibility and adaptability than positional status' (Sparrow, 1996).

Findings consistently show that line manager/supervisor support is critical to employee career motivation and development (for example, Kidd, 2002; Kidd, Jackson, & Hirsh, 2003; Kidd & Smewing, 2001; Maurer et al., 2002; Noc, 1996). A manager is ideally placed to provide career performance feedback by clarifying career goals, communicating organizational expectations and helping the employee establish contacts and development activities. Greenberger and Strasser (1996) add that managerial support can ensure that unanticipated obstacles do not unnecessarily restrict employees' development plans, especially for female employees (see also Kidd & Smewing, 2001). London and Mone's (1987) review of organizations' career management systems, however, showed that often line managers do not feel sufficiently well developed to be able to manage their own careers, let alone support others' career development.

Arnold (1997) points to the potential usefulness of theories of adult cognitive development for informing career self-management intervention. For instance, the role of the career counsellor could be to encourage the use of post-formal logic that recognizes that life is full of contradictions and inconsistencies and in particular that there is no ideal solution to a career problem. This emphasis on logic, however, does not preclude the importance of considering the role of emotion in career development (Kidd, 2002).

Arnold (1998: 13) cautions that at the end of the day:

> even organizational career management is about individuals. If the goals are not clear and/or not valued, if people do not feel competent to carry out the intervention, if there is no reward for doing so, and if the intervention is not tuned to individual needs, then there will be no motivation to do it, no matter what the potential organizational benefits.

Boerlijst (1998: 288) confirms that employees prefer the 'more personal approach' to their development and recent postmodern perspectives build on this in advocacy of an approach to careers based on the idea of creating meaning (Savickas, 2002). Arnold (1997: 14) adds that, to date, there is little evidence for either an individual or organizational benefit of career management schemes, and that there is thus a very real need to 'do more and better evaluation of the impact of attempts to manage careers'. Developing a theoretical basis for career management is integral to this. It is generally agreed that this will need to be undertaken with reference to major rethinks in the theory and practice in careers counselling more generally (for example, Kidd, 2002; Watts, Killen, Law, Kidd, & Hawthorn, 1996).

## Part 2 Summary (III) and Conclusions

- Career management was conventionally undertaken in the form of management development through organizational succession planning. With the economic imperative to be lean and flexible, organizations can no longer support long-term management development. With this has emerged an emphasis on individual career self-management.
- Organizations have begun to realize that they can reconcile individual and organizational goals by actively facilitating careers. In the 'knowledge economy', continuous learning and development is a core corporate asset.
- The career management initiative is not well founded either empirically or theoretically. There are nonetheless many theoretical possibilities that could be used to inform career management practices.

## Work/Family Interface

The work/family interface is now a critical career consideration (Watkins & Subich, 1995), coincidental with changes in the nature and context of work coupled with changes in family demographics, and dynamics (Kodz, Harper, & Dench, 2002). Increased female participation in the workplace has, in particular, increased the profile of the dual earner/dual career family (Study Box 3.27).

**Study Box 3.27**

**The dual-career family**

The dual-career family (Hall & Hall, 1997) challenges 'gender relations' in the home (Parker & Arthur, 2004) with consequences for marital, domestic and childcare attitudes, strategies and practices. For example, if both partners are equally highly involved in their career, who does the home tasks? Neither may be concerned with 'perfection' in the home (employing someone for child-care and to keep 'house'), or one may expect 'the other' to do the home tasks or both may take responsibility. The latter requires management 'acrobatics', whilst the female who still takes on the burden of responsibility at home and for the children may suffer from the inevitable stress associated with trying to be 'superwoman' (Nicholson, 1995).

One of the difficulties in examining the work/family interface as a context in which to understand careers is in determining the criteria for deciding whether the 'career' (or the family/couple) is suffering or not. The criteria could be objective (missing promotion opportunity) and/or subjective (feeling left behind). The work/family interface is also becoming as much a male as a female career consideration (Aryee & Luk, 1996). As Herriot (1992: 131) put it, 'success will be seen more and more as integrating work and family life at whatever level of the organization one finishes up'. Segal (1987) offers suggestions for how organizations can facilitate protean, slow-burn careers among employees with children (Study Box 3.28).

**Study Box 3.28**

**Organizational 'facilitators' of balance**

- flexible working arrangements, including working from home and attractive well-compensated part-time/job share/flexi-time, and flexible career paths;
- high quality child-care facilities;
- maternity/paternity leave if children are ill;
- re-evaluation of relocation procedures/policies;
- job search assistance for partners of employees being relocated;
- refresher courses for those returning to work after a career break;
- more union support in promoting equal opportunities.

## 'Minority' Careers

Theories of career development are increasingly being criticized for their non-applicability to members of minority group populations. Minority may refer to non-white or non-Anglo-Saxon (Alfred, 2001), female (Crozier, 1999), lower social-economic status (Betz, 2000), and/or disabled by physical and/or mental handicap (Beveridge, Craddock, Liesener, Stapleton, & Hershenson, 2002). The move towards accepting that careers are fundamentally subjective, life-relevant and concerned with identity rather necessarily bound to organizations, occupations/professions or even work in the conventional, paid sense, opens up all kinds of career possibilities.

Recent work has argued for a completely different approach to career development inextricably linked with identity theories, fundamentally 'relational' in orientation and concerned with elucidating the process or mechanisms of development (for example, Bird, Gunz, & Arthur, 2002; Study Box 3.29). These trends extend the interest in career development beyond the work organizations into 'rehabilitation' contexts (for example, for those experiencing vocational handicaps) and also into educational contexts to help frame interventions designed to aid the transition from school to work (for example, Kane, 2002).

Clearly organizations do not operate as meritocracies, where each member has an equal chance of progression (Tharanou, 1997, 1999). Thus, any model used to explain development and/or advancement must be able to explain why it is rare for minority group members to progress to the upper echelons of an organization. In her sample of 1000 subordinates, 567 line managers, 344 lower managers and 520 middle managers, Tharanou (1999) found that endorsement of the *masculinity trait* for example was a strong predictor of whether females progressed up the organizational hierarchy in male-dominated companies. Not all individuals have the personal inclination or wherewithal to be so-called 'career capitalists', managing their own portfolio of career investments.

---

### Study Box 3.29

#### 'Relational' career models

Various writers have advocated a relational model of careers more appropriate to the analysis of female careers (for example, Crozier, 1999; Flum & Blustein, 2000). The term 'relational' originates from Gilligan's (1982) work on relational identity. The central idea is that women define themselves in terms of their relationships with others, whereas men define themselves in terms of their independence and achievement. Indeed, the viability of this assumption has since been consistently supported in studies looking at what is important to female careers and to their development more generally (for example, Johnson & Stokes, 2002). One especially fruitful line of enquiry has focused on the use of social and professional networks (for example, Linehan, 2001), the importance of vocational exploration, and the constructive use of role models (for example, Robitschek & Cook, 1999) in the development process.

## Research Challenges

- investigate the role of emotion in careers and career theory;
- explore theoretical and empirical links between developmental appraisal and career management initiatives – for example, through constructs like career self-concept;
- look more closely at the role of self-insight and self-assessment in the career development process, with particular reference to the cognitive skills involved;
- harness mainstream career theories for insights into career management (for example, adult development theories);
- investigate the meaning of careers, and, in particular, of subjective career success;
- explore the viability of career contracting as a conceptual basis for career management.

## Recommended Reading

Arnold, J. (1997). *Managing careers into the 21st century.* London: Paul Chapman Publishing.

Drenth, P.J.D. (1998). Personnel appraisal. In P.J.D. Drenth, H. Thierry, & C.J. de Wolff (Eds), *Personnel psychology. Volume 3: Handbook of work and organizational psychology* (2nd edn, pp. 59–88). Hove, East Sussex: Psychology Press.

Fletcher, C. (2001) Performance appraisal and performance management: The developing research agenda. *Journal of Occupational and Organizational Psychology, 74,* 473–487.

Kidd, J.M. (2002). Careers and career management. In P.B. Warr (Ed.) *Psychology at work* (5th edn). Harmondsworth: Penguin.

Williams, R., & Fletcher, C. (1998). Performance management. In I. Robertson, D. Bartram, & M. Callinan (Eds), *Individual performance and organizational effectiveness.* Chichester: Wiley.

# 4

# Employee Relations and Motivation

'To explore the challenge to the human soul in organizations is to build a bridge between the world or the personal, subjective, and even unconscious element of individual experience and the world of organizations that demand rationality, efficiency, and personal sacrifice.'

(Briskin, 1998: xii)

## Preface

The topic of employee relations 'broadly deals with the relationships encountered by people in their working lives' (Green, 1994: 1), studied by many other disciplines (for example, economists, sociologists), as well as psychologists. The focus of investigation ranges from the individual in relation to the organization through to the 'shop floor'. The 20th century witnessed radical change in the way employee relations are conceptualized and managed. In the first half of the century, a highly formalized system of collective bargaining dominated, consistent with the economic model of the time. This prompted a rise of trade unionism and an ethos of employee regulation through 'labour restraint' (that is, institutionalizing and containing employee grievance), the traditional industrial relations (IR) system.

De-industrialization coupled with increased differentiation of product markets, technological advance, devolved production systems and heterogeneity of the labour force furnished the decentralization of IR practices to organization-specific employment systems. Many companies opted out of multi-employer bargaining systems (for example, IBM). Traditional trade unionism was rooted in a particular type of occupational identity (male, industrial workers). Nowadays there are many different 'voices' from previously excluded non-unionized groups seeking attention for their own particular collective priorities.

The eclipse of the traditional union may reflect the general erosion of societal collectivism. Economic crisis has both afforded and actively encouraged a growth in market liberalism and individualism. Coupled with this, a rise in the importance of consumption, in parallel with the rise in the service sector, has shaped personal identities and interests (Hyman, 1994). In contemporary Britain, however, there is a growth in individualized career expectations and thus a far more complex relationship between collective and individual interests. In combination with this is a tendency for companies to 'personalize' the employment relationship (Herriot, 2001).

The rhetoric of employee involvement has become a means of integrating employees. The companies that model the employee as a strategic asset may introduce arrangements for employee information and consultation. Those that, by contrast, model the employee as a disposable liability may not view employee considerations as part of their strategic framework.

The above provides an important backdrop to understanding the psychology of human relations (HR) which has centred on the issue of performance regulation via the concept of motivation. The chapter is divided into four parts: Part 1 looks at work design as the key to leveraging motivated performance, Part 2 takes a detailed look at individual level theories of motivation, Part 3 looks at groups and teams, and Part 4 investigates leadership as a key to harnessing the motivational potential of employees. Some clear trends are discernible across this literature: (1) an increase in the use and relevance of dispositional concepts to understand motivated behaviour, especially self-regulatory concepts; (2) a move towards integration across different motivational propositions and models; and (3) a heightened emphasis on looking at the cognitive mechanisms and processes involved in self-regulated individual and group/team behaviour. At the meta-level, these trends are indicative of a reformulated model of the individual as actively engaged in a process of sense making, as much a shaper of the environment as shaped by it, combined with a mission to understand and explain, rather than simply predict behaviour. These changes have fundamental implications for the way occupational psychologists intervene in regulatory matters.

# Part 1: Work Design

## Learning Objectives

Studying the contents of this chapter will enable you to:

1  critically discuss the problem of employee performance regulation;
2  critically evaluate the work design approach to managing motivation;
3  debate various individual-level approaches to the topic of employee motivation;
4  examine the significance of the workgroup for employee motivation;
5  critically discuss the concept of team and team effectiveness;
6  consider the role of the leader in the motivation of employees.

## Employee Relations

Nowadays it is not common for employees to strike, but some salient recent UK examples can be cited (for example, fire fighters, train drivers; Study Box 4.1; **www.sagepub. co.uk/millward** for more details).

---

**Study Box 4.1**

**The employee on 'strike'**

Withdrawal of labour is the ultimate employee weapon. A strike strategy is adopted by unions either because disputes apparently cannot be resolved through discussion, when management refuse to engage in discussion or as a reaction to an unsatisfactory pay agreement. Usually, a working compromise is achieved without resorting to strike activity. Most companies have 'dispute procedures' designed to avoid the costs of industrial action. Strikes can be official and unofficial. An official strike runs according to union rules (for example, ballot, called by a full-time trade union official). If a union member is instructed to strike, he or she is obliged to (or risk being disciplined). The unofficial strike works outside union rules and regulations – that is, wild cat – and tends not to last as long as the 'official strike', used primarily as a negotiating tactic to convince the management of the strength of union feeling (Green, 1994).

---

A conflict perspective on employee relations (which acknowledges the reality of different interests between employees and employers) shaped the UK industrial landscape for over 100 or so years. Today, organizations operate with unitary or neo-unitary assumptions, underpinned by the principle of worker–employer collaborations, and as such do not have systematic procedures for dealing with conflict. The *unitarist perspective* predominates in organizations like Kodak, Hewlett Packard, 3M and IBM: the employee–employer relationship is seen as a partnership between the suppliers of capital, management and employees. Neo-unitarist philosophy (1980s) is a market-oriented philosophy with commitment to quality and customer satisfaction. A key component of neo-unitarism is the importance of Human Resource Management (HRM), especially training and development. These two perspectives run counter to the traditional union philosophy of collective bargaining, which tends to determine the terms and conditions of employees on a *group* basis, but are the most dominant contemporary organizational paradigms. Such organizations may even offer various 'strike-free' deals (for example, employee participation).

Yet the fact remains that power differentials and conflicting interests do still prevail in organizational life (Herriot, 2001; Hollway, 1991). Contemporary conflict theorists (that is, so-called pluralists), however, advocate a peaceful resolution of conflict either by collective bargaining (hard pluralism) or joint consultation and problem solving (soft pluralism) (Study Box 4.2). A *psychological contracting* approach to employer–employee relations offers one potential framework in which to pursue consultation and negotiation (Herriot, 2001; see below).

The UK has witnessed a 'diminished mobilizing potential' attributable to shifts in attitudes towards unions and what they represent. Those in the service sector face the fact that any form of industrial action will affect the consumer, with the potential consequence of losing public sympathy. The Royal College of Nursing, for instance, has a 'no strike' clause as a criterion of membership. Younger workers, in particular, are less likely to participate in union activity or take on positions of representation, pursuing instead very different interests and aspirations than those contained within the union agenda (for example, Hyman, 1994).

---

**Study Box 4.2**

**European directives**

The move towards European integration coupled with an increase in the number of Euro-companies parallels the acceleration of cross-border mergers, acquisitions and strategic alliances. Consequently, there is pressure for the development of new forms of European IR regulation (Marginson & Sisson, 1994: 44). Centralization of management at European level in place of national structures (for example, Ford, General Motors, Nestle, Unilever) has afforded the strategic potential to establish 'organization-specific' pan-European systems of IR management. This may be expressed in common policy objectives across countries (for example, common philosophy of HRM as in IBM and Digital, employee involvement programmes as in Ford).

---

Within psychology, 'employee relations' has been addressed as a problem of employee regulation. Contemporary performance problems are more likely to manifest in a relatively silent (or not so silent in some areas of work) way, in, for example, high absence rates than in more overt forms like striking (**www.sagepub.co.uk/millward** for a discussion of some contemporary performance problems).

## Employee Performance Regulation

Hollway (1991) notes the inextricable link between the production of knowledge and politico-economic requirements in the practice of organizational psychology. It is a discipline that has evolved from the need to regulate performance. The idea of regulating performance by managing motivation arose in response to the resistance of workers to Scientific Management (SM) regimes of control (see 'Introduction'). In particular, the notion evolved that optimal performance could be engineered by re-designing or 'enriching' the job to make it more intrinsically satisfying, fostering 'feelings of achievement and worthwhile accomplishment' (Paul & Robertson, 1970: 12; see **www.sagepub.co.uk/millward** for an example from IBM Endicott). In the words of Hollway (1991: 10):

> It was not scientific merit that determined the emergence of Human Relations theory motivation and job satisfaction ... if machine pacing, deskilling, piece rates, and tight supervision had succeeded in achieving optimal productivity, motivation and job satisfaction would never have seen the light of day.

In the USA, the problem of regulation was focused on the individual, whilst in the UK – and also the USA – the workgroup (as a work design option) was seen as the key to 'optimizing' employee work experience. The former is exemplified by the work of Herzberg and colleagues (Herzberg, Mausner, & Snyderman, 1959; Herzberg, 1968) on the notion of 'intrinsic reward' (level of interest in the work). The latter is exemplified by Likert's (1967) linchpin theory of participative workgroups. Both now constitute classic works yielding assumptions about the motivating character of work that still remain strong today. Herzberg's legacy, for instance (whilst not supported in its finer details), is the idea that people are motivated by challenge, responsibility, the opportunity to develop, achieve and attain recognition (Paul & Robertson, 1970).

Thus, since the inception of the HR movement in the 1930s (see 'Introduction and overview'), there has been a drive towards making the nature of work more motivating as a means of regulating performance (for example, Vroom, 1995; Walker, 1950). In the early stages, this was formulated as a problem of satisfaction. The assumption was that by redesigning work, one can increase satisfaction which will in turn provide an indirect (that is, subjectively driven by the employee) means of regulating performance (Figure 4.1).

**Figure 4.1**   The work design principle

This pragmatic approach to managing motivation was later superseded by a more conceptual approach to job enrichment derived from the propositions of Hackman and Oldham (1975) in their job characteristics model (JCM). Nonetheless, the key assumptions remained as follows:

- that work design is the causal antecedent of job satisfaction;
- that work satisfaction is a motivating mechanism; and
- that motivation is the casual antecedent of performance.

It is an incontrovertible fact that motivation is critical to performance (though it is not the only antecedent factor; Campbell, 1999; Kirk & Brown, 2003; Chapter 3, Part 1), but the assumption that work design *determines* satisfaction and that satisfaction is causally prior to motivation are not so easily sustained. These two assumptions will be considered in detail below.

## Assumption 1: Work design as causal antecedent

There are two conventional models of work design: The JCM (Hackman & Oldham, 1975) and socio-technical systems (STS) theory (Emery & Trist, 1969). STS theory assumes that any system has a technical and a human (social) element, both of which must be optimized in an integrated and unitary way to optimize the system as a whole. STS theory (Cooper & Foster, 1971) is outlined in detail on **www.sagepub.co.uk/millward**.

The basic principle of STS theory is that the workgroup should be self-regulating ('the autonomous workgroup') and that the supervisor should facilitate and support this, rather than try to 'interfere' in it. Many organizations in the 1960s and 1970s experimented with this design solution (and variants in the form of the semi-autonomous group), but it is only recently that the autonomous workgroup (or self-managed team) has become a popular design solution (Lawler, Mohrman, & Ledford, 1992). Subsequent research has confirmed the benefits to well-being and motivation of autonomous workgroup designs, but their impact on performance (including absenteeism) has been less conclusively demonstrated (Antoni, 1996; Frese, 1998; Parker & Wall, 1998).

Guzzo, Jette and Katzell (1985) reported evidence from a meta-analysis indicating the greater power of the *semi-autonomous* (rather than completely autonomous) workgroup to enhance productivity, although notably they also found *goal setting and training interventions* to be just as powerful if not more. Frese (1998) points out that to be effective, autonomous and semi-autonomous workgroups should be supported by an appropriately consistent pay structure, consistent with the finding that teamwork is not possible if pay is individually determined and/or where other features of the wider system do not support the autonomous working principle (West & Markiewicz, 2004). STS interventions are also difficult as a whole to evaluate precisely because of 'the lack of specificity about the nature of expected effects' (Parker, Wall & Cordery, 2001: 416). The autonomous workgroup is discussed later.

The JCM was inspired by the work of Lawrence and colleagues (1961) who identified links between specific aspects of the job (for example, number of tasks comprised by the job and the type of skills required to perform them) and job satisfaction and performance. In a nutshell, the JCM assumes that jobs with certain characteristics fulfil important psychological needs, which has a motivating effect (Study Box 4.3).

---

### Study Box 4.3

#### Job characteristics

The three critical psychological states are: experienced responsibility, knowledge of results and experienced meaningfulness. It is proposed that 'an individual experiences *positive affect* to the extent that he/she personally (*experienced responsibility*) has performed well on the task (*knowledge of results*) he/she cares about (*experienced meaningfulness*)'. This 'positive affect' provides the incentive to perform well in the future through a 'self-perpetuating cycle of positive work motivation powered by self-generated rewards' (Hackman & Oldham, 1975). In short, intrinsic work motivation is derived from feelings derived from the job itself and the satisfaction created by performing it well.

The five core job characteristics that create these psychological states are: *skill variety* (degree to which one's job requires the use of several skills), *task significance* (the importance of the task to other people), *task identity* (characteristics that enable a worker to identity with a complete task from beginning to end), *autonomy* (degree to which an employee has discretion in deciding how to perform the job) and *feedback* (whether performance provides feedback). The first three create experienced meaningfulness, autonomy fosters experienced responsibility and feedback fosters knowledge of results. *Autonomy* and *feedback* are not only necessary, but

*(Continued)*

Study Box 4.3    Continued

also *sufficient* to create all three psychological states, meaning that a job comprising these two features which is low on skill variety, task identity and significance will nonetheless still be 'motivating'. Finally, individual differences in 'growth-need-strength' (GNS) will moderate reactions to job characteristics. Those with high GNS will react more positively than those with low GNS. Other proposed moderators are knowledge and skill.

The 'motivating potential' (MPS) of a job is calculated by the following multiplicative (as opposed to additive) equation:

$$\text{MPS} = (\text{skill variety} + \text{task identity} + \text{task significance})/3 \times \text{autonomy} \times \text{feedback}$$

The JCM has spawned an enormous research effort (see reviews by Parker & Wall, 1998, 2001). Parker and Wall (1998) draw two main conclusions from this work: (1) collectively, each of the *job characteristics* are indeed strongly associated with satisfaction and motivation (although this does not support a causal role), but are *not* consistently associated with performance (including absence and turnover); and (2) the critical causal assumption that job characteristics create three psychological states remains unsupported. This has raised theoretical concerns about the proposed causal sequencing in the model. For instance, it could be argued that the experience of job satisfaction creates the critical psychological states rather than vice versa. Finally, there are many criticisms of the Job Diagnostic Survey (JDS), which is central to research conducted in the JCM tradition. The five job characteristics do not always factor into independent dimensions, there is a sole reliance on self-report to obtain all relevant sources of data (that is, common method variance problem), and the calculation of 'motivating potential' is said to be unnecessarily complex.

Although some researchers have advocated alternative (and supposedly improved) job characteristic models (for example, Cummings & Schwab, 1970), none have gained much support. It is nonetheless generally agreed that whilst the five key characteristics are undoubtedly important to the analysis of jobs, they do not adequately represent all psychologically salient aspects of contemporary jobs (for example, Frese, 2000; Parker et al., 2001; Study Box 4.4).

Study Box 4.4

### Contemporary work

Contemporary work is characterized by:

- more work at the interface with the customer (European Commission, 2000);
- growth in the 'knowledge' sector (information systems, education/training, product development, consulting);

---

**Study Box 4.4   Continued**

- increased demands on organizations and individuals to be 'flexible', including the use of teams;
- advances in IT;
- demographic changes (more women, educated employees, diversity of ethnic origin, 'older workers').

Parker and Wall (1998) postulate the following additional job characteristics to be important to contemporary work:

- *the opportunity to acquire new, especially transferable skills* (see Chapter 2);
- *managing multiple roles* within a job and across work and home lives (for example, teleworkers often have to manage the boundaries tightly);
- *cognitive characteristics of work* – problem solving, self-regulatory requirements;
- *emotional demands* (for example, emotional labour) – evidence demonstrates that emotion management can be a source of stress (see Chapter 8).
- *group-level work characteristics* – increased demand for teamwork and other forms of interdependent working.

---

In short, the JCM, whilst supported in *some* aspects, is (Parker et al., 2001):

- *outdated* (does not do justice to the nature of contemporary work; Study Box 4.4);
- *theoretically problematic* in its construct base (assuming that the three proposed psychological states are the only critical states, that people vary in 'growth need strength'), its causal assumptions (that is, that certain job characteristics create the psychological states) and predictive propositions (that is, that satisfaction provides the motivating force, that the psychological states mediate the impact of job characteristics on satisfaction and performance, and that the only moderator of the impact of work design on satisfaction and performance is growth need strength);
- *methodologically problematic* in its reliance on the JDS (including problems of common variance, and the inability to distinguish reliably and validly between different job characteristics).

Above all, it is clear that the assumption that work design is *causally responsible* for satisfaction, motivation and performance is not tenable. Job characteristics impact on employees via their *perceptions and interpretations*. Work design is only one influence on perception, taking the focus away from work design per se, to job perceptions.

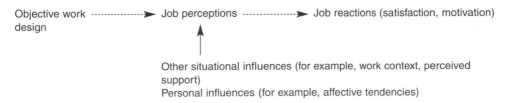

**Figure 4.2**   The job perception principle

Recent work on work design also points to the fact that individuals can to some extent shape their jobs in line with their needs (Parker et al., 2001). In circumstances where jobs are not so highly prescribed, there may be licence to increase autonomy or task variety or to generally enrich one's work. This requires a more dynamic socially constructed depiction of the 'job' inseparable from the person. Even in circumstances where jobs are highly prescribed, instances can be cited where employees 'adjust flexibly and intelligently' by creating *informal* work practices that compensate for the inadequacies of their job (Frese, 1998: 658; Thompson & McHugh, 1995). The extent to which this is possible may, however, depend fundamentally on management style and other organizational factors (Case Study 4.1), a relatively ill-considered yet essential 'design' issue (Cordery, 1999). Jobs may be informally redesigned by changing *how* work is undertaken rather than the nature or content of the work itself (Case Study 4.1). There may, however, be individual variation in the extent of inclination or ability to reshape the job to suit personal needs (for example, proactivity, self-efficacy, cultural values; Parker et al., 2001).

---

### Case Study 4.1: Informal work redesign

Twenty-eight women working in a company that manufactures high-quality sound recording equipment are engaged in the production of 'consoles' involving the construction of thousands of simple electronic circuit boards, by hand, using thin insulated wires. Wiring requires considerable concentration and manual dexterity, with the average console involving half a mile of wiring. The work is intensive and highly repetitive. The design of the jobs is such that the necessary skills (interpretation of wiring diagrams, manual dexterity and fine point soldering) can be learned in less than a day. *None of the women, however, expressed dissatisfaction with the nature of their work. They enjoyed not having to think about their work so they could chat to each other, the prime source of their job satisfaction. A hardworking yet playful and pleasant working atmosphere pervaded the wiring section.* When the manager was replaced however (for being too soft), the 'no nonsense meet production targets' management substitute put a stop to all informal practices and discouraged what he regarded as excessive talking. Things came to a head when he reprimanded three women for returning 10 minutes late from lunch break. Although the women explained that they had finished the morning shift 10 minutes late to complete a batch of consoles, the manager refused to reconsider his decision as the women had failed to seek his approval. Two of the women – the hardest working and most experienced of the team – then handed in their notice.

---

At the same time, work design initiatives can have an important moderating impact on individual outcomes, in relation to wider organizational practices and initiatives. For instance, Parker, Wall, and Jackson (1997) found that downsizing, which increased job demands, did not have the anticipated negative effect because of the counteracting effect of an empowerment initiative that afforded increased autonomy. Work design can also moderate the impact of teamwork, teleworking, close performance monitoring and temporary employment status on individual outcomes (Parker et al., 2001). Thus, work design is of continued importance to our understanding of individual work reactions and outcomes.

The point is that *work design is not the only factor implicated in these outcomes* (see Figure 4.3 – arrows denote influences, not precise relational rules). Also, the three critical psychological states do not appear to be the key mediating factors (see Study Box 4.5). Indeed, the precise mechanisms by means of which job characteristics influence outcomes, and the factors that moderate this association, remain unclear (Mitchell, 1997).

Contemporary research on work design has also expanded the criterion domain to include well-being (Parker & Wall, 1998). Other potential outcomes of importance in the context of work design include safety attitudes and behaviours (Chapter 8), contextual performance (Chapter 3), career outcomes (Chapters 3 and 6) and knowledge transfer (Chapters 2 and 7).

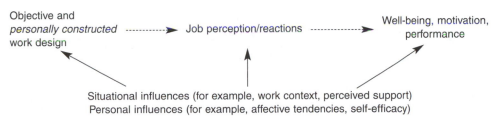

**Figure 4.3**   Work design in context

---

**Study Box 4.5**

**Mediating mechanisms connecting job characteristics with performance**

Psychological empowerment is a state comprising an assessment of meaning, impact, competence and choice or self-determination. Empowerment may arise in association with work characteristics, but denotes a motivational state with a more contextual basis than the critical psychological states, influenced, for instance, by other features of work (for example, 'social-structural changes designed to increase individual mastery and power'; Liden, Wayne, & Sparrowe, 2000: 407). Thus, 'changes in psychological states are expected to follow not only from formal interventions designed to increase power but also from complementary processes in the social milieu that increase efficacy and intrinsic task motivation' (pp. 407–408). Liden et al. (2000) provide evidence demonstrating an association between psychological empowerment and job satisfaction, commitment and performance. The *meaning and competence dimensions* of empowerment were especially important to this association. In fact the *meaning dimension completely mediated the impact of job characteristics on commitment*. However, importantly, the quality of leader member and team members' relations was *more important than empowerment* in accounting for variance in commitment and job performance. This finding suggests that the *quality of social interaction and relationships* in the immediate proximal environment are a critical complement to work design initiatives such as empowerment.

*(Continued)*

> ### Study Box 4.5 Continued
>
> Other mediating mechanisms connecting job characteristics with individual outcomes might be self-efficacy (Parker, 1998), proactive/self-regulating role orientations (Parker et al., 1997), learning opportunities and, thus, cognitive development (Frese & Zapf, 1994), enriched knowledge (Frese & Zapf, 1994; Parker et al., 2001) and engagement (May, Gilson, & Harter, 2004). A recent study reported by Leach, Wall and Jackson (2003) found that an empowerment initiative was associated with increased job knowledge and also self-efficacy, particularly for less experienced employees. Leach et al. (2003) argue that this provides support for the idea that empowerment facilitates cognitive growth and development because, through the experience of control, an individual will feel the need to learn and to know and to gain mastery. This is consistent with action theory's (Frese & Zapf, 1994) key proposition that knowledge and skill are most strongly acquired through action that is within an individual's jurisdiction and control, and with various other models that assume a direct association between control, knowledge and mastery (for example, demand–control model, Herzberg's theory of satisfaction and participative management models; see Leach et al., 2003 for review). Leach et al. (2003) see efficacy and knowledge as inextricably linked, and propose that empowerment may be a mechanism that links job knowledge/self-efficacy with performance.

Potential moderating factors can be divided into organizational, team and individual level considerations. Cummings and Blumberg (1987) propose three organizational level contingencies: technical interdependence, technical uncertainty and environmental uncertainty.

- *Technical interdependence* – if people need to interact to complete a task, it creates an imperative to collaborate. However, evidence suggests that even in situations where there is no such imperative, there may be a benefit to group members to work together in the completion of their tasks (that is, mutual learning and support; Batt, 1999).
- *Technical/environmental uncertainty* – necessitates that people have the jurisdiction to make their own operational decisions. Evidence confirms that in conditions of high uncertainty, employees need to be able to solve their own local problems in the here and now, and to acquire a deeper understanding of what they are doing and why (Wall & Jackson, 1995). In service situations, employees need to be able to respond quickly and to meet a range of demands simultaneously. This requires that employees are appropriately empowered to do this (Batt, 1999). It is generally agreed that to be flexible, an organization needs to decentralize its skills, knowledge and abilities to the frontline. This is one of the key socio-technical systems theory principles that spawned the autonomous teamworking movement (Lawler, Mohrman, & Ledford, 1992).

Broader influences include human resource practices and culture (for example, team working does not work if the culture is individualistic; West & Markiewicz, 2004). National cultural influences may also impact on whether people respond to particular job characteristics (for example, autonomy may conflict with deferential values; for example, Roberts, Probst, Martocchio, Drasgow, & Lawler, 2000).

Team-level moderators include team dynamics (for example, interdisciplinary conflicts may undermine the effectiveness of a team-design solution) and team composition (for example, ability and dispositional mix) (Parker et al., 2001). At the individual level of analysis, proposed moderators (apart from growth need strength) include proactive personality, need for achievement and desire for learning and development (Parker & Wall, 1998).

Whilst this research remains theoretically uninformed, one thing is clear and this is 'that job design is part of [a] package, and to fully appreciate its effects, we need to consider work content in relation to wider HR provision and culture' (Parker et al., 2001). It may be difficult to isolate the impact of a work-design initiative from other organizational changes or other contextual factors, but as Parker et al. (2001) emphasize, this should pose a challenge to researchers to develop more creative but also tighter research designs.

## Part 1 Summary (I) and Conclusions

- Work characteristics have important implications for satisfaction, motivation and performance: it is the assumption that work design *causes* satisfaction/motivation and improved performance that can be challenged.
- The impact of work characteristics depends on how they are perceived and interpreted. Job characteristics can also be formally and informally shaped by the job incumbent. In this way, the person and their work characteristics can become inextricably linked.
- STS theory proposes that the autonomous self-regulating work group is the most effective way of organizing work for reasons of both productivity and satisfaction/well-being. However, evidence suggests that whilst autonomy is generally satisfying for workers, it may not yield objective performance benefits. It is difficult to evaluate STS interventions, because they are highly context bound and multivariate. Nonetheless there has lately been a rise in popularity in the principle of autonomy for organizing group work.
- The JCM postulates five key characteristics (variety, identity, significance, feedback, autonomy) as fundamental to motivation (defined in terms of three critical psychological states) which (via increased job satisfaction) is the causal mechanism underpinning performance improvement. Evidence for the critical states is not strong, but recent conceptual developments include the idea of 'psychological empowerment'.
- Two characteristics in particular (autonomy and feedback) are both necessary and sufficient to afford performance improvement. However, today there are likely to be many other characteristics to consider and many other *outcomes* including well-being.
- Work design is only part of the picture in accounting for individual outcomes; the impact of work design is likely to be *moderated* by many different organizational, team and individual-level factors.

## Assumption 2: Satisfaction as the Motivating Mechanism

The topic of employee satisfaction has attracted longstanding interest (Harter, Schmidt, & Hayes, 2002). Most if not all motivation theories contain a satisfaction component. The JCM assumes that satisfaction is *the motivating mechanism* that causes improved performance.

### What is satisfaction?

Herzberg et al. (1959) extended Maslow's (1954) need theory into the work domain, understanding 'needs' to be prerequisite to understanding motivation and its link with reward. Like Maslow, Herzberg differentiated between two sets of needs: basic 'hygiene' needs (physiological, safety) and uniquely human needs (growth and achievement). Herzberg stipulated that for job content to be motivating it should stimulate 'growth needs' (pp. 56–57), which ties in with the assumptions of the JCM (discussed earlier).

According to Herzberg et al. (1959), job satisfaction and job *dis*atisfaction are two different constructs. Dissatisfaction arises if hygiene needs are not addressed, but their fulfilment will not necessarily increase satisfaction. For satisfaction to increase, employees must be offered challenging work that stimulates growth needs. There has been little formal support for this two-factor proposition. However, in reviewing the field, Staw and Cummings (1996) reported that 81 percent of the factors that contribute to job satisfaction can be categorized as 'motivators' and that 69 percent of factors that contribute to job dissatisfaction can be categorized in 'hygiene' terms, consistent with Herzberg's model. In the strictest sense, however, the notion of two distinct 'satisfaction' constructs is difficult to test (Staw & Cummings, 1996).

Despite the intuitive appeal of Herzberg's model, job satisfaction is generally used to refer to a global affective state arising in association with the appraisal of one's job or job experience (Locke, 1976). However, some maintain a distinction between overall satisfaction (for example, 'job in general') and specific or 'facet' satisfaction with respect to pay, promotion, opportunities, supervision, and co-workers (Brief, 1998; Study Box 4.6). The more important the 'facet', the greater the level of satisfaction/dissatisfaction said to arise from it.

### Study Box 4.6

#### The measurement of job satisfaction

The Minnesota Satisfaction Questionnaire (MSQ) taps both facet and global aspects of satisfaction. The MSQ poses each item as follows: 'On my present job, this is how I feel about …' (for example, being able to keep busy all the time, the chance to do things for other people). Factor analysis of the MSQ has identified two dimensions of facet satisfaction: extrinsic (for example, environmental, supervisory, procedures)

Study Box 4.6    Continued

and intrinsic (for example, recognition and support). Normative data is available for the MSQ, enabling comparison of average levels of satisfaction across different groups of employees (Smither, Collins, & Buda, 1989), Nagy (2002), on the other hand, argues for a single-item approach to measuring job satisfaction as potentially more convenient, face valid and flexible than multi-item measures, performing as well if not better in accounting for variation in work outcomes.

There is a vast literature looking at the association between satisfaction and performance, with performance commonly measured in motivational terms (see Chapter 3, Part 1, and **www.sagepub.co.uk/millward**). The assumption that the satisfied employee is likely to stay longer, be absent less and perform better (that is, 'a happy worker is a good worker') has intuitive appeal, and is of direct practical significance for managers. However, the proposed link is far from simple.

Brayfield and Crockett (1955) concluded from their review that 'there is little evidence that employee attitudes of the type usually measured in morale surveys bear any simple – or for that matter, appreciable – relationship to performance on the job'. Vroom (1964) later concluded likewise. However, recent findings derived from meta-analysis yield more positive results. Judge and Bono (2001) obtained a mean true correlation of 0.30 for the association between satisfaction and performance (defined at the individual level) whilst Harter, Schmidt and Hayes (2002) in a study based on 7939 business units across 36 companies reported a mean true correlation of 0.28 for job satisfaction with business level outcomes (for example, profitability, turnover, safety records). Higher correlations were observed for customer loyalty and turnover.

Lawler and Porter (1967) postulated that the causal relationship, however, may be from performance to satisfaction rather than vice-versa because of the rewards it leads to. Cummings and Schwab (1970) suggested further that performance and satisfaction may only be related to the extent that rewards are *contingent* on performance (see also Brief, 1998). In other words, good performance leads to the attainment of valued goals (like success and achievement), and other rewards like promotion, recognition and high earnings. Some have argued, however, that the satisfaction–performance association is confounded by affective tendencies (dispositional and state; Wright & Staw, 1999).

Recent findings also demonstrate a strong association between 'core self-evaluations' and job satisfaction, motivation and performance (Judge & Bono, 2001). Core self-evaluation is a broad dispositional trait indicated by four specific traits: self-esteem (overall self-ascribed value or worth), self-efficacy (self-estimated ability to cope, perform, and be successful), internal locus of control (sense of personal responsibility), and emotional stability or low neuroticism (tendency to be confident, secure, and steady). The correlations are so similar across satisfaction, motivation and performance criteria (combined with high inter-correlations across core self-evaluation traits) that Judge and colleagues speculate on the existence of the latent trait underlying the two domains.

The above findings suggest that job satisfaction, motivation and performance may be linked *only to the extent that they are all linked with a common dispositional composite.* This puts a different spin on the satisfaction–motivation–performance debate with important theoretical implications (Study Box 4.7).

---

**Study Box 4.7**

**Core self-evaluations and job satisfaction**

Impetus to the study of dispositional correlates of job satisfaction arose from Staw and colleagues (for example, Staw, Bell, & Clausen, 1986). Until recently, however, there has been no clarity on the issue of which traits matter most to satisfaction (Brief, 1998). Narrative reviews have, however, pointed in particular to the relevance of traits making up the 'core self-evaluation' (CSE) construct (for example, Judge and Bono, 2001; Spector, 1997). Judge and Bono (2001) define CSEs as the 'bottom line evaluations that individuals hold about themselves'. Each of the four composite traits are self-evaluative, and refer to broad, fundamental source traits. Judge and Bono (2001) argue that there are good theoretical reasons why these traits should link with job satisfaction. Those with high self-esteem are predisposed to positive job evaluations, especially those involving challenge and mastery, maintaining optimism in the face of failure (making future success and therefore satisfaction more likely). People with high internal locus of control are also more likely to attribute their success to their own efforts and to conduct themselves accordingly, again, self-selecting themselves into more satisfying jobs. Self-efficacy is also associated with persistence and mastery and the attainment of valued and satisfying outcomes. Finally, neuroticism is likely to be associated with low satisfaction because of predispositions to negative affect and negative job evaluations (Brief, 1998; Spector, 1997). Evidence for the association between CSEs and performance also makes sense theoretically. For instance, self-consistency theory (see Brief, 1998) assumes that individuals are motivated to behave in a manner consistent with their self-image, and, if this is positive, they will strive to maintain this. Theories of learned helplessness (Seligman, 1975) also predict that when faced with difficult situations, those with a positive optimistic style are less likely to display motivational deficits.

---

Together, the findings suggest that satisfaction may be a 'symptom' not a cause of motivated performance, linked with performance via other mechanisms. Doyle (2003) makes a good everyday case for not assuming that satisfaction is directly causally linked with either motivation or performance by referring to instances where people remain highly motivated despite feeling extremely job dissatisfied (for example, nurses). She explains this seemingly anomalous finding with reference to identity. A strong professional identity, she says, will in itself be a motivator since, through good performance, it is possible to both express and reinforce this identity. That is, good performance can be intrinsically motivating irrespective of satisfaction. Doyle's (2003) argument points to the need for more research on the *dynamic relationship* between satisfaction, motivation and performance, over time.

## Part 1 Summary (II) and Conclusions

- It is commonly assumed that satisfaction and motivation go together, but whether satisfaction is prerequisite to motivation is a different question. The mechanisms linking the two constructs have not been investigated, and moreover the possibility that the relationship may be a dynamic and changing one has not been contemplated.
- Satisfaction may derive from performance, as much as performance may derive from satisfaction, but it is now generally agreed that other factors are involved. The association between satisfaction and motivation (and performance) may in fact be explicable at a higher-order dispositional level.

# Part 2: The Motivated Individual

## What is Motivation?

Motivation concerns the *direction, intensity and persistence of work behaviour* (Kanfer & Ackerman, 2000). Kanfer and Ackerman (2000) note a growth in emphasis on 'cognitive' theories of motivation, coupled with a move towards *theoretical integration* (for example, goal-setting theory and social-cognitive theory). It is clear, they say, that motivation is a 'multiply-determined, complex and dynamic' phenomenon. Rainey (2001) notes how the term motivation has become an umbrella concept referring to a set of issues rather than a single variable with a precise operational definition.

There are several different ways of looking at motivation. One could focus on the question of 'what' motivates positive workplace behaviour (content theories) or on 'how' motivated behaviour comes about (process theories) (Foster, 2000). Here motivation is examined using Kanfer's (1992) scheme of 'conceptual proximity to action' – that is, the closeness of the proposed underlying motivational mechanism to action. Some theories propose the influence of constructs like basic needs, expectations, outcome evaluations, personality and other such factors 'inferred' from behaviour, denoting indirect (distal) forms of influence on behaviour. Theories proposing factors that have a more direct (proximal) influence on behaviour pertain to mechanisms at the immediate level of behavioural regulation or action (for example, goal setting, self-regulation).

Distal theories have moved from need-based towards being more cognitive in their explanatory basis, with a particular emphasis on how 'choices' are made. However, there has also been a revival of interest in dispositional causes of motivation (for example, Judge & Ilies, 2002). Proximal theories, on the other hand, reflect a revival of interest in 'volitional' concepts (Gollwitzer, 1993).

# Distal Theories

## Need theories

Early theories assumed that all motivated behaviour is need based (Study Box 4.8). McGhee and Thayer (1961) likened motivation to an intrinsic force or tension responsible for directing behaviour. Fundamental needs keep people in a continually 'stirred up' state, although a state of complete satisfaction is largely unattainable. Criticisms of need theories include the problem of measurement, the question of which needs are associated with which particular behaviours and how to use the theory in practice (for example, Foster, 2000). Need theories are nonetheless popular among managers, encouraging them at least to appreciate that different employees have different needs (Rollinson, Broadfield, & Edwards, 1998).

---

**Study Box 4.8**

### Assumptions of content (need) theories of motivation

- People have innate needs that never change. The categories of 'need' postulated by different writers are arbitrary, and largely untestable. McDougall (1932) identified 18 'propensities' and Murray (1938) suggested 20 'psychogenic needs'.
- Needs operate within a closed system, and, if unfulfilled, produce a state of disequilibrium or tension.
- Needs (and values) cannot be instilled by management practices or developed or shaped by cultural or organizational factors. Needs flow from within the individual. Management efforts can, however, help shape the 'goals' that are the object of behaviour arising from unmet needs. This will entail shaping the process of need fulfilment, but not the source of the needs.
- Needs are either met or not. Managers can provide environments that harmonize with the salient needs of an individual employee, and help them channel their efforts in a direction congruent with both personal and organizational goals.

---

## Dispositional approaches

Dispositional approaches refer to the motivational relevance of personality. The concept of personality has largely been in disfavour since the situation-versus-trait debates of the 1970s (for example, Mischel, 1973). However, there has been a dispositional revival in recent years, particularly in connection with ideas about the factor structure of personality and the influence of this on performance, the influence of personality on information-processing style and also on self-regulatory processes (Kanfer & Ackerman, 2000).

It is generally agreed amongst personality researchers that there are five dimensions to personality: extraversion, neuroticism, openness to experience, agreeableness and conscientiousness (McCrae & Costa, 1987). Of particular interest is the dimension of 'conscientiousness', which has been found to be closely associated with motivational processes (that is, hard working, achievement oriented and persevering). The dimension might also be known as 'dependable' (planful, responsible, careful; Barrick & Mount, 1991; Barrick, Mount, & Judge, 2001).

A recent meta-analysis published by Judge and Ilies (2002) integrated 150 correlations from across 65 studies looking at the relationship between the Big Five dimensions and performance motivation (defined as goal setting, expectancy, and self-efficacy). The results yielded an average validity of 0.24 for conscientiousness and, interestingly also, an average validity of –0.31 across all three motivational criteria. These findings are consistent with those reported by Salgado (1997) and Hurtz and Donovan (2000). Overall, the Big Five produced an average multiple correlation of 0.49, suggesting that personality really does matter to performance motivation defined in theoretically, *cognitive* terms. Some writers point out, however, that there are limits to the kind of occupational areas where conscientiousness is relevant (Robertson, Baron, Gibbons, MacIver, & Nyfield, 2000). For example, individual differences in 'conscientiousness' are only likely to be apparent in performance situations where persistence is required.

The pathways via which various dispositions and their interactions can impact on performance are potentially extremely complex, and yet to be unravelled. At its most basic level, it is clear that the performance impact of distal, dispositional variables, such as personality, are likely to be mediated by proximal (goal-oriented, self-regulatory) motivational factors (Barrick, Stewart, & Piotrowski, 2002; and see later discussion).

### Instrumentality theories

Instrumentality theories all assume that wants are turned into actions when some balance of benefit is perceived likely in the foreseeable future. Motivation results from the process of allocating personal resources in the form of time and energy. The most well known and researched example of this is valence-instrumentality expectancy (VIE) theory (Vroom, 1995). VIE theory assumes that likely benefits are broken down into 'expectancies' (perceived likelihood that the effort expended will result in desired outcomes) and 'valences' (desirability of perceived outcome). Individuals are modelled as weighing up 'valences', although this comparative calculation is not necessarily performed consciously.

The motivation to perform an action is conceptualized as a multiplicative function of the valence of the anticipated outcome and the expectancy that these valences will occur. People will expend effort to the extent that it is perceived to pay dividends (that is, it is instrumental). If the pay-off is unclear or the link between effort and outcome is muddy (for example, 'Is it worth the effort?'), motivation to exert effort is unlikely.

Research conducted in both laboratory and field contexts has *not*, however, found much support for VIE theory (Pritchard, Campbell & Campbell, 1977; Study Box 4.9).

---

**Study Box 4.9**

**Testing VIE theory**

The lack of support for VIE theory has been attributed in part to inappropriate testing and analysis of VIE propositions (Pinder, 1984). Vroom (1964, cited in Vroom, 1995) stipulated that the within-subject design is the most optimal enabling consideration of choices made with respect to a particular situation. However, most researchers have tested VIE theory using between-subject designs to examine choices made by different groups of employees (Dipboye, Smith, & Howell, 1994).

The original 'multiplicative' aspect of the theory has also been criticized as too complex. Vroom (1995) has recognized that although much behaviour is goal directed, 'the level of processing required by expectancy theory is rarely possible and would represent one extreme, found mainly on relatively simple choice problems where the alternatives are clear and information is readily available' (p. xix). Vroom (1995) also recognizes that a lot of behaviour is under the control of emotions or habit (see also Beach, 1997). Lord, Hanges and Godfrey (2003), however, argue that VIE theory need not imply a complex process of mental computation if it is reformulated in neural network information processing terms. Evidence from cognitive science is used to demonstrate how 'neural networks operating in parallel can perform many computational activities', including those assumed by VIE theory, *automatically and rapidly, assuming that one has extensive experience with the problem situation*' (Lord et al., 2003: 23). These computational processes occur sub-symbolically (p. 26).

Each of the components within the theory has been demonstrated to have independent motivational force (for example, Tharanou, 2001a). Tharanou (2001a) found that valence and expectancy were subordinated to instrumentality issues in the context of training motivation (see Chapter 2).

---

Contemporary interest in VIE theory has been integrated with other models of motivation such as goal-setting and self-efficacy theory, and also equity theory. It has also been argued, for instance, that the language of expectancy and instrumentality is more appropriately applied to some people (for example, those with high CSEs, including a strong internal locus of control) than others who may, in turn, be more swayed in their efforts by 'external' sources of influence (for example, social norms) (Miller & Grush, 1988).

### *Motive approaches*

Motive approaches postulate universal psychological motives and aim to specify the conditions and the processes that translate motives into action. For example, equity theories postulate a desire for 'equity' in social relationships (Adams, 1965). Perceptions of inequity create psychological tension and prompt attempts to regain balance through cognitive and/or behavioural change. Specifically, people compare their own inputs to a situation with those of other people, and also make similar comparisons of what they may gain. Inputs may include effort, experience, skill, training, hours of work and so on. Gains may include pay, status, esteem, material comforts, and so on.

Two forms of equity have been discussed: *distributive* and *procedural* (Thibaut & Walker, 1978):

- *Distributive fairness* – perceptions of fairness in the allocation of outcomes or *where* valued outcomes are distributed. Studies focus on the cognitive and motivational consequences of perceived unfairness in outcomes created through underpayment or overpayment.
- *Procedural fairness* – perceptions about organizational procedures used to make outcome decisions, or *how* outcomes are distributed. Thibaut and Walker (1978) showed that allowing people to provide input into the decision-making process enhanced perceptions of procedural justice irrespective of the outcome obtained, a basic finding since confirmed in many studies (Sweeney & MacFarlin, 1993). Recent work is concerned with identifying potential mediators (for example, trust in supervisor) of the association between justice perceptions and motivated behaviour (Aryee, Budhwar, & Chen, 2002). Trust in the supervisor might also moderate the likelihood of perceiving a breach of justice expectations in the terms of the employment relationship (Lester, Turnley, Bloodgood, & Bolino, 2002).

Justice theory has been applied to the study of candidate reactions in the context of selection (for example, Gilliland, 1993; Truxillo, Steiner, & Gilliland, 2004; Chapter 1), to the study of survivor reactions to downsizing (for example, Allen, Freeman, Russell, Reizenstein, & Rentz, 2001; Chapter 5) and is being linked with other theoretical considerations (for example, psychological contract theory; Herriot, 2001, see below).

Another claim is that people are intrinsically motivated in certain respects, and that the key to managing motivation is to harness these natural inclinations. For instance, Deci (1975) argues that people have a strong need to feel competent and in control and that being offered external inducements can undermine this (cognitive evaluation theory), an argument reiterated more recently by Collins & Amabile (1999). The question of whether reward can create dependence on external contingencies (undermining personal locus of control) has also been asked in the context of whether it is possible to 'bribe people to be creative' (Hennessey & Amabile, 1998). Findings, however, show that creativity can be enhanced rather than undermined by rewards (Eisenberger & Rhoades, 2001; see **www.sagepub.co.uk/millward** for details).

Whilst Deci and colleagues continue to demonstrate that reward for carrying out a task regardless of performance can decrease intrinsic interest (for example, Deci, Koestner, & Ryan, 1999), independent support is mixed (Eisenberger & Rhoades, 2001). Eisenberger and Rhoades argue that personal control is most likely to be undermined when reward is *non-contingent on performance* (that is, performance is not instrumentally meaningful in association with this reward). However, when reward is contingent on performance, it signals that the task has value, will lead to positive outcomes, and that it is in the performer's hands (self-determination) to achieve them.

Despite mixed support for the idea that reward can squash intrinsic motivation, research has demonstrated that the notion of 'intrinsic motivation' is a viable one. There are nonetheless found to be many different forms of intrinsic motivation (for example, need for information and arousal, for achievement, for self-determination and control, to demonstrate competence), each with different motivational consequences (see Kanfer & Ackerman, 2000 for a review). Different forms of intrinsic motivation may be differentially affected by reward, whether contingent or not on performance. Also, in the work setting, managers are more likely to try to actively motivate only those who are evidently 'demotivated', or only motivated by extrinsic rewards (pay, benefits). Those who are already highly intrinsically motivated are unlikely to be the target of motivational strategies.

## Part 2 Summary (I) and Conclusions

- Distal perspectives on motivation include need, dispositional, instrumentality and motive approaches. Traditional need theories based on homeostatic models have been superseded by other approaches, favouring the idea that motivation has a dispositional (conscientiousness, core self-evaluations) basis, that it may involve some form of conscious calculation of utility (valence, instrumentality and expectancy), and/or is present in some naturally intrinsic form that must be appropriately harnessed.
- Arguably, the dispositional element of motivation may interact with the likelihood and/or quality of cognitive evaluation of whether a particular action is worth the effort, and perhaps also the mechanisms associated with an *intrinsic* motivational impetus (for example, self-determination).

## Proximal Theories

### Goal-setting theory

Locke (1991) has described personal goals as 'often, though not invariably, the most immediate conscious motivational determinants of action' (Locke & Latham, 2002: 709). In 1976, Locke introduced the idea that setting goals provides motivational impetus. At least four mechanisms are proposed by which goals influence performance:

- directing attention and action;
- mobilizing energy expenditure and effort;
- prolonging effort over time (persistence);
- motivating the individual to develop relevant strategies for goal attainment.

By assigning a specific and stated goal, employees are encouraged to focus on achieving something finite and manageable, with tangible consequences. This contrasts with a method of simply encouraging an employee to work harder (Study Box 4.10).

### Study Box 4.10

#### Variations in goal content

The object or result being sought can vary in *clarity or specificity* (degree of quantifiable precision with which aim is specified) and *difficulty* (degree of proficiency or

**Study Box 4.10    Continued**

level of performance sought). The completion of a task may be a goal, but mostly goal refers to a standard or performance as opposed to the nature of a task and task completion per se. Locke (1976) found evidence for a positive, linear relationship between goal difficulty and task performance (assuming sufficient ability). Many subsequent studies have produced the same kinds of conclusions (see Locke, 1997 for a review). Moreover, studies consistently support the proposition that the more specific the difficult goal is, the better the performance relative to 'do your best' (that is, vague, non-specific) or no goals. Whilst there has been extensive research on goal specificity and difficulty, little consideration has been given to the notion of *goal complexity* (that is, the number and interrelation of the results aimed for) and *goal conflict* (that is, the degree to which attaining one goal negates or subverts attaining another).

The basic principles of goal setting have been supported by hundreds of studies, but the benefit to performance of goal setting is said to derive in particular from 'personal goals, including goal commitment and self-efficacy' (Study Box 4.11; Locke, 2001). Thus, assigned goals are mediated by self-set goals (that people choose in response to the assignment) and by self-efficacy. Locke and Latham (2002: 707) note how it is 'a virtual axiom that all action is the result of cognition and motivation, but that these elements can interact in complex ways'. They summarize findings from 35 years of research as follows:

- In relation to task goals, people automatically use existing knowledge and skill relevant to goal attainment.
- If there is no pre-existing knowledge or skill directly pertinent to the goal situation, people will draw on a repertoire of skills acquired from related contexts.
- If the goal is new, people will consciously develop strategies to achieve it.
- People with high self-efficacy are more likely than those with low self-efficacy to develop task strategies (this may incur a time lag, allowing for strategies to develop).
- Faced with a complex task, sometimes 'do your best' goals lead to better strategy development because otherwise a specific goal can create too much anxiety, which is an impediment to effective strategy development and performance (that is, creates evaluative pressure). In this instance, setting challenging learning rather than performance goals may be better (Seijts & Latham, 2001).
- Training in the development of proper strategies adds to the impact of setting specific goals; if the strategy used is inappropriate, then a difficult goal can lead to worse performance than an easy one (Audia, Locke, & Smith, 2000).

Moderators of the goal–performance relationship are summarized in Study Box 4.11.

---

**Study Box 4.11**

### Moderators of the goal–performance association

The relationship is strongest when:

- People are *committed* to their goals, especially when the goals are difficult (Klein, Wesson, Hollenbeck, Wright & Deshon, 2001). Facilitators of commitment include valued outcomes in association with goals (for example, reinforced by leaders, accountability, participation in goal setting), and belief in ability to achieve the goal. However, Woods, Atkins and Bright (1999) found that incentive effects on the goal–performance relationship were mediated by instrumentality or outcome expectancies (rather than efficacy).
- *Feedback* on progress in relation to goals – this will enable adjustment and will maintain focus and a sense of personal control.
- *Task complexity* – requires a higher level of automated skill and/or the ability to develop strategies. Setting proximal goals (learning subgoals) can facilitate performance in this instance. Proximal goals can also increase error management ability whereas distal performance goals in a context of steep learning can have a deleterious effect on performance (Frese & Zapf, 1994; see Chapter 2). From a socio-cognitive perspective, the process of setting and attaining proximal goals is the most effective way of achieving longer-term goals (Bandura, 1997).

---

Since most goal-setting research is conducted in the laboratory setting involving mainly students, direct applications of goal-setting theory to organizations are not common. Evidence from the field, in which there are potentially multiple and conflicting goals, offers more equivocal support (Yearta, Maitlis & Briner, 1995). Locke and Latham (2002) recognize that there are instances where organizational and individual goals may conflict and that this can undermine performance because of incompatible action tendencies. There is also the matter of risk attached to setting difficult goals in complex organizational settings (Knight, Durham, & Locke, 2001; see **www.sagepub.co.uk/millward** for a discussion of the Management by Objectives programme).

Many have argued that the simplicity of goal setting is both its strength and its weakness. As a theory, it is said to be relatively under-developed and rudimentary, perhaps constituting an approach to, rather than a theory of, motivation. Developments within goal-setting theory are largely empirical rather than theoretical. However, efforts by Locke and Latham (2002) in recent years include attempts to integrate goal-setting theory with self-efficacy theory within a socio-cognitive framework (see Locke, 1997 for a review).

Research suggests the need to identify the conditions under which goal setting can contribute an explanation of motivation in organizational contexts (Pinder, 1998). Recent work looking at the more dynamic context of goal setting across time explored, in particular, the driving force of goal–performance discrepancy on performance. Donovan and Williams (2003) found that athletes were highly sensitive to goal–performance discrepancy and that athletes use this information to revise their goals accordingly. Specifically, athletes moderated their goals by lowering both immediate (proximal) and longer-term (distal, seasonal) goals when discrepancies were high. However, this inclination was moderated by attributions of stability (that is, performance is attributed to stable factors) and the progress made so far across the allotted time. Stability attributions may create a sense of performance inevitability. This, combined with being close to the allotted goal attainment time, makes it not surprising that athletes modified their goals. Other research has confirmed that as deadlines approach, self-regulatory strategies are intensified (Raynor & Roeder, 1987).

Issues for future research arising from studies like these include the need to look at the dynamic relationship between proximal and distal goals over multiple performance episodes and, in particular, joint regulatory effects on performance. Donovan and Williams (2003) found that athletes had goal hierarchies in which their long-term goal was the ideal or hoped-for goal, subordinate to which were a lot of proximal or short-term subgoals. Movement within a personal goal hierarchy has not yet been explored in an organizational setting. Another outstanding issue concerns whether goals should be conscious to be effective performance motivators and also the role played by unconscious processes in motivating goal-oriented performance (Wegge & Dibbelt, 2000).

## Self-regulation theories

Several self-regularity concepts have been proposed (Study Box 4.12), but there are three main *models*: German action theory, self-regulation theory, and cybernetic theory.

German action theory is a generic theory of performance (Frese & Zapf, 1994). A core premise is that the human is an 'active rather than a passive being who changes the world through work actions and thereby changes him- or herself' (1994: 286). In short, personal change occurs through action and reflection on this action. There are two main sets of propositions, one pertaining to action processes and the other pertaining to the idea of an action hierarchy. Action processes (activity regulation theory) comprise the following steps: (1) goal setting; (2) orientation; (3) plan development; (4) monitoring of execution; and (5) feedback:

- *Goal setting* – 'an internally represented desired state' (Austin & Vancouver, 1996: 361).
- *Orientation* – development of an appropriate problem representation.
- *Plan development* – conceptually, a plan denotes anything from a momentary (reactionary, 'here and now') strategy, to a detailed action plan. A planning strategy includes preventative actions and an active search for relevant information. Higher performers are found to be more detailed in their plans than low or average performers, but not so detailed that they cannot respond to the more localized requirements of a situation (Sonnentag, 1996).
- *Monitoring of execution* – this stage bridges cognition and action and draws heavily on working memory. Interruptions at this stage can prompt errors or omission.
- *Feedback* – people need to know how they are progressing in relation to their goals, but feedback can also divert attention from the task by creating a tendency to be self-ruminative (Kluger & DeNisi, 1998). The effectiveness of feedback depends on its timing, its delivery, the context of its delivery (for example, learning culture versus sanction-oriented culture), and the person.

The action hierarchy, on the other hand, pertains to levels of regulation, and assumes that higher-level goals regulate lower levels of behaviours (as in cybernetic theory, Carver & Scheier, 1998). Higher-level processes are conscious and general whilst lower-level goals are automatic and specific. Conscious higher-level 'meta-cognitive' processes pertain to knowledge and awareness of cognitive regulation strategies. People prefer to regulate behaviour at a lower automatic level through the use of effortless routines. However, routines can keep people bound to what they know, rather than enabling them to learn new and better ways to do things. Actions may be regulated at a higher level in the face of imperatives to establish new goals and routines. This requires self-reflection. The downside of reflecting on an otherwise automatic action is the potential for performance disruption and cognitive overload.

Action theory assumes that individual differences moderate action processes as well as movement up and down the action hierarchy. For example, a learning-oriented person will be more inclined to set detailed plans for goal achievement, learn from (perhaps also actively seek) negative performance, reflect on and adjust their action routines. Recently, Frese and colleagues have introduced the 'personal initiative' concept, to describe and explain one potentially important dispositional influence on this process (Frese, Kring, Soose, & Zempel, 1996).

It is also assumed that increasing the degree of control someone has over their work and work processes will not only motivate them, but deepen their understanding of the task (through exploration and reflection). Action is the means by which knowledge is acquired and via which learning is possible. This has fundamental implications for work design (for example, increasing personal control), training (for example, learning from errors), individual and organizational change (for example, through facilitated action and reflection) (see Chapter 2 on error training and Chapter 8 on error management).

---

### Study Box 4.12

**The concepts of 'flow-state' and action-state orientation**

*Flow state*

Flow state denotes a psychological state characterized by undivided attention, an organized set of action opportunities, a limited stimulus field (to enable focus), clear goals, and perceptions of personal control (Csikszentmihayli & Lefevre, 1989). The term originates from research on skilled performers such as surgeons and dancers. Once in 'flow state', higher cognitive processes are said to become operational, protecting the individual against competing demands for attention. Csikszentmihayli and LeFevre (1989) investigated flow state in the workplace with 78 employees who kept diaries (two-hourly in response to a pager signal) of their daily motivations, activities and subjective perceptions of the quality of their experiences. More flow-like experiences were reported in work contexts than leisure contexts. The results suggested, however, that flow state per se may be insufficient for sustaining task activity. Others have proposed that this may depend on individual differences in motivational orientation (for example, Cellar & Barrett, 2004).

**Study Box 4.12   Continued**

*Action state*

Action state (Kuhl, 1994) denotes individual differences in the ability to make timely decisions, commit to a course of action, avoid procrastination, handle multiple competing demands, maintain challenging goals, and persist in the face of failure or setback. The action state concept is considered central to issues of self-regulation (Kuhl, 1994). The Action-Control Scale or ACS-90 (revised by Diefendorff, Hall, Lord, & Strean, 2000) yields three robust factors: preoccupation, hesitation and volatility. These subscales do not appear to be tapping into variance otherwise accounted for by personality or ability, and successfully predict self-regulatory (self-consciousness, thought intrusion, cognitive interference, depressive thinking) variables as well as job attitudes (job involvement, job satisfaction) and performance (ratings, organizational citizenship). Notably, the preoccupation subscale showed the strongest relationship with self-regulatory variables, whilst the hesitation subscale was the strongest correlate of job attitudes and performance. However, unexpected findings include a negative association of the preoccupation score with performance ratings. This was explained as being contingent on the task, in that some tasks may benefit from a more diligent and reflective state-orientation. Diefendorff et al. (2000: 260) argue that 'differing combinations of the action-state orientation may be optimal for the performance of different types of jobs'.

*Self-regulation theory*

Kanfer and Ackerman (2000) agree that goals represent a critical feature of self-regulation. Goals may also denote 'possible selves' or representations of self in the future (Markus & Nurius, 1987) indicating a potentially inextricable link between self and one's performance aspirations (see **www.sagepub.co.uk/millward** for more on this). Bandura's (1997) theory of self-regulation proposes that the attainment of difficult and specific goals is accomplished through self-regulation activity involving three major components:

- *Self-observation* (self-monitoring) – refers to the direction and quality of focus or attention. Self-monitoring of activities corresponding to one's goal is assumed to be an essential prerequisite for effective self-regulation (for example, Where am I in relation to my goal?).
- *Self-evaluation* – refers to the comparison of one's current behaviour or circumstances with the goal. These produce self-reactions (that is, positive or negative thoughts, feelings and behaviours).
- *Self-reactions* – include affective responses (for example, feelings of satisfaction/disatisfaction) and self-efficacy expectations for future goal attainment. Self-efficacy refers to the beliefs people hold about their ability to accomplish something. The stronger one's perceived self-efficacy, the more likely it is that they will exert effort and persist at the task concerned (Bandura, 1977, 1997). Also, successful past performance predicts future performance success via the impact of the former on self-efficacy beliefs (Vancouver, Thompson, & Williams, 2001; see Chapter 2 for application of self-efficacy concepts to training; see also **www.sagepub.co.uk/millward** for examples).

Self-evaluation involves comparison of the current situation with the goal state (indicating a level of discrepancy), which in turn leads to self-reactions and self-efficacy expectations for future goal attainment. Person and situation factors mediate the impact of self-evaluation on satisfaction and self-efficacy expectations. Kanfer and Ackerman (2000) also find that the pattern of self-reactions that optimize motivation depends on specific features of the situation (for example, novel task, goal difficulty).

### Cybernetic theory

Carver and Scheier's (1998) theory of self-regulation is based upon the notion of a negative (discrepancy-reducing) feedback loop. Comparison between one's standard (or goal) and perceived performance (the products of self-monitoring) results in cognitive and behavioural output directed towards the reduction of discrepancy between the aspired-to goal and perceived current state.

   Carver and Scheier (1998) also specify a process by which various types of goal become salient. Difficulty in execution of a higher-order goal is expected to shift attention towards a lower-order subcomponent of a goal that is yet to be achieved. As sub-goal performance discrepancy is reduced, attention is expected to shift back to the main goal. This qualifier enables the self-regulation model to explain behaviours pertaining to the attainment of long-term goals.

   Bandura (1997) criticizes the 'cybernetic' model of self-regulation as too preoccupied with discrepancy reduction in contexts where individuals seek to rectify inadequate performance. He argues that there are also 'feed forward processes' by which goals are adjusted upward following successful discrepancy reduction. However, Carver and Scheier (1998) do take heed of the importance of self-efficacy expectations and other individual difference factors (for example, need for achievement) as critical moderators of goal acceptance and commitment. They also acknowledge the role played by variations in self-focus (Study Box 4.13).

---

### Study Box 4.13

#### Dispositional influences on self-regulation processes

Carver and Scheier (1998) describe self-focus as a pattern of preference exhibited with respect to the source and subject of one's attention. People high on self-focus are characterized as attending to self-generated sources of information about the self, whilst people low on self-focus seem to attend more to 'outside' sources of information. Individual differences in self-focus are ascertained using the Self-Consciousness Scale developed by Fenigstein, Scheier, and Buss (1975). Carver and Scheier argue that high self-focus promotes activation of self-regulatory processes by increasing the frequency of comparison processes between the current state of affairs and some standard or goal. There is substantial evidence for these propositions. For example, Hollenbeck, Williams and Klein (1987) examined the impact of self-set goals, goal importance, and self-focus on sales volume performance. Those high on self-focus, for whom goals are important, set harder goals (higher outcome expectations) and also attained the highest levels of performance.

Overall, findings strongly indicate the importance of self-referential goals and goal orientation for mobilizing self-regulatory processes.

## Part 2 Summary (II) and Conclusions

- Proximal theories of motivation are mainly focused on the point of action, with accent on the self-regulating function of goals. Goal-setting theory focuses on what types of goal and goal-setting strategy are the most effective in yielding a performance benefit.
- Much on goal setting remains to be investigated in the field, including the concept of goal hierarchies, and the relationship between proximal and distal goals. Goal-setting theory lacks theoretical specification of the cognitive and motivational processes involved in accounting for why and how goal setting yields performance benefits.
- Action theory specifies the cognitive and meta-cognitive processes involved in goal-oriented behaviour. Self-regulation theory looks at the self-referential mechanisms involved in reflecting on and monitoring behaviour, whilst cybernetic theory focuses on the feedback loops involved in self-regulated behaviour as a function of perceived goal discrepancy. Theories have complementary contributions to make to the understanding of motivated behaviour at the point of action.

## Part 2 Reflection: Integrating Distal and Proximal Considerations

What remains unclear is the exact process by which intentions become goals that in turn become invested with motivational power to facilitate cognitive control over action. Processes of transformation of goals into actual actions may depend on dispositional tendencies (for example, upward striving, positive/negative affectivity, procrastination) and the precise circumstances surrounding goal assignments (for example, feasibility of acting on intention). Van Eerde (2000) also notes how procrastination tendencies (defined as the avoidance of implementation of an intention because of its aversive associations) may prevent the translation of intentions into action (for example, fear of failure may induce procrastination). Activated goals with positive (or non-aversive) associations then may provide the motivational force behind self-regulatory activity (Locke, 2001).

There is some indication that 'mood' – a transitory concept – impacts on self-regulatory activity and behavioural persistence (for example, by mediating self-reactions; Kanfer & Ackerman, 2000). It is clearly important not only to examine the cognitive and meta-cognitive processes involved in motivated behaviour, but also hitherto neglected emotional considerations. This may also involve some consideration of the idea that highly focused and engaged people are more effective at managing their own emotions to avoid task distraction (May, Gilson, & Harter, 2004; and see 'Job involvement' later).

In attempting the task of integration of concepts, Kanfer and Ackerman (2000) point out complications due to differences in terminology across domains, and a lack of precision in the articulation and operationalization of some concepts. They rely heavily on an information processing perspective in their attempts to build links across different conceptual domains in motivation research using the concept of 'choice' and 'volition'.

One example of an integrated approach to motivation is exemplified by Locke and Latham's (1990) model of the 'high performance cycle', based on goal-setting theory (see Locke & Latham, 2002 for a review). This model predicts that high goals and high success expectations lead to high performance. High performance, in turn, is expected to produce rewards, satisfaction and commitment. The impact of person (for example, ability, self-efficacy) and situation (for example, task complexity) factors is also built into the model. Goal orientation is also associated with feedback seeking (through perceived 'low' performance level; Tuckey, Brewer, & Williamson, 2002). Recent research reviewed above suggests that, of the person factors, 'core self-evaluations' (locus of control, self-esteem, self-efficacy beliefs and neuroticism) may be key to understanding goal-oriented high-performance behaviour (for example, Judge & Bono, 2001).

More controversially, Doyle (2003: 110) argues that understanding self-concept or identity holds the key to understanding what motivates different people and that we have been asking the wrong question. It is not 'what is the motivator?' but 'what are people motivated to do?'. Thus, pay might motivate people to work in the first instance, but it will not explain what they do or why, once they are there.

## Organizational and Job Investments

### Job involvement

Job involvement is defined in the literature as the extent to which a person psychologically identifies with his or her job, a relatively stable characteristic based on a personal value orientation (Lodahl & Kejner, 1965). It is described by Janssen (2003: 351) as 'the key that unlocks motivation' to exert extra effort. Behaviours indicative of job involvement include working overtime to meet a deadline, and pride in job accomplishment. It is commonly measured using the Job Involvement Scale (Lodahl & Kejner, 1965).

Research shows that job-involved employees derive self-esteem from successful job performance (Thoits, 1992), suggesting that they may be more sensitive to performance information and feedback than those whose esteem is not so closely tied up with their job (Janssen, 2003). Indeed, Frone, Russell and Cooper (1997) found that job-involved employees typically display more signs of distress (alcohol use, health problems) than less involved employees in response to role ambiguity and pressure.

One possible antecedent of job involvement is engagement (Kahn, 1990: 694), defined as the 'harnessing of organizational selves to their work roles; in engagement people employ and express themselves physically, cognitively, and emotionally during role performance'. The self is conceptualized as driving energy into the role and the role is simultaneously an expression of self. Engagement entails the active engagement of emotion in addition to cognitive skills and behaviour in association with the role (see **www.sagepub.co.uk/millward** for measurement details). Several contemporary researchers have found that engagement in meaningful work was linked with a range of positive individual and organizational outcomes (Britt, Adler, & Bartone, 2001; Brown, 1996; Harter, Schmidt, & Hayes, 2002; May, Gilson, & Harter, 2004).

It is commonly suggested that job involvement is little more than a reflection of variation in 'work centrality'. Using meta-analysis, Brown (1996), however, found a strong association between job involvement and both in-role and extra-role (contextual) performance controlling for work centrality and also other individual difference variables. Brown argues that the association between job involvement and performance is sensitive to variation in the criterion and its measurement.

## Organizational Commitment

The commonest way to investigate dedication is via the concept of organizational commitment (OC) defined as 'the relative strength of an individual's identification with, and involvement in, an organization' (Mowday, Steers, & Porter, 1979; Study Box 4.14). Meyer (1997) argues that OC comprises three distinct components: desire to maintain membership, belief in and acceptance of the values and goals of an organization, and willingness to exert effort on behalf of the organization.

Meyer (1997) also distinguished between three different *types* of commitment. *Affective commitment* is the emotional attachment individuals have to their organization. *Continuance commitment* reflects an individual's perception of the costs and risks associated with leaving their current organization, and *normative commitment* denotes a moral dimension based on a person's felt obligation and responsibility to the employing organization. Employees can exhibit varying degrees of all three forms of commitment.

---

**Study Box 4.14**

**The measurement of OC**

The Organizational Commitment Questionnaire (OCQ; Mowday et al., 1979) is a 15-item scale inviting individuals to respond to questions such as, 'I am proud to tell others that I am part of this organization' and, 'This organization really inspires the very best in me in the way of job performance'. Researchers have reported good reliability and validity data for the OCQ across a wide range of different studies (Meyer & Allen, 1997). This scale, and others like it (for example, Warr, Cook & Wall, 1979), focus only on the affective side of commitment. Meyer and Allen (1997) have also developed a scale for assessing continuance commitment (reflecting perceived costs associated with leaving the organization in terms of personal loss, sacrifice and lack of comparable alternatives) and also for assessing normative commitment. Confirmatory factor analysis demonstrated that the three scales tap relatively distinct constructs, thus demonstrating construct validity. It has also been demonstrated that the three scales correlate differently with variables considered to be antecedents of commitment, demonstrating discriminant validity.

Virtually all research on commitment has focused on 'affective' rather than continuance or normative commitment, using the attitude conceptualization (Mathews & Shepherd, 2002). Mathieu and Zajac (1990) found that the strongest correlates (antecedents) of affective organizational commitment were 'job characteristics' (especially 'job enrichment') and group-leader relations (for example, communication, participative leadership, task interdependence). The strongest 'consequences' of commitment were intention to search, intention to leave, and actual turnover (relative to performance, attendance, lateness, and perceived job alternatives). These 'outcomes' were more strongly predicted by affective than calculative (continuance, normative) indicators of commitment. Also, the more committed the employee, the more likely they are to define their job in broader terms, suggesting that commitment has organizational implications over and above job or task performance.

Despite the 'causal' nature of terms (antecedents, consequences) used in association with commitment, most studies comprise cross-sectional self-reports. Bypassing the issue of causality, Meyer (1997: 180) says that findings point, at best, to the place of commitment 'in a nomonological network of work-related variables'. Also, different types of commitment are likely to have different antecedents and consequences (see also Meyer & Allen, 1997).

Some attempt has been made by Blau and colleagues to integrate the concepts of job involvement and commitment. They classified employees into 'lone wolves' (high job involvement, low organizational commitment) and 'corporate citizens' (low job involvement, high organizational commitment). The interaction of the two constructs is said to explain both turnover and absenteeism (for example, Blau & Boal, 1987; but see Huselid & Day, 1991). Other efforts have been to link the concepts of job–person fit (Mathieu & Zajac, 1990), met expectations (for example, Irving & Meyer, 1994), and organizational justice (for example, Sweeney & McFarlin, 1993) with commitment.

Following Reichers' (1985) comment that too often the organization is treated as a monolithic entity, the question of 'commitment to what' has begun to generate interest. Insofar as the organization is comprised of various 'coalitions and constituencies' (1985: 469), the possibility remains of multiple commitments at different levels of analysis (Cohen, 1993; see **www.sagepub.co.uk/millward** for more on this issue). Cohen (1993) suggested that employees are more likely to develop their strongest attachments to subgroups or teams than to the organization itself, since these are more local in their day-to-day meaning and significance (Bishop & Scott, 2000; van Knippenberg & van Schie, 2000). However, Stinglehamber, Bentein, and Vandenberghe (2002) found that only affective organizational commitment (relative to several other meaningful foci of commitment) predicted actual turnover 18 months later, suggesting no reason to negate the validity and usefulness of the global commitment construct (Meyer & Allen, 1997).

There may be some 'dependence' across both focus and form of commitment. It is clear that the relevance of commitment to performance depends on whether there is some discretion involved (Meyer, 1997). However, there may be a downside to commitment (that is, insufficient turnover, resistance to change, inability to think creatively; see **www.sagepub.co.uk/millward** for a discussion). Commitment is said to be more context independent than job satisfaction, and as such less readily influenced by daily circumstances or events (for example, interpersonal conflict, job-related problems).

Interest has also extended to the association between occupational and organizational commitment. In a meta-analysis comprising 76 samples, Lee, Carswell, and Allen (2000) found that *occupational* commitment was positively associated with *organizational* commitment and, also, job involvement and satisfaction, performance and turnover intentions (through occupational turnover intentions). Of particular interest is the finding that the association between occupational and organizational commitment was moderated by the *compatibility of the occupation and the organization*. These findings suggest that occupational commitment figures as much as organizational commitment in job attitudes and behaviours.

One of the impediments to progress in the field of commitment research is the lack of theory to guide formulation of hypotheses about what predicts commitment, why and how (Meyer, 1997; Study Box 4.15). Meyer and Allen (1997) noted that work experiences such as organizational rewards, procedural justice and supervisor support have demonstrated stronger associations with affective commitment than have structural features of the organization or the personal characteristics of the employee. However, the mechanisms underlying these proposed relationships are unknown.

---

**Study Box 4.15**

**Theories of OC**

***Perceived organizational support theory (POS) (Eisenberger, Huntington, Hutchison, & Sowa, 1986).***

If commitment is understood to be part of a social exchange process, employees can be expected to become more committed to their employing organization if they perceive that the organization values their contributions and cares about their well-being (for example, Eisenberg et al., 1986). When deciding how much an organization values them, employees also judge whether the organization has high discretionary control over this. Employees who perceive themselves to be thus supported are, in turn, more likely to feel obligated to respond in a favourable manner. Several studies have confirmed that POS is a core mediator of employees' affective commitment and intention to leave (for example, Rhoades & Eisenberger, 2002). Armeli, Eisenberger, Fasolo and Lynch (1998) also found that 'need fulfilment' (that is, socio-emotional needs) may in part mediate the relationship between POS and employee contributions. Eisenberger et al. (1986) argued that POS is developed via the same attribution processes that people use generally to infer commitment by others in social relationships – that is, from 'local' support. Consistent with this are findings demonstrating that a strong association between POS is indeed shown to be associated with high quality leader–member exchanges (LMX; Settoon, Bennett, & Liden, 1996), and that employees view the actions by agents of the organization as actions of the organization itself (Rousseau, 1995).

*(Continued)*

> **Study Box 4.15    Continued**
>
> *Interaction and attachment processes*
>
> It could be argued that commitment denotes a particular type of individual–organizational relationship (O'Reilly & Chatman, 1986). As in all relationships, an affective bond evolves between the individual and organization through everyday *interaction* (Bartholomew & Perlman, 1994). Thus, understanding with whom and how one interacts with the organization on a day-to-day basis may be a first step to identifying the proximal and/or psychologically salient factors underpinning the why and how an employee becomes 'committed' to an organization and its interests. However, bonds can also be forged simply through a process of social categorization and identification (Haslam, 2004; see below).

## Part 2 Summary (III) and Conclusions

- Organizational commitment is used mainly to denote an affective investment in an organization, but there are other types of commitment describing investment of an instrumental and normative kind.
- Affective commitment is a strong predictor of many different organization-relevant outcomes including satisfaction, willingness to go the extra mile, turnover intentions and other performance indicators. Findings suggest that commitment is mainly itself predicted by organizational factors, especially local factors (for example, leader–member relations) rather than personal factors.
- Recently, interest in the fact that commitment can have other work-relevant foci has emerged, including occupational, team/group and potentially also supervisor and customers/clients. Each foci of commitment may have different antecedents and consequences.
- Some recent attempts to look at the theoretical mechanisms involved in the commitment process include perceived organizational support theory.

## Psychological Contracts

The assumption of reciprocity between two parties to an exchange relationship is core to organizational support theory (Eisenberger, Armeli, Rexwinkel, Lynch & Rhoades, 2001) and is also integral to the notion of a psychological contract (Argyris, 1962; Aselage & Eisenberger, 2003; Levinson, Price, Munden, Mandl & Solley, 1962; Rousseau, 1995; Herriot, 2004).

Since Rousseau's (1989) seminal work, the term 'psychological contract' has become pivotal to our understanding of the exchange relationship between employees and employers. The term 'psychological contract' is now variously used as a metaphor for describing the contemporary employment relationship (Makin, Cooper, & Cox, 1996), an explanatory construct (Rousseau, 2001) and as an analytic framework for investigating and managing the employment relationship (Coyle-Shapiro & Kessler, 2000; Millward & Herriot, 2000).

The dominant use of the term, however, is in the form of a construct denoting 'an individual's beliefs regarding the terms and conditions of a reciprocal exchange agreement between the focal person and another person' (Rousseau, 2001: 512). Notwithstanding the debates surrounding the conceptualization and measurement of psychological contract (see **www.sagepub.co.uk/millward** for discussion), here it is used to describe three different aspects of the employment relationship: form, content and process (Millward & Cropley, 2003).

Whilst, as Rousseau (1995: 91) points out, contracts can 'take an infinite number of forms', certain aspects 'tend to cluster together'. At the most general level, the *form* of an exchange relationship can be classified as transactional or relational, describing the way an employee interfaces with the employing organization (for example, explicitly and narrowly defined or open-ended and diffuse). The *content* of exchange (deriving from both organizational and personal factors) refers, on the other hand, to 'an individual's beliefs regarding the terms and conditions of a reciprocal exchange agreement between the focal person and another person' (Rousseau & Schalk, 2000: 1). The issue of contract *content* is a matter on which there is little agreement.

It is conventional to examine content through perceived employee and employer obligations with particular obligations associated with particular forms of psychological contract (see Rousseau & Tijoriwala, 1998 for a review). However, different groups of employees engaged in otherwise identical jobs (for example, contractors and core employees, teleworkers and office-based employees) can be party to similar forms of psychological contract (for example, relational or relationship-based) comprising very different contents (for example, Millward & Brewerton, 2000). Moreover, defined in this way, transactional-type relationships need not preclude loyalty (Herriot & Pemberton, 1997).

Transactional relationships denote a strictly defined exchange of goods (that is, one good is exchanged for another), indicating less about the actual content of the exchange (such as preoccupation with pay and benefits) and more about what is valued by the employee (that is, fair exchange of goods). Likewise, the relational contract is about valuing the relationship per se (that is, reciprocity) rather than the particular terms and conditions comprising it (Study Box 4.16).

---

### Study Box 4.16

#### Form and content in psychological contracts

The distinction between form and content affords the possibility that the terms of exchange can change without jeopardizing the form of the relationship. The adjustment of terms (from, say, the exchange of promotion prospects for employee commitment to the exchange of personal development opportunity for job transferability), need have no real impact on the fundamentally relational form of the relationship. Minor breaches perceived in the fulfilment of obligations (for example, during organizational change) might also prompt adjustments in content but not necessarily in

*(Continued)*

---

**Study Box 4.16   Continued**

the form of the contract (for example, Robinson, 1995, 1996). Conway and Briner (2002) found that perceived breaches are common, and occur in association with virtually all aspects of work. This is not to say that a change in content cannot trigger a change in form. Conway and Briner (2002) reported some strong emotional reactions to perceived contract breach, all potentially with longer-term implications for the quality of the employment relationship. This work links the topic of violation with the concept of perceived procedural justice (Korsgaard, Sapienza, & Schweiger, 2002; see Chapter 5).

Clearly, issues of form and content are likely to be inextricably linked, with some exchange terms being indisputably transactional (for example, payment terms) rather than relational. Coyle-Shapiro and Kessler (2000: 906) rather that transactional elements are more likely to pertain to normative or common aspects of an employment relationship like pay and benefits. Relational considerations are, on the other hand, potentially more variable and unique to individuals. In principle, however, a psychological contract may have 'literally thousands of items in it' (Kotter, 1973: 92), implying that it is probably fruitless to attempt to identify and capture the content of psychological contracts in any definitive way (Turnley & Feldman, 2000).

Contract form is more likely to be contingent on how contracts are evolved and managed (involving equity and justice considerations) than contract content (Herriot, Hirsh, & Reilly, 1998). Thus, a change in form resulting in a major withdrawal of investment may arise from a serious violation of trust. By contrast, changes in contract content managed within (and for the maintenance of) a framework of trust need not alter an individual stake in the relationship (Guest, 1998).

---

The product of the contractual process is captured in both the form and content of the current relationship between employer and employee *as perceived by the individual* (Rousseau, 1995). Contract perceptions (irrespective of whether perceptions are mutual) predict employee behaviour, including effort and contribution, frequency of absence and intention to stay or leave (Rousseau & Schalk, 2000).

More research is clearly needed on how 'content' and 'form' interrelate. Rousseau (1995) notes that the content of psychological contracts can be heavily driven by organizational factors, evolving out of common experiences and interpretations of what is on offer as much as what is wanted or desired. For example, the longer the tenure of an employee, the more likely it is his or her 'wants' are likely to be shaped by, and thus are inextricably bound up normatively with, what is 'on offer' (for example, Schneider, Kristof-Brown, Goldstein, & Smith, 1997; Study Box 4.17).

---

**Study Box 4.17**

**Entry expectations**

Many employees today may not be entirely sure what they want from their employing organization until they see what is on offer (Herriot, 1989) and/or experience

**Study Box 4.17    Continued**

breach or violation of otherwise unspoken exchange terms (Robinson, 1996). In the words of Guzzo, Noonan and Elron (1994: 618), 'Just as organizations cannot plan for all types of employee contributions, to the … exchange, individuals cannot form expectations in advance about all the things an employer might contribute.' Thomson and Anderson (1998) confirm that newcomers enter with only rudimentary notions of the exchange relationship they will and/or would like to form with an organization. Within the space of only eight weeks, employees' understandings of their contractual terms and conditions can change in line with organizational reality. Taking a sense-making perspective, De Vos, Buyens, and Schalk (2003) found that changes in newcomers' perceptions of employer promises are affected by their perceptions of the employer inducements they have received.

Finally, the process of exchange pertains to (1) the intra-individual, cognitive and emotional processes involved in contract formation and change (for example, Rousseau, 2001; Conway & Briner, 2002); and (2) the inter-party interplay of wants and offers on the part of both the employee and the organization (Herriot & Pemberton, 1997). The former has been extensively studied in the context of contract breaches and violations (Turnley & Feldman, 2000), but the latter has not (Herriot, Hirsh, & Reilly, 1998), though relevant research has begun to emerge (for example, Dabos & Rousseau, 2004; Millward & Cropley, 2003; Tekleab & Taylor, 2003). The mutuality element of an exchange relationship is arguably critical to the achievement of interdependent individual and organizational goals (Rousseau, 1995). Each of the two sets of process considerations will now be considered in turn with reference to contemporary examples:

- *Intra-individual processes* – Coyle-Shapiro and Nuenan (2004) have shown that a creditor ideology (morally indebted to) was associated with positive perceptions of mutual obligations and their fulfilment, whilst an exchange ideology (quid pro quo) is associated with negative perceptions of their obligations vis-à-vis the employers' obligations. Other important individual process considerations include perceived trust (Chrobot-Mason, 2003), perceived equity and justice (Herriot, Hirsh, & Reilly, 1998), and cultural values (Thomas, Au, & Ravlin, 2003). Taking a more dynamic micro-analytic approach to studying psychological contract processes, Conway and Briner (2002) used diaries to track cognitive and emotional reactions over time in response to contract breach.
- *Inter-party exchange processes* – The process of contracting requires negotiation of wants and offers, and as such cannot be taken for granted. A true psychological contract cannot be imposed: what is wanted from an employment relationship offers a basis for psychological contract fulfilment, and cannot be assumed (Herriot, 2001). Focusing predominantly on the employee-owned aspect of psychological contracts has meant that questions about the other party and about the reciprocal processes involved in contract making have been assumed to be either irrelevant or non-problematic (Herriot, 2001). However, such questions concern the very essence of what is meant by a psychological contract.

One of the problems associated with investigating processes of exchange (and the interplay of wants and offers) is that it may not always be clear *who* is the employer. Coyle-Shapiro and Kessler (2000, 2002) looked at between group perceptions of workers and their managers of perceived obligations as a means of examining mutuality within the exchange relationship. Others have also begun to compare manager (as employer representatives or organizational agents) and employee perceptions of mutual obligations and violations. For example, Tekleab and Taylor (2003) found that a positive leader–member exchange (LMX) was positively related to agreement of perceptions on employee obligations. The perceptions of both managers and employees uniquely contributed to an explanation of employee outcomes, underscoring the importance of considering both sides of the exchange relationship.

Dabos and Rousseau (2004) examined the exchange relationship per se by examining perceptions of mutuality and reciprocity in the context of 80 actual employee–employer relationships in a research centre. They found that the greater the level of mutuality and reciprocity perceived between them, the greater the unit productivity, career advancement, perceptions of met expectation, and intention to stay. Dabos and Rousseau (2004) argued that mutuality was more than a matter of perception; it was a matter of fact. Outstanding issues include looking at the association between mutuality of understanding and reciprocity (which involves exchanges over time), whether there is a time limit on whether reciprocity occurs, beyond which a reciprocal act may be considered 'too little too late' (see also Millward & Cropley, 2003 and Chapter 1 for details of other studies on contracting processes).

There are many outstanding issues in connection with psychological contracts, most of which arise from questions about appropriate conceptualization and measurement (Rousseau, 2001). One continuing debate is whether the term psychological contract pertains to 'old wine in new bottles' – that is, commitment by another name (Millward & Brewerton, 2001). Here, organizational commitment is understood to be 'exchange material' (that is, content; for example, Rousseau, 2001).

## Part 2 Summary (IV) and Conclusions

- A psychological contract refers to the mutual obligations perceived by the employee to bind him or her with the organization, obligations that comprise a promissory element. Psychological contracts have important implications for employee attitudes and behaviours, especially if promises (explicitly or implicitly) made by an employer are deemed by the employee to have been unfulfilled.
- Psychological contracts can be described in terms of form (relational, transactional), content (mutual obligations) and process (cognitive processes of formation, interpersonal processes of formation).
- Researchers are beginning to look more closely at processes of contracting and the impact of various mediators (for example, perceived justice, perceived trust) and moderators (for example, individual differences in exchange ideology) on these. Little work has been undertaken on the inter-party aspects of contracting, but some important research is emerging on the obligations (and violations) perceived by both managers and employees within the same organization, and on also on the dynamics of exchange between two parties using the concepts of mutuality and reciprocity.

# Organizational Identity and Image

Another construct inextricably linked with questions about the employment relationship is organizational identification (OID). The impact of OID on the well-being of the organization and its members has long been recognized (O'Reilly & Chatman, 1986). Recently, however, the question of 'who am I' in connection with organizations has recently been cast 'centre stage' (Brown, 2001: 113).

Harnessing social identity theory (Study Box 4.18), Ashforth and Mael (1989) defined OID as the perception of oneness with, or belonging to, an organization, where the individual defines him- or herself in terms of the organization(s). This cognitive-perceptual conceptualization of OID differentiates it from the term 'commitment' as an affective investment in the organization (Mowday, Steers, & Porter, 1979).

---

### Study Box 4.18

#### Social identity theory

Social identity theory maintains that individuals identify with social categories as a means of enhancing self-esteem (Tajfel, 1978). Through comparison, individuals can vicariously partake in the accomplishments of the group. Members may even engage in activities with detrimental personal consequences for the sake of a larger group cause or interest. The need for positive self-esteem is not, however, the only mechanism driving the identification process. The desire for distinctiveness of the group's values and practices in relation to those of comparable groups (Abrams & Hogg, 1988) provides another motive. In addition, Breakwell (1986) has suggested that the need for continuity across time and situation is important.

---

The intensity of one's *felt identification* with an organizational classification is a matter of degree. One consequence of OID is increased contact and submersion in organizational activities and practices (for example, Haslam, 2004; van Knippenberg, 2000). Moreover, strong OID keeps members attuned to the future viability of the organization insofar as their sense of survival is tied to the organization. A perception that one's fate is interdependent with that of the organization facilitates co-operative behaviour towards other organizational members because of heightened in-group (organizational) trust and reciprocity, social attraction towards in-group members, and presentation of a favourable image of the organization to self and others. Also, individuals tend to choose activities congruent with salient aspects of their identities, and thus support the organizations that embody those activities (Whetten & Godfrey, 1998).

In short, it is generally agreed that OID is positively related to work motivation (task and contextual performance) to the extent that identity is salient and high performance is perceived to be in the interest of the organization (Haslam, 2004; van Knippenberg, 2000).

Research has consistently shown how various organizational artefacts (for example, corporate architecture, dress code, advertisement, branding) may provide a valuable source of implicit information about an organization used by employees and potential employees in the formation of their identities (Dutton, Dukerich, & Harquail, 1994). By actively managing its corporate reputation and identity, an organization can promote employee identification (as well as client identification with a brand or service) and hence the likelihood of pro-organizational behaviour (Dowling, 2001; Fombrun & Rindova, 2000).

Most research has focused exclusively on identification with the organization as a whole. However, there are potentially many other foci of work-related identification, especially workgroup or team (Bishop & Scott, 2000). A key question for future research, as Haslam (2004: 49) puts it, is, 'when will an employee ... see and act in terms of the organization as a whole, or in terms of the department or team to which they belong, or as an individual?' The *particular* level at which employees define themselves has distinctive implications both for their own behaviour and for the functioning of the organization as a whole (Haslam, 2004; Van Knippenberg & Van Schie, 2000).

Researchers have also noted a heightened salience of various organization-independent identities, both social categorical (for example, professional, occupational) and personal (for example, career) (for example, Sparrow, 2000).

## Part 2 Summary (V) and Conclusions

- Organizational identity denotes the cognitive-perceptual alignment of the individual with the organization and its interests. People depend on their social identities, of which organizational identity is one, for self-esteem.
- Perceived organizational image can impact on how employees connect with their organization.
- Organizational identity predicts thoughts, feelings and behaviours consistent with organizational values and goals, including commitment.
- Identity in organizational contexts can have other foci, including team and group foci. Different foci of identity have different implications for attitudes and behaviours.

# Part 3: The Motivated Group

Until the 1990s, organizations made little systematic use of workgroups (Sundstrom, McIntyre, Halfhill, & Richards, 2000). Various writers like Likert (1967) and McGregor (1964) began to call for more worker participation in the work process via workgroup, the assumption being that performance can be enhanced by giving responsibility back to the worker (see also Emery & Trist, 1969). A supportive workgroup was also said to provide an important source of satisfaction and well-being (affiliation, identity, self-esteem, testing social reality, security, mutual support).

However, through both the 1960s and 1970s, workgroups were used only in an occasional experimental way (for example, General Motors). In the 1980s, workgroups were used more often, in the form of 'quality circles' (Sundstrum et al., 2000) and project teams in large manufacturing companies such as Ford, Motorola, and Boeing. Generally, though, the use of workgroups went out of favour in the 1980s, and many 'show case' uses (for example, the Volvo plant in Kalkar) were also disbanded (Frese, 1998). Frese (1998) explains this decline in use with reference to authoritarian management tendencies, anti-autonomous work attitudes in the trade unions, and technological advances affording other equally productive work design options. By the 1990s, however, a revival in the use of workgroups was witnessed across the USA and Europe, though in many different guises (for example, production groups, service groups, management teams, project groups; see **www.sagepub.co.uk/millward** for details).

Most of the early research on workgroups was conducted by social psychologists in the laboratory (McGrath, 1984). However, there are some notable exceptions of some seminal field work conducted by industrial psychologists (for example, Trist & Bamforth, 1951; see **www.sagepub.co.uk/millward** for details).

Sundstrum et al. (2000) reviewed 90 (selected) field studies and experiments involving 4890 groups and more than 37,000 employees, published since the 1980s, to ascertain the identifying features of workgroups, research strategies and questions, criterion of work effectiveness and predictors of effectiveness (**www.sagepub.co.uk/millward** for details). However, they were unable to synthesize the results because of the highly contextual nature of the findings: different factors predicted effectiveness across different criteria across different types of workgroup. Moreover, the concept of workgroup was used to describe both groups and teams. The importance of perceptions of collective efficacy and autonomy did nonetheless stand out as consistent predictors of effectiveness (see below).

One of the problems in making sense of research on groups is that there is no real theory in the area. A team is arguably very different from a group, whose members are not strictly interdependent on each other for achieving the group goal. Various researchers have attempted to model group performance at work in terms of *contributory factors*, as well as the *process* via which groups may become effective. One of the most commonly known of these is Hackman and Morris's (1975) model (see **www.sagepub.co.uk/millward** for details).

Hackman and Morris (1975) propose that members of an effective group must: (1) invest *effort* in the task and *co-ordinate* their efforts; (2) use the *knowledge and skill* of its members in an optimal manner; and (3) employ *task performance strategies* appropriate to the task. Various input variables influence the *interaction process* of a group. Despite the intuitive appeal of input–output models of group performance, their explanatory value is limited.

Evidence also suggests that despite the potential benefits of working in a group for enhancing satisfaction and motivation, 'too many cooks can spoil the broth'. Steiner (1972) argued that this may be due to process loss. Process gains could include an energizing effect deriving from the presence of other group members, increased knowledge, ability and effort, diversity of views and group pressure to conform to norms (see Study Box 4.18). However, each of these possible process gains can also serve as a source of process loss (Study Box 4.19).

> ### Study Box 4.19
>
> ### Sources of process loss
>
> #### *In-group bias and inter-group discrimination*
>
> One of the consequences of self-categorization and identity (Study Box 4.18) is that individuals will favour their group *(in-group)* over other groups to which they do not belong *(out-groups)*, to the extent of out-group prejudice, inter-group conflict and hostility. Even nurses, for whom cooperation is an important part of caring practices, show evidence of in-group bias and inter-group conflict across status differentials (Brown,1988).
>
> #### *Conformity*
>
> Asch (1952) showed very clearly the power of groups to influence individual thinking, feeling and behaviour. Symptoms of conformity can include distortions of perception, judgement and action.
>
> #### *Groupthink*
>
> Janis (1972) analysed American foreign policy decisions made between 1940 and 1970 (for example, the decision to invade Cuba) and identified why they turned out badly for decision makers (American interests were damaged) using the concept of groupthink. Groupthink is marked by five features: the group is very cohesive, typically insulated from information outside the group, decision makers rarely search systematically through alternative policy options to appraise their relative merits, the group is often under some pressure to reach a decision urgently and is nearly always dominated by a very directive leader (see Griffiths & Luker, 1994 and **www. sagepub.co.uk/millward** for a health care example of groupthink). The role of the leader is decisive in whether groupthink is likely or otherwise (that is, encouraging total participation; Brown, 1988).

## Part 3 Summary (I) and Conclusions

- Workgroups have been the focus of mostly social psychological investigation in the laboratory, though a few seminal examples of intensive field study do exist. One of the difficulties in drawing conclusions about the nature and effectiveness of workgroups is that they are often studied as teams, when in some instances there is no objective or perceived interdependence between members.
- A group is said to exist if it is perceived to be as such and can be verified as such by at least one other. A workgroup may be perceived as such for many different functional reasons, including physical proximity and the sheer fact of reporting to the same manager or supervisor.
- It was not popular to organize work using groups (or teams) until the 1980s, despite recognition of their benefits to both the individual and the organization in the 1950s and 1960s.

- A recent review of relevant field work (of both workgroups and teams) identified autonomy and collective efficacy to be important generic predictors of effectiveness. Recent studies confirm the benefits of autonomy to satisfaction and well-being, but not always for performance.
- Models of group performance are limited to basic 'input, process, output' diagrams, comprising lists of important factors rather than testable explanatory propositions. The problem of 'process loss' refers to instances where the group performs worse than expected given its composite qualities, explanations for which include groupthink, social loafing, and conformity, with reference to social identity/self-categorization theory.

## Workplace Teams

A team can be defined as 'a distinguishable set of two or more people who interact dynamically, interdependently, and adaptively towards a common and valued goal/objective/mission and who each have specific roles or functions to perform' (Tannenbaum, Beard, & Salas, 1992: 118). That is, some form of task dependency exists, some coordination is required, and some structure exists within which this coordination is made possible. Thus, one of the defining features of work *teams* as opposed to workgroups is that of *shared goals*. Teams often comprise members of different disciplines or professional groups, thereby adding some complexity to our consideration of the group dynamics surrounding teamwork. Nonetheless, research on group processes can offer understandings about teams, in particular about the kinds of things that can undermine performance in team contexts (Brown, 1988).

The shift to teamwork in recent years assumes that teams have greater production potential than the sum of their individual parts arising from what has been termed a 'synergy bonus'. Some like Sinclair (1992) have questioned the logic of this, given the absence of any clear-cut evidence for the superiority of 'teamwork' over other ways of organizing work. Sinclair (1992) worries that 'the prescriptions of much contemporary management thinking are based on a dominant ideology of teamwork ... supported by researchers who offer the "team" as a tantalizingly simple solution to some of the intractable problems of organizational life'.

There are many 'implicit theories' of the effective versus ineffective team (for example, cooperative, friendly and open climate of communication, task oriented), but little hard evidence. Teambuilding intervention rests on the assumptions of the team as a singular concrete entity characterized by stability, regular interaction, symbiosis and team member proximity. However, a team is arguably a 'psychological' entity expressed through perception and awareness of membership as much as a physical entity (Brown, 1988). In the words of Moreland and Levine (1993), the extent to which a team is socially integrated depends on the extent to which they think, feel and act like a team rather than a mere collection of individuals.

In team contexts, cause-and-effect relationships (for example, between teamwork processes and performance outcomes) have proved difficult to establish. Various models of the successful team have nonetheless been proposed, most pragmatic and purely taxonomic (for example, Buller, 1988). Also, the literature assumes that team process is directly related to team effectiveness. Gladstein (1984), however, found a connection between team process and team effectiveness only when self-report measures are used. When independent measures of team process are used, coupled with objective measures of performance, no relationship between process and outcome was found.

An alternative route to understanding team effectiveness is to ask more fundamental questions about what 'causes' team effectiveness (what the necessary and sufficient factors are), rather than focusing on how it is 'indicated' (that is, process), since different processes may be appropriate in different types of team and team situation. Varney (1989: 7–8), for example, argues that 'successful teams' can be characterized as follows:

- Team roles are clear to each and everyone in the team, individuals are committed to their jobs and accept and support the roles of others.
- Individuals have agreed goals.
- Structure, practices, policies, and systems are understood and agreed to by all members.
- Working relations are seen as an essential part of an effective team; therefore, they are discussed and interpersonal problems are solved and not left to fester.
- The members of the team develop high levels of satisfaction and commitment and they are energized to accomplish the things that need to be done.
- The abilities, skills, talents, and resources of team members are fully harnessed.

Concrete indicators of these success factors include: open communication, few mistakes, low levels of conflict, higher levels of job satisfaction, co-operation, taking responsibility, and few complaints. The critical success factors ('causes') will ensure effective teamwork process ('indicators') that will, in turn, increase the productivity of the team ('results'). Results include the ability of the team to capitalize on opportunity, the meeting of deadlines, decreased costs, effective use of time, innovative and effective problem solving (see Study Box 4.20).

Varney's model is attractive for several reasons:

- It provides a 'standardized' model of team effectiveness that applies irrespective of variations in context (type of team, team task, organizational structure and culture).
- It attributes the causes of team success to the cognition, affect, and self-regulatory abilities of team members – all factors that are within team control.
- It advocates that 'indicators of team effectiveness' are measured independently of 'team results'.
- The model is easily implemented, and as such can be used to frame and focus the team building (TB) intervention effort (for example, focused on the 'causes' of team effectiveness as opposed to 'indicators').

Varney (1989) argues that an effective and productive team does not happen by accident, but requires attention, in particular, to the development of team management skills, a commitment to continuous learning and the development of awareness that teams are dynamic entities. This moves the analysis away from issues of behavioural processes to issues of *cognition and affect* as the root of team effectiveness (Millward & Jeffries, 2001).

Team process can manifest in several ways depending on the task, task structure, team composition and characteristics and such like (Katzenbach & Smith, 1993). Thus, an effective team is essentially a self-managed one with the ability to monitor the situation, diagnose requirement and to act accordingly (Hockey, 2000). Ilgen and Sheppard (2001) describe and provide evidence for a team learning model of effectiveness consistent with the idea of a constantly regenerating and self-organizing team learning about itself, from its successes and mistakes.

---

### Study Box 4.20

#### Shared goals

A major problem with multi-disciplinary teamwork is that certain members may feel that their professional distinctiveness is under threat (Castledine, 1996). This increases the attempts of members to tighten up their professional boundaries, thus creating inter-professional rivalry and competition and problems with cross-disciplinary communication and interaction (Brown, 1988). Divisions of age, sex and ethnic background can have the same effect within teams as professional or disciplinary distinctions (Brown, 1988). In short, differences within teams can reduce the salience and meaning of the team as a whole. Individuals may cling on to familiar identities that service their self-esteem and provide them with meaning.

In their study of nurses, Oaker and Brown (1986, cited in Brown, 1988) found that increasing the clarity, salience and meaning of super-ordinate goals can promote effective teamwork. They argued that, far from requiring a dilution of professional identities within the team, effective teamwork directed towards shared goals depends on each contributing member *retaining their professional distinctiveness*. This means that distinctive professional contributions are recognized and constructively used in the achievement of super-ordinate goals. This requires that the goals are clearly defined and accepted by team members, that they are committed to their achievement, and that the distinctive contributions of team members are 'rewarded'.

---

Millward and Purvis (1998) argue that the intelligent or 'smart' team engineers its own processes to suit requirement. It is goal directed (that is, oriented to the achievement of common goals); able to reflect on and strategically manage its own interpersonal and task processes; able to diagnose the 'process requirements' of a situation and to respond accordingly; able to learn from its experience (that is, 'capturing learning'), maximizing learning opportunity (Argote, 1993); able to harness and to optimize all of its resources as necessary, including 'experience'; able to reconcile individual with organizational and team goals and provide opportunity for personal development (Locke & Latham, 1990); aware of its strengths and its weaknesses (maximizing strengths and overcoming or minimizing weaknesses) and of the need for diversity and openness to outside influence as a prerequisite to flexibility and innovative capacity (Conway & Forrestor, 1997); recognizes and rewards the specific contributions/roles of all its members and is confident in its self-regulatory ability and success (that is, has a collective belief that it can be effective) (Guzzo, Yost, Campbell, & Shea, 1993). Pearce, Gallagher and Ensley (2002) report a strong relationship between team potency and team effectiveness in a longitudinal field study.

The key operational principle is that the team as a self-organizing entity reflects on itself *causally* as well as in terms of its processes. Issues of context and how they are handled are ultimately within the responsibility of the self-organizing team, which in principle has the ability to reflect on itself and to adjust to whatever task or task situation is encountered (Study Box 4.21). In instances of a virtual organization or team, where membership is distributed cross-functionally and is also geographically widely dispersed, organizational focus and orientation may be completely absent (because of low proximity and contact) and will need to be actively engineered and managed by the leader (Millward & Kyriakidou, 2004b).

---

### Study Box 4.21

#### Team role theory

Belbin (1981) found that the most successful (that is, productive) groups were the ones comprising a *mix* of individuals, each contributing to the group in a different way (that is, eight different team roles). The Belbin Team Role Inventory (BTRI) profiles eight (and more recently nine) different roles: chairman, company worker, shaper, resource investigator, plant, monitor-evaluator, teamworker, completer-finisher, specialist. Each person will take on a preferred role or set of roles in a group context. Whilst there is no evidence for the overall model as a predictor of team effectiveness, Makin, Cooper and Cox (1996) argue that there are two main practical uses: acknowledging differences in role preferences, and identifying which roles are missing, especially in a group that is not performing as well as it should (for example, missing completer-finisher). Whilst the BTRI remains one of the most widely used group assessment techniques, its lack of reliability and validity has been criticized (Belbin, 1993; Furnham, Steele, & Pendleton, 1993a, 1993b). However, recent research conducted on a wide range of occupational samples (5003) provides strong support for the validity of all except two (completer-finisher, implementer) of the proposed nine roles, although they suggest that the item wording for at least one other role (shaper) would benefit from some attention (Swailes & McIntyre-Bhatty, 2003).

---

## Part 3 Summary (II) and Conclusions

- Teams are defined by their interdependence. Teams presuppose a group, but pertain to a distinctive dynamic marked by the fact of a shared goal.
- To operate effectively as a team, it is assumed that members must perceive themselves to be a team (that is, interdependent, shared goal and identity) and be able to size up a situation and regulate itself accordingly. This analysis focuses attention on the cognitive-motivational causes of teamwork (in the generative sense) and thus away from description and prediction, towards explanation.

# Part 4: Leadership

There is no agreed-upon framework driving leadership research (Shackleton & Wale, 2000), its multi-disciplinary character making the task of conceptual and empirical synthesis difficult. Terms like 'supervisor', 'manager', and 'leader' are often used interchangeably. Moreover, common currency of the term leader has populated the literature with 'ideal types' and prescriptions for good practice rather than rigorous analysis. In distinguishing between a manager and a leader, Kotter (1990) argues that management is more about bringing order and consistency to the organization (path following), whilst leadership is about engineering constructive and adaptive change (doing the right things). In practice, however, leaders may also be managers and vice versa (see **www.sagepub.co.uk/millward** for a discussion of leadership concepts in the context of the National Health Service).

Bryman (1996) notes, however, that most researchers would not argue with a definition of leadership 'as the process (act) of influencing the activities of an organized group in its efforts towards goal setting and goal achievement' (Stogdill, 1950: 3). The influence process is inextricably linked with groups and the group process. In the early stages of leadership research, the ability to 'lead' was attributed to distinctive traits (so-called 'great man' theory). However, a comprehensive and landmark review by Stogdill (1948) concluded that there was no evidence for this claim, and research took another turn. In particular, the focus shifted towards understanding how exactly leaders behave, and to linking different group processes with different *styles of behaviour.*

## Leadership Style

There are many different models of leadership style, but common to all is the assumption that leadership behaviour can be described in two main ways: *task-oriented* and *relationship-oriented.* The task style is oriented to managing task accomplishment (where the leader defines clearly and closely what subordinates should be doing and how, and actively schedules work for them), whilst the relationship style is oriented to managing the interpersonal relations of group members (by demonstrating concern about subordinates as people, responsiveness to subordinate needs and the promotion of team spirit and cohesion).

Other terms have been used to differentiate between these two distinct sets of orientation, including 'initiating structure' versus 'consideration' (Fleishman, 1953), 'production-oriented' versus 'people-oriented' (Blake & Mouton, 1964), 'production-centred' versus 'employee-centred' (Likert, 1967), 'task emphasis' versus 'relations emphasis' (Fiedler, 1967) and 'performance concern' versus 'maintenance concern' (Misumi, 1985).

The 'initiating structure/consideration' distinction has had a major impact on leadership theory and research since the 1950s. It forms the basis of many leadership measures, for instance the Supervisory Behaviour Description Questionnaire (Fleishman, 1953), the Leadership Opinion Questionnaire (Fleishman, 1953) – a vehicle for asking subordinates how they think their leader should behave as a supervisor – and the Leader Behaviour Description Questionnaire (LBDQ); (Fleishman, 1953), probably the most frequently employed measure of leadership. The two subscales 'consideration' and 'initiating structure' produce moderate to high reliabilities (between 0.68 and 0.90) and have been reproduced in confirmatory factor analyses of subscale scores (Cook, Hepworth, Wall, & Warr, 1981: 229–231).

Bales (1950) claimed that the same person could not occupy both a task and relationship orientation simultaneously. A similar assumption is made by Fiedler (1967) in his concept of the least preferred co-worker (LPC) (Study Box 4.22). Most agree, however, that it is more reasonable to see task and relationship orientations as independent leadership dimensions (Bass, 1990; Stogdill, 1974). Evidence also suggests that leaders can change their style to suit situational demands (for example, Barrow, 1976).

---

### Study Box 4.22

#### The least preferred co-worker

Fiedler (1967) argues that LPC is a reflection of a fixed trait indicative of the relative importance attached by individuals to person and task aspects of group functioning. Those who evaluate their least preferred co-worker favourably (high LPC) habitually adopt a relationship-motivated leadership style, while low LPC leaders are more task motivated. The concept of LPC has been criticized on many grounds. Attempts to demonstrate the empirical correspondence of LPC with the concepts of consideration and initiating structure have yielded equivocal results. Ambiguity surrounding the meaning of LPC has led to varied interpretations and uses of the concept. Graham (1986) refers to LPC as a behavioural disposition reflecting the degree to which leaders are responsive to task-related feedback, whilst Larson and Rowland (1973) treat it as an expression of a need hierarchy or motivational structure. A more popular view is that LPC is an indicator of cognitive complexity (Chemers, Rice, Sundstrom, & Butler, 1975): the high LPC leader is more cognitively complex than the low LPC leader.

---

Whether a leader is task or relationship oriented refers to the *focus* of his or her influence. Another way of describing leadership style concerns the *nature* of a leader's influence (autocratic, democratic; Bass, 1990; Northouse, 2001). Autocratic describes leaders who seek sole possession of authority, power and control, whilst democratic describes leaders who share authority, power and control, with their followers. In a now classic study, Lewin and Lippitt (1938) found that differences in the nature of leadership had a fundamental impact on group morale and effectiveness. The autocratic-led group worked the hardest, but only when the leader was present; group members were self-centred and aggressive. The democratic-led group was a little less productive than the autocratic-led group, but their work activity was not affected by the leader's absence – that is, they demonstrated autonomy. Moreover, group morale was higher in the latter group.

The autocratic leader might also be described as directive and coercive (Bass, 1990). Similarly, a democratic style of leadership is also consultative and consensual. Eagly, Makhijani and Klonsky (1992) argue that the focus and nature of leadership vary independently. Thus, a leader can be directive in both a task-oriented way (telling subordinates how the task is to be done), or people-oriented way (structuring the interaction amongst group members) (Fiedler, 1989). Conversely, a leader can be democratic in a task-oriented as well as people-oriented way. In practice, Eagly and colleagues note that the conceptual distinction between autocratic/democratic and task/people-oriented leadership styles is difficult to maintain in practice (for example, Eagly et al., 1992).

There is some doubt whether the construct 'consideration' is distinct from measures of subordinate satisfaction. There is a 'circularity' to the finding that the satisfied subordinate is more likely than the dissatisfied subordinate to perceive his or her leader as considerate (Bryman, 1996). This can be overcome if ratings of the leader originate from a source independent of ratings from subordinate satisfaction (for example, the leader's superior). There is also the potential confounding of perceived consideration and perceived organizational support.

Many studies rely on leader descriptions of their own behaviour. However, self-reported leadership style does not necessarily correlate with descriptions of the same behaviour by their group members and observers, or with measures of actual behaviour. There are some doubts being raised about the validity of the Ohio State LBDQ scales as well, particularly in regard to the potential impact of people's 'implicit leadership theories' on how they rate the behaviour of leaders (Bryman, 1996).

## Leadership Effectiveness and its Measurement

Central to the difficulty in describing and explaining leader effectiveness is the absence of an established criterion of 'effectiveness': effectiveness is context-specific. Some researchers rely heavily on assessments of leader effectiveness provided by subordinates and/or seniors. Williams, Podsakoff, and Huber (1992), for instance, argue that the dyadic relationship between the leader and each of his/her subordinates is a more appropriate unit of analysis for assessing leadership effectiveness than the entire workgroup. They claim that perceived individual-level variation in leader behaviour continues to predict effectiveness on various attitude criteria (for example, satisfaction with supervision, organizational commitment), even after the effects of group-level leader variation have been controlled.

Many, however, argue that a true test of leadership effectiveness is the performance of the group as a whole using objective measures like productivity and/or quality of output (for example, Hunt, Osborn, & Schuler, 1978). Measures of group outcome are either evaluated, or measured directly (quality of output, number of correct answers), or both (for example, Muringham & Leung, 1976). Unfortunately, most measures of effectiveness are obtained by self-report in the same questionnaire inviting people to rate the style of the leader (Bryman, 1996). This type of measure of effectiveness is thus likely to reflect common variance in association with the measure of leadership style.

## Linear models of effectiveness

Linear models investigate the association between particular styles of leadership and leadership effectiveness. Most find, however, that the association is moderated by various task and/or context factors. Gastil (1994) found, for instance, that the democratic style was most strongly tied to effectiveness when *naturally occurring* rather than experimentally induced, particularly when working on *fairly complex tasks*. However, Paul and Ebadi (1989) note that the power of 'participation' (which presupposes a democratic style of leadership) for increased workgroup effectiveness is by no means clear-cut. There are many degrees of participation and many ways of measuring its effectiveness. They argue that forms of employee participation can be functional when:

- the leader has the authority to make a decision;
- the decision can be made without stringent time limitations;
- subordinates have the relevant knowledge, skills and abilities to discuss and implement the decision made;
- subordinate characteristics (values, needs, attitudes, and so on) are congruent with the decision to participate;
- the leader is skilled in use of participative techniques.

In the words of Gastil (1994), the democratic style entails 'giving group members responsibility, improving the general abilities and leadership skills of other group members, and assisting the group in its *decision-making process*' (p. 403). Clearly, much of the effectiveness of the democratic style depends on task requirements, subordinate capability and subordinate acceptance of responsibility for meeting these requirements.

Bass's (1990) review of the hundreds of studies on leadership style concludes that the relative predictive power of each particular style varies with various organizational, leader and subordinate contingencies.

## Contingency models of leader effectiveness

Whilst agreement exists on the fact of 'contingency', fundamental disagreement exists on the exact nature and impact of these contingencies. A major problem with existing contingency models is that whilst they provide a well structured set of propositions to test, they fail to explain when an interaction is expected (Study Box 4.23; Northouse, 2001).

### Study Box 4.23

### Contingency models of leadership

#### Fiedler's model

Fiedler (1967) proposed that leadership effectiveness depends on the match of a leader's style with the situation. Factors that determine the amount of control required of the leader are: leader–member relationship (acceptability of leader), degree of structure required for the task to be accomplished and investment of power (whether the leader has formal authority by virtue of position). A highly favourable leadership context is one where the leader is acceptable to the group, the task is structured and the leader is in a position of formal authority. In particular, the contingency model predicts that, in situations described as high or low in 'favourableness', low LPC leaders (high task orientation) are most effective. In situations of only moderate favourableness, high LPC leaders (high relationship orientation) are most effective. Support for these predictions is offered by Strube and Garcia (1981) who reviewed 145 tests of Fiedler's model. Schneier (1978), however, argues that measures of 'situational favourableness' conceptually overlap with LPC, making findings difficult to interpret. There are also methodological and measurement debates surrounding the use of LPC and the assignment of leaders to conditions (Northouse, 2001).

### House and Mitchell's path–goal theory

Central to path–goal theory (House & Mitchell, 1975) is that to be effective, leader behaviour must have a motivational impact on subordinates, sufficient to optimize their performance. The leader can do this by: (1) making subordinate need satisfaction contingent on effective performance; and (2) providing guidance, coaching, support and rewards necessary for effective performance (that are not otherwise provided). Four main behavioural practices are described as important: *leader directiveness* (clarifying expectations, assigning tasks), *leader supportiveness* (consideration for subordinate needs); *achievement orientation* (setting challenging goals, faith in others to perform at their best); and *leader participativeness* (consulting others, asking for/taking into account others' suggestions). Overall, there has been mixed support for goal–path theory, much of this attributed to the global nature of the leadership dimensions (Fulk & Wendler, 1982).

### Situational leadership theory

This proposes that the optimal supervisory style varies with level of follower-maturity. Low maturity requires a high task orientation; high maturity, however, requires a low task and relationship orientation (that is, facilitation of autonomy); whereas a follower of intermediate maturity requires a relationship orientation, varying in the requirement for a task orientation. Vecchio (1995) reports evidence involving high school teachers to support the predictions of low and moderate maturity individuals but not high maturity levels, whilst others have not obtained any support for the theory (for example, Goodson, McGee & Cashman, 1989). Vecchio (1995) highlights the difficulty associated with testing the theory rigorously. Only a limited number of occurrences or 'matches' of maturity level and type of supervisory orientation can be obtained in any one study, and there is a reliance on supervisor ratings of follower maturity and performance effectiveness. They note that a more appropriate test of the theory would be a longitudinal study and the development of a sound measure of employee maturity.

The use of style dichotomies to understand leadership processes is nonetheless attractive because of the otherwise bewildering complexity of the leadership literature. Moreover, as Yukl and Van Fleet (1982: 88) note, 'measurement of leadership at a high level of abstraction and with such broadly defined behaviour categories has failed to provide much insight into the reasons why some leaders are more effective than others'. For instance, the concept of 'initiating structure' can be unpacked into several subdimensions like 'initiation', 'planning', 'organization', 'production', 'recognition', 'integration' and 'communication'.

Northouse (2001) likewise notes the potential for a divergence of general style and the skill of expressing it in a manner appropriate to a particular context. Arguably, one of the most important skills for a leader is recognition and appreciation of their resources, in both intra-individual (for example, subordinate competence) and extra-individual (for example, organizational support) forms. He emphasizes the importance of ascertaining 'which type of leader best recognises and implements the "potentialities" within different situations', rather than how to describe their leadership orientation (see also t'Hart & Quinn (1993) on 'paradoxical' leadership).

This suggests that effective leadership is underpinned by a *cognitive and social ability (and motivation)* to 'switch' the style to suit the occasion, perhaps akin to a naturalistic decision-making process (Beach, 1997; see Chapter 8). This requires a shift of research attention away from ascertaining causes and contingencies (that is, which style suits which occasion) towards the *cognitive, social and motivational prerequisites of effective leadership* that make possible an effective leadership process. Research on naturalistic decision making (Beach, 1997; Chapter 8) may be informative here. The latter refers to a growing literature on how experts (often in managerial or leadership roles) make quick but effective decisions in complex situations under time pressure.

As Bales (1950) recognized, the most effective leader is the one best able to assist the group to fulfil its goals *in that context*. This argument is consistent with Hosking's (1988) that leadership is a negotiated process between the leader, subordinates and the particular context in which leadership takes place.

## Effects of Stress on Leadership

Many critical leadership decisions are made under conditions of extreme stress. One hypothesis (Fiedler, 1967) assumes that under stress, a leader will be motivated to (1) restrict the number of goals they try to achieve; and (2) achieve their most important goals first (Larson & Rowland, 1973). Isenberg (1981) argued that this is explained by arousal in that, under stress, the leader may 'impulsively seize upon a hastily contrived solution that seems to promise immediate relief'.

A recent view on this issue is that the leader simply relies more heavily on 'experience' than 'intelligence' under stress. Yukl and Van Fleet (1982: 102) call it the 'conditioned response', such that 'there is less likelihood of panic and immobility in the face of extreme danger' (Study Box 4.24).

### Study Box 4.24

#### Cognitive resource theory

Cognitive resource theory (CRT) (Fiedler, 1989; Gibson, Fiedler, & Barrett, 1993) proposes that a leader's intellectual abilities contribute to group performance only if there is 'an unbroken chain between the generation of plans, decisions and action strategies and their group implementation'. The leader must (1) be able to devote intellectual effort towards development plans and decisions; (2) effectively communicate them in the form of directions and instructions; and (3) have the group support to implement them.

Thus, leader intelligence should correlate more highly with group performance if the leader is directive rather than non-directive, and where the directive behaviour is focused on task performance rather than on the interpersonal relations of group members. Interpersonal stress (rather than task stress) moderates the effective use of intellectual abilities by distracting the leader from task to interpersonal concerns. The distracting effect is particularly strong for intellectually demanding group tasks (Gibson et al., 1993).

Research on those who fail to continue to be successful once they have become leaders (that is, leadership derailment; see Shackleton & Wale, 2000 for a review), suggests a lack of 'practical streetwise intelligence' among the derailed who are otherwise highly conceptually intelligent. What they lack is an awareness of the politics and realities of organizational life, self-awareness and interpersonal skills.

Various writers note how organizations respond to stress by concentrating control and authority for decision making at the highest levels – that is, vertical structuring (Isenberg, 1981: 120). Staw, Sandelands and Dutton (1981) explain that the influence of dominant members prevails more easily under stress as group members are motivated to abdicate task responsibility and defer to authority. Leaders are simultaneously more likely to adopt an authoritarian stance under stress (Fodor, 1976).

There is indeed considerable evidence showing that 'initiating structure' is the most effective strategy under ambiguous or non-routine task conditions (for example, Downey, Sheridan, & Slocum, 1975; Fiedler, 1967). Others, however, find that centralized structures can prematurely lock the group into a pattern of interaction that can inhibit adjustment to change and performance in unfamiliar situations (Foushee, 1984).

The discrepancy in findings may be to some extent explained by the nature of the task and its requirements, as well as the nature of the stressor. Foushee's (1984) case studies revolve around group dynamics in true emergency conditions whilst most others derive their findings from laboratory studies where emergencies are simulated or mild stressors are introduced. Commitment to the group goal is essential, however, to *quick response*s in situations requiring coordinated effort. t'Hart & Quinn (1993), likewise, present case studies demonstrating that loyalty kept soldiers going in terms of combat effectiveness and resistance to enemy propaganda during war. Other field studies in the disaster literature have obtained similar findings (Zander, 1982).

A competing suggestion is that *all* group members under stress (whether high or low in status) become more receptive to task information from others (Driskell & Salas, 1991). A different, but supportive, line of evidence is also provided by Kinicki and Vecchio (1994) who found that, contrary to expectation, the greater the time-based pressure the better the quality of leader–member relations. Yukl and Van Fleet (1982: 101) highlight the importance of inspiration to building group commitment (despite sometimes overwhelming odds) and thereby improving leader effectiveness (Study Box 4.25).

---

### Study Box 4.25

**Inspirational leadership**

The significance of 'inspirational' leadership is central to the recently evolved transformational leadership framework (Bass & Avolio, 1998). Isaac, Zerbe and Pitt (2001) argue that high performance results from a motivational environment that inspires employees to perform beyond expectation. An effective leader also fosters proactivity among employees (information seeking, one-to-one contact) (Madzar, 2001). Such are the skills of the transformational leader. Bass (1998) describes four components of transformational leadership: individualized consideration (demonstrating care and concern for individual needs), intellectual stimulation (challenging employees to think, to question and to use their imagination), inspirational motivation (future-oriented and visionary inspiration) and idealized influence (providing a role model). In short, this leader articulates group goals and visions, demonstrates self-confidence and confidence in group members, provides group members with a personal example of how to behave, communicates faith in group goals and has high performance expectations. The transformational leader – as well as having an instrumental focus (exchanging reward for effort) – elicits positive emotional and motivational responses from group members (the 'augmentation hypothesis').

Bass (1998) reports that leaders rated high on the transformational scales of the MultiFactor Leadership Questionnaire were also rated higher on performance, promotability and ability to manage their seniors. The subordinate is thus inspired to demonstrate commitment and extra effort (Bass & Avolio, 1998). In principle, leaders can be trained in transformational skills (Dvir, Eden, Avolio, & Shamir, 2002). Some, however, have noted that the relationship between transformational leadership and employee motivation might be more complex than is typically assumed (for example, Porter & Bigley, 2001). There are measurement problems in distinguishing between different components of leadership (that is, the common variance problem) and, moreover, it is difficult to obtain a truly independent measure of effectiveness (Yammarino & Bass, 1990). On a more practical note, high levels of transformational behaviour may be difficult to sustain consistently over time and may perhaps not always be necessary or appropriate to maintaining employee motivation.

---

During an emergency, the leader may be justified in being directive. The long-term effectiveness of this, however, is likely to depend on the leader having already built up trust and rapport amongst group members. There are instances where directive leadership can facilitate quick and efficient responding, but also instances where directive leadership is so institutionalized that status barriers inhibit effective communication within the group, even when disaster is imminent (Foushee, 1984).

A group or team has the ability to monitor and regulate its own processes under stress (Hockey, 2000). The issue is whether the leader is an enabler or an inhibitor of self-organizing team practices. Some argue that leaders are not always necessary to effective performance: teams that are self-regulating (where members are highly experienced, knowledgeable and committed) can lead themselves (through 'leadership substitutes' such as high task structure or organization, formal goals and plans) (Kerr & Jermier, 1978).

## Part 4 Summary and Conclusions

- Leadership has a popular ring, but despite over a century of research, few clear conclusions can be drawn. Early research failed to differentiate the dispositional characteristics of effective and ineffective leaders.
- Many different leadership styles have been described, but all maintain a distinction between task-oriented and relationship-oriented styles, and between authoritarian and democratic styles. A democratic style is consistently the most effective. The benefits of being task oriented or relationship oriented are, however, contingent on the situation. None of the contingency theories have unequivocal support.
- Contemporary interest is focused on the idea of a generally effective leader with 'transformational' qualities, and the dynamics of leadership ability and experience under stress. No-one has yet attempted to explain (as opposed to describe) effective leadership. Here can be argued that the effective leader has the ability to diagnose the requirements of a situation and occasion whatever style is appropriate.

## Future Research Challenges

- examine the concept and implications of core self-evaluations for self-regulatory processes;
- test the validity of goal-setting theory and in particular the dynamics of goal setting and goal revision in field settings;
- compare and contrast the concept of a learning goal with a performance goal in terms of the mechanisms involved;
- integrate different theories/models of motivation with a view to developing a more coherent theoretical framework;
- theoretically integrate considerations of identity, commitment and psychological contract;
- investigate processes of psychological contracting;
- explore Rousseau's schema approach to psychological contracts;
- investigate two-party relationships (leader–members, employer–employee) within a psychological contract framework;

- investigate the possibility of conceptual dissociation between content and form of the psychological contract, with particular reference to the idea that there will be a threshold of change to content beyond which a change in form may also follow;
- link justice and equity considerations into the psychological contract framework, with particular attention to processes of exchange;
- investigate the cognitive motivational basis of effective teamwork and of effective leadership;
- examine leadership *processes*;
- investigate the different antecedents and implications of different foci of commitment, identification and psychological contracts;
- investigate the concept of normative contract;
- test theoretical formulations of the commitment process;
- investigate the idea that the effective leader can switch styles to suit the occasion;
- test the proposition that the effective leader can be differentiated from the ineffective leader in their degree of ability, experience and self-regulatory and interpersonal capacity.

## Recommended Reading

Bandura, A. (1997). *Self-efficacy: The exercise of control*. New York: Freeman.

Brief, A.P. (1998). *Attitudes in and around organizations*. Thousand Oaks, CA: Sage.

Carver, C., & Scheier, M. (1998). *On the self-regulation of behavior*. New York: Cambridge University Press.

Haslam, S.A. (2004). *Psychology in organizations: The social identity approach* (2nd edn). London: Sage.

Locke, E.A. (1997). The motivation to work: What we know. In M. Maehr & P. Pintrich (Eds), *Advances in motivation and achievement*. Vol. 10 (pp. 375–412). Greenwich, CT: JAI Press.

Parker, S.K., & Wall, T.D. (1998). *Job and work design*. London: Sage.

Parker, S.K., Wall, T.D., & Cordery, J.L. (2001). Future work design research and practice: Towards an elaborated model of work design. *Journal of Occupational and Organizational Psychology*, 74(4), 413–440.

Rousseau, D.M. (2001). Schema, promise and mutuality: The building blocks of the psychological contract. *Journal of Occupational and Organizational Psychology*, 74, 511–541.

# 5 Organizational Development and Change

... very little, if any, attention has been given to the working through of the potent need of human systems to hold onto the existing order – to that which is – and to avoid the powerful feelings that changed circumstances can trigger.

(Tannenbaum and Hanna, 1985: 99)

## Preface

It has been an enduring quest of many to explain organizational change. The issue has recently been cast centre stage as organizations are increasingly experiencing high-velocity discontinuous change. Downsizing, restructuring, mergers and acquisitions, outsourcing and the introduction of a core/complementary employment structure, coupled with heightened competition and cultural proliferation, have all put their strain on organizations in recent years. Sheer survival has created an imperative for organizations not just to adjust, but to substantially reformulate themselves in alignment with new demands. Unfortunately, the literature is replete with examples of failed change efforts, despite a long history of research on organizational transformation. Managed change has tended to be 'recipe driven', and relatively uninformed by the wider literature, with little dialogue between those who are the 'managers of change' and those who think and write about it.

Organizational development (OD) was a discipline evolved independently of the management tradition, informed by the behavioural sciences and designed to facilitate change by building commitment. The idea of building commitment, which presupposes subjective organizational integration, is of particular interest given the largely disintegrated nature of contemporary organizational life.

Despite this, the OD literature has become littered with recipes for engineering successful change using behavioural principles, to the exclusion of a more micro-level psychological analysis. Moreover, the OD approach evolved mainly on the assumption of organizational stasis, and that change is about moving the organization from one stable state to another (that is, episodic, discontinuous, and intermittent), precipitated by a specific external or internal event (for example, industry deregulation, process redesign, technological change). In short, the deep structure of an organization becomes increasingly misaligned with environmental demands, and is thrown into disequilibrium.

Nowadays, no such assumption can be made: change is something continuous, conditions are turbulent and chaos rules. A new 'organizing' discourse has begun to supersede the metaphor of organization as a stable entity, but little guidance is afforded on the processes that furnish effective transition in these conditions. Nonetheless, organizations continue to experiment with new organizational forms (for example, virtual, self-organizing).

This chapter begins by examining the tradition of OD and its philosophical assumptions. It is argued that one of the reasons why OD concepts, tools and techniques often do not work is because of *the way change itself is conceptualized* (that is, something that happens to people, which they are likely to resist, or a process to become engaged with or a part of), and the lack of attention to *micro-level processes*. The literature on culture is equally problematic to the extent that it is seen as synonymous with the organization, an attribute of organizations which is internalized by people, rather than a set of processes in which people are inextricably involved. However, the literature continues to perpetuate a *content* view of culture. The contribution of the culture literature to the understanding and management of change has been impeded somewhat by paradigm wars concerning which discipline 'owns' the study of culture. Some might say that psychology will never have anything valid to say on culture, it being irreducible to subjectivities. Psychologists may, on the contrary, argue that culture cannot exist 'for real' outside of people's sense-making processes. Such 'navel gazing' may be considered frustrating to the magic-wand change brigade, but the balance to strike is perhaps somewhere in between theoretical reflection and practice.

This chapter also looks at 'the psychology of change' informed by the literature on attitude and behaviour change, identity and also sense-making processes. The implications of micro-level considerations for managing change are identified and discussed. In so doing, topics in particular that pertain to the individual-organizational interface (culture, socialization and identity) are reviewed, all offering an important means of securing leverage in the pursuit of organizational change. Postmodern contributions to the understanding and management of change are considered, including knowledge management, which today is said to hold the key to an organization's competitive edge. The magic potion has yet to be formulated, but there is no shortage of ideas peppering the contemporary change literature.

This is a complex and unwieldy literature to distil, built largely from pragmatic prescription rather than sound theory or evidence.

## Learning Objectives

**Studying the contents of this chapter will enable you to:**

1  explain the OD tradition and its philosophical assumptions;
2  compare and contrast various different OD models;

3  critically review the concept of organizational culture and its relevance to OD intervention;

4  critically discuss the concepts of socialization and organizational identification as forms of 'acculturation';

5  describe and evaluate the success of various OD interventions;

6  distinguish between commitment-based and compliance-based strategies of change management;

7  explain some of the problems associated with OD impact evaluation;

8  describe and comment on the ethical dilemmas faced in the pursuit of OD activity.

# Part 1: The Contemporary Context of Organizational Change

Strategies of organizational change have recently become a byword for maintaining success and creating competitive performance. (Wilson, 1992: 2–3).

There are economic, legal, and technological challenges facing the contemporary organization that have increased organizational complexity, making continuous adjustment and change imperative to survival (Burke, 2002). Change, says Wilson (1992), should not be contrasted with stasis, since in reality no such pure state exists: change is an inextricable part of all contemporary organizational life. The issue is one of whether change is construed as something incremental and emergent (determined by political, economic and legal climate), or whether it is a strategic, transformational and thus planned event. Most management theory assumes that change is a planned event and that it is the responsibility of all managers to become 'change masters' (Burke, 2002).

An abundant literature has emerged on 'the characteristics of highly effective organizations', with various 'model' organizations used as templates against which to gauge success (Study Box 5.1), along with various prescriptions for 'how to' manage the change process (for example, Burke, 2002; McNish, 2002). Various 'happy ending' fairy tales of culture change continue to litter the literature (for example, Hailey & Balogun (2002) on the case of Glaxo Wellcome UK and Hyde & Paterson (2000) on AstraZeneca), but these tend to present 'gloriously simple' pictures ('celebrity fictions') of the change process that in reality is highly complex (for example, Grugulis & Wilkinson, 2002; Senior, 2000).

These approaches give the false impression that changes can be achieved simply by means of whatever the current hot topic (the 'magic wand') may be, rather than addressing the underlying issues within the organization. All such management maxims can be viewed as attempts to 'rationalize' the change situation to bring it under 'managerial control' (Wilson, 1992: 7). Wanburg and Banas (2000) note that when the pace of change threatens to defeat an organization, in panic an organization may take on board whatever, supposedly panacea, initiative might be flavour of the day to help them to cope. Yet, behind the scenes failed change efforts abound (for example, Worrall & Cooper, 1998).

Media-salient organizations struggling to reposition themselves in the contemporary market include some of the oldest and most recognized shops on the UK high street like Marks and Spencer plc and W.H. Smith. The impact of panic restructuring in the late 1980s and 1990s did not yield the expected returns, instead depleting organizations of key skills and experience, and massively undermining staff commitment and morale (Worrall & Cooper, 1998; Study Box 5.1).

---

### Study Box 5.1

#### Reactions to downsizing

Research identifies two sets of factors particularly susceptible to being undermined during downsizing: job-level factors (satisfaction, performance, perceived job security), and organizational-level factors (morale, trust, commitment) (for example, Armstrong-Stassen, 2002; Worrall, Cooper, & Campbell-Jamison, 2000). If employees perceive injustice involved in the lay-off procedures, commitment can take a particularly dramatic nosedive. The higher the pre-lay-off level of commitment (and job involvement), the greater the potential for damage from survivor perceptions of organizational injustice (for example, Allen, Freeman, Russell, Reizenstein, & Rentz, 2001). Among such employees, commitment can be difficult to recover, and may not return to pre-downsizing levels completely (see also, Lind, Greenberg, Scott, & Welchans, 2000 and Rousseau & Wade-Benzioni, 1995).

---

One common financial solution has been to acquire or merge (Lynch & Lind, 2002). However, this has more often than not created more problems than answers and, in some cases, the consequences are disastrous (Clemente & Greenspan, 1998; Study Box 5.2). It is now beyond dispute that the human capital implications of a merger planned and managed in purely financial terms are negative and substantial. The loss or disengagement of human capital through actual or psychological withdrawal of effort and investment can seriously undermine the likelihood of long-term merger success, as for any other change effort.

---

### Study Box 5.2

#### The 'human challenges' of merger

Attention is increasingly on the human challenges posed by corporate mergers and acquisitions (Lynch & Lind, 2002). Evidence highlights the long-term financial costs incurred by deals that do not pay appropriate consideration to the human component, despite making good initial accounting sense (for example, Clemente & Greenspan,

**Study Box 5.2   Continued**

1998). Three to five years post-merger, 50–80 percent of merged entities are described as underperforming, with some said to have completely destroyed their shareholder value (Morosini, 1998).

Researchers have nonetheless consistently argued that the way human capital is managed during merger lies at the heart of its success or failure in financial terms (Buono & Bowditch, 2003; Cartwright & Cooper, 1995; Marks & Mirvis, 2001). Although companies may appreciate the detrimental effects of cultural misfit on employees, it is rarely addressed at a level at which the employee struggles involved in realizing the new organizational paradigm are actively recognized and managed (Ericson, 2001). Merger-induced personal readjustment involves cognitive and emotional severance from the pre-merger organization and a re-alignment of self with a new 'unknown' organizational reality (Weick & Quinn, 1999). Moreover, if pre-existing investments are felt betrayed, it is unlikely that pre-merger attachments will transfer to the post-merger organization (Jetten, O'Brien & Trindall, 2002; Van Knippenberg et al., 2002). Case studies of mergers also indicate reduced job and organizational satisfaction, reduced commitment, increased cynicism, stress, and intention to leave (for example, Marks & Mirvis, 2001; Robinson & Morrison, 2000). See **www.sagepub.co.uk/millward** for more on merger-induced change.

Organizations, realizing that 'the people make the place' (Schneider, 2002), are now struggling to re-incarnate whilst simultaneously also trying to keep abreast of changing economic demands, through continual business re-alignment (Study Box 5.3). This struggle to retrieve and re-harness lost capital in *human* terms is akin to trying to hit a moving target with a defective gun; an image that puts into perspective the harsh reality of organizational survival in contemporary times.

**Study Box 5.3**

**From learning organization to knowledge creation and management**

According to *Fortune* magazine (Charan & Colvin, 1999: 68), 'the most successful corporation … will be something called a learning organization, a consummately *adaptive* enterprise'. Senge (1990) argues, however, that it will also be *generative* – that is, continually expanding its capacity. Although there is currently no such thing as a learning organization, Senge (1990) has articulated a clear view of what it would stand for. In practical terms, a learning organization would comprise 'awakened' workers, who believe in their capacity to learn, take risks in order to learn, and understand how to seek enduring solutions to problems instead of quick fixes. One problem is the utopian vision this 'metaphor' embodies. The concept of organizational learning has nonetheless since become increasingly influential as a way of examining and prescribing how organizations might respond to contemporary

*(Continued)*

> **Study Box 5.3    Continued**
>
> economic and social conditions – globalization, IT, and importance of knowledge as a source of competitive advantage (for example, Dealtry, 2002; Qureshi, 2000).
>
> Yet management and the management of organizational change is a highly contested field where agreement is not always achieved, either about what is possible, or how. It is clear, nonetheless, that knowledge (or intellectual capital), and the learning processes that generate and manage it, have become key factors in creating competitive business advantage (Laszlo & Laszlo, 2002). Many organizations are, today, thus preoccupied with developing strategies for promoting learning and knowledge creation. Writers have argued that progress in knowledge management requires more than just a conversion of tacit into explicit knowledge (or content management), it requires that organizations develop 'self-organizing capabilities' (for example, Bhatt, 2001; Scharmer, 2001; Snowden, 2002). Knowledge denotes both content and process (involving the interaction between technology, techniques and people). Individual 'sense-making' processes are said to be integral to knowledge creation (Thomas, Sussman, Watts, & Henderson, 2001). See **www.sagepub.co.uk/ millward** for more on 'knowledge management'.

The message to pay attention to the 'human' dimension during a change effort has been one that organizational scholars have tried to deliver since the 1930s inception of the human relations (HR) paradigm (see Introduction and overview), yet the message either remains unheard, unaccepted or still 'on-the-shelf'.

The change literature operates in one of two extremes. At the one extreme is 'recipe driven' change, based on some guiding principles, but no solid theory and very little, if any, attention to micro-level 'psychological' considerations. At the other extreme is the esoteric literature which is difficult to distil, let alone apply, especially true of some of the postmodern literature on 'the role of language' in organizational change (for example, Linstead & Brewis, 2004). It is indeed the responsibility of the skilled change master to interpret and apply the principles *in their particular context*, but if the ideas are difficult to penetrate, even the most reflective practitioner may 'give up' before they have even started and refer back to 'the recipe'. Thus the onus is on scholars to make their work *accessible* to its users (for example, West & Markiewicz, 2004).

The OD approach to organizational change is the most well-established approach among the *behaviour sciences*. There are many other 'competing' approaches to managing change, one of the most popular of these in the late 1990s being business process re-engineering (Study Box 5.4) and more recently a 'performance management' ethos has begun its sweep. These approaches are distinctly *managerial* (that is, concerned with regulation and control). The OD tradition has, itself, often been criticized for being too 'managerial', devoid of psychological content (for example, Vaught Hoy & Buchanan, 1985; see Study Box 5.4). However, French, Bell and Zawacki (1994: 11) are ardent in their maintenance of a distinction between OD and management practice.

Study Box 5.4

### From 'business process re-engineering' to 'self-organizing' models

Business process re-engineering (BPR) is a tool for facilitating radical change by 'starting from scratch' to build new structures and processes (for example, job descriptions, reward systems, technological systems, and so on) to engineer improved organizational efficiency and effectiveness (Stewart, 1993). This requires a huge investment in time and resources, driven by a strategic plan. In practice, BPR need not involve the whole organization (for example, re-engineering financial systems, procurement procedures). However, change in the wider system might also be necessary to support re-engineering of subsystems to be successful. The poor success rate (70 percent suboptimal performance) of BPR projects is now well known (for example, Laudon & Laudon, 2002), and other change models have now succeeded this (for example, performance management). The failure of BPR has nonetheless taught some important lessons about the role played by strategy and structure in organizational change. BPR was built on the assumption that structuring the processes in a more efficient manner will achieve better results. However, by allowing structure to dictate process, the process then loses its power to respond flexibly (and more efficiently) to different or changing demands (that is, structural determinism). Total quality management (TQM) initiatives (during the late 1980s and early 1990s) failed for the same reason. There is now a strong postmodern movement within managerial science advocating a 'self-organizing' model. To furnish this, organizations need to allow processes to dictate the structure (for example, hierarchy, matrix, network, and so on) required for the situation (Ciborra, 1996). The military have begun to take up this idea of structuring for the occasion (via front-line initiatives) rather than allow the 'long screwdriver' (bureaucratic structure) to dictate local practices, but psychologists have yet to take up the challenge of looking at the human capital requirements (that is, cognitive ability, social skill) of this new 'self-organizing' principle.

## The Organizational Development Tradition

OD is about how to engineer organizational change (across structure, technology, task and people) by focusing on the *human and social implications* of these elements of organizations (French, Bell, & Zawacki, 1994: 5). Organizations are modelled as social systems and OD refers to the act or process of furthering, advancing or promoting the growth of these systems. Specifically, OD is defined as:

> a powerful set of concepts and techniques for improving organizational effectiveness and individual well-being that had its genesis in the behavioural sciences and was tested in the laboratory of real-world organizations (French et al., 1994: 1)

Other definitions have been offered (for example, Cummings & Worley, 2000: 12), but the above encapsulates best the attempt to reconcile the goal of increased organizational effectiveness with that of also enhancing individual well-being. OD, then, is not just anything done in the name of organizational betterment, it denotes a particular kind of change process designed to produce a particular kind of end result. Specifically, it denotes a 'prescription for a process of planned change' comprising the following elements (Cummings & Worley, 1993: 6–16):

- A long-range, planned, system-wide process requiring sustained effort of a complex and multi-faceted kind.
- Derived from the behavioural sciences (including anthropology and sociology as well as psychology) and framed by an action research model (problem-solving, self-reflexive approach).
- Targets work-related groups of individuals and inter-group configurations as points of leverage, in combination with a more strategic focus on organizational culture and processes.
- Enables the organization to better adapt, cope, solve its own problems and renew itself. For lasting change, the system must be able to master its own fate (must acquire its own competence in managing its structures, processes and culture more effectively).
- Involves one or more consultants who establish an equal and collaborative relationship with the client system, and where the consultant facilitates the change process by asking questions. Expertise is used to facilitate, not to direct or prescribe.

In practice, OD is often conflated with the term 'organizational culture'. Indeed, many OD experts see culture as the main route into management of the organizational change process (French, Bell & Zawacki, 1994). Unfortunately, this model of the organization as a culture may have undermined the flexibility of OD to use other 'metaphors' of the organization to inform the change management process (Morgan, 1997).

## What constitutes an 'OD intervention'?

An intervention involves entering 'into an ongoing system of relationships, to come between or among persons, groups, or objects for the purpose of helping them' (Argyris, 1971: 15). Blake and Mouton (1964) divide OD interventions into nine different categories:

- *discrepancy intervention* – explores contradictions in action or attitude (for example, leadership rhetoric not matched in practice);
- *theory intervention* – behavioural science knowledge is used to define and explain the problem (for example, high turnover explained by psychological contract violation);
- *procedural intervention* – a critique of the way something is being done (for example, promotion procedures);
- *relationship intervention* – focuses attention on interpersonal relationships and identifies issues for exploration and resolution (for example, supervisor/subordinate relationships);

- *experimental intervention* – two or more different interventions are tested for their consequences prior to their full-blown implementation;
- *perspective intervention* – adopts a 'big' picture, enabling examination of the past through to the future;
- *dilemma intervention* – an imposed or emergent dilemma is used to force close examination of various options and the assumptions underpinning them;
- *structural intervention* – examination and evaluation of structural causes of organizational ineffectiveness (for example, management hierarchy);
- *cultural intervention* – examines traditions, precedents and practices.

French et al. (1994: 177) also differentiate between interventions directed at individuals (for example, coaching and counselling), dyads (for example, arbitration), teams (for example, survey feedback, role analysis), inter-group configurations (for example, survey feedback, group-level arbitration) and organizations as a whole (for example, merger). Movement from one level of focus to the next implies that the number of interdependencies and the number of dimensions to be considered are substantially increased.

## Organizational development models

**The intervention model**   The intervention model (Argyris, 1971) assumes that organizations require assistance to diagnose and solve their own problems because they are subsumed by the complexity of the system. For example, contradictions between the espoused (for example, rhetoric of empowerment) and the reality of organizational life (for example, abdication of responsibility) may not be fully appreciated. This is a problem currently being faced in the UK National Health Service. In the inquiry into the death of Victoria Climbié, Lord Laming (2003: 6) said, 'time and time again it was dispiriting to listen to the "buck passing" from those who attempted to justify their positions' (see **www.sagepub.co.uk/millward**).

The interventionist never prescribes: the task is to merely clarify and assist in the decision-making process. Lasting change must come from *within*. However, in practice, organizational pressures for quick fix solutions may mean that consultants are expected to take a more active and directive role than aspired to (Schein, 1999).

**The planned change model**   This involves establishing a working contract with a designated change agent within a broad framework of intervention aims and objectives (Schein, 1999). A diagnostic exercise is undertaken and feedback is given on the basis of which an action plan is evolved, implemented and then evaluated (Senior, 2000; Example Box 5.1). Fordyce and Weil (1979) describe seven basic ways in which diagnostic OD data can be collected including questionnaires, interviews, sensing, group interviews, polling, collages, drawing, and sculpting (see **www.sagepub.co.uk/millward** for more details).

Planned change can be adjustive (for example, changes to the promotion system), transitional (for example, one-shot) or transformational (that is, paradigm-shifting). The type of change required depends on the source of the change imperative (for example, competition, legal, technological, high absenteeism and turnover). In practice, the change process does not happen in quite the linear and progressive way depicted by this model (Cummings & Worley, 2000). Moreover, there has tended to be an emphasis on implementation (for example, recipes for change) without due attention to 'diagnosis'.

---

**Example Box 5.1**

### Using repertory grid methods to facilitate organizational change

Cassell, Close, Duberley and Johnson (2000) developed a practitioner workbook involving a repertory grid (RG) exercise that managers can use for diagnostic purposes at the start of a change management effort. The RG method is couched in personal construct theory (Kelly, 1955) and assumes that people are governed by a need to make sense of the world (in part to make it more predictable). To aid this process, people develop constructions of themselves and their world. Here is not the place to describe how to use repertory grids (see Cassell & Symon, 2004 for details of use in an organizational context), but to report how they can be used to 'surface embedded assumptions about work performance'. Cassell et al. (2000) argue that RGs are especially powerful tools for eliciting deeply held assumptions and values that might otherwise remain untapped, with the potential to 'hold back' the change effort. By surfacing assumptions, the process of 'unfreezing' can begin (see 'The unfreezing model' below) so that movement is possible. The use of grids can also engage people in a reflective dialogue about their assumptions and values (which they may not have been so consciously aware of before) and thus, involves them in the change effort. To this extent, the RG might be described as a useful 'conversational technology' (2000: 572) for engaging people in the change effort as well as a means of diagnosis.

---

*The action research model*   The action research model sees the diagnostic process as an integral part of the intervention, whereby diagnosis leads to action, which in turn affords more diagnostic activity, and so on (see Senior, 2000 for details; Study Box 5.5). All diagnostic activity involves *systematic data gathering and analysis*. The type of techniques used for data gathering can vary from highly structured (for example, questionnaire surveys and audits) through to highly unstructured (for example, face-to-face conversations). The former can help bring structure to bear on a problem and thus to scope it out, whilst the latter can help build up relationships of trust as well as provide a valuable source of data (Example Box 5.1). The way the problem is defined or conceptualized will depend heavily on the theoretical perspective of the consultant.

---

**Study Box 5.5**

### The tradition of survey feedback

Survey feedback describes a tool for summarizing and providing feedback on diagnostic data (Bowers & Franklin, 1994). Data is summarized for each workgroup, for

---

**Study Box 5.5    Continued**

combinations of groups within an organizational division and for the organization as a whole. Each relevant supervisor/manager receives the data as an indicator of how his or her immediate subordinates think and feel about the present state of affairs. A consultant helps the supervisor/manager make sense of the data and then arranges a time for supervisor and subordinates to meet for discussion. The 'feedback' meeting is facilitated by the consultant. In the words of Bowers and Franklin (1994: 94), 'an effective survey feedback operation depicts the organization's groups as moving, by a discussion process, from the tabulated perceptions, through a cataloguing of their implications, to commitment for solutions to the problems that the discussion has identified and defined'.

---

*The appreciative inquiry model*   Most diagnosis assumes something is in need of repair. However, *appreciative inquiry* focuses not on what is, but what *might be*, what *should be*, and what *will be* (Srivastva & Cooperrider, 1990). Specifically, 'appreciative inquiry seeks out the very best of what is to help ignite the imagination of what might be' and 'helps ... envision a collectively desired future and then to carry out that vision' (1990: 129). The method involves an identification and analysis of so-called 'peak experiences' and their bases, as the building block for envisioning how things could be (Fry, Barrett, Seiling, & Whitney, 2002; Srivastva & Cooperrider, 1990; Study Box 5.6).

---

**Study Box 5.6**

**Critical change assumptions of appreciative inquiry**

1  People respond to their map of reality, not to reality itself. Change begins with a change of map.
2  All behaviour is purposeful and has a positive intention. Our intention or purpose is not the action itself. People make the best choice they can at the time. No matter how self-defeating, bizarre or unacceptable the behaviour, it is the best choice available to that person at the time given their map of the world.
3  People work perfectly. No one is wrong and nothing is broken. It is a matter of finding out how they/it functions so that they/it can effectively be changed to something more constructive and desirable.
4  The meaning of a communication is the response you get. This may be different from that you intend. There are no failures in communication, only responses and feedback. If you are not getting the result you want, do something different.
5  We already have all the resources we need or we can create them.
6  Modelling successful performance leads to excellence. If one person can do something, it is possible to model it and teach it to others.
7  If you want to understand, act. The learning is in the doing.
8  Build on what is going well and working well, rather than what is wrong or problematic: be aware of amplifying the problem by making an issue of it and using the language of dysfunction; use positive language (what works, what we are doing well, what we could do more of or better).

Appreciative inquiry highlights the power of language in framing our perception and experiences of the world, and is a pragmatic off-shoot of the broader 'narrative' approach to organizational change (described below). This model of change involves changing the language to change the way reality is perceived. This involves, for example, putting negative stories aside to construct new more positive stories through a process of participation and inquiry. Employees are asked only for positive stories and to invent the narrative they want to live.

### Assumptions of the OD change model

The assumption behind all change management strategies arising from the OD tradition is that organizations, as systems, will strive to maintain a quasi-stationary state of equilibrium. This assumption is rooted in field theory (Lewin, 1951). Changes to the system thus throw the system into disequilibrium and as such *cause resistance* which is the root of all *inertia* during a change effort. The key to effective change is thus to *overcome this resistance* (Cummings & Worley, 2000). Thus change is a problem to be overcome.

*The unfreezing–freezing model*   Lewin (1951) argued that organizational change involves a simple three-step process: unfreezing, moving and freezing. Unfreezing involves opening the system up to change by breaking down or minimizing resistance by confrontation of the need for change (Study Box 5.7). Once changes have been made, freezing or consolidation of changes will stabilize them (for example, a new reward system).

Although, in use by OD consultants, this model may suppose a diagnostic phase to identify the precise causes of resistance and thus a more precisely targeted influence effort, at the bottom line it is a 'top-down' rational model of change. It assumes quite simply that people can be 'persuaded' of the need for imposed change before they will engage with it. In practice, the persuasion may be delivered at the very minimum by a letter or memo and at most by some kind of 'tell and sell' intervention (a launch event). The former is typical of many acquisition scenarios (Case Study 5.1), whilst the latter may be more likely as part of a culture change initiative.

---

**Case Study 5.1: Royal Bank of Scotland acquisition of NatWest**

At 7.30am on 6 March 2000, the Royal Bank of Scotland (RBS) announced its 'acquisition' of NatWest to the stock exchange. This was an unusual acquisition of a larger institution (£186 billion assets, 64,400 staff) by a smaller one (£75 billion assets, 22,000 staff) amongst the Big Five retail banks. The news was relayed to NatWest staff as soon as possible (who had been kept informed of the bidding process, which had also received a lot of media attention), with faxes and emails awaiting them at around 8.30am the same morning. Within three days, RBS had closed down the NatWest head office and chosen only the best employees to remain. The acquisition process was dealt with 'rationally' by keeping staff informed on every aspect of change. In the words of the Group CEO, Fred Goodwin, 'we believe that it is important to remove uncertainty for staff as quickly as possible'. The imposition of the RBS system of technology into 'the NatWest branch' was justified as saving the company around £1 million a day.

---

**Study Box 5.7**

### Force-field analysis

Force-field analysis assumes that an object at rest will remain so unless the forces to move (forces for change) outweigh forces working against change (forces resisting change). Likewise, a behaviour that is positioned between two forces (opposing change and pushing for change) will not change if the forces are equal (cancel each other out). Change will occur, however, if the forces for change are strengthened and/or the forces against change are weakened.

In an organizational context, this may involve identifying the driving forces for and the resisting forces against the desired end state, and identifying strategies and tactics to strengthen forces for change and weaken forces of resistance. However, this assumes that people can readily articulate a finite list of drivers and restraints in a particular set of change circumstances.

---

Most subsequent models of organizational change, whilst generally more elaborate than this, incorporate these basic principles of change. For instance, Weiss (1996) advocates a five-stage model of effective change management as follows: (1) motivating change (creating readiness for change, overcoming resistance); (2) creating a vision; (3) developing political support (including stakeholder support); (4) managing transition (that is, by intervention); and (5) sustaining momentum (installing a new support system, reinforcing new behaviours, developing new competences). None of these models has been systematically tested, however (Dean, Carlisle, & Baden-Fuller, 1999), though it is clear at the very least that 'tell and sell' is not enough in many cases to overcome resistance, or motivate successful change (Porras & Silvers, 1991).

*The participation and involvement model*   This model assumes that resistance can be more effectively overcome if, in addition, employees are given the opportunity to participate and become involved in the change effort (Porras & Silvers, 1991; Tannenbaum & Hanna, 1985). This will furnish a sense of direction, ownership and control, and build commitment to change. Recently, investigations of employee 'reactions to change' have demonstrated the importance of *justice perceptions* as a mediator of change acceptance (Study Box 5.8). 'Involvement', however, has a wide range of meanings and operational formats. In the USA, 'involvement' implies 'direct participation'; in Europe, it usually denotes something more 'indirect' and 'representative' (largely as a legislative necessity or societal obligation) and, in Britain, involvement has tended to be 'reacted to' (more than proactively implemented) as a 'threat to management' (Cotton, 1993: 231).

---

**Study Box 5.8**

### Organizational justice theory

Organizational justice theory (Greenberg, 1990) is about employee perceptions of the fairness of work-related issues. Three different types of justice perception have

*(Continued)*

---

> **Study Box 5.8   Continued**
>
> been investigated: distributive justice (perceived fairness of allocation decisions), procedural justice (perceived fairness of formal procedures that result in decisions), and interactional justice (perception of how fairly one is treated by decision makers). There is some query as to whether interactional justice is an independent construct or whether it denotes simply the interpersonal side of procedural justice (Paterson, Green, & Cary, 2002). Research demonstrates that a fair procedure is perceived as consistently and impartially implemented, where decisions are based on accurate information, and mechanisms exist to correct inappropriate decisions, which is compatible with current ethical moral standards, and which afford employees the opportunity to have input.
>
> Involvement in the change process can promote a sense of procedural justice, resulting in heightened trust and also a greater likelihood of 'signing on' to change goals and outcomes (Korsgaard, Sapienza & Schweiger, 2002; Paterson, Green & Cary, 2002). Folger and Skarlicki (2001) argue that perceived justice mediates employee resistance to change.
>
> One caveat to the concept of justice is that its measurement appears to be highly context sensitive. To overcome this, many researchers use one-item measures, but this impedes comparison across studies. Greenberg (1993) says that this can be resolved by using standardized measures that can be customized to suit the situation (see Paterson et al., 2002 for an example).

Strategies for involvement may include inviting employees to voice ideas, identify ways in which they can each individually help progress or ensure change or even to take an active part in the 'rolling-out' process. As part of the NatWest acquisition process, the RBS (Case Study 5.1) employees were given shares to make them feel collectively involved in the effort to maximize profit (a strategy called 'gain sharing'; Cotton, 1993). Increasingly, organizations are distributing responsibility for change amongst their existing managerial and professional staff and/or appointing internal change agent specialists (Doyle, 2003; Tsoukas & Chia, 2002; see **www.sagepub.co.uk/millward** for examples).

### *Transformational Change Models*

Transformational change usually involves culture change. The issue of culture change within organizational contexts continues to attract both interest and excitement as a means by which an organization can secure a competitive edge (for example, Grugulis & Wilkinson, 2002). This has prompted an uncritical search for the definitive 'success culture', as if everything about organizations can be 'reduced' to, and explained by, culture (see Study Box 5.9). This, unfortunately, has injected the concept of culture with the flavour of a 'religion' (Grugulis & Wilkinson, 2002).

---

**Study Box 5.9**

**'In search of excellence'**

Peters and Waterman (1982) argued on the basis of anecdotal evidence that successful cultures have eight distinctive attributes:

1   action oriented;
2   customer driven;
3   fostering leaders and innovators;
4   respect for individuals;
5   hands-on value driven (for example, high achievement and supportiveness);
6   stick in markets where there is the expertise;
7   simple form, lean staff;
8   elements of both centralization and decentralization.

Others have since disputed that all of these attributes are necessary to success. It also depends on what exactly it means to be 'successful'. Hitt and Ireland (1987) found only one of the attributes to be definitive of success in their own sample – that is, the fostering of leaders and innovators.

---

Over the past 20 years or so, the concept of culture has generated significant research interest within a variety of diverse academic disciplines, including sociology, anthropology, management science and psychology. Despite this:

> there is ... little agreement on what the concept does and should mean, how it should be observed and measured, how it relates to more traditional industrial and organizational theories, and how it should be used in our efforts to help organizations. (Schein, 1999)

There are many competing claims and models of culture, proliferated in part by a huge growth in culture business in the consulting world (Martin & Frost, 1996). Putting this issue into perspective, Van Muijen (1998) says that even in 1952 there were 164 definitions of culture. Definitional issues have also been at the centre of so-called paradigm wars concerning the appropriate way to conceptualize and study culture (for example, quantitative versus qualitative). Example definitions include:

- Kilmann (1985: 62): '... the shared philosophies, ideologies, values, assumptions, beliefs, expectations, attitudes, and norms that knit a community together.'
- Frost, Moore, Louis, Lundberg & Martin (1995: 2): culture is about '... symbolism – of rituals, myths, stories and legends – and about the interpretation of events, ideas and experiences that are influenced and shaped by the groups within which people live.'
- Becker and Geer (1958: 50): 'Set of common understandings, expressed in language.'
- Kroeber and Kluckhohn (1952: 1): 'Transmitted pattern of values, ideas, and other symbolic systems that shape behaviour.'
- Van Maanen and Schein (1979: 209): 'Values, beliefs and expectations that members come to share.'

Schein's (1992; 2004) definition and model of culture was the most commonly cited and used until postmodern thinking on culture started to permeate organizational studies:

> (a) a pattern of basic assumptions, (b) invented, discovered or developed by a given group, (c) as it learns to cope with its problems of external adaptation and internal integration, (d) that has worked well enough to be considered valid and, therefore (e) is to be taught to new members as the (f) correct way to perceive, think and feel in relation to those problems.

Schein (1992; 2004) says that culture has a multi-layered 'onion'-like quality comprising basic assumptions (unconscious, unquestioned, guide reactions), values (about what is important), norms (to guide behaviour in particular settings) and behavioural artefacts (externally visible symbols including rules, procedures and appearance of the organization) (Figure 5.1). Rousseau (1995) and Hofstede (1991) likewise both adopt a similar 'onion-like' conceptual framework.

Rousseau added 'patterns of behaviour' between norms and artefacts. Hofstede, however, elaborated his own multi-layered model involving symbols (for example, status symbols), heroes (real or imaginary personifications of valued aspects of culture including founding fathers) and rituals (organizational activities carried out for their own sake). All of these three elements are subsumed by 'organizational practices' (formal policy, procedures, reward systems, lines of authority and ways of doing business) and all are in turn underpinned by values (the guiding framework or 'glue').

Most conventional writers on culture would not dispute that culture pertains to the essence of an organization (fundamental assumptions, values), which is expressed in its norms, practices and other 'symbols'. This 'onion' metaphor of culture has intuitive appeal, but it provides a framework for organizational research and practice, not a theory of culture. Other similar frameworks have been offered for culture analysis (for example, Vecchio, 1995), which though useful as a means of qualitative 'diagnosis', provide no basis for explanation. Vecchio's (1995) framework includes:

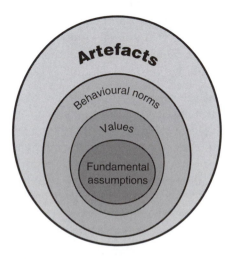

**Figure 5.1**   Adapted from Schein's model of culture

- *Critical decision of founding organizational members* – the vision of pioneers and their influence over culture development through key decisions made (for example, Body Shop is synonymous with its founder, Anita Roddick, who represents non-conformity, social responsibility, tenacity and creativity).
- *Guiding ideas and mission* – mission statements or slogans articulating the purpose and/or identity of the organization (for example, Body Shop is known for its 'natural', 'environmentally friendly', 'animal friendly' products).
- *Social structure* – this denotes patterns of formal and informal interaction within the organization.
- *Norms and values* – behavioural expectations and preferences learnt by members of an organization.
- *Remembered history and symbolism* – includes stories, legends, heroes, rituals and ceremonies that help to exemplify and communicate norms and values.
- *Institutionalized framework* – policies and systems that influence attitudes and behaviours.

Schein (1992: 40) argues, fundamentally, that culture is not amenable to quantification. In Schein's words:

> ... when I see my colleagues inventing questionnaires to measure culture, I feel that they are simply not seeing what is there, and this is particularly dangerous when one is dealing with a social force that is invisible yet very powerful.

Schein (1992) does, however, offer an explanation of how culture 'works' to glue people together, to create consistency in thinking, feeling and behaving. Simply put, the content of culture becomes an inextricable part of the individual mindset, via a process of *socialization* (or *acculturation*). Socialization has itself been defined as the infusion or transmission of culture within a person (Hebden, 1986; Simpson, 1967). The socialization process (which can be formal or informal) assumes a mechanism of *indoctrination* of specifications for behaviour (appropriate rules and norms to follow) and of attitudes (to align them with those of the group) (Ofshe & Singer, 1986; Study Box 5.10).

---

**Study Box 5.10**

**Totalist indoctrination**

Schein's (1992) use of the unfreezing, change and refreezing process of change operates within the same conformity-inducing tradition. Thus, 'unfreezing' involves the destabilization of prior identity to diminish confidence in prior social judgements and to foster a sense of anxiety and powerlessness to reduce resistance to new demands and increasing suggestibility (for example, through degradation ceremonies and a requirement to challenge the adequacy of prior conduct; Ofshe & Singer, 1986). The 'change' process enables the individual to escape punishment by demonstrating the required learning. This involves cognitive restructuring (helping individuals judge things, feel things and react to things differently based on a new

*(Continued)*

---

**Study Box 5.10    Continued**

point of view). Finally, 'refreezing' denotes the attempt to promote and reinforce behaviour acceptable to the controlling organization through social approval, status gains and small privileges. The maintenance of the new identity depends on continual careful management, monitoring and manipulation of the social and emotional environment (through peer pressure) including the prohibition of alternative ways of being and doing. This includes limiting or prohibiting opportunities for criticism or the sharing of doubts and reservations about the group ideology.

---

Whilst most programmes of change may not be quite so coercive in their acculturation strategies and tactics, they will all nonetheless implicitly subscribe to a tradition that culture can be instilled in individuals through various methods of social control. This stance on culture has led to the following research efforts: attempts to describe the 'content' of culture to be instilled, to identify the attributes of culture that are likely to be most conducive to organizational success and to investigate more closely the role of the leader in engineering cultural change.

### *Identifying cultural attributes*

Following in the steps of classical anthropology in which it was common to describe and classify cultures like plants by a botanist (Widdowson, 2003), several different organizational typologies began to emerge (Study Box 5.11).

---

**Study Box 5.11**

**Cultural typologies**

There are many managerial attempts to develop taxonomic systems that allow organizations to be categorized according to their predominant structural features, assuming that organizations can be classified *as a whole*. Example classifications include:

* Deal and Kennedy (1982): Tough-guy macho, Work hard-play hard, Bet-your-company, Process;
* Williams, Dobson and Walters (1989): Power, Role, Task and People orientations;
* Harrison (1972): Power, Role, Achievement, Support cultures.

Furnham and Gunter (1993) argue that theories of classification can be tested empirically and as such can be discarded, revised or supported. Simple 'typing' can also be used to help people become aware of their own culture and how it differs from others, making an otherwise complex and elusive concept potentially more accessible. However, classification merely describes and does not explain culture or its consequences. Moreover, posited cultural types have proved little more than interpretative intuitions that have yet to be validated.

In the effort not only to describe, but to quantify the core attributes of culture, many different psychometric measures also began to appear (Study Box 5.12). Such tools can be easily administered and are probably the least costly option for organizations seeking readily digestible results for both diagnostic and evaluation purposes (Johnson & Scholes, 1997). There is enormous discrepancy, however, in views on what constitutes the crucial cultural dimensions.

---

**Study Box 5.12**

**Culture surveys or 'organometrics' (Furnham & Gunter, 1993)**

- *Organizational Culture Inventory* (Cooke & Szumal, 1993) – profiles culture in terms of 'behavioural norms' and 'expectations'. Cultures are divided into three types: constructive, passive/defensive, or aggressive/defensive.
- *Organizational Culture Scale* (O'Reilly, Chatman & Caldwell, 1991) – focuses on communication processes within an organization across six subscales: teamwork–conflict, climate–morale, information flow, involvement, supervision and meetings.
- *Hofstede's measure of culture and values* (Hofstede, Neuijen, Ohayv & Sanders, 1990) – measures values and practices.
- *Corporate Culture Survey* (Zamanou & Glaser, 1994) – divided into four subscales measuring: values, heroes/heroines, tradition/rituals and cultural network.
- *Organizational Beliefs Questionnaire* (Sashkin, 1984) – measures organizational values on ten subscales: work should be fun, being the best, innovation, attention to detail, worth and value of people, quality, communicating to get the job done, growth/profit/success indicators, hands-on management, and importance of shared philosophy.
- *Culture Gap Survey* (Kilmann, 1985) – measures behavioural norms on four subscales: task support, task innovation, social relations, and personal freedom, and along two dimensions: technical/human concern and short-term/long-term orientation.
- *Diagnosing organizational culture* (Harrison, 1975) – assesses organizational ideologies against four orientations: support orientation, achievement orientation, power orientation, role culture.

---

Most researchers agree that culture is *conceptually different* from climate. Debates centre more on whether culture, like climate, can be measured by survey (Study Box 5.13). Burke, Borucki and Kaufman (2002) define climate as perceptions of organizational characteristics (how it *feels* to be a member of the organization) rather than individual members' interpretations of organizational events. In Schneider's (2000) words, culture focuses on *why* things happen as they do, on the meaning or reasons for what happens, whereas climate tells us *what* is happening. Moran and Volkwein (1992) say that climate is directly observable whereas culture is not.

A common criticism of the climate construct, however, is that it is no more than another way of looking at satisfaction (Baltes, Bauer, Bajdo, & Parker, 2002) and/or commitment (Suliman, 2002). However, others maintain that whilst perceptions of climate are significantly associated with job satisfaction and commitment, they are not reducible to this (Carr, Schmidt, Ford, & DeShon, 2003). Using Ostroff's (1993) model, Carr et al. (2003) found that different climate perceptions predicted different psychological outcomes (satisfaction, commitment, well-being) as a function of whether they were associated with an *affective*, *cognitive* or *instrumental* latent state.

In practice, however, researchers may use the terms culture and climate interchangeably to look at the 'way in which people experience and make sense of their organizational environment' (Schneider, 2000).

---

**Study Box 5.13**

**Culture and climate?**

The difference between the constructs of culture and climate is said perhaps to be largely a difference in epistemological perspective (Denison, 1996). Most culture research has been undertaken from within an anthropological and sociological perspective, although this approach has been largely superseded by a constructivist/ critical theory framework. Climate, on the other hand, has a tradition rooted in Lewinian field theory (Lewin, 1948) and has a more global and intuitive 'affective' flavour (that is, what it feels like, general environmental ambience). Whereas culture is rooted in history, held collectively and difficult to change, climate is subjective, temporal and can be more easily manipulated by those in authority and power (Mearns & Flin, 1999). In practice, whether these concepts really do denote distinct phenomena or whether they are interconnected concepts (for example, climate is a manifestation or symptom of culture) are issues for debate. Some maintain a conceptual and an empirical distinction (for example, Alvesson, & Deetz, 1996) which in the early days was easier to justify in that culture was regarded as a highly qualitative phenomenon irreducible to dimensions in a survey, whereas climate was assessed using quantitative methods. However, nowadays this empirical distinction is more difficult to justify and maintain. For example, Solomon's (1986) Organizational Climate Questionnaire is similar to O'Reilly et al.'s (1991) Organizational Culture Scale, especially the subscales measuring team orientation, involvement and information flow. The pressure on practitioners to 'measure' and 'contain' culture so that it can be more easily 'manipulated' may have contributed to this conflation of the two concepts in empirical terms. On the other hand, findings on safety management suggest that safety climate is in part a culture's expression (Cox & Flin, 1998; Mearns & Flin, 1999; O'Toole, 2002). O'Toole (2002) found, in particular, that there was a positive impact of perceived safety attitudes and values on safety outcomes (including reduction of injury rates), which could suggest that *climate is in fact how culture is perceived* or that *climate is a mediator of cultural phenomena* (see, for example, Zohar, 2003). However, in general, the literature does a lot more describing than explaining (Ong, 2004).

---

***Linking cultural attributes to performance*** It is commonly assumed that a 'strong' culture (well-integrated and effective set of specific values, beliefs and behaviour patterns) is critical to organizational success (Case Study 5.2). However, evidence shows that the link between organizational culture and its success or failure in a given market is not so simple (Marcoulides & Heck, 1993). Moreover, strong cultures might facilitate success in highly reliable organizations involved in life-and-death type work (military, accident and emergency services), but do not afford the essential flexibility required to adapt to new circumstances with efficiency and effectiveness (Sorensen, 2002). Even the ultra-reliable military organization has acknowledged the costs associated with the inability to respond flexibly and fast (Phillips, Loureries, Millward, Kyriakidou & Gore, 2003).

---

**Case Study 5.2 The pottery industry**

Strong traditions of value and belief have passed down through generations of workers since the 1700s and such traditions can still be evidenced in the Staffordshire pottery industry within companies such as Wedgwood, Spode, Mason, Royal Doulton, and Minton. The founder Josiah Wedgwood was – and is still depicted as – an adventurous experimenter and inventor striving for new developments in techniques and standards of creativity and excellence, good to customers, and responsible for the establishment of a humanitarian tradition. All of these values remain strongly evident today not only in the way the factories are run, but also in the involvement of the Wedgwood family in research on elderly mental health and in surgical aid.

---

The precise link between culture and performance will, however, depend heavily on how the concept is studied, whether from an organizational (Marcoulides & Heck, 1993) and/or individual (O'Reilly, Chatman & Caldwell, 1991) perspective. Moreover, perceptions of culture differ according to levels in the organizational hierarchy and the presence of influential subunits within an organization may have either an inhibitory or enhancing influence on performance (Cooke & Rousseau, 1988). Sackmann (1997) points out that any one culture (for example, an organizational culture) comprises diverse and sometimes contradictory elements denoting a conglomeration of co-existing, newly emerging, and continually changing subcultures.

Subcultures may not always necessarily conform to the managerial rhetoric of the proscribed cultural values of the organization. Internal fragmentation can occur even in organizations with a strongly homogeneous external image of uniformity and solidarity, such as the police force. Jermier, Slocum, Fry and Gaines (1991), for instance, described an 'anti-military social work' subcultural cluster espousing a philosophy of service, and a 'peacekeeping moral entrepreneur' cluster espousing a philosophy of peacekeeping and maintaining order. The appearance of a singular mission and uniform conduct, argue Jermier et al. (1991), may be reserved for the 'public', whilst the reality of organizational life is a set of divergent missions and varied practices arising from personal biographies (gender, race, ethnicity) and social histories (family background, social class membership, educational level), positional characteristics (speciality, rank) and task exigencies (technical and/or managerial requirements.

***The role of the cultural leader*** In a conventional 'top-down' driven culture change, the role of leaders is critical. Through rhetoric and practice, leaders can demonstrate the required 'attributes' in the way they conduct themselves on a day-to-day basis (Schein, 1992: 317). The concept of the 'transformational leader' is rooted in this assumption and has generated some significant findings (Study Box 5.14). The appointment of a new leader is often used as a catalyst for immediate change insofar as he or she embodies or personifies the new vision and values (for example, Rank Xerox, British Airways; Furnham, 1997). Caution, however, has been raised by studies showing how a new leader may, on the contrary, be perceived by members as a threat to the stability and identity of an organization (Buono & Bowditch, 2003).

---

### Study Box 5.14

#### The transformational leader

Concepts associated with the 'transformational' leader include charisma, inspiration and vision. Bass (1998) argued that most leadership research conceptualizes the process of leading as transactional, where the relationship between the leader and the follower are based on a series of cost-benefit exchanges, or implicit bargains (for example, path–goal theory, House and Mitchell, 1975; see Chapter 4). This could be in the form of clarifying goals and rewards in return for goal achievement. Whilst this might motivate subordinates to perform expected goals, the transformational leader will inspire people to go further than originally expected.

The transformational leader generates awareness and acceptance of the purpose of change, assists followers in identifying where the future of the organization lies, and gains commitment to that future vision, even if the individual has to put aside self-interest for the greater good of the group. By doing this, the transformational leader can ultimately 'transform' the organization. As Buono and Bowditch (2003) conclude, most people will support the change effort if they can *understand* the need for it.

A relatively neglected consideration, however, is the prerequisite ability of the leader to comprehend a potentially highly complex change situation (termed 'situational awareness'), and to translate it into both meaningful and actionable terms (Gutmann & Pierre, 2000). Also, the transformational ability of a leader assumes positive change beliefs and self-efficacy in connection with the change management task.

---

Consistent with the above analysis, a typical change programme thus involves the top-down manipulation of culture as follows (for example, Williams, Dobson, & Walters, 1989; Study Box 5.15):

- establishing a clear strategic vision underpinned by precise achievable goals;
- secure commitment from the 'top';
- demonstrating 'culture' through appropriate leadership practices;
- supporting change with an appropriate infrastructure (for example, reward structures and mechanisms);

- changing organizational membership (if necessary) or encouraging existing members to 'buy in' to change through consultation, training and development; 'buy in' approaches like this are often little more than 'rubber stamping' exercises.

---

**Study Box 5.15**

**Culture change recipes**

There are many recipes for culture change, but very few of them are theoretically driven or have been evaluated empirically. Recipe approaches assume that change can be unambiguously harnessed and secured. However, it is now generally agreed that recipe-induced change rarely results in lasting change (for example, Herriot, Hirsch, & Reilly, 1998; Ofshe & Singer, 2003) and in many cases can result in hostility, resentment and psychological distancing. Change that requires adjustment to new inter-subjective meanings may be strenuously resisted (Hatch & Schultz, 2002). When Temig, a major Brazilian telecommunications company, tried to introduce a completely new culture and set of practices from the top, it merely succeeded in generating a counter-culture. It was regarded as manipulative and failed to create the desired change. Many now adopt Herriot et al.'s (1998) thinking that the recipe book approach detracts from the complexity and necessary analytical sophistication for characterizing and explaining culture change. Maybe we are beginning to see the last of the recipe book approach to change …

---

Recently, the *attribute-acculturation* approach to culture change has been seriously questioned. Up to 70 percent of organizations are said to have tried to 'transform' their culture using this approach in the 1980s and 1990s, but failed (Burke, 2002). Experiences like that of AT&T, which took 10 years to change its culture, are not uncommon: CEOs like the president cited by Senior (2000) who gave up after only six years of trying need not apply! Findings like this question whether it is desirable to direct either the course or speed of change within an organization. Radical transformational change can often involve quite a *brutal refutation of the meanings* that employees have constructed over many years. It is not surprising, then, that change superimposed on an organization in this way is likely to be 'resisted' (van Muijen, 1998: 119).

The above criticisms stem in the main from a different epistemology of culture and of the interface between culture and individuals, in parallel with developments in anthropology as well as organization science influenced by postmodern thinking (Study Box 5.16).

---

**Study Box 5.16**

**'Cultural psychology'**

There is an emerging field of 'cultural psychology' that is described as having in common nothing other than a 'commitment to the cultural formation of individuals'

*(Continued)*

---

**Study Box 5.16    Continued**

(Squire, 2000). In other words, the individual *is* culture rather than 'in' culture and to this extent the individual cannot be conceived of outside of their cultural context. This newly emerging psycho-cultural approach does not subscribe to the view that culture can be reduced to perception, since this maintains the assumption of dualism (that is, there is a culture 'out there' to perceive). On the contrary, culture is conceptualized as a process involving people. This does not dissolve the relevance of psychology (which some structural postmodernists do by displacing the subject to the status of an epiphenomenon). Culture in psychology, on the contrary, looks at the psychological processes involved in cultural construction. In qualitative research, people give very psychological accounts of self in relation to culture, positioning themselves in it as well as feeling sometimes trapped by it. Squire (2000) argues that we should aim to blend different levels of analysis for a fuller more meaningful account of culture.

---

Millward, Brown and Kyriakidou (2003) identify some fundamental flaws in the assumption of the attribute-acculturation approach as follows:

- *Culture is assumed to be equivalent to reality itself.* Organizational (and national) boundaries are inappropriately used as a surrogate definition of culture, in part attributable to a lack of theory about the relationship between culture and psychological reality within and across organizations (as well as within and across nations).
- *Culture determines attitudes and behaviours.* Culture pre-exists individuals and is imposed on them.
- *Culture is homogeneous and relatively unchanging, describable in the form of typologies.* This has promoted an uncritical and fallacious search for a definitive 'success culture'; a view that has since been consistently disputed since, at its simplest level, what constitutes success varies substantially by circumstance (Martin, 2002). Anthropologists have demonstrated that culture is much more fluid and internally diversified than previously recognized, and that assumptions of cultural homogeneity are the product of perception (for example, cultural stereotyping) and motivation (for example, inter-group boundary carving) rather than reality (Widdowson, 2003). Cultural perceptions and stereotypes fulfil particular functions (for example, categorization and sense-making processes) that precede the phenomenon of culture itself, originating in group and inter-group dynamics (Haslam, 2004).
- *Culture is promulgated and manipulated by leaders.* For example, 'culture and leadership are two sides of the same coin' (Schein, 1992: 2). This view of how culture originates and impacts on people is attractive in its ease of translation into recipes for change, but is now understood to be an oversimplification (Martin, 2002). Evidence from the literature on safety management confirms the importance of the leader – especially their demonstrated commitment and behaviour – for instilling and cultivating safety values and practices (see 'Safety Cultures' in Chapter 8). However, culture is found not to be simply a matter of leaders dictating and enacting a new cultural reality: cultures are co-created by leaders and their followers as they mutually engage in the process of making sense (Clarke & Meldrum, 1999).

- *Culture is acquired through a process of 'acculturation'.* Thus, the individual is assumed to be a passive recipient of socialization practices regulated and controlled by a socializing agent. Research demonstrates, however, that employees actively socialize themselves with reference to pre-existing schemas (Kammeyer-Mueller & Wanberg, 2003). Attention has been too heavily focused on organization-driven socialization practices rather than employee-driven ones, and has, moreover, omitted to consider how pressures to conform may be an impediment to innovation (Jones, 1986).
- *Culture can be assessed through the extent to which people endorse cultural values, norms and practices.* This kind of research has, however, fuelled what Walkerdine (2000) has described as a 'love–hate' relationship between psychologists and scholars of cultural study because of the *reductionism* inherent in the use of cultural surveys. For instance, Wasti (2003) describes individualistic and collectivist cultures as those in which the modal profile across individuals is either 'idiocentric' or 'allocentric', respectively. Thus, culture is reduced to the *frequency* across individuals in their endorsement of particular cultural values and norms. Suffice it to say that despite the availability now of some very sophisticated multi-level modelling techniques for assessing *supra-individual* effects using individual-level data (Griffin, Mathieu, & Jacobs, 2001), the question of whether this is an *epistemologically* appropriate way of conceptualizing and measuring culture has not gone away.

Summarizing recent conceptualizations of culture, Millward et al. (2003) offer a complementary (if not alternative) stance on *culture as process*, as follows:

- *Culture as communication* – culture is a means of communication, rather than a 'super-organic' entity, that offers both a template or guide to existing meanings that facilitate social interaction (for example, to render it intelligible and predictable), whilst at the same time constituting a medium for reinvention and change of meanings through social interaction. Culture, like language, is not reducible to individual minds, but at the same time it is produced by, and can be deemed an emergent property of, interaction between individuals (Giddens, 1984, structuration theory). It allows people to understand each others' actions and to act in ways that convey the meanings they want, but at the same time new meanings can also be created (Geertz, 1983, semiotic view of culture). People recreate culture all the time (and never replicate it entirely), sometimes consciously.
- *Culture as a resource* – whilst we would expect shared meanings amongst those who belong to a particular culture, no one is a blueprint or complete representative of this culture. Culture is a milieu in which people construct themselves (that is, culture does not construct people; they construct themselves in this context). To this extent, culture is a resource that enables people to model reality and their place in it, but is not reality itself. The way culture is used depends on their goals and aspirations. For instance, culture may be used symbolically as a source of group legitimacy or as a political weapon. People behave in particular ways not because of their culture, but they use culture as their means of interaction. Thus, cultural heterogeneity may be glossed over in a power play between groups, involving attempts to legitimize claims to cultural distinctiveness (Haslam, 2004).

Models of culture change within the OD tradition assume that change is 'episodic' (that is, the change, no matter how small, requires a transformation of some kind from a previous to a new state) and that the organization's culture and its composite individuals are separate entities that have to be somehow 'glued' together. Change thus requires 'unfreezing' the old glue and applying a new, more improved version. This model, however, fundamentally ignores the role of people as creators and perpetuators of culture – that is, the inseparability of cultures and individuals (Study Box 5.16). As such, cultures are constantly changing of their own natural accord through an ongoing process of sense making and constructing. This kind of change is of an evolutionary (unplanned, first order) kind (Rugg, Eva, Mahmood, Rehman, Andrews, & Davies, 2002; Schein, 2004). Some change experts are now advocating that culture is 'evolved' and *cannot* be directly 'transformed'.

Even though a radical change may eventually become embedded (for example, 10 years for AT&T), the process may be unnecessarily prolonged due to inertias arising from the sheer fact of having a new 'artificial' culture superimposed on it (Senior, 2000). Facilitating a process of evolutionary/incremental change, not of culture per se, by, for example, establishing new working practices (demanded by a business imperative), culture will evolve in support of these practices through a natural process of sense making (in which practices are 'responded to' – welcomed, rejected, accepted, modified) and socially construction such that these choices become part of the practice itself (Orlikowski, 1993). Change can be actively facilitated and supported, but 'culture' is something that will evolve in conjunction with this change and as such cannot be controlled or imposed. When the relationship between people and context is seen as one of mutual creation and negotiation, the outputs are seen as the emergent product of their interrelation. The reality of the organization/individual interface is, in fact, *naturally one of ongoing adjustment, initiated and carried out by individuals* (Orlikowski, 1993).

### The narrative model

The narrative approach to culture change is rooted in postmodern thinking. It is commonly accepted now that people are driven to make sense of the world (so they can locate themselves within it and create order and meaning; Weick & Quinn, 1999). One way in which people do this is to recount their experiences in the form of a 'story' (Boje, Alvarez, & Schooling, 2001). 'Stories' have long been recognized as a key component of an organization's culture (see Vecchio, 1995 for a review). Communication through telling stories is a basic human activity. A story is an account of a specific event, though stories can be linked together. One crucial aspect of a 'story' is that it has some sort of implicit structure – a middle, a beginning and an end. Within this structure, the story will have a sequence (there is a plot or a point of some kind) all pointing towards an emerging future. This sequencing of experience captures time (past, present, future), and as such enables us to see how the past is transformed into a future (Study Box 5.17).

---

**Study Box 5.17**

**Stories and story telling**

Stories come about mainly in association with departures from the socially acceptable/normative that calls for an explanation. To this extent, the story attempts to reconcile the tension between the expected and the normatively exceptional event. A story, moreover, communicates information about the inner world of the story teller and/or the person about whom the story is being told. In particular, it conveys something about identity, intentions and feelings. Stories refer to specific events at a particular time and place whether the event really happened or not. To some extent, the way a story is told is shaped by the audience. There is no one definitive reading of a story; it depends on the agenda of the listener. A story can be a means of resolving dilemmas and tensions. The act of telling a story in particular can provide a means of re-establishing control and order (through the process of formulating an account). Telling stories can also help bring order to chaos, and thereby enables some kind of understanding to be achieved (for example, of how and why something happened). Through story telling, the teller is not only representing information and experience, but constructing an identity. Stories can also contextualize and locate meaning.

---

As well as a general sense-making function, other functions served by story telling include:

- bringing order, sequence, and a sense of completion to a set of experiences;
- problem solving by providing a causal explanation for something that happened;
- development of a sense of perspective, by placing a singular event into its broader context.

Drawing on narrative forms of therapeutic change (White & Epston, 1989), the 'story' metaphor is now being used in organizational change as a means of gaining access to, and facilitating, change in fundamental underlying 'maps' of the world (for example, Boje et al., 2001; Wilkins & Thompson, 1991).

## Part 1 Summary and Conclusions

- OD is associated with a set of traditions surrounding the change process, framed by a problem-solving approach in which change is viewed as a problem (employee resistance) to be overcome.
- This begins with a diagnostic phase to establish key sources of resistance and then proceeds through a top-down process of change, involving a period of 'unfreezing' of old attitudes and ways of behaving through confrontation and persuasion, followed by a period of 'refreezing' new more desirable attitudes and behaviours.
- Recent additions to the basic model include attempts to make people feel involved in the change, but 'involvement' has many different renditions. Evidence suggests

that feeling involved is successful in engaging people to change because it creates a sense of ownership, control and, above all, a sense of justice in the procedures used to facilitate change.

- Culture change also rests on an assumption that 'culture' is the key to an organization's success, that it is incumbent on researchers to identify the critical performance-enhancing attributes and on practitioners to instil them in employees. Culture change typically follows a recipe consistent with the OD unfreezing–refreezing principle. The leader is seen as key to securing culture change.
- Criticisms of this approach question the concept of culture as a homogeneous set of attributes, and of the principle of acculturation using methods of social control. Recent views on culture see it more as a process of communication and as a source of meaning or resource.
- Some contemporary OD efforts ('appreciative inquiry') may begin by identifying the strengths of an organization with a view to building on them. This approach sees language or narrative as a critical source of leverage for change.

# Part 2: Psychology *of*, and *in*, the Process of Change

One of the main criticisms of change models is their lack of attention to micro-level considerations of change. Arguably, there is a psychology both *of* change (that is, how change can be brought about), and *in* the change itself (that is, the experience, meaning and creation of change), that can be usefully harnessed in the change effort. OD approaches tend to employ a macro-level approach that makes assumptions *about* micro-level processes (for example, resistance, acculturation) but does not explore them further, for example, in the effort to understand why inertia or resistance is likely during a change effort, or what facilitates acceptance of change. Postmodern approaches contribute substantially to understanding the role of language in change, but there is a distinct lack of attention to the *subjective* in this work.

## Reactions to Change

Any change, whether anticipated or actual, can be a major source of stress for individuals, generating fear and inducing resistance (George & Jones, 2001). Resistance has been little studied, but those who have looked closely at this concept say that it is a multi-dimensional consideration. For example, Dawson (2003) proposes that resistance can result from one, or a combination, of the following factors:

- substantive changes in job (change in skill requirements);
- threat to employment;
- psychological threat (perceived or actual);
- lowering of status (redefinition of authority relations).

Management books are replete with suggestions for how to overcome these resistances (for example, ensure quick success, celebrate success, unload old baggage; for example, Bridges, 2001), but no further consideration is given to understanding how these resistances come about or how people work through them, despite the call for urgent attention to this issue by Tannenbaum and Hanna in 1985.

One key psychological consideration in the study of resistance is the potential threat to self-esteem posed by organizational change (Jetten, O'Brien, & Trindall, 2002; van Knippenberg et al., 2002). Coopersmith (1967: 4–5) defines self-esteem as 'the evaluation the individual makes and customarily maintains with regard to the self: it expresses an attitude of approval or disapproval, and indicates the extent to which an individual believes the self to be capable, significant, successful and worthy'. Self-esteem is inextricably linked with self-efficacy: a person will think well of him or herself if he or she is effective in dealing with the outside world. Likewise, Locke (2001: 9) argues that self-esteem comprises two components: a belief in one's ability to deal with life challenges and a belief in one's fundamental worth.

Locke (2001) argues that the realm of work is critical to self-esteem since it is via work that life can be mastered and sustained. Generally, people seek and maintain self-enhancing identities and find it difficult to adjust to identities that make or will potentially make them feel bad about themselves. Identity importance intensifies the experience of something that could severely threaten it. So, for example, the manager might fear loss of status contingent upon the implementation of a policy of employee involvement in decision making, or the loss of identity continuity implied by 'merger' or redundancy (Breakwell, 1986; Chreim, 2002).

People's response to change can also be formulated in terms of whether it involves some gain or loss in value for the individual (Prochaska, Redding & Evers, 1997). Research has shown that a positive decisional balance (in favour of gain) is a good predictor of successful behavioural change across a broad range of situations. That is, if people perceive that the effort is worth the outcome (expectancy theory), they are also more likely to engage with a change effort (Burke, 2002). Change must therefore be perceived as 'attractive' (value enhancing, beneficial) for an individual to engage with it.

Carnall (1990), however, says that there is a finite level of change that self-esteem can cope with before it begins to inhibit functioning. Adams, Hayes and Hopkins (1976) note that the way people cope with change is transitional rather than parabolic. They describe a five-stage model beginning with denial (psychological buffering against information and emotional overload), defensive behaviour (resistant to persuasion as to the needs for change, prone to anxiety and even depression), 'discarding' or 'nostalgic' (appreciation that change is inevitable and necessary), testing the new reality (acknowledging the advantages of the new systems, procedures and so on) and internalization (complete acceptance) (Study Box 5.18).

Kubler-Ross (1969) describes a similar model of responses to traumatic personal loss in that change can also imply 'loss' of an old way of being and doing. Although there has been no direct research to link Parkes's (1972) grief processes with employee experiences of organizational change, many writers make allusions to this link in their recognition that employees exhibit signs of 'grief' during major change (for example, Bridges, 2001). However, there is no evidence that individual change occurs through a series of stages (Segan, Borland, & Greenwood, 2004).

---

**Study Box 5.18**

### Work role transitions

Organizational transitions denote major changes in role requirement (for example, job redesign, change of co-workers, job change), involving role transition. Nicholson and West (1988) describe role transition in four stages: preparation (for example, 'psychological readiness'), encounter (for example, 'shock' and 'surprise'), adjustment (for example, development of new priorities), and stabilization (for example, role maintenance and final adjustment). Psychological defences such as denial and withdrawal are said to be common at the preparation and encounter stages. 'Lay-off survivor sickness' has been used to describe the stress induced post-downsizing (for example, Noer, 1997). However, it is commonly found that this experience does not last long, and the transition may be re-construed in retrospect as a positive one affording growth and development. For instance, Axtell, Wall, Stride, Pepper, Clegg, Gardner, and Bolden (2002) found that increased job complexity following a change event mediated adjustment in their study. Whether this is likely to happen may depend on pre-downsizing attitudes. For example, Mishra and Spreitzer (1998) argued that things such as job involvement and trust in management may moderate reactions to downsizing, by affecting how the event is appraised (see Lazarus, 2000, also 'Stress and Stress Management', in Chapter 8). If job involvement and initial trust is high, a major imposed change may be appraised as a violation of a psychological contract.

　　Looking more closely at the 'preparation stage', Prochaska et al. (1997) argue that readiness for change begins with a perception of the benefits of change, the risks of failing to change or the demands of externally imposed change. Later Prochaska added that the perceived ability to manage change successfully (efficacy for change) also exerts an effect on readiness to change (Prochaska et al., 1997). Research reported by Cunningham, Woodward, Shannon, MacIntosh, Lendrum, Rosenblum and Brown (2002) confirmed that the role of job-change efficacy was the single biggest predictor of whether employees ($N = 654$) in a health-care organization actively engaged with large-scale change. Notably, the greater the efficacy ('readiness'), the higher the emotional exhaustion scores, which could be interpreted as an integral part of an active coping response.

---

　　Both models can be credited with highlighting the emotionally charged nature of the change experience (as opposed to focusing primarily on the rational, cognitive aspects of change) and the need to actively manage affect during the change management process (Kiefer, 2002). There is indeed growing attention to the 'emotional' side of organizational life generally, and emotional management more specifically (Callahan & McCollum, 2002; Weiss, 2002; see 'Stress and Stress Management' in Chapter 8).

　　One other common explanation offered for why people may resist change links with research on the psychological contract (Noer, 1997; Rousseau, 1995). From this perspective, change may leave people feeling betrayed and angry. Stiles, Gratton, Truss, Hope-Hailey and McGovern (1996) provide evidence from three major UK-based firms that survivors perceived that the organization had violated employee psychological contracts during change (whether they had directly experienced this or not). This had a number of negative individual and organizational consequences, including reduced profits. Highly identified and involved employees (with strong relational contracts) are likely to be especially sensitive to how change is handled (Allen, Freeman, Russell, Reizenstein, & Rentz, 2001). Mone and Barker (1996) found that organizational trust mediated the relationship between downsizing and individual and organizational outcomes. The higher the pre-existing degree of organizational trust, the greater the impact of perceived injustice and the more negative the impact of change.

If employees perceive injustices in the lay-off procedures, commitment can take an especially dramatic nosedive: the stronger the pre-lay-off commitment, the greater the potential for damage (Allen et al., 2001; Meyer, 1997). Among such employees, commitment can be difficult to recover, and may not return to pre-downsizing levels completely (Armstrong-Stassen, 2002; Lind et al., 2000; Rousseau & Wade-Benzioni, 1995).

Research on the victims themselves also suggests that their experience of violation may be generally difficult to recover from, affecting their attitudes towards re-employment. Among a sample of 141 lay-off victims, Pugh, Skarlicki and Passell (2003) found that violation was associated with a reduced trust in the new employer and increased cynicism. Worrying (ruminative preoccupation that things might go wrong) about being similarly mistreated mediated the association between violation and both trust and cynicism (an attitude of disillusionment, negative feelings towards and distrust of organization). Brief (1998) has called this 'attitudinal baggage'.

Cynicism is said in particular to be associated with negative implications for organizations, including reduced organizational citizenship (Wanous, Reichers, & Austin, 2000) and the worry associated with this may also be cause for substantial anxiety and emotional discomfort (Morrison & Robinson, 1997). Theoretically, the experience of lay-off is seen as forming a pre-employment schema that has a self-fulfilling aspect to it (because the individual concerned may be defensively guarded and mistrustful), making it difficult for an employee to re-engage or for anyone to try to re-engage him of her (Pugh, Skarlicki, & Passell, 2003).

## Part 2 Summary (I) and Conclusions

- Little is known about the concept of resistance, its sources and its psychological causes and manifestations. One key source of resistance may arise from threats to identity and self-esteem.
- Evidence suggests that people do weigh up the costs and benefits of change relative to their current circumstances and also make judgements about whether the proposed benefits are likely to be achieved.
- Models of individual change propose that people go through a series of stages during a change effort, which may involve working through the 'loss' signified by the change. These models highlight the emotional trauma that can be suffered by people during imposed organizational change.
- Whilst the evidence for stages of change is thin, findings do indicate that people respond better to change if they feel 'ready for it'. Readiness may involve feeling able to change (that is, change efficacy).

## The Sense-Making Model

To understand and manage effective change, contemporary change scholars argue that it is necessary to examine employee sense making that serves to create and legitimate the meaning of change (Dutton, Duckerich & Harquail, 1994). Sense making refers to the attempts of actors to build their own understandings of their context. The assumption is that people are continuously engaged in a sense-making process, which involves the creation of reality by making retrospective sense of the situation in which they find themselves, including their own actions (Weick & Quinn, 1999). 'Making sense' tends to occur with reference to some existing interpretative scheme which, in so doing, perpetuates the schema. However, some inevitable modification will also take place as 'unknown' events are assimilated and accommodated to the scheme.

The schema concept is central to the sense-making perspective on change (George & Jones, 2001; Peterson & Smith, 2000). George and Jones (2001) propose a model of the individual change process that starts with the idea that organizational members use schemas to process information and make sense of what is going on in their organizations'. In this model, affect plays a key role in initiating the change process and directing sense-making activities to pressing concerns (Figure 5.2).

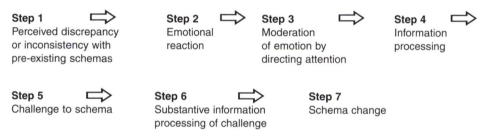

**Figure 5.2**  Sense-making process during change

This model has yet to be empirically evaluated, but resonates closely with Lazarus' model of appraisal processes in relation to stress and coping (Lazarus, 2000; see Chapter 8), which has itself been the focus of considerable research. An important feature of sense making is also the role of sense giving, which concerns attempts to influence the way another party understands or makes sense. Gioia and Chittipeddi (1991) found that sense making and sense giving occur in a reciprocal fashion encompassing progressively expanding audiences.

Weick and Quinn (1999) and others (for example, Peterson & Smith, 2000) argue that language interventions, or sense giving, are fundamental tools for facilitating change. Helping employees make sense of change requires a strong alternative interpretation to be presented clearly and persistently. It is more usual for people to refer back to themselves and their own experience when 'making sense', but this can be complemented by a range of sense-giving interventions to help contextualize personal sense-making efforts (Peterson & Smith, 2000).

It is generally agreed that it is incumbent upon managers or leaders of change to explain the 'who, what, where, why and how' of the change (Burke, 2002). Leaders can indeed help with the sense-making process by drawing attention to particular events and meanings. However, there are many other more powerful sources of sense giving for an employee. Colleagues, for example, may be even more pivotal as trusted every-day sources via which to derive meaning, particularly in instances where everyone is collectively trying to make sense of a radical change. External sources (for example, media) can also play a sense-giving role (for example, big corporate takeovers are often the focus of much media attention, Case Study 5.2). Finally, friends and family can also actively influence the way employees make sense of a change. Different sources of 'sense giving' will need, however, to be reconciled by the employee, which may account for continued resistance or equivocation (Bartunek, 1984).

The above approach to sense making does not explain why it is that employees may be especially resistant to change, why pre-existing interpretative schemas may in fact not engage with change. One explanation for why a schema may resist change is because it is deeply rooted in identity (Dutton, Dukerich, & Harquail, 1994; Study Box 5.19). Organizations have identities (Ashforth & Mael, 1989) that influence interpretations of, and attitudes towards, change through employee perceptions of these identities (Gioia & Thomas, 1996). Using Weick's (1977) concept of enactment, employees actively frame proposed changes as they construct and enact organizational reality through schemas of organizational identity. If a new organizational identity is not perceived to be attractive relative to the present organizational identity, this will constrain an employee's engagement with the change implied.

---

**Study Box 5.19**

### Corporate identity and organizational identity

Carroll (1995) argues that 'corporate identity' can be used as a metaphor for articulating the espoused values and beliefs of an organization during change programmes. Introducing new logos and letterheads, corporate flags and colour schemes may signal the first phase of a longer-term change programme. A clear vision statement gives direction and meaning to an organization's strategy, and enables people to project themselves more securely into the future (Johnson & Scholes, 1997). Such cosmetic alterations serve to prepare employees for the more significant changes that are to follow, though they are not enough in themselves to effect change (Hatch & Schultz, 2002).

Corporate identity 'means different things to different people'. Olins defines corporate identity as 'the explicit management of all the ways in which the organisation presents itself through experiences and perceptions of all its audiences' (1995: 1). In short, corporate identity can be described as the visible, tangible communication of the *external image of an organization* to an audience (whether that audience is internal, or external, to the company). The potential impact of corporate identity on external audiences is consistently demonstrated. Gatewood, Gowan and Lautenschlager (1993) showed how job applicants are motivated to pursue positions with organizations depending in part on their corporate image.

*(Continued)*

> ### Study Box 5.19    Continued
>
> Dutton, Dukerich and Harquail (1994) show how employees infer the reputation of their organization and react to the external image they construe of their organization, proud to belong (for example, basking in reflected glory) to an organization that is believed to have socially valued characteristics (Mael & Ashforth, 1992). Dutton, Dukerich and Harquail (1994) emphasize the importance of distinctiveness and continuity in employees' perceptions of their organization's image when considering the extent to which an individual *identifies* with his/her employing organization. Strong identification is associated with heightened psychological attachment to the organization. This, in turn, is associated with pro-organizational behaviour (motivation, commitment, citizenship). Thus, what individuals think about an organization (organizational identity), coupled with how they think others see it too (construed external image), affects how they see themselves and the way they behave as employees.

A future identity (as articulated through image projections and visionary claims by leaders and change agents) may be perceived threatening (unattractive), for example, if it undermines valued features of a current identity. Zeit (1996) describes how employees at a semiconductor manufacturer regarded the shift from technologically innovative to providing excellent customer service as 'dishonest', concluding that senior management were abandoning innovation. This created resistance.

The perceived future identity must be perceived as desirable (self-enhancing, maintaining continuity of valued organizational attributes) and defensible (perceived legitimate and valid) if employees are to engage with it, forcing them to question the relative unattractiveness of the present identity (Ashforth & Mael, 1996). However, as Millward and Kyriakidou (2004b) found, if the proposed change contradicts valued attributes and is out of step with employee needs for self-enhancement, change is likely to be rejected and resisted.

Millward and Kyriakidou (2004b) also found that if perceived future image was not perceived attractive relative to the perceived current image, there was no imperative on employees to question the adequacy of present organizational identity for fulfilling their identity needs. They concluded that the activation and 'pull' of a future organizational identity requires that employees critically question the viability of the existing identity, whilst simultaneously maintaining the integrity of its valued elements by projecting them forward into the new organizational state. This is consistent with findings demonstrating the importance of organizational identity, particularly the *continuity* of identity, to merger success (van Knippenberg et al., 2002).

The above findings point to the potential for integrating ideas about sense making with theories of organizational identity as a means not only for understanding resistance to change, but also for understanding how to make change 'attractive' and 'engaging' to individuals. The change process can, for example, be sensitively managed by giving due respect to issues of identity and self-esteem. Involvement with, and commitment to, change may be motivated largely by the extent to which an individual can anchor him- or herself meaningfully and positively in relation to the change – as opposed to being threatened by it. People need to make sense of the change and, if not aided in the sense-making process, may construct their own self-protective largely change-inhibitory stories (Ford & Locke, 2002; Ludema, 2002).

## Part 2 Summary (II) and Conclusions

- From a cognitive perspective, the success of a change effort depends on the ability of employees to understand and accept a new conceptualization of the organization.
- During a radical change event, people will experience cognitive and emotional discomfort because of a discrepancy between existing interpretative schemas and the 'unknown' situation that 'makes no sense'. Discrepancy evokes an intense period of sense making as the new situation is either accommodated to existing schemas (thus changing the schema) or new schemas are formed.
- Other people can be instrumental to the sense-making process by sharing their own meanings ('sense giving'). Resistance is likely to come about particularly in response to challenges to identity-relevant schemas. Change to identity schemas can come about if the change or prospect of change is: (1) self-enhancing; and (2) maintains the integrity of valued features of the present schema. A projected future identity will attract employees if they begin to appreciate the relative inadequacy of the present schema.

## Strategies of Change

In the OD literature, commitment-based strategies have evolved out of an assumption that the management task is one of persuading people to commit to a vision of the future (for example, Gallivan, Hofman & Orlikowski, 1994). Compliance-based strategies depend more on an analysis of the 'force-field' operating to either 'drive' or 'restrain' the implementation of change (Lewin, 1951). The management task in this instance is to pave the way for effective implementation by removing underlying 'restraints', thus reducing the probability that change will be 'resisted' by individuals affected by it.

Which strategy is chosen depends on how change is conceptualized – that is, as a process or as an implementation task (Wilson, 1992: 10–11). In short, commitment-based strategies presuppose a view of change as a process, whilst compliance-based strategies are implementation oriented and largely top-down (Study Box 5.20). Compliance is behaviourally driven whilst commitment is attitudinally driven. When people are committed to something, they tend to adopt it as their own. A compliant individual, however, will only undertake the action required of them because they have to.

---

**Study Box 5.20**

**Commitment based strategies of changed**

- explanation of the process of cultural change;
- emphasis on the importance of empathy, communication and participation with workers;
- clear articulation of desired visions and associated practices;
- translation of vision into memorable reality;
- endorsement of top management and 'modelling' by management;
- building a new team, if necessary, to reinforce the new values/approach;
- engaging in symbolic acts, for example, team/company presentations, changing uniforms to symbolize team spirit, and so on;
- explanation of proposed goals and aims to be achieved through change and how these will impact on the organization and, ultimately, on organizational performance, that is, translation of a 'soft' process into 'hard' financial results;
- training management in 'transformational' leadership skills, and in the understanding of group processes and group dynamics.

---

### Commitment-based strategies

Commitment-based strategies involve attitude change. Eagly and Chaiken (1993) describe an attitude as an evaluative reaction, either favourably or unfavourably disposed towards something or someone. Changing attitudes depends on the skill of persuasion. Persuasion is defined as to 'win over by an appeal to one's reasons and feelings'. The ideal scenario is where people have already worked out what they need to do and have started the attitude change process.

Attitudes may be deeply rooted in personal experience and identity and, as such, can be highly invulnerable to change. According to Eagly and Chaiken (1993), who proposed the Elaboration Likelihood Model (ELM) of persuasion, there are two routes to attitude change: central and peripheral. The central route employs *systematic argument*, while the peripheral route employs *mechanisms of association*. The central route depends not just on the clarity of the arguments, but on *how much an individual is stimulated to question their existing stance in detail and depth* (see **www.sagepub.co.uk/millward** for examples). The peripheral route, however, relies on the availability of appropriate cues (for example, images associated with pleasure) – cues that will trigger acceptance of a message without the need for much thinking.

### Compliance-based strategies

The commitment-based approach assumes that in order to change behaviour, we must first change attitudes: we think ourselves into a way of acting. However, the compliance-based approach assumes that we can also *act ourselves into a way of thinking and that our attitudes are created through action*. This proposition links with the *sense-making* principle, that people make sense in retrospect (Weick & Quinn, 1999).

Cognitive dissonance theory (Festinger, 1964), for example, proposes that behaviour change can lead to attitude change via a process of dissonance reduction. People usually internalize attitudes associated with behaviours enacted voluntarily, publicly and repeatedly. The greater the public commitment to the behaviour that they perceive to be their own doing, the greater the need to justify it to the point of genuine attitude change. In short, it is possible to act oneself (verbally or through behaviour) into an attitude or belief just as much as it is possible to think oneself into behaving in a particular way. For example, research on role-playing involving the adoption of behaviours that one perhaps does not ordinarily engage in shows that it can have a significant and enduring effect on attitudes as the behavioural role is internalized (Myers, 1993).

The critical point is that attitudes will align with behaviour change *only to the extent that the behaviour is coaxed but not coerced.* When people agree to do something they take more responsibility for it. The coaxing should be enough to elicit the desired behaviour, yet mild enough to leave someone with a sense of choice. The task for the OD specialist, then, is to work on persuading people to change their behaviour, both willingly and publicly, so that attitude change is self-generated. The process of attitude change can be aided if behavioural imperatives for change are also established (for example, changes in organizational procedures and practices).

## Part 2 Summary (III) and Conclusions

- There are two main strategies of influence: compliance based and commitment based. Commitment-based strategies seek attitude change, whilst compliance-based strategies seek behaviour change.
- Changing attitude occurs through either a fairly unconscious associative process or a central route process, requiring deep cognitive processing and reflection. Attitudes that are self-referential (that is, central to identity) are especially difficult to change.
- Changing behaviour through the creation of imperatives can create compliance, but this is unlikely to be sustained in the long term unless there is an element of choice involved in the process. If, retrospectively, behaviour cannot be attributed to external causes, attitudes are more likely to change in accordance with the behaviour.
- The implication for organization change is to make the imperatives clear, but involve people in deciding how to meet them, and give them the opportunity to reflect on their self-referential consequences by providing them with the necessary information as well as the opportunity to actively *work through* this information.

## Technological Change and 'the Network Organization'

The classic approach to understanding the role of technology in the workplace is known as socio-technical systems (STS) theory (Trist & Bamforth, 1951; see Chapter 4). The overarching mission of STS theory was to achieve an optimal balance between technical (task and technology) and social (people) subsystems. The principle of 'joint optimization' assumes that social and technical systems should be designed in parallel rather than focusing solely on implementing technological developments that could have detrimental human consequences. Adopting this approach meant that intervention should focus on the interdependence of the technical and the social, and, as such, may involve job redesign and organizational restructuring as well as changes in human processes (Buchanan & Boddy, 1983). In practice, however, most technological innovations in organizational contexts are 'technology-led', without consideration of their human consequences (Clegg & Walsh, 1998).

One reason why the human consequences of introducing new technology are often sidetracked is the, perhaps, implicit assumption that technology must dictate organizational structure and process. Indeed, technology is often coupled with structure and those holding determinist assumptions would posit a direct causal relationship between technology and organizational structure. For instance, the introduction of digital systems has given rise to the idea that the organization of the future is necessarily a 'networked' entity (Symon, 2000).

However, others argue that whilst there is indeed a coupling of sorts, it is neither causal nor inevitable (see Majchrzak & Borys, 1998, for a review of the technology–structure association). Some advocate that the relationship between technology and structure depends on various 'contingencies', whilst others advocate an enabling role for structure provided by technology (Symon, 2000). Others take a harder line, arguing that new technology is essential to effective knowledge management in a self-organizing 'knowledge creating' system (Rockart, Earl & Ross, 1996).

An illustration of the dangers of a too tightly coupled understanding of structure and technology is provided by Symon's (2000) critique of the so-called 'network' organization. Military researchers have advocated that the Command and Control organization would benefit by harnessing the 'network' metaphor as a means of conceptualizing the digitalized organization (for example, Almen, Anderson, Lagerlof, & Pallin, 2000). Almen et al., for instance, note that given the critical importance of the ability to seize initiative at the local incident-specific level for fast and flexible action (a so-called 'manoeuvre' approach to warfare), a networked system of information coordination is required. This, in turn, will facilitate a 'common situational awareness' and the possibility of decentralized flexibility of action at all levels of defence.

However, as Symon (2000) notes, the assumed 'informating potential' of new forms technology (enabling better, more informed local decisions, and the ability to respond flexibly to change quickly and with initiative) presupposes a direct causal relationship between technology and structure. In fact, the whole idea of a networked organization dispenses with the notion of structure altogether, seeing it as merely a temporary matter created through communication. Yet this dangerously assumes a strong networking capability involving the ability to:

- access correct usable and realistic information;
- process and assess this information;
- make the right decision at a critical moment.

Information, notes Symon (2000), is a symbolic resource that has to be processed and interpreted and applied, rather than incontrovertible fact. Moreover, evidence shows that IT does not necessarily support effective coordination, flexibility and effective decision making in the way assumed. This may in part be due to the lack of social cues important to the development of shared understandings. Moreover, the use of IT may not be suited to all managerial tasks. Nor is it possible at this stage to identify those tasks and task conditions under which it is the most effective way of managing a situation. Laboratory-based evidence suggests that IT does not always enable more effective communication, although the real-life applicability of such evidence is dubious given the absence of 'context' and reliance on largely student samples (Symon, 2000). In conclusion, IT may well enable flexible working but it does not necessarily create flexible working; under what conditions it does is still unclear (Study Box 5.21).

---

**Study Box 5.21**

**Technology and organizational change**

More specifically, Symon (2000) argues that:

1  Whether new information technologies do or can actually support new ways of working is unclear.
2  There is no straightforward link between new information technologies and new ways of working.
3  Evidence is limited to laboratory-based, largely non-transferable conditions.

Symon (2000) says that new information technologies will only support new ways of working where:

- there are rules for its appropriate use (but does this undermine flexibility?);
- the culture supports its use;
- employees are relatively autonomous and operate within a participative culture;
- work is not standardized;
- employees operate with internalized organizational goals.

In short, she argues that the principle of 'networking' is not a suitable metaphor for all organizations and by no means an inevitable consequence of its use. Clearly there is no simple effect of IT on organizational structure or on the way work is accomplished (Sonnentag, 1996; Symon, 2000).

---

# Part 2 Summary (IV) and Conclusions

- Technology is often coupled with structure, and together they are used to impose new ways of working on people.
- However, a socio-technical systems perspective requires that technological solutions are designed in keeping with the process requirements of work and the

people doing this work. There is always a fine line between *supporting existing processes* and *enabling new ones* to be fashioned. There is no automatic creation of a network organization through the introduction of advanced networking technologies.

- Technology is viewed as an artefact around which people interact and which people have to make sense of before it can be effectively integrated into the workplace. Also the cognitive requirements of effective networking should not be under-estimated.

## Team Development

Team building is one form of OD intervention designed to improve the productivity and/or performance of groups or teams. While team-building interventions are conceptually similar, they vary widely in focus and in their operational form. The 'peculiar circumstances of interventions' (Gavin & McPhail, 1978: 176) mean that each tends to be purpose built to address a 'unique constellation' of precursors and problems.

Common to all definition is the characterization of team building as a forum for problem solving, designed to aid a particular work unit or team to reflect on, and eliminate, blocks to its effectiveness. The emphasis is on the team taking diagnostic responsibility and learning how to reflect on (drawing on different forms of data), and manage, its own processes with the help of an external facilitator (Study Box 5.22). Definitions vary in how much emphasis is put on improving the quality of working relationships within teams, and whether there is recognition of the role of the wider system in which the team is a fundamental part (for example, Boss, McConkie, Ringer & Polok, 1995).

---

**Study Box 5.22**

**Process consultation**

Schein (1999) describes the process consultation model as a means of helping the client perceive, understand and act upon the process events that occur in the client environment, in order to improve the situation as defined by the client. The consultant seeks to give the client insight into the 'problem situation', then helps the client work out what should be done. The client retains both the diagnostic and remedial initiative. The model assumes that most clients/managers have constructive intent to improve things, but need help in identifying what to improve and how; and that most organizations can be more effective if they learn to diagnose and manage their own strengths and weaknesses. Moreover, a consultant cannot, without exhaustive and time-consuming study, know enough about the culture to suggest reliable and valid new courses of action. Unless remedies are worked out jointly with members of the organization who do know what will or will not work, such remedies are likely either to be wrong and/or resisted because they come from an outsider. Finally, unless the client/manager learns to see the problem and think through the remedy, he or she will not be willing or able to implement the solution and, more importantly, will not learn how to fix problems should they recur.

> ### Study Box 5.22    Continued
>
> To be effective, the process consultant must be able to establish trust and demonstrate expertise in process analysis. For example, a process consultant can help a group review its communication patterns, use of resources and time management after a meeting. It also involves teaching organizational representatives of the need to develop skills in 'perpetual diagnosis'. The rationale for process consultation is that groups and organizations too often become locked into issues of content, and fail to reflect on their own processes.

There is no universally accepted definition of TB. Early definitions (1970s/1980s) defined TB typically as 'a process of helping a work group become more effective in accomplishing its tasks and in satisfying the needs of group members' (Huse, 1980: 511). Later definitions acknowledge the potential of the team to champion organizational change, for example, 'one method of creating new structures to aid managing change in organizations, used more specifically to set goals, decide upon strategies, observe group dynamics and explore the quality of working relationships' (for example, Kormanski, 1991).

It is more common to describe the 'typical' team-building intervention (Boss et al., 1995). For instance Boss et al. (1995) describe team building, broadly speaking, as a short-cycle (one to two days) affair involving individuals who are hierarchically and/or functionally involved in some common flow of work, who have real, unresolved issues with one another, geared towards:

- building trust (horizontally, vertically);
- creating an open, problem-solving climate, where problems are confronted and differences are clarified;
- locating decision-making/problem-solving responsibilities;
- increasing the sense of ownership of organizational goals/objectives;
- moving towards collaboration between interdependent persons/groups by developing a shared perspective on the issues to be resolved;
- increasing awareness of group process and its consequences for performance;
- identifying blockages in communication;
- freeing people to communicate openly and thereby setting the stage for authentic interaction and effective problem solving.

Team building (as a process intervention aimed at helping individuals and groups examine and act upon their behaviour and relationships) is also differentiated from team training (the systematic effort to develop relevant knowledge, skill and attitudes within the group). However, in practice, similar concerns may be addressed (for example, communication and decision-making processes; Tannenbaum, Beard, & Salas, 1992).

Team building is also differentiated from T-Group training (Woodman & Sherwood, 1980). Whereas team building aims to improve group performance, T-Groups are more narrowly geared to increasing self-awareness and interpersonal sensitivity. Moreover,

T-Group training focuses on the unstructured exploration of interpersonal processes, whereas team building is usually data based, incorporating diagnostic information from interviews/surveys conducted in advance of the team-building intervention. However, T-Group training methods may be used within a team-building design.

### When is team building appropriate?

Hardingham and Royal (1994: 43) stipulate that 'if it ain't broke don't fix it', warning against the search for the 'Holy Grail of teams'. A team is effective (or ineffective) only with reference to a particular purpose given a particular set of resources within a very particular context. Common team problems include role ambiguity, communication problems, issues of loyalty (for example, 'to which team do I belong?'), team interface conflicts, issues of control versus empowerment, individual personalities and preferences incongruent with the team culture, stress, managing time, low morale, and job insecurities within the team (Varney, 1989). Team building may also be appropriate to establish a new team or to re-form a team after reorganization, for example, where a team takes on self-managed status (Steckler & Fondas, 1995: 20).

### Conditions of effective team building

From their review of the TB literature, Liebowitz and de Meuse (1982: 12–13) identify *nine prerequisites* for an effective TB intervention applicable in *all instances*:

1   There is true 'interdependence', since without it the group may not perceive any 'absolute need' to operate as a team (that is, *symbiotically* versus *associatively linked*).
2   *Formal data collection* is an integral part of the programme, to determine the needs of the team and to establish a benchmark from which change can be measured.
3   There are *realistic expectations of what team building can achieve* and what is expected, including *a continuous process of diagnosis, action planning, monitoring and evaluation*.
4   That *long-term commitment* is necessary to effect lasting improvement, analogous to an 'exercise regimen' (to be continually worked at and maintained), as opposed to a 'headache pill' (that is, a one-shot effort) that can simply be taken, left to take effect and then forgotten. One-shot team-building interventions can be damaging for a team finding itself 'stirred up' by the identification of problems that are not then systematically followed up and dealt with.
5   The *active and explicit support of senior management*.
6   The *team leader is committed* to, and involved in, the team-building effort, demonstrated by a willingness on their part to be reflexive and open to constructive criticism.
7   Team members have a *positive attitude* towards the programme (belief in relevance, involvement). This is easier to achieve in instances where the team is a psychologically relevant reference group for its members, and where members *identify with team goals* (Brown, 1988).

8   Members of the client organization are trained as 'internal OD consultants' to provide a point of contact between internal and external sources of facilitation to aid the weaning-off process once the external facilitator has gone.

9   An *'open systems'* point of view is adopted (for example, What reward principles are in operation in the appraisal system? Are rewards afforded individuals and/or teams? How will the TB effort be influenced by the culture of the organization?). Improved team performance needs to be supported by appropriate changes in appraisal, compensation, training/staffing strategies, amongst other changes.

### Approaches to team building

In 1976 Beer described four team-building approaches: goal setting, interpersonal, role clarification and managerial grid (Study Box 5.23). The problem-solving model can be added to this, which assumes that teams will become more effective by identifying their own problems, generating relevant information, engaging in problem solving and action planning, and then implementing and evaluating these action plans (Buller & Bell, 1986). It is critical that the problems tackled are real and significant, requiring the contribution of the whole team in the problem-solving process. Moreover, the problem(s) selected must be within team competence to solve (as opposed to resource or organizational problems).

---

**Study Box 5.23**

**Team-building approaches**

*The goal-setting approach*

This aims to energize a group to become more goal oriented. The core propositions of Locke's theory (setting clear, specific goals increases focus, effort and persistence) have been supported by many studies, with groups as well as individuals (Cooper, Phillips, Sutherland, & Makin 1994; see Chapter 4). Conditions of effectiveness include: (1) group goals are articulated as individual goals, (2) goals are accepted and there is commitment to their achievement; (3) the goals are measurable and afford knowledge of results; (4) goals are consistent with prevailing performance norms; and (5) multiple goals are internally consistent with each other (that is, there is no goal conflict or goal trade-offs). Tannenbaum, Beard and Salas (1992) note how establishing agreed output levels may help the team link goals to tangible results, and elucidate the resources (including skills, abilities, and personal qualities) needed to accomplish goals. The team can also establish goals to revise their task, task structure and/or process. Finally, the power of superordinate goals to unite otherwise distinctive professional groups within an interdisciplinary team matrix and to override tendencies towards 'loafing' in the performance of a collective task has been documented (Brown, 1995).

*(Continued)*

> ### Study Box 5.23   Continued
>
> #### *The interpersonal approach*
>
> This involves changing team climate (increased trust, cooperation, cohesiveness) and team process (for example, conflict resolution strategies, communication) by improving the way team members feel about each other and the way they interact (Tannenbaum et al., 1992). Techniques commonly used to facilitate positive interpersonal process include the Firo-B, the Myers Briggs Type Indicator, Interaction Process Analysis, therapeutic interventions like psychodrama and Alignment Technique. Whilst the interpersonal approach is popular, actually very little is known about the relationship between team process and performance. Moreover, the otherwise abundant literature on 'group processes' has not been harnessed by the team-building literature (for example, process losses through social loafing, process gains through social facilitation, group think, group polarization, inter-group dynamics).
>
> #### *The role-model approach*
>
> This aims to clarify role expectations and obligations (that is, what team members are expected to give each other and receive such as information, advice, technical consultancy/coaching, services, involvement, response times). A better understanding of roles (own and others) is thought to be essential to reducing unnecessary competition, role conflict and/or ambiguity, thereby releasing energy for task-relevant behaviours and enhancing coordination and communication (Tannenbaum et al., 1992). Commonly used techniques include Belbin's Team Role Inventory (BTRI) (Belbin, 1981, 1993) and 3-D Image Technique. Swailes and McIntyre-Bhatty (2003) evaluated the psychometric properties of the BTRI and concluded that all but the implementer role (one of nine role distinctions) appeared to yield reliable and valid results (see also Senior, 1997 and 1998).
>
> #### *Managerial-grid model (Blake & Mouton, 1964)*
>
> This is designed to create a 9/9 culture (i.e., a pattern of management emphasizing concern for both production and people, through participation). It assumes that: (1) team culture is directly linked to performance; (2) that the team will 'know' how to model themselves on a 9/9 culture, and have the necessary skills to do so.

In practice, team-building interventions rarely rely on one model alone. Beer (1976) argued that a mixed approach, tailored to the specific requirements of a particular team, is likely to be the most effective. Team problems often raise more than one issue (for example, unclear goals, role ambiguity, and interpersonal problems). Also, over-reliance on one particular approach can become prescriptive (imposing an 'ideal' or optimal team standard), with 'narrow' and 'binding' strictures on the way team problems are construed and managed.

It has been advocated (for example, Hardingham and Royal, 1994) that the best way to use 'theory' in the team-building arena is *informatively*, as a means of suggesting hypotheses about what might be going well or badly and to provide new ways of thinking that teams might choose to use in solving their problems. An optimal use of theory is to provide team members with a shared framework and/or language that they can apply to their own situation, facilitating team ownership of the problem-solving process.

### Critique of the 'typical' team-building intervention

Team-building research and practice have largely been conducted in a theoretical vacuum, despite a burgeoning literature on teamwork and team effectiveness. There are many different types of team and of teamwork. The team-building literature, however, presupposes only one type of team (that is, a stable, interacting and fairly closed highly interdependent entity). Moreover, the identifying attributes of the *team* are often confounded with the identifying attributes of the *successful team.*

The team-building literature presupposes that the aim of intervention is to develop particular types of behaviours, stemming from a diagnostic assumption that they are the source of all teamwork problems. This focus on behaviour is equivalent to a focus on symptoms not causes and, as such, is unlikely to produce sustained change. Indeed, long-term team success (as opposed to short-term) following a team-building intervention focused on behaviour is rarely documented. Goal setting can, on the contrary, engineer long-term improvement in team performance purely by motivating and focusing members on 'ends' rather than 'means'. This focus on 'ends' rather than 'means' directs attention away from a prescribed set of behaviours, and affords the team its own responsibility for pursuing those behaviours necessary to achieve the goal.

There is, indeed, no evidence for a relationship between particular types of group processes (or behaviours) and team performance. For example, despite many years of research, cohesiveness has not yet been definitively linked with increased performance or productivity. Despite this, the majority of team-building interventions aim to build teams by building cohesiveness. Moreover, cohesiveness continues to be used as a critical criterion for assessing team-building impact (Study Box 5.24).

---

**Study Box 5.24**

**Team-building impact evaluation**

Several meta-analyses of team-building evaluation studies have been published since the 1970s (Buller & Bell, 1986; de Meuse & Liebowitz, 1981; Nueman, Edwards, & Raju, 1989; Tannenbaum et al.,1992; Terpstra, 1982; Woodman and Sherwood, 1980). All but one (Nueman et al., 1989) did not permit the application of statistical meta-analysis, since few studies provide hard data on team-building impact, and those that do lack sufficient information to produce an estimate of the degree to which team-building actually affects group response. There is agreement, nonetheless, on several important features of team-building research:

*(Continued)*

> **Study Box 5.24    Continued**
>
> - Most typically used with *management teams* and with *established groups* with a history and a future (that is, *relatively stable groups*) and whose members are interdependently related. It is only recently that team building has been used for teams where members are associatively, rather than symbiotically, linked (for example, Carron & Spink, 1993).
> - Team-building interventions generally have a positive impact on *attitudes,* but not necessarily on behaviour or objective performance. Moreover, attitude changes are often documented on indices without established reliability or validity.
> - The relationship between intervention and reported outcomes often remains indeterminate because of poor experimental design: generally, the more stringent the design, the less positive the findings (Tannenbaum et al., 1992).
> - Evidence for goal-setting interventions is stronger overall than for other approaches.
> - Eighty percent of the team-building studies are framed by a problem-solving approach (for example, Murrell and Valsan, 1985) combining two or more approaches (goal setting, interpersonal processes, role clarification), coupled with workplace changes (for example, job redesign, changes in working conditions and incentives). Other miscellaneous approaches include: use of management simulation as a diagnostic stimulus (for example, Fisher & Thomas, 1987), code setting (for example, Armour, 1995), the use of interest surveys (for example, Campbell, 1996), and various therapeutic-style interventions (for example, Bendicsen & Carlton, 1990). The *problem-solving approach*, coupled with an emphasis on engendering *team ownership of the team-building process* and the creation of so-called '*self-managed teams*', is becoming increasingly common (Senior, 2000).
> - Whilst the time-span of team-building evaluation exercises is wide (for example, two weeks to four years), most team-building interventions are assessed for 'impact' within six months or less. Most would agree that the full effects of a team-building intervention are unlikely to be captured in the short term. In studies where long-term 'impact' is followed up, *regression* to the *pre-intervention position* is common.

The prescription of desired behaviour also implies that context is a constant that can mean that the team is ill equipped to respond appropriately to contextual variation and challenge. A competent team, for example, is one that is able to effectively adapt to the requirements of the situation, including an ability to diagnose the requirements of a situation and to harness its resources accordingly (Study Box 5.25). Issues of context (including team type and purpose), and how they are handled, are ultimately within the responsibility of the team, who in principle should have the ability to reflect on and adjust itself to whatever task or task situation is encountered.

The team-building literature has also largely ignored its OD foundations by not specifying the relationship between team-building approaches/technique and 'the change process'. Lewin (1951: 390) argued that the best way to facilitate system change is to create a 'shared perception by members of the need for change, thus making the source of pressure for change lie within the group'.

## Study Box 5.25

### A cognitive-motivational approach to team building

Traditional process theories of the team rely on the assumption that there is only one type of team characterized by collocation, longevity and stability and that there are absolute qualities of the effective team (for example, cohesiveness) that are directly linked with its success. A virtual team, however, refers to a team who, while working together, do not sit face-to-face but interact and communicate over computer-mediated communications networks. The core feature of this team is that they are interdependent group members who work together on a common task while spatially separated (Driskell, Radtke & Salas, 2003). The virtual team is pragmatically and logically incapable of replicating the traditional team characteristics of collocation and longevity. The temporal and spatial context of this type of team mediates team processes and impact on performance. Regular face-to-face interactions cannot therefore be the gold standard for understanding and managing the mechanics of the virtual team. Theories that conceptualize teamwork at the level of observable processes have limited intervention potential in this context and, indeed, arguably also in any context. Behaviour is situation, task, team and individual specific, and, moreover, none of the available theories really tell us what makes a team effective. Millward and Purvis (1998) argue that the best these theories can do is offer a framework for research by listing all the factors that could in principle impact on teamwork.

Drawing on theories of group and team processes with a heavily cognitive basis, Millward and Jeffries (2001) argue that the key to effective team building is to address the 'causes' of optimal team behaviour, rather than team behaviour per se. Whereas traditional team-building interventions are largely preoccupied with changing team process, the cognitive-motivational approach asks more fundamental questions about 'What makes team behaviour *possible*?' and 'How is optimal team functioning *brought about*?' Answers to these questions include reference to 'shared mental models' (for example, Druskat & Pescosolido, 2002), the ability of the team to self-regulate (which requires meta-cognitive skills) and a motivational impetus (for example, identification, team efficacy) (Millward & Jeffries, 2001; see Chapter 4). In this instance, the team-building process involves: (1) the promotion of a *team focus and orientation* as a prerequisite to team effectiveness; and (2) the promotion of *team competence* at cognitive (team mental models), meta-cognitive (higher-order team-regulatory strategies) and motivational levels (team identification and team potency/efficacy). In the case of virtual teams, team development may thus focus on developing a shared sense of identity and understanding of the team task, and to develop communication strategies that help to 'use' and maintain this understanding to optimal effect. This enables the team to operate 'as a team' in cognitive and motivational terms regardless of its spatial and temporal context. Evidence for the predictive power of at least the *shared mental model* and the *team potency* component of the model in accounting for team effectiveness has since been obtained from independent sources. In a longitudinal study, Pearce, Gallagher, and Ensley (2002) demonstrated that team potency ratings obtained from 71 change management teams in an automotive firm in the USA were strongly predictive of team effectiveness as judged by external raters. Evidence also suggests that mental model similarity in the team interaction domain improves coordination processes, which improves team performance overall (Marks et al., 2000; Mathieu, Heffner, Goodwin, Salas, & Cannon-Bowers, 2000; see Chapter 2 on team training).

## Part 2 Summary (V) and Conclusions

- Traditional team-building interventions are based on the assumption that teams are relatively stable entities and that there are absolute process properties of the effective team. However, there are many different types of teams, including non-collocated virtual teams that have a cognitive rather than a physical identity.
- Research has not demonstrated any clear link between particular team processes and team performance. Moreover, team-building interventions are well known for their immediate 'feel good' impact, rather than their sustained impact on team performance.
- An alternative cognitive-motivational model is proposed as the basis for intervention applicable to all types of teams. Intervention based on this approach is directed at the *causes* of team effectiveness rather than team processes, the rationale being that the effective team will *generate the appropriate processes to suit the situation.*

## OD Intervention Impact Evaluation

There is a continuing lack of understanding of how, if at all, OD intervention influences behaviour. The problem-specific, 'diffuse' and eclectic nature of most interventions make them difficult to evaluate. Few OD interventions are hypothesis driven (Wilson, 1992). Even in instances where the intervention is modelled on a particular concept or theoretical principle, the findings are difficult to interpret due to methodological complexities. Vague reporting (lacking detail on intervention process, sample size and characteristics, length of evaluation period, and numerical/statistical data) also makes it difficult to compare intervention activities or techniques.

Choice of intervention often reflects the preferences of the practitioner/researcher, rather than a systematic consideration of the alternatives. It has long been suspected that were it possible to ascertain statistically, there would be a strong *consultant/facilitator and treatment interaction* effect accounting for variation in intervention impact (Maples, 1992).

Questions like: How can change be discerned?', How much change constitutes a successful intervention? What is the most that can be expected? Which techniques are most effective and under what conditions? What is the most appropriate timescale for investigating the sustained impact of an OD intervention? (Gavin & McPhail, 1978: 190) are yet to be systematically addressed. Some advocate the use of 'path analysis' in the development of OD models and their outcomes (for example, Buller, 1988).

Others argue that research on OD will always lack rigour because OD activities are 'clinical' interventions, making it 'almost impossible to measure accurately' what is going on. Moreover, interventions rarely happen in isolation from other activities/system changes, making it difficult to isolate the 'impact' of OD interventions precisely.

Some like Wilson (1992: 3) have argued that 'recipe-book thinking detracts from the complexity and necessary analytical sophistication for characterising change'. For instance, how exactly are culture and change interlinked? The term 'culture' is often used as a catch-all term imbued with elixir-like qualities for facilitating organizational change, which in turn assumes that culture is something tangible that can be broken down into manageable components and then manipulated. Moreover, it assumes that change can be rationalized and unambiguously harnessed once the 'recipe' is known. However, organizational change requires 'appreciation of a vast network of competing theories from many disciplines and perspectives' (Wilson, 1992: 121).

The absence of any form of critical analysis in the change management literature, coupled with the lack of hard evidence to support universal claims, points to the need for healthy scepticism in the application of the OD approach.

## Ethical Issues in OD Intervention

Clearly, the OD approach provides only a partial account of organizational problems and their solutions. It neglects the role that other factors can play in the change management process, such as technology and financial systems. Moreover, there are some contradictions in the use of OD as an intervention framework that pose dilemmas for the consultant. These dilemmas pertain to the fact that the OD approach advocates that organizations should be taught to solve their own problems, and that it is not ethical to foster dependency.

Other ethical problems arise as follows:

- Where the values of OD (the 'truth and love approach', Bennis, 1969) clash with those of the client organization. The principles of openness and collaboration might not be appropriate for all organizational environments (for example, highly competitive, Machiavellian, hard-nosed). In this instance, OD consultants would benefit from lessons in the 'dynamics of power', a consideration rarely taken up within the OD approach.
- Where there is disagreement over problem definition, and/or recommendations for change, the consultant runs the risk of contract termination.
- Where intervention goals pit the interests of the organization against those of employees. In the words of Hollway (1991: 124), 'the more on target and insightful social science research becomes, the more threatening it is and the least likely to be accepted'. In the final analysis, intervention will be shaped by the 'priorities and constraints of the company' (1991: 124). She refers to Hill's (1971) analysis of an intervention conducted at Shell in the mid-1960s as an example of 'failure' to address the real problems of the organization, because of pressures to 'contain' and 'reduce' them to problems of attitude.
- The intervention sphere is inherently 'faddish', which means that consultants may be pressured into pursuing a particular type of intervention for the sake of it rather than because of a real need.
- Lack of quality control, in part due to organizational pressures for instant solutions. This means that OD intervention is conducted in a largely ad hoc, non-scientific way with little 'professional' regulation. In the 'rush to change', it may not be managed properly and lasting change is thus rare (Herriot, 1992: 99).

## Future Research Challenges

- explore the concept of 'resistance' in the context of organizational inertia;
- look closely at how people make sense of change (whether structural, cultural, technological);
- integrate theories of organizational identity with sense-making principles to explore the role played by interpretative schemas in either impeding or facilitating change;
- investigate the role of 'corporate identity' in securing commitment to the change effort;
- compare and contrast commitment-based and compliance-based change strategies;
- compare the effectiveness of a radical transformational change with an evolutionary one;
- investigate how people use and make sense of work technology;
- investigate the concept of 'knowledge' and its management from a distinctly psychological point of view;
- explore the validity of the cognitive-motivational model of team development relative to traditional process models for furnishing effective teamwork in virtual as well as collocated team contexts.

## Recommended Reading

Ashkanasy, C., Wilderom, C., & Peterson, M. (Eds) (2003). *Handbook of organizational culture and climate*. London: Sage.

Burke, W.W. (2002). *Organization change: Theory and practice*. Thousand Oaks, CA: Sage.

Cummings, T.G., & Worley, C.G. (2000). *Organization development and change*. Mason, OH: South Western College Publishing.

French, W., Bell, C., and Zawacki, R. (Eds) (1994). *Organizational development and transformation: Managing effective change*. Burr Ridge, IL: Irwin McGraw Hill.

Weick, K.E. (1995). *Sensemaking in organizations*. London: Sage.

# 6

## Workplace Counselling and Personal Development

... 'I sometimes find, and I'm sure you know the feeling, that I simply have too many thoughts and memories crammed into my mind' ... 'At these times' said Dumbledore, indicating the stone basin, 'I use the Pensieve. One simply siphons the excess thoughts from one's mind, pours them into a basin, and examines them at one's leisure. It becomes easier to spot patterns and links, you understand, when they are in this form.'

J.K. Rowling (2000). *Harry Potter and the goblet of fire (pp. 518–519)*

## Preface

Counselling may denote something intensely personal, pertaining to non-work life. It may be slightly stigmatized, suggesting weakness, failure or incompetence. Whilst the concept of 'employee assistance' brought counselling into the workplace, this was in a remedial capacity, contributing to its 'hush hush' backroom image. Career counselling was likewise something only ever undertaken at the commencement of working life as part of a vocational guidance service, amounting to little more than a single assessment interview involving feedback and prescriptive advice about occupations or jobs to which one is most suited (the so called 'test and tell' method). In exceptional cases, one might consult a career counsellor to address a problem of dissatisfaction with, or exclusion from, an existing occupation or job, underwritten largely by a sense of failure. Otherwise careers were largely the prerogative of managers and professionals, whose careers (defined as upward hierarchic progression) were managed by an organization through succession management and/or through status marking within professional associations.

Nowadays, counselling may be actively pursued by all employees (not just managers or professionals) for development purposes. The somewhat artificial distinction between different types of counselling (for example, personal, stress, career) is also becoming more difficult to sustain. The personal and the work are so inextricably linked that it is rarely viable to focus on one to the exclusion of the other. A career is fundamentally about the person as much as the personal is about the career. Work is acknowledged to be about 'who I am' and 'where I am going in life', as much as 'what I want to do and achieve'. Careers and their management are in fact now a strategic organizational consideration (as well as being internationally high up on the government agenda) and are not just (if at all) about making sure one is suitably matched to a job or occupation, but about life-long learning and development, personal responsibility and self-management (see Chapters 2 and 3).

Similarly, stress counselling can be reformulated within this strategic framework as one of many activities that can be pursued in support of this development. This does not negate or undermine the validity of the use of counselling services to address stress-induced performance and/or mental health problems but it is clear that if companies are to take at least some responsibility for the stress problem (Chapter 8), there are other more effective system-level interventions ('up-stream strategies') for this that can arguably reduce the need for 'downstream' individual remediation. On this issue, an important distinction can be made between counselling as a professional activity, counselling as a style and a set of skills, and also as a philosophy of organizational life. Managers, trainers and consultants can deploy counselling skills as an integral part of their interpersonal repertoire, but this does not make them 'counsellors'. The possibility of 'counselling values' being integrated into organizational life requires a different level of consideration than that ordinarily addressed by the term 'counselling' and involves the creation of development cultures.

Professional counsellors, on the other hand, are specialist trained, may be involved in their own personal therapy and are actively 'supervised' on a regular basis. However, unlike psychotherapeutic forms of counselling, workplace counselling makes no assumptions about the content of problems, difficulties or equivocations nor their origin. Indeed, workplace counselling is increasingly being undertaken in the guise of 'coaching' using 'helping models'. This is primarily a semantic change that removes from the practice of counselling its long-suffering remedial connotations, injecting it with a more proactive performance management edge. Executive coaching has in fact become big business in recent years, and may be associated with mentoring schemes. All of these involve in one form or another (counselling, mentoring, coaching) the constructive use of a one-to-one relationship (for example, akin to the 'personal trainer') for personal development purposes. Psychotherapeutic intervention may be required for those who have become excluded (or risk being excluded) from the economic world (for example, due to stress-induced mental health problems) or may be taken up voluntarily by those who have issues to address that they feel may be an impediment to their success, but this is outside this chapter's remit.

The location of counselling generally within a strategic organizational framework may, however, put the 'counsellor' in a catch-22 position at the interface of two potentially different sets of interests (those of the individual and those of the organization). To this extent the counsellor may take a stand as either primarily working for the organization and its interests, as primarily working for the individual and his/her interests, or playing an important bridging role of 'meta-mediator'. This chapter looks in detail at the place of counselling in an organizational setting and also the skills of helping. The 'organizational' roles, responsibilities and potential contributions of the counsellor are also discussed.

## Learning Objectives

Studying the contents of this chapter will enable you to:

1 critically reflect on the contribution of counselling to organizational life;
2 describe personal/interpersonal, administrative and organizational facets of counselling;
3 discuss the concept of career counselling and explain the trend towards 'personal development' as a philosophy of organizational life;
4 describe and critically discuss forms of career development intervention as a framework in which careers counselling can be conducted in an organizational setting (for example, development centres, career planning workshops, mentoring schemes);
5 examine the concept of stress and stress counselling at both individual and organizational levels of analysis;
6 describe two 'helping models' and explain the assumptions on which they are built, as well as their operational implications;
7 debate the role of the counsellor at the interface between individual and organizational interests, and discuss professional and ethical issues arising from this.

## Counselling in Organizational Settings

### The counselling domain

There are two different ways in which counselling provision can be tied to the workplace:

- career or career development counselling;
- counselling for stress, and/or problems 'impacting' on work efficiency and effectiveness – which may be provided in-house or contracted in (either as an independent service or as part of an 'employee assistance' programme).

These two domains of counselling provision have separate paths of evolution and historical origin. In this chapter, both forms of counselling provision are addressed. The career development angle on counselling builds on the review of career theory in Chapter 3 by examining its 'practice' implications. The 'employee assistance' angle on counselling provision is, on the other hand, inextricably linked with Chapter 8, on 'Health and Safety'. Here the concept of employee assistance provides a backdrop to looking at the place of counselling in the workplace and its evolution as a human resource management (HRM) tool (that is, to improve performance).

The bottom line in the contemporary organization is that counselling for purposes of both career and stress management is about performance as much as well-being. Career development is fast becoming a performance management linchpin as 'development' takes on strategic human capital value in today's knowledge society in which there are no economic or organizational guarantees. Organizational survival depends on employees demonstrating a continuous learning capability, performance self-monitoring, transferable skills, emotional resilience and adaptability, whilst individuals depend on the same things for their own personal employability (Chapter 3). This movement towards performance management via development is not confined to the UK; it has arisen from an international government agenda espousing the benefits to society and to the global economy of life-long learning (Watts, 1996; see Chapter 2).

Stress counselling may also be undertaken in the same vein (either as part of career counselling or career management initiatives, or separately) of facilitating increased coping and resilience. Some advocate discarding the terms 'stress' and 'coping' altogether because they locate stress within a psycho-medical model and, as such, implicitly abdicate the organization of its responsibility for managing stress. Kenny and Cooper (2003: 278) instead prefer to talk about 'occupational stressors' which the organization can and should manage 'because there is a point in which even the most resilient worker will break down', for instance, due to fatigue. This stance on stress makes it an organizational-level issue rather more than an individual-level issue that can be addressed through counselling. Nonetheless, there is still a place for counselling (whether personal, stress or career focused) in facilitating stress self-management as an integral part of an employee's personal development, particularly in high-stress (emotionally demanding as well as potentially risky) service work like fire-fighting and policing (Brown & Campbell, 1998).

The focus of this chapter is mainly on the personal/interpersonal side of counselling, the concept of development and the organizational context that frames it. The reader is referred elsewhere to consider the 'administrative' side of counselling provision – that is, setting it up, marketing it, managing and running it, and evaluating it (for example, Carroll & Walton, 1997); for core skill requirements see **www. sagepub.co.uk/millward**.

## What is counselling?

Counselling as a *professional activity* is distinguishable from counselling as a *style* and a *set of skills,* and counselling as a *philosophy of organizational life.* Increasingly, the concepts of counselling style and skill are upheld as a model of the interpersonal process for supervisors, managers, leaders, consultants and trainers. There is for example a growing literature on the manager as 'quasi-counsellor' (Carroll, 1996: 31; Reddy, 1993). It is consistently found that managers afford enormous benefits to their staff from using a counselling style and skills as part of their interpersonal repertoire (for example, Nixon & Carroll, 1994). Nonetheless, this is not 'counselling' per se.

Formal counselling involves 'confidences' that an employee may not wish to share with his or her manager. Various management situations may well require the use of counselling skills, but not counselling in the professional sense (Martin, 1997) pursued by a specialist and accredited practitioner. Most 'organizational' counsellors are trained in clinical and/or counselling psychology (British Psychological Society (BPS)) and/or have acquired advanced therapeutic skills accredited by either the UKCP (United Kingdom Council for Psychotherapy) or the BAC (British Association for Counselling). Counselling skills, on the other hand, involve the sophisticated use of listening and questioning techniques within a problem-solving or 'helping' framework, which aim to 'help' (via constructive facilitation) the client marshal the necessary resources to handle their problems (by environmental mastery). The latter may also be termed a form of 'coaching' (Carter, 2002). In practice, many workplace counsellors may employ the helping model, bringing to bear various other psychotherapeutic formulations as required (Study Box 6.1).

Counselling also denotes a *philosophy of organizational life* espousing counselling values (that is, valuing people as assets, demonstrating care, with the emphasis on growth and development, on difference and on continuous learning). This approach targets the organization as a whole and will be discussed later. The discussion is prefaced by consideration of the organizational side of the 'problem' (that is, the role of the organization in creating the problems they seek to address; see Chapter 8). It is no good, Carroll (1996) warns, in rescuing an employee from 'drowning' in a system that runs 'downstream'. The organization must be helped to run 'upstream'. This highlights the possibility for counselling intervention at the organizational as well as individual level of analysis. The professional and ethical issues arising from the pursuit of counselling as an expert service (to which people can self-refer or be referred) in an organizational setting will be addressed later.

### A definition of counselling

Counselling has been defined by Nelson-Jones (1993) as an *interactional process* involving a *series of decisions* in pursuit of a particular *goal*. The types of decision made and the goals at stake are influenced not only by the nature of the problem presented by the client, but also the counsellor's theoretical position (see Study Box 6.1). For instance, humanistic theories may advocate *general goals* (like 'self-actualization') whilst behaviourists may advocate *specific goals* (like the acquisition of career decision skills). Also, goals may be primarily client determined and intrinsic (for example, as in the goal of self-realization) or imposed by others (for example, adjustment of the individual required by the organization). If client and counsellor goals are irreconcilable, strictly speaking counselling cannot proceed.

In common to all counselling, whatever theoretical orientation, is the emphasis on wellness and self-realization rather than on sickness, maladjustment and disturbance. The overarching goals of counselling are likely to be *developmental* (helping to achieve 'growth' goals) or *preventative* (lessening the need for remedial counselling interventions) rather than curative or remedial. In practice, developmental and preventative goals overlap and there is also likely to be a remedial element to all improvement efforts.

Study Box 6.1

### Therapeutic orientations

There are five main theoretical orientations, each offering a particular view of human nature and an explanation of how problems can arise.

#### Psychodynamic

These are therapies characterized by a way of thinking about both client and counsellor that includes unconscious conflict, deficits and distortions of intra-psychic structures and internal object relations.

#### Humanistic/experiential (after Rogers, 1951)

Humanistic/experiential therapies emphasize experience as the primary datum for therapy. They are discovery oriented, person centred, and see the therapeutic relationship as central to therapy, all seeking to foster a client's potential for growth, self-determination and choice. Awareness and the generation of new meaning is the basis for change.

#### Cognitive and cognitive-behavioural

This approach seeks to reduce distress by changing maladaptive beliefs and providing new information processing skills. Thus, all cognitive interventions attempt to engineer change by influencing thinking. Rational-emotive therapy (Ellis, 2001) and Beck's (1976) cognitive therapy are prime examples of the cognitive approach. Cognitive-behaviour approaches, by contrast, tend to conceptualize thinking in concrete and behavioural terms, and focus on the development of cognitive strategies and skills (as opposed to examining the validity of beliefs). The stress inoculation technique (Meichenbaum, 1985), for example, combines efforts at cognitive restructuring with training in verbal self-instruction and behavioural self-management. In practice, each approach (whilst coming from a slightly different perspective) combines elements of both cognitive and cognitive-behavioural approaches (Hollon & Beck, 1994).

#### Behavioural

Behavioural approaches emphasize the application of behavioural techniques such as systematic desensitization (Wolpe, 1958), guided exposure (Marks, Hodgson & Rachman, 1975) and aversion therapy (Emmelkamp, 1994).

#### Constructivist

Counselling conducted within this framework (for example, Peavy, 1997) sees the client's world as constructed, and that everyone is in the process of seeking and creating meaning. The constructivist approach describes a philosophy of life and of how counselling can help in this process, rather than a set of techniques. Within this framework it is common to use 'narrative' as the means of helping people construct and enact more meaningful life narratives. Perhaps because they have abdicated

---

**Study Box 6.1   Continued**

responsibility for authoring their own narrative, clients may feel trapped but unable to see beyond others' narratives of their lives (expressed for instance in their use of particular metaphors) and can be helped to see how this has happened and to begin to discard inhibiting or debilitating narratives whilst creating new ones that enable them to progress. For instance, Peavy (1997) describes a case of a woman using language evocative of a 'wheel' metaphor that she used to explain why she felt she could not move out of this position (as the hub of a wheel everything might collapse around her). The constructivist therapist would focus the client's attention on this use of language to explore surrounding meanings, and to facilitate release from inappropriate or limiting metaphors when other more constructive ones are possible. The constructivist approach now strongly permeates the career counselling literature (Chen, 2002; McMahon & Patton, 2000; Richardson, 2002; Savickas, 2002; see below).

---

## Assumptions of Workplace Counselling

### A 'problem-oriented' approach

Workplace counselling tends to be 'problem oriented' and designed to facilitate self-management. Clarkson (1990) distinguishes between different problem origins as follows:

- problems arising from within the individual (for example, personal insecurities concerning personal advancement);
- problems generated by the work environment (for example, client expectations);
- problems generated by the non-work environment which impinge on work in either a visible or invisible way (for example, family demands).

In practice, problems are likely to be interrelated. The employee may need to be referred for more specialist help if problem scope is assessed to fall beyond the counsellor's remit (for example, stress-induced mental health problems). Problems may also include those pertaining to career development.

Most counsellors in organizational settings are eclectic in their approach to problem management (Carroll, 1996), since their client base usually varies widely as do the issues they bring with them, the timeframes they have to work within and the environments they work in.

Workplace counselling may also be pursued on a short-term, 'solution-focused' basis (that is, between one and eight sessions), which means that some therapeutic approaches (which operate with long-term agendas) are hard pushed to achieve their goals. Cynics says that the use of so-called 'brief therapy' (for example, Carroll, 1995) is driven less by client need than by the organizational politics (that is, anxiety about misuse and over-dependence on the counselling service). It is often said that workplace counselling should not concern itself with non-work related problems, the 'goal' (and criteria for success) of counselling being improved performance and productivity.

Yeager (1998: 137) argues, for instance, that the role of the workplace counsellor is not to help an employee to self-actualize but to 'fix the performance problem and ... fix it fast'. This is behaviourist in orientation (that is, work performance) without concern for underlying causes and is antithetical to the development principle fostered through effective self-management.

Carroll (1996: 45) describes workplace counselling along a continuum with business-centred goals at one end and personal-centred goals at the other, with positions along the continuum being more or less person and business centred. Under the jurisdiction of the counsellor, this can mean a 'pick and mix' approach to the problem, depending on particular organizational and individual requirements. Some individuals may seek counselling for 'personal growth' (for example, feeling stifled in their job and unable to 'progress') and others may seek it (or be referred) because of a work-related problem or crisis.

In the final analysis, it is undeniable that counselling conducted in and on behalf of an organization is in an organization's interests (that is, its performance requirements). Yet at the same time this cannot be at the sacrifice of individual needs and interests. As put by Herriot (2001), it is imperative that to survive in the contemporary employment world the individual and the organization must 'cooperate' with each other. Life outside work impinges on work and vice versa; the individual comes with a 'perspective' that cannot easily be divided up into non-work and work. At the same time, some dividing line or 'primary focus' is needed if only as an initial guide for the counselling process.

The problem-solving model underpins the employee assistance approach to counselling and is core to all *models of helping* (see below). Two specialist forms of career counselling conducted within a problem-oriented framework include redundancy counselling and pre-retirement counselling (Example Boxes 6.1 and 6.2).

---

### Example Box 6.1

#### Redundancy counselling

Redundancy counselling is a process by which a nominated employee is trained and counselled in the techniques of self-appraisal and securing a new job appropriate to his/her skills and needs. This may involve:

- clarifying with employees their marketable, transferable, and work skills and helping them to develop short-term plans by which skills might be realistically applied in other situations;
- creating opportunities for displaced employees to vent their feelings about vocational and also personal concerns connected with this;
- helping employees to identify and assess their sources of financial, marital/familial and other types of support;
- helping clients to obtain and use timely information on referral services, employment outlook and available placement services; and
- reinforcing with employees that they are skilled and mature and the job loss they have experienced is not due to personal incompetence.

**Example Box 6.1    Continued**

Different people experience 'dislocation' differently. Career counselling intervention can help dislocated employees maintain career identity and self-esteem, build career resilience and self-efficacy. Studies of redundancy suggest that much of the psychological stress of transition from work to non-work depends on how the 'redundancy process' is handled by organizations. Sometimes this type of counselling is considered part of the nominated employee's support or severance package.

**Example Box 6.2**

### Pre-retirement counselling

Retirement can be construed in terms of 'bereavement' or 'loss', in this case of one's job, one's identity and self-worth. Counselling may be required to prepare for, and help an employee deal with, this major life-transition from work to non-work, particularly in an employment climate where early retirement is seen as one way in which organizations are currently being streamlined. Hopson and Adams (1976) describe the phases of a transition that can be applied to the job loss scenario:

- *Immobilization* – a sense of being shocked and overwhelmed, of being unable to make plans, of being numbed or 'frozen up'.
- *Minimization* – of the change or disruption, sometimes to the point of trivialization. An individual may be inclined to deny the change, affording temporary retreat from reality while internal resources gather strength.
- *Depression* – as the realities of the change begin to hit, individuals realize that they must adjust to the change, and may be inclined to get depressed. This may manifest in feelings of helplessness and powerlessness, including feeling out of control of emotions.
- *Acceptance of reality* – accepting reality for what it is, letting go of the past and orienting oneself to the future. Optimism is possible at this stage, but a clear and definitive letting go of the past is prerequisite to this.
- *Testing* – denotes progression where people become much more active and start testing new behaviours, lifestyles, and ways of coping with reality. As they begin to do this, anger and irritability are likely.
- *Search for meaning* – following a burst of activity and self-testing, the individual may engage in a more gradual shift towards seeking meanings for how things are different and why they are different.
- *Internalization* – This is the final phase and involves the integration of meaning into adaptive behaviour.

These seven phases represent a cycle of experiencing disruption, gradual acknowledgement of its reality, testing oneself, and incorporating change in one's behaviour. Any given individual will progress and regress. For instance, one may become locked into minimization or depression. What is important is *the potential for growth* arising from any major disruption including job loss. Transitions are most stressful when unpredictable and involuntary. It is the counsellor's role to harness one's growth potential. Retirement counselling may also include consideration of leisure time, finances, and health.

## The 'personal development' model

Herr and Cramer (1992) note a shift in emphasis in the employment world from personnel management to *personal development*. Whereas traditional organizations maximize the efficiency of their employees by imposing management control, nowadays there is recognition that organizations must elicit the commitment of their employees if they are to be successful in the future. Whereas, for traditional organizations, career development meant 'fast-tracking' up the hierarchy and providing mentoring schemes for graduates, potential managers and high fliers, the 'development' organization addresses the needs of everyone, including non-managerial staff. Employees are 'corporate resources' and 'human capital' to be nurtured and maintained by means of training, development and counselling. Thus, note Herr and Cramer (1992), companies are trying to reconcile 'high tech' with 'high touch', the latter involving provision for personal growth, for further education, for mobility and challenge. This, coupled with a philosophy of personal development (see Chapter 2), is also recognition of the important link between 'development' and 'health' (Chapters 3 and 7).

Traditionally, career counselling has been oriented to 'economic health', to occupational choice, and preparation for work. It occurred at the margins of the organization but was not a core organizational concern (Watts, 2004). Into the new millennium now, the shift in emphasis foretold by Herr and Cramer in 1992 has come to fruition in that the remit of career counselling has now broadened to include the development of self-efficacy, coping with stress and transition and with organizational life generally (Kidd, 2002).

Thus, 'development' is on the corporate agenda. The concept and focus of careers counselling (and other career development intervention) is no longer confined to the individual at the point of entry to work (Arnold, 1997; Kidd, 2002; Watts, 1996). Social and technological changes mean that people are changing jobs more often and need help with managing the transition process. More and more women are entering the workplace in the pursuit of careers, one implication of this being to change family structures (for example, dual career). This, coupled with a growing recognition of career as a life-long phenomenon (as opposed to a simple process of fitting a person to a job and tracing their progress in status terms), have all increased the salience of individual development which needs to be actively managed (see Chapter 3 for a more detailed discussion).

By contrast with the problem-oriented model of workplace counselling, the development model is about facilitating insight into self in relation to the world of work (Jackson, Arnold, Nicholson & Watts, 2000). The development approach facilitates this by helping individuals obtain a realistic view of their current competence and potential, their personal and life goals, interests and values, and understanding the requirements of various jobs, types of career and job opportunities. This emphasis on 'strength' and 'potential' is consistent with the philosophy and practice of appreciative inquiry (Study Box 6.2 and Chapter 5). It also aims to foster self-management capability.

## Study Box 6.2

### Appreciative inquiry

Most traditional counselling assumes something is in need of repair. However *appreciative, inquiry* focuses not on what is, but what *might be*, what *should be* and what *will be* (Srivastva & Cooperrider, 1990). Specifically, appreciative inquiry 'helps … envision a collectively desired future and then to carry out that vision' (Cooperrider & Srivastva, 1987: 129). The method involves an identification and analysis of so-called 'peak experiences' and their basis, as the building blocks for envisioning how things could be (Fry, Barrett, Seiling, & Whitney, 2002). This is also consistent with recently introduced constructivist approaches to counselling (Study Box 6.1).

Within an organizational context, the network of career development provision can be extended to include the line-manager, trainers and human resource specialists in combination with the career counsellor (see Study Box 6.3).

## Study Box 6.3

### Career development interventions

#### *Career planning workshops*

Career workshops vary in length (for example, 1–5 days) and focus, involving 12–15 people. Common elements include extensive use of self-help materials, an emphasis on networking and an opportunity for one-to-one counselling. Workshops are most often run by independent consultants along with personnel and training staff. An example of a well-organized and well-run career development workshop is provided by Jackson and Barltrop (1994).

#### *Coaching and mentoring*

Both aim to facilitate learning on a one-to-one basis. *Coaching* depends heavily on the skills of the coach and the openness of the individual being 'coached' (in turn depending on whether coaching is an organization-wide strategy). Effective coaching is not about driving the individual, it is about 'facilitation' through questioning and challenging. In the 'facilitation' model, the individual retains responsibility for learning. Many training functions may be devolved to the manager or supervisor in the vein of the 'coach'. Executive coaching is now a hot topic in the contemporary organization (Carter, 2002). Some have wondered whether coaching is just another 'fad' or whether it does actually improve performance (for example, Kampa-Kokesch & Anderson, 2001). Research is yet to evaluate its effectiveness over and above other sources of facilitation and support.

*(Continued)*

| Study Box 6.3    Continued |
| --- |

*Mentoring* is less about performance and results and more about support on a broader more long-term holistic level. Mentors can help an individual to cope with transitions, with decision making and long-term focus. Widespread mentoring on a formal basis (that is, mentoring schemes) is only a relatively recent activity incorporated into UK organizational life, imported from Europe and also Japan. Until now, mentoring has largely been conducted on an informal and non-sytematic basis (see Parsloe, 1992 for detailed commentary; also see Chapter 3).

### Career discussions

This idea originates from Jennifer Kidd's work on career development and is the focus of her current research (Kidd, 2002; Kidd, Jackson & Hirsh, 2003; Kidd & Smewing, 2001) and can be explored further on The Career Learning Network (www.careers-cafe.com/mitw1.pdf). A career discussion involves a serious conversation at work about career issues. Kidd et al. (2003) interviewed over 150 people in five organizations. They found that good career discussions vary widely in terms of how, where and with whom, with most people gravitating towards people they like for career discussion, who cannot always provide the appropriate career support. Kidd et al. (2003) argue that career discussions should be more systematically structured into the performance management system as a distinctive process in its own right, rather than tucked at the back end of an annual performance appraisal interview (see Chapter 3, Part 1).

### Development centres

The development centre is essentially the same as the assessment centre (see Chapter 1), except that in this instance the aim is to identify and develop management potential. Feedback is the primary 'development' tool. Evidence shows how development centres can increase self-awareness among some employees (that is, those who 'underrate' their level of performance) but by no means all employees respond favourably to this form of intervention. There is also much cynicism among managers today as to the benefits of development centres, especially when the competencies they are expected to 'develop' are not the same as those used in performance appraisal contexts (Abraham, Karns, Shaw, & Menon, 2001).

### Computerized career planning

One of the systems developed for use within UK organizations is called Career Builder2 developed by LifeSkills Associates in Leeds, an interactive computer programme that can be used on a stand-alone basis or integrated with other career interventions. It comprises a series of linked modules for self-assessment of occupational interests, skills, work values, preferred career patterns, and work-related stress, objective setting and action planning. More broadly, the Internet can be said to play a major role in computer-assisted career counselling: as a source of information, an electronic book, and a vehicle for assessment (Aalto & Kankaanrana, 1996). Taking a European perspective on this, Plant (2002) argues that whilst the conventional use of computer-assisted careers counselling within some countries

---

**Study Box 6.3    Continued**

(France, Spain, Greece) is to support assessment, in others (UK, Italy, Germany), the client is encouraged to use it to explore 'occupational and educational possibilities' in either a facilitated or self-directed mode. Plant (2002) cautions that the huge number of IT developments appearing across Europe in support of careers counselling are not led by any coherent master plan. Most have been developed for 'assess and tell' type purposes (that is, matching people to occupations and jobs), and assume an outdated picture of the world as presenting predictable and solid possibilities. Plant argues that computer-based tools can on the contrary be designed to help clients (alongside an appropriately qualified counsellor) to explore their own reality (www.careerstorm.com, www.getting-on.co.uk/toolkit/construct.htm and www.enquirewithin.co.nz).

### Self-help tools

The growing emphasis on the use of 'self-help' techniques is part of a society-wide trend towards encouraging self-management (in part because 'expert services' are a scarce resource and in part because of a contemporary political ethos of responsibility and accountability; Watts, 1996). Few self-help programmes and packages have been systematically evaluated. Moreover, without the active provision of external facilitation and support, the individual may also end up establishing unrealistic and unobtainable goals. Self-help tools are most appropriately embedded within other activities (for example, career planning workshops) to help the individual apply the techniques in an informed, systematic and mutually supported manner.

---

One of the key issues to be addressed by future work is how to conceptualize development and how one can tell whether it is really happening or yielding its anticipated corporate and individual benefits. Looking across various subdomains in which 'development' has become an important practical issue (training, performance management, career management), various different sets of foci and emphases can be discerned (Table 6.1). All concur that development is a process, but what this is said to involve, how it comes about and what it might culminate in are matters on which approaches differ widely.

Development research conducted in a performance management framework depicts development initiated by a feedback process that raises personal awareness of a discrepancy between current and expected or desired performance (as perceived by supervisors, peers, subordinates, and perhaps also customers) against various management competences. Development is assessed by 'self-awareness' (increased self-awareness presupposes a high degree of congruence between self and others' perceptions of one's performance) and will be associated with performance improvements (including attitudes towards, and actual uptake of development activities) (Fletcher & Baldry, 2001; see Chapter 3). However, the feedback–self-awareness–performance link is found to be more complex than this model assumes, and, moreover, the self-awareness construct requires further elucidation and validation.

Table 6.1  *Models of development*

| Process | Antecedents/facilitators | Outcomes/markers |
|---|---|---|
| **Performance management** | | |
| Process of reducing discrepancy between self and others' ratings of performance | Feedback from multiple sources Self-efficacy | Self-awareness -> performance improvement |
| **Humanistic/developmental theories** | | |
| Continual self-reflection and adjustment of behaviour | Active facilitation/quality of therapeutic relationship | Self-insight, reflective ability, behavioural adjustment Satisfying occupational identity *free from emotional distortion* Personal responsibility for development and its outcomes Career maturity |
| **Learning (cognitive-behavioural) theories** | | |
| A decision-making process | Active facilitation of personal responsibility, willingness to self-explore | Effective personal decision making |
| Continuous learning | Learning ability, learning attitude, self-management skills | Responsibility for continuous learning, self-efficacy |
| Goal-oriented continuous learning | Learning ability, goal setting, self-management ability Proactive career construction | New skills acquired Effective self-management |
| **Constructivist approaches** | | |
| Continuous pro-active construction and reconstruction of the future | Facilitation in self-authorship through sense-making process (reflection on language, meaning structures, and fostering responsibility for self-construction) | Feeling of 'congruence' in reconciling life goals/interests with contextual requirements Self-authorship (sense of responsibility for constructing a satisfying career) |
| **Emotional resilience approach** | | |
| Continuous self-management including emotion management | Facilitation of self-management ability through reflection and discussion with a trusted confidante (mentor, coach, manager, counsellor) | Career resilience, career efficacy, stress self-management 'Emotional intelligence' |

Nonetheless, the idea of increased self-awareness furnished by performance feedback is consistent with many conventional counselling models within psychotherapeutic, humanistic and cognitive traditions that work on the assumption that 'self-insight' is a pre-requisite to change. In counselling, this insight is furnished not by performance feedback, but by a process of self-reflective inquiry. The concept of 'reflection' is also central to formulations of training in which self-evaluation is the critical medium of learning. However, surprisingly little is known about what this involves, whether it is indeed an effective way of learning, and if it is, how it can be most effectively facilitated (Chapter 2).

Drawing on Roger's 'self theory', Super's (1990) work on vocational development is perhaps most seminal to conceptualizations of 'development' (Chapter 3, Part 2).

According to Super, career choices and decisions are driven by self-concepts. Decisions are being made all the time, not just at the point of entry; initial career choices may be voluntarily or compulsorily reversed.

1 The attainment and implementation of a satisfying occupational identity is an important developmental goal, making a sizeable contribution to emotional stability and psychological well-being.
2 Career development implies helping people to become more effective in such decision making by taking responsibility for the development of, and satisfaction they derive from, their careers.

The goal of developmental careers counselling is to facilitate the client's self-actualization by means of a relationship in which the client feels safe and free to explore, clarify if necessary, and receive help in implementing an occupational self-concept undistorted by emotional factors (Study Box 6.4). The aim of assessment is to use tests to facilitate self-exploration. The most important instrument of change in this instance is the *quality of the therapeutic relationship* (Study Box 6.13). The quality of the relationship depends on the attitude of the counsellor (that is, unconditional positive regard) coupled with their skill in facilitation (listening and questioning skills – see below). The relationship is an empowering one, designed to furnish self-insight and 'career maturity'.

Career maturity is defined by Super (1990) as the readiness to make informed, age-appropriate career decisions and cope with career development tasks appropriate to one's life stage. Vondracek and Reitzle (1998) criticize this reference to 'developmental stages' for its assumption that there are clearly identifiable age-related maturational regularities in an absolute sense (independently of culture, historical time and economic context). Moreover, it is unclear what exactly this construct is referring to. Definitions include 'ability to make appropriate career decisions' and 'degree to which one's choices are both realistic and consistent over time' (Patton & Creed, 2001). Super (1990) also argued for the critical role of 'curiosity' in career development, which he says promotes a sense of autonomy, of being in control of the present and the future and of pursuing one's interests.

---

**Study Box 6.4**

**Elements of developmental counselling**

*A fundamental counselling relationship*

The counsellor strives to create an emotional climate of acceptance and understanding to facilitate occupational self-exploration including needs, conflicts and anxieties, hopes, desires and expectations as they relate to aptitudes, abilities, interests and concepts of work and occupations. The atmosphere should be sufficiently trusting for the client to start acknowledging and clarifying ideas and feelings that may be at variance with current occupational self-conceptions.

*(Continued)*

---

| Study Box 6.4 Continued |
| --- |

### Use of tests to facilitate occupational self-exploration

Developmental counselling differs from the usual person-centred counselling in the use of tests and occupational information. Tests may be used to help the client understand him- or herself rather than to provide information for counsellor evaluation. The client participates in test selection and the counsellor creates a safe environment for the presentation and discussion of results. There is always the risk of tests impeding rather than facilitating self-exploration.

### Use of occupational information to explore the world of work

As with tests, occupational information may be introduced when the client either overtly or covertly seems ready for it, about sources of careers information and ways of making a decision, as well as information about particular careers. The counsellor has no vested interest in what the client chooses. Once again, there should be an emotional climate conducive to the client's feeling safe to express and work through his thoughts and feelings about the information.

### Planning the implementation of an occupational self-concept

Action planning may follow the crystallization of a career decision. Though the responsibility for the planning is that of the client, information about the planning process itself as well as specific information about occupations may be introduced by the counsellor in accord with the client's needs.

### Focused exploration to assist occupational decision making

Some developmental counsellors may focus their exploration on blocks in thinking that can impede effective occupational decision making. This exploration may look at self-standards giving rise to dysfunctional self-evaluations, causal attributions, assumptions of responsibility, and ways in which test information is perceived. Counsellors may use confrontation skills to provide clients with information discrepant with their current self-conceptions.

---

Some might argue that this approach to development is too all encompassing and abstract, providing a framework for career counselling, but not a concrete set of testable or useable propositions. Summerfield and van Oudthoorn (1995) evaluated the heuristic value of six different counselling theories to the organizational setting, concluding that each had something to offer but none could provide an 'entire approach'. In particular, a humanistic developmental approach was valued for its ability to foster rapport between client and counsellor, but its broad-brush 'touchy feely' orientation uncoupled from any kind of problem-solving and action focus was said to limit its usefulness.

In an attempt to pin down the concept of 'career maturity', one of Super's key developmental constructs, Crites (1971) draws heavily on cognitive psychology. He argues that career maturity is about being cognitively equipped with the relevant decision-making skills. The emphasis here is thus on learning generic decision-making skills rather than just solving particular career problems. In this model of development, career maturity is a mark of success in the developmental process (although according to Super, this must be continuously evolved in association with new developmental tasks across the life span).

The idea that development involves the ability to make effective decisions is broadly akin to the cognitive-behavioural approach to career counselling, which views development as a process of learning new skills, especially self-management skills (Study Box 6.5). This emphasis on development as a continuous learning process is consistent with the views of several Canadian speakers at the helm of research and practice in career counselling (Bezanson, 2003; Watts, 1996). Within this framework on 'development', career development is defined as 'a life long process of managing learning and work in order to live and work with a purpose and create careers' (Watts, 1996: 2). No ideal end point is postulated for successful development; development is literally a self-managed learning process. Indeed, the ability to learn, and to learn fast, has emerged as an important topic in the psychology of training, and could be usefully harnessed in this conceptualization of development (for example, Downs, 1996).

---

### Study Box 6.5

#### Tools of the 'cognitive-behaviourist' counselling tradition

##### Modelling (see Chapter 2)

Live, taped or filmed models may be used to demonstrate desired behaviour, for example, information-seeking behaviour, decision-making skills and effective interview behaviour. There must be at least some degree of perceived similarity between observer and model for the influence of the model to be significant.

##### Simulated work experience

Research by Krumboltz and colleagues suggests that presenting clients with occupational problem-solving materials that are life-like and involve active participation may increase career exploration through 'doing' (see Krumboltz, 1996 for review).

##### Behavioural rehearsal (see Chapter 2)

Involves identifying situations in which clients are having difficulty; defining what might be appropriate behaviours, role-playing the appropriate behaviours and encouraging clients to try out the rehearsed behaviours in real life. For example, assertiveness training can help clients in seeking desirable jobs, since they may be inhibited about acknowledging their abilities and afraid of applying and thus risking rejection.

*(Continued)*

---

**Study Box 6.5    Continued**

### *Behavioural self-control*

Thoresen and Ewart (1976) have proposed a behavioural self-control approach to help clients to become better architects of their occupational lives on a continuing basis. Four broad areas in which presence or absence of suitable self-control procedures can affect career decision making are: commitment (for example, sustaining motivation through making self-contracts), awareness (for example, keeping a diary to monitor career-relevant thoughts, feelings and behaviours), restructuring environments (for example, seeking or creating opportunities) and evaluating consequences.

---

All of the above perspectives on development assume some sense of the person in the concrete sense that can be nurtured and evolved by facilitating self-regulatory ability. All assume that development is in one form or another a process of self-regulation or self-management, and that development is fundamentally shaped and constructed by the individual. Taking the idea of self-construction as the key starting point, constructivist approaches question the extent to which realist epistemologies of self-management can truly engage with the issue of development defined in this way (for example, Chen, 2002).

Chen (2002: 314), for instance, says that to conceptualize development as a process of self-management or self-regulation requires detailed consideration of the role of self as 'agent in the process ... a developing and changing variable rather than a developed state'. He argues that conventional career models 'may not be sufficient to conceptualise the mission of self in career making' as they need to reckon with the underlying drive for development being 'a person's quest for meaning finding and meaning making'. The constructivist view, on the other hand, holds that people (1) are self-interpreting beings capable of negotiating and creating their own meanings; (2) have the freedom to explore and construct their own life narrative and reality purposefully; and (3) that human agency is contextualized in life events and alternatives (see Chapter 3, Part 2 for more on the constructivist approach to career counselling; Study Box 6.6).

---

**Study Box 6.6**

### The constructivist approach to career development

The following basic assumptions underpin the constructivist approach to career development:

- *collaboration* – equal participants, client is expert on their own life experience;
- *receptive inquiry* – safe but challenging, involving meaning-generating questions, metaphorical transformations, the use of artwork and objects to create meaning, autobiographical writing, visualization and dialogical discussion;
- *pattern recognition* – counsellor and client try to identify patterns of influence shaping a client's thinking and action, especially relationships.

---

**Study Box 6.6   Continued**

### Primacy of life experience

Counselling works directly with life experience (perceptions and personal meanings as revealed through narrative, interview dialogue, concept mapping, artwork and other self-revelatory activities). Counselling is a matter of influencing change already underway (self is continually evolving). Resistance is not an issue: it is meaningful and relevant to the client's current frame of reference.

### Mindfulness

(1) creation of new categories of construct to help interpret experience; (2) expanding openness and receptivity to new information, both internal and external; and (3) the awareness of more than one perspective on any aspect of one's life world including career. Critical reflection is a key to developing mindfulness (Peavy, 1997).

### Creating meaning through activity

Involves work experience, job shadowing, work site visits, work simulation which can provide a basis for personal meaning. The use of such activities is enhanced through reflection on activity, discussion and dialogue (see Chapter 2 for a discussion about 'on site' learning).

---

On a more practical note, career counsellors may find constructivist theory less easy to implement in an organizational context than, say, more cognitive approaches which have a more tangible leaning on development as one's ability to continuously learn. Nonetheless, there is scope for at least some recognition of the important role of language, dialogue and discussion in facilitating a self-management process (for example, people may use defeatist and fatalistic language in the way they narrate and project their career or in the way they approach learning new skills; Peavy, 1997).

Finally, Kidd (2002, 2004) has continually pointed to the absence of consideration of the role played by emotion in career development. Super (1990) speaks of emotion, but as a block to making effective decisions (that is, a source of distortion) and achieving a satisfactory occupational identity. However, he does not elaborate on this, nor contemplate the possibility that the achievement of some ability to manage emotion (of self and others) might be an integral part of the developmental process. Emotion may also be a constructive, energizing influence and not necessarily posing dysfunctional blocks in the way of developmental progress.

The concept of 'career resilience' has entered into the language of career management and is an integral part of London and Mone's (1987) theory of career motivation (Chapter 3, Part 2). Akin to the concept of self-efficacy, London and Mone define resilience as the ability to persevere at all odds, avoiding setbacks and overcoming obstacles to development. This definition somewhat disengages the concept of resilience from its deeper emotional connotation, which implies that one is able to buffer the impact of career-related (developmental) stressors through the effective use of personal coping resources. This links the issue of development with that of effective emotion and/or stress management (Study Box 6.7).

---

**Study Box 6.7**

### The concept of emotional intelligence

Emotional intelligence (EI) is a concept popularized by Goleman (1996), now generally used to describe the ability to process, understand, and use emotions effectively (Cobb & Mayer, 2000). In the fields of training, career development, and career-technical education, EI has been connected to job skills training (Houghton & Proscio, 2001), leadership development (Dearborn, 2002), team development (Druskat & Wolff, 2001), and organizational development and learning (Callahan & McCollum, 2002). The role of emotions in adult learning is, in particular, a growing area of interest, particularly as contrasted to assumptions that the processes involved are largely rational and instrumental ways of learning. Dirkx (2000), for example, counters the prevailing views of transformative learning that emphasize rational and cognitive processes by highlighting the part played by emotions in transforming meaning perspectives. Leicester (2002) identifies the characteristic 'emotional intelligence and intuitive understanding' as an alternative form of thinking, which is contrasted with the traditional rational forms.

The career development literature has connected emotion to career change, career interventions, and job search (Kidd, 2002). Other than contrasting views of learning that incorporate emotions with the more dominant, rational views of learning, few issues related to the effect of emotions on learning appear in the literature of adult, career, and career-technical education.

---

Given the emphasis across all approaches to development on facilitating self-regulation, it is surprising that the pertinent literature on 'self-regulation' has not yet been sourced from within the psychology of employee motivation (Chapter 4).

### Summary (I) and conclusions

- Counselling has two profiles in organizational settings: career counselling and stress counselling. Career development is synonymous with personal development, and, increasingly, counselling is viewed as a forum in which to facilitate continuous career self-management rather than merely something brief and advisory undertaken at the point of entry into the workforce or for purposes of remediation (for example, redundancy counselling, change of career).
- Stress counselling is usually an integral part of employee assistance undertaken for purposes of remediation, but may now also be undertaken as part of a career management strategy, since nowadays the ability to cope with stress is arguably an integral part of a general ability to self-manage. However, stress counselling is unlikely to be effective if the organization is an unwitting promulgator of stress.

- The development counselling model is contrasted with the problem-oriented counselling model. In practice, the issue is about striking an appropriate balance between performance remediation and developmental progression, which many coaching models try to do.
- A distinction is made between formal counselling, counselling skills that, in principle, anyone can use, and a counselling style which describes an interpersonal empathic orientation. Counselling style and skills can be used by coaches, mentors, and managers to facilitate personal development (and to encourage performance reflection and self-monitoring).
- The end point of all counselling is the client's ability to take responsibility for their performance and its regulation.

## The Role of Assessment in Counselling

The first step in all applications of counselling is always an *assessment* of the individual problem (see Study Box 6.8) and of various options for intervention.

---

**Study Box 6.8**

### Individual and organizational assessment

The term 'assessment' has been criticized for its 'diagnostic' (that is, medical model) implications. However, Carroll (1996: 107) says that whatever it is called, some form of judgement about the nature of the problem and the way it should be handled is required. The term 'formulation' is commonly used to describe the task of defining and circumscribing client problems and involves working towards an *agreed understanding* of the issues to be addressed and how to work with them. Most formulations require an understanding not only of the 'presenting problem' (that is, the difficulties with which a client is currently faced, such as 'work load' or redundancy) but also the *psychological concerns* that surround the problem (for example, dysfunctional interpersonal patterns, inability to hold down a job). For detailed consideration of the client assessment process refer to MacMahon and Palmer (1997). Carroll (1996) also emphasizes the importance of 'organizational assessment' as a necessary complement to 'individual assessment' in the workplace counselling scenario.

Constructivist counsellors argue that 'assessment' assumes something fixed and stable to be uncovered and measured. By contrast, assuming that the client's world is constructed, the issue for the counsellor is not to assess but to *understand* this world by entering into a client's life space and developing a collaborative relationship so that the client can tell his or her story, explore its meaning and reconstruct it. This approach assumes that the client has already pursued a process of self-assessment and that the counsellor can thus help to explore the meaning of this. Traditional assessment tools may be used within this framework, but not with a view to obtaining 'scores' or 'fit' but to furnish understanding (Savickas, 2002). The client is 'expert' on his or her world and, as such, assessment can only be undertaken *with* them not *on* them.

Career counselling has a long tradition of being *assessment dominated* (Brown & Brooks, 1996). Parsons (1909) and later Williamson (1965) provided the historical precedent for this in the principle of matching person to job or occupation. At its inception, Parsons (1909: 26) described the process as follows: 'a fifteen minute interview will often bring the counsellor to a definite opinion as to the advice to be given', especially for those clear about their interests and abilities. Likewise, Williamson (1939, 1965) proposed a model in six stages: analysis (data collection), synthesis (summary of data), diagnosis (identification of career problems), prognosis (predictions about likely success of an individual relative to his or her goals), counselling (if the individual has career problems) and follow-up (examining the viability of the career decision). Together, Parsons and Williamson heralded the career counsellor in the expert 'test and tell' role (Chartrand & Walsh, 2001: 232), which still describes much careers counselling today (Kidd, 2002). Whilst Holland's (1997) 'modern differentialist' approach (Chapter 3, Part 2) aims to help clients towards a process of self-counselling, which seems more 'developmental' than prescriptive, the role of the counsellor is nonetheless built on expert judgement, prediction and advice (Study Box 6.9; Example Box 6.3).

---

### Study Box 6.9

#### The differentialist approach

The 'talent matching' approach originates from Williamson's trait-factor approach, which led the vocational counselling movement between 1926 and 1969. The trait-factor approach assumes that: (1) individuals have a unique and stable pattern of capabilities after adolescence, (2) capabilities are identifiable by objective 'tests', (3) different capacities are significantly associated with different work tasks, and (4) success in work tasks is best predicted by a battery of trait tests. The trait-factor approach involves the analysis of objective and subjective sources of client information, for example, attitudes, interests, family background, knowledge, educational progress and aptitudes and so on, profiling unique capabilities, strengths and weaknesses, predicting the consequences of particular educational and career decisions, vocational instruction and review.

Holland's (1997) differentialist approach assumes that most people can resolve their own vocational problems if they have suitable opportunities for obtaining information and are encouraged in their exploration. Once a person's definition of the problem is accepted, he or she is provided with resources and information to facilitate exploration of self and the world. Ways of helping include *placement and work experience* to help people to explore particular kinds of work, supported *transition* in that many people lack the confidence to translate personal characteristics into opportunities and a counselling service designed to help individuals to understand themselves and their future possibilities. Holland's (1997) model has recently been heavily criticized for its limited focus on matching people to occupations and jobs (Arnold, 2004). Not only do jobs continually change, but the developmental orientation is more concerned with 'where I am going' and 'what I want to achieve' rather than just 'what I want to do now'.

---

**Example Box 6.3**

### The self-directed search

The self-directed search (SDS) includes two booklets: a self-assessment booklet and an occupational classification booklet. Completion of the self-assessment booklet involves describing occupational daydreams, preferences for six kinds of activities (realistic, investigative, artistic, social, enterprising, conventional), competences in these six areas, preferences for six kinds of occupations and estimations of ability in six areas. The booklet is scored to obtain a three-letter occupational code (for example, RIE, or realistic, investigative, enterprising). All permutations of the three letter code are used to locate suitable occupations in the occupational classification booklet, *The Ocupational Finder*. Holland says that the SDS encourages exploration, self-direction and initiative in resolving vocational decisions, helps people who do not have access to professional counsellors and multiplies the number of people a counsellor can serve.

---

In this 'test and tell' approach (McMahon & Patton, 2002):

- assessment is the prerogative of the counsellor, who takes responsibility for the selection, use, scoring, diagnosis, analysis and interpretation of results;
- assessment is primarily quantitative, deploying standardized tests;
- the purpose of testing is to make predictions about how a client might be most appropriately *matched* to particular occupations or jobs (Krumboltz, 1996);
- the client plays little role in either the assessment, interpretation or counselling process and there is little scope to deal with 'other' career issues broader than occupational choice (Betz & Corning, 1993);
- the counselling scenario fails to consider the inextricable link between the issues arising in counselling and the wider *context* (Brown & Brooks, 1996);
- the critical role played by the counselling relationship is not acknowledged, appreciated or harnessed (Savickas, 2002).

Whilst assessment is inevitably part of any counselling process, constructivist critiques of the test and tell approach argue that it is in the way it is practised and used that is problematic. Savickas (2002), in particular, argues that career counselling should move away from scores and fit towards 'stories'. In a modernist context, counselling is said to have taken on a 'technical rationality' (objectivity, neutrality, expertness, quantification and measurement) and aspects of 'instrumental reasoning' (efficiency and accountability speak) (Peavy, 1997). However, social changes have radically altered day-to-day lives and experiences, which are now more ambiguous, uncertain and chaotic than ever. Peavy argues that 'counsellors must comprehend the scope and effect of social changes on the experience of self'. He has been foremost in the advocacy of a constructivist approach to career counselling, hinging on terms like 'self-construction' (versus self-presentation), 'self-as-narrative' (versus self-as-traits), and 'life-planning' (versus career choice) (see Chapter 3, Part 2 for more on this).

Within this general framework, Savickas (2002) and others (for example, Peavy, 1997) describe the role of the counsellor as a 'co-author', helping clients to construct and enact more meaningful career narratives through a process of active engagement and dialogue. In this approach, assessment is primarily qualitative and the end point is not about 'matching' but about *meaning making*. The process is collaborative rather than prescriptive. Chen (2002: 314) points out that the client should be construed as an active agent in the process of career construction. He elucidates a process of 'career projection through narrative'. Basically this means that the client envisions a future story line that reconciles personal goals and objectives with the wider context. They may not necessarily be able to change the context, but they can actively manoeuvre themselves in it to construct a better future. This does not mean ignoring the past; it merely frees clients from these experiences and orients them to the future (Study Box 6.10).

---

### Study Box 6.10

#### Career projection through narrative

Chen (2002) describes and explains each important feature of the 'career projection' process:

- *Retrospectivity* – knowing the self and its relationship with social context;
- *Reflexivity* – facilitating a sense of reflexivity towards the content of narratives unfolding in the story telling process;
- *Sense of development* – emphasis on career development as life development which is a continuous process;
- *Descriptive means* – using a range of qualitative techniques to facilitate the client to construct their stories (for example, genograms, life-lines);
- *Positive uncertainty* – there are always unknowns accompanying life narratives; the client can be encouraged to see this as a positive experience, a catalyst for exploring alternatives;
- *Perspective taking* – the client is encouraged to take different perspectives on the current and future situation;
- *Compromise through negotiation* – the narrative process involves adjustment and revisions following contextual needs.

---

Notably, the goal of both approaches to counselling is to increase congruence of some kind (person and occupation or job, person and context), the difference being that in the 'test and tell' approach congruence is predicted on the basis of a precise quantitative assessment by a counsellor, whereas in the constructivist model congruence is actively constructed by the client in collaboration with the counsellor.

It is generally also agreed among modernist (positivist) and postmodernist approaches to career counselling that making available good quality information is a necessary but not sufficient means of leveraging change, as people need to be helped in the process of making sense of this information in relation to their own life goals, abilities and circumstances, and to converting this into action (Watts, 1996).

## Summary (II) and conclusions

- The traditional 'test and tell' model of career guidance (within a matching framework) is compared with a more qualitative holistic approach in which assessment is either undertaken by the client and/or used to facilitate self-exploration.
- The 'test and tell' approach still dominates much career development counselling today, but is fast becoming outdated as an approach to facilitating the reconfigured career involving life-long learning and development.

# Counselling as 'Employee Assistance'

## Overview of approaches to 'employee assistance'

Counselling as an HRM tool dates back to the early 1900s in the form of 'welfare provision' charged with monitoring employee physical and mental well-being (see Cooper, Dewe, & O'Driscoll (2001) for a review). In the 1920s, welfare provision was supplemented by industrial psychiatry. Both were largely concerned with managing problems of attendance, production and discipline originating from physical and mental distress. Elton Mayo criticized this approach as being too organization centred, without due respect for the psychological needs of employees (Mayo, 1933). Mayo's work heralded the dawning of the human relations (HR) era underpinned by the thesis that the 'happy worker' is the most 'productive worker' (see Chapter 4 for a critique).

Harnessed by the HR movement, the remit of welfare provision widened to address problems of alcoholism, psychosomatic illnesses, the ageing worker and 'executive' emotional problems as well as management and workplace climate generally. The term 'employee assistance' was coined in the 1940s to encompass this widened remit and evolved to include not just psychiatrists and social workers, but also occupational psychologists and personnel officers (Carroll, 1996; Oher, 1999). The guiding framework was nonetheless still one of 'employee regulation' (that is, managed care; Reddy, 1993: 62). Assistance was also largely pursued in the curative medical mode, and as an adjunct to the organization (that is, on the periphery) rather than as an integral part of its corporate agenda and reality.

Today, the concept of employee assistance has gained renewed impetus as a key HRM tool (Oher, 1999). A recent study reported by Sciegaj et al. (2001), presents figures showing that 92 percent of Fortune 500 firms offer employee assistance. Sciegaj et al. (2001) say that such evidence suggests that company use of employee assistance programmes (EAPs) is at an historic high. Evidence also suggests a broadening of the remit for EAPs to include strategies to help employees balance work and family commitments (for example, Hobson, Delunas, & Kesis, 2001), preparation for early retirement (for example, Isaksson & Johansson, 2000), preparation and support during family relocation (for example, Eby, Douthitt, Perrin, Noble, Atchley, & Ladd, 2002), to facilitate diversity awareness and training (for example, Dillard & Harley, 2002), to facilitate the development of strategies to deal with potential violence at work (for example, nurses in mental health contexts) and with the effects of assault (for example, Cummins, 2002), for stress management (for example, Stein, 2001), for health promotion (for example, Elkin & Rosch, 1990), to address the needs of the disabled employee (for example, Chima, 2002), to help employees cope with organizational downsizing (for example, Worster, 2000) and rehabilitation back into the workplace after time out owing to illness or injury (for example, Nuttman-Shwartz & Ginsburg, 2002).

Researchers are arguing for a more multi-faceted, integrated and strategic use of EAPs within a human resource 'organizational development' framework (see Chapter 5), to both pre-empt and address problems at the interface between employer and employee (for example, Sandhu & Longwell-Grice, 2002). To this extent, some say that EAPs would benefit from the use of consultation models rather than being purely crisis driven, geared to helping the troubled employee (for example, Alker & McHugh, 2000). Elliot and Williams (2002) reported that members of the Fire Brigade were, on the whole, satisfied with their EAP, perceiving it to be effective in both human and financial terms. However, staff felt that there could be better communication between the service provider and the client company. Evidence from others does indeed confirm that employees would prefer their company to adopt a more integrated employee assistance solution (Sandhu & Longwell-Grice, 2002).

Systematic evaluation of EAP provision is rare. Quite apart from the methodological and measurement problems associated with measuring human and financial outcomes (for example, issues of confidentiality, restriction of range; Sexner, Gold, Anderson & Williams, 2001), there is a notoriously poor uptake of employee assistance opportunity by staff, and especially managers. Panks (2002) reports that uptake requires not only a recognition by an employee of the need for help, but also tolerance of potential stigma arising from the perceptions of others, interpersonal openness and confidence in EAP professionals. Potential stigma is consistently found to be a block to taking up employee assistance opportunity, especially among male employees.

### Counselling provision

Counselling provision is provided in the form of either an in-house or external EAP. Whilst EAPs are usually delivered by an external agency contractor, funded as an employee benefit (Cooper, Dewe, & O'Driscoll, 2001; Oher, 1999), the 'in-house counsellor' is now becoming much more commonplace, particularly in the UK (Carroll, 1996). There are various factors that have established a need for a specialist counselling service within organizations. These include the realization that employee health and well-being (physical and mental) is fundamental to good performance, legal pressures from the Health & Safety Executive (1998) to ensure that the workplace is a safe and healthy environment for employees, and political pressures on companies to take 'social responsibility' for assisting employees. In the USA, companies are being taken to court for 'emotional damage' to employees and stress-related illnesses (attributable to demanding workloads and also organizational change). As such, many companies are being forced into taking the preventative rather than curative line on employee assistance (see Study Box 6.11).

Reddy (1993) found that 85 percent of the companies surveyed ($N = 400$) reported the provision of some kind of counselling service, and all indicated that steps were being taken actively to manage stress (via in-house or external counselling provision). However, some concern has been raised over whether all those who provide counselling within organizational settings are suitably qualified to do so (the evidence suggests that many are not; Carroll, 1996).

---

### Study Box 6.11

### Managing employee well-being

The current prosperous economic situation appears to have a downside. A recent survey of a random population in the UK showed that about 20 percent of employees report high or extremely high levels of stress at work. The Health & Safety Executive (1998) estimated that between 30 and 60 percent of all sickness from work in the UK is attributable to some form of mental and emotional disturbance. Moreover, 40 million working days are lost every year in the UK through sickness absence caused by stress-related problems (Mental Health Foundation, 2000). The Confederation of British Industry (CBI) estimated the total costs of workplace absence in 1999 to be over £10 billion. Approximately £4–£5 billion is lost annually due to stress-related sickness (Gray, 1999). Department of Social Security (DSS) statistics indicate that on a weekly basis in Britain, around 3000 people move from Statutory Sick Pay (SSP) to Incapacity Benefit, and up to 80 percent of these people are then out of work for several years.

---

The 'in-house' counsellor (that is, where the organization employs both counsellor and client) may be part of a department (for example, Human Resources, Occupational Health) or may operate independently. Other counselling provision may be contracted in by an organization in the form of an EAP (for example, Independent Counselling and Advisory Services), on a full- or part-time basis. Career counselling is also increasingly being drawn into the employee assistance remit. Some organizations might also provide counselling services to clients to supplement their core service (for example, educational institutions which provide formal counselling facilities for students).

Whether in-house or external, counselling provision paid for by the organization raises various ethical issues. Many counsellors ignore the existence of the organization and focus on client well-being, whether the problems presented are work related or not. Others operate as allies of the organization, viewing their work as an essential part of managing employee effectiveness. To this end, counselling is pursued as a means to ensure that problems 'blocking' effective performance are minimized or overcome. Yet other counsellors may work to reconcile individual and organizational needs and interests (Carroll, 1996: 18–19).

## Stress counselling

Counselling in the employee assistance vein has been, and is still, very strongly connected with 'stress management'. The profile of counselling as a means of dealing with stress-related problems has increased in recent years in response to health and safety legislation, which raises issues about what constitutes 'reasonable stress'. For many, the term 'workplace counselling' is used synonymously with the term 'stress counselling' (for example, Reddy, 1993). Carroll (1996: 59) wonders whether this interchangeable use of terms is appropriate. Not all workplace counselling is concerned with stress. Moreover, there are lots of ways of handling stress (Ross & Altmaier, 1994) that may or may not involve counselling in some form.

A rapid increase in interest in stress management has been witnessed in recent years, with various forms of individual and organizational intervention being advocated (Palmer & Dryden, 1996). No one 'technique' or set of techniques is considered panacea. Reynolds and Briner (1996) have noted that most stress management intervention is based on a multi-modal form of cognitive therapy. However, this view is gleaned from a review of published research rather than actual practice, which Palmer and Dryden (1996) reckons is much more varied and probably atheoretical due to the consumer-led basis on which most stress management interventions are run. Practitioners note that people want to know about the physiology of stress. To this extent interventions usually incorporate an explanation of the biology of stress, coupled with an emphasis on how individuals can then cope with the stress they experience (for example, relaxation exercises; for example, Milner & Palmer, 1998). In some instances the client may need pharmacological intervention too.

## Models of stress counselling

***The multi-modal model***   Various 'models' of stress counselling have been proposed. One such model described by Palmer (1996) as 'multi-modal' draws on the work of Monat and Lazarus (1991) on stress appraisal and coping (see Chapter 8) and also Cox and MacKay's (1981) transactional model of stress. It assumes that how an individual reacts to stress is due more to his or her perceptions of it coupled with an appraisal of his or her ability to handle it than the event or situation itself. Specifically, one will experience stress to the extent that one perceives one cannot cope with perceived demands. Palmer's (1996) multi-modal approach to stress management assumes that stress manifests itself in a multitude of specific problems across a range of modalities (behaviour, affect, sensation, imagery, cognition, interpersonal, biology), each of which requires a different form of treatment. For example, the client in 'stress' may experience sleep disturbance (behavioural), anger and irritability (affect), tension (sensation), nightmares (imagery), self-deprecating thoughts (cognition), interpersonal difficulties (interpersonal) and constant headaches (biology). The possibility of a stress reaction is likely to be moderated by self-efficacy perceptions. Thus, individuals with high perceived self-efficacy (for example, 'I am in control', 'I can handle it') in dealing with 'stressors' are less likely to perceive that the demands they face outweigh their ability to deal with them.

Application of the model begins with a therapeutic assessment across the seven modalities described above comprising an initial interview and the completion of a multi-modal life history inventory (Monat & Lazarus, 1991). This inventory also examines client expectations about the therapy, the therapist and what both will achieve. The point of this is to help therapists to match their approach to client needs (for example, some will want the therapist to be tough and no-nonsense, whereas others will prefer the therapist to be rather more touchy-feely; Palmer, 1996: 551). The assessment process enables the formulation of a 'comprehensive modality profile' (see Palmer, 1996: 551 for an example). At the most basic level, the therapist can then help the client to identify which intervention or technique is likely to be appropriate for tackling each particular problem. Ultimately, however, it is up to the client to select the treatment(s) he or she think will be most appropriate. Referral to other therapists or stress specialists may be indicated.

If basic-level interventions are not successful, a second-order approach can be used that concentrates on each specific problem in more detail. Palmer (1996: 534–535) describes a tracking sequence involving examination of the way stress that manifests in one modality can 'fire off' stress in another. Thus, a rapid heartbeat can prompt a cognition of having a panic attack which in turn can afford an image of collapsing in public, prompting an individual to want to escape. Palmer (1996) describes a range of techniques that can be harnessed for addressing stress arising from each of the seven modalities. For example a behavioural technique might constitute 'behavioural rehearsal' (for example, for a presentation), anxiety management and relaxation training, coping imagery, the use of positive self-statements, thought stopping, role play and referral to a physician for medical treatment. The usefulness of this model is in its potential to help target intervention (for example, to moderate perceptions and appraisals of one's ability to cope, and to improve coping resources).

***The rational-emotive model***   Another approach to stress known as 'rational-emotive' aims to change client philosophies, attitudes and beliefs underpinning their distress or disturbance (Ellis, 2001). Like Palmer, Ellis argues that stress does not exist per se, only via the perceptions and reactions of the individual. On the other hand they do recognize that there are instances where trauma is inevitable (for example, rape). Nonetheless they argue that the prime determinant of stress is the individual's irrational (that is, absolute), inflexible and dogmatic beliefs and self-defeating styles manifest as 'musts', 'shoulds', 'oughts', 'have tos' and so on. It is not suggested that there is a linear correspondence between stress-related illness and irrational beliefs, merely that irrational belief can generate prolonged anguish and arousal. Irrational beliefs can take the form of unconditional demands (for example, 'I have to be successful') and 'awfulizing' ('It would be really awful if I didn't get promoted'). As Ellis (2001: 67) puts it, 'people create traps for themselves with musts that often cannot be satisfied'. Such beliefs can operate unconsciously to generate extreme emotional reactions.

Thus, the aim of the therapy is to change the detrimental personal philosophies harboured by individuals to bring the stress reaction under control (see Study Box 6.12). Rational-emotive behavioural therapy is also multi-modal insofar as it harnesses a range of intervention techniques, and is known to have been successfully applied to the organizational setting (for example, Neenan, 1993).

## Study Box 6.12

### Rational-emotive techniques

The guiding questions for the rational-emotive therapist are: 'is this belief logical?', 'what is the evidence on which this belief is based?' and 'what are the consequences of this belief?' Techniques include:

- 'active-directive disputing' of client beliefs (for example, disputing absolute 'musts', disputing 'I can't stand its', disputing feelings of worthlessness);
- re-framing (that is, to find good things in some of the bad things that have happened to them);
- cognitive homework (comprising self-help techniques and materials);
- emotive-evocative dramatic techniques (to help individuals cope with stressful situations); and
- action methods to help individuals overcome stress reactions.

### Individual or organizational responsibility for stress?

Both the multi-modal and rational-emotive approaches emphasize the client as responsible for his or her own stress. Both may thus be criticized for neglecting the possibility that the organization is contributing to, generating and/or maintaining experienced stress (Cooper & Cartwright, 1996; Newton, 1995; Reynolds & Briner, 1996). Indeed, most writing on how to manage stress in organizational contexts emphasizes the individual nature of the problem (that is, personal responsibility for recognizing and managing stress; for example, Newton, 1995). Newton (1995) argues that stress dealt with as a counselling issue decontextualizes the problem of stress, which is fundamentally an organizational responsibility. Individualizing stress also pathologizes it and makes people vulnerable to unwarranted organizational influence and control.

Carroll (1996: 61) argues that stress is *both* an organizational and an individual problem and that its management cannot be reduced to either. It is clear nonetheless that little is known about what constitutes an effective stress intervention at both individual and organizational levels of analysis and that no definitive recommendations can be made about how best to cope with employee stress (Semmer, 2003). Few interventionists operate with a systematic working model of stress. Evidence does not look good for stress management interventions generally, as few culminate in any real benefit to either individuals or the organization (Giga, Cooper, & Faragher, 2003; Kenny & Cooper, 2003; Taris et al., 2003; see Chapter 8). Arthur (2000) argues that declaration of a stress experience disguises mental health problems, and that practitioners need to be aware that the 'emperor is wearing no clothes'.

*An integrative model*  Milner and Palmer (1998) advocate an integrative approach involving the 'flexible' use of many different theoretical principles and models. An

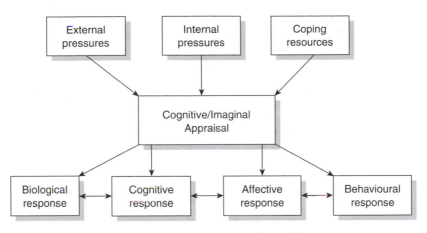

**Figure 6.1**   Milner and Palmer's Integrative Stress Model
(adapted from Milner and Palmer, 1998: 17)

integrative approach is built on the theory of helping and the 'relationship' or process factors that facilitate client change. To this extent it is less concerned with the content of the problem than the process of helping clients to solve or manage it. This goes beyond eclecticism, involving the use of whatever technique is deemed appropriate to address the problem. It is built on a model of what constitutes effective helping and, to this end, various techniques can be harnessed (that is, systematic eclecticism). Milner and Palmer (1998) describe a problem-focused stress counselling model within the framework of the 'skilled helper' advocated by Egan (1998, see below for a brief outline of this model). The fundamental assumptions of the model (see Figure 6.1) are that the client is at the heart of the issue, that counselling is a collaborative learning encounter where power is shared and that stress counsellors are professional and accountable for the quality of their work (Milner & Palmer, 1998: 17).

The approach assumes that clients are able to take responsibility for their own learning. It also assumes that the counsellor's resources are 'impotent' without the contributions of the client. The model integrates humanistic principles with behavioural theory moving from a client-focused 'here-and-now' approach to a more future-focused action-oriented approach (in the skilled helper tradition): 'the concepts underpinning the counselling process are those of a therapeutic relationship providing the core conditions for growth and change, integrated with the asumptions and explanations which underlie a problem management process' (Milner & Palmer, 1998: 21). The reader is advised to consult Milner and Palmer (1998) directly for the integrative problem-focused approach in action, coupled with illustrative case material, a description of various techniques and therapeutic tools.

Without clear guidelines on stress counselling, coupled with scepticism as to the value of stress management interventions generally (for example, Palmer & Dryden, 1996: 11; Reynolds & Briner, 1996), Milner and Palmer (1998) argue that stress counsellors should, *overall*, be competent in the following areas:

- cognitive-behavioural techniques;
- rational-emotive behavioural techniques;
- counselling and listening skills;
- group facilitation (since stress counselling may address groups as well as individuals);
- problem-solving skills;
- educating people about stress and its management;
- the use of psychometric tests;
- knowledge of relevant research;
- knowledge of various lifestyle options, for example, diet, exercise;
- understanding of occupational, organizational change, management, family and social issues.

### Summary (III) and conclusions

- Stress counselling has conventionally been undertaken within a framework of managed care underwritten by a philosophy of employee assistance as a means of addressing performance problems and difficulties induced by 'personal' problems.
- Nowadays, some EAPs may be more well-being oriented than problem oriented, which may put the counsellor into a difficult ethical position as to whose interests he or she is serving.
- Health and safety legislation provides the backdrop to corporate attempts to ensure that their employees do not suffer more than a 'reasonable' level of stress (which is heavily dependent on whether the work is in itself intrinsically stressful), and may thus be undertaken defensively rather than as part of a strategic stress-management package.
- Three different stress-counselling models are reviewed in detail: multi-modal, rational-emotive and integrative. All are highly oriented to achieving change in how stress is appraised, reacted to and coped with.
- Sadly, evidence suggests that stress management interventions are generally not that effective in addressing the 'stress problem' because they pay too little attention to organizational factors, focusing too much on individual coping skills.

## The Helping Approach

General helping models (for example, Egan, 1998; Nelson-Jones, 1993) applicable to a variety of contexts and problem domains can be compared with those specific to workplace counselling (for example, Carroll, 1996). The difference between the 'general helping model' and more specific counselling models is that the former can be used by anyone who has acquired the appropriate skill base, including coaches, mentors, managers and supervisors. The two self-reflection activities designed to bring the concept of helping alive (your counselling attitude and counselling style) can be located on **www.sagepub.co.uk/millward**.

## The concept of helping

The helping approach assumes that the client can be facilitated to marshal his or her own resources to alleviate, rid oneself of or manage a problem. In short, the client retains ownership of the problem and its remedial responsibility. As well as helping the client to 'frame' or indeed 'reframe' the problem into something manageable, the skilled helper may also 'resource' the client with practical help and support, and/or guide him or her on where to find necessary resources. Ultimately, however, the client actually solves or manages the problem.

This model contrasts with the prescriptive 'doctor–patient' approach. It construes the counsellor as expert in process facilitation as opposed to problem resolution – that is, in helping the client to solve or manage the problem rather than prescribe or provide a 'potted' solution. The centrality of the empathic relationship and its role in facilitating client change is emphasized (see Study Box 6.13) as is the action-oriented component. There are various 'helping' models available for the counsellor to draw upon in a workplace setting, some of which are briefly outlined below. The reader is, however, advised to consult the source direct for detailed information about the models described and for illustrative 'case material'.

---

**Study Box 6.13**

### The empathic relationship

The empathic relationship is understood by most therapists/counsellors to be fundamental to the generation of client change (Clarkson, 1990), particularly in the early stages. The person-centered tradition assumes that for a client to move towards psychological growth they must be able to experience the counsellor as:

- demonstrating empathy (through an understanding of their problems and concerns);
- demonstrating genuineness and authenticity in the therapeutic relationship; and
- demonstrating respect or unconditional acceptance of them as persons.

Skilful communication of these attitudes comprises the foundation of all counselling work even in the case of cognitive-behavioural therapy (Milner & Palmer, 1998). These 'attitudes' help the client to develop trust in the counsellor and in the counselling process. The relationship between counsellor and client helps form the therapeutic alliance (that is, a pragmatic partnership).

---

## Helping models

There is broad agreement amongst practitioners operating with the 'problem-solving' approach that a nurturing or facilitative phase, focused on improving the client's

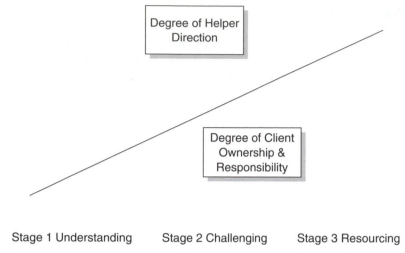

Stage 1 Understanding     Stage 2 Challenging     Stage 3 Resourcing

**Figure 6.2**   Egan's Helping Model

capacity for experiencing, precedes a more action-oriented phase, focused on thinking and acting. The first helping model is generic in its applicability whilst the second is specific to workplace counselling.

***Gerard Egan's 'The skilled helper'***   According to the Egan (1998) model, counselling is:

- a set of techniques, attitudes and skills
- to help people manage their problems
- using their own resources as far as possible.

Egan (1998) describes a three-stage model in which the counsellor and the client are each depicted as having particular goals or tasks to achieve (see Figure 6.2). The first task is for the counsellor to facilitate problem definition by 'demonstrating understanding'. The second task is for the counsellor to engineer problem redefinition (if necessary) such that the client takes 'ownership' of the problem and that affords various options for its solution (the client may at first disown the problem and/or perceive it to be unmanageable). To do this, the counsellor will need to 'challenge' the client's way of construing the problem and to help them reframe it. Finally, the counsellor may be required to 'resource' the client (that is, actively empower him/her) to take action to solve or manage the problem (see Example Box 6.4).

   Overall, the aims of the counselling in the form of the 'skilled helper' are understood to be:

- to provide a quiet confidential environment for those who have a problem, concern or anxiety;

- to enable them to talk openly about themselves and their feelings without being judged;
- to help them to gain a clearer and more positive understanding of themselves and their situation
- to focus on ways to help them to manage their problems.

The three-stage model can be progressed in the short-term (one or two sessions) or long-term (across many sessions), depending on the type of problems clients bring with them. The problem-solving process may also be pursued on a *cyclical basis* (that is, as one 'problem' is being 'resourced' another related problem is being scoped out). The client may also regress from one stage to the next, particularly if, in the process of re-framing the problem, other psychological concerns are raised and start to 'block' progress. Some clients only require help with problem definition (in itself this can help empower the client and motivate the necessary initiative to manage it). Others will need help with re-framing the problem, but once this is achieved and the client can readily see a way forward, he or she may be appropriately inspired to take action on their own initiative. Other clients will require the full three-stage process.

---

**Example Box 6.4**

### Egan's three-stage model in action

#### *Exploration by demonstrating understanding*

Involves establishing a relationship to enable the client to explore his or her thoughts, feelings and behaviours through open questions, active listening and appropriate responses. The aim is to help the client to define the nature and scope of the problem in his or her own terms. This involves the attitudes of genuineness (authenticity) and respect (non-evaluative, non-judgemental), and the technique of demonstrating understanding of what has been communicated as accurately as possible (for example, playing back in simple concrete language the experiences, behaviours and feelings that are being conveyed, active listening and open questions that help the client to explore the problem; see **www.sagepub.co.uk/millward**).

#### *Problem redefinition through challenging*

Involves helping the client to piece together the picture that has emerged at phase 1, to see all the issues involved and to develop self-understanding of strengths/weaknesses and the resources available. Phase 1 provides a basis for the development of mutual trust and respect. It focuses on the individual's frame of reference. Phase 2 represents a shift in perspective to assist the client to see his/her world from a different, more

*(Continued)*

---

**Example Box 6.4   Continued**

'objective' point of view. This phase must be constructive rather than overwhelming and destructive. It may require (in addition to the basic counselling attitude) *judicious self-disclosure* (sharing your own private feelings and experiences of a similar nature with the client, taking care not to burden him/her), *caring* (with the individuals needs in mind) and *tentative challenge.* The skill in this phase is similar to that for phase 1, but with the additional use of *interpretation* – that is, playing back to the individual an understanding not only of what is said but of what is implied through verbal and non-verbal signals. It involves summarizing in a concrete way what the individual has presented only fragmentally, identifying themes, and making links between them by filling in the missing blanks and helping to draw conclusions. This phase might also involve the use of *immediacy* – that is, direct mutual 'you and me' talk to eliminate blocks to progress (for example, defensive games). It will also most definitely involve the use of *advanced listening* skills.

### Resourcing for action

Involves helping the person to act or cope with the problem or difficulty via his or her own self-understanding and/or by developing the appropriate coping strategies and drawing on relevant resources. This is the action-planning phase with three main aims: to help the client to establish concrete viable goals, to establish concrete viable means, and to provide support and direction as the individual pursues these goals. Counselling involves emotional re-education so clients can see things more realistically with a better picture of their resources. Techniques that can be used by the counsellor include objective/goal setting, action planning, progress review and the provision of support.

---

If continuing assistance is required, the thrust should be to emphasize action. It is critically important that the client retains the remedial initiative. Forms of support may include guidance (for example, rehearsing something), information/advice, practical service (for example, compiling a CV), use of expertise, referral, feedback on behaviour (for example, giving a presentation) and training. Various techniques can be used by counsellor's to help clients to check the viability of their action plans (for example, force-field analysis – see Example Box 6.5). As noted earlier in this chapter, the importance of facilitating client action and self-management has been given more emphasis in recent years as a necessary part of workplace counselling strategy (Chen, 2002).

---

**Example Box 6.5**

### Force-field Analysis

Force-field analysis comprises the following steps:

1   Client lists all restraining forces as obstacles he or she might experience during the implementation of their action plans (for example, reactions of others, client's own feelings, lack of skills).

---

**Example Box 6.5   Continued**

2   Identify all facilitating forces or resources that will contribute to the implementation of the plan.
3   Identify the most significant forces in each list.
4   Identify ways of reducing the impact of restraining forces and of maximizing the effects of facilitating forces.

Prompts to help generate action include: *people* (who might help?), *models* (what have others done in similar situations?), *places* (where might help be available?), *things* (what might help? for example, books, activities, equipment, training).

---

*Carroll's (1996) 'integrative' model of workplace counselling*   Carroll's model is unique in that it is specifically addressed to the issue of workplace counselling. This model is only briefly summarized here. For detail the reader can consult Carroll (1996) directly, who also advises on how to set up, administrate/manage and evaluate counselling provision in a workplace context. Carroll describes the model as atheoretical, process oriented and competence based, which means that it can be readily applied in an organizational setting and used eclectically (that is, the counsellor can draw on any theoretical orientation or method of intervention depending on informed judgement as to what is required). Carroll (1996: 102–133) outlines a five-stage model as follows:

1   *Preparation* – establishing aims and objectives, formulating policy and procedures with respect to the place of counselling in the setting concerned, establishing clear roles and responsibilities and a network for referral, providing information about the service to clients and establishing the parameters of confidentiality. The client needs to know what counselling will involve, the kinds of services available, location and interface (including confidentiality) with the organization. In short, the service must inspire confidence and trust in the clients it serves.
2   *Assessment* – formulation (that is, what is happening?, what is the source of the problem?) and decision making about how the client might be most appropriately helped (that is, what is the best form of help 'right now'?). The client will also need to decide whether to continue to see the counsellor. Carroll (1996) describes four main methods of individual assessment (see Study Box 6.10) and also provides advice on organizational assessment (see Study Box 6.11).
3   *Contracting/referral* – establishing a working agreement between counsellor and client that the client will continue to work with the counsellor or will need to be referred to another counsellor or source of help. This will cover issues of confidentiality (including who has access to client notes), what counselling is all about and what the client can expect to get out of it, what to do if the session needs to be cancelled, how often to meet, how to contact the counsellor and so on. Procedures for referral also need to be agreed, including a point of contact interfacing between the counselling service and the referral agency.

4 *Counselling* – the personal/interpersonal side of the counselling situation itself as well as administrative and organizational considerations. Most of the literature on counselling focuses on the interpersonal dimension – that is, counselling theory, therapeutic techniques, therapeutic relationships and the counselling process. However, Carroll (1996) argues that there are also *administrative* (that is, the arrangements surrounding counselling provision including the point of contact and location of counselling, note keeping and so on; see, for example, Towler, 1997) and *organizational* considerations (that is, how does the context affect the counselling event?, are there clear boundaries between the counsellor's responsibility to the client and to the organization?). Issues of 'reentry' of a client (after long absence) into the workplace are also an integral part of the counselling scenario in the workplace.

5 *Termination* – requires planned and systematic management. Carroll (1996: 128) argues that termination must be built into the contract itself – that is, when agreeing on the number of sessions that will be required. Carroll also advises on how to work towards termination (by preparing the client) and how to actually manage the process of termination itself.

Assessment involves the counsellor and Carroll (1996: 114) argues that matching intervention to client is a fundamental skill for workplace counsellors. Decision about how best to intervene (that is, whether to refer, which method to use) will depend on a whole host of factors including theoretical orientation and preferences, the needs of the workplace, the extent of inter-professional involvement in the provision of employee assistance, and so on.

---

### Study Box 6.14

#### Methods of individual assessment

##### Diagnostic

Medical, clinical and counselling assessment may involve the application of diagnostic criteria such as the DSM (Diagnostic and Statistical Manual for Mental Disorders) or ICL (International Classification of Diseases). The ICL is more commonly used in Britain than the DSM. Counsellors may be criticized for not considering the possibility that a client may need 'medical' or 'psychiatric' help (for example, Malan, 1976). For example, a client may need to be referred for medical consultation to check whether his or her constant headaches are attributable to something organic or neurological (for example, brain tumour) rather than psychological (for example, stress). Malan (1976) notes that counsellors may also need to think in terms of 'practical' help (for example, training in assertiveness).

##### Psychometric

The counsellor may draw on various standardized psychological tests such as the Occupational Stress Inventory or the State/Trait Anxiety Inventory, for example, or

## Study Box 6.14    Continued

personality inventories like the MMPI (Minnesota Multiphasic Personality Inventory; see McNally, Bryant & Ehlers, 2003 for more on this). Career counsellors rely heavily on psychometric tests as their way of understanding a client's 'growth' needs and as the starting point for dialogue.

### Interpersonal assessment

This is conducted as an integral part of the counselling process through questioning and listening. This type of assessment may be informed by a particular theoretical orientation or may rely on a combination of theory and intuition.

### Presenting problems and underlying psychological concerns

This aims to get behind the problem to ascertain its deeper roots (for example, perpetuating life-patterns and recurrent interpersonal problems).

## Study Box 6.15

### Methods of organizational assessment

Counsellors are short on methods of assessment appropriate to an organizational level of analysis because of the largely interpersonal nature of their work. Carroll (1996) argues that assessment of the individual will need to take into consideration the role of the organization in generating client problems. Is the problem specific to the individual, arising largely irrespective of the workplace (for example, recurrent depression)? Or is the problem highly specific to the workplace (for example, sexual harassment or bullying)? Is it a problem arising from outside work (for example, marital, medical)? Or is it an organization-induced problem (for example, reorganization, redundancy)? Carroll (1996) refers to the work of Clarkson (1990), who talks about individual and organizational levels of 'growth' and 'dysfunction' as a framework for understanding client problems.

Milner and Palmer (1998: 43–49) describe in detail how counsellors can establish the 'core conditions' for a constructive therapeutic relationship to emerge. Core skill requirements include active listening and questioning (see **www.sagepub.co.uk/millward** for detailed coverage and self-development activities).

### Summary (IV) and conclusions

- The helping approach can be used by anyone with the appropriate inclination and skill base, including managers and supervisors, to help someone take responsibility for their problems or difficulties and also, if necessary, help them to formulate a plan of action and provide the appropriate support.

- The key to 'helping' is to enable clients to look at their problems or difficulties with new eyes and with a sense of ownership. By contrast, counselling models like Carroll's specific to workplace counselling adopt a more formal therapeutic stance.
- All models are 'modal' (that is, applicable to the prototypical client) and as such need to be applied flexibly such that they can be tailored to individual needs.

## Organizational and Ethical Issues in Counselling

### The 'ecology' of the organization in which counselling provision is located

The increased profile of counselling in organizational settings has prompted some to advocate a new species of counsellor dubbed the 'organizational counselling psychologist' (Gerstein & Shullman, 1992). There are three different but overlapping considerations arising from the organizational angle on workplace counselling: the organizational context of counselling including the impact of the organization on the counselling dynamic, the role of the counsellor at an organizational level of analysis and professional/ethical considerations.

Key questions include: How does the organization construe counselling and its role? Where do loyalties reside? How congruent are counsellor values with those of the organization? What are the politics and policies surrounding the counselling service and which characterize the organization in general? To what extent can one manage/is one prepared to manage problems generated by the organization (for example, poor management, sexual harassment, prejudice, bullying) – that is, symptoms of organizational dysfunction? To what extent is the counsellor part of the same dysfunctional system?

Counsellors work in organizational settings of all kinds and must appreciate the context in which they work (for example, Gray, 1984; Walton, 1997). The counsellor may be under pressure to achieve results and fast, creating confidentiality dilemmas and posing a threat of 'failure' when particular clients do not respond to their interventions. The organization not only provides a forum in which particular 'practicalities' become salient (for example, number of sessions, location of counselling service), but it also provides a context in which problems are generated and derive meaning (Walton, 1997). Egan (1998) calls this 'organizational messiness' and 'organizational stupidity' (see also Newton, 1995).

Many counsellors/therapists have adopted a stance on this by construing the problems individuals take on as reflections of organizational ills (for example, Hirschhorn & Barnett, 1993; see Study Box 6.16). At the other extreme, some counsellors take the view that counselling is a fundamentally personal/interpersonal event, a kind of 'insulated alliance' (Carroll, 1996: 65) whereby people are empowered to cope within the systems in which they operate (Nelson-Jones, 1993).

**Study Box 6.16**

**The psychodynamic approach to organizations and organizational life**

Hirschhorn and Barnett (1993) picture organizations as being driven by an unconscious source of motivation in the way postulated by psychodynamic approaches to the individual, described as the 'shadow' side of an organization. Specifically, an organization is described as:

- developing defences against anxiety and other difficult emotions – that is, keeping emotions under wraps;
- developing organizational procedures and processes that serve as defences against anxiety;
- operating largely as an 'irrational' entity;
- having irrational processes that influence the way work is organized and conducted.

Individuals are said to be attracted to particular types of organizations and organizational cultures, which provide them forums in which to deal with 'unresolved' intra-psychic issues. Troubled individuals are also described as 'containers' for organizational anxiety who are often 'scapegoated' because they are acting out organizational problems in their own life. This reflects in the illnesses they take up, the kinds of 'informal' roles they adopt and the emotions they express. The work of Menzies (1954) is a classic of its kind, describing the kind of organizational defences that evolve to contain anxiety among nurses, and which influence the way that nurses interact with their clientele.

In between these extremes are those taking into consideration both individual and organization. Systemic approaches to counselling, for example, construe the individual as an integral part of a wider system (Carroll & Walton, 1997) whereby each is a mirror of the other. The systems approach advocates that all client problems are context specific (that is, Whose problem is it? How is the problem 'framed'? What is it a symptom of? What is the 'hidden agenda' at work?). This approach requires an appreciation that an individual is also part of many other systems (family, friends, educational systems and so on).

It is thus strongly advocated that the counsellor take an 'upstream' stance on the organization (that is, intervene at the organizational level of analysis) as well as a 'downstream' one (that is, involving individual 'rescue'). In the words of Clarkson (1990: 4):

employee counselling should not be tackled on a piecemeal basis, but should be coherently and effectively integrated with assessment, training and consultancy endeavours to form part of a coherent overall strategy for the whole organization.

## The role of the counsellor in an organizational setting

The workplace counsellor can operate in potentially high-profile organizational roles and not only in the capacity of 'clinician'. Gerstein and Shullman (1992) described 18 different 'hats' worn by the workplace counsellor including trainer, welfare officer, advocate, adviser, change agent and so on. Some worry about workplace counsellors becoming 'jacks of all trades', though at the same time understand the potential for counsellors to pursue an 'organizational development' role (for example, Carroll, 1997; Walton, 1997; see Study Box 6.14). Hampden-Turner (1994), for instance, describes the role of counselling in organizational culture change by introducing new ways of working with people, how to facilitate change and how to deal with blocks that make constructive change difficult. Clarkson (1990) also talks about the 'organization as client' and describes a framework (underpinned by notions of 'myth and narrative') within which counsellors can work at this level of complexity.

---

### Study Box 6.17

#### The role of counselling in facilitating organizational change

- *Listening forum* – where people are listened to, trusted, respected and helped to make important life decisions.
- *Training* – educating the organization into new more 'healthy' practices that prevent the generation of stress and distress.
- *Management consultation* – helping managers work more effectively with individuals and their teams.
- *Managing change* – aiding with transitions and with the integration of old with new, with handling loss and facilitating flexibility, and helping to cope with uncertainty and ambiguity.
- *Helping with bad news* – communicating and helping employees cope with 'bad news', for example, redundancy, early retirement, change imperatives, relocation, and so on.
- *Modelling professional relationships* – for example, the demonstration of respect, compassion and concern, the ability to harness potential.
- *Empowering individuals and groups* – facilitating personal power and the harnessing of personal and group potential.
- *Creating awareness and respect for individual differences* – arising from biographical, social and cultural circumstances.

(Carroll, 1996: 38–41).

---

### Ethical issues in workplace counselling

To operate effectively in an organizational setting, the counsellor is required to 'build bridges' between individual and organization through a sophisticated process of 'mediation' (Carroll & Walton, 1997; Shea & Bond, 1997). This can create many professional and ethical dilemmas for the counsellor. For example, the client may be drinking on the job or may admit committing a serious error. These problems are unique to counselling pursued in an organizational setting, and are coupled with all the ethical dilemmas facing all counsellors in general (for example, a client admits to abusing his partner or child, or to committing theft).

Carroll (1996: 151) notes how dilemmas for the counsellor in the workplace nearly all involve issues of loyalty and to whom. When do counsellors break confidentiality agreements? When do they 'tell' on the organization if it is in breach of legislation? When do they become involved at an organizational level? Some of these dilemmas can be pre-empted by establishing clear policy and procedures to deal with conflicts of loyalty including answers to questions like: What is my relationship with the employee? Are employees aware of my responsibilities? Unfortunately there are no ethical guidelines for the workplace counsellor, other than those pertaining to EAPs generally (that is, UK Standards of Practice and Professional Guidelines for Employee Assistance Programmes, 1995). Most ethical decisions are made intuitively (see Carroll, 1996: 154–171 for guidelines on a more systematic process of ethical decision making, and also Shea & Bond, 1997). In M. Carroll's (1995: 23) words:

> the employee counsellor has one of the most difficult counselling jobs, and has a thin line to tread between the organization and the individual.

### *Summary (V) and conclusions*

- The organization is the context that can help make sense of individual problems and difficulties: it is inappropriate to deal with them outside of a system-level perspective. Unfortunately, it may not be possible or reasonable to involve all relevant parties in a counselling event, so more often than not *individuals* are the focus of a counselling intervention.
- Workplace counselling may pose a dilemma for counsellors who are trained to facilitate the well-being of individuals. Issues of confidentiality may arise that could make salient the accountability of the counsellor to the organization. Conversely, accountabilities to the employee may mean that the counsellor will sometimes need to act against the interests of the organization.
- Some argue that counselling can play a strategic organizational role in, for example, the facilitation of change or the creation of an organization-wide counselling philosophy or culture. Stress management interventions (including counselling) are far more likely to be successful if there is a system level supportive infrastructure. Thus, a role for the counsellor in more upstream system-level work may be fitting.

## Future Research Challenges

- integrate the relevant literature and research on the construct 'development' with view to conceptual and empirical clarification;
- conceptualize and investigate the central role played by self-insight and self-awareness in development;

- conceptualize and investigate the concept of self-reflection as the central mechanism postulated to be a key facilitator of development (see also Chapter 2 on the proposed role of reflection in the learning process);
- investigate informal as well as formal helping roles in organizational contexts and, in particular, evaluate their effectiveness within the context of coaching, mentoring and manager–employee relations;
- conceptualize and investigate the self-management process and, in particular, the construct of self-regulation (perhaps with reference to the wider literature on motivation);
- look closely at the concept of emotional intelligence in the self-management process;
- explore the role played by emotion in development;
- clarify the concepts of coaching and mentoring and their key psychological ingredients;
- explore the idea of manager–employee 'career discussion';
- evaluate the effectiveness of executive coaching (is coaching just another form of 'helping' dressed up in business terms?);
- investigate the effectiveness of career counselling interventions based on a conceptualization of the key processes involved;
- investigate the effectiveness of stress counselling in an organizational context;
- explore the role of counselling at a system-wide level of analysis.

## Recommended Reading and Resources

Carroll, M. (1996). *Workplace counselling*. London: Sage.
Carroll, M., & Walton, M. (1997). *Handbook of counselling in organizations*. London: Sage.
Egan, G. (1998). *The skilled helper*. Monterey, CA: Brooks/Cole Publishing.
Ellis, A. (2001). *Stress counselling: A rational emotive behavioural approach*. London: Sage.
Holland, J.L. (1997). *Making vocational choices: A theory of vocational personalities and work environments* (3rd edn). Odessa, FL: Psychological Assessment Resources.
Peavy, R.V. (1992). A constructivist model of training for career counsellors. *Journal of Career Development*, 18, 215–228.

### *Internet resources*

'Careers work for the 21st century' from The Career Learning Network, www.careers-cafe.com/mitw1.pdf – this resource offers a rich format in which the learner can develop self-insight in relation to the working world.
Other useful resources are offered at the following sites:

- www.careerstorm.com
- www.getting-on.co.uk/toolkit/construct.htm
- www.enquirewithin.co.nz

# 7

# Human–Machine Interaction

If one views technology not simply as hardware but as a process in which flows of knowledge and artefacts are generated and diffused through the process of invention, use and exchange, it is clear that an individual organisation is itself but one site for the shaping of the technology that it applies.

(Corbett, 1994: 207)

## Preface

Widespread adoption of computer technology for everyday work, coupled with increased automation of jobs (across manufacturing and service sectors) and advances in microprocessor-based technology, have heightened the salience of the interface between employees and machines. The design of human–machine systems and artefacts is ever more critical to individual and, ultimately, organizational performance. The study of the human–machine interface can be approached from a range of disciplines such as engineering, physics, mathematics, design, computing, and cognitive, environmental, experimental and social psychology. Here the study of human–machine interaction in workplace settings is examined from an occupational psychology perspective. The increased use of computer technology has prompted attention in particular to the *cognitive* elements of ergonomic 'fit' between humans and machines, in addition to the traditional focus on physical and physiological factors. This includes the study of the impact of automation as well as other more advanced technologies on human users. Hence, whilst some may assign the topic of human–machine interaction to the ergonomics expert, psychologists are to be encouraged to take a unitary approach to this issue, taking into account human factors at both a job and organizational level as well as the machine side of the equation.

Cognitive developments in connection with understanding the human–machine interface have burgeoned interest in the mental model concept, and the possibility that mental models can be distributed across both people and artefacts comprising a single cognitive system. The optimal use of technology is inextricably tied up with cognition. A digital scenario in particular requires a prerequisite cognitive capability. As stressed by Jafee (2001), new forms of skill and knowledge may be required to exploit new technology. Intelligence is *not* the technology but the people using the technology. A litany of failures can be cited where technological solutions have been imposed on organizations to drive them, some of them with disastrous consequences. Evidence from a more organizational level of analysis demonstrates how issues of attitude and social context, as well as the cognitive capabilities of the users, dictate whether a new technological system will be accepted and used as intended. There is a fine balance to be achieved between enabling new processes and supporting existing processes.

This module begins by describing the human–machine interaction system, progressing to issues of automation, human error, usability, control and display design. The potential interface implications of new advanced technologies are then reviewed. The chapter ends with a more organizational level of analysis, within a socio-technical systems framework. The human implications of the digital organizational solution are considered at the level of the social system as well as in terms of the increased requirement for cognitive capability.

## Learning Objectives

**Studying the contents of this chapter will enable you to:**

1   examine the issues underpinning the development of the human factors movement;
2   provide an ergonomic rationale for the design of a human–machine system;
3   explain the concept of usability in the context of user-centred design of an artefact or product;
4   examine the cognitive basis of human error, mental models and learnability in relation to systems design, training and computer-based tasks;
5   discuss the human factors issues arising from advanced microprocessor technologies including virtual workplace realities;
6   examine technological innovation within the context of the organization as a social system (or so-called 'soft system') within a socio-technical systems framework.

## The Systems Approach to Human–Machine Interaction – An Individual User Perspective

Human factors is the formal study of the *human* aspects of machine use, in the broader context of 'human factors' research. Human factors research emerged from the need for increased efficiency and sustained performance under stressful conditions (e.g. excessive noise/vibration, complete darkness) during World War II (Chmiel, 1998). For example, pilot confusion between the cockpit system operating landing gear and that responsible for aircraft lift and altitude is said to have been responsible for more than 400 Royal Air Force accidents (Sanders & McCormick, 1993). Wartime design solutions were later transposed onto peacetime industries. A field of research termed 'ergonomics' (or 'human factors' in North America) was thus born.

The discipline has been variously defined but Shackel's (1996) view is perhaps one of the most apt, placing accent less on the 'design' aspect and more on the study of the interface between user and artefact:

> the study of the relation between people and their occupation, equipment and environment, and particularly the application of anatomical, physiological and psychological knowledge to the problems arising therefrom. (p. 1)

The field harnesses the study of human anatomy and physiology (for example, bio-mechanics, anthropometry and perceptual systems) and of the physics of the external environment (for example, noise, light, heat, cold, radiation, vibration) as well as the cognitive elements of human functioning (for example, skills, learning, human error, individual differences). Contemporary human factors specialists thus model the human–machine interface as a 'system' of interacting components (Howell, 1991).

Early ergonomic study failed to fully appreciate this multi-disciplinary perspective, focusing on the ergonomic *detail* of machines (for example, readability and aesthetics of oil pressure displays on car dashboards) without addressing the human–machine 'system' as a whole (for example, the information provided on oil pressure displays was not mean-ingful to the driver). A systems approach, however, requires consideration of whether, for example, the information provided by an oil pressure display generates action (for exam-ple, warning light) even if the *technical* meaning of the light is not fully understood.

Howell's (1991) depiction of the systems approach is illustrated in Figure 7.1 with the example of a telesales operator in a call-centre at a computer, communicating with callers via a headset. A call is received and the operator calls up the customer's details on screen using the keyboard and mouse ('controls'). This 'action' sends a message to the central processing unit (CPU) of the computer and the machine carries out the required action ('machine information processing and decision making'). The caller's details then appear on the monitor ('displays') and are read from the screen ('sensing'). Any requests by the caller are then considered by the operator ('human information processing and decision making').

The critical features of any human–machine system are that they are:

- composed of several interacting components and may comprise subsystems and/or be integral to larger systems;
- the *interface* between human and machine is a critical consideration (e.g. if a car's brakes are not responsive the driver will be neither efficient nor safe); and
- both the worker and the machine may perform similar information processing functions (Chmiel, 1998).

The 'acceptability' of any given system is determined by a number of parameters com-mon to *any* system in *any* setting (Nielsen, 1995). Figure 7.2 highlights areas of direct ergonomic input (that is, usefulness and its subparameters, as well as system reliabil-ity), in addition to social acceptability and more technically driven issues such as cost and compatibility.

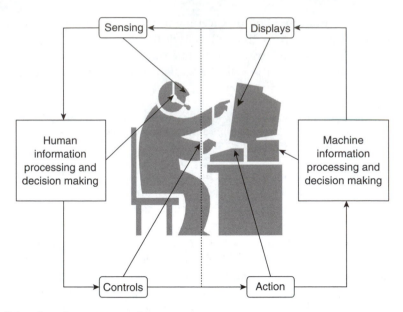

**Figure 7.1** A systems perspective

Adapted from Howell, W.C. (1991). Human factors in the workplace. In M.D. Dunnette and L.M. Hough (Eds), *Handbook of industrial and organizational psychology* (Vol. 2). Palo Alto, CA: Consulting Psychologists Press.

Human factor specialists are likely to form one element of a multi-disciplinary team comprising engineers and other organizational forces such as accountants, marketing specialists and client representatives. In such cases, multi-disciplinary design teams may shift the design process away from human factors considerations and towards cost or production-centred approaches, ignoring the 'human' operation element.

### Summary (I) and conclusions

- The human–machine interaction system emphasizes the importance of the fundamentally 'human' aspects of the interface, which is otherwise easily marginalized in organizational settings amidst preoccupations with design issues and matters of cost.
- Taking account of the human dimension, however, is essential insofar as compromising on system usability, for example, may ultimately increase costs, because of a concomitant increase in error likelihood.

## Automation

Many civilian and military aircraft are now automated to such a degree that human pilots and flight deck crew are not absolutely necessary to safe flight. Wickens (1992) argues that purposes of automation can be assigned to one of three categories:

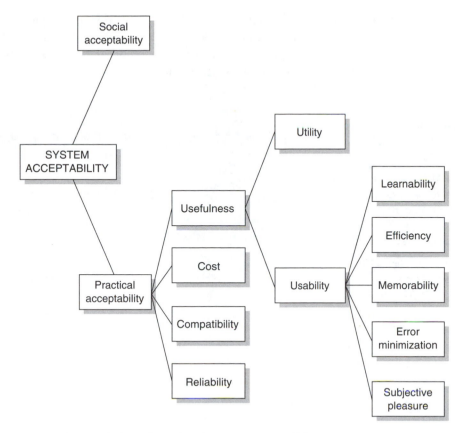

Figure 7.2   Nielsen's (1995) model of system acceptability

Adapted from Nielsen, J. (1995). *Multimedia and hypertext: The internet and beyond.*
Cambridge, MA: Academic Press.

- performing functions that the human operator cannot, due to inherent limitations
  (for example, complex mathematical/computational calculations);
- performing functions that the human operator can do but performs poorly or at
  the cost of high workload (for example, autopilot functions in aircraft);
- augmenting or assisting performance in areas in which humans show limitations
  (for example, human working memory, prediction/anticipation).

Automation has had a significant impact on the workplace through increased computerization of technical/administrative tasks and mechanization (and computer-
mediated supervision) of manufacturing tasks. At a base level, automation improves
organizational performance by cutting human labour costs and increasing efficiency
through use of hardware (photocopiers, fax machines, and so on). Over-automation,
however, is said to be the cause of many catastrophic accidents. For instance, in 1981,
a DC-10 crashed into Mount Erebus in Antarctica (Mackley, 1982). The cause was
attributed to an incorrectly programmed ground-based computer that had down-
loaded erroneous flight path data to the plane's automatic navigation system. The

pilot had been briefed that whilst his route would take him close to Mount Erebus, the aircraft would clear it by a safe margin (Study Box 7.1). Recent research has accordingly focused on the potential threat of automation to situation awareness and user self-regulation (for example, Endsley & Kaber, 1999; Kaber, Riley, & Tan, 2002).

### Study Box 7.1

#### The cost of automation

Sarter, Woods & Billings, (1997) outline a number of drawbacks of automation if the human needs of the operator are not fully considered.

#### Operator attitudes

If an operator's job is reduced to monitoring alone or a collection of arbitrary tasks, de-skilling may lead to lowered feelings of achievement, which in turn can increase errors and absenteeism.

#### Attentional demands

A fundamental problem with automating manual system tasks is the attention requirements of the monitoring-only task. Effective visual attention may only be maintained by humans for around 30 minutes, after which it will degrade and task efficiency will degrade with it.

#### Overtrust and mistrust

The attitudes of human operators towards automated systems have been shown to 'flip' from complete, near complacent trust in a newly automated system to complete mistrust once an automated system has shown itself to be fallible (Singh, Sharma, & Parasuram, 2001). Researchers are arguing for a distinction between automation trust (a subjective phenomenon) and automation reliance (a behavioural phenomenon) (Weigmann, Rick, & Zhang, 2001).

#### Reduced teamwork

The synergistic relationship between skilled human operators can be markedly reduced when dialogue shifts from human–human to human–machine.

#### Higher-level operator error

Automation may not eliminate human error from a given system, but may simply relocate it to another part of that system. In designing out human *operator* error, human *designer* error is invariably designed *in*, which may lead to any number of inefficiencies with the human–machine system.

#### System complexity

Automated systems are not limited in their information processing bandwidth, which increases their complexity including the number of things that could fail. The

## Study Box 7.1    Continued

so-called 'glass cockpits' typical of the Airbus A320 and all new Boeing series aircraft, in which all cockpit information is provided to pilots via the *visual* perceptual channel, presents a vast array of system status displays. Since feedback is limited to a single perceptual channel there is an increasing risk of mental overload, and human error.

### Workload unevenly distributed

'Clumsy automation' can result in the development of automated systems requiring the input by operators of numerous additional data pertaining to the outside world. For instance, during take-off and landing phases, the pilot's job may be reduced to a translation function between the automated system and the air traffic controller (ATC), clearing every action with the system and then with the ATC. Thus, workload is not necessarily reduced, but is merely redistributed over time.

### Out-of-the-loop unfamiliarity

When an operator's tasks are replaced with automation, the experienced level of inter-action with the system is reduced. Recent reports of pilots flying newly constructed civil aircraft (for example, Airbus A320, Boeing 757, 767 and 777 series) allude to a loss of control engendered by automated systems. Error is caused by minor manual adjust-ments by pilots still in the 'mindset' of traditional cockpit control systems.

Norman (1990) says that automation per se is not responsible for human–machine interface errors, but poor feedback mechanisms. This leads to a 'miscalibration' of system users' perceptions of their levels of competence with newly automated equip-ment. 'Well-calibrated' users are aware of the circumstances for which they have accu-rate knowledge and those in which their knowledge is limited or incomplete. 'Miscalibrated' users, however, are those who are over-confident and wrongly believe that they understand all aspects of a system.

### Case Study 7.1: The London Ambulance Service

The London Ambulance Service installed a new centralized computer-aided despatch system in October 1992, intended to increase service efficiency by centralizing commu-nications and control across a previously fragmented and locally operated organization. However, the system performed poorly throughout the first month of operation and then failed completely less than a month after its introduction. The subsequent inquiry concluded that a number of factors contributed to the failure:

- staff (who had not been consulted during the design process) found the new system to be an operational 'straitjacket', and still attempted to operate local flexibility which overloaded the system;
- training given to control staff and ambulance crews was incomplete and inconsistent;

*(Continued)*

---

**Case Study 7.1    Continued**

- changes to the layout of the control room meant that staff were working in unfamiliar positions and were physically prevented from working with close colleagues;
- there had been no attempt to foresee fully the effect of inaccurate or incomplete data available to the system.

---

Wickens (1992) advocates the of 'flexible automation' approaches that allow the user to retain a real sense of control (responsive to the external environment and can be swithced on or off by the user), but which switch between user and machine-operated system functioning when the situation demands (Figure 7.3). The automated system also communicates to the user in the form of recommendations or advice (for example, 'suggest that autopilot control be implemented') rather than assertions (for example, 'autopilot control has been taken').

Pinzel, Freeman, Scerbo, Mikulka and Pope (2000) have demonstrated how flexible or 'dynamically adaptive automation' (rather than automation per se) can enhance pilot engagement and self-regulation by promoting an intuitive interface between the pilot and the flight management system. Others have reported similar benefits from part-automated systems (for example, Endsley & Kaber, 1999; Haas, Nelson, Repperger, Bolia & Zacharias, 2001).

The decision to switch tasks to automation may be based on external task conditions (for example, in piloting an aircraft, take-off and landing involve greater human operator workload than does level flight) and/or direct measures of system performance that suggest that performance has, or is about to, decline. However, the automated system must accommodate different underlying reasons for poor performance, for example, departure from assigned altitude due to excessive workload, as opposed

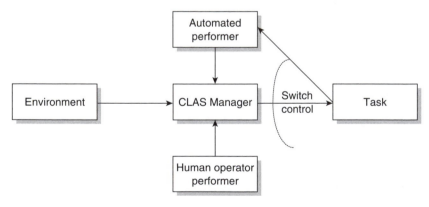

**Figure 7.3**   Wickens' (1992) closed-loop adaptive system

Adapted from Wickens, C.D. (1992). *Engineering psychology and human performance* (2nd edn). New York: Harper-Collins.

to departure due to a lack of vigilance in low arousal conditions (Bennett, Cress, Hettinger, Stautberg, & Haas, 2001).

Lee (2002) argues that function allocation within systems design should *not* be regarded as a simple division of labour between human and machine, but should take into consideration the multitude of contextual and domain-specific factors that make up the system's environment. A 'user centred' approach appreciates that new technology must be sensitive to the constraints and pressures acting in the operational world, and acknowledges that there are multiple actors at different levels with different scopes of responsibility embedded in a larger operational system. Some of these agents are human and some machines, and designers must consider automation as *part of a multi-agent control and management system* (Study Box 7.2).

Several models and methods have since been advocated to aid function allocation in dynamically adaptive automated work systems (see Tattersall & Morgan (1997) and Tattersall, Morgan, & Newman (1997) for comprehensive reviews of the issue of dynamic function allocation). Tattersall (2000) argues that the concept of 'mental workload' is central to the theory and practice of function allocation. The focus of investigation is directed towards issues such as attention allocation, effort control and affective state. Thus workload assessment (using subjective and physiological measures) should form a critical part of any system design. The 'workload' concept also affords scope for theoretical integration of an otherwise piecemeal literature in this domain.

---

**Study Box 7.2**

**The design gap**

Designers may:

- oversimplify the pressures and task demands from the users' perspective;
- assume that people can and will call to mind all relevant knowledge;
- be over-confident that they have taken into account all meaningful circumstances and scenarios;
- assume that machines never err;
- make assumptions about how technology impacts on human performance without checking for empirical support or despite contrary evidence;
- define design decisions in terms of what it takes to get the technology to work;
- sacrifice user-oriented aspects first when problems arise;
- focus on building the system first, then try to integrate the results with users.

---

Recent debates have suggested that, ironically, the aims of automation, that is, to reduce human operator input due to unreliability and inefficiency, may, in some cases, be diluted by the unreliability and inefficiency of *systems designs*, which create favourable conditions for error occurrence. Thus, rather than designing human error out of a system, over-automation may increase human error by failing to appreciate the human element within that system (Tattersall, 2000).

### Summary (II) and conclusions

- Whilst one of the aims of automation is to reduce the likelihood of human error, the unintended consequence of automation may in fact be an increase in error likelihood because of the unreliability and inefficiency of *systems design*.
- Attitudes based on the assumption of machine infallibility, combined with reduced vigilance arising from the difficulty sustaining the 'monitoring' role for long periods of time, can reduce perceived ownership and control of the system and its effectiveness.

## Human Error

Responsibility for major disaster ascribed to human error include Chernobyl (Reason, 1988; USSR State Committee, 1986); Bhopal (Bellamy, 1986); the Challenger Space Shuttle (Rogers, 1986); the King's Cross fire (Donald & Canter, 1992); the Channel Tunnel fire (Department of the Environment, Transport and the Regions, 1997); Three Mile Island (United States Nuclear Regulatory Commission, 1980); the Herald of Free Enterprise car ferry disaster; and the Kegworth 737 air crash (Department of Transport, 1990). Pheasant (1991) cites the role of human error in up to 45 percent of critical incidents in nuclear power plants, 60 percent of aircraft accidents, 80 percent of marine accidents and 90 percent of road traffic accidents.

The identification, isolation and measurement of error is thus critical to attempts to improve human reliability in system design. Human error can be defined as a failure on the part of the human to perform a prescribed act (or the performance of a prohibited act) accurately, resulting in damage, disruption or accident.

### Error taxonomies

Human errors have been categorized in a variety of ways, each deriving from a different disciplinary approach. For instance, Kantowitz and Sorkin (1987) categorize errors as those of omission (operator fails to perform), commission (incorrect action carried out), extraneous acts (incorrect action selected), sequential (actions out of order) and time (actions carried out at wrong time). Payne and Altman (1962, cited in Reason, 1990) on the other hand, propose three types of error: input (sensory or perceptual input), mediation (information processing) and output (or response).

Whilst these are useful design-oriented taxonomies, they do not elucidate the underlying cognitive causes of error; they merely describe it (O'Hare, Wiggins, Batt, & Morrison, 1995). A more cognitive approach is offered by Norman (1983a, 1983b) as follows:

- *slip* – failure in the execution phase of an action sequence (for example, a person entering a shop to buy an ink cartridge but buying a magazine instead; Study Box 7.3);
- *mistake* – failure in the planning or intention phase (for example, buying an ink cartridge for the wrong pen).

Chmiel (1998) gives examples of both slips and mistakes, citing an incident at the Davis-Besse plant in the USA, where an operator wanting to start the steam and feedwater rupture control system manually inadvertently pressed the wrong two buttons on the error control panel (a *slip*). The Chernobyl accident (Reason, 1988) involved a previous operator having reduced reactor power to well below 10 percent of maximum. Despite safety procedures prohibiting any operation below 20 percent of maximum power, a team of electrical engineers and operators continued with a planned test programme, contributing to a double explosion in the reactor core (a *mistake*).

Reason (1990) argues that this basic distinction between slips and mistakes does not account for all available research on human error. He proposed the 'generic error modelling system approach' (GEMS), drawing on Rasmussen's (1987) 'skill–rule–knowledge' framework to distinguish between:

- *skill-based slips;*
- *rule-based mistakes;*
- *knowledge-based mistakes.*

These levels of analysis reflect decreasing familiarity with the activity or situation (Chmiel, 1998; 2000; Study Box 7.3). Salminen and Tallberg (1996) found that the majority of human errors (responsible for around 90 percent of serious/fatal accidents) were skill-based, followed by rule-based errors and then knowledge-based errors. There were no age differences in the proportion of human errors, but in general, less experienced workers made more knowledge-based errors, while experienced workers made more rule-based errors.

---

### Study Box 7.3

#### Generic error modelling system approach

*Skill-based slips* are generally associated with monitoring failures, and may be caused by:

- *inattention* – failing to make a high-level check on behaviour at some critical point beyond which actions may take a number of different paths, causing actions to follow frequently used paths, even if the original intention was otherwise;
- *overattention* – making an attentional check at an inappropriate point in an automatized action sequence, typically resulting in omissions, repetitions and reversals of parts of the action sequence.

*Rule-based mistakes* are associated with problem solving failures, especially when the problems are familiar ones whose solutions are governed by stored rules. Mistakes fall into two categories: misapplication of good rules (for example, 'it always worked before', availability bias) and application of bad rules (halo effect, like relates to like).

*Knowledge-based mistakes* come into play in novel situations for which actions must be planned 'on line' using consciously analytic processes and stored knowledge. Mistakes themselves originate from either bounded rationality, where the ability to think laterally within a 'problem space' is not possible, or from inaccurate/incomplete mental models of the problem space and its boundaries. Specific difficulties are caused by: memory limitation (for example, people cannot hold and evaluate multiple hypotheses simultaneously), misinterpretation of communication, reasoning by analogy, matching and availability biases and overconfidence (in evaluating correctness of judgement).

### Measurement of human reliability and error

Human reliability analysis (HRA) is a relatively new field deriving from the disciplines of ergonomics and psychology, which attempts to model and quantify the behaviour of human operators within a system. Reliability in this context is concerned with the probability of successful completion of a given task or parts of a task (Sanders & McCormick, 1993), as opposed to internal consistency reliability of a measure. It is generally reported as a probability value, due to its roots in probabalistic safety analysis (PAS) – an engineering approach to design safety into systems. For example, if the probability of an airline pilot correctly interpreting his/her altimeter dial reading is .995, then the pilot will correctly interpret the reading 995 times in every 1000, and incorrectly interpret the reading 5 times in every 1000.

This engineering-derived approach to HRA has pervaded much of the research and practical application over the last 50 years. However, more recent approaches have integrated the inherent variability of the human operator within a given system, in order to model human–machine system operation more accurately (Kirwan, 1995; Study Box 7.4).

---

**Study Box 7.4**

### Techniques of error measurement

#### THERP – technique for human error rate prediction

This is the best known suite of methods for assessment of human reliability, including event-tree analysis, fault-tree analysis and quantification of system errors. It allows system experts to 'weight' these errors by including 'performance shaping factors' or PSFs. It requires heavy time and resources, and the consistency of the method has been questioned in terms of different assessors adopting substantively different approaches to error assessment due to the complex nature of the modelling technique.

#### HEART – human error assessment and reduction technique

Calculations are quick and do not require experts as the technique derives its component factors from existing research findings. It also includes error-reduction techniques.

#### SLIM – success likelihood index method

SLIM and its software-based counterpart SLIM-MAUD has high face validity within industrial settings largely due to their reliance on the opinion of experts. Cost effectiveness of ergonomic solutions can be estimated due to the inclusion of PSFs in assessing human error probability. It is extremely resource heavy, relying on a panel of 'experts' (whose verification as experts may also be difficult to achieve) and on detailed knowledge of at least two human error probability values prior to assessment.

### *Error reduction – preventative measures*

System-oriented approaches include improving the work situation, or the ergonomics of the system, providing in-built system memory aids, and reducing system impact. Person-oriented approaches include training and changing personnel.

The causes of incidents and accidents in the workplace, whilst often attributed to human error, are in many cases due to poor system design, where the limitations of human operators have not been fully addressed, leading to an increased probability of slips or mistakes (Norman, 1983b). Human error can be reduced to a low level by designing 'redundancy' into the system, in order that the system is tolerant and forgiving of human error. If human errors occur, the system will degrade, but will not fail, and if adequate feedback systems are included, the error's consequences can be rectified fairly rapidly, without the system being required to go off-line.

In addition to addressing possible system design problems, error reduction and prevention may require analysis of work methods, operating procedures, job tasks, job aids, ambient environmental conditions, and so on. When applying this analysis, it is important to involve the system users via one or more approaches including in-depth interviews, focus groups, survey-based methods or critical incidents technique. Worker participation programmes such as quality control circles and error-cause removal programmes (Swain, 1973) can be useful as a method for identifying error-producing conditions, and for continued monitoring of a system following re-design.

Other considerations include the use of memory aids (Reason, 1990), improved personnel selection and/or improved training (King, Fisher, & Garg, 1997). Poor performance may be due to individual-level factors such as inadequate skills, deficient sensory abilities, or poor attitude (Park, 1997). In such cases, the human operator's abilities may need to be matched to a more suitable task, and job rotation may be required in order to identify the most appropriate combination of operators and machines.

### *Summary (III) and conclusions*

- Errors have been classified into types, providing a description but not an explanation of error. Research on the causes of error, yields only a list of potential antecedent factors, including task complexity, human characteristics and design characteristics.
- Much attention has been devoted to the technical issue of error measurement in human–machine systems, and error prevention or reduction. It is generally agreed that human error can be prevented by improving the 'fit' between machine and human operator on a number of different levels (cognitive, affective and behavioural).

## Systems Training

To successfully interact with an automated system or artefact, human users must fully understand all elements of the system, how they interact, implications for their interactions with the system, and a whole host of additional issues allowing the user to build up an accurate 'mental model' of the system. The 'learnability' of new systems, and the technique of mental modelling to assist in the learning process, are crucial issues within the area of systems training, and have attracted particular attention within human–*computer* systems research.

## Mental models and 'learnability' of systems

The relevance of the mental models concept to human–computer interaction (HCI) has been well documented (for example, Waern, 1987). Mental models are commonly used as the basis for system design and training based on the principle that they allow trainees to 'map' system features at a cognitive level, thus assisting the transition from Anderson's (1987) declarative learning to proceduralized knowledge stages (Study Box 7.5).

---

### Study Box 7.5

### Anderson's learning model

Anderson (1987) argues that learning begins with factual knowledge about a task (declarative knowledge) and then moves into a phase characterized by accelerated performance. As the trainee gains a high degree of knowledge compilation, automaticity of previously acquired declarative knowledge occurs, freeing the memory for processing of new knowledge and movement towards proceduralized knowledge. Kanfer and Ackerman (1989) used this model to train a group of air traffic controllers, who learned to accept or land planes on given runways according to a number of rules relating to factors such as weather conditions and amount of fuel (effectively a series of procedural 'if-then' rules). During the first stage, trainees acquired a basic understanding of the tasks involved via lectures and observation. In the second phase trainees actively tried out the various rules and methods. The final phase focused on skill automation, with attentional and memory demands reduced, and rapid information-processing on the part of trainees to accurately apply rules learned to 'real' situations.

---

Some of the characteristics of mental models are as follows:

- They are internal representations of objects, actions, situations, people, and so on.
- They are built on experience and observation of the world and of specific systems.
- They allow people to describe, predict and explain behaviour, and also underpin people's understanding and behaviour.
- They are simulations run to produce qualitative inferences and constitute topography, structure, function or operation of the system.
- They may also contain spatial, causal and/or contingency relations.
- They are constantly evolving through the interaction of the learner and particular environments.
- They are usually not accurate representations of a phenomenon; they typically contain errors and contradictions.

- They provide simplified explanations of complex phenomena.
- They often contain measures of uncertainty about their validity that allow them to be used even if incorrect.
- Because they are parsimonious and are invoked whenever required, they are often incomplete, unstable and often multiple.

Trainees can be aided to develop effective mental models by providing them with structured experiences (such as learning to troubleshoot), by presenting functional representations of systems (such as Kieras's (1987) device models), or by suggesting analogies (such as the 'water through a pipe' analogy for electron flow). Craik (1943) suggests that 'if [a user] carries a "small-scale model" of external reality and of its own possible actions within his head, he is able to try out various alternatives, conclude which is the best of them, react to future situations before they arise, utilize the knowledge of past events in dealing with the present and future ...'. Thus, planning is facilitated by mental modelling of a system – if the model is accurate, the alternatives available to the user in any given situation should be accessible and actionable.

Models allow people to generate descriptions of system purpose and form, to explain system functioning and observed states, and to make predictions of future states. These models thus provide a means for organizing and reorganizing memory to assist in decision making (Study Box 7.6).

---

**Study Box 7.6**

**Mental model training**

Carroll and Olson (1988) found that mental models training helped delegates to build expectations of aircraft cockpit system behaviour, and contributed to the adequate allocation of attention across and within information-rich aircraft cockpit displays. They discovered that training to actively explore available options and dynamics of an automated system was preferable to explicit teaching of a system model, as users need to obtain dynamic knowledge which they can then activate and apply in unusual situations, rather than being tied to following prescribed non-context-specific procedures. The mental model concept has also been applied to team training (or 'cross training'), the idea being that team members can develop shared mental models more effectively if they are given the opportunity to experience each others' roles (see Chapter 2, 'Training').

---

The term 'learnability' describes the intersection of usability, productivity, human performance factors, and learning. Many researchers have subsumed the term under the broader heading of usability (for example, Shackel, 1990), where a number of criteria, including learnability, are included as crucial elements of the usability of a system. It denotes the relative ease with which new users are able to learn the new motor, perceptual and/or cognitive skills and strategies required to operate a system efficiently (for example, Colet & Aaronson, 1995).

Users must be able to learn how to use the system following a certain amount of training, and users who do not frequently use the system must be able to re-learn it after a certain amount of re-training. Mitta and Packebusch (1995) found that 'learning rate' for successful completion of a number of computer tasks was a very useful indicator of interface quality.

The concept is inextricably linked with that of mental models, in that it is often the accuracy and accessibility of trainees' mental models which determines how quickly and efficiently they are able to learn use of a new system.

Colet and Aaronson (1995) conducted research into the learnability of computer-based statistical software packages that presented data in a graphical format. They found that those display formats that employed gestalt and other human factors' principles in display output were far more *learnable* than those that contravened these principles (see also, Sauer, Wastell, Hockey, Crawshaw, Ishak, & Downing, 2002 on display design in ship navigation systems; Study Box 7.7).

---

### Study Box 7.7

#### Mental models and learnability

Research has focused on developing systems that promote the development of mental models in users, both via training, and via direct interaction with the system itself, in order to assist in planning, problem solving, communicating ideas and stimulating creative thinking. For example, problem solving requires the user to interrogate his/her mental model in response to an unexpected event, in order to develop and evaluate various problem-solving options. Newell and Simon's (1972) notion of 'problem-spaces' within which an individual may search for a variety of solutions may be analogized to a mental model (Young, 1983), since it is within the 'space' of the mental model that the user must search for and select an appropriate solution. Expert system users are likely to develop various strategies, based on their understanding of the system's strengths and limitations, for carrying out particular tasks. The model may not be explicitly accessed by the user, but alternative models are *triggered* and *run* 'automatically' when needed.

---

### *Mental models and performance*

The manner in which knowledge structures are developed and maintained is a significant determinant of performance. For instance, studies have shown that differences between the knowledge structures of 'experts' and 'novices' may in part explain differences in performance of these two groups (Lord & Maher, 1990; Study Box 7.8). Experts are said to hold accurate mental models consistent with the functional structure of the system, whereas novices' mental models are often found to be inaccurate or incomplete. Experts also demonstrate more comprehensive declarative knowledge (about various system functions and elements) and procedural knowledge (about system processes), and recall relevant information better than novices.

## Study Box 7.8

### Mapping expertise

Cognitive task analysis (CTA) is the claim of many fields that seek to identify how experts perform cognitive tasks, although there is no accepted definition and the techniques employed vary widely. Most common methods include interviews, verbal think-aloud protocols, retrospective verbal protocols, analysis of previous incidents and observation of task performance (Hoffman, 1998).

Since the seminal works of, for example, Walsh (1995) and Eden and Spender (1998), cognitive mapping research has made a number of important advances (for example, Huff & Jenkins, 2002). However, the success of these various techniques is difficult to evaluate and some of the methods are highly complex.

One of the main criticisms of CTA is the complexity of the methods or techniques employed making them difficult and time consuming to use. This prompted the development of applied cognitive task analysis (ACTA) by Klein Associates (Militello & Hutton, 1998), the intention being to make cognitive mapping techniques more accessible to practitioners. Like CTA, the ACTA technique is intended to assist the identification of key cognitive elements required to perform a task proficiently. The cognitive requirements that cognitive task analysis address are difficult judgements and decisions, attention demands, identifying critical cues and patterns, and problem- solving strategies. ACTA offers a knowledge elicitation (interviews, observations) and a knowledge representation (cognitive mapping) technique (see **www.sagepub.co.uk/millward** for details).

Goldstein (1993) advises the use of 'organizers' (or mental models) – verbal, quantitative or graphical cues – which can be used to present new knowledge to a trainee by taking advantage of existing knowledge. Thus, explicit, graphical models of systems may act as organizing cues to trainees in the formation of their own mental models. Mayer (1988) suggests that these organizers are important for a number of reasons: first, they focus attention on important components and relationships; second, they help the trainee to organize incoming information; third, they assist in illustrating relationships between incoming information and existing relevant knowledge.

Koubek and Salvendy (1991) propose that knowledge structures or mental models begin with surface feature information (explicit, physical, salient, dominant features, and involving little understanding of system process), become more task specific (allowing for more complex cognitive activity such as decision making, but which are 'bound' to the task) and finally abstract/hierarchical (denoting a conceptual understanding of the domain and the overall system, organized in a hierarchical sense). Abstract mental models are said to enable problem solving on a system-wide basis (Koubek, Benysh, & Tang, 1997).

### Mental models in systems design

The mental representation of a system can be absolutely critical during its design and user-trials. Pheasant (1991) describes instances of incompatibility between designers' and users' mental models of a system (see Figure 7.4, below):

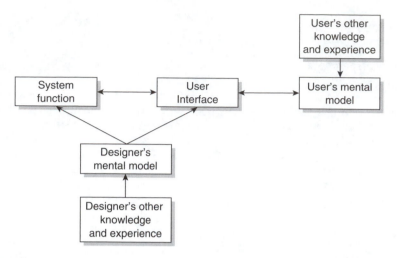

**Figure 7.4** Mental model conflicts

Adapted from Pheasant, S. (1991). *Ergonomics, work and health.* Basingstoke: Macmillan

Figure 7.4 represents the conflict that may occur if a designer's mental model differs from that of the user (perhaps because of different experiences or views of the world), resulting in the system being unusable for the intended user (Case Study 7.2). Mental model incompatibility in systems design commonly arises from the different ways in which the user and the designer view the system. In nuclear and other process control plants, he argues, the systems are best understood by engineers in terms of functional decomposition into sub-systems and components, whereas this is entirely inappropriate for users.

---

**Case Study 7.2: Clash of mental models in design and implementation**

Kantowitz and Sorkin (1987) describe a situation in which computer specialists designed a computer software package for secretaries in a telecommunications company, but subsequently found that, in the main, secretaries were unable to use it. The only secretaries who were able to puzzle out the system were those who had had prior computer programming experience. The designers had used a computer expert's mental model when developing the software, although their target population (secretaries) operated with novices' mental models. The system succeeded only when the designers tweaked the software to produce an inelegant, inefficient but understandable system interface more compatible with the novices' orientation and level of understanding.

---

'Motion stereotypes' are small-scale examples of the importance of compatibility in systems' and users' mental models. Pheasant (1995) outlines some of the most common conventions:

- Turning a control clockwise is expected to result in similar movements of physical objects or pointers of displays.
- Moving a control forward or to the right is expected to result in an increase in some functional quality, for example, speed, volume, time, etc.

Pheasant (1991) argues that the novice user's performance would be faster and more accurate with a system compatible with convention. Under conditions of stress, the non-compatible system would see greater deterioration and a higher error rate. Moreover, in emergency situations, the user would tend to revert to stereotype, thus increasing the chances of an accident with the incompatible system.

As suggested by Moran (1981), 'to design the user interface of the system is to design the user's [mental] model'.

### Summary (IV) and conclusions

- The concept of mental model has been used to inform systems training, by encouraging users to develop accurate cognitive representations of system components and actions that can then be accessed when required during day-to-day operation.
- Mnemonics, real-world analogies and other memory aids can be used to increase the learnability of a new system via training.
- It is generally accepted that to facilitate learnability (and useability), the systems designer must hold a conceptual model of the product or system and use this as the basis for design to facilitate the interface between the machine model and the user model.

## User-Centred Design and Usability

User-centred design principles are critical to the design of any product or artefact intended for use by human operators. Most are likely to agree with Pheasant (1995), that user-centred design is:

- *Empirical* – basing the decisions of the design process on hard data concerning the physical and psychological characteristics of human users, rather than relying on intuitive judgement or 'grand theory'.
- *Iterative* – a cyclical process incorporating feedback loops and re-design where necessary. Plach and Wallach (2002) distinguish between two different usability evaluation methods: guideline-based methods and methods based on the mental generation of scenarios and anticipation of user goals. They advocate the latter as the most effective and efficient, requiring 'perspective taking' on the part of evaluators and designers.
- *Participative* – enrolling the end-user as an active participant in the design process.
- *Non-procrustean* – dealing with people as they are rather than as they might be and fitting the product to the user rather than the user to the product. Kaber, Riley and Tan (2002) argue that the future of interface design might be one in which people are encouraged to employ existing skills rather than to learn new ones.

- *Accommodates human diversity* – achieving the best possible match for the greatest possible number of people.
- *Accommodates the user's task* – recognizing that the match between product and user is commonly task specific.
- *Systems-oriented* – recognizing that the interaction between product and user takes place in the context of a larger socio-technical system, in turn operating within the context of economic and political systems.
- *Pragmatic* – recognizing that there may be limits to what is reasonable and practicable in a given design situation, and seeking to reach the optimal outcome within these constraints.

The importance of usability across the computer hardware and software industries is well established (Zirkler & Ballman, 1994). If a software product is not easily learned and used by its target market, it will fail; products that do poorly in the market are those that have been poorly defined and reflect a lack of end-user testing. On the other hand, companies who have developed successful products have a clear understanding of their end-user community. Microsoft, Lotus, Oracle, for instance, test their products in carefully controlled conditions known as 'usability laboratories'.

### Usability testing

Salzman and Rivers (1994) and others (for example, Nielsen, 1997) have discussed the preparation of usability labs for successful usability measurement. Shackel (1990) proposes a simple structured process for usability testing. The *research* phase requires objective study of the match between human capabilities and system operational concepts. Pilot studies can be undertaken to explore the users' operational needs and to study possible effects of system operational concepts on organizational, team and other social structures. By including end users at the earliest stage possible in the design process, synthesis of potentially disparate models between designers and users is most likely to be achieved.

  Booth and Marshall (1990) suggest that a 'user needs analysis' should include:

- *user characterization* (capturing all data concerning the target user group relevant to system design; Study Box 7.9);
- *task analysis* (listing the end results that a user wishes to achieve using the system);
- *situational analysis* (concerning the workplace context in which the system will ultimately operate, and considering a variety of situations which may render the system less usable); and
- *acceptance criteria* (the users' stated requirements and preferences for the system, which promote the chances of the system being accepted into the intended work environment as a valued tool). The importance of this criterion for assessing usability is reflected in the technology acceptance model (TAM) (Thong, Hong, & Tam, 2002). Thong et al. (2002) note how millions have been spent on building usable digital libraries, yet potential users may still not use them. Their research showed that 'ease of use' was a key factor in predicting user acceptance and use of digital libraries.

> **Study Box 7.9**
>
> **Checklist for user characterization**
>
> - *User data* – identify target user group, proportion of males and females, average age/age range, cultural characteristics (including language, and so on);
> - *Job characteristics* – job role description, main activities, main responsibilities, reporting structure, reward structure, schedules, status, turnover rate;
> - *User background* – relevant education/knowledge/experience, skills, training;
> - *Usage constraints* – voluntary versus mandatory use, motivators versus de-motivators;
> - *Personal references* – learning style, interactional style, aesthetic preference, personality traits.

*System development* requires detailed analyses to be carried out of all functions, tasks and operations involving or affecting human users. Preliminary test results may be used as a basis for redesign and retest. At this stage, Shackel (1990) recommends that the design team also commence development of training and user support materials in order that these may utilize the iterative nature of the design process to build system understanding into the training programme.

*Prototype development* may require laboratory evaluation and/or full field trials with representative samples of end users in the working context for which the system is being designed. Finally, *introduction and operation* of the system within its intended workplace setting should be prefaced with user support functions such as training, provision of 'local experts' on-site (either fully-trained existing staff experts, or out-sourced system troubleshooters retained for the first few weeks of system operation), off-site 'help-lines', and so on.

### User participation

Vink and Kompier (1997) argue that users should be involved in the design process from the outset, offering their views and getting involved, in order to provide more accurate information about job tasks, to present a fresh focus on design issues and arguments, and to increase the chances of user acceptance of the system by providing users with a sense of participation in the process.

However, the counter-arguments for full user participation include the exclusion of the majority of the target population resulting in resentment and reduced 'buy-in' from that population, that management may also be unwilling to allow their staff to participate due to temporal and financial constraints (Kontogiannis & Embrey, 1997) and that designers may be forced to compromise their design to satisfy incompetent participants (Olson & Ives, 1981). Heinbokel, Sonnentag, Frese and Stolte (1996), in a study of 29 commercial software products, found that user participation was negatively related to process and product quality and to project success.

Shneiderman (1992) cites the example of warehouse managers who see their positions threatened by the introduction of an interactive system that provides senior managers with up-to-date information. He suggests that intentional sabotage of the system's processes may be one possible outcome of such a scenario if the warehouse managers are not consulted during the design process. Thus, he suggests, the practitioner should take into account the effects on users, and should secure their participation to ensure that all concerns are made explicit early enough to avoid 'counter-implementation' (Keen, 1981).

Wider organizational and political considerations, then, should form a focus for choice of usability test participants (Axtell, Waterson, & Clegg, 1997). Keates, Langdon, Clarkson and Robinson (2002) also point out that existing interface design practices are based on user models derived almost exclusively from studies of able-bodied users, who are only at one point on a wide scale of potential physical capabilities. They argue a case for identifying differences in interface design for users varying in physical capability, not least because the user population is ageing.

## Usability criteria and measurement

Briggs (1987), in the context of user interface with computers, outlines several usability criteria:

- *Increased efficiency* – in terms of speed, accuracy (that is, reduced error), and user adoption of all available system features;
- *Increased user satisfaction* – in terms of users' reported levels of endorsement of the system;
- *Training costs* – in many cases, new software/hardware will be introduced into office environments with little or no training for some staff; therefore, systems should be designed to require as little formal training as possible to reduce associated costs;
- *User understanding* – the level of required user understanding of a given system will vary according to the target population and their job requirements. It is important for the practitioner to ensure a match between the usability aim (for example, user satisfaction; decreased errors; simple cognitive model) and the measurement method adopted (for example, qualitative survey/interview; quantitative measurement of errors; qualitative interviews/focus groups/direct observation of users' cognitive models, respectively).

It is important in the measurement process to ensure a match between the usability aim (for example, user satisfaction; decreased errors; simple cognitive model) and the method adopted (for example, qualitative survey/interview; quantitative measurement of errors; qualitative interviews/focus groups/direct observation of users' cognitive models, respectively).

**Performance measurement**   McLelland (1995) lists a number of measures of performance commonly used in user trials: time (Study Box 7.10), speed of response, activity rate, and so on, accuracy and errors, convenience and ease of use, comfort, satisfaction, physical health and safety, physical 'fit', physical effort and workload, stress and mental workload.

---

**Study Box 7.10**

**Measures of time**

- Time taken to perform a task (Booth & Marshall, 1990).
- The number of tasks of various kinds that can be completed within a given time limit (Nielsen, 1997).
- Time taken to train users to perform adequately with the system (Shackel, 1990).
- Time taken to warm-up after period of non-use of system (Shackel, 1990).
- Time spent using training manuals/other help/support systems (Nielsen, 1997).
- Time taken to recover from errors (Shackel, 1990).
- 'Dead-time' when the user is not interacting with the system (Nielsen, 1997). Includes two kinds of dead-time: response-time delays where the user is waiting for the system; and thinking-time delays, where the system is waiting for the user.
- Work-rate metric (Whiteside, Jones, Levy, & Wixon, 1985, cited in Booth & Marshall, 1990), for example, $S = 1/T \, PC$, where $S$ = the user's performance score, $T$ = time spent on task, $P$ = percentage of task completed and $C$ = constant based on fastest possible task solution for practised system expert.

---

***Self-report measurement***   Self-report techniques can be used to assess such system/product features as mental workload (for example, the Cooper-Harper Scale, in Wilson & Corlett, 1995) and perceived physical exertion (for example, Borg's Rating of Perceived Exertion Scale, Borg, Bratfisch & Dorinc, 1971), which provide internal robustness (in terms of reliability and validity) and quantitative comparability. There are a number of more generic usability questionnaires (Lin, Choong, & Salvendy, 1997) including the Computer System Usability Questionnaire (CSUQ) and Questionnaire User Interaction Satisfaction (QUIS).

***Other quantitative assessment techniques***   Booth and Marshall (1990), within the context of HCI, cite a number of further performance/behavioural measures that may be measured quantitatively:

- *Visual scanning patterns* – 'saccadic' eye movement studies provide data on what information the user was looking at, at what time, and for how long. Can assist in identifying pre-determinants of errors, as it is possible to identify which part of the screen the participant was attending to just prior to making an error.
- *System use patterns* – by placing prototype systems in work environments and studying users' patterns of use, it is possible to assess which parts of a system are more frequently used, suggesting perhaps that these system elements are more usable or more accessible, or that certain tasks are more amenable to automation.
- *Cognitive complexity measures* – Booth and Marshall (1990) outline a rationale for measuring the 'cognitive grammar' used by participants and analysing this to infer the relative cognitive complexity of different parts of a system.

***Qualitative methods***   Qualitative methods are numerous and include observational approaches (descriptive, evaluative, diagnostic), data structuring techniques (card sorts,

Kelly's (1955) repertory grid, critical incident technique (CIT)) and interviews (group, one-to-one) (Study Box 7.11).

---

### Study Box 7.11

#### Qualitative methods of usability assessment

##### *Observational approaches (Meister, 1985)*

- *Descriptive techniques* – observer records events taking place (for example, time, frequency of events, postures, controls used and so on).
- *Evaluative techniques* – observer evaluates outcome or consequence of events that have taken place (for example, degrees of difficulty, errors of judgement, incidence of hazardous events and so on).
- *Diagnostic techniques* – observer identifies the causes that give rise to the observed events (for example, positioning of controls, inadequacy of displays, poor user instructions and so on).

##### *Data structuring techniques*

These approaches may be used at any stage of the design process in order to provide structure to potentially complex series of instructions or actions.

- *Affinity-diagrams or card sorts* – these involve listing of errors, instructions, control actions, system functions, and so on, or any area of system operation where a large number of categories have developed (for example, Nielsen, 1997). Each of the items on the list are then transposed onto a card or sticky notes and 'sorted' by participants into related groups. Can provide an insight into the cognitive models being developed by users.
- *CIT* – Flanagan's (1954) approach can be useful in identifying precursors to error and grouping these data into helpful categories to allow the system to take account of these problems (Briggs, 1987).
- *Kelley's repertory grid* – personal construct technique has been demonstrated to be particularly useful in providing an overview of the user's understanding of a system, indicating those areas in which the user is well or poorly informed about the system. Thus, aspects of the system may be pinpointed that are poorly understood and consequently under-utilized (for example, Boose, 1985).

##### *Interview techniques*

Structured interviews are useful for eliciting from participants a variety of data pertaining to specific issues; for example, McLelland's (1995) suggested areas for interview are: users evaluating the product/system in general terms, explaining difficulties they may have experienced during the course of the user trial, explaining why they undertook certain actions, assessing their own physical or psychological condition and commenting on how the product might be improved. However, prone to post-hoc rationalization by users, and the user's reconstruction of events may be inaccurate or incomplete.

One common method known as 'verbal protocol analysis' (see Bainbridge & Sanderson, 1995, for a comprehensive treatment of this subject) invites participants to say what they are thinking or doing, for example, what they believe is happening, what they are trying to do, why they took a particular action, and so on. Use of this method allows the practitioner to understand how the user approaches the interface and what considerations the user keeps in mind when using the interface. If, for example, the user expresses that the sequence of steps dictated by the product to accomplish the task goal is different from the one they expected, the interface may be convoluted or inconsistent with their mental representation.

Problems with this approach include the 'unnaturalness' and awkwardness of thinking aloud, the possibility that thinking aloud may confound behaviour or other cognitive processes, and the difficulty of articulating thought/perceptual processes while concentrating on a task.

A variation on this involves co-participation, where two people work together on a given task. Normal conversation between participants is recorded, thereby removing the awkwardness of thinking aloud. The interaction between the two participants can also bring out more insights than a single participant vocalizing his/her thoughts. Co-participation has been used for the computer-supported cooperative work (CSCW) product study, as well as the study of groupware, and other products designed to be used by workers in team environments (see later).

A variant on this technique is the 'co-discovery learning' approach (Mack & Burdett, 1992) in which a semi-knowledgeable 'coach' and a novice participant work together, with the novice using the interface. This technique results in the novice asking questions and the 'coach' responding, thereby providing insights into the cognitive processes of both beginner and intermediate users.

To fully evaluate a system or product, it is likely that qualitative and quantitative research methods will be required. Nielsen (1997) proposed a number of usability heuristics derived from a factor analysis of around 250 user-reported usability problems (Study Box 7.12).

---

### Study Box 7.12

#### Usability heuristics

- *Visibility of system status* – keep users informed about what is going on, via feedback within a reasonable timeframe.
- *Match between system and real world* – system should 'speak the user's language', with words, phrases and concepts familiar to the user, rather than system-oriented terms.
- *User control and freedom* – users often choose system functions by mistake, therefore needing a clearly marked 'emergency exit' to leave the unwanted function without having to go through an extended dialogue.

*(Continued)*

> ### Study Box 7.12   Continued
>
> - *Consistency and standards* – use of function keys in different elements of the same system must mean the same thing.
> - *Error prevention* – for example, prompt boxes that ask the user to confirm whether he/she is sure he/she wants to complete the selected action.
> - *Recognition rather than recall* – objects, actions and options should be made visible. Users should not have to transfer memorized information from one part of the system to another.
> - *Aesthetic and minimalist design* – dialogues should not contain irrelevant or rarely needed information.
> - *Help users recognize, diagnose and recover from errors* – error messages expressed first in plain language (with codes relegated to less visible locations and to be used only when consulting a system expert) precisely indicate the problem and constructively suggest a solution.
> - *Help and documentation* – documentation should be easy to search, focused on the user's task and list concrete steps to be undertaken.

### Summary (V) and conclusions

- Usability is a major topic within the field of human–machine interaction. The literature is littered with heuristic prescriptions for system design.
- Whilst some important usability considerations are now well catered for in the design agenda (for example, user control and freedom, help and documentation and 'recognizability' of function), others have yet to be systematically addressed (for example, recovery from errors and match between system and the real world).

## Control and Display Designs

Many major air traffic, marine and other accidents have in part been caused by poor control and/or display design (Darnell, 1998). For instance, in the Herald of Free Enterprise disaster, a display was not available to the ship's captain to indicate that the bow doors were open. Also, amongst the multiple causes of the BP Oil Refinery explosion and fire at Grangewood in 1987 were:

- inaccurate gauge readings due to physical effects of wax and cold;
- a display which read higher than true because the dial was offset without the operator's knowledge;
- displays going off-scale;
- operators having to estimate flow rates due to lack of displays;
- controls for similar functions being of similar appearance; and
- breakdown of expectations in relationship between movement of controls and valve actions

(Health & Safety Executive, 1999).

**Figure 7.5**   Car dashboard design 1

**Figure 7.6**   Car dashboard design 2

Photographs courtesy of www.baddesigns.com.

More everyday examples of deficiency in control and display are provided by Darnell (1998). These include oven hob controls (where it is not obvious to the human operator which control knob corresponds with which hot plate), lamp switch design requiring the user to defy natural logic with an 'off' setting requiring the switch to be centred (as opposed to 'off' as fully switched either upwards or downwards), and TV remote controls on which there are conflicting cues (the 'up' volume button effectively has a 'down' symbol – 'V').

The positioning of car speedometers and tachometers together on a car dashboard are apt to cause confusion if arranged as shown in Figure 7.5. The two displays are similar in appearance. This flaw can be addressed in part by visual separation of the two displays, perhaps with other system feedback displays, as illustrated in Figure 7.6.

### Control

Bullinger, Kern and Braun (1997) state that design, arrangement and required task of *control* mechanisms have a considerable influence on the strain to which human operators are exposed, as well as on the effectiveness and safety of a system.

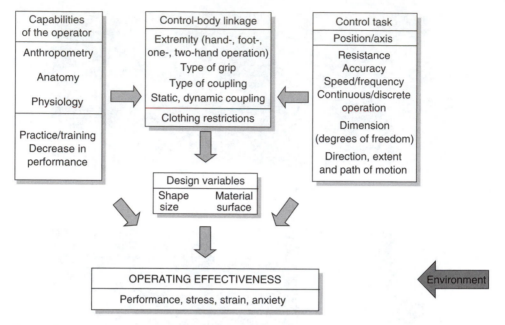

**Figure 7.7**   Integrated systems approach to control design

Adapted from Bullinger, H.J., Kern, P., & Braun, M. (1997). Controls. In G. Salvendy (Ed.), *Handbook of human factors and ergonomics*. New York: Wiley.

Figure 7.7 illustrates the importance of control task analysis (including nature of the control device and its operation), operator capabilities (anthropometric, physiological, competency training), and the interface between operator and control (including types of grip or coupling required) in the design and integration of a control mechanism.

Sanders and McCormick (1993) outline a number of factors that may influence the overall utility of a given control or set of controls. These include:

- *Ease of identification of controls* – primarily a function of control coding, which may be achieved using methods such as shape, texture, size, location, operational method, colour and labels. Any of these approaches must conform to the principles of detectability, discriminability, compatibility, meaningfulness and standardization. Confusion between landing gear and flap controls was found to be the cause of over 400 air force accidents during a 22 month period of World War II. Unique combinations of, say, shape *and* size may be used to distinguish between different control types.
- *Control-response (C/R) ratio* – describes the relationship between the movement of a control device by the operator and the movement of the system in response, often fed back to the operator via a system display. Low C/R ratio control devices are 'sensitive' in nature, in that a very small movement of the control results in a marked change in the controlled feature. This can lead operators to 'overshoot' the precise location required. Optimal C/R ratios depend on the gross and fine motor movements required of the operator to achieve the desired control setting.

- *Resistance in controls* – the 'resistance' of any control device provides the kinaesthetic 'feel' of the control (for example, elastic or spring-loaded, viscous and promoting smooth control, inertia – slow to accelerate but once started difficult to stop; Case Study 7.3).
- *Deadspace* – amount of control movement around the null, home or neutral position resulting in no movement of the controlled system device. Where the control may not always spring back to the same place, some deadspace is desirable. However, in other forms of control device, significant amounts of deadspace may be detrimental to performance.
- *Location and component arrangement* – Sanders and McCormick (1993) argue that important (critical controls) and frequently used components should be placed in a convenient location, that components should be grouped by function and commonly used sequences should be reflected in control positioning.

---

**Case Study 7.3: Cockpit design**

The issue of resistance is particularly salient to the 'glass cockpit' design of many modern civilian aircraft. A principal cockpit design feature is to provide pilots with a 'joystick' control for manual steering of the plane, similar in size to a video game joystick. This design has been criticized by current and ex-pilots due to the associated reduction in kinaesthetic feedback provided by this control. It is reported not to have the 'feel' of the traditional steering column, which would allow the pilot to gauge the status of the aircraft, either visually or by touch (by resting one or both hands on the steering wheel at all times during flight). It has also been relegated to a side-of-pilot position, rather than being situated between the pilot's legs as with conventional steering apparatus, making it less accessible to the pilot.

---

## Display

Displays can be used to present both static (textual, graphical or coded) and dynamic (quantitative or qualitative) information to the human operator. These different display types present various challenges to the display designer, although the underpinning rationale for display design remains the same: to optimize human user efficiency by designing to the cognitive and perceptual strengths and limitations of the user.

Given the heavy use of computer technology in the contemporary workplace, it is no surprise that much research has focused on the design of computer monitor/VDU displays in order to maximize the usability and usefulness of data presented to operators. Bennett, Nagy and Flach (1997) introduced a number of factors of importance to display design (particularly in relation to computer monitor displays), including the reflective nature of the display, colour contrast, brightness, and so on. They pointed out that these factors, whilst crucial to promoting data availability, that is, ensuring that the operator has access to required information by being able to see it, are largely mechanical in terms of the display design process.

However, Woods (1991) draws an important distinction between design for '*data availability*' and design for '*information extraction*' (which provides the operator with more than just raw data via the display, rather presenting it in a way that is user-friendly and affords the operator easy access to the information he/she requires). Woods suggests that display designs that consider only data *availability* often impose unnecessary burdens on the operator, including active extraction of data, retention of data in memory and cognitive integration of data to arrive at a decision.

Bennett at al. (1997) summarize four alternative approaches to static display design: aesthetic (for example, data-ink ratio, data density, irrelevant information, effective labels/proportion and scale); psychophysical (cognitive processes involved in perceiving and understanding information); attention-based (for example, factors controlling the distribution of attention to visual stimuli); and problem solving and decision making (for example, how information via displays can be represented to aid human operators in problem solving and decision making) (Study Box 7.13).

---

### Study Box 7.13

#### Attention

Research into attention in connection with display design has found that a 'continuum' of attention exists, ranging from 'focused' tasks (which require selective responses to specific elements in the display) to 'integration' tasks (which require the distribution of attention across many features that must be considered together in order to select a suitable response). A focused task, for example, may require an operator to read the value of a single bar within a bar graph; an integrated task may require the operator to read the relative points of a number of bars within the graph prior to making a decision.

Two basic types of display have been proposed to deal with the attention continuum – object-based and separate. Object-based displays are solid graphical representations of a variety of information, differentiated within the object by use of colour, shading, labelling, and so on. Research has found that object-based displays lead to better performance for integration tasks, although there is a suggestion that this is because the display maps directly onto the task (Bennett, Nagy, & Flach, 1997).

---

Problem-solving research (for example, Newell & Simon, 1972) focuses on the *representation* of problems and the impact of this representation on ease of solution. Decision research has focused on developing models that describe the generation of multiple alternatives, the evaluation of these alternatives and the selection of the most appropriate alternative, generally in the absence of perceptual variables (Bennett et al., 1997).

Recent developments in the area have also considered *recognition* of problem types/categories as a crucial component of good 'expert' decision making (for example, Klein, Orasanu, & Zsambok, 1993). Recognition has a basis firmly within the research field of perception and this has led to the synthesis of the two areas in the context of naturalistic decision-making research.

Kirlik, Walker, Fisk and Nagel (1996) provided some support for this proposition by examining the efficacy of an augmented display design in supporting perception of task-relevant information for decision making. Twenty-four male undergraduates estimated the perceived threat of simulated moving vehicles and launched attacks at those judged to be hostile. Results indicated that perceptual augmentation of displays facilitates decision-making acquisition and performance. The researchers concluded that skilled performance acquisition in dynamic environments can be accelerated by supporting perceptual decision-making activities.

**Dynamic displays**  Dynamic information displays may be used for a number of general applications (Sanders and McCormick, 1993), including: *quantitative readings* (precise numeric value), *qualitative readings* (approximate value or trend, rate of change or change in direction), *check readings* (whether parameters are within some 'normal' bounds or that several parameters are equal) and *situation awareness* (project forward in time/space to predict future event, for example, an air traffic controller's display allows prediction of plane positions over the next few minutes). Sanders and McCormick (1993: 133–148) provide a detailed discussion of the various elements of display design (for example, pointer, scale, scale markers).

### Contemporary developments in control and display

Recent research has also raised the possibility of three-dimensional dynamic displays. Wickens, Liang, Prevett and Olmos (1996) conducted a number of trials with computer-simulated aircraft flight desk displays and found that three-dimensional displays could assist in the visualization of the external environment in a simulated landing task. Clearly, the part played by three-dimensional displays for presentation of dynamic information would be to model the system environment more accurately and facilitate a better match between user mental models of the display and the physical elements of the system itself.

Control and display devices have altered enormously in the past few decades, with the advent of increased automation and widespread use of microprocessor-based technology. Many jobs now involve employees spending a substantial portion of their day working at a desktop, or other computer, interacting via existing control mechanisms, for example, mouse and keyboard, and receiving feedback via a monitor screen. Current control technologies have likewise developed rapidly. This is particularly true for computer input devices, such as the keyboard, mouse, joystick, trackball, touch screen, graphic tablet, and light pen (Bullinger, Kern, & Braun, 1997; Study Box 7.14).

---

**Study Box 7.14**

**Advances in control device**

New technology has promoted the development of a number of control devices that have no direct linkage between human and machine, blurring the distinction between control *inputs* and consequent actions. Some of these technologies also blur the distinction between display and control – touch-screen menus, for example, employ such a technology, where a menu is initially displayed to the user via a screen,

*(Continued)*

---

**Study Box 7.14    Continued**

then switching to a control mechanism when the operator selects an option by touching the screen. McMillan, Eggleston and Anderson (1997) outline a number of new control/display technologies including speech and EEG-based control.

For example, automatic speech recognition (ASR) systems are widely used within the telecommunications industry, where limited vocabulary 'word-spotting' technology is used to increase the speed of connection by users speaking the name of the party they wish to call. ASR systems represent a powerful enabling technology for disabled users, with voice control of home appliances, computer software, telephones, hospital beds and motorized wheelchairs all now commercially available. The wider marketplace has also benefited from these enabling technologies in the shape of voice-programmable video recorders, voice-operable TVs, voice-controlled computer systems and carphones.

EEG measurements taken from the surface of the scalp represent electrical activity of the brain. By analysing specific rhythms and patterns of synchronized electrical activity of large groups of neurones, the sources of sensory processing, cognitive activity and motor control may be tapped into and used to control a human–system interface. Research has also focused on EEG-based control as a surrogate for conventional control, with control of computer cursors and light pen movements successfully trialled over the last decade (for example, Pfurtscheller, Flotzinger, & Neuper, 1994). Simple flight simulators have been controlled using this approach following only 30 minutes of training, with more complex simulator actions, for example, roll angle commands, requiring five to six hours of training.

---

An application attracting research attention at present is radio frequency selection by pilots using EEG-based control. More sinister would be the ability for the system to recognize the human user's cognitive or emotional states, intentions and desires. Whilst such a facility is perhaps crucial to the development of truly *intelligent* interfaces (McMillan et al., 1997), a number of ethical issues must also be addressed in terms of the availability of this information to outside parties, including the system itself.

### Summary (VI) and conclusions

- Control and display design that accounts for the human dimension is critical to successful system operation and functioning.
- Many catastrophic events can be attributed to poor control and/or display design that do not match the information-processing capacities of human operators, do not provide sufficient relevant feedback to the user on the state of the system and do not take account of basic principles of human perception (that is, placement of controls, and in the organization of visual display data).

# Advanced Technologies

A meteoric growth in user base has been the result of the increase in computer power and versatility, and a reduction in cost. With regard to Internet and intranet use, that is, global and internal business communication, people are beginning to use computers as a general-purpose tool to gather and distribute information, to communicate with others and to perform long-distance group work (Waterson, 2000). New advanced technologies associated with this boom in computer-driven workplace applications include: multimedia; virtual environments (VEs); CSCW and groupware.

## Multimedia

'Multimedia' alludes to the interactivity of computer-based systems, within the context of a *media-rich* environment. Chignell and Waterworth (1997) criticize narrow definitions of the term, which focus solely on the multiple media (visual and auditory) that may make up a multimedia application rather than as a bridge (or interface glue) between different media, database environments and text environments. In addition, they suggest, multimedia can provide a structural (often spatial) metaphor within which information can be embedded.

Chignell and Waterworth (1997) propose three main approaches to multimedia, as follows:

- *performance* – concerned with creating a sensory experience through the use of various actors and events, for example, walkthrough tours of tourist destinations (hotels, cities, and so on);
- *presentation* – creating links between slides and intersperse standard slides with animations, video clips and sound clips;
- *document* – an 'interactive' book, allowing the user to move fairly freely within the document, rather than being tied to a linear reading order.

*Navigation*   Navigation around effectively non-linear environments presents problems for some users (Boechler & Dawson, 2002). Although long-term memory is associative, learnability is better for material structured in a linear way (McKnight, Dillon, & Richardson, 1991). Confusion and disorientation can be quite typical of new Internet users who attempt to 'surf' for the first time.

Features that can aid navigation include 'cognitive organizers', such as site maps, tables of contents and path lists: these reduce the cognitive load on working memory by summarizing information about structure and organization. Tversky's (1981) work on cognitive representations of physical space suggests that items contained within perceptual space should be organized in a way congruent with the principles of perceptual organization. Chignell and Waterworth (1997) suggest the use of 'landmarks' to allow users to orient themselves easily by checking their 'position' in space relative to known features (that is, route knowledge). Ruddle, Payne and Jones (1997) found that computer-generated 'virtual' buildings with landmarks were just as easy to navigate as their real-world counterparts. Likewise, Charoenkitkarn, Chignell and Golovchinsky (1996) report evidence showing that concept maps in a multimedia context can be helpful to information retrieval.

***Multi-sensory modality*** The use of multiple sensory modalities, that is, auditory and visual, in multimedia applications can be advantageous in terms of maintaining focus and concentration on the part of the user, but may also lead to information 'overload' (Wickens, 1992). Analysis of multi-sensory media is atypical for ergonomists, who tend to focus on single channel information presentation, for example, display, auditory feedback, and so on. For instance, research on auditory feedback and typing performance is typical of this approach (for example, Gerard, Armstrong, Rempel, & Woolley, 2002). However, calls for a more integrated multi-modal approach to interface research are increasingly being voiced (Popescu, Burdea, & Trefftz, 2002).

Chignell and Waterworth (1997) advocate the use of ecological interface design (EID), which conveys task- and goal-relevant information in an easily assimilated perceptual form. The possible utility of multi-sensory and multi-modal presentation in training and learning environments has been highlighted by Waterworth (1995), who found that the visual display of information enhanced piano training by providing feedback to the user on various elements of his/her performance, including dynamics, tempo and articulation.

Whilst user navigation has been a central theme in hypertext research and development, progress is limited by a heavy reliance on indirect measures of navigation. Darken and Peterson (2002) provide a detailed review of the concept of navigation in virtual environments with particular emphasis on understanding how people navigate in the real world and how this information can be used to design more navigable virtual environments.

### Virtual environments

Virtual environments are now used widely for a variety of applications by developing fully interactive, three-dimensional environments that users may manipulate and interact with. Typical applications include:

- cockpit/car design;
- product design;
- education and training in health care (by producing fully interactive human 'bodies' that may be manipulated through 360 degrees by trainees; see for example, Riva, 2002);
- clinical neuro-psychological assessment and rehabilitation (for example, Holden & Todorov, 2002);
- medical diagnosis (for example, Satava & Jones, 2002);
- clinical intervention (for example, treatment of anxiety disorders through exposure therapy; for example, Difede, Hoffman, & Jaysinghe, 2002);
- social skills training (for example, for people with autistic spectrum disorder; for example, Parsons & Mitchell, 2002);
- education, that is, general problem solving, mastery of facts and concepts and improvement of the learning process, second language acquisition (for example, Cobb, Neale, Crosier, & Wilson, 2002);

- driving, flight (Iovine, 1994), building layout (Witmer, Bailey, Knerr, & Parsons, 1996), and psychological research methods training (Colle & Green, 1996);
- navigation in hypertext systems and the modelling of cognitive information spaces to assist in information resource management (Nilan, 1992);
- team training (for example, Salas, Oser, Cannon-Bowers, & Daskarolis-Kring, 2002);
- military training (for example, Knerr, Breaux, Goldberg, & Thurman, 2002);
- to enhance the social richness of telecommuting systems (Venkatesh & Johnson, 2002);
- social-psychological research (for example, to manage the control-mundane realism trade-off) (Blascovich, Loomis, Beall, Swinth, Hoyt, & Bailenson, 2002);
- usability testing (Hix & Gabbard, 2002) and performance measurement (Lampton, Bliss, & Morris, 2002).

## *Virtual Environment*

The term virtual environment (VE) describes:

> A computer-based generation of an intuitive, perceivable and experiential scene of a natural or abstract environment. (Bullinger, Bauer & Braun, 1997: 698)

VEs exhibit the following characteristics:

- visual realism – three-dimensional perspective view, often stereoscopic;
- time-varying, animated;
- user-centred, immersive view;
- user-centred, or closed-loop, interaction;
- multi-sensory interaction:
  - action *from* user – speech, whole-body movement, gesture;
  - feedback *to* user – visual, auditory, kinaesthetic, force, tactile.

The term 'virtual environment' is preferred by contemporary researchers over and above 'virtual reality', which is argued to have become too all-embracing and bound up with media and populist terminology (for example, Wan & Mon-Williams, 1996). Object representations within VEs can possess various qualities and behaviours by incorporating graphical, auditory and physical force feedback into VE systems, thereby utilizing human sensory channels to provide 'realistic' feedback to the user about a computer-generated environment.

The way in which such complex three-dimensional 'virtual' worlds are generally transmitted to the user is via a head-mounted display (HMD), and other interaction devices such as gloves and full body suits. Critical to the user's experience of a VE is his/her 'belief' in the system. VE system designers generally endeavour to provide system users with an experience that incorporates a sense of presence, a feeling of immersion and a high level of engagement (Witmer & Singer, 1998).

Witmer and Singer (1998) suggest that experiencing presence in a remote operations task or in a VE requires the ability to focus on one meaningfully coherent set of stimuli (in the virtual environment), to the exclusion of unrelated stimuli (in the physical location). They argue that presence is likely to be influenced by the perceived 'reality' of the VE, that is, the level of integration of system objects and actions within the overall system itself, particularly in relation to the continuities, connectedness and coherence of the stimulus flow within a VE system.

Contemporary research is concerned with assessing the effect of user movement control, exposure duration, and scene complexity on performance. Stanney, Kingdon, Graeber and Kennedy (2002) examined performance on a set of basic tasks representative of human interaction in most virtual environments and found that providing users with complete control affords better performance on both stationary tasks and those requiring only head movement. For tasks involving both head and body movement, Stanney et al. (2000) say that user movement control should be more sensitively synchronized to minimize feelings of motion sickness without compromising performance.

The use of VEs also raises a whole host of cognitive issues including perception, attention, learning and memory, problem solving and decision making and motor cognition (Munro, Breaux, Patrey, & Sheldon, 2002). Research has begun to clarify some cognitive aspects of VE usage, but many questions remain.

Developments such as the ability of computers to respond to human 'brain waves' (or EEG signals) and to emotional state (Bianchi-Berthouze & Lisetti, 2002) potentially complicate the interface issue, but in the long term enhance the likelihood of optimizing the 'fit' between people and computers. For instance, future cockpit design (especially, instrument display) might incorporate a means of adaptation to detected variation in pilot anxiety (Hudlick & McNeese, 1994). Research on emotion coupled with detailed knowledge of the emotional components of the task and task context is thus critical to development in this field. This increased interest in emotion might be usefully integrated with contemporary work on emotion in the context of stress and coping (Lazarus, 1999; Chapter 8).

### Computer-supported Cooperative work and Groupware

**Groupware**    Interacting with computers is different from interaction with others via computers (Bubb-Lewis & Scerbo, 1999). 'Groupware' is an umbrella term describing the electronic technologies that support intra- and inter-group collaboration. The term derives its meaning from its two root components: a socio-organizational meaning ('group') – a collective way of working and collaborating, and a technical meaning ('ware') – the artefact or tool (Ciborra, 1996). While traditional technologies such as the telephone qualify as groupware, the term is ordinarily used to refer to a specific class of technologies relying on modern computer networks, such as email, newsgroups, video-conferencing and electronic meeting systems, as well as systems for workflow and business process re-engineering. Groupware has been defined as:

> Computer-mediated collaboration that increases the productivity *or functionality of person-to-person processes*. (Coleman, 1996)

Groupware technology may be used to communicate, cooperate, coordinate, problem solve, compete, or negotiate (Attaran & Attaran, 2002). Groupware technologies are typically categorized along two primary dimensions:

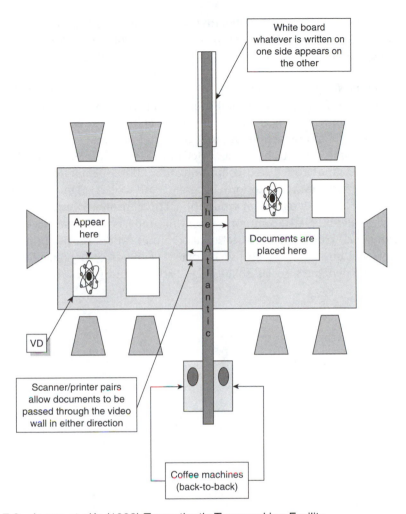

**Figure 7.8** Lyons et al.'s (1993) Transatlantic Teamworking Facility

Adapted from Lyons, M.H., Cochrane, P. & Fisher, K. (1993). Teleworking in the 21st century.
*IEE Computing and Control Engineering Journal*, August.

- whether users of the groupware are working together at the same time ('real-time' or 'synchronous' groupware like video communication, chat systems, decision support systems and shared whiteboards) or different times ('asynchronous' groupware like email, newsgroups and mailing lists, workflow systems, group calendars, collaborative writing systems); and
- whether users are working together in the same place ('collocated' or 'face-to-face') or in different places ('non-collocated' or 'distanced').

Lyons, Cochrane and Fisher (1993) described such a facility, designed to encourage feelings of team membership in two halves of a multi-disciplinary project group working on either side of the Atlantic (see Figure 7.8).

Other models of web-based collaborative systems are also beginning to appear in the literature. For instance, Jang, Steinfield and Pfaff (2002) describe a system called TeamSCOPE, designed to support awareness of globally distributed teams.

***Computer-Supported Cooperative Work*** CSCW refers to research examining the design, adoption, and use of groupware. Sproull and Kiesler (1986) noted that, to some extent, all communication technologies (including the telephone, for example) reduce feedback and social cues in interaction, but that computer mail and computer conferences do so more than all other technologies. McGuire, Kiesler and Siegel (1987) reported that although computer-mediated communication allows people to work in groups they would not have been able to form otherwise and to exchange information more quickly and easily, the dynamics of group interaction are altered, too.

Use of computer-mediated communication thus impacts on the *mechanics* and *structure* of individual, group and organizational communication, on the process of communication and on certain social psychological elements of organizational life, for example, group dynamics, social isolation, and so on (Study Box 7.15).

---

### Study Box 7.15

#### Impacts of electronic messaging systems on communication structure

Andriessen (1991) outlined the following impacts of electronic communication on co-operative work within and between work-based groups:

- reductions in telephone calls and letters;
- speeding up exchange of information;
- exchange of new information;
- many more people receive information than through traditional channels;
- expanded horizontal and diagonal contacts;
- easier to reach people by email and voice messaging than through normal channels;
- senior personnel easier to communicate with since there is far less screening by their secretaries for electronic messages than for letters and face-to-face meetings;
- less waiting time for colleagues and customers;
- better coordination by supervisors of employees who are often out of the office;
- within existing groups, the network 'connectedness' increases;
- inter-organizational communication is enhanced – conducive for transfer of innovation.

---

The following research findings relate to CSCW group communication (for example, Wigan, 1991):

- Participants engage in less overt agreement and more opinion-giving than comparable face-to-face groups.

- Groups take longer to reach agreements.
- Changes in group roles, hierarchies and structures have been reported. Computer-mediated group discussion is less likely to produce polarization or shifts to extremities on a risk-caution dimension than in face-to-face interaction.
- Group members are more honest in expressing their feelings (Tidwell & Walther, 2002).
- US findings suggest a greater incidence of hostilities, profanities and insults (termed 'flaming') than occur in comparable face-to-face exchanges (for example, Siegel, Dubrovsky, Kiesler & McGuire, 1986). UK-derived findings suggest the contrary (PATRA, 1992–94).

Social influence is communicated through verbal, paralinguistic and social context cues (for example, seating position). A number of experiments have been conducted (for example, McGuire et al., 1987) into group or team effects of computer-mediated communication. Experiments demonstrate that the consequent reduction in paralinguistic and social context cues prevented the full exchange of views and feedback possible in face-to-face interaction. When discussion time is held constant, the number, length, complexity and novelty of arguments is less in computer-mediated discussions than in face-to-face discussions.

McGuire et al. (1987) posited that the difference found in social influence by media was due to the difference in fullness of verbal and non-verbal exchange. One design issue mentioned in their study concerns decision making, as they found that computer-mediated communication permitted wider information searches and fostered more equal participation. They suggested that group interactions via computer might also increase the influence of those who initially have minority or deviant views, possibly leading to increased group innovation, or, alternatively, to group fragmentation and divisiveness.

Jirotka and Luff (2002) argue that the future of systems development to aid collaborative working depends on being able to relate naturalistic (ethnographic) studies of work practice and interaction to those involved in software design.

Some note how the distinction between face-to-face and virtual teams (geographically dispersed members who work across boundaries of time and space using computer-driven communication technology) is becoming increasingly blurred due to the invasive nature of technology throughout most contemporary organizations (for example, Arnison & Miller, 2002). A key task for future research is to harness existing theory in pursuit of a more conceptually driven approach to system design in a team context. One fruitful line of work along these lines is informed by Hutchin's (1995) 'distributed cognition' approach (McCarthy, Healey, Wright, & Harrison, 1998; Study Box 7.16).

The distributed cognition approach regards the group or team as a single interconnected cognitive system of people and artefacts rather than as a collection of individuals (Banks & Millward, 2000; Cannon-Bowers & Salas, 2001; Hutchins, 1995; Larson & Christensen, 1993). Of particular interest is how teams coordinate themselves in relation to both technology and task by distributing the cognitive load (Banks, 2001).

---

**Study Box 7.16**

**Distributed cognition and mental models**

Banks (2001) argues that the word 'shared' has two quite different meanings. Either it can mean that something is jointly owned or it can mean that something is apportioned amongst people. So far, the expression shared mental models has been used to refer to the former meaning, mental models that all the team has a copy of. However, mental models can be distributed in a coordinated fashion amongst a team (that is, 'distributed mental model'). The distributed cognition (DC) (Hutchins, 1995) approach is one that argues that cognitive processes are distributed between both individuals and artefacts (materially distributed cognition) and other people (socially distributed cognition). The central tenet of DC is that it *redefines the boundaries of the unit of analysis for cognition.* Traditionally within cognitive psychology, the unit of analysis has been the individual, however this is not necessarily the most appropriate unit. To illustrate this, Hutchins (1995) analysed the cockpit of a plane as one socio-technical system of pilot, co-pilot and aeroplane. He argued that the positioning of the markers on a dial indicating the range, the speed, and so on must be kept within when landing a plane constitutes cockpit 'memory'. These values are maintained by the position of the markers and can be referred to by pilot or co-pilot. Thus, if the co-pilot sets them and the pilot refers to them, this is effectively a communication of the representation of the values from one person to another. Hutchins (1995) presents a detailed case study describing the task of navigating a US Navy ship as a distributed task. No single person completes this computation; one person takes the bearing, another configures the chart and so on. The state of the computation (the location of the boat) can move through the system of individuals and artefacts. The cognitive processes, therefore, involve the 'propagation of representational state across a series of representational media' (Hutchins, 1995: 117). Applied to mental models, O'Malley and Draper (1992) found that in order to navigate through a piece of software, users did not retain a complete mental model of the word processor, but a mental model of how to access information allowing them to use the program. The cognitive system in this instance thus contains both the individual and the artefact.

---

## *Summary VII and conclusions*

- Advanced technologies are *advancing* so rapidly it is difficult to keep apace of the human implications. The consequence of this is that the technological possibilities afforded by advancement may well enable new processes, but if these are not at least consistent with the requirements of the situation and its users, they will be difficult to embed in human terms.
- Moreover, the cognitive and social requirements of new technologies may be unanticipated, and instead of reducing the need for cognition through a deskilling process, they can end up causing overload.
- Questions are raised about the damage to health and well-being furnished by the introduction of new technologies surrounding which the human implications are unclear, as well as about the damage to performance.

# An Organizational-level 'Socio-Technical Systems' Perspective

The dangers to organizations of a technology oriented procurement culture (where technology is seen as the driver for change and performance improvement) can be illustrated by many 'disaster' cases (for example, London Ambulance Service, Case Study 7.1). The ambulance staff union claimed that imposition of a new system into an organization without taking account of its context as a whole cost 11 lives, because ambulances were delayed in reaching patients. The official report into the collapse of systems at London Ambulance Service said of the procurement: 'The size of the programme and the speed and depth of change were simply too aggressive for the circumstances' (Finkelstein & Dowell, 1993). The report also said that management had 'ignored or chose not to accept advice provided to it from many sources outside of the service on the tightness of the timetable or the high risk of the comprehensive systems requirement' (see **www.sagepub.co.uk/millward** for other case examples).

Contemporary organizations are preoccupied with doing everything faster, better and cheaper (Damanpour, 2001). Boddy and Gunson (1996) note, however, the dangers of assuming automatic success in developing information and communication technologies for the benefit of organizations. They demonstrate how the outcomes of these technological innovations frequently have an emergent rather than a planned character. Outcomes are often very different to what is planned, for these are not simply technological innovations; they are socio-technical interventions in which disturbances set off perplexing and unpredictable ripples. When these interventions take place in a volatile environment, what the organization requires will also frequently change. The paradox of increasing availability of information and communications technology alongside a persistent inability to implement projects successfully has encouraged considerable academic reflection on project success factors.

The basic premise of socio-technical systems (STS) theory (Trist & Bamforth, 1951) is that new technology cannot be imposed; a technological innovation should always take into consideration the 'human' dimension (psychological and social). Cooper and Foster (1971) define the concept of the STS theory as based on the simple fact that any production system requires both a technology (machinery, plant, material) and a work relationship structure that relates the human operation both to the technology and to each other. The technology makes demands and places limits on the kind of structure possible, whilst the work structure itself has social and psychological properties that generate their own unique requirements with regard to the task to be done (see Chapter 4 for details on STS theory).

The extent to which technologies 'disturb' the organizations into which they are admitted varies with the degree of interaction between people and the new technology. In soft-systems terminology, the degree of coupling between human and technological components of 'people–machine' systems varies (Eason, 1996). The adoption of communication technologies within organizations has been the subject of a number of different theoretical models. Dating back to the early work in computing by Leavitt and Whisler (1958) and more recently in relation to studies of the Internet by Caincross (1997), there is what has been called a 'technological imperative' model in which organizations adopt available new technologies, almost inevitably, to survive in a competitive economy.

An illustration of the dangers of a too tightly coupled understanding of structure and technology is provided by Symon's (2000) critique of the so-called 'network' organization (see also Chapter 5 for more on technology in the context of organizational change). Many contemporary organizations have harnessed the 'network' metaphor (Network Enabled Capability) as a means of implementing their organization in a digital form, sometimes called 'e-commerce'. Even the military has adopted this metaphor (for example, Almen, Anderson, Lagerlof, & Pallin, 2000). Almen et al., for instance, note that given the critical importance of the ability to seize initiative at the local incident-specific level for fast and flexible action (a so-called 'manoeuvre' approach to warfare), a networked system of information coordination is required. This, in turn, will facilitate a 'common situational awareness' and the possibility of decentralized flexibility of action at all levels of defence.

However, there are many well-documented stories of business-transforming Information Technology (IT) projects that have failed under the technological imperative model. The human factors perspective on this issue raises fundamental questions about the lack of fit between the technology and the social context within which it is used. Failures in association with e-commerce solutions abound, despite organizations making a significant financial investment in associated information and communication technologies (Study Box 7.17).

---

### Study Box 7.17

#### The digital imperative ...

The planning and implementation of an integrated IT infrastructure to support effective decision making in distributed/virtual enterprises for the successful deployment of assets/resources is found to be highly complex, with significant re-design implications for all human aspects of an organization (Scott-Morton, 1991). To this end, many have signed up to an e-commerce strategy underwritten by a network-centric rationale, on the assumption that this will enable them to do things better and more competitively (Wang, 2000), for example, Barclay's Bank, IBM, Pegasus Solutions, Rolls Royce and Whitbread. However, despite the advocated benefits of ecommerce to organizations such as:

- better information management;
- better integration of suppliers and vendors;
- better channel partnership;
- lower transaction costs;
- better market understanding;
- expanded geographical coverage;

it is clear that 'enablement' is more of a hypothetical ideal than a reality (Wang, 2000).

**Study Box 7.17   Continued**

It is not enough to solely demonstrate an IT infrastructure. *Decision making effectiveness across organizational hierarchies, processes and other various organizational coalitions, such as project teams, assumes there is a common understanding based on shared meaning and mental models* (Senge, 1990). Therefore, semantic interoperability/harmonization is a key soft/human factors enabler of effective joint decision making. This is especially important for tasks where 'unity of thought' is essential (Thackray, 2000). It is generally agreed that significant effort is required to ensure that new technologies 'make sense' to people in terms of their everyday tasks and task circumstances, and to some extent processes must 'emerge' (rather than be imposed from top-down) from grass roots level to ensure that new technologies become embedded into everyday thinking and action.

The extent of capacity to use information from a technological point of view may blind organizations to the risks faced by organizations and projects in developing systems that harness this information capacity. As Symon (2000) notes, the assumed 'informating potential' of new forms of technology (enabling better, more informed local decisions, the ability to respond flexibly to change quickly and with initiative) is not an automatic consequences of a digital networking solution.

In contrast, the 'strategic choice' model (Macdonald, 1985) emphasizes the influence that people in an organization have on shaping how the resulting technologies are used. People within organizations decide which technologies to use and install according to what seems most rational, but others decide how the technologies will be used (or modified in use) in the light of the pursuits they are engaged in. Consistent with this, Symon (2000) describes information as a symbolic resource that has to be interpreted and applied, rather than an incontrovertible fact.

Finally, Orlikowski (1993) talks of a structuration model in which the products of IT investments depend on interactions of people and technology over extended periods. Different groups of people initiate, plan and design IT. Users then respond to it by welcoming it, rejecting it, learning to live with It or modifying it. In doing so, they 'socially construct the technology in the sense that, with continued use, these human choices become established features of the operation'. As Corbett (1994) also says, technology derives from and enlists subjective experience, and to that extent can be influenced by the ideas and meanings which make sense of that experience (see also Symon, 2000). This model sees technology as an inextricable part of the meaning system within an organization, rather than a separate material entity.

The application of a strategic choice or structuration model to the understanding of technological innovation first requires a deep understanding of the actual processes currently at work in an organization (Study Box 7.18; see also Chapter 5).

> **Study Box 7.18**
>
> ### Organizational ethnography
>
> The goal of organizational ethnography is to understand work from the perspective of those who do it and the principles they use to get work done. There is a big difference in what people are supposed to do in their jobs with what they actually do. The emphasis here is on understanding the social dimensions of work and the informal practices and processes used as opposed to the ways in which formal job specifications, documented processes and managerial overviews may assume that work is done. One major research effort, pioneered by Xerox Global Services, the consultancy arm of Rank Xerox, provided a major thrust into the design of technology by studying the 'knowledge ecology' within an organization. This entailed focusing on the qualitative real-life work practices that exist amongst people at work, rather than on the quantitative generalizations about cost-savings or on formal documented processes.

Contemporary digital solutions also require serious consideration of the *cognitive capability* underpinning successful 'enablement' of a network centric principle of organizing. A digital solution has an informational and physical component, but these are 'technological' considerations embodied within the concept of digitization. However, the dominant consideration is the process to be 'enabled' by digitization, which is increased flexibility. A physical and informational 'enablement' is not sufficient in itself to support the realization of this. The cognitive capability is a necessary prerequisite for both the informational and physical enablement. Information has no meaning outside of its use by people and the physical coordination of both information and people also requires cognitive coordination. Thus, information superiority requires cognitive superiority.

Figure 7.9 depicts these considerations in graphic form (Phillips, Louveries, Millward, Kyriakidou, & Gore, 2003). A full realization in practice of a network capability requires human capital (cognitive superiority) as well as information capital (information superiority) as expressed by cell 4. Note that cognitive superiority does not automatically arise from physical or information superiority (structural capital); cognitive superiority both incorporates and supersedes physical and information superiority.

The cognitive superiority required to furnish a genuine realization of a network-enabled capability is discussed further at **www.sagepub.co.uk/millward**.

### Summary (VIII) and conclusions

- Lessons from industry inform us that if technology is used to drive change in structure and process, the intervention will most often fail. Socio-technical systems theory has long maintained that technological systems should be *integrated* with social and human systems, and to this extent, a technological solution that does not take human considerations into account can be costly in the long term.

Human capital                                         Structural capital

                          Stable form

| | |
|---|---|
| **Cell 1** Stable form, cognitive superiority | **Cell 2** Stable form, physical and information superiority |
| **Cell 4** Dynamic form, cognitive superiority *(genuine realization of a network enabled capability)* | **Cell 3** Dynamic form, physical and information superiority *(network enabled capability in principle only)* |

Dynamic form

**Figure 7.9**   Digital superiority = cognitive superiority

- Technological innovations are most effectively evolved with users or in parallel with a deep understanding of both formal and informal organizational practices to ensure that they can be appropriately embedded into everyday functioning. Technology is best seen as an enabler rather than a driver of new processes.

## Future Research Challenges

- explore more formally the concepts of mental model, shared mental model, distributed cognition and distributed mental models in the context of human–machine interaction involving several people;
- investigate the human implications of new technologies, including virtual environments, teleworking and other digital work solutions;
- examine the problem of automation from a cognitive motivational perspective;
- investigate how people make sense of, and embed, new technologies into everyday practice;
- examine the cognitive superiority requirements of new technologies;
- investigate causes of error taking into consideration both person, machine and situational/organizational factors.

## Recommended Reading

Bullinger, H.J., Bauer, W., & Braun, M. (1997). Virtual environments. In G. Salvendy (Ed.), *Handbook of human factors and ergonomics* (pp. 1727–1759). New York: Wiley.

Chmiel, N. (1998). *Jobs, technology and people*. London: Routledge.

Symon, G. (2000). Information and communication technologies and the network organization: A critical analysis. *Journal of Occupational and Organizational Psychology*, 73, 389–414.

Tattersall, A.J. (2000). Workload and task allocation. In N. Schmiel (Ed.), *Introduction to work and organizational psychology: A European perspective* (pp. 181–205). Oxford: Blackwell.

Waterson, P.E. (2000). The design and use of work technology. In N. Schmiel (Ed.), *Introduction to work and organizational psychology: A European perspective* (pp. 231–254). Oxford: Blackwell.

# 8

# Design of Work and Work Environments: Health and Safety

Many firms think that investing in health and safety is an extra cost to their business … they do not calculate the employees' work experience which might be priceless.

(Source: News.scotsman.com).

## Preface

The topic of employee health and safety has recently gained currency, probably furnished in part by a fear of litigation incurred by a growth in compensation claims. Some companies have acknowledged that by actively managing employee health and safety (physical and psychological), they can simultaneously reduce sickness absence and promote employee well-being. It may also improve 'emotional capital' (for example, emotional investment, energy and resilience), itself anticipated to reap performance benefits. Other companies may marginalize health, viewing it as largely a personal not a public matter, but most may at least pay some lip service to it on health and safety grounds. In countries where health (along with safety) is on the executive agenda, societal pressures (political, economic, cultural) and concerns (for example, unacceptably high disability-induced social security costs) have been instrumental in creating imperatives to ensure employers take seriously their role in generating health problems and take steps to rectify this (for example, the Netherlands). The UK is beginning to take heed of the increasing burden to society imposed by health problems arising from work-related stress. Addressing the issue is now high on the political agenda.

This chapter considers in detail the topic of stress and stress management, and ends with a review of psychological approaches to the study of workplace accidents and safety management. The focus will then turn to the way organizations *react and deal with health and safety matters* rather than the health and safety matters per se. There are undoubtedly many 'physical dangers' inherent to certain industries and lines of work (for example, fire-fighting, policing, military, construction), even in jobs which do not ordinarily involve a physical component (for example, physical abuse during a service encounter, exposure to toxic substances). However, these 'risks' are *not* addressed here.

The focus instead is on how the psychological perspective, a relative infant in the field of health and safety, can make a distinctive and useful contribution to reconciling employee welfare needs with organizational goals. This may be through the development of appropriate diagnostic tools, the production of a scientific knowledge base, and the design of effective interventions. Winnubst and Diekstra (1998: 399) describe the work and health psychologist as a 'more generally oriented psychologist whose expertise embraces organizational theory and industrial psychology, group dynamics, psycho- and organizational diagnostics, stress intervention, psychopathology and advice on social security'. Adding safety management to this remit will also benefit from a background in ergonomics. The rather all-encompassing role of the psychologist in health and safety management, it would seem, will harness many different aspects of occupational and organizational psychology, a not insubstantial bit of health and clinical psychology, a ring of occupational psychiatry (a growing field in the UK), and perhaps also, even a touch of social work.

In short, this chapter focuses on the *psychological issues* arising specifically from, and pertinent to, the management of healthy and safe work environments. The topic of work design, though briefly touched upon, is otherwise addressed in detail in Chapters 4 and 7. Relevant material on culture change can also be drawn from Chapter 5, 'Organizational Development and Change', to inform the discussion on health and safety cultures. The literature on decision making will also be critically reviewed. As Wagenaar and Hudson (1998: 68) say, an accident is the end of a long chain of events beginning with a 'fallible decision'.

## Learning Objectives

Studying the contents of this chapter will enable you to:

1 explain the implications of the Health and Safety at Work Act 1974 and the Disability Discrimination Act 1996 for employers and organizations;
2 describe and explain the influence on worker health and performance of auditory, thermal, visual and social environments at work;
3 describe and explain the concept of workplace stress and its health implications;
4 on the basis of a sound theoretical and empirical defence, propose methods for both assessing and managing workplace stress;
5 critically assess the various theories proposed to explain workplace accidents from an integrative perspective;
6 again, with sound theoretical and empirical defence, propose methods for both assessing and managing workplace safety;
7 critically review various approaches to the study of decision making in organizational contexts.

## Introduction to Health and Safety

Case Study 8.1 illustrates both the health and the safety issues facing organizations today in the way they design and organize work. It also highlights that, despite increased industry regulation and a climate of increased worker litigation, the health risks in particular facing workers may still not be taken seriously by organizations. An accident can occur in the here and now, with immediate consequences, whereas health is a relatively invisible and insidiously long-term issue. Health is also over-shadowed by debate about who should take responsibility, and whether in retrospect an illness or disease *really* is caused by work and its conditions. Accountabilities are by no means clear cut.

---

**Case Study 8.1: Chronic illness and construction sites**

The death toll in the building industry receives a lot of media attention but the level of disabling injury and chronic disease goes almost unreported. There are 3000 cases every year of vibration white finger (or hand–arm vibration syndrome – HAVS), a crippling condition caused by operating hand-held power tools, and more of disabling cement dermatitis, a painful, disfiguring and sometimes disabling skin disease. Ten percent of workers have been forced to give up their jobs because of this condition. A known cause of this is high-chromium cement; most cement in the UK thus presents a significant risk to workers' health. There are simple practical precautions, such as proper toilet facilities, where workers can wash off cement dust, and glove wearing, known to greatly reduce the risk of cement dermatitis. Guidelines to protect workers from HAVS include job rotation, use of low vibration machinery and breaking up periods of continuous use (workers report working on these machines for at least three hours at any one time). In March 2004, safety visits to 200 construction sites revealed inadequate washing facilities and a total lack of awareness of health risks. Workers were concerned that wearing gloves would prove restricting and could not conceive of reducing their stints on hand-held tools to half an hour because of reduced productivity which might jeopardize their jobs. There is prejudice against change because of anticipated slowing up in production.

(Edited transcript from *Nice Work*, BBC Radio 4, hosted by
Phillipa Lamb, Tuesday 17 March 2004)

---

Even in the instance of an accident, precise 'cause' is difficult if not impossible to establish (Sheehy & Chapman, 1988). Enquiries into recent rail disasters (for example, Wolmar, 2003) and shuttle disasters (for example, Vaughn, 1996) are a highly perti-nent illustration of this (Case Study 8.2). The public demand a neat causal explana-tion, but in most cases an accident may be the culmination of many 'latent' factors (with accumulative long-term effect), which do not necessarily meet the pragmatic need for instant action (Brotherton, 1999; Wagenaar & Hudson, 1998).

---

**Case Study 8.2: 'Design flaws, mistakes and bad management – the truth behind the Central line crash'**

An *Evening Standard* investigation into the Central line derailment, which shut the line six weeks ago, today pinpoints the cause. The train's revolutionary design, combined with its high speed, caused it to vibrate so much that bolts holding one of the motors in place were weakened. It eventually fell off on to the track, causing the train to derail … The *Standard* also reveals a catalogue of mistakes and management failings in the two years leading up to the incident… (Wolmar, 2003).

Likewise, in a highly complex organization like the National Health Service (NHS), said to be 'riddled with violence, bullying, work-related stress, accidents and excessive overtime' (Carvel, 2004), the 'causes' of stress and ill-health are likely to be both multiple and layered, a product of both individual and organizational factors.

It is generally agreed that health and safety is a matter of both attitude *and* behaviour, and this requires ownership and responsibility (Mearns & Flin, 2001; Redmill, 1997), necessitating a total cultural solution. Legislation provides an essential backdrop to this, heightening the strategic salience of health and safety matters, as an unavoidable imperative. Winnubst and Diekstra (1998: 396) provide many examples across the continent of legislative initiatives designed to 'encourage' if not 'urge' employees to 'treat more seriously the questions of the quality of work and the welfare of the workers in his or her company' (see **www.sagepub.co.uk/millward** for background information on pertinent health and safety legislation).

### Summary (I) and conclusions

- Health is the Cinderella of the health and safety equation, a less tangible, subterranean organizational issue, where the accountabilities are unclear and highly debatable.
- Legislation can help create the appropriate organizational imperatives, but this is clearly not a sufficient basis on which to leverage any true or meaningful change in company practices.

## Stress and Stress Management

It is well established now that stress plays a central role in health (physical, psychological) and well-being (Quick, 1999; Warr, 1999). Amongst its physical implications, stress is directly associated with heart disease, stroke, accidental injury, and indirectly with cancer, liver disease, and bronchitis. It is also strongly implicated in mental health, especially anxiety and depression. Between 30 and 60 percent of all sickness absence from work in the UK is attributable to some form of mental and emotional disturbance caused by stress (Cooper, 2001; Mental Health Foundation, 2000).

Work-induced stress is said by many to have increased dramatically in the developed world, arising from the enormous changes in society generally and the workplace in particular (Cooper, Dewe, & O'Driscoll, 2001; Sparks, Faragher, & Cooper, 2001; Study Box 8.1). A UK survey published in 2001 noted that 20 percent of those employees sampled reported high or extremely high levels of stress at work (Cooper et al., 2001). In financial terms, the Confederation of British Industry (CBI) estimated approximately £24–£25 billion is lost annually due to stress-related sickness. Indeed, work-related stress is now said to be the biggest occupational health problem in the UK, after musculo-skeletal disorders (Kompier, Cooper, & Geurts, 2000). Thus, in the words of Le Blanc, de Jonge and Schaufeli (2000: 175), 'job stress is a scientific as well as a social problem'. The heightened salience of legal imperatives to take responsibility for stress, coupled with the growth in performance costs incurred by stress-induced employee problems, has increasingly put stress on the 'strategic' boardroom agenda (Giga, Cooper, & Faragher, 2003).

---

**Study Box 8.1**

## Contemporary workplace correlates of occupational health and well-being

From a comprehensive review of the literature, Sparks, Faragher and Cooper (2001) identify the factors below to be implicated in occupational health and well-being.

### Job insecurity

Whilst there has been little actual change in degree of job insecurity, employees *perceive* that their jobs are insecure (for example, Smithson & Lewis, 2000). Pelfrene, Vlerick, Moreau, Mak, Kornitzer and De Backer (2003) found that it was perceived job insecurity (rather than actual job insecurity) that was significantly associated with job strain and self-reported health status, amongst their sample of 16,335 men and 5084 women (aged 35–39 years) from 25 companies across Belgium between 1994 and 1998.

### Working hours/pace of work

Perceived job insecurity has increased the tendency for 'presenteeism' (an increase in working hours). The pace of work has also increased. Working long hours and/or intensively for long periods of time has been associated with poor lifestyle habits (for example, heavy smoking/drinking, poor diet, lack of exercise) all with health implications. Longitudinal studies confirm that working persistently long hours over a number of years is predictive of poor health and well-being (for example, higher blood pressure, chronic headaches, chronic fatigue, sleep problems, and limb problems). Work–family conflict (which has an established negative impact on health) is also more likely in association with working excessive hours under time pressure.

### Control at work

'Perceived control' has been extensively investigated for its impact on health and well-being. Very low levels of perceived control are said to be psychologically harmful, whereas high perceived control is associated with positive health (and reduced likelihood of ill-health). An important qualifier of whether perceived control has positive outcomes are individual differences in whether control is perceived as desirable or not. For example, one study found that job autonomy was associated with reduced emotional exhaustion and health complaints *only* among employees with a high need for autonomy. Moreover, whether perceived control is beneficial to health may also depend fundamentally on whether employees can use it (that is, perceived self-efficacy; Spector, 2000). Control is clearly a multi-dimensional construct, so the impact may depend on which type it is, and whether it tallies with employee needs and desires (van der Doef & Maes, 2000). In other words, increasing control will not necessarily and automatically improve health and well-being.

Study Box 8.1   Continued

### Managerial style

When managers themselves are under pressure, their style of management can change towards being more 'inconsiderate', even bullying. Management support, however, is well established to be critical to employee well-being.

Other considerations include the need to address the implications of workplace changes for employees at the lower end of the hierarchy (most affected yet also most neglected), the training needs of managers called to manage an increasingly diverse workforce (including cross-cultural management), and to consider the impact of technology on health (for example, musculo-skeletal problems, visual problems, general fatigue), including the cognitive intensity of work associated with the increased use of computers. The health and well-being implications of all of the factors considered in their review depend fundamentally on how they are *perceived and reacted to by employees*.

Not everyone agrees that the workplace is more stressful now. Whilst things have changed, whether things *are* worse is a different issue, especially relative to when employees were working long monotonous hours in the factory or down the mines (Jones & Bright, 2002; Warr, 2000). Some say that the experience of work has become generally more positive (comprising more opportunities and challenge) than in the past (Jones & Bright, 2002). There is also mounting evidence for the mental health benefits (for example, increased self-esteem) of working over unemployment, and that it can decrease the service usage of people with mental health problems (Department of Health, 1999; Secker & Membrey, 2003). Nonetheless, the reality is that stress is now much more of *an issue* for employees and employers alike (Cooper, 2001; Cooper, Dewe, & O'Driscoll, 2001). There is no straightforward definition of stress. The term has been variously used in both the scientific and popular literature. It may refer to a broad range of events that may happen to a person known as stressors, individual reactions to such events (subjective feelings of stress, actual physical/physiological distress), and/or an imbalance between the person and the environment (a problem of coping) (Wilkinson, Campbell, Coyle & Davis, 1997: 195). These varied uses reflect century old deliberations as to whether stress is a stimulus (stressor), a response (strain) or a process (cognitive appraisal, coping) or, in fact, *all* of these things (for example, Quick, 1998). It is not surprising then that Quick (1999) has defined stress as a 'fuzzy set concept'.

Stress has physical (for example, lack of appetite, insomnia, headaches) and behavioural symptoms (for example, irritability, difficulty in making decisions) that can lead to more serious ailments (for example, heart disease, high blood pressure) and social problems (for example, alcohol or drug abuse, marital and family problems) (Cooper et al., 2001), all of which can seriously impede effective life functioning. Stress may also lead to burnout (Siegrist, 1996; Study Box 8.2).

## Study Box 8.2

### Burnout syndrome

Burnout refers to a situation in which people have been over-stretched for a long period without sufficient opportunities to recover from stress. The result is a dysphoric and dysfunctional state with profound consequences, yet without major psychopathology. The syndrome is characterized by high levels of (emotional or psychological) exhaustion, and feelings of reduced personal competence and a cynical attitude towards one's work and work objects (patients, clients, students, colleagues) (Maslach & Jackson, 1986). Burnout also inhibits coping, thus causing a negative spiral. People usually do not recover from burnout without outside help or environmental rearrangement. Current perspectives on burnout suggest that people are at risk when they perceive a chronic dis-balance between their input (effort, time) and the output (material and immaterial rewards) in their work (Siegrist, 1996). Leiter and Maslach (1988) model the stress process in accounting for burnout as follows: emotional exhaustion leads to depersonalization, which in turn causes a reduced sense of personal accomplishment. Others have proposed alternative sequences. For instance, Golembiewski and Stevenson (1986) say burnout starts with depersonalization, followed by reduced personal accomplishment, and finally emotional exhaustion. Testing the viability of each of these two models, results obtained from Lee and Ashforth's (1996) longitudinal study were in favour of the Leiter and Maslach model. Burnout is especially problematic amongst service workers.

### Theories of stress

There are many different models of stress across the medical, health and occupational literatures, each with a slightly different emphasis. Health psychologists try to explain the physiological and psychological basis of stress in relation to various health and medical outcomes, whilst occupational psychologists have sought to identify stress-inducing work characteristics ('stressors') linked with occupational outcomes (job satisfaction, performance). Here the focus is specifically on work stress (for a comprehensive contemporary review of the broader stress literature, see Jones & Bright, 2002). The review is framed nonetheless by a brief overview of early stress models, to provide a context for understanding contemporary formulations of work stress.

Early stress models were rooted in a stimulus-based 'engineering' metaphor describing it as an external 'force' or pressure on an individual that causes 'strain'. Work conducted in this tradition is that of Holmes and Rahe (1967) on stressful life events, the argument being that experiencing a series of 'significant life events' within a short period of time makes individuals prone to disease (for example, moving house, divorce, bereavement; see **www.sagepub.co.uk/millward** for details). Some of the organizational literature on stress is still couched in this basic stressor–strain model correlating 'work characteristics' such as long working hours with the experience of job strain. However, evidence does not support a direct association between objective work characteristics and subjective strain, as it depends on individual differences in perception and interpretation (Sparks et al., 2001).

The response-based conceptualization of stress views it as an adrenergenic response leading to either a 'flight' or 'fight' reaction. For instance, Selye's (1956) general adaptation syndrome (GAS) views stress as a non-specific natural response to a stressor occurring in three temporal phases: hormonal arousal by an alarm (shock, leading to counter-shock), resistance (maximum adaptation and return to equilibrium), and exhaustion if coping efforts are inadequate (failure to adapt, resulting in illness or death).

This model has been described as too simplistic for both health and occupational purposes, concerned solely with physiological (that is, non-specific vulnerability to illness) rather than psychological stress, and failing to take account of the complexity of the interaction between stressor and individual. The same stressor can have a different effect depending on individual perceptions. Both stimulus and response models promulgate the view that stress is always negative. Yet stress can have a positive impact on some individuals and moreover felt stress does not necessarily mean distress or illness (Wilkinson, Campbell, Coyle & Davis, 1997). The possibility that individuals can recognize and modify stress reactions is also ignored (Lazarus, 1999).

More recent work incorporates the physiological response to stressors as an integral part of the stress experience, examining the various individual and situational factors that may contribute to, and mediate, the stress experience, response and outcome (for example, Kalimo, Lindström, & Smith, 1997). This is known as the *transaction* approach to stress defined as a process or relational phenomenon at the interface of both individual and environment (Monat & Lazarus, 1991). The notion of *transaction* is different from *interaction* in that the latter is purely a statistical term describing a relationship between variables whilst the former focuses on understanding the *dynamic stress process* itself (Cooper et al., 2001).

Transactional definitions are concerned in particular with the psychological mechanisms of cognitive appraisal and coping involved in a stressful encounter (Monat & Lazarus, 1991). First the individual evaluates the situation and makes a subjective judgement about whether an event may involve personal harm, threat of harm or challenge (primary appraisal). Next, the individual evaluates whether he/she can cope with this event (secondary appraisal). Primary appraisal can lead to perceptions that the impact is benign (that is, nothing to be lost or gained), positive (for example, excitement, exhilaration) or negative (for example, harm, loss, threat or challenge). Secondary appraisal can lead to either acceptance, recognition of the need to change, the need to know more, or holding back. The role of appraisal in the *coping* aspects of the stress process is elaborated further below.

Stress does not therefore reside in either the individual or the environment, it is a dynamic cognitive state (involving appraisal), an imbalance within normal functioning and an attempt to manage or resolve this imbalance (coping). In short, stress denotes a transactional process comprising stressors (events or stimuli), strains (physiological, psychological, behavioural) and outcomes (coping responses and their consequences for individual and organization) (Cooper et al., 2001; Case Study 8.3).

Recent work on stress, spawned largely by theoretical developments in the coping literature (Lazarus, 1999), as well as disillusionment with the all-inclusive nature of the stress concept, is looking more closely at the role played by *emotion* in stress and the appraisal of stressors (Ashforth & Tomiuk, 2000; Buunk, de Jonge, Ybema, & de Wolfe, 1998; Dormann & Zapf, 2002; Harris, Daniels, & Briner, 2003).

Buunk et al. (1998: 149), for example, define stress as 'the occurrence of negative emotions evoked by demanding situations'. They propose that negative emotions come about because the situation is perceived as threatening, evoking either anxiety (ranging from tension, apprehension, nervousness to fear and panic) or anger (varying from irritation to rage), each with their own physiological response pathways. Conway and Briner's (2002) diary study found that broken promises (perceived by employees to occur regularly and with respect to nearly every area of work) were systematically related to fluctuations in emotion and daily mood. They point to the usefulness of the concept of psychological contract as a theoretical basis for understanding emotional reaction in the workplace.

Speculating on the other emotions that might be evoked by a situation, they add resentment, depression, grief, disappointment, jealousy, shame and embarrassment to the list. Initial evidence for the possibility that these emotions may be implicated in a stress reaction is derived from Warr's (1987) Vitamin Model of mental health at work (Study Box 8.3). The initial emotional reaction may be non-specific (and ambiguous), thus evoking an attempt to make sense of the situation (akin to an attribution process) using a meaningful emotional label (itself a process open to social influence).

### Study Box 8.3

#### Warr's Vitamin Model

Warr (1987) proposed that mental health is affected by job characteristics analogous to the impact of vitamins on physical health. Vitamins promote health and well-being, but beyond a threshold of input there are no additional benefits; in fact, an overdose of certain vitamins can cause ill-health. Metaphorically, Warr (1987) proposes nine essential job features, six of which (job demands, autonomy, social support, skill utilization, skill variety and task feedback) have curvilinear effects (that is, lack or excess will be bad for health) and three (safety, salary, task significance) with a linear effect (that is, more is better). He sees mental health comprising three affective dimensions: discontent/content (that is, job satisfaction and job attachment), anxious/comfortable (that is, job anxiety, tension and strain), and depressed/actively pleased (fatigue, burnout, job-related depression). In 1994, Warr added three individual moderators of the impact of these nine job features on mental health: ability, values and pre-existing mental health. The more matched the individual characteristics with those of the job, the stronger the moderator effect (for example, value autonomy → heightened impact of job autonomy). Unfortunately, evidence is inconsistent and support is not strong. Buunk et al. (1998) say that the model fails to consider the impact of different combinations of 'job features' on mental health.

Consistent with this, Dormann and Zapf (2002) found that 'irritation' substantially accounted for the impact of social stressors (arising from problematic workplace relationships) on depressive symptoms. Irritation was said to cause an increase in anxiety and decrease in self-esteem. With regard to anger, Schulz, Cowan, Pape Cowan and Brennan (2004) found that negatively arousing work days were, for women, linked to angrier marital behaviour, with its own equally stressful consequences.

---

**Case Study 8.3: Relationship between stressors and stress**

It is common to describe the effects of stress (for example, high staff turnover, low levels of job satisfaction, lack of motivation, burnout) and 'causes' of stress (for example, low level of control over one's job, scheduled staff breaks, electronic performance monitoring, the attitude that human resources are expendable) in the call centre, assuming a direct relationship between them. This assumption that stressors exist that in absolute terms cause 'stress' is overly simplistic and misleading. It assumes that there is something inherently stressful about, for example, electronic performance monitoring and that all employees react in the same way. Also the concept of stressor is much more complex than this (Wheaton, 1996: 29), perhaps manifest in the form of daily hassles (or micro-events) built into the fabric of everyday life (some occurring ritually, others more episodically), influenced, in turn, by macro-system stressors.

---

To date, the role of emotion in the study of stress is a surprisingly neglected area of investigation. Emotional exhaustion, on the other hand, has been associated in particular with *'emotional labour'* (EL) (Hoschild, 1983), describing the process of regulating expressed emotions to meet organizational expectations, particularly among service employees. During EL, employees *may* (though not necessarily) experience emotional dissonance owing to an incompatibility between expectations and actual feelings (Morris & Feldman, 1996). An employee can deal with this dissonance by altering the displayed emotion (surface acting) or 'conjuring up' (deep acting) the required emotion (Hoschild, 1983). This requires considerable emotional effort. Many studies have shown that emotional labour can undermine health, well-being and performance (Morris & Feldman, 1996). Brotheridge and Lee (2003) found in particular that surface acting (which involves the suppression of genuine emotions) was related to emotional exhaustion and depersonalization (both symptomatic of burnout) (Ashforth & Tomiuk, 2000). Grandey, Dickter and Sin (2004) review the topic of emotional regulation in the workplace more generally, offering some insightful theoretical links to the concept of emotional intelligence, as well as providing a more integrated framework for future research and practice.

## Summary (II) and conclusions

- Stress now has a well established link with health. Organizations have long been seen as comprising many sources of strain, called stressors.
- Over recent years, radical changes (in society generally and in organizational life in particular) are said to have imposed an inordinate degree of strain on people.

Others say there is not more stress, just *different* types of stress, some of which we have yet to fully explore and understand.

- The concept of stress is fuzzy, comprising many elements. Stress has been variously conceptualized as a physiological response, an experience of distress (strain), a stressor–strain relationship, an emotional process, and a transactional process involving many factors. Most now agree that *stress is a process* beginning with an emotional reaction to a negative event, involving a stress response, a cognitive appraisal, an experience of distress (or strain) and a coping effort.
- Recent work has begun to look more closely at the role of emotion in the stress process.

## A General Psycho-social Model of the Job Stress Process

Smith and Carayon's (1996) model of the psycho-social job stress process (Figure 8.1) comprises the following two core assumptions:

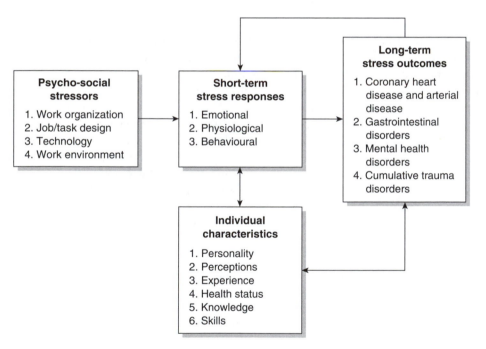

**Figure 8.1** Model of psycho-social job stress process

Adapted from Kalimo, R., Lindström, K., & Smith, M.J. (1997). Psychosocial approach in occupational health. In G. Salvendy (Ed.), *Handbook of human factors and ergonomics* (2nd edn). New York: Wiley.

1    Work makes demands on the worker which he/she responds to according to his/her skills, motivations and other individual-level characteristics. This assumption is derived from the *Person Environment Fit Model* (French, Caplan, & Van Harrison, 1982), which states that job demands are threatening when a misfit is perceived between these demands (and the rewards derived from meeting these demands) and one's capacity to meet them.
2    The worker has expectations regarding work, for example, decision-making autonomy, opportunity for development and availability of peer and management support.

Kalimo et al. (1997) argue that when a mismatch occurs between environmental stressors and the worker's perceived ability to cope with these stressors, one is mobilized to cope by, for example:

- changing the external situation to mediate the stressors;
- interpreting the external situation in a new way to avoid perception of the situation as stressful;
- alleviating stress outcomes with mediating measures, for example, relaxation, medication, reliance on social support.

If coping fails, negative stress reactions are likely, including frustration, dissatisfaction, fear or anger. These reactions may lead to physiological changes, which may in turn manifest themselves as chronic physical or mental states. Such an outcome is likely to feed back into the perception of, and reaction to, the original stressors and the dysfunctional stress response is exacerbated, allied with a lowered perception of future coping ability.

This process of comparing capacity with demand and weighing this against expectation is akin to that proposed by the *Cybernetic Model* (Carver & Scheier, 1998; Edwards, 1998), within the framework of control theory. Components of the Cybernetic Model include the input function (perception of own state relative to that of the environment), a reference value (desires, values and goals), a comparator (which compares input with the reference value), and an output function (behaviour). The output function is activated when a discrepancy is perceived between input function and reference value (either because of a change in environment and/or reference value). The output function, which is sensed as stressful, is designed to rectify the discrepancy (that is, coping) to restore well-being (see **www.sagepub.co.uk/millward** for details of the Cybernetic Coping Scale, Edwards & Baglioni, 1993).

Arnold, Robertson and Cooper (1995) identify five types of workplace stressor: intrinsic to the job, organizational role, work relationships, career development, and organizational structure and climate (see also Buunk et al., 1998: 157–161 for an extensive review; Study Box 8.4). In contemporary times we can add to this the impact of transformational organizational change (for example, downsizing, merger; for example, Vahtera, Kivimaki, Koskenvus, & Pentti, 1997) and of working/relocating abroad (Shaffer & Harrison, 2001).

## Study Box 8.4

### Workplace stressors

#### Factors intrinsic to the job

(1) These are aspects of the job involving risk or danger to life, as encountered, for example, by firemen, soldiers, and deep sea divers; and (2) actual conditions in which a job is carried out, such as noise, lighting, temperature, long hours, shift work, work overload and work underload. Noise is a common workplace stressor, and whilst there are tight restrictions and regulations in association with this, *even moderate noise* can have adverse physical (for example, elevated blood pressure) and psychological (for example, sleep disturbances) consequences (for example, Babisch, 1998). Fried, Melamed and Ben-David (2002) found that the joint effect of noise and job complexity was a strong predictor of sickness absence (controlling for somatic complaints) in their sample of 802 white-collar employees in Israel.

#### Organizational role

(1) These are role ambiguity (when a person is unclear about how he or she fits into the organization and is unclear about expectations); and (2) role conflict (when a person may have conflicting job requirements, may be asked to do things out of kilter with their values and beliefs, or when the demands of work conflict with demands faced by other life domains) and degree of role responsibility (especially, responsibility for people) (Rizzo, House, & Lirtzman, 1970). There is vast literature on role-related stress in the occupational and organizational literature. Jackson and Schuler's (1985) meta-analysis found that an increase in role conflict and ambiguity led to decreased work-related participation, organizational commitment, and a correspondent increase in tension, anxiety and staff turnover. Recent work has confirmed that role ambiguity and conflict are implicated in a number of stress-related psychological and physiological outcomes (Meyerson, 1994; see **www.sagepub.co.uk/millward** for examples).

#### Work relationships

Dormann and Zapf (2002) lament the relative lack of research on 'social stressors' (conflicts between co-workers and supervisors, social animosities) at work, despite being more strongly associated with psychological strain (especially burnout) than task-specific stressors. Bullying at work has attracted significant recent attention. Bullying can be defined as being exposed repeatedly and over time to negative actions on the part of one or more persons at the workplace. Edelmann and Woodall (1997) found that 19 percent of the teachers they sampled indicated that they were currently being bullied (for example, verbal threats, shouting, anger, being undermined and receiving overly negative feedback) resulting in loss of confidence (44 percent), physical ailments (38 percent), stress (37 percent), feeling sad or let down (32 percent) and feeling anxious or depressed (29 percent).

#### Career development

The discrepancy between career goals and actual achievement relative to life stage have been found to be a significant source of experienced stress (for example, Arnold, 1997; Kidd, 2002; see Chapter 3 for more on this).

---

**Study Box 8.4   Continued**

### *Organizational structure and climate*

Kotter and Heskett (1992) have talked of workplace cultures as 'healthy' or otherwise. In a people-oriented culture that cares for and supports its employees, affords some participation and choice in the way they organize and conduct their work, and appreciates that they have lives outside of the workplace, employees are more likely to thrive than if their work is highly regulated and controlled, where they are treated as 'cogs in a wheel'.

---

Another key source of contemporary stress arises at the interface between work and family life. The increased incidence of the dual-career family, for instance, brings with it many different kinds of potential strain (Parker & Arthur, 2004). Schulz, Cowan, Pape Cowan and Brennan (2004) used diaries to look at changes in workday pace and end of workday mood in association with withdrawn and angry marital relations. They found that more negatively arousing days were linked with angrier marital behaviour for women and less angry but more withdrawn behaviour from men. This is commonly known as a 'spill-over' of stress from work to family life. Spill-over, however, can also occur from family to work. Frone, Russell and Cooper (1997) found that both forms of work–family conflicts (family-to-work and work-to-family) were strongly predictive of physiological, psychological and behavioural disorders in family members, across a four-year period.

Behson (2002) found that 'informal work accommodations' to family life (IWAF) can attenuate the likelihood of conflict at the work–family interface. IWAF is defined as 'a set of behaviours in which employees temporarily and informally adjust their usual work patterns in the attempt to balance their work and family responsibilities' (p. 326). Strategies include modifying how, when, or where work gets done without incurring any changes to work output (see **www.sagepub.co.uk/millward** for further details).

### *Moderators of the stressor–strain relationship*

A moderator is defined as a variable that affects the direction and/or strength of a relationship between a predictor variable and a criterion variable (Baron & Kenny, 1986: 1174). In stress research, moderators can be classified as demographic (for example, gender), personal/dispositional (for example, self-efficacy, locus of control, Type A behaviour), and social (for example, social support). Many have criticized existing theories of stress for being male oriented and thus gender biased (for example, Bell & Lee, 2002; Iwasaki, MacKay, & Ristock, 2004).

### *Demographic moderators*

Gender, age, and social class (see Fletcher, 1988, for a comprehensive review of the 'epidemiology of stress') are some of the variables that contribute to differentials in levels of stress. With the exception of work on gender, very little research has been done in the effort to explain these differences (Iwasaki et al., 2004). Some (for example, Bell & Lee, 2002; Zalcquett & Wood, 1998) have begun to question whether existing theories of stress (and stress measures) are sufficient for the study of women's stress experiences. For example, Brown and Campbell (1998) found that female police officers 'not only suffer adversely from the same job stressors as ... males ... but in addition suffer *gender specific stressors*', for example, sexual harassment, and career blocks. Other findings confirm that the stress experiences of working women may be attributable to their 'token' status in non-traditional jobs (Davidson & Cooper, 1992), especially women from ethnic minorities (that is, double-jeopardy).

Research also shows that women are far more likely to be emotionally affected by multiple role responsibilities than men (for example, Iwasaki et al., 2004). Women still take most of the responsibility for child-care and for household chores (Greenhaus, Collins & Shaw, 2003), are expected to do so (Armstrong & Armstrong, 1990) and experience more guilt when they feel they are *not* meeting role expectations in the family domain (Iwasaki et al., 2004). Iwasaki et al. explain these gender differences with reference to societal role expectations surrounding the way gender (masculinity/femininity) is socially constructed (that is, females taking the caring role).

### *Dispositional moderators*

Research conducted within a diathesis-stress model looks in particular at the role of individual differences in predisposition to stress (Wilkinson, Campbell, Coyle & Davis, 1997). Such factors can influence exposure to stressful effects (for example, certain people may actively position themselves in stressful situations), their reactivity to stressors (for example, appraisal processes, choice of coping mechanism) or both. A classic example of a dispositional factor is the now infamous Type A behavioural pattern (Study Box 8.5). Another factor is self-efficacy on the assumption that beliefs about self and one's abilities may render one more or less susceptible to the adverse effects of stressful conditions (Ganster & Schaubroeck, 1995).

---

### Study Box 8.5

#### The Type A behavioural pattern

The Type A behavioural pattern is also known as the 'stress prone' personality (Rosenman, Swan & Carmelli 1988) and is typified by strong endorsement (for example) of the following statements: 'never late', 'very competitive', 'always rushed', 'anticipates what others are going to say', 'impatient while waiting', 'tries to do many things at once, thinks about what will do next', 'emphatic in speech, fast and forceful', 'ambitious', 'eager to get things done', 'hides feelings', and 'hard driving' (of self/others). Research shows that Type A behaviour has been implicated in heart disease (Smith & Pope, 1990). The Type A profile can, however, be changed (see Roskies, 1987).

Kobasa's (1979) research into 'career hardiness' found that individuals varied in their resistance to stressors. Highly resistant individuals were high on internal locus of control (perceive a strong sense of personal control over self and events), job and life commitment, and perception of change as a challenge rather than a threat. Spector (2000) cautions against assuming that an internal locus of control is always pre-emptive of stress. He reports research showing how stress was greater amongst tele-workers who 'internalized' work-related problems, particularly problems concerning communication and computer systems.

## Social moderators

The importance of social support in 'buffering' occupational and organizational stress is clearly documented (Cohens & Wills, 1985). Support may buffer stress by attenuating the physiological and psychological reaction to stressors, and/or by facilitating active coping behaviours. However, availability of social support per se may not automatically moderate the stress experience (Cazals, Almudever, & Fraccaroli, 1995). There are many different types of support (for example, emotional comfort, social integration, informational and practical) including actual and perceived support, each of which may have different effects. Kalimo et al. (1997) found that supervisors were perceived as a more potent source of support at work than peers in moderating the effect of management/supervisory style on perceived stress (see also Sparks et al., 2001, and Chapter 4 on local foci of commitment and identification). Research has also tended to confound the support available, with the support used and its effectiveness.

Cooper et al. (2001: 152) argue that the role of support (and other moderators) must be considered 'within the context of the dynamic transaction between the individual and the environment. This will require theoretical models that integrate moderators more explicitly into the coping process'.

Recent interest has extended to the concept of trust in management as a potential buffer between workload and experienced stress (for example, Harvey, Kelloway, & Duncan-Leiper, 2003), with trust defined as 'a psychological state comprising the intention to accept vulnerability based upon positive expectations of the intentions or behaviour of another' (Rousseau, Sitkin, Burt, & Camerer, 1998: 2). Harvey et al. (2003) predicted and found that trust in managers will reduce the perceived impact of their workload on various measures of distress. However, there was also an upper limit on the extent to which trust had an attenuating effect, suggesting a threshold of tolerance or acceptability beyond which no increase in trust will buffer stress. Harvey et al. (2003) speculate that excessive increases in workload can push trusting relationships to a limit, which may then undermine trust.

These findings hold some promise for the integration of theories of stress (effort–reward imbalance theory, Siegrist, 1996), with theories from studies of organizational behaviour (for example, justice theory, psychological contract theory, Rousseau, 1995). Research on merger-induced change has demonstrated, for instance, that trust relationships in the workplace have higher thresholds of tolerance for the breaking of contractual agreements than transactional relationships, but that *gross violations* of previous agreements (for example, perceived injustice, threats to identity), can change the fundamental basis of the relationship (Millward & Kyriakidou, 2004b). These findings tie in nicely with the idea that trust might also moderate (within reason) the effect of other stressors (workload, job change).

### Summary (III) and conclusions

- The general job stress model assumes that an experience of stress will arise from having failed to cope with a perceived mismatch between capability and perceived demand (which is the basic assumption of the person–environment fit model), relative to personal expectations. The postulated process is akin to the Cybernetic Model of stress.
- Five different categories of workplace stressor have been identified: job, role, relationships, career development and organizational culture. Work–family conflict is now also a major source of contemporary stress.
- Known moderators of the stressor–strain relationship include gender, certain individual differences, and social support. Gender differences in the experience of stress are said to be *qualitative* rather than quantitative, raising questions about stress assessment. Social support is itself a difficult concept to pin down, comprising many different facets, including trust. The buffering mechanism of variables such as social support is still not well understood.

## Coping Strategies

Coping is clearly fundamental to the stress process (Le Blanc, de Jonge, & Schaufeli, 2000). There is a burgeoning interest in this topic, and, correspondingly, a move away from classifying, measuring and comparing the relative efficacy of different types of coping strategies, towards investigating *coping processes* and in particular elucidating the role of emotion and appraisal in these processes (for example, Dewe, 2003).

This shift has been underwritten in part by elaborations of the theory of stress appraisal (Lazarus, 1999, 2000; Monat & Lazarus, 1991), in part by disillusionment with the all inclusive 'fuzzy' nature of the stress concept (for example, Reynolds & Briner, 1996), a growing general interest in the study of emotion in everyday organizational life (for example, Fineman, 2003), and by long-standing psychometric difficulties in identifying distinct, stable coping strategies (for example, Dewe, 2003). Maybe, also, there is no small contribution furnished by the realization that stress has become a somewhat inevitable part of contemporary working life, bringing with it an imperative to understand how people can better cope with (for example, Wainwright & Calnan, 2002), and recover from, stress (for example, Cropley & Millward, 2004).

Seminal to coping research in the early days was Lazarus and Folkman's (1984) work on stress, appraisal and coping processes (see Lazarus, 2000 for review). In their appraisal theory, coping was defined as cognitive and behavioural attempts to master, reduce, or tolerate the internal/external demand created by the stressful transaction.

This theory strongly emphasized the dynamic nature of coping as reflecting an interaction between internal and external contextual factors. Lazarus and Folkman's early legacy, however, is most strongly associated with their description of two types of coping strategy: problem focused and emotion focused (Study Box 8.6).

---

**Study Box 8.6**

### Coping strategies

#### *Problem focused*

Describes attempts to confront and deal directly with the demands of the situation itself using 'mastery' strategies such as systematic problem diagnosis and solution generation. Solutions may involve changing goals and aspirations, more effective time-management, confronting the problem directly, and/or changing the situation.

#### *Emotion focused*

Describes strategies used when we believe there is nothing we can do to manage or to change the situation, aimed at managing the physiological component of the response. Such strategies include venting anger, drinking, seeking emotional support and reappraising the situation in a way that minimizes its anxiety-inducing impact. In the reappraisal of the situation, we are often prone to distort the reality of the situation as a way of dealing with anxiety.

---

On the basis of this coping distinction, Lazarus and Folkman (1984) developed the Ways of Coping Checklist (WCCL), since revised (Folkman, Lazarus, Dunkel-Schetter, DeLongis, & Gruen, 1986), and in this 67-item form now one of the most widely used coping measures (Guppy, Edwards, Brough, Peters-Bean, Sale, & Short, 2004). Research, however, started to become heavily preoccupied with measurement matters, including the fastidious application of factor-analytic techniques to ascertain the relative validity of each proposed coping strategy as a *description* of coping behaviour and as a basis for *predicting* adjustment (for example, Endler & Parker, 1994). As part of these psychometric efforts, alternative coping schemes have also been proposed including the Coping Strategies Inventory (Tobin, Holroyd, Reynolds, & Wigal, 1989), the COPE (Carver, 1997), the Coping Inventory for Stressful Situations (Endler & Parker, 1994) and the Cybernetic Coping Scale (CCS) (Edwards & Baglioni, 1993). Different measures are rooted in different conceptualizations of coping behaviour, but these alternative theoretical formulations have been largely neglected in research, overshadowed by descriptive and technical concerns.

Despite this psychometric effort, it is clear that most if not all of the available coping measures, including the classic WCCL (revised), do not yield factor structures that are theoretically consistent with prediction, or that have any kind of factorial stability or consistency across studies or over time. Moreover, apparently meaningful factors, on the surface, most commonly fail to achieve satisfactory internal consistencies when composite items are tested for reliability (Dewe, 2003). Predictive research has also failed to yield consistent findings for the relative efficacy of different coping strategies for buffering stress, though few studies have properly tested the buffering hypothesis (relying primarily on main effects rather than statistical interactions; Ingledew, Hardy, & Cooper, 1997).

One explanation for the lack of solid findings on coping (adopting the psychometric line) is that coping behaviour is highly contextual (thus accounting for the absence of any cross-situational stability of derived factors). Within the psychometrics of coping, researchers have advocated that one way round this is to adopt a dispositional approach to coping (for example, Carver & Scheier, 1998; Rick & Guppy, 1994). However, measures like the COPE and the CCS (both looking at coping generally) do not yield consistent findings either (De Ridder, 1997). One recent attempt to modify the CCS (from 20 to 15 items) has yielded better findings (a reasonably stable factor structure and good reliabilities; Guppy, Edwards, Brough, Peters-Bean, Sale, & Short, 2004), but this work has yet to be replicated and the support (though better than for other coping scales) was more moderate than strong.

Others have argued that the reason why coping research is so messy is because it is barking up the wrong tree. Findings suggest not only that it might be inappropriate to investigate coping in the form of discrete, stable factors (because coping is highly complex and contextual; Dewe, 2003), but it is not appropriate (for theoretical as well as empirical reasons) to pit one type of coping against another (to ascertain which is best), since all may play some role in the coping process. Arguably, whilst conceptually distinct, they are empirically interdependent, working together 'as a single coping unit' (Lazarus, 2000: 669). Ingledew et al. (1997) demonstrated in a longitudinal study that *both* problem and emotion focused coping had beneficial effects on well-being. Moreover, predictive research (investigating the main effects of coping on adjustment) obscures the complexity of the relationship between coping strategies and health outcomes (Oakland & Ostell, 1996). A more *ecological perspective on coping* is thus evolving, moving away from psychometric matters towards looking more closely at the nested complexity of coping processes, as originally envisaged by Lazarus and colleagues (Lazarus & Folkman, 1984).

This ecological movement has also reinvigorated interest in the role of emotion in coping (Dewe, 2003; Harris et al., 2003; Lazarus, 2000) in connection with appraisal processes (Lowe & Bennett, 2003). Simply put, coping can be described within this perspective as 'a process by which an individual attempts to minimize the negative emotions that arise from the experience of negative events. The exact nature of these emotions is a result of the individual's cognitive appraisal of the precipitating event' (Lowe & Bennett, 2003: 393; Study Box 8.7).

This coping process is now believed to be most coherently explained and described within Lazarus's recent '*cognitive–motivational–relational*' theory of emotion (Lazarus, 1999, 2000; Monat & Lazarus, 1991). The motivational aspect of this theory proposes that personal goals are important to understanding affective experiences (Lazarus, 1999). Research has started to emerge in support of both cognitive (appraisal processes; Lowe & Bennett, 2003; Study Box 8.7) and motivational (personal goals) aspects of this theory (for example, Harris et al., 2003). Harris et al. (2003) found, in particular, that goal attainment (assessed in daily diaries across two weeks) was positively associated with pleasurable affect, especially for more important goals.

---

### Study Box 8.7

#### Appraisal of emotion

Monat and Lazarus (1991) describe two categories of appraisal: primary and secondary appraisal. Primary appraisal assesses the *valence of the situation* but appraising the personal relevance of a situation (motivational relevance) relative to the extent to which the situation is consistent with personal goals (motivational congruence). Negative situations are both relevant and incongruent. Secondary appraisal evaluates coping options and outcomes, taking into consideration: accountability (who/what is responsible for the situation), future expectancy (likelihood of change), problem-focused coping potential (options for influencing the situation), and emotion-focused coping potential (ability to emotionally adapt to the situation). The two appraisal processes combine to determine the emotion experienced from which different appraisal configurations can be identified. For instance, anger is associated with other-accountability, guilt by self-accountability, and anxiety by pessimistic/ uncertain emotion focused coping potential (Lowe & Bennett, 2003: 394).

Appraisal influences emotion and also coping, because actual coping behaviour will in part be a function of how different coping options are appraised (including whether one feels able to use a particular strategy given opportunities relative to efficacy beliefs). Lowe and Bennett (2003) investigated the role played in particular by secondary appraisal in coping among 107 female nurses in relation to a recent work stressor. Observed appraisal–emotion–coping configurations made sound theoretical sense. For instance, active coping was associated with optimistic appraisals of problem-focused coping potential, whilst behavioural disengagement was associated with pessimistic appraisals (predicted by high other-accountability, and low self-accountability perceptions) of problem-focused coping potential. Anger and anxiety were the strongest and most commonly reported emotions. Notably, appraisal was directly linked with coping independently of emotion (supporting the proposition that appraisal is an antecedent of coping), but emotion was not linked with coping independently of appraisal (consistent with the proposition that emotion drives coping efforts).

Another noteworthy finding is that motivational congruence (personal goal congruence) was associated with positive reframing (associated in turn with optimistic emotion-focused coping potential combined with pessimistic future expectancy), confirming that appraisal itself may also constitute a coping mechanism (see also findings on the use of reappraisal processes in coping reported by Ingledew et al., 1997). In other words, if one perceives the situation to be relevant to one's personal goals, it is more likely to be re-evaluated (that is, re-appraised; Harris et al., 2003).

---

Evidence, then, points to a more dynamic coping process involving interrelated strategies, cognitive, affective and motivational components, harnessed in complex but theoretically meaningful configurations.

This has fuelled debates about the most appropriate way to measure coping – whether quantitative/self-report or qualitative (Aldwin, 2000; Coyne & Racioppo, 2000). Cooper et al. (2001: 183) suggest that both approaches are needed to capture the richness and idiosyncratic nature of the coping process. However, Coyne and Racioppo (2000) and more recently Dewe (2003) say that if quantitative research is to progress in the study of coping, different more ecologically sensitive ways of capturing coping patterns and sequences over time are needed. Dewe (2003), for instance, illustrates the 'rich description' of coping over time afforded by 'sequential tree analysis'. Researchers call in particular for the use of longitudinal designs (consistent with methodological developments in stress research generally) combined with a more intra-individual person-centred approach using diaries, narrative interviews, and other similarly 'provocative' techniques for looking at the micro-dynamics of coping works (Lazarus, 2000). The growth in popularity of diaries as a means of studying emotion and coping in context is testament to this call (for example, Harris et al., 2003; Tennen, Affleck, Armeli, & Carney, 2000).

Apart from being more theoretically informed (Aldwin, 2000), future research is said to be most fruitfully focused on elucidating the role of affect in coping, including positive affect, which could prevent breakdown under conditions of severe and prolonged stress (Dewe, 2003; Folkman & Moskowitz, 2000; Lazarus, 2000), the role of personal goals (for example, Lazarus, 1999; Harris et al., 2003), dispositional variables (Ingledew et al., 1997) and ego-defence in stress and coping (Lazarus, 2000) and coping efficacy (Somerfield & McCrae, 2000).

Whilst the concept of ego-defence is conceptually and empirically obscure (Cramer, 2000), it would seem appropriate to at least consider the possibility that some coping might be oriented to self-protection. Lowe and Bennett (2003) found that nurses used denial in negative situations in which one has some personal goal investment (which was not associated with any of their appraisal variables) and Ingledew et al. (1997) found in their research that avoidance coping had a direct deleterious effect on well-being. Other types of defensive mechanism that could come into play are repression (exclusion of painful memories), rationalization (assigning of logic), projection (re-assigning undesirable behaviour/qualities onto others), reaction formation (concealing through expressing an apparently opposite view), and displacement (re-channelling of motives) (Wilkinson, Campbell, Coyle & Davis, 1997).

Coping efficacy is another difficult issue (Somerfield & McCrae, 2000). In particular, determining an appropriate time-lag is an important consideration in coping research using longitudinal designs (for example, Fay & Sonnentag, 2002). Fay and Sonnentag (2002) looked at the role of personal initiative in preventing a looming or re-occurring stressor. They found that a negative stress experience in the short term was associated with the use of personal initiative in the long term, which moderated how the stressor itself was appraised and reacted to (that is, the stressor was removed or minimized). An important caveat to this conclusion, though, is that it may crucially depend on whether an employee has sufficient control over their work to be able to take such initiative.

Finally, Lazarus's (1999, 2000) notion of coping as a process of individuals constructing 'relational meaning' may inspire social constructionists to investigate processes of sense making in association with stress, emotion and coping.

## Summary (IV) and conclusions

- There is a burgeoning interest in the topic of coping. Research has moved away from identifying different strategies of coping and their relative efficacy towards looking at coping processes. The role of emotion, and also appraisal, in this process is of particular interest.
- Coping research that has been heavily reliant on the use of questionnaires has been strongly criticized as missing the real point about coping. Coping is a dynamic, fundamentally unstable process that may not be amendable to capture and quantification.
- The shift in coping research towards the use of more ecologically and temporally sensitive methods of investigation is notable.

## Specific Models of Work Stress

It has been suggested that when control over work and job processes is high, there is a 'buffering' effect on other job demands. This idea is central to the *demand–control* model (Karasek & Theorell, 1990), now perhaps the most commonly known testable conceptualization of job-induced stress. The original demand–control model predicts that four types of psycho-social work experience are generated by the interaction of high and low levels of psychological demand and decision-latitude (Figure 8.2). Note that the 'job' denotes the unit of analysis in this model, not the individual, which means that, strictly speaking, the former is in some way objectively classified, independently of employee perceptions. This is an important consideration when evaluating the contribution of this model (Morrison, Payne, & Wall, 2000).

Karasek and Theorell (1990) describe various prototypical job types ranging from 'active' (high psychological demand and decision latitude such as engineering, teaching

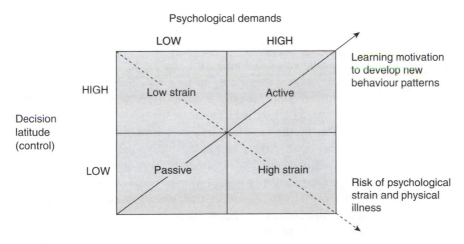

**Figure 8.2**   Demand–control model

Adapted from Karasek, R.A., & Theorell, T. (1990). *Healthy work: Stress, productivity and the reconstruction of working life.* New York: Basic Books.

and medicine) through passive (where both psychological demands and decision-making autonomy are low) such as miner and caretaker, low strain (high control, but low psychological demand) such as mechanic and machinist, and high strain (low control and high psychological demand) such as telephone operator and assembly-line operator.

Karasek and Theorell (1990) argue that high-strain jobs are the most likely to lead to 'psychological strain' since they involve low levels of decision-making latitude coupled with a requirement for prolonged periods of information-processing activity, leading to fatigue, anxiety and uncertainty. Active jobs, he argues, may lead to negative stress-related outcomes, but only when the worker is unable to employ suitable coping mechanisms such as increasing feelings of competence.

Passive jobs can also lead to negative outcomes since the worker is likely to experience *role underload* and de-motivation. Tepas (1994) says that it is possible to experience under-load in connection with the performance of automated computerized tasks. He suggests that psychological health may be affected by poor application of computer-based technology, especially when this restricts the input of, and deskills, the operator, resulting in feelings of lowered self-esteem.

It is well established that control over the environment is important to employee health and well-being (for example, see Jones & Fletcher, 1996 for a comprehensive critique). However, there is some continuing debate about how control should be operationalized (for example, perceived control, actual control, decision latitude), whether perceived control is a moderator (interaction model) of the association between job demands (stressors) and individual outcomes (strain), and whether it 'adds' to the effect of the stressor (Morrison, Payne, & Wall, 2000; Study Box 8.8). Social support has also been factored into the demand–control model as an additional 'buffer' of high work demand (Payne, 1979).

A recent review of studies affords strong support for the model, but only to the extent that they measure job-specific psychological well-being as opposed to general well-being (Van Der Doef & Maes, 1999). Notably, studies that did *not* support the model all relied on *self-report measures of both independent and dependent variables* (that is, they had resorted to an individual rather than job level of analysis). None of the studies in which the job was independently classified offered any support; nor were findings derived from nine longitudinal studies supportive. It would also seem that the use of self-report measures is the more common way of investigating the model.

Some recent studies have looked specifically at *job-level effects* within the demand–control framework, but this accounts for only a small degree of variance in stress outcomes (that is, average of 7 percent; Morrison, Payne, & Wall, 2000). Sceptical of whether these studies really do (on methodological and statistical grounds) demonstrate a job-level impact, Morrison et al. (2000) compared individual (job perception) and job-level effects (aggregated perceptual data rather than independent classification) against individual and job level psychological outcomes respectively. Using a sample of 6700 across 81 different jobs, they found that only job *perception* effects were significantly associated with psychological outcomes.

Morrison et al. (2000) speculate on whether this implies that the demand control model should be reformulated as an individual- (perceptual) rather than job- (objective) level consideration. Alternatively, more attention to a job-level conceptualization and measurement may be required to refine the way the model is tested (for example, perhaps using consensus rather than data aggregation methods; for example, Kirkman, Tesluk, & Rosen, 2001). On the other hand, the 'job' is now rather an outdated concept. Even the conventional job analyst has begun to query the viability of this unit of analysis relative to the role or team level, consistent with more contemporary work structures and arrangements (Chapter 1). Morrison et al. (2000) themselves wonder whether the concept of role or role set is a more appropriate unit of investigation for demand–control research.

Recently, however, attention has switched from studying the negative health effects (for example, psychosomatic health, high cholesterol, general ill health) of low control to those associated with *high effort/low reward* (de Jonge, Landeweerd & Nijhuis, 2000; Siegrist, 1996; Study Box 8.8). Some have argued that the two models (job demand–control/effort–reward) may identify different aspects of stressful job conditions (for example, Tsutsumi, Nagumi, Morimoto & Matoba, 2002) and that a combination of them may be the best predictor of mental distress (for example, Calnan, Wainwright, Forsythe, Wall & Almond, 2001). However, the predictive validity of each model may vary from occupation to occupation.

---

### Study Box 8.8

#### Effort–reward model of stress

The effort–reward model emphasizes the importance of reciprocity in the effort–reward process. Two sources of high effort at work are described: extrinsic (the demands of the job) and intrinsic (individual motivation). Rewards are understood to be distributed by three transmitter systems: money, esteem and status control. Siegrist (1996: 30) hypothesizes that stress occurs when a combination of high costs and low gains exists, suggesting that: '... lack of reciprocity between costs and gains (that is, high-cost/low-gain conditions) define a state of emotional distress with special propensity to autonomic arousal and associated strain reactions'. An example of a high-effort, low-reward situation is a person in a demanding but unstable job or a person who is achieving a high level without being offered promotion prospects. Another example is instances where people may continue in a job where they experience high efforts and low rewards, for example: (1) lack of alternative choice (for example, losing job); (2) strategic reasons (for example, the acceptance of an unfair job arrangement in order to improve chances of promotion later); and (3) 'over commitment' (that is, a personal pattern of coping characterized by a set of attitudes, behaviours and emotions reflecting excessive striving and strong desire to be approved).

The Effort–Reward Imbalance Questionnaire was developed in Germany by Siegrist (1996). It measures three main constructs: extrinsic effort referring to demanding aspects of the work environment (for example, 'I have constant time pressure due to heavy workload'), reward (referring to 'esteem' and 'status') and need for control (competitiveness, need for approval, disproportionate irritability and inability to withdraw from work). The reliability of this measure is said to be good. Hanson, Schaufelli, Vrijkotte, Plomp, and Godaert (2000) have also validated the scale for Dutch samples. Such international studies have demonstrated the validity of this measure for predicting health outcomes amongst white-collar employees and service professionals as well as blue-collar employees.

### Summary (V) and conclusions

- The demand–control model assumes that jobs can be objectively classified into high or low strain, high or low control. High-strain, low-control jobs are said to be especially stressful. Support is said to attenuate the impact of stressful jobs on health and well-being.
- Most researchers, however, have treated the demand–control variable as a matter of perception rather than an objective feature of jobs. At this level of analysis, there is good support for the model. At the job level of analysis there is little or no support for the model. Critics say that either the model needs to be reformulated in perceptual terms, or, alternatively, more sophisticated means of job classification need to be developed.
- Research confirms that perceived control plays an important role in stress, but that this role is not straightforward. Control has many different facets and, moreover, not everyone desires control.
- Recent interest in stress being a function of effort–reward imbalance has yielded some positive results, which may be explained with reference to theories of exchange.

## Stress Assessment

There is no established set of measures for stress just as there is no agreed-on definition (Quick, 1998: 291). It is also important to distinguish between a normal physiological stress response and an 'unhealthy' one, which may fail to properly recover (Cropley & Millward, 2004). It is the latter not the former that has negative health consequences (Cropley, Steptoe, & Joekes, 1999). A chronic stress experience arises because an acute response may become 'too intense, too frequent, too prolonged, or mismanaged' (Quick, 1998: 291). This can be described as an occasion where 'stress goes wrong and becomes distress' (Spector & Jex, 1998).

Distilling the literature on stress assessment is no easy matter since stress may be variously investigated as an independent variable, dependent variable, moderator or mediator (Cassidy, 1999). Most popularly in occupational psychology, stress is measured in the form of 'job strain' (Job Content Questionnaire) which signals both a stressor (perceived demand) and a stress reaction (perceived control) (Karasek & Theorell, 1990), although others maintain that strain is strictly a stress reaction (physiological and psychological; Hurrell, Nelson, & Simmons, 1998). The relevant measurement literature can be divided up by type of assessment (self-report, interview, observation, physiological, diary), but this may obscure and conflate otherwise important conceptual distinctions. For instance, the self-report inventories measure different aspects of the stress process ranging from perceived sources of stress to stress reactions (Study Box 8.9). Measures like the Performance Management Indicator (PMI) (Williams & Cooper, 1998) also attempt to measure a wide range of stress phenomena all inclusively across 22 different subscales (demands, moderators, reactions).

## Study Box 8.9

### Self-report stress measures

#### *General Health Questionnaire (Goldberg, 1978)*

Used as a psychiatric screening instrument, the 28-item version assesses somatic symptoms, anxiety, insomnia, social dysfunction, and depression. Scores are associated with other forms of clinical assessment.

#### *Job Content Questionnaire (Karasek & Theorell, 1990)*

A perceptual measure of job strain informed by the demand–control model, looking at the social and psychological character of jobs and job content. This measure has been extensively validated in a cross-cultural context (Karasek, Brisson, Kawakami, Houtman, Bongers & Amick, 1998).

#### *Job-Related Tension Index (Kahn, Wolfe, Quinn, Snoek, & Rosenthal, 1964)*

Acceptable levels of reliability and validity are reported for this scale (Eden & Jacobson, 1976) which taps into four stable factors of ambiguity and conflict on a five-point scale, ranging from 'Never' to 'Nearly all the time'. This measure, coupled with the Job Strain Index (Indik, Seashore, & Slesinger, 1964), was the first to look at work stressors, in so doing providing a major launch pad for the stress assessment enterprise.

#### *Work Environment Scale (Moos, 1981)*

A 90-item true/false survey designed to assess perceptions of general climate across 10 dimensions (for example, work pressure, supervisory support, peer cohesion, control, peer cohesion). The short form comprises 40 items.

#### *Stress Diagnostic Survey (Ivancevich & Matteson, 1998)*

Comprising the Job-Related Tension Index , this survey identifies specific areas of high stress at work (there is also a version looking at personal stressors). Validated on a wide range of occupational samples, Hurrell et al. (1998) say that this measure has good reliability.

#### *Anxiety-Stress Questionnaire (House & Rizzo, 1972)*

Looks at psychosomatic reactions. Test–retest and internal consistency reliability levels as well as discriminant validity levels have been reported as acceptable for this scale (Cook, Hepworth, Wall, & Warr, 1981), which includes items relating to 'job-induced tension', 'somatic tension' and 'general fatigue and uneasiness'. Measures of burnout syndrome (Maslach & Jackson, 1986) can be cast in this assessment tradition.

#### *Psychological Work Stressors Observation Method (Elo, 1994)*

This validated observation method is intended for non-practitioner use and comprises a 13-dimension checklist for the observer.

*(Continued)*

---

### Study Box 8.9    Continued

#### *Ways of Coping Checklist (Lazarus & Folkman, 1984)*

This includes items covering problem-focused and emotion-focused coping styles, and has been adapted to work situations by Dewe (1992).

#### *Occupational Stress Indicator (OSI) (Cooper, Sloan, & Williams, 1988)*

This comprises computerized scales that include items on stress responses and individual-level mediating factors, designed in conjunction with the Cooper and Marshall (1976) stress model. These two measures have also recently been succeeded by the Pressure Management Indicator (Williams & Cooper, 1998).

#### *Occupational Stress Inventory (Osipow & Davis, 1988)*

This looks at three domains of occupational adjustment: occupational stress (occupational environment scale), personal strain, and coping resources. The occupational scale measures role overload, role ambiguity, role insufficiency, role boundary, responsibility and the physical environment.

#### *Stress Assessment Profile (published by Western Psychological Services)*

This measures 14 scales including: perceived stress, lifestyle habits, social support network, coping style, cognitive hardiness, psychological well-being, and response bias. The tool's psychometric properties have been reported in Greene and Nowack (1996).

#### *Job Stress Survey (Vagg & Speilberger, 1998)*

This is designed to assess generic sources of occupational stress, some not considered in previous measures (for example, frequent change, dealing with crisis, critical on-the-spot decisions, frequent interruptions) and assessing both frequency and severity. The items factor into two sets: job pressure and lack of organizational support.

#### *General Well-Being Questionnaire (see Cox & Griffiths, 1995)*

A two-factor measure, including items relating to tiredness, emotional lability and cognitive confusion (this first factor is termed 'worn out'), as well as items relating to worry, fear, tension and physical signs of anxiety (the second factor is termed 'up tight and tense').

#### *Perceived Stress Questionnaire for Young Women (Bell & Lee, 2002)*

This is designed specifically to redress the balance in questionnaires designed on the basis of male stress experiences, looking at the sources and levels of stress among 18–23 year olds.

Quick (1998: 291) offers a taxonomy of what he calls 'construct categories' to help with the process of distinguishing between different aspects of the stress process:

1   demands and stressors;
2   the normal stress response (acute stress);

3   modifiers of the stress response; and

4   the experience of distress (medical, psychological, behavioural) or health out-
    comes, defined as 'enduring negative health states' (Hurrell et al., 1998: 368).

There is also a growing literature on *stress mechanisms* (for example, cognitive appraisal
process, the role of emotion). Occupational *health* psychology has been focused
mainly on identifying workplace demands and stressors and linking them with health
outcomes. Occupational psychology has, on the other hand, been more concerned
with measuring stressors and demands in association with various employee performance variables, including job satisfaction and well-being.

*Demands and stressors*   This construct category pertains to sources of stress known as
'stressors' in the occupational context, defined as 'exposures' within the work environment (associated with certain work conditions) with the potential to impact on
workforce health and well-being (Hurrell et al., 1998: 368). Hurrell et al. (1998)
describe three distinct levels of analysis in association with the study of stressors: physiological, psychological and sociological.

Physiological indicators, including measures of blood pressure, heart rate, serum
cholesterol, cortisol, lipids, catecholamines and insulin function, were originally used
as objective markers of the 'stressor' potential of various work stimuli that bypassed
the need for subjective assessment (for example, Herd, 1988). Nowadays, attempts are
made to distinguish the acute physiological stress response from the chronic response
(Cropley & Millward, 2004).

At the psychological level of analysis, there have been many different attempts to
look at work stressors using self-report and observational methods. Some of the self-
report measures are described in Study Box 8.9, but a more exhaustive and detailed
review of available scales and surveys is provided by Hurrell et al. (1998). These measures vary according to their theoretical orientation, whether they assess global (for
example, Job Stress Survey) or specific (for example, Stress Diagnostic Survey) job
demands, whether they have been evolved to measure stress per se (for example,
Occupational Stress Indicator) or as an integral part of a word design assessment (for
example, Job Content Inventory). There are also many occupation-specific measures
peppering the stress literature (for example, The Doctor Stress Inventory described
by Deary, Blenkin, Agius, Endler, Zealley & Wood, 1996). Choice of measure depends
largely on the purpose of the assessment, as well as the preferred theoretical
perspective.

A common criticism of self-report measures is that they usually only assess the frequency of stress (with the exception of the Job Stress Survey), yet the experience of
stress may normally be a function of severity and/or duration. Another problem is in
the abstract and disconnected nature of stress assessed in this way. For instance, in one
study cited by Hurrell et al. (1998), an interview investigation suggested that for police
officers the experience of job ambiguity was high, which a general stress questionnaire
did not pick up. Interviews were able to identify different sources of job ambiguity
(arising from community, organizational and societal expectations) that are not
tapped by questionnaire measures.

Finally, most of the available measures, with the exception of the Job Stress Survey, are now quite old. Hurrell et al. (1998) question whether they are still relevant today, given radically changed work conditions (for example, continual change, increased cognitive complexity, job uncertainty) and working populations (for example, increased working profile of women, older workers, ethnic minorities). Sarafino (1998), for example, has closely scrutinized the Social Readjustment Rating Scale and second generation Life Events Scale, concluding that they are both culture and gender biased (see also Bell & Lee, 2002). Recently, Iwasaki, MacKay, and Ristock (2004) have argued more forcefully that existing measures are not sufficient for tapping into the *qualitative differences* emerging in research between male and female employees in their experiences of stress.

Observational methods for assessing stressors include the checklist technique (Elo & Vehvilaienen, 1983), the Job-Stress Analysis instrument (Greiner & Lietner, 1989), the Position Analysis Questionnaire (McCormick, Jeanneret & Mecham, 1972) (Study Box 8.10). The main attraction to observational methods is in their supposed objectivity but there are also some drawbacks. For example, observers need to be specially trained and the protocols may need to be adapted to different occupational environments.

---

**Study Box 8.10**

**Observational methods**

*Checklist Method*

Designed for use by occupational health specialists at the Finnish Institute for Occupational Health and Safety, this method requires ratings on 12 different potential stressors on a four-point scale supplemented by interviews with workers and supervisors. The measure has not been widely used outside of Finland.

*Job-Stress Analysis*

Developed at the Technical University of Berlin and based on action regulation theory (Frese & Zapf, 1994), this measure involves worksite observation by a trained observer, using a standard protocol (2–6 hours; Greiner, 1994). The instrument is reported to have good validity and reliability (Greiner, Ragland, Krause, Syme, & Fisher, 1997).

---

*The stress response*   There are various ways in which stress manifests physiologically: cardiovascular problems (increased heart rate, raised blood pressure), stress hormones (for example, increase in catecholamines, cortisol), and immunological indicators (lymphocyte cell counts indicating immunosuppression) (Ogden, 2000). Job strain, for instance, has been associated with higher blood pressure levels in teachers (Cropley et al., 1999), but the validity of this particular indicator of stress per se has been questioned. Using a sample of working adults, Costa et al. (1999) caution that the use of ambulatory blood pressure monitoring can be associated with reduced physical activity during the monitoring day (in part due to self-imposed restrictions) that may seriously undermine the validity of the measure. Heart rate is also affected by many other factors (for example, caffeine intake, dietary influences). Measures of stress hormones and immunological assays are, on the other hand, quite invasive and, moreover, similar issues of construct validity also arise. Stress hormones, for example, work differently in that some react quickly but recover slowly and others react slowly but recover quickly. Important questions of both *sensitivity* and *specificity* of physiological measurement remain to be addressed.

Recent innovations include the use of serum lipids that are found to be associated with emotional and physical burnout (Shirom, Westman, Shamai & Carel, 1997) and plasma fibrinolytic activity (implicated in cardiovascular disease and independent of other risk factors like raised blood pressure, obesity and smoking, making it a relatively 'pure' stress indicator; for example, Ishizaki et al., 1996). Actigraphy has also been recently acknowledged to be a potential source of objective data in the study of stress, enabling activity levels to be monitored across selected environments (Thierry & Jansen, 1998). Essentially, actigraphy records levels of physical activity via a motion-monitoring wristwatch device, and allows a profile of individual activity levels (including sleep patterns) to be constructed and analysed. Advocates of objective measurement generally agree, however, that it is wise to employ a combination of both objective and subjective forms of assessment to ensure validity check (Quick, 1998).

**Stress modifiers**   There are two main categories of stress moderators investigated by researchers: dispositional and situational (as discussed above). Moderators are usually investigated by questionnaire. Whilst there are a number of potential moderators (that can either substantially reduce or increase the relationship between a stressor and its distressing impact), research is said to have yielded 'few substantial conclusions' (Ingledew et al., 1997: 119). Methodological debates surround, in particular, how to measure a 'buffering' effect, especially over time, and sufficiently independently of measures of both the stressors and the strain.

Some have suggested that moderator effects may be *qualitative* not quantitative, and that attempts to test for moderation statistically may miss the point. For instance, *qualitative* differences have been observed between male and female employees in their experiences of stress (Iwasaki et al., 2004; Study Box 8.11).

---

**Study Box 8.11**

**Qualitative approaches to exploring stress experiences**

Iwasaki et al. (2004) used focus groups to look at stress experiences of male and female managers, consistent with the view that this forum offers an effective means of eliciting in-depth information. Iwasaki et al. argue that focus groups also provide a social context for meaning making unique to the study of gender differences in the stress experience. Interestingly, they found that different 'meanings' were inclined to

*(Continued)*

> **Study Box 8.11   Continued**
>
> emerge in different focus group contexts (single-sex, mixed groups) that the authors attributed to different social dynamics. For instance, female managers were more open about the emotional distress they experienced from juggling work and home responsibilities in the female-only groups, whilst male managers were more explicit about their stress experiences in the male-only groups. Other qualitative methods that could be usefully employed for the study of stress include one-to-one in-depth interviews, participant observation, open-ended diaries and case studies (for example, Cohen, Kessler & Underwood, 1997).

*Strain or the Experience of Distress*   Some of the measures described in Study Box 8.9 pertain to the experience of distress. Categories of distress include anxiety (for example, State-Trait Anxiety Inventory), depression (for example, Beck Depression Inventory), burnout (for example, Maslach Burnout Inventory), general psychological distress (for example, General Health Questionnaire), and medical symptoms (for example, Daily Log of Stress Symptoms) (see Hurrell et al., 1998 for a detailed description and review). Other forms of clinical assessment include the Revised Clinical Interview Schedule (CIS-R) (Lewis & Pelosi, 1990). The CIS-R was designed for use by non-clinicians to assess neurotic symptoms (for example, depression, anxiety, fatigue, irritability). Using this interview in a study of 160 teachers, Cropley et al. (1999) looked at the association between job strain and mental health. Findings showed that the prevalence of neurotic symptoms was greater in the high-strain than the low-strain teacher group.

Problems arise in the use of self-report measures of the stress experience when other self-report measures are also used to assess the stressors. In instances like this, it is arguable that measures of the independent and dependent variable are tapping into the same latent construct. For instance, self-report measures of stressors and also distress may comprise items that tap into negative affective (NA), thus confounding the observed stressor–strain association (Costa & MacCrae, 1990). NA describes a pervasive tendency towards negative emotions (Watson & Clark, 1984), which has been directly linked with a predisposition to become emotionally exhausted (direct, additive effect), as well as moderating the association between workload and exhaustion over time (Houkes, Janssen, de Jonge, & Bakker, 2003). Most researchers have, however, concluded that NA is more likely to be a dispositional moderator than a mediator of the stressor–strain equation, although others more cautiously acknowledge that its specific role is unclear (Spector, Chen, & O'Connell, 2000). Buunk et al. (1998) have pointed out that people prone to NA may also be inclined to wrongly attribute 'strains' to the work situation and that, in this instance, sometimes the measure of both stressor and strain may simply be a reflection (at latent level) of their personality.

For this reason, most contemporary stress researchers would advocate a triangulated approach to assessment involving multi-level assessment or 'measurement convergence', particularly given the increasing theoretical emphasis on integrating organizational, psychological and physiological aspects of the occupational stress process (for example, Williams & Cooper, 1998). Triangulation may also involve seeking the views of the worker's employer and his/her family in addition to observed or self-reported results. Kalimo, Lindström & Smith (1997) also point out that measuring other factors such as job design, availability of social support and efficacy of coping strategies may also inform an individual's reported stress experience.

Outstanding issues in the assessment domain concern construct validity (for example, does the measure assess a stressor or strain?), reconciling the importance of reliability with relevance, and how to most appropriately investigate the stress *process* (see Dewe, 2000 for a review and critique). Studies on stress often fail to offer a theoretical rationale for the proposed predictive or associative relationships obtained in, for example, structural equation research. On the issue of process, some have begun to look more closely at the cognitive appraisal processes involved during stress exposure. Dewe (1992) used a critical incident method to elicit written accounts of stressful experiences. Others have introduced a diary component to their study of stress for exploring the dynamics of stress (for example, Cropley & Millward, 2004; Jones & Fletcher, 1996). Diaries can be used to look at both quantitative and qualitative aspects of stress as a daily fluctuating process including so-called spill-over effects from work to home and vice versa (Cohen, Kessler & Underwood, 1997). Longitudinal studies are also appearing, looking in particular at the role of both mediators and moderators on the experience of stress over time (for example, Ingledew et al., 1997). This is consistent with recommendations of looking more closely at within-subject effects in a more detailed way (Buunk et al., 1998). Finally, the impact of stressors on strains is nearly always tested as if the relationship is linear (rather than curvilinear). Yet there are instances where we might otherwise expect a U-shaped relationship (for example, anxiety in association with both high and low job demands).

In a review of over 25 different stress measures, Rick and Briner (2001) argue that there is a need for a fundamental rethink of the way stress is measured at work and how more reliable and valid tools for assessing stress can be developed. Commonly used measures may not be valid. Few, they conclude, have any strongly documented link with health outcomes.

## Summary (VI) and conclusions

- Stress assessment is no easy matter. 'Stressors' are most commonly investigated by questionnaire, as are 'strains'. There is a plethora of measures of both these aspects of stress, choice of which is largely dictated by purpose and theoretical orientation.
- Criticisms of self-report measures of both stressors and strains include the possibility of common underlying variance explained by individual differences in affective tendencies. Measuring and assessing the role of moderators using self-report measures has also been criticized for similar reasons of potential confound and common variance.
- Advocates of a bio-physiological approach argue that there are many objective indicators of stress that can be used as a double check on self-report measures. However, as yet there are no pure bio-physiological measures of stress.

- Others argue that we need to start looking at stress in a more qualitative, ecologically sensitive way using more innovative techniques. Most, however, advocate a more triangulated approach including both qualitative and quantitative methods.

## Stress Management Intervention

The development and implementation of interventions to prevent or ameliorate stress has been a slow process (Kompier et al., 2000). As apparent from the above discussion, diagnosing stress, and in particular burnout, is a complicated matter. It is becoming increasingly popular for organizations to attempt to actively contain and manage 'occupational stress' (Cooper, 2001; Kenny & Cooper, 2003). The British Post Office, for example, introduced an organization-wide employee welfare and counselling scheme in the late 1980s, as a means of tackling stress and improving employee health and well-being (for example, Allison, Cooper, & Reynolds, 1989). Clearly, however, not all employers are so enlightened (Study Box 8.12).

---

### Study Box 8.12

**Organizational cynicism**

In the UK, many organizations have been cynical about stress and have either doubted whether it truly exists or have taken the view that if 'employees cannot stand the heat, they should get out of the fire'. Stress is thus often seen as a weakness and thus a criterion for distinguishing between a good and a bad performer. The term 'stress' is indeed over-used: cynicism may arise in part from its umbrella nature. Both the causes of, and reactions to, stress can be almost anything that one finds difficult to deal with. Vagueness coupled with extreme complexity has meant that it is difficult for organizations to both audit and measure the impact of stress. Nonetheless, the stress issue is a serious one. Recently, Northumberland County Council had to pay £200,000 in compensation for failing to take responsibility for a stressed employee.

---

Some concern has been expressed that so-called 'stress management' interventions (SMIs) are merely temporary solutions (that is, individual-level, empowering workers to cope better) to more fundamental problems of stress generated and maintained by the organization (Giga et al., 2003; see also Chapter 6). Stress management interventions also tend to assume homogeneity of stress reaction, yet evidence indicates that different groups of employees are differentially exposed to stress and also vary widely in their reactions (Ross & Altmaier, 1994; see also Schabracq, Cooper, Travers, & van Maanen, 2001 for a review).

Bunce (1997), Schabracq et al. (2001) and Jones and Bright (2002) all describe in detail the various individual- (Study Box 8.13) and organizational-focused approaches to stress management within the workplace (Study Box 8.14).

## Study Box 8.13

### Individual-focused stress management interventions

- *Educational* – provide a conceptual overview of stress, its causes and its outcomes.
- *Stress counselling* – see Chapter 6.
- *Cognitive–behavioural* – address individuals' interpretations and reactions to stress experiences. Murphy (1988) explains that these interventions assume that cognition, emotion and behaviour are causally related, and that an individual's expectancies, beliefs and attributions can predict behavioural consequences. An example intervention is provided by Meichenbaum's (1985) stress inoculation training.
- *Arousal reduction* – involves relaxation training to reduce arousal responses to the stress stimulus. Variants include Benson's (1985) Respiratory One Meditation (ROM), Clinically Standardised Meditation (Carrington, 1978), Progressive Muscle Relaxation (Bernstein & Borkovec, 1983) and biofeedback, in the form of electromyography, electroencephalography or blood pressure measurement (Ivancevich & Matteson, 1998).
- *Personal skills training* – to reduce experienced stress by enhancing self-esteem and self-efficacy (which act as mediators of the stress experience). Interventions may include assertiveness, time management or negotiation skills, although these are matched closely with the underlying source of stress for each individual.
- *Debriefing* – specific to post-accident or near accident scenarios involving any number of workers (who may be emergency services personnel, or victims of accidents or violence at work) intended to avert severe post-traumatic stress disorders in workers by debriefing each individual within two hours post-event (Flannery, 2001). Violence at work is increasingly of concern within the general domain of health and safety research (Watson, Williams, & Ball, 2001). Kalimo et al. (1997) suggest that similar interventions may equally well be applied to serious organizational 'traumas', such as downsizing and mergers, where employees may experience elevated stress levels and need to be briefed as to the nature of the crisis.

## Study Box 8.14

### Organization-focused stress management interventions

Sauter, Murphy and Hurrell (1990) divide organizational-level interventions into four:

- *Job design* – to improve working conditions (that is, addressed to role and job characteristics, interpersonal relationships, organizational structure and climate and human resource management (HRM) systems). Bunce (1997) suggest that workers should be encouraged to identify workplace stressors and then alleviate or modify them by altering their work methods, their approach to interacting and dealing with others, or their work environment. Jobs can be enriched

*(Continued)*

> **Study Box 8.14　Continued**
>
> quantitatively (for example, reduced number of clients) and qualitatively (for example, mixing case loads so that no one staff member is left to deal with one particular type of 'difficult' client). Job redesign may also involve a change in work schedules (for example, compressed working week, flexitime, job sharing), which allows employees the opportunity to realign themselves with their non-work responsibilities.
> * *Surveillance of psychological disorders and risk factors*
> * *Information dissemination* (for example, newsletters on coping with stress and on how to promote wellness)
> * *Training* (for example, training in stress management techniques for self and others (see Chapter 2))

Ross and Altmeier (1994) advocate an organizational intervention model comprising four elements, each argued to influence the relationship between stress and performance (and addressing many of the areas discussed earlier): task stress; operation of other stressors; a coping process; and an indicator of stress.

Intervention is targeted accordingly:

* *Task stress* – stress associated with a primary task (for example, responsibility for people, ambiguity, physical danger). Intervention may include job and role clarification to alleviate role ambiguity (for example, Ivancevich & Matteson, 1998).
* *Surrounding stressors* – 'surrounding' stressors associated with the job though not directly (for example, poor co-worker relationships, career concerns, home–work conflict). Three strategies for dealing with stressors are: decentralization (devolution of decision making and responsibility downwards), participative decision making (strategies encouraging involvement in decision making) and climate surveys (to elicit employee reactions and preferences to aid managers in identifying key issues and problems) (Ross & Altmeier, 1994: 102–107).
* *Coping process* – a behaviour that reduces the stress experienced by an individual (for example, developing a more efficient method of task completion, negotiating help or support).
* *Stress indicator* – observation of task performance by a manager to estimate 'stress' experiences (for example, increased errors, increased length of time taken to complete a task).

Changes to HRM systems in connection with stress can include: ensuring new employees know what to expect (for example, through the use of realistic preview), systematic socialization (or 'breaking in'), goal setting and performance feedback (affording a sense of movement and progress and reduced feelings of uncertainty), stress-management training, career-development strategies, work–family programmes and special employee assistance programmes (EAPs) (see Chapter 6 for details).

Unfortunately many organizations rely solely on either one or other specific strategy as the basis for intervention (Ross & Altmeier, 1994). Giga et al. (2003) maintain that stress management that only teaches coping skills (Study Box 8.13) does not warrant being called *stress* management. All intervention, however, must be built into a larger organizational intervention strategy along the lines described by Murphy, Hurrell, Sauter and Keita (1995).

However, it should be said that even organizations that do try to address 'organizational level' stress do not necessarily demonstrate much beneficial impact either (for example, Hart & Cotton, 2003; Taris et al., 2003). These findings may in part be attributable to methodological difficulties (Taris et al., 2003), but it may also be because of 'fundamental flaws' in the way stress management is conducted (Kenny & Cooper, 2003). For instance, organizations implementing family-responsive policies without underpinning these policies with any true cultural change (valuing work–family balance, supportive supervisor referrals) are unlikely to be sufficient for stress reduction (Casper, Fox, Sitzmann, & Landy, 2004).

Cox and Howart (1990) conceptualize healthy organizations at the 'cultural' level: those organizations that truly invest in the development of staff, in providing a reasonable level of job security and promotional prospects, in introducing people-centred technology to the workplace, and in equitably recognizing and rewarding staff are likely to experience lower staff stress levels than those companies who do not invest in such things.

Sadly, reviewing the evidence on 'occupational stress and its management', Kenny and Cooper (2003: 275) end with a pessimistic statement that whilst there is generally 'a lack of good research on stress management interventions', what little evidence does exist indicates that currently 'there are few benefits to workplaces' implementing stress-management programmes (see also Giga et al., 2003). Resignedly, they contemplate discarding the concept of occupational stress (because it 'has had its day') and that from an intervention point of view, a focus on occupational stressors and worker fatigue might be more productive (since 'there is a point where even the most resilient worker will break down'; Kenny & Cooper, 2003: 278). In other words, intervention, simply put, will involve removing the offending stressor.

## Summary (VII) and conclusions

- Organizations have been slow to take their responsibility for stress prevention and management seriously. Whether intervention is individually or organizationally focused, many depend on the organization's position on this matter.
- Conceptualized as a personal matter, intervention will be designed to facilitate better coping. Conceptualized as at least in part an organizational-level responsibility, a more preventative approach may be taken, involving a shift in culture from survival of the fittest to collective support.
- Whilst most of the interventions are directed at the individual level, even those taking a more preventative line do not appear to yield the intended benefits. This may, in part, be attributable to difficulties with evaluation. Key players in the field are now wondering whether stress management has become too complicated.

## Stress recovery after Work

It has recently been suggested that speed of recovery following a stress response may be more important to the aetiology of ill-health than the reactions themselves. Findings show that it is accumulated stress that is associated with health problems (Kuper & Marmot, 2003). Evidence also suggests that this can occur when employees experience impaired physiological recovery during non-work time (Cropley et al., 1999). Failure to recover may be explained in part by difficulty 'unwinding' after work from high-strain jobs (for example, Cropley & Millward, 2004; Sluiter, van der Beek, & Frings-Dresen, 1999).

Cropley and Millward (2004) operationalized difficulty unwinding with reference to the concept of cognitive rumination (perseverative thinking about work), and tested the unwinding hypothesis using a diary method with a sample of teachers whose jobs are well known to be stressful. High-strain teachers did indeed find it difficult to stop thinking about work, thought more about future work-related tasks, and thought more about something that had happened at work over the last few days, in comparison with low-strain teachers. They also took longer to disengage from work-related matters over the course of the evening. In this study, rumination was conceptualized as a proxy for insufficient recovery, but it might also be a mediator in the stressor-strain relationship.

### Returning to work after absence

A relatively understudied yet critical issue also concerns that of 'returning to work' after long-term sickness absence (Noordsy, Torrey, Mueser, Mead, O'Keefe, & Fox, 2002; Study Box 8.15). Research suggests both organizational and personal factors are involved in whether an employee returns to work. For example, when supervisors are more considerate and supportive, return to work programmes are more likely to be successful (Secker & Membery, 2003). Return to work is also facilitated when there is a 'return to work action plan' in which specific strategies and resources are identified (Shrey & Mital, 2000). Such an action plan should explore the physical and psychosocial dimensions of the job, the receptivity of the employer, and the accommodations needed to facilitate a safe and timely return to work. On a more personal front, Borkin and colleagues (2000) found that an optimistic attitude ('recovery is possible and needs faith') is more frequently associated with successful rehabilitation than a pessimistic attitude ('recovery is difficult and differs among people').

### Summary (VIII) and conclusions

- Research on recovery has begun to look closely at the stress response, and factors that switch it from being a normal and healthy reaction to being a chronic source of ill-health.
- On another little studied area of investigation, not much is known about the processes of returning to work after long-term absence.

# Workplace Accidents and Safety

The topic of workplace safety and accident involvement is inextricably linked with research on human error, system design and automation (Chapter 7). Pheasant (1995) reports around 400 industrial fatalities per year in the UK, equating to a death rate of 1.5 per 100,000 across the UK population. In addition, there are many thousands of instances of workplace accidents every year. Pheasant reports that 16,000 workers in the UK are seriously injured every year, with more than 150,000 sustaining injuries serious enough to prevent them from coming into work for three days or more.

Over 50 percent of workplace fatalities occur from either a fall from height, or by workers being struck either by moving vehicles or moving/falling objects. For non-fatal accidents on the other hand, manual handling/carrying tasks and slips, trips and falls appear to be responsible for over 50 percent of reported accidents. Despite the availability of 'causal' accident data such as this, it says little about the *underlying pre-determinants*.

## Accidents: Definitions and critical factors

An accident can be defined as the *unplanned outcome* of inappropriate action – that is, accidents are avoidable. Pheasant (1991, 1995) describes two main perspectives on accident analysis, as follows:

- *Theory A* – accidents are caused by *unsafe behaviour* (for example, lack of risk awareness, foolhardy attitude to risks, lack of training in safe practice, lack of supervision) and can be prevented by modifying the ways in which people behave (that is, fitting the person to the job). Pheasant (1995) says that human error is responsible for the majority of accidents at work. However, not all errors or unsafe behaviours result in accidents. Errors are frequent and often go unnoticed (Frese, 1998: 644). If errors become associated with benefits (for example, increasing output rate and associated financial return), unsafe behaviours are *reinforced* over time.
- *Theory B* – accidents are caused by *unsafe systems of work*; they may therefore be prevented by redesigning the working system. This includes a safe working environment, plant and equipment, procedures and working practices and assigning competent personnel.

Pheasant (1995) describes two classes of error: errors of judgement in the appraisal of risk and errors of execution in the performance of the working task. Errors of execution, however, are most commonly system induced, in that deficiencies in the design of the working system (most typically at the human–machine interface) make the operator's working task more difficult and render him/her more error-prone. Errors are distinct from violations (which are deliberate) or faults (which arise from the machine itself) (Frese & Zapf, 1994).

## Theories of accident causation

Theoretical models of accident causation can be discussed under the following headings: accident proneness, risk perception, learning models, and stress models.

***Accident proneness***  Sanders and McCormick (1993) identify two versions of 'accident prone' theory, both assuming unequal initial liability: one that says that certain individuals are innately prone to accidents irrespective of task, working conditions, time or other factors, and the other that says that all individuals vary in their propensity to accidents depending on their 'functional state'. However, it has been demonstrated that when factors like exposure to job hazards, age and type of job are controlled for, there is no evidence at all for the concept of an 'accident prone' individual (Mohr & Clemmer, 1988). Also the use of temporal reliability calculations to infer the individual stability of accident proneness tends to conflate association with cause.

A more realistic view of accident proneness is that people are more or less prone to accidents in specific situations and that this changes over time, depending on the interaction between the person and the environment (Garis, 2001). This has been termed 'accident-liability theory' and finds evidence in data which shows higher accident rates, for example, in younger relatively inexperienced, rather than older workers. Also, whilst no single measure of personality has been found to consistently predict accident occurrence (Chmiel, 2000), Hansen (1989) reported that two personality variables, social maladjustment and neuroticism, were good predictors of accident occurrence in a study of chemical plant workers.

***Risk perception***  Perceived probability or likelihood of injury or death predicts the degree to which an individual takes precautionary actions to prevent accidents (Sanders & McCormick, 1993). The perception and evaluation of risk (for example, likelihood of injury) or the frequency of injury associated with technological risks has been extensively studied by Slovic, Fischoff, & Lichtenstein (1980). Whilst risk perception for more common accidents and injuries has been less widely studied, Slovic et al.'s (1980) risk perception principles may still apply (Study Box 8.15).

---

**Study Box 8.15**

**Decision biases in risk perception**

Many decisions made in organizational contexts are programmed (that is, pursued using standard operating procedures, rule books and manuals), but there are also many others that are not (that is, non-routine, ill-structured) (Vecchio, 1995). It is important to distinguish between ideas about how people *should* make decisions (normative theories) and ideas about *how they actually make decisions in practice* (normative versus descriptive theories). The classical decision making (CDM) approach is built on two sets of theoretical assumptions: formal theory (which focuses on the decision event, prescribing the optimal choice from a fixed set of known alternatives) and normative role (which represents CDM as an abstract system of propositions designed to describe the choices of an ideal hypothetical decision maker, for example, one who is computationally omnipotent and motivated by economic utility). The implication of these models is that decision making is rational and utilitarian.

| Study Box 8.15   Continued |
| --- |

Simon (1957), however, argued that rationality is bounded by cognitive limitations, especially in highly complex decision environments. He said that people largely use a 'satisficing' approach, choosing 'good enough' solutions. Evidence from some of the classic work, however, also pointed to deviations from normative theory even in simple tasks that do not tax people cognitively (for example, Kahneman, Slovic, & Tversky, 1982). Research has also shown that the way a problem is presented (or framed) can radically change the decision that is made. If a decision outcome is presented and perceived as positive, a risk-averse decision is more likely. If the same outcome is presented and perceived negatively, then a risk-taking decision is more likely.

In the context of risk judgement, there is a tendency to overestimate low-frequency events and underestimate high-frequency events. This bias is driven by the use of heuristics, or rules of thumb, to make decisions, including the following:

- the *availability heuristic* – refers to the use of readily available cognitive 'schemas' about events or risks (for example, aircraft crash media coverage will increase the accessibility of available schema and consequently increase biases in probabilistic judgements of their occurrence);
- *illusory bias* in self-judgements – for example, unrealistic optimism, assumptions of invincibility which make people more likely to engage in risky behaviour in the mistaken belief that they have mastery of the situation;
- *acceptability of risk* – people will accept a higher level of risk if an activity is voluntary, the level of risk is controllable, the hazards are known and understood and the consequences are immediate.

Naturalistic decision making (NDM) openly acknowledges and applauds the use of heuristics in the decision-making process in difficult situations, as having been built from valid experience rather than being indicative of failure and poor decision making (see **www.sagepub.co.uk/millward** for more details on NDM). As Klein (1998: 13) points out, NDM is much less concerned than classic approaches are with the 'moment of choice' (that is, choosing between various decision options). The issue for the experienced person is to appropriately 'categorize the situation'. Thus NDM researchers are interested in the way people represent situations within context. Heuristics include recognition/meta-cognition (Cohen, Freeman & Thompson, 1997) and the so-called RAWFS heuristic (where each letter denotes a coping strategy for dealing with uncertainty). Recognition/meta-cognition is used when recognition fails (and the stakes are high), as a means of identifying and correcting the gaps in situation awareness, to check unwarranted assumptions, and to reconcile multiple goals. RAWFS, on the other hand, stands for reducing uncertainty, assumption-based reasoning, weighing up the pros and cons, forestalling and suppressing. The application of NDM approaches to risk perception and judgement is yet to be explored in the context of accident analysis, perhaps because the emphasis is less on error than on expertise.

Sanders and McCormick (1993) suggest that judgement biases may explain people's overestimation of risks attached to aircraft and nuclear power accidents, in that these risk sources are regarded as being outside people's perceived control. Biased judgements of controllability may have the adverse impact of inappropriate engagement in high-risk activities. Flin, Mearns, Fleming and Gordon (1996) found that a sample of offshore workers perceived greater risk from a platform explosion or a strike from a passing ship than from slipping, tripping and falling accidents. These findings suggest that perceived level of control over risk is instrumental in perceptions of overall risk.

*Learning models* Learning models draw on the idea that unsafe work behaviours are more socially acceptable than safe work behaviours. Case Study 8.1 highlighted the risk to construction workers of cement dermatitis that can be easily prevented by wearing gloves. However, workers who were made aware of this risk were nonetheless reluctant to wear gloves because they are seen as a sign of weakness in a male-dominated environment. In this way, unsafe behaviour is culturally reinforced and perpetuated.

Östberg (1980) demonstrated how unsafe behaviour can be socially perpetuated in a study of tree-fellers. Despite their wide knowledge and understanding of the risks involved in unsafe work behaviours, fellers often broke safety rules due to the encouragement of the existing piecework system which rewarded unsafe behaviour with increased remuneration. Östberg reported that the lenient attitude towards safety of supervisors also compounded this situation.

*Stress/arousal models* Arousal theory (Brown, 1995) posits that accidents happen when arousal is either lower (for example, when a worker is under-loaded, bored or drowsy) or higher than average (for example, when a worker is anxious or excessively motivated) (Moore, 1995; Figure 8.3). Brown (1995), however, cautions that stress and arousal should not be confused. In this context, he argues that stress is by definition harmful, whilst arousal may or may not be harmful depending on its level.

Pheasant (1991) points to other transient states as potential contributors to accident occurrence, including alcohol use and certain drugs, which both slow the individual's reactions and change his/her attitude towards risk and fatigue (MacDonald, 1997). Although the exact link between accidents and stress is not clear, many writers postulate a role played by stress and anxiety in accident causation. Cox and Cox (1993) speculate on a mediating role. There is some evidence to suggest that 'tension' can mediate the impact of organizational factors on safe behaviour (Tomas, Melia, Oliver & Sese, 1993).

Oliver, Cheyne, Tomas, and Cox (2002) tested the hypothesis that one's current state of health may create a predisposition to an accident using a measure of general health (anxiety and depression subscales) across a range of industries in the Valencia region of Spain. They confirmed that general health was a significant *mediator* (along with safe behaviour) of the impact of organizational and environmental factors on accident rate.

## Integrative models of accident causation

Mearns and Flin (1995) developed an integrative model of accident causation incorporating both individual- and organizational-level factors (Figure 8.4). Numerous factors

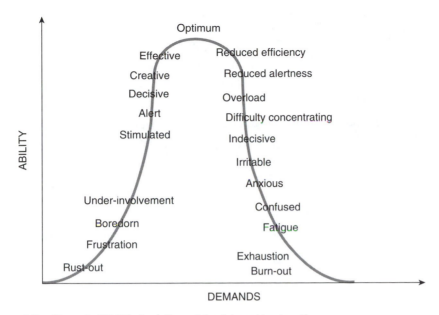

**Figure 8.3**  Moore's (1995) depiction of the 'stress' trade-off

Moore, R.S. (1995). *Improving organisational performance through the management of stress.*
Copyright © 1995 Richard Moore MBA/Anglia Polytechnic University

are said to influence an individual's response to a hazardous situation. At the risk assessment phase, for example, an individual's knowledge, perceptions of self-efficacy, past experience and adaptation to the work environment are critical. Attitudes to risk (mediating the relationship between risk assessment and selected behaviour) may include affective responses to the workplace (for example, general satisfaction with job and with existing safety processes) but may also be influenced by management's and co-workers' demonstrated commitment to safety (the predominant safety culture existing within the workplace).

Hofmann and Stetzer (1996) have found likewise that both group-organizational-level (group process, safety climate, and intentions to approach other team members engaged in unsafe acts) and individual-level factors (perceptions of role overload) are involved in accident causation in their research within a chemical processing plant.

It is generally agreed that accidents and errors are most likely to be 'caused' by a number of contributory factors that may interact in unexpected and unpredictable ways. This is based on the rationale that accidents are caused by *latent failures* in the system, perhaps building up over a long time. As Wagenaar and Hudson (1998: 68) put it, 'accidents are at the end of a long chain starting with a fallible decision' (Study Box 8.16). That is, latent failures come from managerial decisions (or indecisions) 'taken earlier, and often elsewhere' ... 'hidden from view, waiting to create a failure when it is least wanted' (p. 83). Formal enquiries into, for example, the Three Mile Island accident (Rogovin, 1979) revealed many 'latent failures' that pointed to the inevitability of the accident. Accidents occur either when local problems (or triggers)

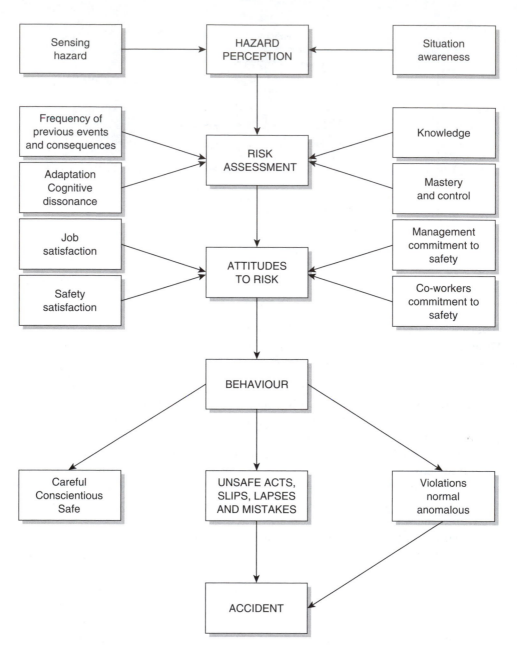

**Figure 8.4** Mearns and Flin's (1995) socio-cognitive model of risk perception

Adapted from Mearns, K. & Flin, R. (1995). Risk perception and attitudes to safety by personnel in the offshore oil and gas industry: a review. *Journal of Loss Prevention in the Process Industries, 8,* 299–305.

occur that mismatch with system-level factors, or because of 'latent errors' occurring after the error has taken place that furnish the likelihood it will have negative and even disastrous consequences (Frese, 1998).

---

**Study Box 8.16**

**Group think at the root of some major disasters**

In principle, group decision making allows for the pooling of resources, the genera-tion of more and better solutions and wider acceptance within the group. However, group decisions are not always of a better quality. For instance Janis (1972), whose work on *groupthink* is described in Chapter 4, showed that closely knit groups pose pressures on members to achieve consensus, even if this means sacrificing one's own critical thinking in favour of what the group demands. Group process may be dominated by certain members within the group, resistance against which can cause conflict. Groupthink is said to be responsible for many political (for example, Bay of Pigs) and technical disasters (for example, shuttle disasters) (see Brotherton, 1999 for a review). Similarly, Foushee (1984) noted the reluctance of cockpit officers to question the decisions of the pilot, in many instances with often fatal results. This reluctance was attributed to the culture of hierarchy and authoritarian leader-ship. Ultimately, the benefits of group decision making over individual decision mak-ing are likely to depend heavily on several factors, including the quality of the leadership and the composition of the group itself (for example, expertise, resource, personality).

There are many prescriptions for how to optimize the quality of decisions made in group contexts (see **www.sagepub.co.uk/millward** for examples), but little evi-dence to suggest either that they work or that one particular technique is any better than another.

---

Latent failures include (Wagenaar & Hudson, 1998: 79–80):

- *design* (equipment, work areas) – that does not take account of the human factor;
- *lack of optimal fit between human and machine* (see Chapter 7);
- *defences* – missing pieces of the most obvious defence including protective clothing (see Case Study 8.1), alarms, rescue plans, and so on;
- *error enforcing conditions* – the working conditions are suboptimal (for example, working under extreme conditions, shift work, insufficient knowledge or skill);
- *housekeeping* – management has little practical grip on what is going on;
- *procedures* – no clear, accurate or comprehensible procedures available to reduce or contain risks, or perhaps even too many procedures and not enough initiative taking;
- *maintenance management* – failure to perform maintenance, no proper maintenance strategy (for example, as in the Piper Alpha disaster);
- *training* – under- or over-qualified workers;
- *communication* – systems that break down or communication system not clear (for example, as in the Piper Alpha disaster when satellite platforms continued to pump oil and gas into the burning platform because they were unaware of the disaster);
- *organization* – the structure may not be appropriate for the task and/or the people; too much structure can mean over reliance on procedures and abdication of responsibility;

- *incompatible goals* – inappropriate balance between production and safety because of cost-cutting (that is, production norms prevail).

The above constitutes a means for diagnosing an organization's 'failure state' (or accident likelihood). Some argue, like Redmill (1997), that 'the best chance of safety occurs not simply when a special effort is made but when a pervasive safety culture exists in an organisation', thereby reducing the likelihood of 'an accident simply waiting to happen'.

## Safety cultures

Corporate safety and health consultants suggest that, in recent times, most organizations' safety strategies have been entrenched in 'safety by compliance', rather than 'prevention by planning'. This translates into after-the-fact hazard detection. The Health and Safety Commission (1993) described safety cultures as:

> the product of the individual and group values, attitudes, competencies and patterns of behaviour that determine the commitment to, and the style and proficiency of, an organisation's health and safety programmes. (p. 4)

As Redmill (1997) points out, short-lived interventions may not lead to long-term accident reduction since such approaches do not address the values and norms that underpin behaviour at work (see Chapter 5 for a detailed discussion of the culture concept). Hofmann & Stetzer (1996), for example, reported that perceptions of safety climate within a chemical processing plant were found to be directly related to incidence of unsafe behaviours (at individual and team level), and to incidence of accidents at team level. Recent work on safety culture in a nuclear processing plant by Harvey and colleagues has since reported likewise (Harvey, Erdos, Bolam, Cox, Kennedy, & Gregory, 2002).

Redmill (1997) suggests that safety cultures can only be achieved with the full support of senior management, integration into company policy decisions, and propagation and maintenance by all levels of staff within the company. He argues that three elements are necessary for the successful introduction and retention of a safety culture:

- *Awareness* – designing for functionality may often be at the expense of safety. The King's Cross underground disaster in the UK is a catastrophic illustration of the effects of chronic under-staffing of a station and under-training of station staff (both results of cost-saving measures) when faced with an emergency situation (Donald & Canter, 1992). Thus, awareness of safety issues must be introduced into the design process, the training and day-to-day operation of safety-critical systems of any kind, from factory floor, to office environment, to underground railway system (Case Study 8.4).

**Case Study 8.4: Safety awareness programme**

Davies, Haines, Norris and Wilson (1998) describe a safety awareness programme run by Greater Manchester Police to heighten awareness of psychological and safety factors involved in police driving. The programme included the following stages:

1  explanation of the nature of traffic accidents in general and of police vehicle accidents in particular, supported by an illustrative video;
2  discussion of the consequences of accidents underpinned by Sutton's (1982) work on fear arousal and behavioural change;
3  examining how driver attitude may impact on driving performance in terms of risk-taking and speed;
4  exploring facets of attention relevant to driving and fatigue;
5  stress and impact on driving – including stress management ideas;
6  evaluating transfer of training.

Wilson reports that following introduction of the training programme in 1994, emergency 'blameworthy' accidents (accidents where police drivers were at fault) fell by 3 percent between 1993 and 1994 and by a further 2 percent between 1994 and 1995. In addition, two to three times the number of blameworthy accidents were reported in staff groups who had not been trained than in those who had received the training.

- *Commitment* – Redmill (1997) argues that 'the development of a culture can be directed and led, but it cannot be forced' (see Chapter 5 on culture change). Accident reporting and analysis is said to be a visible demonstration of managerial commitment to safe work environments (Study Box 8.17; Chmiel (2000) and O'Toole (2002)). Vredenburgh (2002) found that a proactive (as opposed to reactive) approach to managing accidents significantly differentiated between hospitals with low and high injury rates. Shared perception among managers and staff of the importance of safety is an integral part of this proactive approach (Clarke, 1999; Gillen, Baltz, Gassel, Kirsch, & Vaccaro, 2002; Mearns, Flin & O'Connor, 2001). In a proactive safety environment, supervisors are more likely to demonstrate they care about safety, employees are made aware of dangerous working practices and have received detailed safety instruction, and there are regular safety meetings.
- *Competence* – Redmill (1997) argues that there is a need for organizations to appreciate and address their limitations and constraints, whether of knowledge, experience, facilities, or resources, and so on. Safety competence may require training, retraining, a wide and detailed knowledge of the working system, and human appreciation of the limits of their competence with the system. In the Kegworth air crash in 1989, the pilots misinterpreted a cockpit display and shut down the wrong engine and then failed to notice the reading on the left-hand engine vibration indicator, largely due to a lack of simulator training with this new equipment (DoT, 1990).

Zohar (2003) describes a multi-level model of safety climate (as opposed to culture) that links it to safety behaviour, injury rates and also health outcomes. The model details various contextual correlates of safety climates including leadership style, job characteristics and technological factors. Leadership style is consistently found to be critical to safety climate (for example, Barling, Lughlin, & Kelloway, 2002). Pertinent job characteristics include job autonomy, role overload, job control, supervisor support, training adequacy and communication quality (Parker, Axtell, & Turner, 2001). Along similar lines, Varonen and Mattila (2000) found a significant association between safety climate and accident rate across eight wood-processing companies. Mearns and Flin (2001) maintain a distinction between safety culture and safety climate (see Chapter 5). Their review of the literature showed that whilst the two terms are often used interchangeably, they are conceptually distinct (albeit related) constructs and should be treated accordingly. Mearns and Flin (2001) describe safety climate as employee perceptions, attitudes and beliefs about risk and safety. Safety culture, on the other hand, pertains to more enduring values, norms, assumptions and expectations surrounding safety, and may reflect in safety climate. For example, Mearns, Whitaker and Flin (2001) found that unsafe behaviour in the offshore industry was predicted by perceptions of pressures for production.

O'Toole (2002) demonstrates how culture and climate work together to promote safety by prevention as a core company value. The most significant factor O'Toole (2002) linked with reduced injury rates was change in senior management attitude with particular emphasis on safety leadership and commitment to safety. The company culture (comprising perceived organizational commitment to safety, participation in safety management initiatives, effective education and training) was visible through surveys that tapped 'climate' (perceptions and attitudes towards management practices). O'Toole (2002) argued that safety climate was, in this instance, reflective of deeper cultural processes.

Oliver et al. (2002) evaluated directly the relative power of individual and organizational factors in accounting for safe individual behaviour across a range of industries in the Valencia area of Spain. Safe behaviour was strongly predicted by employees' evaluations of their organizational involvement in safety. Employees also perceived organizational and work environment variables to be closely interrelated, suggesting that organizational involvement may provide a context in which to assess physical hazards. The findings were interpreted as highlighting once again the critical importance of management commitment to, and action on, safety issues. Note also that, in this study, both *safe behaviour* (taking shortcuts, following rules, safety versus speed, using safety equipment) and *general health* predicted accident rate (near misses, minor accidents, up to three days off, and severe accidents).

Chalk, Donald and Young (1997) describe a major team-level intervention in a UK electricity generating company. Goal-setting techniques were adopted within teams to address and improve each area of safety of concern. Self-reported accident rates fell from just under 24 percent to 9 percent in the years prior to, and following, the introduction of the intervention. Interestingly, absenteeism and sick leave figures also dropped markedly over the same period. Chalk et al. (1997) suggest that the intervention succeeded due to its democratic inclusion of all staff levels and disciplines.

Geller, Roberts & Gilmore (1996) likewise found that employees must perceive a certain level of control or mastery over the safety system if they are to commit to implementing and maintaining it.

---

**Study Box 8.17**

### Accident Reporting and Analysis

Accident reporting systems are a legal obligation of employers. Data can then inform subsequent analysis and, ultimately, be fed back into safety systems (and to employees) and assist in identifying the remaining needs of the organization or system in achieving its desired safety culture (in terms of, for example, training, system design and communication needs; Chmiel, 2000). Brown (1995) argues that accident reporting must be *purposeful* (useful and useable), *adequate* (pertaining to all types of accident and *not only those which result in human injury), factual* (versus attributing blame) and *task-specific*.

The recording of antecedent behaviour is crucial to purposeful accident recording (for example, black box flight recorders). Accident analysis can then examine the range of behaviours exhibited during an accident, its causes, and its context (Smith et al., 2001).

Brown (1995) advocates the use of human error modelling techniques by safety practitioners. For instance, Edkins and Pollack (1997) used Reason's Generic Error Modelling System (GEMS) to investigate rail mishaps, finding that 'skill-based' errors (that is, reduced driver vigilance) were more common than rule-based or knowledge-based errors. Hobbs and Williamson (2002), by contrast, found that rule-based and knowledge-based errors were more common than skill-based errors in aircraft mechanics.

---

### *Behavioural change approaches*

Grindle, Dickinson and Boettcher (2000) provide a comprehensive, largely positive review of 18 behavioural safety programmes in manufacturing settings. Geller and colleagues (Geller, 2002; Boyce & Geller, 2001) suggest a number of behaviour-based interventions designed to encourage employees to take responsibility for their own safety performance and to foster self-monitoring (Olson & Austin, 2002). These include:

- *Procedural checklists* – checklists have now been introduced as a standard procedure in many industries, including aircraft and military operations.
- *Error management* – this 'damage limitation' approach derives from action theory (Frese & Zapf, 1994) and requires that employees are trained to actively *avoid the negative consequences of error* by dealing with them quickly, and learning from the experience to reduce the likelihood of error reoccurrence (Frese, 1998). This approach relies on the distinction between an 'error' (for example, drug miscalculation in medicine) and the 'error consequences' (for example, there may be no noticeable impact but the implications of drug overdose could have been fatal). Error prevention attempts to reduce the likelihood of action errors, whilst error

management focuses on reducing the negative consequences of error when it does occur. Effective error management requires a learning attitude and an ability (and motivation) to detect error early (Frese, 1998).

- *Training* – in safe behaviours (not just the avoidance of unsafe behaviour; Goldenhar, Moran, & Colligan, 2001).
- *Feedback/praise* – following desired safe working behaviour, to act as reinforcement (see also, Cooper, Phillips, Sutherland, & Makin, 1994).
- *Communication of risk* – Sell (1997), for instance, found that posters placed in areas where the target safety behaviour was to be adopted (in a steel mill) resulted in a 15–20 percent improvement in workers adopting the target behaviour, which continued across a series of follow-up trials. On this basis, Sell recommended that risk communication must be specific to a particular task/situation, backed up by training, instructional, positioned close to where the target behaviour is to be promoted, and built on existing attitudes and knowledge. Communication should not involve shock tactics (arousing defensive behaviour) or be too general (lessening the applicability of the communication) (see Chapter 5).

Frese (1998) argues that an appropriate balance must be struck between error prevention and error management. Organizations that focus on error prevention without paying attention to error management tend to sanction error and assign blame (Case Study 8.5). This may mean that errors are not detected or the error and its potential consequences are denied. The agenda behind this might even be a sinister one, to maintain professional power and credibility. In the medical professional, there is a long-established history of 'error' concealment. Frese (1998) cautions that organizations like this lose the ability to detect and take responsibility for error, and to respond constructively to error when it noticeably does arise.

---

**Case Study 8.5: A case of 'blame'...**

The consistent and reliable reporting of errors in the UK NHS is critical to the smooth running of hospitals, since shortcomings in any area (for example, prescription dispensing, identification or administration) can be potentially life-threatening for patients. However, in many UK hospitals, the error reporting system does not encourage nursing staff to accurately report the number of errors or 'critical incidents' that have occurred during a given work period. A 'blame' culture exists, such that whilst nursing staff may *not* be at fault for an erroneous dosage of medication (for example, the original prescription may have been incorrect), nurses invariably take the 'blame' since they are at the front line. As a result, nurses are often reticent to report errors in the belief that doing so may damage their career or reputation.

---

### Summary (VIII) and conclusions

- Safety management has become an important topic for psychologists in recent years. Accident analysis provides a descriptive benchmark for organizations against which to pursue improvements.

- Analyses of accident causation point to individual sources of unsafe practice (accident proneness, stress, bad habits, risky behaviour) as well as system-level failures in that the accident is merely a symptom of various latent organizational factors (arising from poor managerial decision making).
- Error management (as a complement to error prevention) requires the development of a culture that is prepared to actively detect errors, deal with them quickly and learn from them. An organization that sanctions errors will cultivate a climate of error concealment, which may be the immediate cause of an accident (because of error escalation), rather than the error itself.
- As with many areas of intervention, it is generally agreed that it is at the *organizational* level of analysis that attention should be focused when addressing safety management.

## Future Research Challenges

- aspects of the *physical environment* in association with health and well-being, including the idea of a 'sick building' and the 'green office';
- the role of emotion in stress and coping;
- the concept of emotional labour in association with burnout;
- compare the relative validity of different models of workplace stress (for example, demand–control relative to effort–reward);
- link effort–reward theory with the concept of psychological contract;
- investigate appraisal theory;
- develop innovative ways of assessing stress and coping that are ecologically sensitive and allow for the temporal dimension;
- apply social constructionist ideas to the concept of coping;
- explore further the moderating role of gender in the stress process;
- look closely at the concept of perceived control and its role in the stress process;
- explore further the concept of support, its assessment and practical implications;
- evaluate different types of stress intervention;
- investigate the health and safety issues of teleworkers;
- evaluate the impact of computerization on health and well-being;
- assess the role played by health in accidents;
- compare and contrast the concepts of culture and climate as a means of safety management;
- apply social constructionist ideas to the field of safety management;
- investigate the idea that most accidents are just 'waiting to happen';
- explore the concept of 'sense making' in the context of decision making;
- test propositions about decision making in the field derived from recognition primed decision making and image theory;
- apply naturalistic decision making ideas to team decision making.

## Recommended Reading

Chmiel, N. (2000). Safety at work. In N. Chmiel (Ed.), *Work and organizational psychology: A European perspective* (pp. 255–273). Oxford: Blackwell.

Cooper, C.L. (2001). *Managerial, occupational and organizational stress research*. Aldershot: Ashgate.

Cooper, C.L., Dewe, P.J., & O'Driscoll, M.P. (2001). *Organizational stress: A review and critique of theory, research, and applications*. London: Sage.

Jones, F., & Bright, J. (2002). *Stress: Myth, Theory and Research*. Harlow: Pearson Education.

Lazarus, R.S. (1999). *Stress and emotion: A new synthesis*. London: Free Association.

Wagenaar, W.A., & Hudson, P.T.W. (1998). Industrial safety. In P.J.D. Drenth, H. Thierry, & C.J. de Wolff (Eds), *Work psychology. Volume 2. Handbook of Work and Organizational Psychology* (pp. 65–87; 2nd edn). Hove: Psychology Press.

Winnubst, J.A.M., & Diekstra, R.F.W. (1998). Work and health psychology: Methods of intervention. In P.J.D. Drenth, H. Thierry & C.J. de Wolff (Eds), *Personnel psychology. Vol 3. Handbook of work and organizational psychology* (pp. 395–408). Hove: Psychology Press.

# References

Aalto, P., & Kankaanranta, K. (1996). *Towards an information society: Information technology applications in guidance and counselling.* Helsinki: CIMO.

Abraham, S.E., Karns, L.A., Shaw, K., & Menon, M.A. (2001). Managerial competencies and the managerial performance appraisal process. *Journal of Management Development*, 20(10), 842–852.

Abrams, D., & Hogg, M.A. (1988). Comments on the motivational status of self-esteem in social identity and intergroup discrimination. *European Journal of Social Psychology*, 18, 317–334.

Adams, J.D., Hayes, J., & Hopkins, B. (1976). *Transition: Understanding and managing personal change.* London: Martin Robertson.

Adams, J.S. (1965). Inequity in social exchange. In L. Berkowitz (Ed.), *Advances in experimental social psychology* (Vol. 2, pp. 267–299). New York: Academic Press.

Adler, N. (2002). Women joining men as global leaders in the new economy. In M. Gannon & K. Newman (Eds), *The Blackwell handbook of cross cultural management.* Oxford: Blackwell Business.

Aldwin, C.M. (2000). *Stress, coping and development: An integrative perspective.* New York: Wiley.

Alfred, M.V. (2001). Expanding theories of career development: Adding the voices of African American women in the White academy. *Adult Education Quarterly*, 51(2), 108–127.

Algera, J.A., & Greuter, M.A.M. (1989). Job analysis for personnel selection. In M. Smith and I.T. Robertson (Eds), *Advances in selection and assessment* (pp. 7–30). Chichester: Wiley.

Ali, H., & Davies, D.R. (2003). The effect of age, sex and tenure on the job performance of rubber tapers. *Journal of Occupational and Organizational Psychology*, 76(3), 381–391.

Alker, L., & McHugh, D. (2000). Human resource maintenance. *Journal of Managerial Psychology*, 15(4), 303–323.

Allen, T.D., Freeman, D.M., Russell, J.E.A., Reizenstein, R.C., & Rentz, J.O. (2001). Survivor reactions to downsizing: Does time ease the pain? *Journal of Occupational and Organizational Psychology*, 74(2), 145–164.

Alliger, G.M., Tannenbaum, S.I., Bennett, W. Jr., Traver, H., & Shotland, A. (1997). A meta-analysis of relations among training criteria. *Personnel Psychology*, 50, 341–358.

Allison, T., Cooper, C.L., & Reynolds, P. (1989). Stress counselling in the workplace – the post office experience. *The Psychologist*, 2, 384–388.

Almen, A., Anderson, M., Lagerlof, J., & Pallin, K. (2000). *The role of command in network centric warfare.* Paper presented at 5th International Command and Control Research and Technology Symposium, Orlando, Florida.

Alvesson, M. (2001). Knowledge work: Ambiguity, image and identity. *Human Relations*, 54(7), 863–886.

Alvesson, M., & Deetz, S. (1996). Critical theory and postmodernism approaches to organization studies. In S.R. Clegg, C. Hardy & W.R. Nord (Eds), *Handbook of organizational studies*, (pp. 191–217). London: Sage.

Anderson, J.R. (1982). Acquisition of cognitive skill. *Psychological Review*, 89, 369–406.

Anderson, J.R. (1987). Skill acquisition: Compilation of weak-method problem solutions. *Psychological Review*, 94, 192–210.

Anderson, N. (2001). Towards a theory of socialization impact: Selection as pre-entry socialization. *International Journal of Selection and Assessment*, 9(1/2), 84–91.

Anderson, N. (2003). Applicant and recruiter reactions to new technology in selection: A critical review and agenda for future research. *International Journal of Selection and Assessment*, 11(2–3), 121–136.

Anderson, N. (2004). Editorial – The dark side of the moon: Applicant perspectives, negative psychological effects (NPEs), and candidate decision making in selection. *International Journal of Selection and Assessment*, 12, 1–8.

Anderson, N., & Herriot, P. (Eds) (1997). *International handbook of assessment and selection*. London: Wiley.

Anderson, N., & Ostroff, C. (1997). Selection as socialisation. In N. Anderson & P. Herriot (Eds), *International handbook of selection and assessment* (pp. 413–440). Chichester: Wiley.

Anderson N., & Shackleton, V. (1996). Decision making in the graduate selection interview: A filed study. *Journal of Occupational Psychology*, 63, 63–76.

Anderson, N., Born, M., & Cunningham-Snell, N. (2001). Recruitment and selection: Applicant perspectives and outcomes. In N. Anderson, D.S. Ones, H.K. Sinangil & C. Viswesvaran (Eds), *Handbook of industrial, work and organizational psychology* (Vol. 1, pp. 200–218). London: Sage.

Anderson, N.R. (1991). Eight decades of employment interview research: A retrospective meta-review and prospective commentary. *European Work and Organizational Psychologist*, 2, 1–32.

Anderson, N.R., Herriot, P., & Hodgkinson, G.P. (2001). The practitioner-researcher divide in industrial, work and organizational (IWO) psychology: Where we are now, and where do we go from here? *Journal of Occupational and Organizational Psychology*, 74(4), 391–411.

Anderson, S.L., & Betz, N.E. (2001). Sources of social self-efficacy expectations: Their measurement and relation to career development. *Journal of Vocational Behavior*, 58(1), 98–117.

Andriessen, J.H.E. (1991). Mediated communication and new organizational forms. In C.L. Cooper & I.T. Robertson (Eds), *International review of industrial and organizational psychology* (Vol. 6, pp. 17–70) Chichester: Wiley.

Annett, J., & Sparrow, J. (1985). Transfer training: A review of research and practical implications. *Journal of Programmed Learning and Educational Technology*, 22, 116–124.

Antoni, C. (1996). Lean production in Europe: A matter of technical adjustment or cultural change? *Applied Psychology: An International Review*, 45(2), 139–142.

Antonioni, D. (1994). Designing an effective 360-degree appraisal feedback process. *Organizational Dynamics*, 25(2), 24–38.

Argote, L. (1993). Group and organizational learning curves. Individual, system, and environmental components. *British Journal of Social Psychology*, 32, 31–51.

Argyris, C. (1962). *Interpersonal competence and organizational behaviour*. Homewood, IL: Richard D. Irwin.

Argyris, C. (1971). *Management and organizational development: The path from XA to YB*. New York: McGraw-Hill.

Argyris, C., & Schon, D.A. (2002). *Organizational Learning II*. Reading, MA: Addison Wesley.

Armeli, S., Eisenberger, R., Fasolo, P., & Lynch, P. (1998). Perceived organizational support and police performance: The moderating influence of socioemotional needs. *Journal of Applied Psychology*, 83, 288–297.

Armour, N.L. (1995). The beginning of stress reduction: Creating a code of conduct for how team members treat each other. *Public Personnel Management*, 24(2), 127–132.

Armstrong, P., & Armstrong, H. (1990). *Theorizing women's work*. Toronto: Garamond Press.

Armstrong-Stassen, M. (2002). Designated redundant but escaping lay-off: A special group of lay-off survivors. *Journal of Occupational and Organizational Psychology*, 75(1), 1–14.

Arnison, L., & Miller, P. (2002). Virtual teams: A virtue for the conventional team. *Journal of Workplace Learning*, 14(4), 166–173.

Arnold, J. (1985). Tales of the unexpected: Surprises experienced by graduates in the early months of employment. *British Journal of Guidance and Counselling*, 13, 308–319.

Arnold, J. (1997). *Managing careers into the 21st century*. London: Paul Chapman.

Arnold, J. (2004). The congruence problem in John Holland's theory of vocational decisions. *Journal of Occupational and Organizational Psychology*, 77, 95–113.

Arnold, J., Robertson, I.T., & Cooper, C.L. (1995). *Work psychology: Understanding human behaviour in the workplace* (3rd edn). London: Pitman.

Arthur, M.B. (2000). The boundaryless career: A new perspective for organisational enquiry. *Journal of Organisational Behaviour*, 15, 295–306.

Arthur, M.B., Hall, D.T., & Lawrence, B.S. (1989). *Handbook of career theory*. Cambridge: Cambridge University Press.

Arthur, W. Jr., Bennett, W. Jr., Edens, P.S., & Bell, S.T. (2003). Effectiveness of training in organizations: A meta-analysis of design and evaluation features. *Journal of Applied Psychology*, 88(2), 234–245.

Aryee, S., & Luk, V. (1996). Balancing the two major parts of adult life experience: Work and family identity among dual career couples. *Human Relations*, 49, 465–487.

Aryee, S., Budhwar, P.S., & Chen, Z.-X. (2002). Trust as a mediator of the relationship between organizational justice and work outcomes: Test of a social exchange model. *Journal of Organizational Behavior*, 23(3), 267–286.

Aselage, J., & Eisenberger, R. (2003). Perceived organizational support and psychological contracts: A theoretical integration. *Journal of Organizational Behavior* 24 (5, Special Issue), 491–509.

Asch, S.E. (1952). *Social psychology*. Englewood Cliffs, NJ: Prentice-Hall.

Ash, A. (1994). Participants reactions to appraisal of managers: Results of a pilot. *Public Personnel Management*, 23(2), 237–256.

Asher, J. (1972). The biographical item: Can it be improved? *Personnel Psychology*, 25(2), 251–269.

Ashforth, B.E., & Mael, F. (1989). Social identity theory and the organization. *Academy of Management Review*, 14, 20–39.

Ashforth, B.E., & Mael, F.A. (1996). Organizational identity and strategy as a context for the individual. *Advances in Strategic Management*, 13, 19–64.

Ashforth, B.E., & Tomiuk, M.A. (2000). Emotional labour and authenticity: Views from service agents. In S. Fineman (Ed.), *Emotion in organization* (2nd edn, pp. 184–203). London: Sage.

AshKanasy, C., Wilderom, C., & Peterson, M. (Eds). (2003). *Handbook of organizational culture and climate*. London: Sage.

Atkinson, R.K., Renkl, A., & Merrill, M.M. (2003). Transitioning from studying examples to solving problems: Combining fading with prompting fosters learning. *Journal of Educational Psychology*, 95, 774–783.

Attaran, M., & Attaran, S. (2002). Collaborative computing technology: The hot new managing tool. *Journal of Management Development*, 21(8), 598–609.

Atwater, L., Waldman, D., Atwater, D., & Cartier, P. (2000). An upward feedback field experiment: Supervisors' cynicism, reactions, and commitment to subordinates. *Personnel Psychology*, 53, 275–297.

Audia, G., Locke, E.A., & Smith, K.G. (2000). The paradox of success: An archival and laboratory study of strategic persistence following a radical environmental change. *Academy of Management Journal*, 43(5), 837–854.

Austin, J.T., & Vancouver, J.B. (1996). Goal constructs in psychology: Structure, process, and content. *Psychological Bulletin*, 120, 338–375.

Axtell, C.M., Wall, T., Stride, C., Pepper, K., Clegg, C., Gardner, P., & Bolden, R. (2002). Familiarity breeds content: The impact of exposure to change on employee openness and wellbeing. *Journal of Occupational and Organizational Psychology*, 75(2), 217–232.

Axtell, C.M., Waterson, P.E., & Clegg, C.W. (1997). Problems integrating user participation into software development. *International Journal of Human-Computer Studies*, 47(2), 323–345.

Babisch, W. (1998). Epidemiological studies of the cardiovascular effects of occupational noise a critical appraisal. *Noise & Health*, 1, 24–39.

Bailey, C., & Fletcher, C. (2002). The impact of multiple source feedback on management development: Findings from a longitudinal study. *Journal of Organizational Behavior*, 23(7), 853–867.

Bailey, C.T. (1983). *The measurement of job performance*. Hampshire: Gower Publishing Company Ltd.

Bailey, J.S., & Austin, J. (2002). Productivity in the workplace. In M.A. Mattaini & B.A. Thyer (Eds), *Finding solutions to social problems: Behavioral strategies for change* (2nd edn, pp. 179–200). Washington, DC: American Psychological Association.

Bainbridge, L., & Sanderson, P. (1995). Verbal protocol analysis. In J.W. Wilson & E.N. Corlett (Eds), *Evaluation of human work: A practical ergonomics methodology* (2nd edn, pp. 169–201). London: Taylor & Francis Ltd.

Bales, R.F. (1950). *Interaction process analysis: A method for the study of small groups*. Reading, MA: Addison-Wesley.

Ballantyne, I., & Hind, P. (1995). So you want to get chartered? *The Occupational Psychologist*, No. 25.

Baltes, B.B., Bauer, C.C., Bajdo, L.M., & Parker, C.P. (2002). The use of multitrait-multimethod data for detecting nonlinear relationships: The case of psychological climate and job satisfaction. *Journal of Business and Psychology*, 17(1), 3–17.

Bandura, A. (1977). *Social learning theory*. New York: General Learning Press.

Bandura, A. (1997). *Self-efficacy: The exercise of control*. New York: Freeman.

Banks, A. (2001). *Mental models in groups*. Unpublished PhD Thesis, Guildford, University of Surrey.

Banks, A., & Millward, L.J. (2000). Running shared mental models as a distributed cognitive process. *British Journal of Psychology*, 91, 513–53.

Banks, M., Bates, I., Breakwell, G., Bynner, J., Emler, N., Jamieson, L., & Roberts, K. (1992). *Careers identities*. Milton Keynes: Open University Press.

Bannister, S., Hilliard, R., Regehr, G., & Lingaard, L. (2003). Technical skill in paediatrics: A qualitative study of acquisition, attitudes, and assumptions in the neonatal intensive care unit. *Medical Education*, 37(12), 1082–1090.

Barley, R. (1989). Careers, identities, and institutions: The legacy of the Chicago School of Sociology. In M.B. Arthur, D.T. Hall & B.S. Lawrence (Eds), *Handbook of career theory*. (pp. 41–65). Cambridge: Cambridge University Press.

Barling, J., Loughlin, C., & Kelloway, E.K. (2002). Development and test of a model linking safety-specific transformational leadership and occupational safety. *Journal of Applied Psychology*, 87(3), 488–496.

Barnard, C. (1938). *The functions of the executive*. Cambridge, MA: Harvard University Press.

Barnes, J.L. (2001). Person perception processes and challenges. In M. London (Ed.), *How people evaluate others in organizations* (pp. 135–153). Mahwah, NJ: Lawrence Earlbaum Associates.

Baron, H., & Janman, K. (1996). Fairness in the assessment centre. In C.L. Cooper & I.T. Robertson (Eds), *International review of industrial and organizational psychology* (pp. 61–113). Chichester: Wiley.

Baron, R.M., & Kenny, D.A. (1986). The moderator-mediator variable distinction in social psychological research: Conceptual, strategic, and statistical considerations. *Journal of Personality and Social Psychology*, 51(6), 1173–1182.

Barrett, P., Kline, P., Paltiel, L., & Eysenck, H.J. (1996). An evaluation of the psychometric properties of the concept 5.2 Occupational Personality Questionnaire. *Journal of Occupational Psychology*, 69, 1–19.

Barrick, M.R., & Mount, M.K. (1991). The Big Five personality dimensions and job performance: A meta-analysis. *Personnel Psychology*, 44, 1–26.

Barrick, M.R., Mount, M.K., & Judge, T. (2001). Personality and performance at the beginning of the new millennium: What do we know and where do we go next? *International Journal of Selection and Assessment*, 9, 9–30.

Barrick, M.R., Stewart, G.L., & Piotrowski, M. (2002). Personality and job performance: Test of the mediating effects of motivation among sales representatives. *Journal of Applied Psychology*, 87(1), 43–51.

Barrow, J.C. (1976). Worker performance and task complexity as causal determinants of leader behaviour style and flexibility. *Journal of Applied Psychology*, 61, 433–440.

Bartholomew, K., & Perlman, D. (Eds). (1994). *Attachment processes in adulthood: Advances in personal relationships*, Vol. 5. London: Jessica Kingsley.

Bartram, D. (2001). Internet recruitment and selection: Kissing frogs to find princes. *International Journal of Selection and Assessment*, 8, 261–274.

Bartunek, J.M. (1984). Changing interpretative schemes and organizational restructuring: The example of a religious order. *Administrative Science Quarterly*, 29, 355–372.

Bass, B.M. (1990). *Bass and Stogdill's Handbook of Leadership* (3rd edn). New York: Free Press.

Bass, B.M. (1998). *Transformational leadership: Industry, military and educational impact*. Mahwah, NJ: Erlbaum.

Bass, B.M., & Avolio, B.J. (Eds). (1998). *Improving organizational effectiveness through transformational leadership*. Thousand Oaks, CA: Sage.

Bass, B.M., & Vaughan, J.A. (1967). *Training in industry: The management of learning*. Belmont, CA: Wadsworth.

Batt, R. (1999). Work organization, technology, performance in customer service sales. *Industrial and Labour Relations Review*, 52, 539–564.

Beach, L.R. (1997). *The psychology of decision making: People in organizations. Foundations for organizational science*. London: Sage.

Bechtoldt, H.P. (1947) Selection. In S.S. Stevens (Ed.), *Handbook of experimental psychology* (pp. 1237–1267). New York: Wiley.

Beck, A.T. (1976). *Cognitive therapy and emotional disorders*. New York: International Universities Press.

Becker, H.S., & Geer, B. (1958). The fate of idealism in medical school. *American Sociological Review*, 23, 50–56.

Becker, T.E., & Strauss, A.L. (1956). Careers, personality and adult socialization. *American Journal of Sociology*, 62, 253–263.

Bedeian, A.G. (2002). Issues in the dimensional structure of career entrenchment. *Journal of Occupational and Organizational Psychology*, 75(2), 247–250.

Beer, M. (1976). On gaining influence and power for OD. *Journal of Applied Behavioral Science*, 12(1), 44–51.

Behson, S.J. (2002). Coping with family-to-work conflict: The role of informal accommodations to family. *Journal of Occupational Health Psychology*, 7(4), 324–341.

Belbin, R.M. (1981). *Management teams: Why they succeed or fail*. London: Heinemann.

Belbin, R.M. (1993). *Team roles at work*. Oxford: Butterworth Heinemann.

Bell, B.S., Ryan, A.M., & Wiechmann, D. (2004). Justice expectations and applicant perceptions. *International Journal of Selection and Assessment*, 12(1–2), 24–38.

Bell, S., & Lee, C. (2002). Development of the Perceived Stress Questionnaire for young women. *Psychology, Health and Medicine*, 7(2), 189–201.

Bellamy, L.J. (1986). *The safety management factor: An analysis of human aspects of the Bhopal disaster*. Paper presented at the 1986 Safety and Reliability Symposium, Southport, UK.

Bendicsen, H., & Carlton, S. (1990). Clinical team building: A neglected ingredient in the therapeutic milieu. *Residential Treatment for Children and Youth*, 8(1), 5–21.

Bennett, K.B., Nagy, A.L., & Flach, J.M. (1997). Visual displays. In G. Salvendy (Ed.), *Handbook of human factors and ergonomics* (pp. 659–696). New York: John Wiley.

Bennett, K.B., Cress, J.D., Hettinger, L.J., Stautberg, D., & Haas, M.W. (2001). A theoretical analysis and preliminary investigation of dynamically adaptive interfaces. *International Journal of Aviation Psychology*, 11(2), 169–195.

Bennis, W.G. (1969). *Organization development: Its nature, origins, and prospects*. Reading, MA: Addison-Wesley Publishing Company.

Ben-Shakhar, G., et al. (1986). Can graphology predict occupational success? Two empirical studies and some methodological ruminations. *Journal of Applied Psychology*, 71(4), 645–653.

Benson, L. (1985). Theoretical perspectives. *American Behavioral Scientist*, 29(1), 25–39.

Berger, P., & Luckman, T. (1967). *The social construction of reality*. New York: Doubleday.

Bernardin, H., & Buckley, M.R. (1981). Strategies in rater training. *Academy of Management Review*, 6, 205–212.

Bernstein, D.A., & Borkovec, T.D. (1983). *Progressive relaxation training*. Champaign, IL: Research Press.

Betz, N.E. (2000). Self-efficacy theory as a basis for career assessment. *Journal of Career Assessment*, 8, 205–222.

Betz, N.E., & Corning, A. (1993). The inseparability of 'career' and 'personal' counselling. *The Career Development Quarterly*, 42, 137–142.

Beveridge, S., Craddock, S.H., Liesener, J., Stapleton, M., & Hershenson, D. (2002). INCOME: A framework for conceptualizing the career development of persons with disabilities. *Rehabilitation Counselling Bulletin*, 45(4), 195–206.

Bezanson, L. (2003). Career development: Policy, proof and purpose. Career Development and Guidance (UK), October.

Bhatt, G.D. (2001). Knowledge management in organizations: Examining the interaction between technologies, techniques, and people. *Journal of Knowledge Management*, 5(1), 68–75.

Bianchi-Berthouze, N., & Lisetti, C.L. (2002). Modeling multimodal expression of user's affective subjective experience. *User Modeling and User-Adapted Interaction*, 12(1), 49–84.

Bird, A., Gunz, H.P., & Arthur, M.B. (2002). Careers in a complex world: The search for new perspectives in the 'new science.' *Management*, 5(1), 1–14.

Bishop, J.W., & Scott, K.D. (2000). Organizational and team commitment in a team environment. *Journal of Applied Psychology*, 85, 439–450.

Blake, R.R., & Mouton, J.S. (1964). *The managerial grid*. Houston, TX: Gulf.

Blascovich, J., Loomis, J., Beall, A., Swinth, K.R., Hoyt, C.L., & Bailenson, J.N. (2002). Immersive virtual environment technology as a methodological tool for social psychology. *Psychological Inquiry*, 13(2), 103–124.

Blau, G., & Boal, K. (1987). Conceptualizing how job involvement and organizational commitment affect turnover and absenteeism. *Academy of Management Review*, 12, 288–300.

Bliesener, T. (1996). Methodological moderators in validating biographical data in personnel selection. *Journal of Occupational and Organizational Psychology*, 69(1), 107–120.

Blinkhorn, S., & Johnson, C. (1990). The insignificance of personality testing. *Nature*, 348, 671–672.

Blum, M., & Naylor, J. (1968). *Industrial psychology: Its theoretical and social foundation*. New York: Harper and Row.

Blumberg, M., & Pringle, C.D. (1982). The missing opportunity in organizational research: Some implications for a theory of work performance. *Academy of Management Review*, 7(4), 562–565.

Blustein, D., & Noumair, D.A. (1966). Self-development in career development: Implications for theory and practice. *Journal of Counselling and Development*, 74, 433–441.

Boddy, D., & Gunson, N. (1996). *Organizations in the network age*. London: Routledge.

Boechler, P.M., & Dawson, M.R.W. (2002). Effects of navigation tool information on hypertext navigation behavior: A configural analysis of page-transition data. *Journal of Educational Multimedia and Hypermedia*, 11(2), 95–115.

Boerlijst, J.G. (1998). Career development and career guidance. In P.J.D. Drenth, H. Thierry, & C.J. de Wolff (Eds), *Personnel psychology. Vol. 3. Handbook of work and organizational psychology* (2nd edn, pp. 273–296). Hove: Psychology Press Ltd.

Boje, D.M., Alvarez, R.C., & Schooling, B. (2001). Reclaiming story in organization: Narratologies and action sciences. In R. Westwood & S. Linstead (Eds), *The language of organization* (pp. 132–175). London: Sage.

Boose, J.H. (1985). A knowledge acquisition programme for expert systems based upon personal construct psychology. *International Journal of Man-Machine Studies*, 5, 495–526.

Booth, P. (1990). Cognitive models in human-computer Interaction. In P. Booth (Ed.), *An introduction to human-computer interaction*. Hove: Lawrence Erlbaum Associates.

Booth, P., & Marshall, C.J. (1990). Usability in human-computer interaction. In P. Booth (Ed.), *An introduction to human-computer interaction*. Hove: Lawrence Erlbaum Associates.

Borg, G., Bratfisch, O., & Dorinc, J. (1971). On the problem of perceived difficulty. *Scandinavian Journal of Psychology*, 12, 249–260.

Borkin, J.R., Steffen, J.J., Ensfield, L.B., Krzton, K., Wishnick, H., Wilder, K., Yangarber, N. (2000). Recovery Attitudes Questionnaire: Development and evaluation. *Psychiatric Rehabilitation Journal*, 24(2), 95–102.

Borman, W.C. (1991). Job behaviour, performance and effectiveness. In M.D. Dunnette & L. Hough (Eds), *Handbook of industrial & organizational behaviour* (Vol. 2, pp. 271–326). Palo Alto, CA: Consulting Psychologists Press, Inc.

Borman, W.C., Walter, C., Campbell, C.H., & Pulakos, E.D. (2001). Analyzing jobs for performance measurement. In J.P. Campbell & D.J. Knapp (Eds), *Exploring the limits in personnel selection and classification* (pp. 157–180). Mahwah, NJ: Lawrence Erlbaum Associates.

Boss, R.W., McConkie, M.L., Ringer, R.C., & Polok, N. (1995). Building productive teams in cross cultural settings: An intervention with Hispanic and non-Hispanic managers. *Organization Development Journal*, 13(2), 59–69.

Boswell, W.R., & Boudreau, J.W. (2001). Separating the developmental and evaluative performance appraisal uses. *Journal of Business and Psychology*, 16(3), 391–412.

Bowers, D.G., & Franklin, J.L. (1994). Survey-guided development: Using human resources measurement in organizational change. In W.L. French, C.H. Bell, & R.A. Zawacki (Eds), *Organization development and transformation: Managing effective change* (4th edn, pp. 43–55). Homewood, IL: Richard D. Irwin, Inc.

Boyce, T.E., & Geller, E.S. (2001). Encouraging college students to support pro-environment behavior: Effects of direct versus indirect rewards. *Environment and Behavior*, 33(1), 107–125.

Boydell, T.H. (1970). *A guide to job analysis*. London: British Association for Commercial and Industrial Education.

Bradley, M. (2002). *IBM's Digitisation Transformation Story*. Cynefin Centre for Organizational Complexity, IBM Global Services. IBM Corporation.

Brant, B., Farmer, J., & Buckmaster, A. (1993). Cognitive apprenticeship approach to helping adults learn. In D. Flannery (Ed.), *Applying cognitive learning theory to adult learning* (pp. 69–78). San Franciso, CA: Jossey-Bass.

Brayfield, A.H., & Crockett, W.H. (1955). Employee attitudes and employee performance. *Psychological Bulletin*, 52, 396–424.

Breakwell, G.M. (1986). *Coping with threatened identity*. London: Methuen.

Breakwell, G.M., & Millward, L. (1995). *Basic evaluation methods: Analysing performance, practice and procedure*. Leicester: BPS Books and Methuen.

Brett, J.F., & Atwater, L.E. (2001). 360 degree feedback: Accuracy, reactions, and perceptions of usefulness. *Journal of Applied Psychology*, 86(5), 930–942.

Bretz, R.D., & Judge, T.A. (1998). Realistic job previews: A test of the adverse self-selection hypothesis. *Journal of Applied Psychology*, 83(2), 330–337.

Bretz, R.D., & Thompsett, R.E. (1997). Comparing traditional and integrative learning methods in organizational training programs. In D.F. Russ-Eft, F. Darlene, H.S. Preskill et al. (Eds), *Human resource development review: Research and implications* (pp. 57–84). Thousand Oaks, CA: Sage.

Bridges, W. (2001). *Managing transitions*. London: Nicholas Brealey Publishing.

Brief, A.P. (1998). *Attitudes in and around organizations*. London: Sage.

Brief, A.P., & Motowildo, S.J. (1986). Prosocial organizational behaviours. *Academy of Management Review*, 11, 710–725.

Briggs, P. (1987). Usability assessment for the office: Methodological choices and their implications. In M. Frese, E. Ulich & W. Dzida (Eds), *Psychological issues of human–computer interaction in the workplace* (pp. 381–442). Amsterdam: Elsevier Science Publishers.

Bright, J.E.H., & Hutton, S. (2000). The impact of competency statements on resumes for short-listing decisions. *International Journal of Selection and Assessment*, 8(2), 41–53.

Brindle, L., & Ridgeway, C. (1995). Occupational Assessment Survey. *The Occupational Psychologist* (pp. 17–23).

Briskin, A. (1998). *The striving soul in the workplace*. San Francisco: Berrett-Koehler.

British Psychological Society (2004). *What do occupational psychologists do?* www.bps.org.uk/careers/areas/occupational.cfm.

Britt, T.W., Adler, A.B., & Bartone, P.T. (2001). Deriving benefits from stressful events: The role of engagement in meaningful work and hardiness. *Journal of Occupational Health Psychology*, 6, 53–63.

Brookfield, M. (1986). *Understanding and facilitating adult learning*. Milton Keynes: Open University Press.

Brothen, T., Warnbach, C., & Hansen, G. (2002). Accommodating students with disabilities: PSI as an example of universal instructional design. *Teaching of Psychology*, 29(3), 229–240.

Brotheridge, C.M., & Lee, R.T. (2003). Development and validation of the Emotional Labour Scale. *Journal of Occupational and Organizational Psychology*, 76(3), 365–380.

Brotherton, C. (1996). Guidelines on recording the activities of an affiliate member of the division. *The Occupational Psychologist*, 29 (August), 50–56.

Brotherton, C. (1999). *Social psychology and management: Issues for a changing society*. Milton Keynes: Open University Press.

Brown, A.D. (2001). Organization studies and identity: Towards a research agenda. *Human Relations*, 54(1), 113–121.

Brown, D., & Brooks, L. (1996). *Career choice and development*. San Francisco, CA: Jossey-Bass Publishers.

Brown, I.D. (1995). Accident reporting and analysis. In J.W. Wilson and E.N. Corlett (Eds), *Evaluation of human work: A practical ergonomics methodology* (2nd edn, pp. 309–316). London: Taylor & Francis Ltd.

Brown, J., Collins, A., & Duguid, P. (1989). Situated cognition and the culture of learning. *Educational Researcher*, January–February, 32–42.

Brown, J.M., & Campbell, E.A. (1998). *Stress and policing: Sources and strategies*. Chichester: J Wiley & Sons.

Brown, R. (1988). *Group processes: Dynamics within and between groups*. Oxford: Blackwell.

Brown, S.P. (1996). A meta-analysis and review of organizational research on job involvement. *Psychological Bulletin*, 120, 235–255.

Brutus, S., London, M., & Martineau, J. (1999). The impact of 360–degree feedback on planning for career development. *Journal of Management Development*, 18(8), 676–693.

Brutus, S., Ruderman, M.N., Ohlott, P.J., & McCauley, C.D. (2000). Developing from job experiences: The role of organization-based self-esteem. *Human Resource Development Quarterly*, 11(4), 367–380.

Bryman, A. (1996). Leadership in organizations. In S.R. Clegg, C. Hardy & W.R. Nord (Eds), *Handbook of organizational studies* (pp. 276–292). Thousand Oaks, CA: Sage.

Bubb-Lewis, C., & Scerbo, M.W. (1999). Does desire for control affect interactions in an adaptive automated environment? In M.W. Scerbo & M. Mouloua (Eds), *Automation technology and human performance: Current research and trends* (pp. 15–26). Mahwah, NJ: Lawrence Erlbaum Associates.

Buchanan, D.A., & Boddy, D. (1983). Advanced technology and the quality of working life: The effects of computerized controls on biscuit-making operators. *Journal of Occupational Psychology*, 56(2), 109–119.

Buller, P. (1988). For successful strategic change: Blend OD practices with strategic management. *Organizational Dynamics*, Winter, 42–45.

Buller, P.F., & Bell, C.H. (1986). Effects of team building and goal setting on productivity: A field experiment. *Academy of Management Journal*, 29(2), 305–328.

Bullinger, H.J., Bauer, W., & Braun, M. (1997). Virtual environments. In G. Salvendy (Ed.), *Handbook of human factors and ergonomics* (pp. 1727–1759). New York: Wiley.

Bullinger, H.J., Kern, P., & Braun, M. (1997). Controls. In G. Salvendy (Ed.), *Handbook of human factors and ergonomics* (pp. 697–728). New York: John Wiley.

Bunce, D. (1997). What factors are associated with the outcome of individual-focused worksite stress management interventions? *Journal of Occupational and Organizational Psychology*, 70, 1–17.

Buono, A.F., & Bowditch, J.L. (2003). *The human side of mergers and acquisitions* (3rd edn). San Francisco, CA: Jossey-Bass.

Burke, M.J., & Day, R.R. (1986). A cumulative study of the effectiveness of managerial training. *Journal of Applied Psychology*, 71, 232–245.

Burke, M.J., Borucki, C.C., & Kaufman, J.D. (2002). Contemporary perspectives on the study of psychological climate: A commentary. *European Journal of Work and Organizational Psychology*, 11, 325–340.

Burke, W.W. (2002). *Organizational change: Theory and practice*. Thousand Oaks, CA: Sage.

Buttner, E.H., & McNally, M. (1996). The interactive effect of influence tactic, applicant gender, and type of job on hiring recommendations. *Sex Roles*, 34(7–8), 581–591.

Buunk, B.P., de Jonge, J., Ybema, J.F., & de Wolfe, C.J. (1998). Psychosocial aspects of occupational stress. In P.J.D. Drenth, H. Thierry & C.J. de Wolff (Eds), *Work psychology, vol. 2: Handbook of work and organizational psychology* (2nd edn, pp. 145–173). Sussex: Psychology Press Ltd. UK.

Caincross, F. (1997). A connected world. Telecommunications survey. *The Economist*, 13 Sept: 3–4.

Callahan, J.L., & McCollum, E.E. (2002). Conceptualizations of emotion research in organizational contexts. *Advances in Developing Human Resources*, 4(1), 4–21.

Calnan, M., Wainwright, D., Forsythe, M., Wall, B., & Almond, S. (2001). Mental health and stress in the workplace: The case of general practice in the UK. *Social Science and Medicine*, 52(4), 499–507.

Camara, W.J., & Schneider, D.L. (1995). Integrity tests – facts and unresolved issues. *American Psychologist*, 49(2), 112–119.

Campbell, D.P. (1996). The use of interest surveys with groups: A useful team-building technique. *Measurement & Evaluation in Counselling and Development*, 29(3), 153–162.

Campbell, J.P. (1971). Personnel training and development. *Annual Review of Psychology*, 22, 565–602.

Campbell, J.P. (1991). Modelling the performance prediction problem in industrial and organizational psychology. In M.D. Dunnette & L.M. Hough (Eds), *Handbook of industrial and organizational psychology* (Vol. 1, 2nd edn, pp. 687–732). Palo Alto, CA: Consulting Psychologists Press.

Campbell, J.P. (1999). The definition and management of performance in the new age. In D.R. Ilgen & E.D. Pulakos (Eds), *The changing nature of performance: Implications for staffing, motivation, and development* (pp. 154–191). San Francisco: Jossey-Bass.

Campbell, J.P., Houston, M-A., & Oppler, S.H. (2001). Modeling performance in a population of jobs. In J.P. Campbell & D.J. Knapp (Eds), *Exploring the limits in personnel selection and classification* (pp. 307–333). Mahwah, NJ: Lawrence Erlbaum Associates.

Campbell, J.P., McCloy, R.A., Oppler, S.H., & Sager, C.E. (1993). A theory of performance. In N.E. Schmitt & W.C. Borman (Eds), *Personnel selection in organizations* (pp. 35–70). San Francisco, CA: Jossey-Bass.

Campion, M.A., Cheraskin, L., & Stevens, M.J. (1994). Career-related antecedents and outcomes of job rotation. *Academy of Management Journal*, 37(6), 1518–1542.

Cannon-Bowers, J.A., Salas, E., Blickensderfer, E., & Bowers, C.A. (1998). The impact of cross-training and workload on team functioning: A replication and extension of initial findings. *Human Factors*, 40(1), 92–101.

Cannon-Bowers, J.A., & Salas, E. (2001). Reflections on shared cognition. *Journal of Organizational Behaviour*, 22, 195–202.

Cardy, R.L., & Dobbins, G.H. (1994). *Performance appraisal: Alternative perspectives*. Cincinnati, OH: South-Western Publishing.

Carey, A. (1967). The Hawthorne studies: A radical criticism. *American Sociological Review*, 32, 403–416.

Carlson, K.D., Scullen, S.E., Schmidt, F.L., Rothstein, H., & Erwin, F. (1999). Generalizable biographical data validity can be achieved without multi-organizational development and keying. *Personnel Psychology*, 52(3), 731–755.

Carnall, C. (1990). *Managing change in organizations*. London: Prentice Hall International.

Carnevale, A.J. (1992). *America and the new economy*. Washington, DC: American Society for Training and Development, & U.S. Department of Labour.

Carr, J.Z., Schmidt, A-M., Ford, J.K., & DeShon, R.P. (2003). Climate perceptions matter: A meta-analytic path analysis relating molar climate, cognitive and affective states, and individual level work outcomes. *Journal of Applied Psychology*, 88(4), 605–619.

Carrington, P. (1978). *Freedom in meditation*. New York: Anchor Press.

Carroll, C.E. (1995). Rearticulating organizational identity: Exploring corporate images and employee identification. *Management Learning*, 26(4), 463–482.

Carroll, J.M., & Olson, J.R. (1988). Mental models in human-computer interaction. In M. Helander (Ed.), *Handbook of human-computer interaction* (pp. 45–65). New York: Elsevier Science Publishers.

Carroll, M. (1995). The counsellor in organizational settings: Some reflections. *Employee Counselling Today*, 7(1), 23–29.

Carroll, M. (1996). *Workplace counselling*. London: Sage.

Carroll, M., & Walton, M. (1997). *Handbook of counselling in organizations*. London: Sage.

Carron, A.V., & Spink, K.S. (1993). Team building in an exercise setting. *Sport Psychologist*, 7(1), 8–18.

Carson, K.P., & Gilliard, D.J. (1993). Construct validity of the Miner Sentence Completion Scale. *Journal of Occupational and Organizational Psychology*, 66, 171–175.

Carter, A. (2002). *Executive coaching: Inspiring performance at work*, IES Report 379. Brighton: Institute for Employment Studies.

Cartwright, S., & Cooper, C.L. (1995). The impact of mergers and acquisitions on people at work: Existing research and issues. *British Journal of Management*, 1, 65–76.

Carvel, J. (2004). Life in the NHS: Violence, stress and pride. *The Guardian*, 10 March.

Carver, C.S. (1997). You want to measure coping but your protocol's too long: Consider the brief COPE. *International Journal of Behavioural Medicine*, 4(1), 92–100.

Carver, C.S., & Scheier, M.F. (1981). *Attention and self-regulation: A control-theory approach to human behaviour*. New York: Springer-Verlag.

Carver, C.S., & Scheier, M. (1998). *On the self-regulation of behavior*. New York: Cambridge University Press.

Cascio, W.F. (1991). *Applied psychology in personnel management* (4th edn). Englewood Cliffs, NJ: Prentice Hall.

Cascio, W.F. (1995). Whither industrial and organizational psychology in a changing world of work. *American Psychologist*, 50(11), 928–939.

Cascio, W.F., & Morris, J.R. (1990). A critical reanalysis of Hunter, Schmidt, and Coggin's (1988) 'Problems and pitfalls in using capital budgeting and financial accounting techniques'. *Journal of Applied Psychology*, 75(4), 410–417.

Casper, W.J., Fox, K.E., Sitzmann, T.M., & Landy, A.L. (2004). Supervisor referrals to work-family programs. *Journal of Occupational Health Psychology*, 9(2), 136–151.

Cassell, C., & Symon, G. (Eds). (2004). *Essential guide to qualitative methods in organizational research* (2nd edn). London: Sage.

Cassell, C., Close, P., Duberley, J., & Johnson, P. (2000). Surfacing embedded assumptions: Using repertory grid methodology to facilitate organizational change. *European Journal of Work and Organizational Psychology*, 9(4), 561–573.

Cassidy, T. (1999). *Stress, cognition and health. Psychology focus*. Florence, KY: Taylor & Francis/Routledge.

Castledine, G. (1996). Extremes of the nurse practitioner role. *British Journal of Nursing*, 5(9), 581.

Cattell, R.B. (1965). *The scientific analysis of personality*. Harmondsworth: Penguin.

Cattell, R.B., Eber, H.W., & Tatsuoka, M.M. (1970). *The 16–Factor Personality Questionnaire*. Champaign, IL: IPAT.

Cawley, B.D., Keeping, L.M., & Levy, P.E. (1998). Participation in the performance appraisal process and employee reactions: A meta-analytic review of field investigations. *Journal of Applied Psychology*, 83, 615–631.

Cazals, M-P., Almudever, B., & Fraccaroli, F. (1995). Social support, coping strategies, and psychological well-being among young people awaiting employment. In J.M. Peiro & F. Prieto et al. (Eds), *Work and organizational psychology: European contributions of the nineties* (pp. 89–100). Oxford: Taylor & Francis.

Cederblom, D. (1982). The performance appraisal interview: A review, implications and suggestions. *Academy of Management Review*, 7(2), 219–227.

Cellar, D.F., & Barrett, G.V. (2004). Script processing and intrinsic motivation: The cognitive sets underlying cognitive labels. *Organizational Behavior and Human Decision Processes*, 40(1), 115–135.

Chalk, J., Donald, I., & Young, S. (1997). Safety teams: Using team work to improve organizational performance. *Occupational Psychologist*, 5–10 April.

Chan, C., & Latham, G.P. (2004). The relative effectiveness of external, peer and self-coaches. *Applied Psychology*, 53(2), 260–278.

Chan, D. (1996). Criterion and construct validation of an assessment centre. *Journal of Occupational and Organizational Psychology*, 69, 167–181.

Chan, D., & Schmitt, N. (2004). An agenda for future research on applicant reactions to selection procedures: A construct-oriented approach. *International Journal of Selection and Assessment*, 12(1–2), 9–23.

Charan, R., & Colvin, G. (1999). Why CEOs fail. *Fortune*, 139(12), 68.

Charoenkitkarn, N., Chignell, M.H., & Golovchinsky, G. (1996). Proceedings of the TREC-4. Gaithersburg, MD: National Institute of Standards and Technology.

Chartrand, J.M., & Walsh, W.B. (2001). Career assessment: Changes and trends. In F.T.L. Leong & A. Barak (Eds), *Contemporary models in vocational psychology* (pp. 231–255). Malwah, NJ: Erlbaum.

Chemers, M.M., Rice, R.W., Sundstrom, E., & Butler, W.M. (1975). Leader esteem for the least preferred co-worker score, training, and effectiveness: An experimental examination. *Journal of Personality and Social Psychology*, 31(3), 401–409.

Chen, C. (2002). Enhancing vocational psychology practice through narrative inquiry. *Australian Journal of Career Development*, 1, 14–21.

Cheng, E.W.L., & Ho, D.C.K. (2001). A review of transfer of training studies in the past decade. *Personnel Review*, 30(1–2), 102–118.

Chignell, M., & Waterworth, J. (1997). Multimedia. In G. Salvendy (Ed.), *Handbook of human factors and ergonomics* (pp. 1808–1861). New York: John Wiley.

Child, J. (1977). *Organization: A guide to problems and practice*. London: Harper & Row.

Chima, F.O. (2002). Employee assistance and human resource collaboration for improving employment and disabilities status. *Employee Assistance Quarterly*, 17(3), 79–94.

Chmiel, N. (1998). *Jobs, technology and people*. London: Routledge.

Chmiel, N. (2000). Safety at work. In N. Chmiel (Ed.), *Work and organizational psychology: A European perspective* (pp. 255–273). Oxford: Blackwell.

Chreim, S. (2002). Influencing organizational identification during major change: A communication-based perspective. *Human Relations*, 55(9), 1117–1137.

Chrobot-Mason, D.L. (2003). Keeping the promise: Psychological contract violations for minority employees. *Journal of Managerial Psychology*, 18(1), 22–45.

Chung-Yan, G.A., & Cranshaw, S.F. (2002). A critical re-examination and analysis of cognitive ability tests using the Thorndike model of fairness. *Journal of Occupational and Organisational Psychology*, 75(4), 489–509.

Church, A.H., & Waclawski, J. (2001). A five phase framework for designing a successful multi-source feedback system. *Consulting Psychology Journal: Practice and Research*, 53(2), 82–95.

Ciborra, C.U. (1996). Introduction: What does groupware mean for the organizations hosting it? In C. Ciborra (Ed.), *Groupware and teamwork: Invisible aid or technical hindrance?* (pp. 1–19). Chichester: Wiley.

Clarke, M., & Meldrum, M. (1999). Creating change from below: Early lessons for agents of change. *The Leadership and Organizational Development Journal*, 20, 70–80.

Clarke, S., (1999). Perceptions of organizational safety: Implications for the development of safety culture. *Journal of Organizational Behaviour*, 20, 185–198.

Clarkson, P. (1990). The scope of stress counselling in organizations. *Employee Counselling*, 2(4), 3–6.

Cleary, T.A. (1986). Test bias: Prediction of grades of Negro and white students in integrated colleges. *Journal of Educational Measurement*, 23, 33–41.

Clegg, C.W., & Walsh, S. (1998). Soft systems analysis. In G. Symon & C. Cassell (Eds), *Qualitative methods and analysis in organizational research* (pp. 107–112). London: Sage.

Clemente, M.N., & Greenspan, D.S. (1998). *Winning at mergers and acquisitions: The guide to market-focused planning and integration*. New York: Wiley.

Cloke, K. (2004). *The end of management and the rise of organizational democracy*. San Francisco, CA: Jossey-Bass.

Cobb, C.D., & Mayer, J.D. (2000). Emotional intelligence: What the research says. *Educational Leadership*, 58(3), 14–18.

Cobb, S., Neale, H., Crosier, J., & Wilson, J.R. (2002). Development and evaluation of virtual environments for education. In K.M. Stanney (Ed.), *Handbook of virtual environments: Design, implementation, and applications. Human factors and ergonomics* (pp. 911–936). Mahwah, NJ: Lawrence Erlbaum Associates.

Cohen, A. (1993). Organizational commitment and turnover: A meta-analysis. *Academy of Management Journal*, 36, 1140–1147.

Cohen, S., Kessler, R., & Underwood Gordon, L. (Eds). (1995). *Measuring stress: A guide for health and social scientists*. New York: Oxford University Press.

Cohen, M.S., Freeman, J.T., Thompson, B.B. (1997). Training the naturalistic decision maker. In G. Klein & C. Zsambok (Eds), *Naturalistic decision making* (pp. 257–268). Hillsdale, NJ: Lawrence Erlbaum.

Cohens, S., & Wills, T.A. (1985). Stress, social support, and the buffering hypothesis. *Psychological Bulletin*, 98(2), 310–357.

Coleman, D. (1996). *Groupware – the changing environment*. http://www.collaborate.com/publications/chapt_toc.html.

Colet, E., & Aaronson, D. (1995). Visualization of multivariate data: Human factors considerations. *Behavior Research Methods, Instruments and Computers*, 27(2), 257–263.

Colle, H.A., & Green, R.F. (1996). Introductory psychology laboratories using graphic simulations of virtual subjects. *Behavior Research Methods, Instruments and Computers*, 28(2), 331–335.

Collins, J.M., Schmidt, F.L., Sanchez-Ku, M., Thomas, L., McDaniel, M.A., & Le, H. (2003). Can basic individual differences shed light on the construct meaning of assessment center evaluations? *International Journal of Selection and Assessment*, 11(1), 17–29.

Collins, M.A., & Amabile, T.M. (1999). Motivation and creativity. In R. Sternberg (Ed.), *Handbook of creativity* (pp. 297–312). Cambridge: Cambridge University Press.

Colquitt, J.A., & Simmering, M.J. (1998). Conscientiousness, goal orientation, and motivation to learn during the learning process: A longitudinal study. *Journal of Applied Psychology*, 83(4), 654–665.

Colquitt, J.A., Le Pine, J.A., & Noe, R.A. (2000). Towards an integrative theory of training motivation: A meta-analytic path analysis of 20 years of research. *Journal of Applied Psychology*, 85, 678–707.

Comte, A. (1853). *The positive philosophy of Auguste Comte*. London: Chapman.

Confederation of British Industry (CBI) (1989). *Towards a skills revolution – A youth charter*. London: Confederation of British Industry.

Connerley, M.L., & Rynes, S.L. (1997). The influence of recruiter characteristics and organizational recruitment support on perceived recruiter effectiveness: Views from applicants and recruiters. *Human Relations,* 50, 1563–1586.

Contu, A., Grey, C., & Ortenblad, A. (2003). Against learning. *Human Relations,* 56(8), 931–952.

Conway, J.M., Jako, R.A., & Goodman, D.F. (1995). A metaanalysis of interrater and internal consistency reliability of selection interviews. *Journal of Applied Psychology,* 80(5), 565–579.

Conway, N., & Briner, R.B. (2002). A daily diary study of effective responses to psychological contract breach and exceeded promises. *Journal of Organizational Behaviour,* 23, 287–302.

Conway, S., & Forrestor, R. (1997). *Innovation and teamwork: Combining perspectives through a focus on team boundaries.* Paper presented at the International Workshop on Teamwork, University of Nottingham, UK, 17–18 Sept.

Cook, J.D., Hepworth, S.J., Wall, T.D., & Warr, P.B. (1981). *The experience of work: A compendium and review of 249 measures and their use.* London: Academic Press.

Cooke, N.J., Kiekel, P.A., Salas, R., Bowers, C., Stout, R., & Cannon-Bowers, J. (2003). Measuring team knowledge: A window to the cognitive underpinnings of team performance. *Group Dynamic* 7, 179–199.

Cooke, R.A., & Rousseau, D.M. (1988). Behaviour norms and expectations: A quantitative approach to the assessment of culture. *Group and Organizational Studies,* 13, 245–273.

Cooke, R.A., & Szumal, J.L. (1993). Measuring normative beliefs and shared behavioural expectations in organizations: Validation of the organizational culture inventory. *Psychological Reports,* 72(3), 1299–1330.

Cooper, C.L. (2001). *Manageral, occupational and organizational stress research.* Aldershot: Ashgate.

Cooper, C.L., & Cartwright, S. (1996). Stress management interventions in the workplace: Stress counselling and stress audits. In S. Palmer & W. Dryden (Eds), *Stress management and counselling* (pp. 89–98). London: Cassell.

Cooper, C.L., & Marshall, J. (1976). Sources of managerial and white collar stress. In C.L. Cooper & R.Payne (Eds), *Stress at Work.* (pp. 301–341). Chichester: J. Wiley and Sons.

Cooper, C.L., Dewe, P.J., & O'Driscoll, M.P. (2001). *Organizational stress: A review and a critique of theory, research and applications.* London: Sage.

Cooper, C.L., Phillips, R.A., Sutherland, V.J., & Makin, P.I. (1994). Reducing accidents using goal-setting theory and feedback: A field study. *Journal of Occupational and Organizational Psychology,* 67, 219–240.

Cooper, C.L., Sloan, S.J., & Williams, S. (1988). *Occupational stress indicator management guide.* Windsor: NFER-Nelson.

Cooper, R., & Foster, M. (1971). Sociotechnical systems. *American Psychologist,* 26, 467–474.

Cooperrider, D.L., & Srivastva, S. (1987). Appreciative inquiry in organizational life. In R.W. Woodman & W.A. Pasmore (Eds), *Research in organizational change and development: An annual series featuring advances in theory, methodology and research,* Vol. 1. (pp. 129–169). Stamford, CT: JAI Press, Inc.

Coopersmith, S. (1967). *The antecedents of self-esteem.* San Francisco: W.H. Freeman.

Corbett, J.M. (1994). *Critical cases in organizational behaviour.* London: Macmillan.

Cordery, J.L. (1999). Job design and the organizational context. In M. Griffin & J. Langham-Fox (Eds), *Human performance and the workplace* (pp. 49–68). Melbourne: Australian Psychological Society.

Costa, M., Cropley, M., Griffith, J., Steptoe, A. (1999). Ambulatory blood pressure monitoring is associated with reduced physical activity during everyday life. *Psychosom Med,* 61(6), 806–811.

Costa, P.T., Jr., & MacCrae, R.R. (1990). *The NEO Personality Inventory Manual.* Odessa, FL: Psychological Assessment Resources.

Cotton, J.L. (1993). *Employee involvement: Methods for improving performance and work attitudes.* Thousand Oaks, CA: Sage.

Cox, S., & Flin, R. (1998). Safety culture: Philosopher's stone or man of straw? *Work and Stress,* 12, 189–201.

Cox, T., & Cox, S. (1993). *Psychosocial and organizational hazard: Control and monitoring in the workspace.* European Occupational Health Series No. 5. Copenhagen: World Health Organization.

Cox, T., & Griffiths, A. (1995). The nature and measurement of work stress: Theory and practice. In J.W. Wilson & E.N. Corlett (Eds), *Evaluation of human work: A practical ergonomics methodology* (2nd edn, pp. 783–803). London: Taylor & Francis Ltd.

Cox, T., & Howart, I. (1990). Organizational health, culture and caring. *Work and Stress*, 4, 107–110.

Cox, T., & MacKay, C.J. (1981). A transactional approach to occupational stress. In E.N. Corlett & J. Richardson (Eds), *Stress, work design and productivity*. Chichester: Wiley.

Coyle-Shapiro, J., & Kessler, I. (2000). Consequences of the psychological contract for the employment relationship: A large scale survey. *Journal of Management Studies*, 37, 903–930.

Coyle-Shapiro, J.A.M., & Neuman, J.H. (2004). The psychological contract and individual differences: The role of exchange and creditor ideologies. *Journal of Vocational Behaviour*, 64(1), 150–164.

Coyne, J.C., & Racioppo, M.W. (2000). Never the twain shall meet? Closing the gap between coping research and clinical intervention research. *American Psychologist*, 55(6), 655–664.

Craik, K. (1943). *The nature of explanation*. Cambridge: Cambridge University Press.

Cramer, D. (2000). Social desirability, adequacy of social support and mental health. *Journal of Community and Applied Social Psychology*, 10(6), 465–474.

Crites, J.O. (1971). Acquiescence response style and the vocational development inventory. *Journal of Vocational Behavior*, 1(2), 189–200.

Cropley, M., & Millward, L.J. (2004). Job strain and rumination about work issues during leisure time: A diary study. *European Journal of Work and Organizational Psychology*, 12(3), 195–207.

Cropley, M., Steptoe, A., & Joekes, K. (1999). Job strain and psychiatric morbidity. *Psychological Medicine*, 29, 1411–1416.

Crozier, S.D. (1999). Women's career development in a 'relational context.' *International Journal for the Advancement of Counselling*, 21(3), 231–247.

Csikszentmihalyi, M., & LeFevre, J. (1989). Optimal experience in work and leisure. *Journal of Personality and Social Psychology*, 56, 815–822.

Cullen, R. (1999). Does performance measurement improve organisational effectiveness? A post-modern analysis. *Performance Measurement and Metrics*, 1(1), 9–30.

Cummings, L.L., & Schwab, D.P. (1970). Evaluation of theories linking employee satisfaction and performance. *Proceedings of the Annual Convention of the American Psychological Association*, 5(2), 581–582.

Cummings, T.G., & Blumberg, M. (1987). Advanced manufacturing technology and work design. In T.D. Wall, C.W. Clegg & N.J. Kemp (Eds), *The human side of advanced manufacturing technology* (pp. 37–60). Chichester: Wiley.

Cummings, T. G., & Worley, C.G. (1993). *Organization development and change* (3rd edn). St Paul, MN: West Publishing Company.

Cummings, T.G., & Worley, C.G. (2000). *Organization development and change*. Mason, OH: South Western College Publishing.

Cummins, Paige N. (2002). Violence in the workplace: Preventing and managing the effects of critical incidence stress in the workplace. In D.S. Sandhu (Ed.), *Counselling employees: A multi-faceted approach* (pp. 323–336). Alexandria, VA: American Counseling Association.

Cunningham, C.E., Woodward, C.A., Shannon, H.S., MacIntosh, J., Lendrum, B., Rosenblum, D., & Brown, J. (2002). Readiness for organizational change: A longitudinal study of workplace, psychological and behavioural correlates. *Journal of Occupational and Organizational Psychology*, 75, 377–392.

Dabos, G.E., & Rousseau, D.M. (2004). Mutuality and reciprocity in the psychological contracts of employees and employers. *Journal of Applied Psychology*, 89(1), 52–72.

Dalessio, A., Crosby, M., & McManus, M. (1996). Stability of biodata keys and dimensions across English speaking countries: A test of the cross-situational hypothesis. *Journal of Business and Psychology*, 10(3), 289–296.

Damanpour, F. (2001). E-business e-commerce evolution: Perspective and strategy. *Managerial Finance*, 27(7), 16–33.

Daniel, C., & Valencia, S. (1991). Structured interviewing simplified. *Public Personnel Management*. 20(2), 127–134.

Darken, R.P., & Peterson, B. (2002). Spatial orientation, wayfinding, and representation. In K.M. Stanney (Ed.), *Handbook of virtual environments: Design, implementation, and applications*. (pp. 493–518). Mahwah, NJ: Lawrence Erlbaum Associates.

Darnell, M.J. (1998). *Bad human factors designs*. www.baddesigns.com.

Darrah, C. (1994). Skill requirements at work: Rhetoric versus reality. *Work and Occupations*, 21(1), 64–84.

Davidson, M.J., & Cooper, C.L. (1992). *Shattering the glass ceiling: The woman manager*. London: Paul Chapman Publishing.

Davies, S., Haines, H., Norris, B., & Wilson, J.R. (1998). Safety pictograms: Are they getting the message across? *Applied Ergonomics*, 29(1), 15–23.

Dawis, R.V., & Lofquist, L.H. (1984). *A psychological theory of work adjustment*. Minneapolis: University of Minnesota Press.

Dawson, P. (2003). *Understanding organizational change: The contemporary experience of people at work*. London, Sage.

Day, E.A., Arthur, W. Jr., & Gettman, D. (2001). Knowledge structures and the acquisition of a complex skill. *Journal of Applied Psychology*, 86(5), 1022–1033.

De Jong, J.A., Thijssen, J.G.L., & Versloot, B.M. (2001). Planned training on the job: A typology. *Advances in Developing Human Resources*, 3(4), 408–414.

De Jonge, J., Landeweerd, J.A., & Nijhuis, F.J.N. (2000). Testing reciprocal relationships between job characteristics and psychological outcomes: A cross-lagged structural equation model. *Journal of Occupational and Organizational Psychology*, 74, 29–46.

De Meuse, K.P., & Leibowitz, S.J. (1981). An empirical analysis of team-building research. *Group and Organization Studies*, 6(3), 357–378.

De Wolff, C.J. (1989). The changing role of psychologists in selection. In P. Herriot (Ed.), *Assessment and selection in organizations* (pp. 81–92). Chichester: Wiley.

De Wolff, C.J., & Van den Bosch, G. (1998). The selection process. In P.J.D. Drenth, H. Thierry & C.J. de Wolff (Eds), *Personnel psychology. Vol. 3. Handbook of work and organizational psychology* (2nd edn, pp. 33–58). Hove: Psychology Press.

Deadrick, D.L., & Madigan, R.M. (1990). Dynamic criteria revisited: A longitudinal study of performance stability and predictive validity. *Personnel Psychology*, 43(4), 717–744.

Deal, T.E., & Kennedy, A. (1982). *Corporate cultures*. Reading, MA: Addison-Wesley.

Dealtry, R. (2002). Managing the corporate university watershed. *Journal of Workplace Learning*, 14(6), 256–262.

Dean, A., Carlisle, Y., & Baden-Fuller, C. (1999). Punctuated and continuous change: The UK water industry, *British Journal of Management*, 10, S3–S18.

Dearborn, K. (2002). Studies in emotional intelligence redefine our approach to leadership development. *Public Personnel Management*, 31(4), 523–530.

Dearing, Sir, R. (1996). Review of qualification for 16–19 year olds. School Curriculum and Assessment Authority Publications, PO Box 235, Hayes, Middlesex, UB3 1HF.

Deary, I.J., Blenkin, H., Agius, R.M., Endler, N.S., Zealley, H., & Wood, R. (1996). Models of job-related stress and personal achievement among consultant doctors. *British Journal of Psychology*, 87(1), 3–29.

Deci, E.L. (1975). *Intrinsic motivation*. New York: Plenum Press.

Deci, E.L., Koestner, R., & Ryan, R.M. (1999). A meta-analytic review of experiments examining the effects of extrinsic rewards on intrinsic motivation. *Psychological Bulletin*, 125, 627–668.

Dehnbostel, P. (2001). Learning bays in German manufacturing companies. *Advances in Developing Human Resources*, 3(4), 471–479.

Dench, S., Perryman, S., & Giles, L. (1998). *Employers perceptions of key skills* (IES Report 349). Brighton: Institute for Employment Studies.

DeNisi, A.S., & Peters, L.H. (1996). Organization of information in memory and the performance appraisal process: Evidence from the field. *Journal of Applied Psychology*, 81(6), 717–737.

Denison, D.R. (1996). What is the difference between organizational culture and climate? A native's point of view on a decade of paradigm wars. *Academy of Management Review*, 21(3), 619–654.

Department of Environment, Transport and the Regions (1997). *The Channel Tunnel Fire*. http://www.railways.detr.gov.uk/ctsa/french/chap9.htm.

Department of Health (1999). HSC 1999/191: *Fire safety and health and safety targets*. Department of Health Circular.

Department of Transport (1987). *Herald of Free Enterprise*. Report of Court no. 8074. London: HMSO.

Department of Transport (1990). *Air Accidents Investigations Branch, Department of Transport. Report on the accident to Boeing 737–400 G-OBME near Kegworth, Leicestershire on 8th January 1989*. Number 4/90. London: HMSO.

De Ridder, D. (1997). What is wrong with coping assessment? A review of conceptual and methodological issues. *Psychology and Health*, 12(3), 417–431.

Derous, E., Bom, M.Ph., & De Wittte, K. (2004). How Applicants want and expect to be treated: Applicants' selection treatment beliefs and the development of the social process questionnaire on selection. *International Journal of Selection and Assessment*, 12(1/2), 99–119.

Derous, E., De Witte, K., & Stroobants, R. (2003). Testing the social process model on selection through expert analysis. *Journal of Occupational and Organizational Psychology*, 76, 179–199.

De Vos, A., Buyens, D., & Schalk, R. (2003). Psychological contract development during organizational socialization: Adaptation to reality and the role of reciprocity. *Journal of Organizational Behavior*, 24(5, Special Issue), 537–559.

Dewe, P. (2000). Measures of coping with stress at work: A review and critique. In P. Dewe, M. Leiter & T. Cox (Eds), *Coping, health and organizations* (pp. 3–28). Washington, DC: Tayor & Francis.

Dewe, P. (2003). A closer examination of the patterns when coping with work-related stress: Implications for measurement. *Journal of Occupational and Organizational Psychology*, 76, 517–524.

Dewe, P.J. (1992). Applying the concept of appraisal to work stressors: Some explanatory analysis. *Human Relations*, 45, 143–164.

Diefendorff, J.M., Hall, R.J., Lord, R.G., & Strean, M.L. (2000). Action-state orientation: Construct validity of a revised measure and its relationship to work-related variables. *Journal of Applied Psychology*, 85(2), 250–263.

Difede, J.A., Hoffman, H., & Jaysinghe, N. (2002). Innovative use of virtual reality technology in the treatment of PTSD in the aftermath of September 11. *Psychiatric Services*, 53(9), 1083–1085.

Dillard, J.M., & Harley, D.A. (2002). Working with ethnic minority employees in the workplace. In D.S. Sandhu (Ed.), *Counseling employees: A multifaceted approach* (pp. 131–149). Alexandria, VA: American Counseling Association.

Dipboye, R.L., Smith, C., & Howell, W.C. (1994). *Understanding industrial and organizational psychology: An integrated approach*. Fort Worth, TX: Harcourt Brace & Jovanovich.

Dipboye, R.L., Smith, C.S., & Howell, W.C. (1999). *Understanding industrial and organizational psychology: An integrated approach* (2nd edn). Fort Worth, TX: Harcourt Brace & Jovanovich.

Dirkx, J.M. (2000). *Transformative learning and the journey of individuation*. ERIC Digest No. 223.

Division of Occupational Psychology (2003). *Guidelines on Becoming a Chartered Occupational Psychologist*. Leicester, UK: The British Psychological Society. www.bps.org.uk/

Division of Occupational Psychology (2004). *Career Management for Occupational Psychologists*. Leicester, UK: The British Psychological Society. www.bps.org.uk/

Donald, I., & Canter, D. (1992). Intentionality and fatality during the King's Cross underground fire. *European Journal of Social Psychology*, 22(3), 203–218.

Donovan, J.J., & Radosevich, D.J. (1999). A meta-analytic review of the distribution of practice effect: Now you see it, now you don't. *Journal of Applied Psychology*, 84(5), 795–805.

Donovan, J.J., & Williams, K.J. (2003). Missing the mark: Effects of time and causal attributions on goal revision in response to goal performance discrepancies. *Journal of Applied Psychology*, 88(3), 379–390.

Dooley, C.R. (1945). *The training within industry report (1940–1945): A record of the development of management techniques for improvement of supervisors, their use and the results*. Washington, DC: War Manpower Commission, Bureau of Training, Training within Industry Service.

Dormann, C., & Zapf, D. (2002). Social stressors at work, irritation, and depressive symptoms: Accounting for unmeasured third variables in a multi-wave study. *Journal of Occupational and Organizational Psychology*, 75(1), 33–58.

Dormann, T., & Frese, M. (1994). Error training: Replication and the function of exploratory behavior. *International Journal of Human-Computer Interaction*, 6(4), 365–372.

Dornan, T., Scherper, A., & Boshuizen, H. (2003). Clinical learning: Towards valid measures of self-directed clinical learning. *Medical Education*, 37(11), 983–991.

Douge, B., & Hastie, P. (1993). Coach effectiveness. *Sports Science Review*, 2(2), 14–29.

Dowling, G.R. (2001). *Creating corporate reputations*. Oxford: Oxford University Press.

Downey, H.K., Sheridan, J.E., & Slocum, J.W. (1975). Analysis of relationships among leader behavior, subordinate job performance and satisfaction: A path-goal approach. *Academy of Management Journal*, 18(2), 253–262.

Downs, S. (1996). Learning to learn. In S. Truelove (Ed.), *The handbook of training and development* (pp. 79–112). Oxford: Blackwell Business.

Downs, S., & Perry, P. (1987). *Developing skilled learners: Helping adults to be better learners. Research and Development* No. 40. Sheffield: Manpower Services Commission.

Doyle, C. (2003). *Work and organizational psychology: An introduction with attitude.* Hove: Psychology Press.

Drakeley, R.J. (1989). Biographical data. In P. Herriot (Ed.), *Handbook of assessment in organizations* (pp. 439–453). Chichester: Wiley.

Drenth, P.J.D. (1998). Personnel appraisal. In P.J.D. Drenth, H. Thierry & C.J. de Wolff (Eds), *Personnel psychology, Vol. 3. A handbook of work and organizational psychology* (pp. 59–88). Hove: Psychology Press.

Driskell, J., Hogan, R., & Salas, E. (1987). Personality and group performance. *Review of Personality and Social Psychology,* 9, 91–112.

Driskell, J.E., & Salas, E. (1991). Group decision-making under stress. *Journal of Applied Psychology,* 76(3), 473–478.

Driskell, J.E., Radtke, P.H., Salas, E. (2003). Virtual teams: Effects of technological mediation on team performance. *Group Dynamics,* 7(4), 297–323.

Driskell, J.E., Willis, R.P., & Cooper, C. (1992). Effective over learning on retention. *Journal of Applied Psychology,* 77, 615–622.

Druskat, V.U., & Pescosolido, A.T. (2002). The content of effective teamwork mental models in self-managing teams: Ownership, learning and heedful interrelating. *Human Relations,* 55(3), 283–314.

Druskat, V.U., & Wolff, S.B. (2001). Building the intelligence of groups. *Harvard Business Review,* 79(3), 81–90.

Dunnette, M.D. (1963). A note on the criterion. *Journal of Applied Psychology,* 47, 251–254.

Dutton, J.E., Dukerich, J.M., & Harquail, C.V. (1994). Organisational images and member identification. *Administrative Science Quarterly,* 39, 239–263.

Dvir, T., Eden, D., Avolio, B.J., & Shamir, B. (2002). Impact of transformational leadership on follower development and performance: A field experiment. *Academy of Management Journal,* 45(4), 735–744.

Dweck, C.S., Hong, Y., & Chiu, C. (1993). Implicit theories: Individual differences in the likelihood and meaning of dispositional inferences. *Personality and Social Psychology Bulletin,* 19, 644–656.

Eagly, A.H., & Chaiken, S. (1993). *The psychology of attitudes.* San Diego, CA: Harcourt Brace Jovanovich.

Eagly, A.H., Makhijani, M.G., & Klonsky, B.G. (1992). Gender and the evaluation of leaders: A meta-analysis. *Psychological Bulletin,* 111(1), 3–22.

Eason, K.D. (1996). *Information technology and organizational change* (2nd edn). London: Taylor & Francis.

Eby, L.T., & Buch, K. (1995). Job loss as career growth: Responses to involuntary career transitions. *The Career Development Quarterly,* 44 (September), 26–42.

Eby, L.T., Douthitt, S.S., Perrin, T., Noble, C.L., Atchley, K.P., & Ladd, R.T. (2002). Managerial support for dual-career relocation dilemmas. *Journal of Vocational Behaviour,* 60(3), 354–373.

Edelmann, R.J., & Woodall, L. (1997). Bullying at work. *The Occupational Psychologist,* 32, 28–31.

Eden, D., & Jacobson, D. (1976). Propensity to retire among older executives. *Journal of Vocational Behavior,* 8, 145–154.

Eden, C., & Spender, J.C. (1998). *Managerial and organizational cognition.* London: Sage.

Edkins, G.D., & Pollack, C.M. (1997). The influence of sustained attention on railway accidents. *Accident Analysis and Prevention,* 29(4), 533–539.

Edwards, J.R. (1992). A cybernetic theory of stress, coping and well-being in organizations. *Academy of Management Review,* 17, 238–274.

Edwards, J.R. (1998). Cybernetic theory of stress, coping and well-being: Review and extensions to work and family. In C. Cooper (Ed.), *Theories of organizational stress* (pp. 122–152). Oxford: Oxford University Press.

Edwards, J.R., & Baglioni, A.J.Jr (1993). The measurement of coping with stress: Construct validity of the Ways of Coping Checklist and the Cybernetic Coping Scale. *Work & Stress,* 7, 17–31.

Egan, G. (1998). *The skilled helper: A problem management approach to helping* (6th edn). Monterey, CA: Brooks/Cole.

Eisenberger, R., & Rhoades, L. (2001). Incremental effects of reward on creativity. *Journal of Personality and Social Psychology*, 81(4), 728–741.

Eisenberger, R., Armeli, S., Rexwinkel, B., Lynch, P.D., & Rhoades, L. (2001) Reciprocation of perceived organizational support. *Journal of Applied Psychology*, 86, 42–51.

Eisenberger, R., Huntington, R., Hutchison, S., & Sowa, D. (1986). Perceived organizational support. *Journal of Applied Psychology*, 71, 500–507.

Elen, J., & Lowyck, J. (1999). Metacognitive instructional knowledge: Cognitive mediation and instructional design. *Journal of Instructional Learning and Intelligent Systems*, 13(3–4), 145–169.

Elkin, A., & Rosch, P. (1990). Promoting mental health at the workplace: The prevention side of stress management. *Occupational Medicine: State of the Art Review*, 5, 739–754.

Elliot, M.S., & Williams, D.I. (2002). A qualitative evaluation of an employee counselling service from the perspective of client, counsellor and organisation. *Counselling Psychology Quarterly*, 15, 201–208.

Ellis, A. (2001). *Stress counselling: A rational emotive behaviour approach*. London: Sage.

Elo, A.L. (1994). Assessment of mental stress factors at work. In O.B. Dickerson & E.P. Horvath (Eds), *Occupational medicine* (pp. 945–959). St Louis: Mosby.

Elo, A.L., & Vehvilaienen, M.R. (1983). *Method for occupational health personnel to assess psychic stress factors at work: A study of reliability and validity of the method*. Helsinki: Institute of Occupational Health.

Emery, R.E., & Trist, E.L. (1969). *Socio-technical systems*. London: Penguin.

Emmelkamp, P.M.G. (1994). Behaviour therapy with adults. In S.L. Garfield & A.E. Bergin (Eds), *Handbook of psychotherapy and behaviour change* (4th edn, pp. 379–427). New York: Wiley.

Endler, N.S., & Parker, J.D.A. (1994). Assessment of multidimensional coping: Task, emotional and avoidance strategies. *Psychological Assessment*, 6, 50–60.

Endsley, M.R., & Kaber, D.B. (1999). Level of automation effects on performance, situation awareness and workload in a dynamic control task. *Ergonomics*, 42(3), 462–492.

Epstein, S., Pacini, R., Denes Raj, V., & Heier, H. (1996). Individual differences in intuitive-experimental and analytical-reasoning thinking styles. *Journal of Personality and Social Psychology*, 71, 390–405.

Ericson, T. (2001). Sensemaking in organizations: Towards a conceptual framework for understanding strategic change. *Scandinavian Journal of Management*, 17, 109–131.

Ernst and Young (2004). Home Page. /www.ey.com/global/content.nsf/

Evetts, J. (1996). *Gender and career in science and engineering*. London: Taylor and Francis.

Eysenck, M.W. (1982). *Attention and arousal*. New York: Springer-Verlag.

Facteau, J.D., & Bartholomew, S. (2001). Are performance appraisal ratings from different rating sources comparable? *Journal of Applied Psychology*, 86(2), 215–227.

Farnham, D.S. (1994). Paradigms of knowledge and instruction. *Review of Educational Research*, 64(3), 463–477.

Fay, D., & Sonnentag, S. (2002). Rethinking the effects of stressors: A longitudinal study on personal initiative. *Journal of Occupational Health Psychology*, 7(3), 221–234.

Feldman, D.C. (1976). A contingency theory of socialisation. *Administrative Science Quarterly*, 21, 433–452.

Fenigstein, A., Scheier, M.F., & Buss, A.H. (1975). Public and private self-consciousness: Assessment and theory. *Journal of Consulting and Clinical Psychology*, 43, 522–527.

Ferguson, E., Payne, T., & Anderson, N. (1994). Occupational personality assessment: Theory, structure and psychometrics of the OPQ FMX5– student. *Personality and Individual Differences*, 17(2), 217–225.

Festinger, L. (1954). A theory of social comparison processes. *Human Relations*, 7, 117–140.

Festinger, L. (1964). *Conflicts, decisions and dissonance*. Stanford, CA: Stanford University Press.

Fiedler, F.E. (1967). *A theory of leader effectiveness*. New York: McGraw-Hill.

Fiedler, F.E. (1989). The effective utilization of intellectual abilities and job-relevant knowledge in group performance: Cognitive resource theory and an agenda for the future. *Applied Psychology: An International Review*, 38(3), 289–304.

Finegold, D., & Soskice, D. (1990). The failure of training in Britain: Analysis and prescription. In D. Gleeson (Ed.), *Training and its alternatives* (pp. 18–57). Milton Keynes: Open University Press.

Fineman, S. (2003). *Understanding emotion at work*. London: Sage.

Finkelstein, A. & Dowell, J. (1993). *A comedy of errors: The London Ambulance Services Case Srudy*. Report of the inquiry into the London Ambulance Service. International Workshop on Software specification and Design Case Study. The Communication Directorate, South West Thames Regional Health Authority.

Fisher, C.D., and Boyle, G.J. (1997). Personality and employee selection: Credibility regained. *Asia Pacific Journal of Human Resources*, 35(2), 26–40.

Fisher, R.C., & Thomas, B. (1987). The application of a task oriented team building model to a 'newly large' organization. *Consultation: An International Journal*, 6(3), 175–186.

Flanagan, B., Nestel, D., & Joseph, M. (2004). Making patient safety the focus: Crisis resource management in the undergraduate curriculum. *Medical Education*, 38(1), 56–66.

Flanagan, J.C. (1954). The critical incident technique. *Psychological Bulletin*, 51, 327–358.

Flannery, R.B.Jr. (2001). The Assaulted Staff Action Program (ASAP): Ten year empirical support for Critical Incident Stress Management (CISM). *International Journal of Emergency Mental Health*, 3(1), 5–10.

Flavell, J.H. (1979). Metacognition and cognitive monitoring: A new area of cognitive-developmental inquiry. *American Psychologist*, 34(10), 906–911.

Fleishman, E.A. (1953). The measurement of leadership attitudes in industry. *Journal of Applied Psychology*, 37, 153–158.

Fleishman, E.A., & Quaintance, M.K. (1984). *Taxonomies of human performance: The description of human tasks*. New York: Academic Press.

Fleming, D. (1991). *The concept of meta-competence. Competence and assessment* (Issue 16). Sheffield. Employment Department Group.

Fletcher, B.C. (1988). The epidemiology of occupational stress. In C.L. Cooper & R. Payne (Eds), *Causes, coping and consequences of stress at work* (pp. 3–50). Chichester: Wiley.

Fletcher, C. (1997). Self-awareness – A neglected attribute in selection and assessment. *International Journal of Selection and Assessment*, 5, 183–187.

Fletcher, C. (2001). Performance appraisal and performance management: The developing research agenda. *Journal of Occupational and Organizational Psychology*, 74, 473–487.

Fletcher, C. (2002). Appraisal – An individual psychological analysis. In S. Sonnentag (Ed.), *The psychological management of individual performance: A handbook in the psychology of management in organizations*. Chichester: Wiley.

Fletcher, C. (2004). *Appraisal and feedback: Making performance review work* (3rd edn). Chartered London: Institute of Personnel and Development.

Fletcher, C., & Baldry, C. (2001). Multi-source feedback systems: A research perspective. In I. Robertson & C. Cooper (Eds), *Personnel psychology and HRM* (pp. 117–162). Chichester: Wiley.

Flin, R.H., Mearns, K.J., Fleming, M., & Gordon, R. (1996). *Risk perception in UK offshore workers*. Report OTH 94454 to OSD, HSE. Suffolk: HSE Books.

Flum, H., & Blustein, D.L. (2000). Reinvigorating the study of vocational exploration: A framework for research. *Journal of Vocational Behavior*, 56(3), 380–404.

Fodor, E.M. (1976). Group stress, authoritarian style of control and use of power. *Journal of Applied Psychology*, 61(3), 313–318.

Folger, R., & Skarlicki, D.P. (2001). Fairness as a dependent variable: Why tough times can lead to bad management. In R. Cropanzano (Ed.), *Justice in the workplace: From theory to practice* (Vol. 2, pp. 97–118). Mahwah, NJ: Lawrence Erlbaum Associates.

Folkman, S.K., & Moskowitz, J.T. (2000). Positive affect and the other sides of coping. *American Psychologist*, 55, 647–654.

Folkman, S., Lazarus, R.S., Dunkel-Schetter, C., DeLongis, A., & Gruen, R.J. (1986). The dynamics of a stressful encounter. Key reading in social psychology. In A.W. Kruglanski & E.T. Higgins (Eds), *Motivational science: Social and personality perspectives* (pp. 111–127). Philadelphia, PA: Psychology Press/Taylor & Francis.

Fombrun, C., & Rindova, V. (2000). The road to transparency: Reputation management at Royal Dutch/Shell. In M. Schultz & M.J. Hatch (Eds), *The expressive organization*. Milton Keynes: Open University Press.

Ford, J., Smith, E., Weissbein, D., Gully, S., & Salas, E. (1998). Relationships of goal orientation, metacognition activity, and practice strategies with learning outcomes and transfer. *Journal of Applied Psychology*, 83, 213–233.

Ford, J.K., & Kraiger, K. (1995). The application of cognitive constructs and principles to the instructional systems model of training: Implications for needs assessment, design, and transfer. In C. Cooper & I.R. Robertson (Eds), *International Review of Industrial and Organizational Psychology* (pp. 1–48). Chichester: Wiley & Sons.

Ford, L.R., & Locke, K. (2002). Paid time off as a vehicle for self-definition and sense-making. *Journal of Organizational Behaviour*, 23 (Special Issue), 489–509.

Fordyce, J.K., & Weil, R. (1979). *Managing with people: A manager's handbook of organization development methods* (2nd Edn). Oxford: Addison-Wesley.

Foster, J.J. (2000). Motivation in the workplace. In N. Chmiel (Ed.), *Work and organizational psychology: A European perspective* (pp. 302–326). Oxford: Blackwell Publishers.

Foushee, H. (1984). Dyads and triads at 35,000 feet – factors affecting group process and aircrew performance. *American Psychologist*, 39(8), 885–893.

Frayne, C.A., & Geringer, J.M. (2000). Self-management training for improving job performance: A field experiment involving sales people. *Journal of Applied Psychology*, 85(3), 361–372.

Freid, Y., Melamed, S., & Ben-David, H.A. (2002). The joint effects of noise, job complexity, and gender on employee sickness absence: An exploratory study across 21 organizations – the CORDIS Study. *Journal of Occupational and Organizational Psychology*, 75, 131–144.

French, J.R.P., Caplan. R.D., & Van Harrison, R. (1982). *The mechanisms of job stress and strain.* New York: Wiley.

French, W., Bell, C., & Zawacki, R. (Eds). (1994). *Organizational development and transformation: Managing effective change.* Burr Ridge, IL: Irwin McGraw Hill.

Frese, M. (1998). Work and organizational psychology. In M. Eysenck (Ed.), *Psychology: An integrated approach* (pp. 624–667). London: Longman.

Frese, M. (2000). The changing nature of work. In N. Chmiel (Ed.), *Introduction to work and organizational psychology: A European perspective* (pp. 424–439). Oxford: Blackwell.

Frese, M., & Zapf, D. (1994). Action as the core of work psychology: A German approach. In M.D. Dunnett, L.M. Hough & H.C. Triandis (Eds), *Handbook of industrial and organizational psychology* (Vol. 4, 2nd edn, pp. 271–340). Palo Alto, CA: Consulting Psychologists Press.

Frese, M., Kring, W., Soose, A., & Zempel, J. (1996). Personal initiative at work: Differences between East and West Germany. *Academy of Management Journal*, 39(1), 37–63.

Fried, Y., Tiegs, R.B., & Bellamy, A. (1992). Personal and interpersonal predictors of supervisors' avoidance of evaluating subordinates. *Journal of Applied Psychology*, 77, 462–468.

Fritzsche, B.A., & Brannick, M.T. (2002). The importance of representative design in judgement tasks: The case of resume screening. *Journal of Occupational and Organizational Psychology*, 75(2), 163–170.

Frone, M.R., Russell, M., & Cooper, L.M. (1997). Relation of work-family conflict to health outcomes: A four-year longitudinal study of employed parents. *Journal of Occupational and Organizational Psychology*, 70, 325–335.

Frost, P., Moore, L., Louis, M., Lundberg, C., & Martin, J. (Eds). (1991). *Reframing organizational culture.* Newbury Park, CA: Sage.

Fry, R., Barrett, F., Seiling, J., & Whitney, D. (2002). Appreciative inquiry and organizational transformation: Reports from the field. *Personnel Psychology*, 55(4), 1022–1025.

Fulk, J., & Wendler, E.R. (1982). Dimensionality of leader-subordinate interaction: A path-goal investigation. *Organizational Behaviour and Human Performance*, 30, 241–264.

Furnham, A. (1997). *The psychology of behaviour at work.* Hove: Psychology Press.

Furnham, A., & Gunter, B. (1993). *Corporate assessment: Auditing a company's personality.* London: Routledge.

Furnham, A., Steele, H., & Pendleton, D. (1993a). A psychometric assessment of the Belbin Team Role Self-Perception Inventory. *Journal of Occupational and Organizational Psychology*, 66, 245–247.

Furnham, A., Steele, H., & Pendleton, D. (1993b). A response to Dr Belbin's reply. *Journal of Occupational and Organizational Psychology*, 70, 241–258.

Gabris, G.T., & Rock, S.M. (1991). Situational interviews and job-performance – The results in one public agency. *Public Personnel Management*, 20(4), 469–483.

Gagne, R., & Driscoll, M. (1988). *Essentials of Learning for Instruction* (2nd edn). Englewood Cliffs, NJ: Prentice-Hall.

Gagne, R., Briggs, L.J., & Wager, W. (1992). *Principles of instructional design.* Orlando, FL: Harcourt Brace.

Gagne, R.M. (1974). *Essentials of learning for instruction* (2nd edn). Hinsdale, IL: Dryden Press.

Gallivan, M.J., Hofman, D., & Orlikowski, W. (1994). Implementing radical change: Gradual versus rapid pace. ICIS, 325–339.

Gallois, C., Callan, V.J., & Palmer, J.A.M. (1992). The influence of applicant communication style and interviewer characteristics on hiring decisions. *Journal of Applied Social Psychology*, 22(13), 1041–1060.

Ganster, D.C., & Schaubroeck, J. (1995). Work stress and employee health. *Journal of Management*, 17, 235–271.

Garis, J.N. (2001). Individual differences in safe behavior: A safety practitioner's viewpoint. *Journal of Prevention and Intervention in the Community*, 22(1), 81–84.

Gastil, J. (1994). A meta-analytic review of the productivity and satisfaction of democratic and autocratic leadership. *Small Group Research*, 26(3), 384–410.

Gatewood, R.D., Gowan, M.A., & Lautenschlager, G.J. (1993). Corporate image, recruitment image, and initial job choice decisions. *Academy of Management Journal*, 36(2), 414–427.

Gaugler, B.B., Rosenthal, D.R., Thornton, G.C., & Bentson, C. (1987). Meta-analysis of assessment center validities. *Journal of Applied Psychology Monograph*, 72, 493–511.

Gavin, J., & McPhail, S.M. (1978). Intervention and evaluation: A proactive team approach to OD. *Journal of Applied Behavioural Science*, 14(2), 175–194.

Geertz, C. (1983). *Local knowledge: Further essays in interpretive anthropology*. New York: Basic Books.

Geller, E.S. (2002). Organizational behavior management and industrial/organizational psychology: Achieving synergy by valuing differences. *Journal of Organizational Behavior Management*, 22(2), 111–130.

Geller, E.S., Roberts, D.S., Gilmore, M.R. (1996). Predicting propensity to actively care for occupational safety. *Journal of Safety Research*, 27(1), 1–8.

George, J.M., & Jones, G.R. (2001). Towards a process model of individual change in organizations. *Human Relations*, 54, 419–444.

Gerard, M.J., Armstrong, T.J., Rempel, D.A., & Woolley, C. (2002). Short term and long term effects of enhanced auditory feedback on typing force, EMG, and comfort while typing. *Applied Ergonomics*, 33(2), 129–138.

Gerstein, L.W., & Shullman, S.L. (1992). Counselling psychology and the workplace: The emergence of organizational counselling psychology. In R. Brown & R.W. Lent (Eds), *The handbook of counselling psychology* (2nd edn, pp. 581–625). New York: Wiley.

Gibb, S. (2003). What do we talk about when we talk about mentoring? *British Journal of Guidance and Counselling*, 31(1), 39–49.

Gibson, F.W., Fiedler, F.E., & Barrett, K.M. (1993). Stress, babble and the utilization of leader's intellectual abilities. *Leadership Quarterly*, 4(2), 189–208.

Giddens, A. (1984). *The constitution of society*. London: Polity Press.

Giga, S.I., Cooper, C.L., & Faragher, B. (2003). The development of a framework for a comprehensive approach to stress management interventions at work. *International Journal of Stress Management*, 10, 280–296.

Gill, R.W.T. (1979). The in-tray (in-basket) exercise as a measure of management potential. *Journal of Occupational Psychology*, 52, 185–197.

Gillen, M., Baltz, D., Gassel, M., Kirsch, L., & Vaccaro, D. (2002). Perceived safety climate, job demands, and coworker support among union and nonunion injured construction workers. *Journal of Safety Research*, 33(1), 33–51.

Gilligan C. (1982). *In a different voice: Psychological theory and women's development*. Cambridge, MA: Harvard University Press.

Gilliland, S.W. (1993). The perceived fairness of selection systems – An organizational justice perspective. *Academy of Management Review*, 18(4), 694–734.

Gilliland, S.W., & Chan, D. (2001). *Justice in organizations: Theory, methods, and applications*. London: Sage.

Ginzberg, E. (1972). Toward a theory of occupational choice: A restatement. *Vocational Guidance Quarterly*, 20, 169–176.

Ginzberg, E., Ginsberg, S.W., Axelrad, S., & Herma, J.L. (1951). *Occupational choice: An approach to general theory*. New York: Columbia University Press.

Gioia, D.A., & Chittipeddi, K. (1991). Sensemaking and sensegiving in strategic change initiation. *Strategic Management Journal*, 12, 443–468.

Gioia, D.A., & Thomas, J.B. (1996). Identity, image, and issue interpretation: Sensemaking during strategic change in academia. *Administrative Science Quarterly*, 41, 370–403.

Gist, M.E., & Mitchell, T.R. (1992). Self-efficacy: A theoretical analysis of its determinants and malleability. *Academy of Management Review*, 17(2), 183–211.

Gladstein, D. (1984). Groups in context: A model of task group effectiveness. *Administrative Science Quarterly*, 29, 499–517.

Glennon, J.R., Albright, L.E., & Owens, W.A. (1966). *A catalog of life history items*. Greensboro, NC: The Richardson Foundation.

Goffman, E. (1961). The moral career of the mental patient. In E. Goffman (Ed.), *Asylums* (pp. 125–170). New York: Anchor.

Goldberg, D. (1978). *Manual of the General Health Questionnaire*. Windsor: National Foundation for Educational Research.

Goldenhar, L.M., Moran, S.K., & Colligan, M. (2001). Health and safety training in a sample of open-shop construction companies. *Journal of Safety Research*, 32(2), 237–252.

Goldstein, A.P., & Sorcher, M. (1974). *Changing supervisor behavior*. New York: Pergamon Press.

Goldstein, I.L. (1980). Training in work organizations. *Annual Review of Psychology*, 31, 229–272.

Goldstein, I.L. (1991). Training in work organizations. In M.D. Dunnette & L.M. Hough (Eds), *Handbook of Industrial and organizational psychology*. (Vol. 2). Palo Alto, CA: Consulting Press, Inc.

Goldstein, I.L. (1993). *Training in organizations: Needs assessment, development and evaluation* (3rd edn). Belmont, CA: Wadsworth.

Goldstein, I.L., & Ford, J.K. (2002). *Training in organizations: Needs assessment, development, and evaluation* (4th edn). Belmont, CA: Wadsworth.

Goleman, D. (1996). *Emotional intelligence*. New York: Bantam Books.

Golembiewski, R.T., & Stevenson, J.G. (1998). *Cases and applications in nonprofit management*. Itasca, IL: F. E. Peacock.

Gollwitzer, P.M. (1993). Goal achievement: The role of intentions. *European Review of Social Psychology*, 4, 141–185.

Gomez-Mejia, B.L.R., Balkin, D.B., & Cardy, R.L. (2001). *Managing human resources*. Englewood Cliffs, NJ: Prentice Hall.

Goodman, J.S., Wood, R.E., & Hendrickx, M. (2004). Feedback specificity, exploration, and learning. *Journal of Applied Psychology*, 89(2), 248–262.

Goodson, J.R., McGee, G.W., & Cashman, J.F. (1989). Situational leadership theory: A test of leadership prescriptions. *Group and Organization Studies*, 14(4), 446–461.

Goodstone, M.S., & Lopez, F.E. (2001). The frame of reference approach as a solution to an assessment center dilemma. *Consulting Psychology Journal: Practice and Research*, 53(2), 96–107.

Gottfredson, G.D., & Holland, J.L. (1996). *Dictionary of Holland occupational codes*. Odessa, FL: Psychological Assessment Resources.

Gouldner, A.W. (1957). Cosmopolitans and locals: Towards an analysis of latent social roles. *Administrative Science Quarterly*, 2, 282–292.

Graham, J.W. (1986). Principled organizational dissent: A theoretical essay. *Research In Organizational Behavior*, 8, 1–52.

Grandey, A.A., Dickter, D.N., & Sin, H.P. (2004). The customer is not always right: Customer aggression and emotion regulation of service employees. *Journal of Organizational Behavior*, 25(3), 397–418.

Graves, J.P. (1982). Let's put appraisal back in performance appraisal: II. *Personnel Journal*, 61(12), 918–923.

Gray, J.J. (1999). Techniques to cool the anger. *Cognitive and Behavioural Practice*, 6(3), 284–286.

Gray, K. (1984). Counselling interventions in organizations. In W. Dryden & A.G. Watts (Eds), *Guidance and counselling in Britain: A 20 year perspective*. Cambridge: Hobson.

Gray, W.D., & Orasanu, J.M. (1987). Transfer of cognitive skills. In Stephen M. Cormier, & Joseph D. Hagman (Eds), *Transfer of learning: Contemporary research and applications. The educational technology series* (pp. 183–215). San Diego, CA: Academic Press.

Green, G.D. (1994). *Industrial relations: Text and case studies*. London: Pitman Publishing.

Greenberg, J. (1990). Organizational justice: Yesterday, today, and tomorrow. *Journal of Management*, 16, 399–432.

Greenberg, J. (1993). Stealing in the name of justice: Informational and interpersonal moderators of theft reactions to underpayment inequity. *Organizational Behaviour and Human Decision Processes*, 54, 81–103.

Greenberger, D.B., & Strasser, S. (1986). Development and application of a model of personal control in organizations. *Academy of Management Review*, 11(1), 164–177.

Greene, R., & Nowack, K. (1996). Stress, hardiness and absenteeism: Results of a 3–year longitudinal study. *Work and Stress*, 9, 448–462.

Greenhaus, J.H., Collins, K.M., & Shaw, J.D. (2003). The relation between work-family balance and quality of life. *Journal of Vocational Behavior*, 63(3), 510–531.

Greiner, B.A. (1994). *Work analysis instrument to identify objective stress factors in service work: Observer manual and response sheets*. Berkeley: University of California, School of Public Health.

Greiner, B.A., & Lietner, K. (1989). Assessment of job stress: RHIA instrument. In K. Landau & W. Roohmert (Eds), *Recent developments in work analysis* (pp. 53–66). Philadelphia: Taylor and Francis.

Greiner, B.A., Ragland, D.R., Krause, N., Syme, S., & Fisher, J.M. (1997). Objective measurement of occupational stress factors: An example with San Francisco urban transit operators. *Journal of Occupational Health Psychology*, 2, 325–342.

Griffin, M.A., Mathieu, J.E., & Jacobs, R.R. (2001). Perceptions of work contexts: Disentangling influences at multiple levels of analysis. *Journal of Occupational and Organizational Psychology*, 74(5), 563–580.

Griffiths, J., & Luker, K. (1994). Intraprofessional teamwork in district nursing: In whose interests? *Journal of Advanced Nursing*, 20(6), 1038–1045.

Grindle, A.C., Dickinson, A.M., & Boettcher, W. (2000). Behavioral safety research in manufacturing settings: A review of the literature. *Journal of Organizational Behavior Management*, 20(1), 29–68.

Grugulis, I., & Wilkinson, A. (2002). Managing culture at British Airways: Hype, hope and reality. *Long Range Planning: International Journal of Strategic Management*, 35(2), 179–194.

Grzeda, M.M., & Prince, J.B. (1997). Career motivation measures: A test of convergent and discriminant validity. *The International Journal of Human Resource Management*, 8(3), 172–196.

Guest, D. (1998). Is the psychological contract worth taking seriously? *Journal of Organizational Behaviour*, 19, 649–664.

Guest, D., & Mackenzie Davey, K. (1996). Don't write off the traditional career. *People Management*, 2 February, pp. 22–25.

Guion, R.M. (1961). Criterion measurement and personnel judgments. *Personnel Psychology*, 14, 141–149.

Guion, R.M. (1998). *Assessment, measurement and prediction for personnel decisions*. Mahwah, NJ: Lawrence Erlbaum.

Gully, S.M., Payne, S.C., Koles, K.L.K., & Whiteman, J.K. (2002). The impact of error training and individual differences on training outcomes: An attribute-treatment interaction perspective. *Human Performance*, 15(4), 381–410.

Gumuseli, A.I., & Ergin, B. (2002). The manager's role in enhancing the transfer of training: A Turkish case study. *International Journal of Training and Development*, 6, 80–97.

Gunzol, H. (1989). The dual meaning of managerial careers: Organizational and individual levels of analysis. *Journal of Management Studies*, 26, 225–250.

Guppy, A., Edwards, J.A., Brough, P., Peters-Bean, K.M., Sale, C., & Short, E. (2004). The psychometric properties of the short version of the Cybernetic Coping Scale: A multi-group confirmatory factor analysis across four samples. *Journal of Occupational and Organizational Psychology*, 77(1), 39–67.

Gutmann, David, & Pierre, Ronan (2000). Consultation and transformation: Between shared management and generative leadership. In Edward B. Klein, & Faith Gabelnick (Eds), *Dynamic consultation in a changing workplace* (pp. 3–31). Madison, CT: Psychosocial Press.

Guzzo, R.A., Jette, R.D., & Katzell, R.A. (1985). The effects of psychologically based intervention programs on worker productivity: A meta-analysis. *Personnel Psychology*, 38(2), 275–291.

Guzzo, R.A., Noonan, K.A., & Elron, E. (1994). Human resource practices as communications and the psychological contract. *Journal of Applied Psychology*, 79, 617–626.

Guzzo, R.A., Yost, P.R., Campbell, R.J., & Shea, G.P. (1993). Potency in groups: Articulating a construct. *British Journal of Social Psychology*, 32, 87–106.

Haas, M.W., Nelson, T., Repperger, D., Bolia, R., & Zacharias, G. (2001). Applying adaptive control and display characteristics to future Air Force crew stations. *International Journal of Aviation Psychology*, 11(2), 223–235.

Haccoun, R.R. (1997). Transfer and retention: Let's do both and avoid dilemmas. *Applied Psychology: An International Review*, 46, 340–344.

Haccoun, R.R., & Saks, A.M. (1998). Training in the 21st century: Some lessons from the last one. *Canadian Psychology*, 39(1–2), 33–51.

Hackett, R.D. (2002). Understanding and predicting work performance in the Canadian military. *Canadian Journal of Behavioural Science*, 34(2), 131–140.

Hackman, J.R., & Morris, C.G. (1975). Group tasks, group interaction process and group performance: A review and proposed integration. In L. Berkowitz (Ed.), *Advances in experimental social psychology* (Vol. 8, pp. 45–99). New York: Academic Press.

Hackman, J.R., & Oldham, G.R. (1975). Motivation through the design of work: Test of a theory. *Organizational Behaviour and Human Performance*, 16, 250–279.

Hailey, V.H., & Balogun, J. (2002). Devising context sensitive approaches to change: The example of Glaxo Wellcome. *Long Range Planning: International Journal of Strategic Management*, 35(2), 153–178.

Hakel, M.D. (1986). Personnel selection and placement. *Annual Review of Psychology*, 37, 351–380.

Hall, D.T., & Mirvis, P.H. (1995). The new career contract: Developing the whole person at midlife and beyond [Special Issue: Careers from midlife]. *Journal of Vocational Behaviour*, 47, 269–289.

Hall, F.S., & Hall, D.T. (1997). *The two-career couple*. Reading, MA: Addison-Wesley.

Hampden-Turner, C. (1994). The structure of entrapment: Dilemmas standing in the way of women managers and strategies to resolve these. *Deeper News*, 5(1), 1–43.

Handy, C. (1987). *The making of managers*. London: NEDO/HMSO.

Hanges, P.J., Schneider, B., & Niles, K. (1990). Stability of performance: An interactionist perspective. *Journal of Applied Psychology*, 75(6), 658–667.

Hansen, C. (1989). A causal model of the relationship among accidents, biodata, personality, and cognitive factors. *Journal of Applied Psychology*, 74, 458–464.

Hanson, E.K.S., Schaufelli, W., Vrijkotte, T., Plomp, N.H., & Godaert, G.L.R. (2000). The validity and reliability of the Dutch Effort–Reward Imbalance Questionnaire. *Journal of Occupational Health Psychology*, 5(1), 142–155.

Hardingham, A., & Royal, J. (1994). *Pulling together: Teamwork in practice*. London: IPD Books.

Harris, C., Daniels, K., & Briner, R.B. (2003). A daily diary study of goals and affective well-being at work. *Journal of Occupational and Organizational Psychology*, 76(3), 401–410.

Harris, M.M., Lievens, F., & Van Hoye, G. (2004). 'I think they discriminated against me': Using prototype theory and organizational justice theory for understanding perceived discrimination in selection and promotion situations. *International Journal of Selection and Assessment*, 12(1–2), 54–65.

Harrison, B. (1989). Class and gender in modern british labour. *History Journal Past and Present*, (124), 121–158.

Harrison, R. (1972). Understanding your organization's character. *Harvard Business Review*, 50(23), 119–128.

Hart, P.M., & Cotton, P. (2003). Conventional wisdom is often misleading: Police stress within an organizational health framework. In M.F. Dollard, A.H. Winefield & H.R. Winefield (Eds), *Occupational stress in the service professions* (pp. 118–127). London: Taylor & Francis.

Harter, J.K., Schmidt, F.L., & Hayes, T.L. (2002). Business-unit level relationship between employee satisfaction, employee engagement, and business outcomes: A meta-analysis. *Journal of Applied Psychology*, 87, 268–279.

Harvey, S., Kelloway, E.K., & Duncan-Leiper, L. (2003). Trust in management as a buffer of the relationships between overload and strain. *Journal of Occupational Health Psychology*, 8(4), 306–315.

Harvey, J., Erdos, G., Bolam, H., Cox, M.A., Kennedy, J.N.P., & Gregory, D.T. (2002). An analysis of safety culture attitudes in a highly regulated environment. *Work and Stress*, 16(1), 18–36.

Haslam, S.A. (2004). *Psychology in organizations: The social identity approach* (2nd edn). London: Sage.

Hatch, M.J., & Schultz, M. (2002). Relations between organizational culture, identity and image. *European Journal of Marketing*, 31, 5/6, 356–365.

Hatchuel, A., Le Masson, P., & Weil, B. (2002). From knowledge management to design-oriented organisations. *International Social Science Journal* (NWISS) 54(171), 25–37.

Hayes, J., Allinson, C.W., Hudson, R.S., & Keasey, K. (2003). Further reflections on the nature of intuition-analysis and the construct validity of the cognitive style index. *Journal of Occupational and Organizational Psychology*, 76(2), 269–278.

Hayes, J., Rose-Quirie, A., & Allinson, C.W. (2000). Senior managers' perceptions of the competencies they require for effective performance: Implications for training and development. *Personnel Review*, 29(1–2), 92–101.

Health & Safety Executive (1995). *A guide to the reporting of injuries, diseases and dangerous occurrences regulations.* Sudbury: HSE Books.

Health & Safety Executive (1998). *Stress at work: A guide for employers.* Sudbury: HSE Books.

Health & Safety Commission (HSC) (1993). *Third report of the Advisory Committee on the Safety of Nuclear Installations – Organising for Safety.* London: Health & Safety Commission.

Health & Safety Executive (HSE) (1989). Reducing noise at work. *Guidance on the Noise at Work Regulations.* Sudbury: HSE Books.

Health and Safety Executive (1999). *Understanding health surveillance at work.* (2nd edn). London: HSE Books.

Hebden, J.E. (1986). Adopting an organization's culture: The socialization of graduate trainees. *Organizational Dynamics*, 15(1), 54–72.

Heinbokel, T., Sonnentag, S., Frese, M., & Stolte, W. (1996). Don't underestimate the problems of user centredness in software development projects—there are many! *Behaviour and Information Technology*, 15(4), 226–236.

Helwig, A.A. (2001). A test of Gottfredson's theory using a ten-year longitudinal study. *Journal of Career Development*, 28(2), 77–95.

Hennessey, B.A., & Amabile, T.M. (1998). Reality, intrinsic motivation, and creativity. *American Psychologist*, 53(6), 674–675.

Henwood, K.L., & Pidgeon, N.F. (1992). Qualitative research and psychologial theorizing. *British Journal of Psychology*, 83, 97–111.

Herbig, B., Bussing, A., & Ewert, T. (2001). The role of tacit knowledge in the work context of nursing. *Journal of Advanced Nursing*, 34(5), 687–695.

Herd, J.A. (1988). Physiological indices of job stress. In J.J. Hurrell, Jr., L.R. Murphy, S. Sauter & C. Cooper (Eds), *Occupational stress: Issues and developments in research* (pp. 124–148). New York: Taylor & Francis.

Herr, E.L. (1997). Super's life-span, life-space approach and its outlook for refinement. *Career Development Quarterly*, 45(3), 238–246.

Herr, E.L., & Cramer, S.H. (1992). *Career guidance and counselling through the life span.* New York: Harper Collins.

Herriot, P. (1989). Selection as a social process. In M. Smith & I. Robertson (Eds), *Advances in selection and assessment* (pp. 171–187). Chichester: Wiley.

Herriot, P. (1992). *The career management challenge.* London: Sage.

Herriot, P. (1995). The changing context of assessment and its implications. *International Journal of Selection and Assessment*, 3(3), 197–201.

Herriot, P. (2001). *The employment relationship.* London: Routledge.

Herriot, P. (2002). Selection and self: Selection as a social process. *European Journal of Work and Organizational Psychology*, 11(4), 385–402.

Herriot, P. (2003). Assessment by groups: Can value be added? *European Journal of Work and Organizational Psychology*, 12(2), 131–145.

Herriot, P. (2004). Social identities and applicant reactions. *International Journal of Selection and Assessment*, 12(1–2), 75–83.

Herriot, P., Hirsch, W., & Reilly, P. (1998). *Trust and transition: Managing today's employment relationship.* Chichester: Wiley.

Herriot, P., & Pemberton, C. (1995). Career contracting. *Human Relations*, 49, 757–90.

Herriot, P., & Pemberton, C. (1996). Contracting careers. *Human Relations*, 49(6), 757–790.

Herriot, P., & Pemberton, C. (1997). Facilitating new deals. *Human Resource Management*, 7(1), 45–56.

Herriot, P., Hirsh, W., & Reilly, P. (1998). *Trust and transition: Managing today's employment relationships.* Chichester: Wiley.

Herzberg, F. (1968). One more time: How do you motivate employees? *Harvard Business Review*, 46, 53–62.

Herzberg, F., Mausner, B., & Snyderman, B. (1959). *The motivation to work*. New York: Wiley.

Heslin, P.A. (2003). Self- and other-referent criteria of career success. *Journal of Career Assessment*, 11(3), 262–286.

Higuera, A.Z.L. (2001). Adverse impact in personnel selection: The legal framework and test bias. *European-Psychologist*, 6(2), 103–111.

Hill, W.P. (1971). Cited in Hollway, W. (1991). *Work psychology and organizational behaviour*. London: Sage.

Hirschhorn, L., & Barnett, C.K. (1993). *The psychodynamics of organizations*. Philadelphia: Temple University Press.

Hirsh, W., & Carter, A. (2000). *New directions in management development*. Brighton: Institute for Employment Studies.

Hitt, Michael A., & Ireland R. Duane (1987). 'Building competitive strength in international markets.' *Long Range Planning*, 20 February, 115–122.

Hix, D., & Gabbard, L. (2002). Usability engineering of virtual environments. In K.M. Stanney (Ed.), *Handbook of virtual environments: Design, implementation, and applications* (pp. 681–699). Mahwah, NJ: Lawrence Erlbaum Associates.

HMSO. (1964). *Industrial training act*. London: HMSO.

Hobbs, Alan, Williamson, & Ann (2002). Unsafe acts and unsafe outcomes in aircraft maintenance. *Ergonomics*, 45(12), 866–882.

Hobson, C., Delunas, L., & Kesis, D. (2001). Compelling evidence of the need for corporate work-life balance initiatives. *Journal of Employment Counselling*, 38, 38–44.

Hochschild, A. (1983). *The managed heart*. Berkeley: University of California Press.

Hockey, G.R.J. (2000). Work environment and performance. In N. Chmiel (Ed.), *Introduction to work and organizational psychology: A European perspective*, Oxford: Blackwell.

Hodgkinson, G.P., & Maule, A.J. (2002). The individual in the strategy process: Insights from behavioural decision research and cognitive mapping. In A.S. Huff & M. Jenkins (Eds), *Mapping strategic knowledge* (pp. 196–219). London: Sage.

Hodgkinson, G.P. & Sadler-Smith, E. (2003). Reflections on reflections … . On the nature of intuition, analysis and the construct validity of the cognitive style index. *Journal of Occupational and Organizational Psychology*, 76(2), 243–268.

Hoffman, H. (1998). Virtual reality: A new tool for interdisciplinary psychology research. *Cyber Psychology and Behaviour*, 1(2), 195–200.

Hoffman, K.G., & Donaldson, J.F. (2004). Contextual tensions of the clinical environment and their influence on teaching and learning. Medical Education, 38(4), 448–454.

Hofmann, D.A., & Stetzer, A. (1996). A cross-level investigation of factors influencing unsafe behaviors and accidents. *Personnel Psychology*, 49(2), 307–339.

Hofmann, D.A., Jacobs, R., & Baratta, J.E. (1993). Dynamic criteria and the measurement of change. *Journal of Applied Psychology*, 78(2), 194–204.

Hofstede, G. (1991). *Cultures and organisations: Software of the mind*. London: McGraw-Hill Book Company.

Hofstede, G., Neuijen, B., Ohayv, D., & Sanders, G. (1990). Measuring organizational cultures: A qualitative and quantitative study across twenty cases. *Administrative Science Quarterly*, 35, 286–316.

Hogan, R., & Hogan, J. (1995). *Hogan Personality Inventory manual* (2nd edn). Tulsa, OK: Hogan Assessment Systems.

Holbeche, L. (2003). Aligning human resources and business strategy. *International Journal of Training and Development*, 7(1), 78–79.

Holden, M.K., & Todorov, E. (2002). Use of virtual environments in motor learning and rehabilitation. In K.M. Stanney, (Ed.), *Handbook of virtual environments: Design, implementation, and applications* (pp. 999–1026). Mahwah, NJ: Lawrence Erlbaum Associates.

Holland, J.L. (1959). A theory of vocational choice. *Journal of Counselling Psychology*, 6, 35–45.

Holland, J.L. (1973). *Making vocational choices: A theory of careers*. Englewood Cliffs, NJ: Prentice Hall.

Holland J.L. (1996). Exploring careers with a typology. What we have learned and some new directions. *American Psychologist*, 51, 397–406.

Holland, J.L. (1997). *Making vocational choices: A theory of vocational personalities and work environments* (3rd Edn). Odessa, FL: Psychological Assessment Resources.

Holland, J.L., & Nichols, R.C. (1964). Explorations of a theory of vocational choice: III. A longitudinal study of change in a major field of study. *Personnel and Guidance Journal*, 43(3), 235–242.

Holland, J.L., Fritzsche, B.A., & Powell, A.B. (1997). *The self-directed search technical manual*. Odessa, FL: Psychological Assessment Resources.

Hollenbeck, J.R., Williams, C.R., & Klein, H.J. (1987). Goal commitment and the goal setting process: Problems, prospects, and proposals for future research. *Journal of Applied Psychology*, 72, 212–220.

Hollon, S.D., & Beck, A.T. (1994). Cognitive and cognitive-behavioural therapies. In A.E. Bergin & S.L. Garfield (Eds), *Handbook of psychotherapy and behaviour change* (4th edn, pp. 428–466). New York: Wiley.

Hollway, W. (1991). *Work psychology and organizational behaviour*. London: Sage.

Holman, D., Epitropaki, O., & Fernie, S. (2001). Understanding learning strategies in the workplace: A factor analytic investigation. *Journal of Occupational and Organizational Psychology*, 74(5), 675–682.

Holmes, T.H., & Rahe, R.H. (1967). The social readjustment rating scale. *Journal of Psychosomatic Research*, 11, 213–218.

Hopson, B., & Adams, J. (1976). *Transition: Understanding and managing personal change*. London: Martin Robertson.

Hopson, B., & Hayes, J. (1972). *The theory and practice of vocational guidance* (pp. 359–373). Oxford: Pergamon Press.

Hosking, D.M. (1988). Organizing, leadership and skilful processes. *Journal of Management Studies*, 25(2), 147–166.

Hough, L.A. (1984). Development and evaluation of an 'accomplishment record' method of selecting and promoting professionals. *Journal of Applied Psychology*, 69, 135–146.

Hough, L.M., & Oswald, F.L. (2000). Personnel selection: Looking toward the future – remembering the past. *Annual Review of Psychology*, 51, 631–664.

Houghton, T., & Proscio, T. (2001). *Hard work on soft skills: Creating a 'culture of work' in workforce development*. Philadelphia, PA: Public/Private Ventures (Ed. 461737).

Houkes, I., Janssen, P.P.M., de Jonge, J., & Bakker, A.B. (2003). Specific determinants of intrinsic work motivation, emotional exhaustion and turnover intention: A multisample longitudinal study. *Journal of Occupational and Organizational Psychology*, 76, 427–450.

House, R.J., & Mitchell, T.R. (1975). Path–goal theory of leadership. *Journal of Contemporary Business*, 3, 81–97.

House, R.J., & Rizzo, J.R. (1972). Role conflict and ambiguity as critical variables in a model of organizational behavior. *Organizational Behavior and Human Performance*, 7, 467–505.

Howell, W.C. (1991). Human factors in the workplace. In M.D. Dunnette and L.M. Hough (Eds), *Handbook of industrial and organizational psychology* (Vol. 2). Palo Alto, CA: Consulting Psychologists Press.

Hoxie, R.F. (1915). *Scientific management and labour*. New York: D. Appleton & Company.

Huddart, S. (1994). Employee stock options. *Journal of Accounting and Economics*, 18, 207–231.

Hudlick, E., & McNeese, M.D. (1994). Assessment of user affective and belief states for interface adaptation: Application to an Air Force pilot task. *User Modeling and User Adapted Interaction*, 12(1), 1–47.

Huff, A.S., & Jenkins, M. (2002). *Mapping strategic knowledge*. London: Sage.

Huffcutt, A.I., & Arthur, W. (1994). Hunter and Hunter (1984) revisited – Interview validity for entry-level jobs. *Journal of Applied Psychology*, 79(2), 184–190.

Huffcutt, A.I., Conway, J.M., Roth, P.L., & Stone, N.J. (2001). Identification and meta-analytic assessment of psychological constructs measured in employment interviews. *Journal of Applied Psychology*, 86, 897–913.

Humphreys, L.G. (1986). An analysis and evaluation of test and item bias in the prediction context. *Journal of Applied Psychology*, 71(2), 327–333.

Hunt, J.G., Osborn, R.N., & Schuler, R.S. (1978). Relations of discretionary and non-discretionary leadership to performance and satisfaction in a complex organization. *Human Relations*, 31(6), 507–523.

Hunter, J.E. & Hunter, R.F. (1984). Validity and utility of alternative predictors of job performance. *Psychological Bulletin*, 96, 72–98.

Hunter, J.E., & Schmidt, F.L. (1996). Intelligence and job performance: Economic and social implications. *Psychology, Public Policy, and Law*, 2(3/4), 447–472.

Hunter, J.E., & Schmidt, F.L. (2000). Fixed effects vs. random effects meta-analysis models: Implications for cumulative research knowledge. *International Journal of Selection and Assessment*, 8(4), 275–292.

Huo, Y.P., Huang, H.J., & Napier, N.K. (2002). Divergence or convergence: A cross-national comparison of personnel selection practices. *Human Resource Management*, 41(1), 31–44.

Hurrell, J.J. Jr., Nelson, D.L., & Simmons, B.L. (1998). Measuring job stressors and strains: Where we have been, where we are, and where we need to go. *Journal of Occupational Health Psychology*, 3(4), 368–389.

Hurtz, G.M., & Donovan, J.J. (2000). Personality and job performance: The big five revisited. *Journal of Applied Psychology*, 85, 869–879.

Huse, E. (1980). *Organizational development and change* (2nd edn). St Paul, MN: West.

Huselid, M.A., & Day, N.E. (1991). The impact of human resource management practices on turnover, productivity, and corporate financial performance. *Academy of Management Journal*, 38, 635–672.

Hutchins, E. (1995). *Cognition in the wild*. Cambridge, MA: MIT Press.

Hyde, A., & Paterson, J. (2000). Leadership development as a vehicle for change during merger. *Journal of Change Management*, 2(3), 266–271.

Hyman, R. (1994). Introduction: Economic restructuring, marlet liberalism and the future of national industrial relations systems. In R. Hyman, & A. Fernier (Eds), *New frontiers in European industrial relations* (pp.1–14). Oxford: Blackwell.

Ilgen, D.R., & Davis, C.A. (2000). Bearing bad news: Reactions to negative performance feedback. *Applied Psychology: An International Review*, 49(3), 550–565.

Ilgen, D.R., & Sheppard, L. (2001). Motivation in work teams. In Miriam Erez & Uwe Kleinbeck, *Work motivation in the context of a globalizing economy* (pp. 169–179). Mahwah, NJ: Lawrence Erlbaum Associates.

Impara, J.C., Plake, B.S., & Spies, R.A. (Eds). (2004). *The fifteenth mental measurements yearbook*. Lincoln, NB: Buros Institute of mental measurements.

Indik, B., Seashore, S.E., & Slesinger, J. (1964). Demographic correlates of psychological strain. *Journal of Abnormal and Social Psychology*, 69(1), 26–38.

Ingledew, D.K., Hardy, L., & Cooper, C.L. (1997). Do resources bolster coping and does coping buffer stress? An organizational study with longitudinal aspect and control for negative affectivity. *Journal of Occupational Health Psychology*, 2(2), 118–133.

Iovine, J. (1994). *Step into virtual reality*. New York: McGraw-Hill.

Irving, G.P., & Meyer, J.P. (1994). Reexamination of the met-expectations hypothesis: A longitudinal analysis. *Journal of Applied Psychology*, 79, 937–949.

Isaac, R.G., Zerbe, W.J., & Pitt, D.C. (2001). Leadership and motivation: The effective application of expectancy theory. *Journal of Managerial Issues*, 13(2), 212–226.

Isaksson, K., & Johansson, G. (2000). Adaptation to continued work and early retirement following downsizing: Long-term effects and gender differences. *Journal of Occupational and Organizational Psychology*, 73(2), 241–256.

Isenberg, D.J. (1981). Some effects of time pressure on vertical structure and decision making accuracy in small groups. *Organizational Behavior and Human Performance*, 27(1), 119–134.

Ishizaki, M., Tsuritani, I., Noborisaka, Y., Yamada, Y., Tabata, M., & Nakagawa, H. (1996). Relationship between job stress and plasma fibrinolytic activity in male Japanese workers. *Int Arch Occup Environ Health*, 68, 315–320.

Ivancevich, J.M., & Matteson, M.T. (1998). Promoting the individual's health and physical well-being. In C. Cooper & R. Payne (Eds), *Causes, coping and consequences of stress at work* (pp. 267–300). London: J. Wiley & Sons.

Iwasaki, Y., MacKay, K.J., & Ristock, J. (2004). Gender-based analyses of stress among professional managers: An exploratory study. *International Journal of Stress Management*, 11(1), 56–79.

Jackson, C., & Barltrop, J. (1994). Career workshops. Presented at Improving Career Development in Organizations conference, London, February.

Jackson, C., Arnold, J., Nicholson, N., & Watts, P. (2000). *Managing careers in 2000 and beyond*. IES Report 304 Brighton: Institute for Employment Studies.

Jackson, C.J., & Furnham, A. (2001). Appraisal ratings, halo, and selection: A study using sales staff. *European Journal of Psychological Assessment*, 17(1), 17–24.

Jackson, S.E., & Schuler, R.S. (1985). A meta-analysis and conceptual critique of research on role ambiguity and role conflict in work settings. *Organizational Behavior and Human Decision Processes*, 36, 16–28.

Jacobs, R.L., & Jones, M.J. (1995). *Structured on-the-job training: Unleashing employee expertise in the workplace*. San Franscisco., CA: Berrettt-Koehler.

Jacobs, R.L., & Russ-Eft, D. (2001). Cascade training and institutionalising organizational change. *Advances in developing Human Resources*, 3(4), 496–503.

Jaffee, D. (2001). *Organization theory: Tension and change*. Boston: McGraw-Hill.

Jang, C-Y., Steinfield, C., & Pfaff, B. (2002). Virtual team awareness and groupware support: An evaluation of the TeamSCOPE system. *International Journal of Human Computer Studies*, 56(1), 109–126.

Janis, I.L. (1972). *Group Think: Psychological studies of policy decisions and fiascos*. Boston, MA: Houghton.

Janssen, O. (2003). Innovative behaviour and job involvement at the price of conflict and less satisfactory relations with co-workers. *Journal of Occupational and Organizational Psychology*, 76(3), 347–364.

Janz, T. (1982). Initial comparisons of patterned behaviour description interviews versus unstructured interviews. *Journal of Applied Psychology*, 67, 577–580.

Jawahar, I.M. (2001). Attitudes, self-monitoring, and appraisal behaviours. *Journal of Applied Psychology*, 86(5), 875–883.

Jermier, J., Slocum, J., Fry, L., & Gaines, J. (1991). Organizational subcultures in a soft bureaucracy: Resistance behind the myth and façade of an official culture. *Organizational Science*, 2, 170–194.

Jetten, J., O'Brien., A., & Trindall, N. (2002). Changing identity: Predicting adjustment to organizational restructure as a function of subgroup and superordinate identification. *British Journal of Social Psychology*, 41(2), 281–297.

Jirotka, M., & Luff, P. (2002). Representing and modelling collaborative practices for systems development. In Y. Dittrich & C. Floyd (Eds), *Social thinking – software practice* (pp. 111–139). Cambridge, MA: MIT Press.

Johnson, C.D., & Stokes, G.S. (2002). The meaning, development, and career outcomes of breadth of vocational interests. *Journal of Vocational Behavior*, 61(2), 327–347.

Johnson, G., & Scholes, K. (1997). *Exploring corporate strategy: Texts and cases*. Hemel Hempstead: Prentice Hall.

Johnson, J. & Pratt, D. (1998). The apprenticeship perspective: modelling ways of being. In D. Pratt & Associates (Eds), *Five perspectives on teaching in adult and higher education* (pp. 93–104). Malaber, FL: Krieger.

Johnson, P., & Cassell, C. (2001). Epistemology and work psychology: New agendas. *Journal of Occupational and Organizational Psychology*, 74(2), 125–144.

Joireman, J.A., Parrott, L.P., & Hammersla, J. (2002). Empathy and the self-absorption paradox: Support for the distinction between self-rumination and self-reflection. *Self and Identity*, 1, 53–65.

Jones, A., Herriot, P., Long, B., & Drakeley, R.J. (1991). Attempting to prove the validity of a well-established assessment centre. *Journal of Occupational and Organizational Psychology*, 64, 1–64.

Jones, F., & Bright, J. (2002). *Stress: Myth, theory and research*. Harlow: Pearson Education Ltd.

Jones, F., & Fletcher, B.C. (1996). Taking work home: A study of daily fluctuations in work stressors, effects on moods and impacts on marital partners. *Journal of Occupational and Organizational Psychology*, 69(1), 89–106.

Jones, G.R. (1986). Socialization tactics, self-efficacy, and newcomers' adjustments to organizations. *Academy of Management Journal*, 29, 262–279.

Jones, J.W., Slora, K.B., & Boye, M.W. (1990). Theft reduction through personnel selection: A control group design in the supermarket industry. *Journal of Business and Psychology*, 5, 275–279.

Jones, J.W., Joy, D.S., Werner, S.H., & Orbon, J.A. (1991). Criterion related validity of a pre-employment integrity inventory: Large scale between groups comparison. *Perceptual and Motor Skills*, 72, 131–136.

Jones, L., & Fletcher, C. (2002). Self-assessment in a selection situation: An evaluation of different measurement approaches. *Journal of Occupational and Organizational Psychology*, 75(2), 145–162.

Jordan, R., & Millward, L.J. (2004). *A daily diary study of reflective appraisal and its implications for emotional well-being among mental health professionals*. University of Surrey, Guildford, UK.

Judge, T.A., & Bono, J.E. (2001). Relationship of core self-evaluations traits – self-esteem, generalised self-efficacy, locus of control, and emotional stability – with job satisfaction and job performance: A meta-analysis. *Journal of Applied Psychology*, 86(1), 80–92.

Judge, T.A., & Ilies, R. (2002). Relationship of personality to performance motivation: A meta-analytic review. *Journal of Applied Psychology*, 87(4), 797–807.

Kaber, D.B., Riley, J.M., & Tan, J.M. (2002). Improved usability of aviation automation through direct manipulation and graphical user interface design. *International Journal of Aviation Psychology*, 12(2), 153–178.

Kacmar, K.M., Delery, J.E., & Ferris, G.R. (1992). Differential effectiveness of applicant impression management tactics on employment interview decisions. *Journal of Applied Social Psychology*, 22, 1250–1272.

Kahn, R.L. (1990). Psychological conditions of personal engagement and disengagement at work. *Academy of Management Journal*, 33, 692–724.

Kahn, R.L., Wolfe, D.N., Quinn, R.P., Snoek, J.D., & Rosenthal, R. (1964). *Organizational stress: Studies in role conflict and ambiguity*. New York: Wiley.

Kahneman, D.P. Slovic, & A. Tversky (Eds). (1982). *Judgement under uncertainty: Heuristics and biases*. Cambridge: Cambridge University Press.

Kald, K., & Nilsson, F. (2000). Performance management at Nordic companies. *European Management Journal*, 25, 349–358.

Kalimo, R., Lindström, K., & Smith, M.J. (1997). Psychosocial approach in occupational health. In G. Salvendy (Ed.), *Handbook of human factors and ergonomics* (2nd edn). New York: John Wiley and Sons.

Kammeyer-Mueller, J.D., & Wanberg, C.R. (2003). Unwrapping the organizational entry process: Disentangling multiple antecedents and their pathways to adjustment. *Journal of Applied Psychology*, 88(5), 779–794.

Kampa-Kokesch, S., & Anderson, M. (2001). Executive coaching: A comprehensive review of the literature. *Consulting Psychology Journal: Practice and Research*, 53, 205–228.

Kane, M. (2002). Validating high-stakes testing programs. *Educational Measurement: Issues and Practice*, 21(1), 31–41.

Kanfer, R. (1992). Motivation theory and Industrial and organizational psychology. In M. Dunnette & L.M. Hough (Eds), *Handbook of industrial and organizational psychology* (2nd edn, Vol. 1, pp. 75–170). Palo Alto, CA: Consulting Psychologists Press.

Kanfer, R., & Ackerman, P.L. (1989). Motivation and cognitive abilities: An integrative/aptitude-treatment interaction approach to skill acquisition. *Journal of Applied Psychology – Monograph*, 74, 657–690.

Kanfer, R., & Ackerman, P.L. (2000). Individual differences in work motivation: Further explorations of a trait framework. *Applied Psychology: An International Review*, 49(3), 470–482.

Kantowitz, B., & Sorkin, R. (1987). Allocation of functions. In G. Salvendy (Ed.), *Handbook of human factors* (pp. 355–369). New York: Wiley.

Karasek, R.A., & Theorell, T. (1990). *Healthy work: Stress, productivity and the reconstruction of working life*. New York: Basic Books.

Karasek, R., Brisson, C., Kawakami, N., Houtman, I., Bongers, P., & Amick, B. (1998). The Job Content Questionnaire (JCQ): An instrument for internationally comparative assessments of psychosocial job characteristics. *Journal of Occupational Health Psychology*, 3(4), 322–355.

Katzenbach, J.R., & Smith, D.K. (1993). *The wisdom of teams*. New York: McKinney.

Keates, S., Langdon, P., Clarkson, P.J., & Robinson, P. (2002). User models and user physical capability. *User Modeling and User Adapted Interaction*, 12(2–3), 139–169.

Keen, P.G.W. (1981). Information systems and organizational change. *Communications of the ACM*, 24(1), 24–33.

Keenan, T. (1995). Graduate recruitment in Britain: A survey of selection methods used by organizations. *Journal of Organizational Behavior*, 16(4), 303–317.

Keeping, L.M., & Levy, P.E. (2000). Performance appraisal reactions: Measurement, modelling, and method bias. *Journal of Applied Psychology*, 85(5), 708–723.

Kelly, G. (1955). *The psychology of personal constructs*. New York: Norton.

Kenny, D.T., & Cooper, C. (2003). Introduction: Occupational stress and its management. *International Journal of Stress Management*, 10(4), 275–279.

Kenny, N.P., Mann, K.V., & MacLeod, H. (2003) Role modelling in physicians' professional formation: Reconsidering an essential but untapped educational strategy. *Academic Medicine*, 78, 1203–1210.

Kerr, S., & Jermier, J.M. (1978). Substitutes for leadership: Their meaning and measurement. *Organizational Behaviour and Human Performance*, 22, 375–403.

Kettley, P., & Strebler, M. (1997). *Changing roles for senior managers* (IES Report No. 327). Brighton: Institute for Employment Studies.

Kidd, J.M. (2002). Careers and career management. In P.B. Warr (Ed.), *Psychology at work* (5th edn). Harmondsworth: Penguin.

Kidd, J.M. (2004). Emotion in career contexts: Challenges for theory and research. *Journal of Vocational Behavior*, 64(3), 441–454.

Kidd, J.M., Jackson, C., & Hirsh, W. (2003). The outcomes of effective career discussion at work. *Journal of Vocational Behaviour*, 62, 119–133.

Kidd, J.M., & Smewing, C. (2001). The role of the supervisor in career and organizational commitment. *European Journal of Work and Organizational Psychology*, 10(1), 25–40.

Kiefer, T. (2002). Understanding the emotional experience of organizational change: Evidence from a merger. *Advances in Developing Human Resources*, 4(1), 39–61.

Kieras, D.E. (1987). What mental model should be taught: Choosing instructional content for complex engineered systems. In J. Psotka, D. Massey and S. Mutter (Eds), *Intelligent tutoring systems: Lessons learned* (pp. 315–324). Hillsdale, NJ: Erlbaum Associates.

Kilmann, R.H. (1985). Corporate culture. *Psychology Today*, 15, 62–68.

King, P.M., Fisher, J.C., & Garg, A. (1997). Evaluation of the impact of employee ergonomics training in industry. *Applied Ergonomics*, 28(4), 249–256.

King, Z. (2001). Career self-management: A framework for guidance of employed adults. *British Journal of Guidance and Counselling*, 29(1), 65–78.

Kinicki, A.J., & Vecchio, R.P. (1994). Influences on the quality of supervisor-subordinate relations: The role of time-pressure, organizational commitment and locus of control. *Journal of Organizational Behavior*, 15, 75–82.

Kinicki, A.J., Hom, P.W., Trost, M.R., & Wade, K.J. (1995). Effects of category prototypes on performance-rating accuracy. *Journal of Applied Psychology*, 80(3), 354–370.

Kirk, A.K., & Brown, D.F. (2003). Latent constructs of proximal and distal motivation predicting performance under maximum test conditions. *Journal of Applied Psychology*, 88(1), 40–49.

Kirk, J.J., Downey, B., Duckett, S., & Woody, C. (2000). Name your career development intervention. *Journal of Workplace Learning*, 12(5), 205–216.

Kirkman, B.L., Tesluk, P.E., & Rosen, B. (2001). Alternative methods of assessing team-level variables: Comparing the predictive power of aggregation and consensus methods. *Personnel Psychology*, 54, 645–667.

Kirlik, A., Walker, N., Fisk, A.D., & Nagel, K. (1996). Supporting perception in the service of dynamic decision making. *Human Factors*, 38(2), 288–299.

Kirman, B.L., Rosen, B., Gibson, C.B., Tesluk, P.E., & McPherson, S.M. (2001). Five challenges to virtual team success: Lessons from Sabre, Inc. *Academy of Management Executive*, 16(3), 67–79.

Kirpatrick, D.L. (1976). Evaluation of training. In R.L. Craig (Ed.), *Training and development handbook: A guide to human resource development* (2nd edn, pp. 301–319). New York: McGraw Hill.

Kirwan, B. (1995). Human reliability assessment. In J.W. Wilson & E.N. Corlett (Eds), *Evaluation of human work: A practical ergonomics methodology* (2nd edn). London: Taylor & Francis.

Klein, G. (1998). *Sources of power: How people make decisions*. Cambridge, MA: MIT Press.

Klein, G.A., Orasanu, J., & Zsambok, C.E. (Eds). (1993). *Decision making in action: Models and methods*. Norwood, NJ: Ablex Publishing Corp.

Klein, H.J., Wesson, M.J., Hollenbeck, J.R., Wright, P.M., & DeShon, R.P. (2001). The assessment of goal commitment: A measurement model meta-analysis. *Organizational Behavior and Human Decision Processes*, 85(1), 32–55.

Klimoski, R., & Brickner, M. (1987). Why do assessment centers work? The puzzle of assessment center validity. *Personnel Psychology*, 30, 243–260.

Kline, P. (1986). *Handbook of test construction*. London: Routledge.

Kline, P., & Lapham, S.L. (1992). Personality and faculty in British universities. *Personality and Individual Differences*, 13(7), 855–857.

Klingner, Y., & Schuler, H. (2004). Improving participants' evaluations while maintaining validity by a work sample-intelligence test hybrid. *International Journal of Selection and Assessment*, 12(1–2), 120–134.

Kluger, A.N., & DeNisi, A. (1998). Feedback interventions: Toward the understanding of a double-edged sword. *Current Directions in Psychological Science*, 7(3), 67–72.

Knefelkamp, L.L., & Slepitza, R. (1976). A cognitive-developmental model of career development: An adaptation of the Perry scheme. *Counseling Psychologist*, 6(3), 53–58.

Knerr, B.W., Breaux, R., Goldberg, S.L., & Thurman, R.A. (2002). National defense. In K.M. Stanney (Ed.), *Handbook of virtual environments: Design, implementation, and applications. Human factors and ergonomics* (pp. 857–872). Mahwah, NJ: Lawrence Erlbaum Associates.

Knight, D., Durham, C.C., & Locke, E.A. (2001). The relationship of team goals, incentives, and efficacy to strategic risk, tactical implementation and performance. *Academy of Management Journal*, 40, 1089–1121.

Knowles, M. (1972). *The modern practice of adult education*. Chicago: Association Press.

Kobaska, S.C. (1979) Stressful life events, personality and health: An inquiry into hardiness. *Journal of Personality and Social Psychology*, 37(1), 1–11.

Kodz, J., Harper, H., & Dench, S. (2002). *Work-life balance: Beyond the rhetoric*. Brighton: Institute for Employment Studies.

Kodz, J., Kersley, B., & Bates, P. (1999). *The fifties revival*. IES Report 359. Brighton: Institute for Employment Studies.

Kolb, D.A. (1984). *Experiential learning*. Englewood Cliffs, NJ: Prentice Hall.

Kompier, M.A.J., Cooper, C.L., & Geurts, S.A.E. (2000). A multiple case study approach to work stress prevention in Europe. *European Journal of Work and Organizational Psychology*, 9, 371–400.

Kontogiannis, T., & Embrey, D. (1997). A user-centred design approach for introducing computer-based process information systems. *Applied Ergonomics*, 28(2), 109–119.

Kormanski, C. (1991). Using theory as a foundation for group training designs. *Journal for Specialists in Groupwork*, 16(4), 215–222.

Korsgaard, M.A., Sapienza, H.J., & Schweiger, D.M. (2002). Beaten before begun: The role of procedural justice in planning change. *Journal of Management*, 28(4), 497–516.

Kotter, J. (1990). *A force for change: How leadership differs from management*. New York: Free Press.

Kotter, J.P. (1973). The psychological contract: Managing the joining-up process. *California Management Review*, 15, 91–99.

Kotter, J.P. & Heskett, J.L. (1992). *Corporate culture and performance*. New York: The Free Press.

Koubek, R.J., & Salvendy, G. (1991). Cognitive performance of super-experts on computer program modification tasks. *Ergonomics*, 34(8), 1095–1112.

Koubek, R.J., Benysh, S.A.H., & Tang, E. (1997). Learning. In G. Salvendy (Ed.), *Handbook of human factors and ergonomics* (pp. 130–149). New York: John Wiley.

Koumoundourou, G.A. (2004). The reliability and validity of the Greek version of the task specific occupational self-efficacy scale. *British Journal of Guidance and Counselling*, 32(1), 75–92.

Kraiger, K., & Ford, J.K. (1985). A meta-analysis of ratee race effects in performance ratings. *Journal of Applied Psychology*, 70, 56–65.

Kraiger, K., Ford, J., & Salas, E. (1993). Application of cognitive, skill-based and effective theories of learning outcomes to new methods of training evaluation. *Journal of Applied Psychology*, 78, 311–328.

Kravitz, D.A., & Balzer, W.K. (1992). Context effects in performance appraisal: A methodological critique and empirical study. *Journal of Applied Psychology*, 77(1), 24–31.

Kroeber, A.L., & Kluckhohn, F. (1952). *Culture: A critical review of concepts and definitions*. New York: Vintage Books.

Krumboltz, J.D. (1996). A learning theory of career counseling. In M.L. Savickas & W.B. Walsh (Eds), *Handbook of career counseling theory and practice* (pp. 55–80). Palo Alto, CA: Davies-Black.

Krumboltz, J.D., Mitchell, A.M., & Jones, G.B. (1976). A social learning theory of career selection. *Counseling Psychologist*, 6(1), 71–81.

Kubler-Ross, E. (1969). *On death and dying*. London: Tavistock/Routledge Publications.

Kuhl, J. (1994). Volitional aspects of achievement orientation and learned helplessness: Toward a comprehensive theory of action control. In B.A. Maher (Ed.), *Progress in experimental personality research* (Vol. 13, pp. 99–171). New York: Academic Press.

Kulik, C.T., & Ambrose, M.L. (1993). Category based and feature based processes in performance appraisal: Integrating visual and computerised sources of performance data. *Journal of Applied Psychology*, 78, 821–830.

Kuper, H., & Marmot, M. (2003). Job strain, job demands, decision latitude, and risk of coronary heart disease within the Whitehall II study. *Journal of Epidemiology and Community Health*, 57(2), 147–153.

Laming, Lord (2003). *The Victoria Climbié Inquiry*. London: HMSO.

Lampton, D.R., Bliss, J.P., & Morris, C.S. (2002). Human performance measurement in virtual environments. In K.M. Stanney (Ed.), *Handbook of virtual environments: Design, implementation, and applications* (pp. 701–720). Mahwah, NJ: Lawrence Erlbaum.

Landy, F.J. (2003). Validity generalization: Then and now. In K.R. Murphy (Ed.), *Validity generalization: A critical review* (pp. 155–195). Mahwah, NJ: Lawrence Erlbaum Associates.

Landy, F.J., & Farr, J.L. (1980). *Performance rating*. New York: Academic Press.

Larson, J.R., & Christensen, C. (1993). Groups as problem solving units: Toward a new meaning of social cognition. *British Journal of Social Psychology*, 32, 5–30.

Larson, L., & Rowland, K. (1973). Leadership style, stress and behavior in task performance. *Organizational Behavior and Human Performance*, 9(3), 407–420.

Laszlo, K.C., & Laszlo, A. (2002). Evolving knowledge for development: The role of knowledge management in a changing world. *Journal of Knowledge Management*, 6(4), 400–412.

Latham, G.P. (1988). Human resource training and development. *Annual Review of Psychology*, 39, 545–582.

Latham, G.P., & Wexley, K.N. (1977) Behavioral observation scales for performance appraisal purposes. *Personnel Psychology*, 30(2), 255–268.

Latham, G.P., & Saari, L.M. (1984). Do people do what they say? Further studies on the situational interview. *Journal of Applied Psychology*, 69, 569–573.

Latham, G.P., Millman, Z., & Miedema, H. (1998). Theoretical, practical and organizational issues affecting training. In H. Thierry & P. Drenth (Eds), *Handbook of work and organizational psychology Vol. 3: Personnel psychology*. (2nd edn. pp. 185–206). Hove: Psychology Press.

Latham, G.P., Saari, L.M., Russell, E.P., & Campion, M.A. (1980). Training managers to minimise rating errors in the observation of behaviour. *Journal of Applied Psychology*, 60, 550–555.

Laudon, C.L., & Laudon, J.P. (2002). *Management information systems: Managing the digital firm* (7th Edn), Saddle River, NJ: Pearson Education.

Lave, J., & Wenger, E. (1991). *Situated learning*. New York: Cambridge University Press.

Lawler, E.E., Mohrman, S.A., & Ledford, G.E. (1992). *Employee involvement and total quality management*. San Francisco, CA: Jossey-Bass.

Lawrence, P.R., Bailey, J.C., Katz, R.L., Seiler, J.A., Orth, C.D., Clark, J.V., Barnes, L.B., & Turner, A.N. (1961). *Organizational behavior and administration: Cases, concepts, and research findings*. Oxford: Dorsey Press & Richard D. Irwin.

Lawrence, P.R., & Lorsch, J.W. (1967). *Organizations and environment: Managing differentiation and integration*. Boston: Graduate School of Business Administration, Harvard University Press.

Lawrence et al., 1961

Lazarus, R.S., & Folkman, S. (1984). *Stress, appraisal and coping*. New York: Springer.

Lazarus, R.S. (1999). *Stress and emotion: A new synthesis*. London: Free Association.

Lazarus, R.S. (2000). Towards better research on coping and stress. *American Psychologist*, 55, 665–673.

Lazlo, K.C., & Lazlo, S. (2002). Evolving knowledge for development: The role of knowledge management in a changing world. *Journal of knowledge management*, 6(4), 400–412.

Leach, D.J., Wall, T.D., & Jackson, P.R. (2003). The effect of empowerment on job knowledge: An empirical test involving operators of complex technology. *Journal of Occupational and Organizational Psychology*, 76(1), 27–52.

Leavitt, H.J., & Whisler, T.L. (1958). Management in the 1980's. *Harvard Business Review*, (November–December), 41–49.

Le Blanc, P., de Jonge, J., & Schaufeli, W.B. (2000). Job stress and health. In N. Chmiel (Ed.), *Introduction to work and organizational psychology: A European perspective* (pp. 148–177). Malden, MA: Blackwell Publishers.

Lefkowitz, J. (2000). The role of interpersonal affective regard in supervisory performance ratings: A literature review and proposed causal model. *Journal of Occupational and Organizational Psychology*, 73(1), 67–85.

Lee, K., Carswell, J., & Allen, N. (2000). A meta-analytic review of occupational commitment: Relations with people and work-related variables. *Journal of Applied Psychology*, 85, 799–811.

Lee, K.S. (2002). Building intergroup relations after September 11. *Analyses of Social Issues and Public Policy*, 2(1), 131–141.

Lee, R.T., & Ashforth, B.E. (1996). A meta-analytic examination of the correlates of the three dimensions of job burnout. *Journal of Applied Psychology*, 81(2), 123–133.

Lee, S., & Klein, H.J. (2000). Relationships between conscientiousness, self-efficacy, self-deception, and learning over time. *Journal of Applied Psychology*, 87(6), 1175–1182.

Leicester, M. (2002). Two decades of feminist thought-and beyond. *International Journal of Lifelong Education* 20(1–2), 55–62.

Leiter, M.P., & Maslach, C. (1988). The impact of interpersonal environment on burnout and organizational commitment. *Journal of Organizational Behaviour*, 9, 297–308.

Lent, R.W., & Worthington, R.L. (2000). On school-to-work transition, career development theories, and cultural validity. *Career Development Quarterly*, 48(4), 376–384.

Lester, S.W., Turnley, W.H., Bloodgood, J.M., & Bolino, Mark C. (2002). Not seeing eye to eye: Differences in supervisor and subordinate perceptions of and attributions for psychological contract breach. *Journal of Organizational Behavior*, 23(1), 39–56.

Levine, A.S., & Zachert, V. (1951). Use of biographical inventory in the Air Force Classification Programme. *Journal of Applied Psychology*, 35, 241–244.

Levinson, D.J. with Darrow, C.N., Klein, E.N., Levinson, M.H., & McKee, B. (1978). *The seasons of a man's life*. New York: Knopf.

Levinson, H., Price, C.R., Munden, K., Mandl, H.J., & Solley, C.M. (1962). *Men, management and mental health*. Cambridge, MA: Harvard University Press.

Lewin, K. (1951). *Field theory in social science*. London: Tavistock.

Lewin, K., & Lippitt, R. (1938). An experimental approach to the study of autocracy and democracy: A preliminary note. *Sociometry*, 1, 292–300.

Lewis, G., & Pelosi, A.J. (1990). The case-control study in psychiatry. *British Journal of Psychiatry*, 157, 197–207.

Liden, R.C., Wayne, S.J., & Sparrowe, R.T. (2000). An examination of the mediating role of psychological empowerment on the relations between the job, interpersonal relationships, and work outcomes. *Journal of Applied Psychology*, 85(3), 407–416.

Liebowitz, S.J., & De Meuse, K.P. (1982). The application of team building. *Human Relations*, 35(1), 1–18.

Lievens, F., & Klimoski, R.J. (2001). Understanding the assessment center process: Where are we now? In C.L. Cooper & I.T. Robertson (Eds), *International review of industrial and organizational psychology* (Vol. 16, pp. 245–286). Chichester: Wiley.

Likert, R. (1967). *The human organization*. New York: McGraw-Hill.

Lin, H.X., Choong, Y.Y., & Salvendy, G. (1997). A proposed index of usability: A method for comparing the relative usability of different software systems. *Behavior and Information Technology*, 16(4–5), 267–278.

Lind, E.A., Greenberg, J., Scott, K.S., & Welchans, T.D. (2000). The winding road from employee to complainant: Situational and psychological determinants of wrongful termination claims. *Administrative Science Quarterly*, 45, 557–590.

Linehan, M. (2001). Women international managers: The European experience. *Cross Cultural Management*, 8(3–4), 68–84.

Linstead, A., & Brewis, J. (2004). Beyond boundaries: Towards fluidity in theorizing and practice. *Gender, Work and Organization*, 11(4), 355–362.

Locke, E.A. (1976). The nature and causes of job satisfaction. In M.D. Dunnette (Ed.), *Handbook of industrial and organizational psychology* (pp. 1297–1349). Chicago: Rand McNally.

Locke, E.A. (1991). Goal theory vs. control theory: Contrasting approaches to understanding work motivation. *Motivation and Emotion*, 15(1), 9–28.

Locke, E.A. (1997). The motivation to work: What we know. In M. Maehr & P. Pintrich (Eds), *Advances in motivation and achievement* (Vol. 10, pp. 375–412). Greenwich, CT: JAI Press.

Locke, E.A. (2001). Self-set goals and self-efficacy as mediators of incentives and personality. In M. Erez & U. Kleinbeck (Eds), *Work motivation in the context of a globalizing economy* (pp. 13–26). Mahwah, NJ: Lawrence Erlbaum Associates.

Locke, E.A., & Latham, G.P. (1990). *A theory of goal setting & task performance*. Upper Saddle River, NJ: Prentice-Hall, Inc.

Locke, E.A., & Latham, G.P. (2002). Building a practically useful theory of goal setting and task motivation: A 35 year odyssey. *American Psychologist*, 57(9), 705–717.

Lodahl, T., & Kejner, M. (1965). The definition and measurement of job involvement. *Journal of Applied Psychology*, 49, 24–33.

Lofquist, L.H., & Dawis, R.V. (1969). *Adjustment to work*. New York: Appelton-Century-Crofts.

Loo, R. (2004). Kolb's learning styles and learning preferences: Is there a linkage? *Educational-Psychology*, 24(1), 99–108.

London, M. (1993). Relationships between career motivation, empowerment and support for career development. *Journal of Occupational and Organizational Psychology*, 66, 55–69.

London, M., & Mone, E.M. (1987). *Career management and survival in the workplace: Helping employees make tough decisions, stay motivated, and reduce career stress*. San Francisco: Jossey-Bass Inc.

London, M., & Smither, J.W. (1995). Can multi-source feedback change perceptions of goal accomplishment, self-evaluations, and performance related outcomes? Theory based applications and directions for research. *Personnel Psychology*, 48, 803–839.

Lord, R.G., Hanges, P.J., & Godfrey, E.G. (2003). Integrating neural networks into decision-making and motivational theory: Rethinking VIE theory. *Canadian Psychology*, 44(1), 21–38.

Lord, R.G., & Maher, K.J. (1990). Alternate information-processing models and their implications for theory, research and practice. *Academy of Management Review*, 15, 9–28.

Louis, M.R. (1981). Surprise and sense-making What newcomers experience in entering unfamiliar organizational settings. *Administrative Science Quarterly*, 25, 226–251.

Lowe, R., & Bennett, P. (2003). Exploring coping reactions to work stress: Application of an appraisal theory. *Journal of Occupational and Organizational Psychology*, 76(3), 393–400.

Ludema, J.D. (2002). Appreciative storytelling: A narrative approach to organization development and change. In R. Fry & F. Barrett (Eds), *Appreciative inquiry and organizational transformation: Reports from the field* (pp. 239–261). Westport, CT: Quorum Books/Greenwood.

Luzzo, D.A. (Ed.) (2000). *Career counseling of college students: An empirical guide to strategies that work*. Washington, DC: American Psychological Association.

Lynch, J.G., & Lind, B. (2002). Escaping merger and acquisition madness. *Strategy and Leadership*, 30(2), 5–12.

Lyons, M.H., Cochrane, P., & Fisher, K. (1993). Teleworking in the 21st century. *IEE Computing and Control Engineering Journal*, August.

Mabey, C. (1986). Black pupils' achievement in inner London. *Educational Research*, 28(3), 163–173.

Macdonald, J.M. (1985). Market exchange or vertical integration: An empirical analysis. *Review of Economics and Statistics*, 67, 327–331.

Macdonald, S. (1997). Work-place alcohol and other drug testing: A review of the scientific evidence. *Drug and Alcohol Review*, 16(3), 251–259.

Mack, R.L., & Burdett, J.M. (1992). When novices elicit knowledge: Question-asking in designing, evaluating and learning to use software. In R. Hoffman (Ed.), *The Psychology of expertise: Cognitive research and empirical AI* (pp. 245–268). New York: Springer-Verlag.

Mackley, W.B. (1982). Aftermath of Mt. Erebus. *Flight Safety Digest*, 1, 3–7.

Madzar, S. (2001). Subordinates information inquiry: Exploring the effect of perceived leadership style and individual differences. *Journal of Occupational and Organizational Psychology*, 74(2), 221–232.

Mael, F., & Ashforth, B.E. (1992). Alumni and their alma mater: A partial test of the reformulated model of organisational identification. *Journal of Organisational Behaviour*, 13, 103–123.

Mael, F.A., & Ashforth, B.E. (1995). Loyal from day one: Biodata, organizational identification, and turnover among newcomers. *Personnel Psychology*, 48(2), 309–333.

Maertz, C.P. Jr., Bauer, T.N., Mosley, D.C. Jr., Posthuma, R.A., Campion, M.A. (2004). Do procedural justice perceptions in a selection testing context predict applicant attraction and intention toward the organization? *Journal of Applied Social Psychology*, 34(1), 125–145.

Mafi, S.L. (2001). Planned on the job managerial training. *Advances in Developing Human Resources*, 3(4), 488–495.

Magnuson, C.S., & Starr, M.F. (2000). How early is too early to begin life career planning? The importance of the elementary school years. *Journal of Career Development*, 27(2), 89–101.

Majchrzak, A., & Borys, B. (1998). Computer aided technology and work: Moving the field forward. In C. Cooper & I. Robertson (Eds), *International review of industrial and organizational psychology* (Vol. 13, pp. 305–354). Chichester: Wiley.

Makin, P.J., Cooper, C.L., & Cox, C.J. (1996). *Organizations and the psychological contract: Managing people at work*. Leicester: British Psychological Society.

Malan, D.H. (1976). *The frontier of brief psychotherapy*. New York: Plenum Press.

Manpower Services Commission (1987). *TVEI: Progress report on the 16–18 Phase*. NSF/86/11. London.

Maples, M.F. (1992). Steamwork: An effective approach to teambuilding. *Journal for Specialists in Group Work*, 17(3), 144–150.

Maran, N.J., & Glavin, R.J. (2003). Low- to high-fidelity simulation – A continuum of medical education? *Medical Education*, 37(Suppl 1), 22–28.

Marcoulides, G.A., & Heck, R.H. (1993). Organizational culture and performance: Proposing and testing a model. *Organization Science*, 4(2), 209–225.

Marginson, P., & Sisson, K. (1994). The structure of transnational capital in Europe: The emerging Euro-company and its implications for industrial relations. In R. Hyman & A. Fernier (Eds), *New frontiers in European industrial relations* (pp. 15–51). Oxford: Blackwell.

Marks, I.M., Hodgson, R., & Rachman, S. (1975). Treatment of chronic obsessive-compulsive neurosis by in-vivo exposure: A two-year follow-up and issues in treatment. *British Journal of Psychiatry*, 127, 349–64.

Marks, J. (1996). Britain out of training for world success. *The Sunday Times*, 2 January.

Marks, M.A., Sabella, M.J., Burke, C.S., & Zaccaro, S.J. (2002). The impact of cross-training on team effectiveness. *Journal of Applied Psychology*, 87, 3–13.

Marks, M.L., & Mirvis, P.H. (2001). Making mergers and acquisitions work: Strategic and psychological preparation. *Academy of Management Executive*, 15(2), 80–95.

Marks, M.M., Sabella, M.J., Burke, C.S., & Zaccaro, S.J. (2002). The impact of cross-training on team effectiveness. *Journal of Applied Psychology*, 87(1), 3–13.

Markus, H., & Nurius, P. (1987). Possible selves: The interface between motivation and the self-concept. In K. Yardley & T. Honess (Eds), *Self and identity: Psychosocial perspectives* (pp. 157–172). Chichester: Wiley.

Martin, B.L., & Reigeluth, C.M. (1999). Affective education and the affective domain: Implications for instructional design theories and models. In C.M. Reigeluth (Ed.), *Instructional design theories and models: A new paradigm of instructional theory* (Vol. II). Hillsdale, NJ: Lawrence Erlbaum.

Martin, J. (2002). *Organizational culture*. London: Sage.

Martin, J., & Frost, P. (1996). The organizational culture war games: A struggle for intellectual dominance. In S.R. Clegg & C. Hardy (Eds), *Handbook of organizational studies* (pp. 345–367). London: Sage.

Martin, P. (1997). Counselling skills training for managers in the public sector. In M. Carroll & M. Walton (Eds), *Handbook of counselling in organizations* (pp. 240–259). London: Sage.

Marshall, H. (1994). Discourse analysis in an occupational context. In C. Cassell & G. Symon (Eds), *Qualitative methods in organizational research: A practical guide* (pp. 91–106). London: Sage.

Maslach, C., & Jackson, S.E. (1986). *Maslach Burnout Inventory: Manual* (2nd edn). Palo Alto, CA: Consulting Psychologists Press.

Maslow, A.H. (1954). *Motivation and personality*. New York: Harper & Row.

Mathews, B.P., & Shepherd, J.L. (2002). Dimensionality of Cook and Wall's (1980) British Organizational Commitment Scale revisited. *Journal of Occupational and Organizational Psychology*, 75, 369–375.

Mathieu, J., & Martineau, J. (1997). Individual and situational influences in training motivation. In K. Ford & Associates (Eds), *Improving Training Effectiveness in Organizations*. Hillsdale, NJ: Erlbaum.

Mathieu, J.E., & Zajac, D.M. (1990). A review and meta-analysis of the antecedents, correlates, and consequences of organizational commitment. *Psychological Bulletin*, 108, 171–194.

Mathieu, J.E., Martineau, J.W., & Tannenbaum, S.I. (1993). Individual and situational influences on the development of self-efficacy: Implications for training effectiveness. *Personnel Psychology*, 46, 125–147.

Mathieu, J.E., Tannenbaum, S.I., & Salas, E. (1992). Influences of individual and situational characteristics on measures of training effectiveness. *Academy of Management Journal*, 35(4), 828–847.

Mathieu, J.E., Heffner, T.S., Goodwin, G.F., Salas, E., & Cannon-Bowers, J.A. (2000). The influence of shared mental models on team process and performance. *Journal of Applied Psychology*, 85, 284–293.

Maurer, T. (2001). Career-relevant learning and development, worker age, and beliefs about self-efficacy for development. *Journal of Management*, 27, 123–140.

Maurer, T.J., Mitchell, D.R.D., & Barbeite, F.G. (2002). Predictors of attitudes towards 360-degree feedback system and involvement in post-feedback management development activity. *Journal of Occupational and Organizational Psychology*, 75(1), 87–107.

May, D.R., Gilson, R.L., & Harter, L.M. (2004). The psychological conditions of meaningfulness, safety and availability and the engagement of the human spirit at work. *Journal of Occupational and Organizational Psychology*, 77, 11–37.

Mayer, R.E. (1988). Learning strategies: An overview. In E.T. Goetz & C.E. Weinstein (Eds), *Learning and study strategies: Issues in assessment, instruction, and evaluation* (pp. 11–22). San Diego, CA: Academic Press.

Mayfield, E.C. (1964). The selection interview: A reevaluation of research. *Personnel Psychology*, 17, 239–260.

Mayo, E. (1933). *The human problems of industrial civilization*. New York: Macmillan.

MCI (1987). *The Management Charter Initiative*. London: Management Charter Group.

McCarthy, J.C., Healey, P.G.T., Wright, P.C., & Harrison, M.D. (1998). Accountability of work activity in high-consequence work systems: Human error in context. *International Journal of Human Computer Studies*, 47(6), 735–766.

McCloy, R.A., Campbell, J.P., & Cudeck, R. (1994). A confirmatory test of a model of performance determinants. *Journal of Applied Psychology*, 79, 493–505.

McCormick, E.J., Jeanneret, P.R., & Mecham, R.C. (1972). A study of job characteristics and job dimensions as based on the Position Analysis Questionnaire (PAQ). *Journal of Applied Psychology*, 56(4), 347–368.

McCrae, R.R., & Costa, P.T. (1987). Analysis of a five-factor model of personality across instruments and observers. *Journal of Personality and Social Psychology*, 52, 81–90.

McCredie, H., & Shackleton, V. (1994). The development and interim validation of a dimension-based senior management assessment centre. *Human Resource Management Journal*, 5, 91–101.

McDaniel, M.A., Rothstein Hirsch, H., Schmidt, F.L., Raju, N.S., & Hunter, J.E. (1997). Interpreting results of meta-analytic research: A comment on Schmitt, Gooding, Noe and Kirsch. (1984). *Personnel Psychology*, 39, 141–148.

McDaniel, M., Whetzel, D., Schmidt, F., & Maurer, S. (1994). The validity of employment interviews: A comprehensive review and meta-analysis. *Journal of Applied Psychology*, 79(4), 599–616.

McDougall, W. (1932). Of the words character and personality. *Character and Personality. A Quarterly for Psychodiagnostic and Allied Studies*, 1, 3–16.

McGhee, W., & Thayer, P.W. (1961). *Training in business and industry*. New York: Wiley.

McGrath, J.E. (1984). *Groups: Interaction and performance*. Englewood Cliffs, NJ: Prentice Hall.

McGregor, D. (1964). *The human side of enterprise*. New York: McGraw-Hill.

McGuire, T.W., Kiesler, S., & Siegel, J. (1987). Group and computer-mediated discussion effects in risk decision making. *Journal of Personality and Social Psychology*, 52(5), 917–930.

McIntosh, C.N. (2001). Report on the construct validity of the Temporal Satisfaction With Life Scale. *Social Indicators Research*, 54(1), 37–56.

McKenna, E., & Beech, N. (1995). *Essence of human resource management.* London: Prentice Hall.

McKnight, C., Dillon, A., & Richardson, J. (1991). *Hypertext in context.* Cambridge: Cambridge University Press.

McLelland, I. (1995). Product assessment and user trials. In J.W. Wilson & E.N. Corlett (Eds), *Evaluation of human work: A practical ergonomics methodology* (2nd edn). London: Taylor & Francis Ltd.

McMahon, G., & Palmer, S. (Eds). (1997). *Client assessment.* Thousand Oaks, CA: Sage.

McMahon, M., & Patton, W. (2002). Beyond 2000: Incorporating the constructivist influence into career guidance and counselling. *Australian Journal of Career Development,* 9(1), 25–29.

McMillan, G.R., Eggleston, R.G., & Anderson, T.R. (1997). Nonconventional controls. In G. Salvendy (Ed.), *Handbook of human factors and ergonomics* (pp. 729–771). New York: John Wiley.

McNally, R.J., Bryant, R.A., & Ehlers, A. (2003). Does early psychological intervention promote recovery from post traumatic stress? *Psychological Science in the Public Interest,* 1(2), 45–80.

McNish, M. (2002). Guidelines for managing change: A study of their effects on the implementation of new information technology projects in organizations. *Journal of Change Management,* 2(3), 201–211.

Meara, N.M., Day, J.D., Chalk, L.M., Phelps, R.E. (1995). Possible selves: Applications for career counseling. *Journal of Career Assessment,* 3(3), 259–277.

Mearns, K., & Flin, R. (1995). Risk perception and attitudes to safety by personnel in the offshore oil and gas industry: A review. *Journal of Loss Prevention in the Process Industries,* 8, 299–305.

Mearns, K.J., & Flin, R. (1999). Assessing the state of organizational safety culture or climate? *Current Psychology,* 18(1), 5–13.

Mearns, K., Whitaker, S.M., & Flin, R. (2001). Benchmarking safety climate in hazardous environments: A longitudinal, interorganizational approach. *Risk Analysis,* 21(4), 771–786.

Mearns, K., Flin, R., & O'Connor, P. (2001). Sharing 'worlds of risk': Improving communication with crew resource management. *Journal of Risk Research,* 4(4), 377–392.

Mearns, K.J., & Flin, R. (2001). Assessing the state of organizational safety—Culture or climate? In H. Ellis & N. Macrae (Eds), *Validation in psychology: Research perspectives* (pp. 5–20). New Brunswick, NJ: Transaction Publishers.

Meglino, B.M., Ravlin, E.C., & DeNisi, A.S. (2001). A meta-analytic examination of realistic job preview effectiveness: A test of three counterintuitive propositions. *Human Resource Management Review,* 10(4), 407–434.

Meichenbaum, D. (1985). *Stress inoculation.* New York: Pergamon Press.

Meister, D. (1986). *Human factors testing and evaluation.* Amsterdam: Elsevier Science Publishers.

Mental Health Foundation (2000). *The cost of mental health problems. The fundamental facts.* (www.mentalhealth.org.uk/ffcost.htm).

Menzies, I. (1954). The functioning of social systems as a defence against anxiety. *Human Relations,* 13, 95–121.

Mero, N.P., Motowidlo, S.J., & Alexandra, L. (2003). Effects of accountability on rating behaviour and rater accuracy. *Journal of Applied Social Psychology,* 33(12), 2493–2514.

Merrill, M.D. (2002). First principles of instruction. *Educational Technology Research and Development,* 50(3), 43–59.

Meyer, J.P. (1997). Organizational commitment. In C. Cooper & I. Robertson (Eds), *International review of industrial and organizational psychology* (pp. 289–341). Chichester: Wiley.

Meyer, J.P., & Allen, N.J. (1997). *Commitment in the workplace: Theory, research and application.* Thousand Oaks, CA: Sage.

Meyerson, D.E. (1994). Interpretations of stress in institutions: The cultural production of ambiguity and burnout. *Administrative Science Quarterly,* 39, 628–653.

Mezirow, J. (1985). A critical theory of self-directed learning. In S. Brookfield (Ed.), *Self-directed learning: From theory to practice* (pp. 17–30). San Francisco, CA: Jossey-Bass.

Militello, L.G., & Hutton, R.J.B. (1998). Applied cognitive task analysis (ACTA): A practitioner's toolkit for understanding cognitive task demands. *Ergonomics,* 41(11), 1618–1641.

Miller, L.E., & Grush, J.E. (1988). Improving predictions in expectancy theory research: Effects of personality, expectancies, and norms. *Academy of Management Journal,* 31(1), 107–122.

Mills, A.J., & Tancred, P. (Eds). (1992). *Gendering organizational analysis*. Newbury Park, CA: Sage Publications.

Millward, L.J., & Brewerton, P. (1999). Contractors and their psychological contract. *British Journal of Management*, 10, 253–274.

Millward, L.J., & Brewerton, P. (2000). The psychological contract: employment relations in the 21st century. In C. Cooper & I. Robertson (Eds), *International Review of Industrial & Organizational Psychology* (Vol. 15, pp.1–62). Chichester: Wiley.

Millward, L.J., & Cropley, M. (2003). Psychological contracting: Processes of contract formation during interviews between nannies and their 'employers'. *Journal of Occupational and Organizational Psychology*, 76(2), 213–242.

Millward, L.J., & Herriot, P. (2000). Psychological contracts in the UK. In R. Schalk & D. Rousseau (Eds), *International Psychological Contracts*. Thousand Oaks, CA: Sage.

Millward, L.J., & Jeffries, N. (2001). The team survey: A tool for health care service development. *Journal of Advanced Nursing*, 35(2), 276–287.

Millward, L.J., & Kyriakidou, O. (2004a). Effective virtual teamwork: A socio-cognitive and motivational model. In P. Ferris & S. Godar (Eds), *Virtual and collaborative teams: Process, technologies and practice* (pp. 20–34). London: Idea Group Inc.

Millward, L.J., & Kyriakidou, O. (2004b). Linking pre- and post-merger identities through the concept of career. *Career Development International*, 9(1), 12–27.

Millward, L.J., & Purvis, R.G. (1998). *Team building techniques – A critical evaluation and conceptual model*. Report for Defence Evaluation Research Agency under contract CHS7330.

Millward, L.J., Brown, D., & Kyriakidou, O. (2003). *Managing diversity in multi-national teams*. Report under contract for Quinetiq, Farnborough, UK.

Millward, L.J., Flyn, C., & Anderton, J. (2004). *Career self-concept – A model and a measurement tool*. Manuscript submitted for publication in *Journal of Career Guidance and Counselling*.

Millward, L.J., Bryan, K., Collins, R., & Everatt, J. (2005). Clinicians and dyslexia – a computer based assessment of one of the key cognitive skills involved in drug administration. *International Journal of Nursing Studies*. In press.

Millward, L.J., Uzzell, D., Webb, C., & Rolph, J. (2004). *Hotdesking, interaction salience and affective commitment*. Under review for publication. University of Surrey, UK.

Milner, P., & Palmer, S. (1998). *Integrative stress counselling: A humanistic problem solving approach*. London: Cassell.

Miner, J.B. (1964). *Scoring guide for the miner sentence completion scale*. Atlanta, GA: Organizational Measurement Systems Press.

Ministry of Labour and National Service. (1958). (The Carr Report) *Training for skill: Recruitment and training of young workers in industry*. London: HMSO.

Mischel, W. (1973). Toward a cognitive social learning reconceptualisation of personality. *Psychological Review*, 80, 252–283.

Mishra, A.K., & Spreitzer, G.M. (1998). Explaining how survivors respond to downsizing: The roles of trust, empowerment, justice, and work redesign. *Academy of Management Review*, 23, 567–588.

Misumi, J. (1985). *The behavioral science of leadership*. Ann Arbor, MI: University of Michigan Press.

Misumi, J., & Peterson, M.F. (1985). *The behavioral science of leadership: An interdisciplinary Japanese research program*. Ann Arbor, MI: University of Michigan Press.

Mitchell, T.R. (1997). Matching motivational strategies with organizational contexts. In B.M. Staw & L.L. Cummings (Eds), *Research in organizational behaviour* (Vol. 19, pp. 57–149). Greenwich, CT: JAI Press.

Mitta, D.A., & Packebusch, S.J. (1995). Improving interface quality: An investigation of human-computer interaction task learning. *Ergonomics*, 38(7), 1307–1325.

Mohr, D.L., & Clemmer, D.I. (1988). The 'accident prone' worker: An example from heavy industry. *Accident Analysis and Prevention*, 20, 123–127.

Monat, A., & Lazarus, R.S. (Eds). (1991). *Stress and coping: An anthology* (2nd edn). New York: Columbia University Press.

Mone, M.A., & Barker, V.L., III (1996). A postmodern Dr. Strangelove: Or how we got along after the downsizing. In S.M. Sommer (Chair), *The role of trust in understanding workplace cooperation and competition*. Symposium conducted at the annual meeting of the Academy of Management, Cincinnati, OH, August.

Moore, R.S. (1995). *Creating public value: Strategic management in government*. Cambridge, MA: Harvard University Press.

Moorrees, V. (1933). Industrial psychology at Rowntree's Cocoa Works. I. The work of the psychological department. *Human Factor, 7*, 159–166.

Moos, R.H. (1981). *Work environment scale manual*. Palo Alto, CA: Consulting Psychologists Press.

Moran, E.T., & Volkwein, J.F. (1992). The cultural approach to the formation of organizational climate. *Human Relations, 45*(1), 19–47.

Moran, T. (1981). The command language grammar: A representation for the user interface of interactive computer systems. *International Journal of Man-Machine Studies, 15*, 3–50.

Moray, N. (1997). Models of models of ... mental models. In T.B. Sheridan, T. Van Luntern et al., (Eds), *Perspectives on the human controller: Essays in honor of Henk G. Stassen* (pp. 271–285). Mahwah, NJ: Lawrence Erlbaum Assoc.

Moreland, R.L., & Levine, J.M. (1993). Group staffing levels and responses to prospective and new group members. *Journal of Personality and Social Psychology, 65*(4), 723–734.

Morgan, Gareth (1997). *Images of organization* (2nd edn). Thousand Oaks, CA: Sage.

Morin, L., & Latham, G.P. (2000). Effect of mental practice and goal setting as a transfer of training intervention on supervisors' self-efficacy and communication skills: An exploratory study. *Applied Psychology: An International Review, 49*, 566–578.

Morosini, P. (1998). *Managing cultural differences*. New York: Pergamon Press.

Morris, J.A., & Feldman, D.C. (1996). The dimension, antecedents, and consequences of emotional labour. *Academy of Management Review, 21*, 986–1010.

Morrison, D., Payne, R.L., & Wall, T.D. (2000). Is job a viable unit of analysis? A multi-level analysis of demand-control-support models. *Journal of Occupational Health Psychology, 8*(3), 209–219.

Morrison, E.W., & Robinson, S.L. (1997). When employees feel betrayed: A model of how psychological contract violation develops. *Academy of Management Review, 22*, 226–256.

Moscoso, S. (2000). Selection interview: A review of validity evidence, adverse impact and applicant reactions. *International Journal of Selection and Assessment, 6*, 240–240.

Moscoso, S., & Salgado, J.F. (2004). Fairness reactions to personnel selection techniques in Spain and Portugal. *International Journal of Selection and Assessment, 12*(1–2), 187–196.

Motowidlo, S.J., & Tippins, N. (1993). Further studies of the low-fidelity simulation in the form of a situational inventory. *Journal of Occupational and Organizational Psychology, 66*(4), 337–344.

Motowidlo, S.J., Dunnette, M.D., & Carter, G.W. (1990). An alternative selection procedure: The low fidelity simulation. *Journal of Applied Psychology, 75*, 640–647.

Mount, M.K., Barrick, M.R., & Strauss, J.P. (1994). The joint relationship of conscientiousness and ability with performance: Test of the interaction hypothesis. *Journal of Management, 25*, 707–721.

Mount, M.K., Witt, L.A., & Barrick, M.R. (2000). Incremental validity of empirically keyed biodata scales over GMA and the Five Factor Personality Constructs. *Personnel Psychology, 53*(2), 299–323.

Mowday, R.T., Steers, R.M., & Porter, L.W. (1979). The measurement of organizational commitment. *Journal of Vocational Behavior, 4*, 224–247.

Mumford, M.D., & Stokes, G.S. (1992). Developmental determinants of individual action: Theory and practice in applying background measures. In M.D. Dunnette & L.M. Hough (Eds), *Handbook of industrial and organizational psychology* (2nd edn, Vol. 3, pp. 61–138). Palo Alto, CA. Consulting Psychologists Press.

Munro, A., Breaux, R., Patrey, J., & Sheldon, B. (2002). Cognitive aspects of virtual environments design. In K.M. Stanney (Ed.), *Handbook of virtual environments: Design, implementation, and applications* (pp. 415–434). Mahwah, NJ: Lawrence Erlbaum Associates.

Murnighan, J.K., & Leung, T.K. (1976). The effects of leader involvement and the importance of the task on subordinates' performance. *Organizational Behaviour and Human Performance, 17*, 299–310.

Murphy, L.R. (1988). Workplace interventions for stress reduction and prevention. In C.L. Cooper and R. Payne (Eds), *Causes, coping and consequences of stress at work* (pp. 301–342). Chichester: Wiley.

Murphy, K.R., & Cleveland, J.N. (1995). *Understanding performance appraisal: Social, organizational and goal-based perspectives*. Thousand Oaks, CA: Sage.

Murphy, K.R., & Cleveland, J.N., Skattebo, A.L., & Kinney, T.B. (2004). Raters who pursue different goals give different ratings. *Journal of Applied Psychology, 89*(1), 158–164.

Murphy, K.R., Cronin, B.E., & Tam, A.P. (2003). Controversy and consensus regarding the use of cognitive ability testing in organizations. *Journal of Applied Psychology,* 88(4), 660–671.

Murphy, K.R., Jako, R.A., & Anhalt, R.L. (1993). Nature and consequences of halo error: A critical analysis. *Journal of Applied Psychology,* 78(2), 218–225.

Murphy, L.R., & De Shon, R.P. (2000). Inter-rater correlations do not estimate the reliability of job performance ratings. *Personnel Psychology,* 53, 873–900.

Murphy, L.R., Hurrell, J.J. Jr., Sauter, S.L., & Keita, G-P. (Eds). (1995). *Job stress interventions.* Washington, DC: American Psychological Association.

Murray, H.A. (1938). *Explorations in personality.* Boston: Houghton-Mifflin.

Murrell, K.L., & Valsan, E.H. (1985). A team building workshop as an OD intervention in Egypt. *Leadership and Development Journal,* 6(2), 11–16.

Myers, D.G. (1993). *Social Psychology* (4th edn). New York: McGraw-Hill.

NCVQ (1991). *General National Vocational Qualifications.* London: NVCQ.

Nagy, M.S. (2002). Using a single-item approach to measure facet job satisfaction. *Journal of Occupational and Organizational Psychology,* 75, 77–86.

Neenan, M. (1993). Using RET in the workplace. *Stress News,* 5(1), 7–10.

Nelson-Jones, B. (1993). *Lifeskills helping: Helping others through a systematic people-centred approach.* London: Brooks-Cole.

Neuman, G.A., Edwards, J.E., & Raju, N.S. (1989). Organizational development interventions: A meta-analysis of their effects on satisfaction and other attitudes. *Personnel Psychology,* 42(3), 461–489.

Newell, A., & Simon, H.A. (1972). *Human problem-solving.* Englewood Cliffs, NJ: Prentice-Hall.

Newton, T. (1995). *Managing stress.* London: Sage.

Nicholson, N. (1987). *The transition cycle: A conceptual framework for the analysis of change and human resources management,* Vol. 5. Greenwich, CT: JAI Press.

Nicholson, N., & West, M. (1988). *Managerial job change.* London: Cambridge University Press.

Nicholson, P. (1995). *Gender, power and organisation.* London: Routledge.

Niedenthal, P.M., Cantor, N., & Kihlstrom, J.F. (1985). Prototype matching: A strategy for social decision making. *Journal of Personality and Social Psychology,* 48, 575–584.

Nielsen, J. (1995). *Multimedia and hypertext: The internet and beyond.* Cambridge, MA: Academic Press.

Nielsen, J. (1997). Usability testing. In G. Salvendy (Ed.), *Handbook of human factors and ergonomics* (pp. 1543–1568). New York: John Wiley.

Niendenthal, P.M., Cantor, N., & Kihlstrom, J.K. (1985). Prototype matching: A strategy for social decision-making. *Journal of Personality and Social Psychology,* 48(3), 575–584.

Nilan, M.S. (1992). Cognitive space: Using virtual reality for large information resource management problems. *Journal of Communication,* 42(4), 115–135.

Nixon, J., & Carroll, M. (1994). Can a line manager also be a counsellor? *Employee Counselling Today,* 6(1), 10–15.

Noe, R.A. (1986). Training attributes and attitudes: Neglected influences on training effectiveness. *Academy of Management Review,* 11(4), 736–749.

Noe, R.A. (1996). Is career management related to employee development and performance? *Journal of Organizational Behaviour,* 17, 119–133.

Noer, D.M. (1997). *Healing the wounds: Overcoming the trauma of layoffs and revitalizing downsized organizations* (2nd edn). San Franscisco, CA: Jossey-Bass.

Noordsy, D., Torrey, W., Mueser, K., Mead, S., O'Keefe, C., & Fox, L. (2002). Recovery from severe mental illness: An intrapersonal and functional outcome definition. *International Review of Psychiatry,* 14, 318–326.

Nord, W.R. (1969). Beyond the teaching machine: The neglected area of operant conditioning in the theory and practice of management. *Organizational Behavior and Human Decision Processes,* 4(4), 375–401.

Nordstrom, C.R., Wendland, D., & Williams, K.B. (1998). An examination of the effectiveness of error management training. *Journal of Business and Psychology,* 12(3), 269–282.

Norman, D.A. (1983a). Some observations on mental models. In D. Gentner & A. Stevens (Eds), *Mental models* (pp. 15–34). Hillsdale, NJ: Erlbaum.

Norman, D.A. (1983b). Design rules based on an analysis of human error. *Communications of the ACM,* 26(4), 254–258.

Norman, D.A. (1990). The problem with automation: Inappropriate feedback and interaction, not 'over-automation'. *Philosophical Transactions of the Royal Society of London*, B327, 585–593.

Northouse, P.G. (2001). *Leadership: Theory and practice*. London: Sage.

Norton, S.D., & Edinger, J.A. (1978). Assessment centers versus traditional methods for predicting managerial success: Empirical and content validity. *Catalog of Selected Documents in Psychology*, 8(1786), 100.

Nuttman-Shwartz, O., & Ginsburg, R. (2002). Injuries. *Employee Assistance Quarterly*, 17(3), 17–32.

O'Hare, D., Wiggins, W., Batt, R., & Morrison, D. (1995). Cognitive failure analysis for aircraft accident investigation. *Ergonomics*, 37(11), 1855–1869.

O'Malley C.E., & Draper, S.W. (1992). Representation and interaction: Are mental models all in the mind? In Y. Rogers, A. Rutherford & P.A. Bibby (Eds), *Models in the mind* (pp. 73–92). London: Academic Press.

O'Reilly, C.A., & Chatman, J. (1986). Organizational commitment and psychological attachment: The effects of compliance, identification and internalisation on prosocial behaviour. *Journal of Applied Psychology*, 71, 492–499.

O'Reilly, C.A., Chatman, J., & Caldwell, D. (1991). People and organizational culture: A profile comparison approach to assessing person-organization fit. *Academy of Management Journal*, 34, 487–516.

O'Toole, M. (2002). The relationship between employees' perceptions of safety and organizational culture. *Journal of Safety Research*, 33(2), 231–243.

Oakland, S., & Ostell, A. (1996). Measuring coping: A review and critique. *Human Relations*, 49, 133–155.

Offermann, L.R., & Phan, L.U. (2002). Culturally intelligent leadership for a diverse world. In F.J. Pirozzolo (Ed.), *Multiple intelligences and leadership* (pp. 187–214). Mahwah NJ: Lawrence Erlbaum Associates.

Ofshe, R., & Singer, M.T. (1986). Attacks on peripheral versus central elements of self and the impact of thought reforming techniques. *Cultic Studies Journal*, 3(1), 3–24.

Ogden, J. (2002). *Health and the construction of the individual*. New York: Routledge.

Oher, J.M. (1999). *The employee assistance handbook*. New York: Wiley.

Olins, W. (1995). *The new guide to corporate identity*. Aldershot: Gower.

Oliver, A., Cheyne, A., Tomas, J.M., & Cox, S. (2002). The effects of organizational and individual factors on occupational accidents. *Journal of Occupational and Organizational Psychology*, 75, 473–488.

Olson, M.H., & Ives, B. (1981). User involvement in system design: An empirical test of alternative approaches. *Information and Management*, 4, 183–195.

Olson, R., & Austin, J. (2001). Behavior-based safety and working alone: The effects of a self-monitoring package on the safe performance of bus operators. *Journal of Organizational Behavior Management*, 21(3), 5–43.

Ondrack, D.A. (1975). Socialization in professional schools: A comparative study. *Administrative Science Quarterly*, 20, 97–103.

Ones, D.S., & Viswesvaran, C. (1996). Bandwidth-fidelity in personality measurement for personnel selection. *Journal of Organisational Behaviour*, 17, 609–626.

Ones, D.S., Viswesvaran, C., & Schmidt, F.L. (1993). Comprehensive meta analysis of integrity test validities – findings and implications for personnel-selection and theories of job-performance. *Journal of Applied Psychology*, 78(4), 679–706.

Ones, D.S., Viswesvaran, C., & Schmidt, F.L. (1995). Integrity tests: Overlooked facts, resolved issues, and remaining questions. *American Psychologist*, 50(6), 456–457.

Ong, S. (2004). *Substitutes for culture. A critical review of the culture change literature*. Essay prepared for MSc in Occupational and Organizational Psychology, University of Surrey, UK.

Organ, D.W. (1998). The motivational basis of organizational citizenship behavior. In L.L. Cummings & B.M. Staw (Eds), *Research in Organizational Behavior* (Vol. 12, pp. 43–72). Greenwich, CT: JAI Press.

Orlikowski, W. (1993). CASE tools organizational change: Investigating incremental and radical changes in systems development. *MIS Quarterly*, 17(3), 309–340.

Ornstein, S., & Isabella, L.A. (1993). Making sense of careers: A review 1989–1992. *Journal of Management*, 19, 243–267.

Osipow, S.H., & Davis, A.S. (1988). The relationship of coping resources to occupational stress and strain. *Journal of Vocational Behaviour*, 32, 1–15.

Östberg, O. (1980). Risk perception and work behaviour in forestry: Implications for accident prevention policy. *Accident Analysis and Prevention*, 12, 189–200.

Ostroff, C. (1991). Training effectiveness measures and scoring schemes: A comparison. *Personnel Psychology*, 44, 353–374.

Ostroff, C. (1993). The effects of climate and personal influences on individual behavior and attitudes in organizations. *Organizational Behaviour and Human Decision Making Processes*, 56(1), 56–90.

Pahl, J.M. (1995). *After success*. Cambridge: Polity Press.

Pajak, E. (1993). Change and continuity in supervision and leadership. In G. Cawelti (Ed.), *Challenges and achievements of American education* (pp. 158–186). Alexandria, VA: Edward Brothers.

Palmer, C.I., Boyles, W.R., Veres, J.G., & Hill, J.B. (1972). Validation of a clerical test using work samples. *Journal of Business and Psychology*, 7(2), 239–257.

Palmer, S. (1996). Developing a stress management programme. In R. Woolfe & W. Dryden (Eds), *Handbook of counselling psychology* (pp. 528–552). London: Sage.

Palmer, S., & Dryden, W. (1996). *Stress management and counselling: Theory, practice, research and methodology*. London: Cassell.

Panks, J.G. (2002). The utilization of employee assistance program services by managers. *Dissertation Abstracts International Section A: Humanities and Social Sciences*, 62(12–A), 4035.

Pannone, R. (1994). Blue collar selection. In M. Mumford & G.S. Stokes (Eds), *Biodata handbook: Theory, research, and use of biographical information in selection and performance prediction* (pp. 261–273). Palo Alto, CA: CPP Books.

Park, K.S. (1997). Human error. In G. Salvendy (Ed.), *Handbook of human factors and ergonomics* (pp. 163–225). New York: John Wiley.

Parker, P., & Arthur, M. (2004). Giving voice to the dual career couple. *British Journal of Guidance and Counselling*, 32(1), 3–23.

Parker, S.K. (1998). Role breadth self-efficacy: Relationship with work enrichment and other organizational practices. *Journal of Applied Psychology*, 83, 835–852.

Parker, S.K., & Wall, T.D. (1998). *Job and work design*. London: Sage.

Parker, S.K., & Wall, T.D. (2001). Work design: Learning from the past and mapping a new terrain. In N. Anderson, D.S. Ones, H.K. Sinangil & C. Viswesvaran (Eds), *Handbook of Industrial, Work and Organizational Psychology* (Vol. 1, pp. 90–109). London: Sage.

Parker, S.K., Axtell, C.M., & Turner, N.A. (2001). Designing a safer workplace: Importance of job autonomy, communication quality, and supportive supervisors. *Journal of Occupational Health Psychology*, 6, 211–228.

Parker, S.K., Wall, T.D., & Jackson, P.R. (1997). 'That's not my job': Developing flexible employee work orientations. *Academy of Management Journal*, 40, 899–929.

Parker, S.K., Wall, T.D., & Cordery, J.L. (2001). Future work design research and practice: Towards an elaborated model of work design. *Journal of Occupational and Organizational Psychology*, 74(4), 413–440.

Parkes, C.M. (1972). *Bereavement: Studies of grief in adult life*. New York: International Universities Press.

Parsloe, E. (1992). *Coaching, mentoring and assessing: A practical guide to developing competence*. New York: Kogan Paul.

Parsons, F. (1909). *Choosing a vocation*. Boston: Houghton-Mifflin.

Parsons, S., & Mitchell, P. (2002). The potential of virtual reality in social skills training for people with autistic spectrum disorders. *Journal of Intellectual Disability Research*, 46(5), 430–443.

Pascale, R., Millemann, M., & Gioja, L. (2000). *Surfing the edge of chaos: The new art and science of management*. New York: Crown Publishers.

Paterson, J.M., Green, A., & Cary, J. (2002). The measurement of organizational justice in organizational change programmes: A reliability, validity and context-sensitivity assessment. *Journal of Occupational and Organizational Psychology*, 75(4), 393–408.

PATRA (1992–94). *Psychological and social aspects of teleworking in rural areas*. CEC/DGXIII 02004, Opportunities for Rural Areas (ORA Programme).

Patrick, J. (2000). Training. In N. Chmiel (Ed.), *Work and organizational psychology* (pp. 100–124). Oxford: Blackwell Publishers.

Patton, W., & Creed, P. (2001). Developmental issues in career maturity and career decision status. *The Career Development Quarterly*, 49, 336–351.

Paul, R.J., & Ebadi, Y.M. (1989). Leadership decision-making in a service organization: A Fields test of the Vroom Yetton model. *Journal of Organizational Psychology*, 62, 201–211.

Paul, W.P., & Robertson, K.B. (1970). *Job enrichment and employee motivation*. London: Gower.

Payne, D., & Altman, J. (1962). *An index of electronic equipment operability: Report of development, Report AIR-C-43–1/62*. Pittsburgh: American Institutes for Research.

Payne, R.L. (1979). Demands, supports, and constraints and psychological health. In C.J. Mackay & T. Cox (Eds), *In response to stress: Occupational aspects* (pp. 85–105). London: IPC Business Press.

Pearce, C.L., Gallagher, C.A., & Ensley, M.D. (2002). Confidence at the group level of analysis: A longitudinal investigation of the relationship between potency and team effectiveness. *Journal of Occupational and Organizational Psychology*, 75(1), 115–119.

Pearn, M., Roderick, C., & Mulrooney, C. (1995). *Learning Organisations in Practice*. Maidenhead: McGraw-Hill Book Co.

Pearn, M., & Kandola, R. (1993). *Job analysis: A manager's guide*. London: Institute of Personnel Management.

Peavy, R.V. (1992). A constructivist model of training for career counsellors. *Journal of Career Development*, 18, 215–228.

Peavy, R.V. (1997). *Sociodynamic counselling: A constructivist perspective*. Victoria, Canada: Trafford.

Pelfrene, E., Vlerick, P., Moreau, M., Mak, R.P., Kornitzer, M., & De Backer, G. (2003). Perceptions of job insecurity and the impact of world market competition as health risks: Results from Belstress. *Journal of Occupational and Organizational Psychology*, 76(4), 411–425.

Peluchette, J., & Jeanquart, S. (2000). Professionals' use of different mentor sources at various career stages: Implications for career success. *Journal of Social Psychology*, 140(5), 549–564.

Pervin, L.A. (1997). *The Science of personality*. Chichester and New York: Wiley.

Peters, R., & Waterman, R. (1982). *In search of excellence*. New York: Harper & Row.

Peterson, M.F., & Smith, P.B. (2000). Sources of meaning, organizations and culture. In N. Ashkanasy, C. Wilderom & M. Peterson (Eds), *Handbook of organizational culture and climate* (pp. 101–115). London: Sage.

Pettijohn, L.S., Parker, R., Pettijohn, C.E., & Kent, O.L. (2001). Performance appraisals: Usage, criteria and observations. *Journal of Management Development*, 20(9), 754–771.

Pfurtscheller, G., Flotzinger, D., & Neuper, C. (1994). Differentiation between finger, toe and tongue movement in man based on 40Hz EEG. *Electroencephalography and Clinical Neurophysiology*, 90, 456–460.

Pheasant, S. (1991). *Ergonomics, work and health*. Basingstoke: Macmillan.

Pheasant, S. (1995). Anthropometry and the design of workspaces. In J.W. Wilson & E.N. Corlett (Eds), *Evaluation of human work: A practical ergonomics methodology* (2nd edn, pp. 23–27). London: Taylor & Francis Ltd.

Phillips, J. (1990). *Handbook of training evaluation and measurement issues*. London: Kogan Page.

Phillips, P., Louveries, P., Millward, L.J., Kyriakidou, O., & Gore, J. (2003). *Examining organizational change and its measurement in future C2 organizations and identifying the nature of the digitalised organization*. Report for QuinetiQ under contract. October.

Pinder, C.C. (1984). *Work motivation*. Glenview, IL: Scott, Foresman.

Pinder, C.C. (1998). Human nature: Emotions at work. In *Work Motivation in Organizational Behaviour*, NJ: Prentice Hall. Englewood Cliffs.

Pinzel, L.J., Freeman, F.G., Scerbo, M.W., Mikulka, P.J., & Pope, A.T. (2000). A closed loop system for examining psychophysiological measures for adaptive task allocation. *International Journal of Aviation Psychology*, 10(4), 393–410.

Plach, M., & Wallach, D. (2002). Toward methods for supporting the anticipation-feedback loop in user interface design. *Theoretical Issues in Ergonomics Science*, 3(1), 26–46.

Plant, P. (2002). *IT in careers guidance: Constructs and learning: Computer-assisted careers guidance – Some European perspectives*. Danish University of Education, Copenhagen.

Ployhart, R.E., & Harold, C.M. (2004). The Applicant Attribution-Reaction Theory (AART): An integrative theory of applicant attributional processing. *International Journal of Selection and Assessment*, 12(1–2), 84–98.

Ployhart, R.E., & Schneider, B. (2002). A multi-level perspective on personnel selection: When will practice catch up? Research in multi-level issues, Vol. 1. In F. Dansereau & F.J. Yammarino (Eds), *The many faces of multi-level issues* (pp. 165–175). New York: Elsevier Science/JAI Press.

Popescu, G.V., Burdea, G.C., & Trefftz, H. (2002). Multimodal interaction modeling. Human factors and ergonomics. In K.M. Stanney (Ed), *Handbook of virtual environments: Design, implementation, and applications* (pp. 435–454). Mahwah, NJ: Lawrence Erlbaum.

Porras, J., & Silvers, R. (1991). Organizational development and transformation. *Annual Review of Psychology*, 42, 51–78.

Porteous, M. (1997). *Occupational psychology*. London: Prentice Hall.

Porter, L.W., & Bigley, G.A. (2001). Motivation and transformational leadership: Some organizational context issues. In U. Kleinbeck & E. Miriam (Eds), *Work motivation in the context of a globalizing economy* (pp. 279–291). Mahwah, NJ: Lawrence Erlbaum Associates.

Premack, S.L., & Wanous, J.P. (1985). A meta-analysis of realistic job preview experiments. *Journal of Applied Psychology*, 70, 706–719.

Pritchard, R.D., Campbell, K.M., & Campbell, D.J. (1977). Effects of extrinsic financial rewards on intrinsic motivation. *Journal of Applied Psychology*, 62(1), 9–15.

Prochaska, J.O., Redding, C.A., & Evers, K. (1997). The transtheoretical model of change. In K. Glanz, F.M. Lewis & B.K. Rimer (Eds), *Health behaviour and health education: Theory, research, and practice* (pp. 60–84). San Francisco: Jossey-Bass.

Pugh, S.D., Skarlicki, D.P., & Passell, B.S. (2003). After the fall: Layoff victims' trust and cynicism in re-employment. *Journal of Occupational and Organizational Psychology*, 76, 201–212.

Pulakos, E.D., Arad, S., Donovan, M.A., & Plamondon, K.E. (2000). Adaptability in the workplace: Development of taxonomy of adaptive performance. *Journal of Applied Psychology*, 85(4), 612–624.

Pulley, M.L. (1994). Navigating the evaluation rapids. *Training and Development*, Sept., p. 19.

Qureshi, S. (2000). Organizational change through collaborative learning in a network form. *Group Decision and Negotiation*, 9(2), 129–147.

Quick, J.C. (1998). Introduction to the measurement of stress at work. *Journal of Occupational Psychology*, 3(4), 291–293.

Quick, J.C. (1999). Occupational health psychology: Historical roots and future directions. *Health Psychology*, 18(1), 82–88.

Rafaeli, A., & Klimoski, R.J. (1983). Predicting sales success through handwriting analysis: An evaluation of the effects of training and handwriting sample content. *Journal of Applied Psychology*, 2, 212–217.

Rafiq, A., Moore, J.A., Zhao, X., Doarn, C.R., & Merrell, R.C. (2004). Digital video capture and synchronous consultation in open surgery. *Ann Surg*, 239(4), 567–73.

Rainey, H.G. (2001). Work motivation. In R.T. Golembiewski (Ed.), *Handbook of organizational behavior* (2nd edn, pp.19–42). New York: Marcel Dekker.

Rasmussen, J. (1987). The definition of human error and a taxonomy of technical system design. In J. Rasmussen, K. Duncan & J. Leplat (Eds), *New technology and human error*. Chichester: John Wiley.

Raynor, T.O., & Roeder, G.P. (1987). Motivation and future orientation: Task and time effects for achievement motivation. In F. Halisch & J. Kuhl (Eds), *Motivation, interaction and volitions* (pp. 61–71). Berlin: Springer.

Reason, J.T. (1988). Errors and violations: The lessons of Chernobyl. Paper presented at the IEEE Conference on Human Factors in Nuclear Power, Monterey, CA.

Reason, J.T. (1990). *Human error*. Cambridge: Cambridge University Press.

Reddy, M. (1993). *The manager's guide to counselling at work*. London: IPM.

Redmill, R. (1997). Practical risk management. In F. Redmill and C. Dale (Eds), *Life cycle management for dependability*. London: Springer-Verlag.

Ree, M.J., & Carretta, T.R. (1996). Central role of g in military pilot selection. *International Journal of Aviation Psychology*, 6(2), 111–123.

Reichers, A.E. (1985). A review and reconceptualization of organizational commitment. *Academy of Management Review*, 10, 465–476.

Reid, A.M., & Barrington, H. (1997). *Learning and training in training interventions: Managing employee development* (5th edn). London: IPD.

Reile, D.M., & Harris-Bowlsbey, J.A. (2000). Using the Internet in career planning and assessment. *Journal of Career Assessment*, 8(1), 69–84.

Reynolds, S., & Briner, R.B. (1996). Stress management at work: With whom, for whom and to what ends? *British Journal of Guidance and Counselling*, 22(1), 75–89.

Rhoades, L., & Eisenberger, R. (2002). Perceived organizational support: A review of the literature. *Journal of Applied Psychology*, 87(4), 698–714.

Richardson, M.S. (2000). A new perspective for counsellors: From career ideologies to empowerment through work and relational practices. In A. Collin & R. Young (Eds), *The future of career* (pp. 69–82). Cambridge: Cambridge University Press.

Rick, J., & Briner, R. (2001). Trauma management vs stress debriefing: What should responsible organizations do? In *The British Psychological Society occupational and organizational psychology conference book of proceedings* (pp. 126–130). Liecester: British Psychological Society.

Rick, J., & Guppy, A. (1994). Coping strategies and mental health in white collar public sector employees. *European Work and Organizational Psychologist*, 4, 1–16.

Riva, G. (2002). Communicating in CMC: Making order out of miscommunication. Studies in new technologies and practices in communication. In R. Ciceri & L. Anolli (Eds), *Say not to say: New perspectives on miscommunication* (pp. 197–227). Amsterdam: IOS Press.

Riverin-Simard, D. (2000). Career development in a changing context of the second part of working life. In R.A. Young & A. Collin (Eds), *The future of career* (pp. 115–129). New York: Cambridge University Press.

Rizzo, J.R., House, R., & Lirtzman, S. (1970). Role conflict and role ambiguity in complex organizations. *Administrative Science Quarterly*, 15, 150–163.

Roberts, C., Probst, T.M., Martocchio, J.J., Drasgow, F., & Lawler, J.L. (2000). Empowerment and continous improvement in the United States, Mexico, Poland, and India: Predicting fit on the basis of the dimensions of power distance and individualism. *Journal of Applied Psychology*, 85, 643–658.

Roberts, K. (1977). The social conditions, consequences, and limitations of career guidance. *British Journal of Guidance and Counselling*, 5, 1–9.

Roberts, G.E., & Pavlak, T. (1996). Municipal government personnel professionals and performance appraisal: Is there a consensus on the characteristics of an effective appraisal system? *Public Personnel Management*, 25(3), 379–408.

Robertson, I.T., & Kandola, R.S. (1982). Work sample tests: Validity, adverse impact and applicant reaction. *Journal of Occupational Psychology*, 55, 171–183.

Robertson, I.T., & Smith, M. (Eds). (1987). *Advances in selection and assessment*. Chichester: Wiley.

Robertson, I.T., & Smith, M. (2001). Personnel selection. *Journal of Occupational and Organizational Psychology*, 74, 441–472.

Robertson, I.T., Baron, H., Gibbons, P., MacIver, R., & Nyfield, G. (2000). Conscientiousness and managerial performance. *Journal of Occupational and Organizational Psychology*, 73, 171–180.

Robinson, G.S., & Wick, C.W. (1992). *A Human Resource Planning*, 15(1), 63–76.

Robinson, S.L. (1996). Trust and breach of the psychological contract. *Administrative Science Quarterly*, 41, 574–599.

Robinson, S.L., & Morrison, E.W. (2000). The development of psychological contract breach and violation: A longitudinal study. *Journal of Organizational Behaviour*, 21, 525–546.

Robitschek, C., & Cook, S.W. (1999). The influence of personal growth initiative and coping styles on career exploration and vocational identity. *Journal of Vocational Behavior*, 54(1), 127–141.

Rockart, J.F., Earl, M.J., & Ross, J.W. (1996). Eight imperatives for the new IT organization, *Sloan Management Review*, 38(1), 43–54.

Roddy, K. (2004). *Organizational cognition: A shared mental model approach to military organization*. Farnborough: QinetiQ.

Rodger, A. (1968). The seven point plan. In B. Hopson & J. Hayes (Eds), *The theory and practice of vocational guidance* (pp. 359–373). Oxford: Pergamon Press.

Roethlisberger, F.J. (1964). Contributions of the behavioural sciences to a general theory of management. In H. Leavitt & L.R. Pondy (Eds), *Readings in managerial psychology* (pp. 518–541). Chicago and London: University of Chicago Press.

Roethlisberger, F.J., & Dickson, W.J. (1939). *Management and the worker*. Cambridge, MA: Harvard University Press.

Rogers, C.R. (1951). *Client-centered therapy*. Boston: Houghton-Mifflin.

Rogers, William P. (1986). *Report of the Presidential Commission on the Space Shuttle Challenger Accident* (5 vols). Washington, DC: Government Printing Office.

Rogovin, B. (1979). *Three Mile Island: A Report to the Commissioners and to the Public* (The Rogovin Report). USNRC Report Nureg/CR-1250–V. Washington, DC: USNRC.

Rollinson, D., Broadfield, A., & Edwards, D.J. (1998). *Organizational behaviour and analysis*. Harlow: Addison-Wesley.

Rosenman, R.H., Swan, G.E., & Carmelli, D. (1988). Definition, assessment, and evolution of the Type A behavior pattern. In C.R. Snyder & B. Houston (Eds), *Type A behavior pattern: Research, theory, and intervention* (pp. 8–31). Oxford: John Wiley & Sons.

Roskies, E. (1987). *Stress management for the healthy type A: Theory and practice*. New York: Guilford Press.

Ross, R.R., & Altmaier, E.M. (1994). *Counselling for occupational stress: A handbook of counselling for stress at work*. London: Sage.

Roth, P.L., BeVier, C.A., Switzer, III, F.S., & Schippmann, J.S. (1996). Meta-analysing the relationship between grades and job performance. *Journal of Applied Psychology*, 81, 548–556.

Rothstein, H., Erwin, F., Schmidt, F., Owens, W., & Sparks, C. (1990). Biographical data in employment selection – Can validities be made generalizable? *Journal of Applied Psychology*, 75(2), 175–184.

Rotundo, M., & Sackett, P.R. (2002). The relative importance of task, citizenship, and counterproductive performance to global ratings of job performance: A policy capturing approach. *Journal of Applied Psychology*, 87(1), 66–80.

Rousseau, D.M. (1989). New hire perceptions of their own and their employer's obligations: A study of psychological contracts. *Journal of Organizational Behaviour*, 11, 389–400.

Rousseau, D.M. (1995). *Psychological contracts in organizations: Understanding written and unwritten agreements*. London: Sage.

Rousseau, D.M. (2001). Schema, promise and mutuality: The building blocks of the psychological contract. *Journal of Occupational and Organizational Psychology*, 74, 511–541.

Rousseau, D.M., & Schalk, R. (Eds). (2000). *Psychological contracts in employment: Cross-National perspectives*. Thousand Oaks, CA: Sage.

Rousseau, D.M., & Tijoriwala, S.A. (1998). Assessing psychological contracts: Issues, alternatives and measures. *Journal of Organizational Behavior*, 19, 649–695.

Rousseau, D.M., & Wade-Benzioni, K.A. (1995). Changing individual-organizational attachments: A two-way street. In A. Howard (Ed.), *The changing nature of work* (pp. 290–322). San Francisco: Jossey-Bass.

Rousseau, D.M., Sitkin, S.B., Burt, R., & Camerer, C. (1998). Not so different after all: A cross-disciplinary view of trust. *Academy of Management Review*, 23, 1–12.

Rowley, J. (2002). From learning organization to knowledge entrepreneur. *Journal of Knowledge Management*, 4(1), 7–15.

Rowling, J.K. (2000). *Harry Potter and the goblet of fire*. London: Bloomsbury.

Ruddle, R.A., Payne, S.J., & Jones, D.M. (1997). Navigating buildings in 'desk-top' virtual environments: Experimental investigations using extended navigational experience. *Journal of Experimental Psychology Applied*, 3(2), 143–159.

Rugg, G., Eva, M., Mahmood, A., Rehman, N., Andrews, S., & Davies, S. (2002). Eliciting information about organizational culture via laddering. *Information Systems Journal*, 12(3), 215–229.

Russell, C.J. (2001). A longitudinal study of top-level executive performance. *Journal of Applied Psychology*, 86(4), 560–573.

Russell, C.J., & Domm, D.R. (1995). Two field tests of an explanation of assessment center validity. *Journal of Occupational and Organizational Psychology*, 68, 25–47.

Russell, C.J., Mattson, J., Devlin, S.E., & Atwater, D. (1990). Predictive validity of biodata items generated from retrospective life experience essays. *Journal of Applied Psychology*, 75, 511–520.

Rust, J. (1999). Discriminant validity of the 'big five' personality traits in employment settings. *Social Behavior and Personality*, 27(1), 99–108.

Ryan, A.M., & Ployhart, R.E. (2000). Applicants' perceptions of selection procedures and decisions: A critical review and agenda for the future. *Journal of Management*, 26, 565–606.

Rynes, S.L. (1993). Who's selecting whom? Effects of selection practices on applicant attitudes and behaviour. In N. Schmitt & W.C. Borman (Eds), *Personnel selection in organizations* (pp. 240–274). San Franscisco, CA: Jossey-Bass.

Rynes, S.L., & Cable, D.M. (2003). Recruitment research in the twenty-first century. In D. Ilgen, R. Daniel & W.C. Borman (Eds), *Handbook of psychology: Industrial and organizational psychology*, Vol. 12. (pp. 55–76). New York: John Wiley & Sons.

Rynes, S.L., & Connerley, M.L. (1993). Applicant reactions to alternative selection procedures. *Journal of Business and Psychology*, 7, 261–277.

Sackett, P.R. (1987). Assessment centres and content validity: Some neglected issues. *Personnel Psychology*, 40, 13–25.

Sackett, P.R., & Harris, M.M. (1984). Honesty testing for personnel selection – A review and critique. *Personnel Psychology*, 37(2), 221–245.

Sackmann, S.A. (1997). *Cultural complexity in organizations: Inherent contrasts and contradictions*. Thousand Oaks, CA: Sage.

Sadler-Smith, E., Spicer, D.P., & Tsang, F. (2000). The cognitive style index: A replication and extension. *British Journal of Management*, 11, 175–181.

Sagie, A., & Magnezy, R. (1997). Assessor type, number of distinguishable dimension categories, and assessment centre construct validity. *Journal of Occupational and Organizational Psychology*, 70, 103–108.

Saks, A.M., & Ashforth, B.E. (2002). Is job search related to employment quality? It all depends on the fit. *Journal of Applied Psychology*, 87(4), 646–654.

Sala, F., & Dwight, S. (2002). Predicting executive performance with multi-rater surveys: Whom to ask makes a difference. *Journal of Consulting Psychology, Research and Practice*, 54(3), 166–172.

Salas, E., & Cannon-Bowers, J.A. (2001). The science of training: A decade of progress. *Annual Review of Psychology*, 52, 471–499.

Salas, E., Cannon-Bowers, J.A., Rhodenizer, & Bowers, C.A. (1999). Training in organizations: Myths, misconceptions and mistaken assumptions. In G. Ferris (Ed.), *Research in personnel and human resources management* (Vol. 17, pp. 123–161). Greenwich, CT: JAI Press Inc.

Salas, E., Oser, R.L., Cannon-Bowers, J.A., & Daskarolis-Kring, E. (2002). Team training in virtual environments: An event-based approach. Human factors and ergonomics. In K.M. Stanney (Ed.), *Handbook of virtual environments: Design, implementation, and applications* (pp. 873–892). Mahwah, NJ: Lawrence Erlbaum Associates.

Salgado, J.F. (1997). The Five Factor Model of personality and job performance in the European Community. *Journal of Applied Psychology*, 82, 30–43.

Salgado, J.F. (1999). Personnel selection methods. In C.L. Cooper & I.T. Robertson (Eds), *International review of industrial and organizational psychology* (Vol. 14). Chichester: Wiley.

Salgado, J.F. (2003). Predicting job performance using FFM and non-FFM personality measures. *Journal of Occupational and Organisational Psychology*, 76(3), 323–346.

Salgado, J.F., Anderson, N., Moscoso, S., Bertua, C., de Fruyt, F., & Rolland, J.P. (2003). A meta-analytic study of general mental ability validity for different occupations in the European Community. *Journal of Applied Psychology*, 88(6), 176–184.

Salminen, S., & Tallberg, T. (1996). Human errors in fatal and serious occupational accidents in Finland. *Ergonomics*, 39(7), 980–988.

Salzman, M.C., & Rivers, S.D. (1994). Smoke and mirrors: Setting the stage for a successful usability test. *Behavior and Information Technology*, 13(1–2), 9–16.

Sandberg, J. (2000). Understanding human competence at work: An interpretive approach. *Academy of Management Journal*, 43, 9–25.

Sanders, M.S., & McCormick, E.J. (1993). *Human factors in engineering and design* (7th edn). New York: McGraw-Hill.

Sandhu, D.S., & Longwell-Grice, R.M. (2002). Reasons, considerations, and strategies for developing and implementing employee assistance programs. In D.S. Sandhu (Ed.), *Counselling employees: A multifaceted approach* (pp. 143–156). Alexandria, VA: American Counselling Association.

Sarafino, E.P. (1998). *Health psychology: Biopsychosocial interactions* (3rd edn). New York: Wiley.

Sarter, N.B., Woods, D.D., & Billings, C.E. (1997). Automation surprises. In G. Salvendy (Ed.), *Handbook of human factors and ergonomics* (pp. 1926–1943). New York: John Wiley.

Sashkin, M. (1984). *Group and organization studies: An international journal.* Beverly Hills, London, New Delhi: Sage.

Satava, R.M., & Jones, S.B. (2002). Medical applications of virtual environments. Human factors and ergonomics. In K.M. Stanney (Ed.), *Handbook of virtual environments: Design, implementation, and applications* (pp. 937–957). Mahwah, NJ: Lawrence Erlbaum Associates.

Sauer, J., Wastell, D.G., Hockey, G.R.J., Crawshaw, C.M., Ishak, M., & Downing, J.C. (2002). Effects of display design on performance in a simulated ship navigation environment. *Ergonomics*, 45(5), 329–347.

Sauter, S., Murphy, L., & Hurrell, J. (1990). Prevention of work-related disorders. *American Psychologist*, 45, 1146–1158.

Savickas, M.L. (2002). Reinvigorating the study of careers. *Journal of Vocational Behaviour*, 61, 381–385.

Saville, P., Holdsworth, R., Nyfield, G., Cramp, L., & Mabey, W. (1984). *Occupational Personality Questionnaire Manual.* Thames Ditton: Saville–Holdsworth, Ltd.

Schabracq, M., Cooper, C., Travers, C., & van Maanen, D. (2001). *Occupational health psychology: The challenge of workplace stress.* Leicester: BPS Books.

Schaefer, J.J. (2004). Simulators and difficult airway management skills. *Paediatric Anesthesia*, 14(1), 28.

Scharmer, C.O. (2001). Self-transcending knowledge: Sensing and organizing around emerging opportunities. *Journal of Knowledge Management*, 5(2), 137–150.

Schein, E. (1992). *Organizational culture and leadership.* San Francisco, CA: Jossey-Bass.

Schein, E.H. (1978). *Career dynamics: Matching individual and organizational needs.* Reading, MA: Addison-Wesley.

Schein, E.H. (1990). *Career anchors: Discovering your real values.* San Diego, CA: Pfeiffer and Co.

Schein, E.H. (1999). *Process consultation revisited: Building the helping relationship.* Reading, MA: Addison-Wesley.

Schein, E.H. (2004). *Organizational culture and leadership* (3rd edn). New York: Wiley.

Schinkel, S., van Dierndonck, D., & Anderson, N. (2004). The impact of selection encounters on applicants: An experimental study into feedback effects after a negative selection decision. *International Journal of Selection and Assessment*, 12(1–2), 197–205.

Schippman, J.S., Prien, E.P., & Katz, J.A. (1990). Reliability and validity of in-basket performance measures. *Personnel Psychology*, 43, 837–859.

Schmidt, A.M., & Ford, J.K. (2003). Learning within a learner control training environment: The interactive effects of goal orientation and metacognitive instruction on learning outcomes. *Personnel-Psychology*, 56, 405–429.

Schmidt, F.L. (2002). The role of general cognitive ability and job performance: Why there can be no debate. *Human Performance*, 15, 187–210.

Schmidt, F.L., & Hunter, J.E. (1993). Tacit knowledge, practical intelligence, general mental ability, and job knowledge. *Current Directions of Psychological Science*, 2, 8–9.

Schmidt, F.L., & Hunter, J.E. (1998). The validity and utility of selection methods in personnel psychology: Practice and theoretical implications of 85 years of research findings. *Psychological Bulletin*, 124(2), 262–274.

Schmidt, F.L., & Hunter, J. (2004). General mental ability in the world of work: Occupational attainment and job performance. *Journal of Personality and Social Psychology*, 86(1), 162–173.

Schmidt, F.L., Hunter, J.E., McKenzie, R.C., & Muldrow, T.W. (1979). The impact of valid selection procedures on work-force productivity. *Journal of Applied Psychology*, 64, 609–626.

Schmitt, N. (1989). Fairness in employment selection. In M. Smith & I.T. Robertson (Eds), *Advances in selection and assessment* (pp. 133–153). Chichester: John Wiley.

Schmitt, N., & Chan, D. (1998). *Personnel selection: A theoretical approach.* Thousand Oaks, CA: Sage.

Schmitt, N., & Noe, R.A. (1986). On shifting standards for conclusions regarding validity generalization. *Personnel Psychology*, 39, 849–852.

Schmitt, N., Gooding, R.Z., Noe, R.A., & Kirsch, M. (1984). Meta-analyses of validity studies. *Journal of Applied Psychology*, 70, 280–289.

Schmitt, N., Oswald, F.L., Kim, B.H., Gillespie, M.A., & Ramsay, L.J. (2004). The impact of justice and self-serving bias explanation of the perceived fairness of different types of selection tests. *International Journal of Selection and Assessment*, 12(1–2), 160–171.

Schneider, B. (2000). The psychological life of organizations. In N.M. Ashkanasy, C.P.M. Wilderom & M.F. Peterson (Eds), *Handbook of organizational culture and climate* (pp. xvii–xxi). Thousand Oaks, CA: Sage.

Schneider, B., Kristof-Brown, A.L., Goldstein, H.W., & Smith, D.B. (1997). What is this thing called fit? In N. Anderson & P. Herriot (Eds), *International handbook of selection and assessment*. Chichester: Wiley.

Schneider, R.J., Hough, L.M., Dunnette, M.D. (1996). Broadsided by broad traits: How to sink science in five dimensions or less. *Journal of Organisational Behaviour*, 17(6), 639–655.

Schneier, C.E. (1978). The contingency model of leadership: An extension to emergent leadership and leader's sex. *Organizational Behavior and Human Performance*, 21, 220–239.

Scholarios, D., & Lockyer, C. (1999). Recruiting and selecting professionals: Context, qualities and methods. *International Journal of Selection and Assessment*, 7(3), 142–156.

Schott, F., Grzondziel, H., & Hillebrandt, D. (2001). What kind of instructional theory do we need for instructional technology in the 21st century? Possible directions of further developments— UCIT. *Journal of Structural Learning and Intelligent Systems*, 14(4), 371–383.

Schuler, H. (1989). Construct validity of a multi-model procedure. In B.J. Fallon, H.P. Pfister & J. Brebner (Eds), *Advances in industrial and organizational psychology* (pp. 343–354). New York: North Holland.

Schuler, H. (1993). Social validity of selection situations: a concept and some empirical results. In H. Schuler, J. Farr & M. Smith (Eds), *Personnel selection and assessment: Individual and organizational perspectives* (pp. 11–26). Hillsdale, NJ: Laurence Erlbaum.

Schuler, H., & Guldin, A. (1991). Methodological issues in personnel selection research. In C. Cooper & I. Robertson (Eds), *International review of industrial and organizational psychology* (Vol. 6, pp. 213–263). Chichester: Wiley.

Schulz, M.S., Cowan, P.A., Pape Cowan, C., & Brennan, R.T. (2004). Coming home upset: Gender, marital satisfaction, and the daily spillover of workday experience into couple interactions. *Journal of Family Psychology*, 18(1), 250–263.

Sciegaj, M., Garnick, D.W., Horgan, C.M., Merrick, E.L., Goldin, D., Urato, M., & Hodgkin, D. (2001). Employee assistance programs among Fortune 500 firms. *Employee Assistance Quarterly*, 16(3), 25–35.

Scott-Morton, M. (Ed.). (1991). *The corporation of the 1990s*. New York: Oxford University Press.

Scriven, M. (1967). The methodology of evaluation. In R.W. Tyler, R.M. Gagné & M. Scriven (Eds), *Perspectives of curriculum evaluation* (pp. 39–83). Chicago, IL: Rand McNally.

Scullen, S.E., Mount, M.K., & Goff, M. (2000). Understanding the latent structure of job performance ratings. *Journal of Applied Psychology*, 85(6), 956–970.

Secker, J., & Membrey, H. (2003). Promoting mental health through employment and developing healthy workplaces: The potential of natural supports at work. *Health Education Research*, 18(2), 207–215.

Sedikides, C., Herbst, K.C., Hardin, D.P., & Dardis, G.J. (2002). Accountability as a deterrent to self-enhancement: The search for mechanisms. *Journal of Personality and Social Psychology*, 83(3), 592–605.

Segal, L. (1987). *Is the future female? Troubled thoughts on contemporary feminism*. London: Virago.

Segan, C.J., Borland, R., & Greenwood, K.M. (2004). What is the right thing at the right time? Interaction between stages and processes of change among smokers who make an attempt to quit. *Health Psychology*, 23, 86–93.

Seijts, G.H., & Latham, B.W. (2001). Creativity through applying ideas from fields other than one's own: Transferring knowledge from social psychology to industrial/organizational psychology, *Canadian Psychology*, 44(3), 232–239.

Sekaran, U. (1986). *Dual career families: Contemporary organizational and counselling issues*. San Francisco: Jossey-Bass.

Seligman, M.E.P. (1975). *Learned helplessness: On depression, development and death.* San Francisco: Freeman.

Sell, J. (1997). Gender, strategies, and contributions to public goods. *Social Psychology Quarterly,* 60(3), 252–265.

Selye, H. (1956). *The story of the adaptation syndrome.* Montreal: Acta.

Semmer, N.K. (2003). Job stress interventions and organization of work. In J.C. Quick & L.E. Tetrick (Eds), *Handbook of occupational health psychology* (pp. 325–354). Washington, DC: American Psychological Association.

Senge, P. (1990). *The fifth discipline: The art and practice of the learning organization.* London: Century Business.

Senior, B. (2000). Organizational change and development. In N. Chmiel (Ed.), *Introduction to work and organizational psychology: A European perspective* (pp. 347–382). Oxford: Blackwell Publishers.

Setterlund, M.B., & Niedenthal, P.M. (1993). 'Who am I? Why am I here?': Self-esteem, self-clarity, and prototype matching. *Journal of Personality and Social Psychology,* 65, 769–80.

Settoon, R.P., Bennett, N., & Liden, R.C. (1996). Social exchange in organizations: Perceived organizational support, leader-member exchange, and employee reciprocity. *Journal of Applied Psychology,* 81(3), 219–227.

Sexner, S., Gold, D., Anderson, D., & Williams, D. (2001). The impact of a worksite health promotion program on short term disability usage. *Journal of Occupational and Environmental Management,* 43(1), 25–29.

Sfard, A. (1998). On two metaphors for learning and on the dangers of choosing just one. *Educational Researcher,* 27(2), 4–13.

Shackel, B. (1990). Human factors and usability. In J. Preece & L. Keller (Eds), *Human-computer Interaction.* Cambridge: Prentice Hall.

Shackel, B. (1996). Ergonomics: scope, contribution and future possibilities. *The Psychologist,* 9(7), 304–308.

Shackleton, V., & Newell, S. (1997). International assessment and selection. In N. Anderson & P. Herriot (Eds), *International handbook of selection and assessment* (pp. 81–95). Chichester: Wiley.

Shackleton, V., & Wale, P. (2000). Leadership and Management. In N. Chmiel (Ed.), *Work and organizational psychology: A European perspective* (pp. 277–301). Oxford: Blackwell Publishers.

Shaffer, M.A., & Harrison, D.A. (2001). Forgotten partners of international assignments: Development and test of a model of spouse adjustment. *Journal of Applied Psychology,* 86(2), 238–254.

Shea, C., & Bond, T. (1997). Ethical issues for counselling in organizations. In M. Carroll & M. Walton (Eds), *Handbook of counselling in organizations* (pp. 187–205). London: Sage.

Sheehy, N., & Chapman, A. (1988). Reconciling witness accounts of accidents. In R. de Bruin & T. Rothengatter (Eds), *Road user behaviour: Theory and research* (pp. 20–25). Assen, Netherlands: Van Gorcum & Co B.V.

Shiffrin, M., & Schneider, W. (1977). Controlled and automatic human information processing: II. Perceptual learning, automatic attending, and a general theory. *Psychological Review,* 84, 127–190.

Shirom, A., Westman, M., Shamai, O., & Carel, R.S. (1997). Effects of work overload and burnout on cholesterol and triglycerides levels: The moderating efffects of emotional reactivity among male and female employees. *Journal of Occupational Health Psychology* (4), 275–288.

Shneiderman, B. (1992). *Designing the user interface: Strategies for effective human-computer interaction* (2nd edn). Reading, MA: Addison-Wesley.

Shrey, D.E., & Mital, A. (2000). Accelerating the return to work (RTW) chances of coronary heart disease (CHD) patients: Part 2: development and validation of a vocational rehabilitation programme. *Disability and Rehabilitation: An International Multidisciplinary Journal,* 22(13–14), 621–626.

Siegel, L.S., Dubrovsky, V., Kiesler, S., & McGuire, T. (1986). Group processes in computer-mediated communication. *Organizational Behavior and Human Decision Processes,* 37(2), 157–187.

Siegrist, J. (1996). Adverse health effects of high effort-low reward conditions. *Journal of Occupational Health Psychology,* 1, 27–41.

Silvester, J. (1997). Spoken attributions and candidate success in graduate recruitment interviews. *Journal of Occupational and Organizational Psychology,* 70(1), 61–73.

Silvester, J., & Anderson, N. (2003). Technology and discourse: A comparison of face-to-face and telephone employment interviews. *International Journal of Selection and Assessment*, 11(2–3), 206–214.

Silvester, J., Anderson, N., Haddleton, E., Cunningham-Snell, N., & Gibb, A. (2001). A cross-modal comparison of telephone and face-to-face selection interviews in graduate recruitment. *International Journal of Selection and Assessment*, 8, 16–21.

Simon, H. (1957). *Models of man*. New York: Wiley.

Simpson, C.H. (1967). Patterns of socialisation into the professions: The case study of student nurses. *Sociological Inquiry*, 37, 47–54.

Sinclair, A. (1992). The tyranny of a team ideology. *Organizational Studies*, 13, 611–626.

Sinclair, S. (1997). *Making doctors: An institutional apprenticeship*. Oxford/New York: Berg.

Singh, I.L., Sharma, H.O., & Parasuram, R. (2001). Effects of manual training on automation reliability on automation-induced complacency in a flight simulation task. *Psychological Studies*, 46 (1–2), 21–27.

Sitkin, S.B. (1992). Learning through failure: The strategy of small losses. In B. Staw & L.L. Cummings (Eds), *Organizational learning* (pp. 231–266). Thousand Oaks, CA: Sage.

Skinner, B.F. (1957). *Verbal behaviour*. New York: Appelton-Century-Crofts.

Slovic, P., Fischoff, B., & Lichtenstein, S. (1980). Facts and fears: Understanding perceived risk. In R. Schwing & W. Albers, Jr. (Eds), *Societal risk assessment* (pp. 235–249). New York: Plenum.

Sluiter, J.K., van-der-Beek, A.J., & Frings-Dresen, M.H.W. (1999). The influence of work characteristics on the need for recovery and experienced health: A study on coach drivers. *Ergonomics*, 42(4), 573–583.

Smith, C.A., Organ, D.W., & Near, J.P. (1983). Organizational citizenship behaviour: Its nature and antecedents. *Journal of Applied Psychology*, 68, 453–463.

Smith, C.S., Silverman, G.S., Heckert, T.M., Brodke, M., Hayes, B., Silverman, M.K., & Mattimore, L.K. (2001). A comprehensive method for the assessment of industrial injury events. *Journal of Prevention and Intervention in the Community*, 22(1), 5–20.

Smith, E.M., Ford, J.K., & Kozlowski, S.W.J. (1997). Building adaptive expertise: Implications for training design strategies. In A. Ehrenstein & M.A. Quinones (Eds), *Training for a rapidly changing workplace: Applications of psychological research* (pp. 89–118). Washington, DC: American Psychological Association.

Smith, M., & George, D. (1992). Selection methods. In C.L. Cooper & I.T. Robertson (Eds), *International review of industrial and organizational psychology* (Vol. 7, pp. 55–97). Chichester: Wiley.

Smith, M.J., & Carayon, P. (1996). Work organization, stress and cumulative trauma disorders. In S.D. Moon & S.L. Sauter (Eds), *Beyond biomechanics: Psychosocial aspects of musculoskeletal disorders in office work* (pp. 23–42). London: Taylor & Francis.

Smith, P.C., & Kendall, L.M. (1963). Retranslation of expectations. *Journal of Applied Psychology*, 47, 149–155.

Smith, T.W., & Pope, M.K. (1990). Cynical hostility as a health risk: Current status and future directions. *Journal of Social Behavior and Personality*, 5(1), 77–88.

Smither, J.W., Collins, H., & Buda, R. (1989). When ratee satisfaction influences performance evaluations: A case of illusory correlation. *Journal of Applied Psychology*, 74(4), 599–605.

Smither, J.W., Reilly, R.R., Millsap, R.E., Pearlman, K., & Stoffey, R.W. (1993). Applicant reactions to selection procedures. *Personnel Psychology*, 46(1), 49–76.

Smithson, J., & Lewis, S. (2000). Is job insecurity changing the psychological contract? *Personnel Review*, 29, 680–698.

Snowden, D. (2002). Complex acts of knowing: Paradox and descriptive self-awareness. *Journal of Knowledge Management*, 6(2), 100–111.

Snyder, M. (1987). *Public appearances, private realities: The psychology of self-monitoring*. New York: W.H. Freeman.

Solomon, E.E. (1986). Private and public sector managers: An empirical investigation of job characteristics and organizational climate. *Journal of Applied Psychology*, 71(2), 247–259.

Somerfield, M.R., & McCrae, R.R. (2000). Stress and coping research: Methodological challenges, theoretical advances, and clinical applications. *American Psychologist*, 55(6), 620–625.

Sonnentag, S. (1996). Planning and knowledge about strategies: Their relationship to work characteristics in software design. *Behaviour and Information Technology*, 15(4), 213–225.

Sorensen, J.B. (2002). The strength of corporate culture and the reliability of firm performance. *Administrative Science Quarterly*, 47(1), 70–91.

Sparks, K., Faragher, B., & Cooper, C.L. (2001). Well-being and occupational health in the 21st century workplace. *Journal of Occupational and Organizational Psychology*, 74, 489–509.

Sparrow, P.R. (1996). Careers and the psychological contract: Understanding the European context. *European Journal of Work and Organizational Psychology*, 5(4), 479–500.

Sparrow, P.R. (2000). New employee behaviours, work designs and forms of work organization. *Journal of Managerial Psychology*, 15, 202–218.

Spearman, C. (1904). 'General intelligence' objectively determined and measured. *American Journal of Psychology*, 15, 201–293.

Spector, P.E. (1997). *Job satisfaction: Application, assessment, cause and consequences*. Thousand Oaks, CA: Sage.

Spector, P.E. (2000). A control theory of job stress process. In C.L. Cooper (Ed.), *Theories of organizational stress* (pp. 15–69). Oxford: Oxford University Press.

Spector, P.E. (2002). Research methods in industrial and organizational psychology: Data collection and data analysis with special consideration to professional issues. In D.S. Ones & N. Anderson (Eds), *Handbook of industrial, work and organizational psychology, Volume 1: Personnel psychology* (pp. 10–26). London: Sage.

Spector, P.E. (2003). Taking the measure of work: A guide to validated scales for organizational research and diagnosis. *Personnel Psychology*, 56(3), 813–816.

Spector, P.E., Chen, P.Y., & O'Connell, B.J. (2000). A longitudinal study of relations between job stressors and job strains while controlling for prior negative affectivity and strains. *Journal of Applied Psychology*, 85(2), 211–218.

Spector, P.E., & Jex, S.M. (1998). Development of four self-report measures of job stressors and strain: Interpersonal Conflict at Work Scale, Organizational Constraints Scale, Quantitative Workload Inventory, and Physical Symptoms Inventory. *Journal of Occupational Health Psychology*, 3, 356–367.

Speelman, C.P., & Kirsner, K. (2001). Predicting transfer from training performance. *Acta Psychologica*, 108(3), 247–281.

Spilsbury, M. (1995). *Measuring the effectiveness of training. personnel and human resources management*. Brighton: Institute for Employment Studies.

Sproull, L.S., & Kiesler, S. (1986). Reducing social context cues: The case of electronic mail. *Management Science*, 32, 1492–1512.

Squire, C. (Ed.) (2000). *Culture in psychology*. London/Philadelphia: Routledge.

Srivastva, S., & Cooperrider, D.L. (1990). *Appreciative management and leadership: The power of positive thought and action in organizations*. San Francisco, CA: Jossey-Bass.

Stanney, K.M., Kingdon, K.S., Graeber, D., & Kennedy, R.S. (2002). Human performance in immersive virtual environments: Effects of exposure duration, user control and scene complexity. *Human Performance*, 15(4), 339–366.

Staw, B.M., Bell, N.E., & Clausen, J.A. (1986). The dispositional approach to job attitudes: A lifetime longitudinal test. *Administrative Science Quarterly*, 31, 56–77.

Staw, B.M., & Cummings, L.L. (Ed.). (1996). *Research in organizational behavior: An annual series of analytical essays and critical reviews*, Vol. 18. New York: Elsevier Science/JAI Press.

Staw, B.M., Sandelands, L.E., & Dutton, J.E. (1981). Threat-rigidity effects in organizational behavior: A multilevel analysis. *Administrative Science Quarterly*, 26(4), 501–524.

Steckler, N., & Fondas, N. (1995). Building team leader effectiveness: A diagnostic tool. *Organizational Development*, 23(3), 20–35.

Steedman, H., & Hawkins, J. (1994). Shifting the foundations: The impact of NVQ's on youth training for the building trades. *National Institute Economic Review*, August, 93–102.

Stein, D.S. (2001). Situated learning and planned training on the job. *Advances in Developing Human Resources*, 3(4), 415–424.

Steiner, I.D. (1972). *Group process and productivity*. New York: Academic Press.

Sternberg, R.J., & Wagner, R.K. (1995). *Practical intelligence in everyday life*. Cambridge: Cambridge University Press.

Stewart, T.A. (1993). Re-engineering, the hot new management tool. *Fortune*, 127, 23 August, pp. 41–48.

Stiles, P., Gratton, L., Truss, C., Hope-Hailey, V., & McGovern, P. (1996). Performance management and the psychological contract. *Human Resource Management Journal*, 7(1), 57–66.

Stinglehamber, F., Bentein, K., & Vandenberghe, C. (2002). Extension of the three-component model of commitment to five foci. *European Journal of Psychological Assessment*, 18(2), 123–138.

Stogdill, R.M. (1948). Personal factors associated with leadership: A survey of the literature. *Journal of Psychology*, 25, 35–71.

Stogdill, R.M. (1950). *Individual behaviour and group achievement*. New York: Oxford University Press.

Stogdill, R.M. (1974). *Handbook of leadership: A survey of theory and research*. New York: Free Press.

Stokes, G., Mumford, M., & Owens, W. (Eds). (1989). *Biodata handbook: Theory, research, and use of biographical information in selection and performance prediction*. Palo Alto, CA: Consulting Psychologists Press.

Stokes, G.S., & Reddy, S. (1992). Use of background data in organizational decisions. In C. Cooper & I. Robertson (Eds), *International review of industrial and organizational psychology* (pp. 287–321). Chichester: Wiley.

Strauss, A.L. (1959). *Mirrors and masks*. New York: Free Press.

Strauss, J.P., Barrick, M.R., & Connerley, M.L. (2001). An investigation of personality similarity effects (relational and perceived) on peer and supervisory ratings and the role of familiarity and liking. *Journal of Occupational and Organizational Psychology*, 74(5), 637–658.

Strebler, M.T., Robinson, D., & Bevan, S. (2002). *Performance review: Balancing objectives and content*. Brighton: Institute for Employment Studies.

Strube, M.J., & Garcia, J.E. (1981). A meta-analytic investigation of Fiedler's contingency model of leadership effectiveness. *Psychological Bulletin*, 90, 307–321.

Struthers, C.W., Colwill, N.L., & Perry, R.P. (1992). An attributional analysis of decision making in a personnel selection interview. *Journal of Applied Social Psychology*, 22(10), 801–818.

Sue-Chan, C., & Latham, G.P. (2004). The relative effectiveness of external, peer, and self-coaches. *Applied Psychology: An International Review*, 53(2), 260–278.

Suliman, A.M.T. (2002). Is it really a mediating construct?: The mediating role of organizational commitment in work climate-performance relationship. *Journal of Management Development*, 21(3), 170–183.

Suls, J., Lemos, K., & Lockett Stewart, H. (2002). Self-esteem, construal, and comparisons with the self, friends and peers. *Journal of Personality and Social Psychology*, 82(2), 252–261.

Summerfield, J., & van Oudthoorn, L. (1995). *Counselling in the workplace*. London: Chartered Institute of Personnel & Development.

Sundstrom, E., McIntyre, M., Halfhill, T., & Richards, H. (2000). Work groups: From the Hawthorne Studies to work teams of the 1990's and beyond. *Group Dynamics: Theory, Research and Practice*, 4(1), 44–67.

Super, D.A. (1990). A life-span, life-space approach to career development. In D. Brown & L. Brooks (Eds), *Career choice and development: Applying contemporary theories to practice* (2nd edn, pp. 197–261). San Francisco: Jossey-Bass.

Sutton, S.R. (1982). Fear-arousing communication: A critical examination of theory and research. In J.R. Eaiser (Ed.), *Social psychology and behavioural medicine*. Chichester: Wiley.

Swailes, S., & McIntyre-Bhatty, T. (2003). Scale structure of the team role self-perception inventory. *Journal of Occupational and Organizational Psychology*, 76(4), 525–529.

Swain, A. (1973). An error-cause removal programme for industry. *Human Factors*, 15(3), 207–221.

Swanson, J.L., & Woitke, M.B. (1997). Theory into practice in career assessment for women: Assessment and interventions regarding perceived career barriers. *Journal of Career Assessment*, 5(4), 443–462.

Sweeney, P., & McFarlin, D. (1993). Workers evaluations of the 'ends' and the 'means': An examination of four models of distributive and procedural justice. *Organizational Behaviour and Human Decision Processes*, 55, 23–40.

Symon, G. (2000). Information and communication technologies and the network organization: A critical analysis. *Journal of Occupational and Organizational Psychology*, 73, 389–414.

Symon, G., & Cassell, C. (1998). Reflections on the use of qualitative methods. In G. Symon & C. Cassell (Eds), *Qualitative methods and analysis in organizational research: A practical guide* (pp. 1–9). London: Sage.

t'Hart, S.L., & Quinn, R.E. (1993). Roles executives play: CEO's, behavioural complexity, and firm performance. *Human Relations*, 46(5), 543–576.

Tajfel, H. (1978). *Differentiation between social groups: Studies in the social psychology of intergroup relations*. London: Academic Press.

Talbot, M. (2004). Good wine may need to mature: a critique of accelerated higher specialist training. Evidence from cognitive neuroscience. *Medical Education*, 38(4), 399–408.

Tamkin, P., Yarnall, J., & Kerrin, M. (2002). *Kirkpatrick and beyond: A review of models of training evaluation*. IES Report 392. Brighton: Institute for Employment Studies.

Tamkin, P., & Pollard, E. (2002). *Making race and diversity training work*. Brighton: Institute for Employment Studies.

Tamkin, P., Hillage, J., Cummings, J., Bates, P., Barber, L., & Tackey, N.D. (2000). Doing business better: The long-term impact of investors in people. *Institute of Employment Studies*, Focus London. February. www.employment-studies.co.uk/summary/

Tannenbaum, R., & Hanna, R. (1985). Holding on, letting go, and moving on: Understanding a neglected perspective on change. In R. Tannenbaum, N. Margulies, & F. Massarik (Eds), *Human Systems Development* (pp. 95–121). San Francisco: Jossey-Bass.

Tannenbaum, S.I., & Yukl, G. (1992). Training and development in work organizations. *Annual Review of Psychology*, 43, 399–441.

Tannenbaum, S.I., Beard, R., & Salas, E. (1992). Team building and its influence on team effectiveness: An examination of conceptual and empirical development. In K. Kelley (Ed.), *Issues, theory, and research in industrial and occupational psychology: Advances in psychology* (pp. 117–153). San Francisco: Jossey-Bass.

Taris, T.W., Kompier, M.A.J., Geurts, S.A.E., Schreurs, P.J.G., Schaufeli, W.B., de-Boer, E., Sepmeijer, K.J., & Watterz, C. (2003). Stress management interventions in the Dutch domiciliary care sector: Findings from 81 organizations. *International Journal of Stress Management*, 10(4), 297–325.

Tate, D.S. (1994). Restructuring agency job descriptions using realistic job previews. *Administration and Policy in Mental Health*, 22(2), 169–17.

Tattersall, A.J. (2000). Workload and task allocation. In N. Chmiel (Ed.), *Introduction to work and organizational psychology: A European perspective* (pp. 181–205). Oxford: Blackwell Publishers.

Tattersall, A.J., & Morgan, C.A. (1997). The function and effectiveness of dynamic task allocation. In D. Harris (Ed.), *Engineering psychology and cognitive ergonomics: Integration of theory and application*. Aldershot: Avebury.

Tattersall, A.J., Morgan, C.A., & Newman, M.D. (1997). Investigations of operator and system control of dynamic task allocation. In D. Fallon, M. Hogan, L. Bannon, & J. McCarthy (Eds), *Revisiting the allocation of functions Issue*, vol. 1. Louisville, KY: IEA Press.

Taylor, F. (1947). *Scientific management*. London: Harper and Row.

Taylor, G.S. (1994). Realistic job previews in the trucking industry. *Journal of Managerial Issues*, 6, 457–473.

Teixeira, M.A.P., & Gomes, W.B. (2000). Autonomous career change among professionals: An empirical phenomenological study. *Journal of Phenomenological Psychology*, 31(1), 78–96.

Tekleab, A.G., & Taylor, M.S. (2003). Aren't there two parties in an employment relationship? Antecedents and consequences of organization-employee agreement on contract obligations & violations. *Journal of Organizational Behavior*, 24, 585–608.

Ten Cate, O., Snell, L., Mann, K., & Vermunt, J. (2004). Orienting teaching towards the learning process. *Academic Medicine*, 79(3), 219–28.

Tennant, M. (1988). *Psychology and adult learning*. London: Routledge.

Tennen, H., Affleck, G., Armeli, S., & Carney, M.A. (2000). A daily process approach to coping. *American Psychologist*, 55, 626–636.

Tennyson, R.D. (1999). Goals for automated instructional systems: Analysis of content. *Journal of Structural Learning and Intelligent Systems*, 13(3–4), 215–226.

Tepas, D.I. (1994). Technological innovation and the management of alertness and fatigue in the workplace. *Human Performance*, 7(3), 165–180.

Terpstra, D.E. (1982). Evaluating selective organization development interventions: The state of the art. *Group and Organization Studies*, 7(4), 402–417.

Tett, R.P., & Burnett, D. (2003). A personality trait-based interactionist model of job performance. *Journal of Applied Psychology*, 88, 500–517.

Tett, R.P., & Guterman, H.A. (2000). Situation trait relevance, trait expression, and cross-situational consistency: Testing a principle of trait activation. *Journal of Research in Personality*, 34, 397–423.

Tett, R.P., Steele, J.R., & Beauregard, R.S. (2003). Broad and narrow measures on both sides of the personality job performance relationship. *Journal of Organizational Behavior*, 24, 335–356.

Thackray, J. (2000). *Future Army Command Structures*. Com Dev SO1: Comd Concepts. D/DG/DD/2/126/8/1.

Tharanou, P. (1997). Managerial career advancement. In C. Cooper & I.L. Robertson (Eds), *International Review of Industrial and Organizational Psychology* (pp. 39–94). New York: Wiley.

Tharanou, P. (1999). Gender differences in advancement to the top. *International Journal of Management Reviews*, 1, 111–132.

Tharanou, P. (2001a). The relevance of industrial and organisational psychology to contemporary organisations: How far have we come and what needs to be done post-2000? *Australian-Psychologist*, 36(3), 200–210.

Tharanou, P. (2001b). The relationship of training motivation to participation in training and development. *Journal of Occupational and Organizational Psychology*, 74(5), 599–622.

Thibaut, J.W., & Walker, L. (1978). *Procedure justice: A psychological analysis* (2nd edn). Hillsdale, NJ: Erlbaum.

Thierry, H., & Jansen, B. (1998). Work time and behaviour at work. In H. Thierry & P.J.D. Drenth (Eds), *Handbook of work and organizational psychology, Vol. 2: Work psychology* (2nd edn, pp. 89–119). Hove: Psychology Press.

Thoits, P.A. (1992). Identity structures and psychological wellbeing: Gender and marital status comparisons. *Social Psychology Quarterly*, 55, 236–256.

Thomas, J.B., Au, K., & Ravlin, E.C. (2003). Cultural variation and the psychological contract. *Journal of Organizational Behaviour*, 24, 451–471.

Thomas, J.B., Sussman, S., Watts, S., & Henderson, J.C. (2001). Understanding strategic learning: Linking organizational learning, knowledge management, and sensemaking. *Organization Science*, May–June 12(3), 331–345.

Thompson, P., & McHugh, D. (1995). *Work organizations: A critical introduction* (2nd edn). Chatham: Macmillan Business.

Thomson, H., & Anderson, N. (1998). Changes in newcomers' psychological contracts during organizational socialisation: A study of recruits entering the British Army. *Journal of Organizational Behaviour*, 19, 745–767.

Thong, J.Y.L., Hong, W., Tam, K.Y. (2002). Understanding user acceptance of digital libraries: What are the roles of interface characteristics, organizational context, and individual differences? *International Journal of Human Computer Studies*, 57(3), 215–242.

Thoresen, C.E., & Ewart, C.K. (1976). Behavioural self-control and career development. *Counselling Psychologist*, 6(3), 29–43.

Thorndike, R.L. (1949). *Personnel selection: Test and measurement technique*. New York: Wiley.

Thorndike, R.L. (1971). *Educational measurement* (2nd edn). Washington, DC: American Council on Education.

Thorndike, R.L., & Woodworth, R.S. (1901). The influence of improvement in one mental function upon the efficiency of other functions. *Psychological Review*, 8, 247–261.

Thornton, G. III., & Mueller-Hanson, R.A. (2004). *Developing organizational simulations: A guide for practitioners and students*. Mahwah, NJ: Lawrence Erlbaum Associates.

Tidwell, L.C., & Walther, J.B. (2002). Computer-mediated communication effects on disclosure, impressions, and interpersonal evaluations: Getting to know one another a bit at a time. *Human Communication Research*, 28(3), 317–348.

Tiederman, D.V., O'Hara, R.P., & Baruch, R.W. (1963). *Career development: Choice and adjustment*. Princeton, NJ: Princeton University Press.

Tinsley, H.E.A. (2000). The congruence myth: An analysis of the efficacy of the person-environment fit model. *Journal of Vocational Behaviour*, 26, 306–343.

Tobin, D.L., Holroyd, K.A., Reynolds, R.V., & Wigal, J.K. (1989). The hierachical factor structure of the Coping Strategies Inventory. *Cognitive Therapy and Research*, 13, 343–361.

Tomas, J.M., Melia, J.L., Oliver, A., Sese, A. (1993). Multisample confirmatory factor analysis: A study of the Middle and Lower Management Safety Response Questionnaire. *Psicologica*, 14(2), 137–149.

Towler, J. (1997). Managing the counselling process in organizations. In M. Carroll & M. Walton (Eds), *Counselling in organizational settings* (pp. 166–186). London: Sage.

Trist, E., & Bamforth, K. (1951). Some social and psychological consequences of the longwall method of coal-getting. Human Relations, 4, 3–38.

Truxillo, D.M., Steiner, D.D., & Gilliland, S.W. (2004). The importance of organizational justice in personnel selection: Defining when selection fairness really matters. *International Journal of Selection and Assessment*, 12(1–2), 39–53.

Tsoukas, H. (1991). The missing link: A transformational view of metaphors on organizational science. *Academy of Management Review*, 16(3), 566–585.

Tsoukas, H., & Chia, R. (2002). On organizational becoming: Rethinking organizational change. *Organisational Science*, 13, 567–582.

Tsutsumi, A., Nagami, M., Morimoto, K., & Matoba, T. (2002). Responsiveness of measures in the effort—reward imbalance questionnaire to organizational changes: A validation study. *Journal of Psychosomatic Research*, 52(4), 249–256.

Tuckey, M., Brewer, N., & Williamson, P. (2002). The influence of motives and goal orientation on feedback seeking. *Journal of Occupational and Organizational Psychology*, 75(2), 195–216.

Turban, D.B. (2001). Organizational attractiveness as an employer on college campuses: An examination of the applicant population. *Journal of Vocational Behaviour*, 58, 293–312.

Turnley, W.H., & Feldman, D.C. (2000). Re-examining the effects of psychological contract violations: Unmet expectations and job dissatisfaction as mediators. *Journal of Organizational Behaviour*, 21, 25–42.

Tversky, B. (1981). Distortions in memory for maps. *Cognitive Psychology*, 13, 497–533.

Tziner, A., & Kopelman, R.E. (2002). Is there a preferred rating format? A non-psychometric perspective. *Applied Psychology*, 51(3), 479–503.

Tziner, A., Latham, G.P., Price, B.S., & Haccoun, R. (1996). Development and validation of a questionnaire for measuring perceived political considerations in performance appraisal. *Journal of Organizational Behaviour*, 17, 179–190.

Uggerslev, K.L., & Sulsky, L.M. (2002). Presentation modaility and indirect performance information: Effects on ratings, reactions, and memory. *Journal of Applied Psychology*, 87(5), 940–950.

Ulrich, L., & Trumbo, D. (1965). The selection interview since 1949. *Psychological Bulletin*, 63, 100–116.

United States Nuclear Regulatory Commission (1980). *Three Mile Island: A report to the Commissioners and to the public*. Special Inquiry Group. Washington, DC: Nuclear Regulatory Commission, Special Inquiry Group, 2 vols in 4 [Rogovin Report] Available at www.three-mileisland.org

USSR State Committee (1986). *The utilisation of atomic energy: The accident at the Chernobyl nuclear power plant and its consequences*. Information compiled for the IAEA Experts' meeting, 19–25 August, Vienna (Part 1).

Vagg, P.R., & Spielberger, C.D. (1998). Occupational stress: Measuring job pressure and organizational support in the workplace. *Journal of Occupational Health Psychology*, 3(4), 294–305.

Vahtera, J., Kivimaki, M., Koskenvuo, M., & Pentti, J. (1997). Hostility and registered sickness absences: A prospective study of municipal employees. *Psychological Medicine*, 27(3), 693–701.

Van Der Doef, M., & Maes, S. (1999). The job demand (-support) model and psychological well-being: A review of 20 years of empirical research. *Work and Stress*, 13, 87–114.

Van Eerde, W. (2000). Procrastination: Self-regulation in initiating aversive goals. *Applied Psychology: An International Review*, 49, 372–389.

Van Iddekinge, C.H., Raymark, P.H., Eidson, C.E. and Attenweiler, W.J. (2003). What do structured selection interviews really measure? The construct validity of behavior description interviews. *Human Performance*, 17(1), 71–93.

Van Knippenberg, D. (2000). Work motivation and performance: A social identity perspective. *Applied Psychology: An International Review*, 49, 357–371.

Van Knippenberg, D., & Van Schie, E.C.M. (2000). Foci and correlates of organizational identification. *Journal of Occupational and Organizational Psychology*, 73, 137–147.

Van Knippenberg, D., van Knippenberg, B., Moden, L., & de Lima, F. (2002). Organizational identification after a merger: A social identity perspective. *British Journal of Social Psychology*, 41, 233–252.

Van Maanen, J. & Schein, E.H. (1979). Toward a theory of organizational socialisation. *Research in Organizational Behaviour*, 1, 209–264.

Van Merrienboer, J.J.G., & Kirschner, P.A. (2001). Three worlds of instructional design: State of the art and future directions. *Instructional Science*, 29, 429–441.

Van Muijen, J.J. (1998). Organizational culture. In P.J.D. Drenth, H. Thierry, & C.J. de-Wolff (Eds), *Organizational psychology, Vol. 4. Handbook of work and organizational psychology* (pp. 113–133). Hove: Psychology Press.

Van Vianen, A.E., & Van Schie, E.C.M. (1995). Assessment of male and female behaviour in the interview. *Journal of Community and Applied Social Psychology*, 5(4), 243–257.

Van Vianen, A.E.M., Taris, R., Scholten, E., & Schinkel, S. (2004). Perceived fairness in personnel selection: Determinants and outcomes in different stages of the assessment procedure. *International Journal of Selection and Assessment*, 12(1–2), 149–159.

Vance, R.J., Coovert, M.D., MacCallum, R.C., & Hedge, J.W. (1989). Construct models of task performance. *Journal of Applied Psychology*, 74(3), 447–455.

Vancouver, J.B., Thompson, C.M., & Williams, A.A. (2001). The changing signs in the relationships between self-efficacy, personal goals and performance. *Journal of Applied Psychology*, 86, 605–620.

Vandenberg, R., & Scarpello, V. (1990). The matching model: An examination of the processes underlying realistic job previews. *Journal of Applied Psychology*, 75(1), 64–67.

Van-der-Doef, M., Maes, S., & Diekstra, P. (1999). The Job Demand-Control (-Support) model and psychological well-being: A review of 20 years of empirical research. *Work and Stress*, 13(2), 87–114.

Varney, G.H. (1989). *Building productive teams: An action guide and resource book*. San Francisco, CA: Jossey Bass.

Varonen, U., & Mattila, M. (2000). The safety climate and its relationship to safety practices, safety of the work environment and occupational accidents in eight wood-processing companies. *Accident Analysis and Prevention*, 32(6), 761–769.

Vaughn, D. (1996). *The Challenger launch decision: Risky technology, culture and deviance at NASA*. Chicago: Chicago University Press.

Vaught, B.C., Hoy, F., & Buchanan, W. (1985). *Employee development programs: An organizational approach*. Westport, CT: Quorum Books/Greenwood Publishing Group.

Vecchio, R.P. (1995). *Organizational behaviour* (3rd Edn). New York: The Dryden Press, Harcourt Brace.

Venkatesh, V., & Johnson, P. (2002). Telecommuting technology implementations: A within and between subjects longitudinal field study. *Personnel Psychology*, 55(3), 661–688.

Vink, P., & Kompier, M.A.J. (1997). Improving office work: A participatory ergonomic experiment in a naturalistic setting. *Ergonomics*, 40(4), 435–449.

Viswesvaran, C. (1993). *Modelling job performance. Is there a general factor?* Doctoral dissertation. Iowa City: University of Iowa.

Viswesvaran, C., & Ones, D.S. (2000). Perspectives of models of job performance. *International Journal of Selection and Assessment*, 8, 216–225.

Viswesvaran, C., & Ones, D.S. (2004). Importance of perceived personnel selection system fairness determinants: Relations with demographic, personality, and job characteristics. *International Journal of Selection and Assessment*, 12(1–2), 172–186.

Viswesvaran, C., Schmidt, F.L., & Ones, D.S. (2002). The moderation influence of job performance dimensions on convergence of supervisory and peer ratings of job performance: Unconfounding construct-level congruence and rating difficulty. *Journal of Applied Psychology*, 87, 345–354.

Volpe, C., Cannon-Bowers, J., Salas, E., & Spector, P.E. (1996). The impact of cross-training on team functioning: An empirical investigation. *Human Factors*, 38, 87–100.

Vondracek, F.W. & Reitzle, M. (1998). The viability of career maturity theory: A developmental-contextual perspective. *Career Development Quarterly*, 47(1), 6–15.

Vredenburgh, A.G. (2002). Organizational safety: which management practices are most effective in reducing employee injury rates? *Journal of Safety Research*, 33(2), 259–276.

Vroom, V.H. (1995). *Work and motivation*. San Franscisco, CA: Jossey-Bass.

Waern, Y. (1987). Mental models in learning computerized tasks. In M. Frese, E. Ulich & W. Dzida (Eds), *Psychological issues of human computer interaction in the work place*. Amsterdam: Elsevier Science Publishers.

Wagenaar, W.A., & Hudson, P.T.W. (1998). Industrial safety. In P.J.D. Drenth, H. Thierry, & C.J. de Wolff (Eds), *Work psychology, Vol. 2. Handbook of Work and Organizational Psychology* (pp. 65–87). Hove: Psychology Press.

Wagner, J.A., Leana, C.R., Locke, E.A., & Schweiger, D.A. (1997). Cognitive and motivational frameworks in research on participation: A meta-analysis of effects. *Journal of Organizational Behaviour*, 18, 49–65.

Wainwright, D., & Calnan, M. (2002). *Work stress: The making of a modern epidemic*. Milton Keynes: Open University Press.

Walker, A.G., & Smither, J.W. (1999). A five year study of upward feedback: What managers do with their results matters. *Personnel Psychology*, 52, 393–423.

Walker, C.R. (1950). *Steeltown: An industrial case history of the conflict between progress and security*. Oxford: Harper.

Walkerdine, V. (Ed.) (2000). *Challenging subjects: Critical psychology for a new millennium*. London: Macmillan.

Wall, T.D., & Jackson, P.R. (1995). New manufacturing initiatives and shopfloor work design. In A. Howard (Ed.), *The changing nature of work* (pp. 139–174). San Francisco, CA: Jossey-Bass.

Walsh, J.P. (1995). Managerial and organizational cognition: Notes from a trip down memory lane. *Organization Science*, 6(3), 280–321.

Walton, M. (1997). Counselling as a form of organizational change. In M. Carroll & M. Walton (Eds), *Handbook of counselling in organizations* (pp. 129–146). London: Sage.

Wan, J., & Mon-Williams, M. (1996). What does virtual reality NEED?: Human factors issues in the design of three-dimensional computer environments. *International Journal of Human-Computer Studies*, 44(6), 829–847.

Wanburg. C.R., & Banas, J.T. (2000). Predictors and outcomes of openness to changes in a reorganising workplace. *Journal of Applied Psychology*, 85, 132–142.

Wang, S., (2000). Managing the organisational aspects of electronic commerce. *Human Systems Management*, 19(1), 49–59.

Wanous, J.P. (1973). Effects of a realistic job preview on job acceptance, job attitudes, and job survival. *Journal of Applied Psychology*, 58, 327–332.

Wanous, J.P. (1980). *Organizational entry: Recruitment, selection and socialization of newcomers*. Reading, MA: Addison-Wesley.

Wanous, J.P., Reichers, A.E., & Austin, J.T. (2000). Cynicism about organizational change: Measurement, antecedents, and correlates. *Group and Organization Management*, 25, 132–153.

Warr, P. (1987). *Work, unemployment and mental health*. Oxford: Clarendon Press.

Warr, P. (1999). Well-being in the workplace. In D. Kahneman, E. Diener, & N. Schwarz (Eds), *Wellbeing: The foundations of hedonic psychology* (pp. 392–412). New York: Russell Sage Foundation.

Warr, P. (2000). Work performance and the ageing workforce. In N. Chmiel (Ed.), *Introduction to work and organizational psychology: A European perspective* (pp. 407–423). Oxford: Blackwell.

Warr, P., & Allan, C. (1998). Learning strategies and occupational training. In C.L. Cooper & I.T. Robertson (Eds), *International review of industrial and organizational psychology*, Vol. 13 (pp. 83–121). Chichester: Wiley.

Warr, P., & Bunce, D. (1995). Trainee characteristics and the outcomes of open learning. *Personnel Psychology*, 48, 347–375.

Warr, P., & Downing, J. (2000). Learning strategies, learning anxiety and knowledge acquisition. *British Journal of Psychology*, 91, 311–333.

Warr, P., Cook, J., & Wall, T. (1979). Scales for the measurement of some work attitudes and aspects of psychological wellbeing. *Journal of Occupational Psychology*, 63, 193–210.

Wasti, S.A. (2003). Organizational commitment, turnover intentions and the influence of cultural values. *Journal of Occupational and Organizational Psychology*, 76(3), 303–346.

Waterson, P.E. (2000). The design and use of work technology. In N. Chmiel (Ed). *Introduction to Work and Organizational Psychology* (pp. 231–253). Oxford: Blackwell.

Waterworth, J.A. (1995). *HCI design as sensory ergonomics: Designing synaesthetic media*. In D. Dahlbom, F. Kämmerer, F. Ljungberg, J. Stage and C. Sorensen (Eds), Proceedings of IRIS 18 Conference, Denmark, August. Gothenburg Studies of Informatics, Report 7, 744–753.

Watkins, C.E., & Subich, L.M. (1995). Annual review, 1992–1994: Career development, reciprocal work/non-work interaction, and women's workforce participation. *Journal of Vocational Behavior*, 47(2), 109–163.

Watson, A.L., Williams, J.E., & Ball, A. (2001). Workplace violence: Another face of the crisis. In Daya Singh Sandhu (Ed), *Faces of violence: Psychological correlates, concepts, and intervention strategies* (pp. 3–21). Huntington: Nova Science, NY.

Watson, D., & Clark, L. (1984). Negative affectivity: The disposition to experience aversive psychological states. *Psychological Bulletin*, 96, 465–490.

Watts, A.G. (1996). *Careerquake*. London: Demos.

Watts, A.G., Killen, J., Law, B., Kidd, J.M. & Hawthorn, R. (1996). *Rethinking careers education and guidance: Theory, policy and practice*. London: Routledge.

Watts, T. (2004). *Bridging policy and practice in career development: an international perspective*. Keynote address delivered to the National Consultation on Career Development, Ottawa, Canada. 26th January.

Wegge, J., & Dibbelt, S. (2000). Effects of goal-setting or information processing in letter-matching tasks. *Zeitschrift fuer Experimentelle Psychologie*, 47(2), 89–114.

Weick, K.E. (1977). Organization design: Organizations as self-designing systems. *Organizational Dynamics*, 6(2), 30–46.

Weick, K.E. (1995) *Sensemaking in organizations*. London: Sage.

Weick, K.E., & Quinn, R.E. (1999). Organizational change and development. *Annual Review of Psychology*, 50, 361–386.

Weigmann, D.A., Rick, A., & Zhang, H. (2001). Automated diagnostic aids: The effects of aid reliability on users' trust and reliance. *Theoretical Issues in Ergonomics Science*, 2(4) 352–367.

Weinstein, C.E., & Mayer, R.E. (1986). The teaching of learning strategies. In M.C. Wittock (Ed.), *Handbook of research on teaching* (3rd edn, pp. 315–327). New York: Macmillan.

Weiss, J. (1996). *Organizational behavior & change: Managing diversity, cross-cultural dynamics, and ethics*. Minneapolis/St. Paul, MN: West Publishing.

Weiss, H.M. (2002). Deconstructing job satisfaction: Separating evaluations, beliefs and affective experiences. *Human Resource Management Review*, 12(2), 173–194.

Wernimont, P.F., & Campbell, J.P. (1968). Signs, samples, and criteria. *Journal of Applied Psychology*, 52, 372–376.

West, M.A., & Markiewicz, L. (2004). *Building team-based working: A practical guide to organizational transformation*. Oxford: BPS Blackwell.

Wexley, K.N. (1984). Personnel training. *Annual Review of Psychology*, 35, 519–551.

Wexley, K.N., & Latham, G.P. (2002). *Developing and training human resources in organizations* (3rd edn). Upper Saddle River, NJ: Prentice Hall.

Wheaton, B. (1996). The domains and boundaries of stress concepts. In Howard B. Kaplan (Ed.), *Psychosocial stress: Perspectives on structure, theory, life-course, and methods* (pp. 29–70). San Diego, CA: Academic Press, Inc.

Whetten, D., & Godfrey, P.C. (Eds). *Identity in organizations: Building theory through conversations. Foundations for organizational science*. Thousand Oaks, CA: Sage.

White, M. (1995). *Re-authoring lives: Interviews and essays*. Adelaide: Dulwich Centre Publications.

White, M., & Epston, D.T.I. (1989). *Literate means to therapeutic ends*. Adelaide: Dulwich Centre Publications.

Wichroski, M.A. (1994). The secretary: Invisible labour in the workworld of women. *Human Organization*, 53(1), 33–41.

Wickens, C.D. (1992). *Engineering psychology and human performance* (2nd edn). New York: Harper-Collins.

Wickens, C.D., Liang, C.C., Prevett, T., & Olmos, O. (1996). Electronic maps for terminal area navigation: Effects of frame of reference and dimensionality. *International Journal of Aviation Psychology*, 6(3), 241–271.

Widdowson, M. (2003). *A scientific foundation for the study of culture in the military*. Work Package 1.2. QuinetiQ. Farnborough, UK.

Wiegmann, D.A., Rich, A., & Zhang, H. (2001). Automated diagnostic aids: The effects of aid reliability on users' trust and reliance. *Theoretical Issues in Ergonomics Science*, 2(4), 352–367.

Wigan, M. (1991). Computer co-operative work: Communications, computers and their contributions to working in groups. In R. Clarke & J. Cameron (Eds), *Managing information technology's organisational impact*. Amsterdam: Elsevier Science Publishers.

Wilkins, A.L., & Thompson, M.P. (1991). On getting the story crooked (and straight). *Journal of Organizational Change Management*, 4/3, 18–26.

Wilkinson, J.D., Campbell, E.A., Coyle, A., & Davis, A. (1997). *Psychology in counselling and therapeutic practice*. New York: John Wiley & Sons, Inc.

Wilkinson, L.J. (1997). Generalizable biodata? An application to the vocational interests of managers. *Journal of Occupational and Organizational Psychology*, 70(1), 49–60.

Williams, A., Dobson, P., & Walters, M. (1989). *Changing culture: New organizational approaches.* London: IPA.

Williams, J.S., & Cooper, C.L. (1998). Measuring occupational stress: Development of the pressure management indicator. *Journal of Occupational Health Psychology*, 4, 306–321.

Williams, M.L., Podsakoff, P.M., & Huber, V. (1992). Effects of group-level and individual-level variation in leader behaviours on subordinate attitudes and performance. *Journal of Occupational and Organizational Psychology*, 65, 115–129.

Williams, R.C., & Fletcher, C. (1998). Performance management. In I. Robertson, D. Bartram & M. Callinan (Eds), *Individual performance and organizational effectiveness.* Chichester: Wiley.

Williamson, E.G. (1939). The clinical method of guidance. *Review of Educational Research*, 9, 214–217.

Williamson, E.G. (1965). Vocational counselling: Trait-factor theory. In B. Stefflre (Ed.), *Theories of Counselling* (pp. 193–195). New York: McGraw-Hill.

Williamson, E.G. (1972). Trait factor theory and individual differences. In B. Stefflre & W.H. Grant (Eds), *Theories of Counselling* (2nd ed. pp. 172–174). New York: McGraw-Hill.

Wilson, D.C. (1992). *A Strategy of change: Concepts and controversies in the management of change.* London: Routledge.

Wilson, J.W., & Corlett, E.N. (1995). *Evaluation of human work: A practical ergonomics methodology* (2nd edn). London: Taylor & Francis Ltd.

Winnubst, J.A.M., & Diekstra, R.F.W. (1998). Work and health psychology: Methods of intervention. In P.J.D. Drenth, H. Thierry & C.J. de Wolff (Eds), *Personnel psychology. Vol. 3. handbook of work and organizational psychology* (pp. 395–408). Hove: Psychology Press.

Witmer, B.G., & Singer, M.J. (1998). Measuring presence in virtual environments: A presence questionnaire. *Teleoperators and Virtual Environments*, 7(3), 225–240.

Witmer, B.G., Bailey, J.H., Knerr, B.W., & Parsons, K.C. (1996). Virtual spaces and real world places: Transfer of route knowledge. *International Journal of Human-Computer Studies*, 45(4), 413–428.

Wnuk, S.M., & Amundson, N.E. (2002). Using the Intelligent Careers Card Sort ® with university students. *Career Development Quarterly*, 51(3), 274–284.

Woehr, D.J., & Feldman, J. (1993). Processing objective and question order effects on the causal relation between memory and judgment in performance appraisal: The tip of the iceberg. *Journal of Applied Psychology*, 78(2), 232–241.

Wohlers, A.J., & London, M. (1989). Ratings of managerial characteristics: Evaluation difficulty, co-worker agreement and self-awareness. *Personnel Psychology*, 42(2), 235–261.

Wohlers, A.J., Hall, M.J., & London, M. (1993). Subordinates rating managers: Organizational and demographic correlates of self/subordinate agreement. *Journal of Occupational and Organizational Psychology*, 66(3), 263–275.

Wolmar, M. (2003). Design flaws, mistakes, and bad management – the truth behind the Central line crash. *Evening Standard*, 6 March, p. 8.

Wolpe, J.E. (1958). *Psychotherapy and reciprocal inhibition.* Stanford, CA: Stanford University Press.

Wood, R., & Bandura, A. (1989). Social cognitive theory of organizational management. *Academy of Management Review*, 14, 361–384.

Woodman, R.W., & Sherwood, J.J. (1980). The role of team development in organizational effectiveness: A critical review. *Psychological Bulletin*, 88(1), 166–186.

Woodruff, C. (2000). *Development and assessment centres.* London: IPS.

Woods, D.D. (1991). The cognitive engineering of problem representations. In G.R.S. Weir & J.L. Alty (Eds), *Human-computer interaction and complex systems* (pp. 169–188). London: Academic Press.

Woods, R.E., Atkins, P.B., & Bright, J. (1999). Bonuses, goals and instrumentality effects: A recommended change in research methods. *Australian Journal of Management*, 84(5), 703–720.

Worrall, L., & Cooper, C.L. (1998). *Quality of working life 1998 survey of managers' changing experiences.* London: Institute of Management.

Worrall, L., Cooper, C.L., & Campbell-Jamison, F. (2000). The impact of organizational change on the work experiences and perceptions of public sector managers. *Personnel Review*, 29, 613–636.

Worster, D. (2000). An EAP approach to managing organizational downsizing. *Employee Assistance Quarterly*, 16(1–2), 97–115.

Wright, O.P. (1969). Summary of research on the selection interview since 1964. *Personnel Psychology*, 22, 391–413.

Wright, T.A., & Staw, B.M. (1999). Affect and favorable work outcomes: Two longitudinal tests of the happy-productive worker thesis. *Journal of Organizational Behavior*, 20, 1–23.

Yammarino, F.J., & Atwater, L.E. (2001). Understanding agreement in multisource feedback. In D.W. Bracken, C.W. Timmreck et al. (Eds), *The handbook of multisource feedback: The comprehensive resource for designing and implementing MSF processes* (pp. 204–220). San Francisco, CA: Jossey-Bass/Pfeiffer.

Yammarino, F.J., & Bass, B.M. (1990). Transformational leadership at multiple levels of leadership. *Human Relations*, 43, 975–995.

Yamnill, S., & McLean, G.N. (2001). Theories supporting transfer of training. *Human Resource Development Quarterly*, 12(2), 195–208.

Yeager, E.A. (1998). Democracy, social studies, and diversity in the elementary school classroom: The progressive ideas of Alice Miel. *Theory and Research in Social Education*, 26(2), 198–225.

Yearta, S.K., Maitlis, S., & Briner, R.B. (1995). An explanatory study of goal setting in theory and practice: A motivational technique that works? *Journal of Occupational and Organizational Psychology*, 68, 237–252.

Young, R.M. (1983). Surrogates and mappings: Two kinds of conceptual models for interactive devices. In D. Gentner & A. Stevens (Eds), *Mental models* (pp. 51–85). Hillsdale, NJ: Lawrence Erlbaum.

Yukl, G.A., & Van Fleet, D.D. (1982). Cross-situational, Multi-method research on military leader effectiveness. *Organizational Behavior and Human Performance*, 30, 87–108.

Zaal, J.N. (1998). Assessment centre methods. In P.J.D. Drenth, H. Thierry & C.J. de Wolff (Eds), *A handbook of work and organizational psychology* (Vol. 3. pp. 89–122). *Personnel psychology*. Hove: Psychology Press.

Zalcquett, C.P., & Wood, R.J. (Eds). (1998). *Evaluating stress: A book of resources* (2 vols). Lanham, MD: Scarecrow.

Zamanou, Sonia, & Glaser, Susan R. (1994). Moving toward participation and involvement: Managing and measuring organizational culture. *Group and Organization Management*, 19(4), 475–502.

Zander, A. (1982). *Making groups effective*. San Francisco: Jossey-Bass.

Zedeck, S., & Kafry, D. (1977). Capturing rater policies for processing evaluation data. *Organizational Behavior and Human Performance*, 18, 269–294.

Zeit, G. (1996). Employee attitudes toward total quality management. *Administration and Society*, 28(1), 120–143.

Zirkler, D., & Ballman, D.R. (1994). Usability testing in a competitive market: Lessons learned. *Behavior and Information Technology*, 13(1–2), 191–197.

Zohar, D. (2003). Safety climate: Conceptual and measurement issues. In J.C. Quick, L.E. Tetrick & E. Lois (Eds), *Handbook of occupational health psychology* (pp. 123–142). Washington, DC: American Psychological Association.

# Index

Main author references (more than one textual reference) are included: multi-author works are indexed under first author, two-part works are indexed under both authors. References in italics indicate diagrams